W9-ATY-499

Inland Waterways
of France

Inland Waterways of France

DAVID EDWARDS-MAY

Imray Laurie Norie & Wilson Ltd
St Ives Cambridgeshire England

Published by
Imray, Laurie, Norie & Wilson Ltd
Wych House, St Ives, Huntingdon, Cambridgeshire PE17 4BT, England
☎ (0480) 62114 *Fax* (0480) 496109

First published 1956
5th edition, 1984
6th edition, 1991

British Library Cataloguing in publication data.
A catalogue record for this book is available from the British Library.

ISBN 0 85288 152 5

CAUTION
While every care has been taken to ensure accuracy, neither the Publishers
nor the Author will hold themselves responsible for errors, omissions or
alterations in this publication. They will at all times be grateful to receive information which tends to the improvement of the work.

The detailed town and junction plans are based on blown-up extracts of the
1:25,000-scale maps produced by the Institut Géographique National.
Authorisation n° 90-1059.

Printed in Great Britain at The Bath Press, Avon

The photographs (by the author except where indicated) on the cover are, from right to left:
Auxerre on the Yonne, Josselin Château on the Canal de Nantes à Brest, the Canal de Bourgogne
(Hugh Potter), a characteristic lock on the Oust section of the Canal de Nantes à Brest between
Josselin and Redon.

Contents

Foreword

TO THE SIXTH EDITION

This new edition of *Inland Waterways of France* appears at a crucial time in the history of the French waterways system. Commercial traffic is declining, a victim of competition from roads and railways. The small 300-ton barges are slowly disappearing, either cut up for scrap or converted into accommodation.

But with the general increase in leisure activities, the canals and rivers are finding a new purpose. Yachts crossing from the Channel to the Mediterranean, hotel barges, passenger boats and no more than 2000 hire boats are all helping to give a new lease of life to a waterways network once doomed to disappear.

Those who have already discovered French waterways realise how important it is to prepare their cruise. Plenty of questions arise. Which waterway will I choose? What is the quickest way from Le Havre to Sète? Which towns will I go through on the way...? No one is better qualified to answer these questions than the author, David Edwards-May, who studied in detail the whole French network and who has often been called upon by the French authorities to advise on new waterways projects.

Those reading this book who knew the waterways twenty years ago, will be astounded to see the changes that have taken place. To cater for the new pleasure traffic, water points have been installed and many river and canal ports have been built. Some locks have been electrified and new modern waterslopes have replaced, more or less successfully, the old lock staircases.

But even more important, the advent of pleasure boats has tempted the regional authorities to revive old waterways which had not been used for years. For example, the Lot has been put back into service between Luzech and St Cirq La Popie. This ambitious scheme was commenced following a study led by David Edwards-May and despite the reticence of some and frank opposition from others, it has proved a great success. David is also participating in another development scheme in southwest France which, if completed, will add hundreds of kilometres of navigable waterways.

Those of us who are involved in the waterways welcome these new schemes. With new towns to discover and new regions to explore, the future of inland boating in France is ensured.

But there are clouds on the horizon. With the decline of commercial traffic, the French government wishes to transfer responsibility for the waterways to the regions. The regions are reluctant to take on this burden and canals such as the Canal du Midi, badly in need of basic maintenance, wait anxiously until their fate is decided.

The beginning of a solution appears to have been found with the institution of a new toll via *Voies Navigables de France*. The privilege of free passage for pleasure boats has now disappeared and, from now on, anyone using the canals and rivers will pay. Those who know and love French waterways are pleased that these funds will be made directly available for their maintenance. But there is also reason for concern. In past centuries, the application of unreasonable tolls has all but destroyed waterways navigation. We can only hope that this does not happen again.

John Riddel
Crown Blue Line
France
November 1991

ACKNOWLEDGEMENTS FOR THE SIXTH EDITION

Thanks are due in the first place to the engineers and technicians of the waterway authorities (*Services de la Navigation*) throughout the country, who kindly devoted much time and effort to reading and correcting the texts and distance tables which make up the bulk of the guide. Their contributions have been most valuable. I would particularly like to pay a tribute to the dedication and efforts of the staff of the Direction Régionale de la Navigation in Lille, especially Jean-Pierre Ledoux, whose forthcoming retirement will be a great loss for the waterways in northern France.

For assistance in designing the new plans and in finding my way around unfamiliar software, I am indebted to Graham Sumner and Jean-Yves Debernardy. Pascale Reveret also helped in the early stages, and it was Patrick Rigaud who come up with the final solution. Marie-Christine Vasseur gave help in obtaining maps and data, and moral support. Thanks also to Paul Hobart of Australia for some valuable suggestions as we came down the home straight. While the last edition paid due tribute to E. E. Benest, I would like this time to recall the memory of Tom Wilson, with whom I first discussed producing continental waterways guides at the 1968 Earl's Court Boat Show in London, and who was always more than supportive.

Photographs were kindly supplied by Hugh Potter, Bill Greenhalgh, Derek Bowskill, Rod Heikell and John Riddel.

For providing boats for all the cruises undertaken in recent years, I am grateful to the hire firms Locaboat Plaisance, Snaily at Seveux on the Saône, Nautic Voyage on the Belgian river Sambre and Blue Line (for the first cruise on the newly-opened river Lot), and to my friend Marie Thirion and Gil Michelin for the use (and, in one unfortunate instance, abuse) of their ex-Blue Line boat.

Top of the list of long-suffering and nonetheless ever-eager crew members are my daughters Emilie and Charlotte, who have brightened many a day on the cut, and my mother Meg.

Finally, the author and publishers are indebted to Elizabeth Cook who compiled the index.

DAVID EDWARDS-MAY
Genoble, France 1991

Introduction

During the 1980s the French waterways established themselves as one of the country's main tourist assets. Development of high-capacity waterways continues, but inland shipping is no longer the exclusive justification for maintaining and extending the network. The multiple functions of inland waterways are now officially recognised, under new legislation introduced in 1990, representing a quiet revolution. The idea behind the new law is to secure additional income from the various users, thus complementing the State budget for waterway maintenance, operation and development. The budget has thus been almost doubled from its pre-1990 level of around 400 million francs.

Voies Navigables de France

For this purpose, management of the whole State network is handed over to the *Office National de la Navigation*, founded in 1912 essentially as a regulatory body for the water transport industry, but now reorganised as a commercial undertaking and renamed *Voies Navigables de France*. The largest new source of income is the electricity generating board *Electricité de France*, which for 50 years had been reaping alone the benefits of low-cost hydropower, especially on the Rhône. Its contribution of about 200 million francs will specifically enable faster progress in construction of the new waterway links between the Rhine and Rhône and between the Seine and northern France. Water pumped from rivers and canals will also now be paid for at more realistic rates.

Boat licences and tolls

Most important for readers, however, is the system of tolls applicable to all boats using the waterways. Tolls and licences were originally to be introduced for the 1991 season, but the complications of the task and characteristic government procrastination delayed the process, and the system is not to become effective until the 1992 season. Full details will be published in a supplement as soon as they are available, but it is already apparent that there will be a basic choice between

a. a full annual licence (such as the boat hire firms will pay), the cost of which is to be approximately 100F per square metre (length by beam), or roughly 1500F to 3500F for a typical range of boat sizes, or
b. a temporary licence based on a lump sum charge of about 5F per square metre per week of navigation anywhere on the network, which works out at 75F to 175F for the same range of boat sizes. The temporary licence will be purchased at the first control lock encountered, and displayed subsequently at other control locks, where it will presumably be possible to purchase a licence for a further period if necessary.

There is an important distinction between time spent navigating and time spent at a long-term mooring. The cruising licence gives the right to moor for up to 48 hours anywhere on the network (although charges are made at harbours leased to a public or private operator). Long-term moorings is subject either to the charges applied by the harbour concessionary, or to a mooring lease or *autorisation d'occupation temporary (AOT)* to be obtained from the *Service de la Navigation*.

New junction maps

This new edition includes a number of new general waterway maps (especially for the Lot, the Upper Rhône and the Sèvre Nantaise), and no less than 180 detailed junction plans, based on the 1:25,000 IGN maps, enlarged to 1:20,000. These are designed to be of the greatest use to boaters by giving the maximum topographical detail, especially at locations where the configuration of the waterways is too complex to be readily understood from the textual description alone.

High-capacity waterways and extensions

The situation of the high-capacity waterways has changed only slightly since the last edition of this work was published. An additional length of the upper river Seine is being opened up to 1000-tonne barges, to serve the busy cereals ports of Nogent. In the north the upgrading of the Escaut down to the Belgian border has been completed, and improvement works are nearing completion on the last section of the Bauvin-Lys branch of the Dunkerque-Escaut waterway. There has been no progress, however, on the Seine-Nord link.

The Rhine and Moselle have seen no major change, although there is talk of deepening the latter river to allow barges and push-tows to carry greater loads. Works continue on the Saône, and 1991 will see opening of the Mâcon bypass, avoiding the historic St Laurent bridge and allowing 3000-tonne push-tows to trade on up the river to Chalon-sur-Saône and beyond. On the Rhône-Rhine link itself, a timid start has made been made at the Mulhouse end and at Sochaux, where extension of the Peugeot car works provided the opportunity to widen a short length of the old canal, now conveying the natural flow of the river Allan, infilled where it ran through the factory.

The Secretary of State for road and water transport created a surprise in early 1991 by announcing a new comparative study of the two alternative routes from the Saône to the Rhine, the Alsace option on which works have started, and the Moselle option, which although possibly more beneficial for France would completely transform the upper Saône, and bypass much of the southern branch of the Canal de l'Est. It is true that the ecology and scenic attraction of the river Doubs also stand to suffer from transformation for high-capacity inland shipping, but arguably less so, as a steep-sided valley. The announcement of a new study may simply be part of a Government policy to avoid committing itself to development of the waterways, which will obviously have an adverse effect on the freight operating results and the deficit of French Railways.

Projects on the Upper Rhône suffered a setback when the Government refused authorisation of the Loyettes scheme designed by the Compagnie Nationale du Rhône, which together with the Miribel-Saint-Clair scheme nearer Lyon would have brought inland shipping to the Plaine de l'Ain industrial development zone. Environmentalists were concerned at the impact which the Loyettes scheme would have had on the unique ecology of the Ain-Rhône

confluence. At the other end of the Rhône, a first stage of upgrading of the Canal du Rhône à Sète has been completed, with bypasses designed for 600-tonne barges at Aigues-Mortes and Frontignan.

In the meantime, upgrading of the central section of the Canal du Midi to 250-tonne barge standards, involving lengthening of the locks from 30 to 38.50m, has been shelved, and is now unlikely ever to be authorised.

That more or less completes the picture of six years of investment on the French waterways, excepting of course various reconstruction and modernisation projects which do not affect the actual routes. Under this category comes the ongoing programme of equipment of locks for automatic operation. Six years after we wrote of recurring failures, the system has still not been made foolproof, and numerous incidents arise from failure of the radar detection system to detect smaller boats. Hence the replacement of the radar detectors at certain locks by the more conventional and well-tried suspended poles.

Kembs Lock on the Grand Canal d'Alsace, which forms the Rhine Navigation between Bâle and Breisach.
Hugh Potter

New waterways for tourism
A substantial effort is being made by local and regional councils to improve and extend the network of smaller waterways that are now devoted exclusively to pleasure traffic and other leisure uses. In many cases this development now takes place quite independently of the State, wherever the waterways have been transferred to the *départements*. The Brittany canals, the rivers of Anjou, the Charente and the Canal du Nivernais are all now managed by the respective *départements* or by regional bodies grouping the *départements* concerned.

The most spectacular development in recent years has been the reopening of a 64km section of the canalised river Lot, with 13 locks restored and a new one built (where the old lock had been converted into a small hydropower plant, a fate alas commonly occurring to disused locks on river navigations in France). There is thus a new entry for this river, which may eventually be made navigable again throughout its 275km length from the Garonne into the heart of the Massif Central. This would involve substantial works to bypass the five large dams that have been built on the river. Curiously, this river, already one of the most popular destinations for boating holidays in France, is operated in a kind of jurisdictional limbo. As a disused and abandoned waterway, it falls under the responsibility of the Ministry of the Environment, and the *département* of Lot has so far refused to take over from the State. It is reassuring in a sense to observe that such legal niceties did not prevent the project from going ahead, but hopefully the councils of the three *départements* concerned by the canalised river Lot will get their act together more forcefully as the restoration effort proceeds.

Also contributing to the creation of an extensive waterway network in South West France is the continuing restoration of the river Baïse. A further 9km length is open, up to the bastide of Vianne, and Nérac, a further 18km, is expected to be reached by 1993. This scenic river, with much of tourist interest, is giving a welcome boost to the Canal latéral à la Garonne, which is attracting far fewer boaters than hirers on the canal expected. Can this canal afford to keep its singularly uninspiring name?

Péniches on the Oise at Conflans-Ste-Honorine. *Hugh Potter*

Further up the Atlantic coast, the Charente is another popular cruising river, with extensions planned. Downstream, the tidal section gives access to the canalised river Boutonne, with a tide sluice and four locks giving access to the small town of Saint-Jean-d'Angély, a distance of 29km. This tributary is added under the Charente, although conditions of access through the tide sluice are delicate. Hence the project to build a lock on a separate channel bypassing the sluice. At the upstream end, restoration of the Charente is projected over a distance of 22km from Chalonne weir north of Angoulême up to the village of Montignac.

On the canals of Brittany efforts have recently been concentrated on restoring the original navigable depth, fitting new lock gates and providing addi-

Canal de la Marne au Rhin. Lock No. 40 and Chanteraines aqueduct near Bar-le-Duc. *Hugh Potter*

tional water supply on the Canal de Nantes à Brest. 1991 should thus see boats again crossing the heavily-locked watershed section of the canal between Rohan and Pontivy (55 locks in 24km!), which in practice has been inaccessible for years.

On the other side of France, the upper Rhône has been developed by the Compagnie Nationale du Rhône, with three new hydropower schemes between the Lake Bourget link canal and Sault-Brénaz, at each of which a boat elevator is available to transfer boats between the upstream and downstream reaches. This possibility, together with the attractions of the Canal de Savières, its do-it-yourself entrance lock and Lake Bourget itself, justified including the Upper Rhône as a separate entry, with cruising possible over 110km from Loyettes to the southern end of the lake.

The Canal d'Arles à Fos, indicated in the previous edition as closed beyond the first 2.5km, in fact remains navigable over the entire distance of 31km down to the salt barrier at the junction with the Rhône-Fos link. Navigation in this section, under the responsibility of the Marseille Port Authority, is officially discouraged by horror stories of low bridges, high banks excluding all views, miscellaneous refuse and wrecked cars under bridges. As on all waterways threatened with closure, navigation is strongly recommended!

A boost to the cruising potential of the Lower Rhône and Camargue region will be the projected reopening of Beaucaire lock at the end of the Canal du Rhône à Sète, with another lock on the spit of land between the bypassed river Rhône and the tailrace canal of the Beaucaire hydropower dam and lock. Work has still to start on this project, but it is worth mentioning, for it would open up an attractive circular route in southern France, at the same time restoring Beaucaire's traditional importance as a port of call on the route to the Languedoc-Roussillon coast and the Midi canals.

Contrasts in northern France

Another error to be confessed to in the previous edition concerns the Canal de Roubaix, a short cross-border canal between the Deûle (Bauvin-Lys waterway) north of Lille and the Belgian Canal de l'Espierre, connecting with the Escaut. The waterway authority had been discreet about the fact that the lift bridges through the industrial town of Roubaix were out of order, and unlikely to be repaired in view of the virtual disappearance of commercial traffic. The canal remains navigable up to Tourcoing, but restoration prospects through Roubaix are poor.

Northern France tries very hard to attract tourism to its dense river and canal network, and the smaller waterways are invariably fascinating, but the network suffers from the insensitive treatment of key sites during construction of the high-capacity Dunkerque-Escaut link and its branch down to the Lys, and from the closure of several abandoned navigations which would be ideal for cruising, especially the Hazebrouck canals and the Canal de la Colme. Among the key locations, Saint-Omer, Aire-sur-la-Lys, Lille, Douai, Béthune, Condé-sur-Escaut and Denain are all less accessible to boats than they could have been.

Whither the Midi?

The main question mark hanging over the French waterways, after the new organisation of *Voies Navigables de France*, the system of licences and tolls to be introduced and the future high-capacity waterway link between the Rhine basin and the Mediterranean, concerns Riquet's Canal du Midi and its extension, the Canal latéral à la Garonne, forming what is variously termed the

Canaux du Midi or the Canal des Deux Mers. A combination of chronic budget shortages and the gradual deterioration of lock gates, aqueducts, embankments, spillways and other structures, many of them more than 300 years old, has produced a situation where an estimated 260 million francs needs to be spent, simply to ensure safety of the various structures and to restore the original navigable characteristics.

After two years of closure of the central section (between Toulouse and Carcassonne) due to severe drought and the increasingly heavy demands made on limited water resources for irrigation, the Canal du Midi is again open throughout in 1991, and the authorities and canalside towns must now try to win back the tourist traffic they have lost in the meantime. The French Government and the three regions concerned must also agree on a financial package to get the canal in proper working order throughout. Historians and preservationists will be delighted at least to learn that there is now very little risk of any further disfigurement of Riquet's heritage by continued upgrading of the Canal du Midi to 250-tonne barge standards.

Pontoonitis

While the smaller State-controlled waterways struggle to survive, local authorities throughout the network have been jumping on the great *tourisme fluvial* bandwagon, frenetically establishing boat moorings at every opportunity, often using subsidies from another compartment of the same State budget that cannot cope with the backlog of maintenance work. In the worst cases, this apparently laudable initiative in fact involves nothing more than throwing a couple of pontoons into the canal, sticking up a flag and hoping boats will stop, assuming of course that there are boats in the canal at all, which is not always the case.

It is extraordinary how disconnected officials and elected representatives can be from the realities of cruising and stopping to take on provisions, visit places of interest or spend the night. This is not to say that all development of dedicated boat moorings is ill advised, far from it, but simply that the ap-

A *carabarge* on the Saône. Once popular, these pontoon boats are now rarely encountered.
Hugh Potter

proach is often rather pompous, if not incoherent. In short, the partnership of waterway authorities and local councils has been good at providing hardware, but poor to hopeless at developing the tourist potential and attractiveness of the sites as such.

Wine, gastronomy and unspoilt countryside

These are minor quibbles, however, and should not distract from the overall picture, which is that of a whole network of waterways and waterside towns and villages at last awakening to their vast tourist potential, and gradually developing a combination of information, water-oriented animations and services that will make cruising through France – enjoying the fascinating diversity of French regions, their history and culture, their gastronomy and wines – all the more eventful and satisfying.

Castets-en-Dorthe locks, where navigation leaves the Canal latéral à la Garonne to enter the Garonne.
The Author

Part I
General

8500 KILOMETRES OF CRUISING WATERWAYS

France has the most extensive waterway network in Western Europe, offering the greatest variety of scenery, tourist interest and cruising conditions. Transport of bulk goods remains the most important function over about a third of the network, and continues to survive over another third, while the remainder is now maintained essentially for tourism and other functions not related to commercial navigation. The current situation and recent developments are described in the foreword. The point to be made here is that tourism is now accepted as one of the main justifications for maintaining the waterways, and that considerable development has taken place accordingly. There are thus no longer any grounds for reservations about venturing on the French waterways, whether in privately-owned or hired boats. Even the industrial waterways of northern France are much less austere in appearance than 10 or 20 years ago, when mining and heavy industry were still predominant, and harbours and attractive moorings for boats have sprung up at an astonishing rate in recent years, here as well as on all the busiest waterways: Rhine, Seine, Moselle, Saône and Rhône. In short, commercial traffic is no obstacle to safe and pleasant cruising, provided certain precautions are taken, and adapted moorings are available at regular intervals.

This having been said, it is obvious that readers without previous cruising experience (or having only cruised on the English canals, for example) would be wise to keep to the smaller waterways where commercial traffic has ceased or is very slight, and the cost of the few inevitable mistakes is not too high, especially the canals of Brittany, the rivers of Anjou, the canals in Burgundy, the river Charente, the Southwest waterways and the Canal du Midi. The pressure of traffic on the last-mentioned canal has lessened significantly in recent years, partly thanks to the development of other cruising areas, and partly on account of the difficulties mentioned in the introduction.

OFFICIAL FORMALITIES

Customs formalities for boats entering France have been greatly simplified compared to the situation a few years ago. Under the conditions for free temporary importation laid down by the customs code, foreign residents may bring a boat into France and use it for up to six months in any 12-month period without being liable for TVA (the French VAT). There is no reporting requirement, provided that there are no goods to be declared and no paying passengers on board (use of the boat is limited to co-owners and their immediate family, a condition designed to avoid disguised charters). To benefit from free importation while keeping the boat in France, it is obligatory to deposit the boat's registration documents 'in bond' at the customs office nearest to the harbour where the boat is moored or laid up, for a single period of six months in the year or for separate periods totalling six months. Otherwise, the boat must either be exported out of France or be cleared by the customs, by payment of import duty on the value of the boat.

The 'bonding' system has been replaced on the Mediterranean coast by a more convenient *titre de séjour*, a temporary resident's permit, issued free of charge by customs offices on arrival in France, and the system may be extended to all points of entry.

If on the other hand the boat or yacht, or goods carried on board are to be imported, the 'Q' flag must be flown by day, or a red light over a white light shown by night. In this case a visit to the customs office with the ship's papers and the passports of all on board should be made as early as possible, at the same time asking the customs officer to issue a *passeport de navire étranger* or otherwise to register temporary importation.

Boats with inboard engines or unpowered boats must have a certificate of registration, either full *Part 1* registration (the 'blue book') or the *Small Ships Register* papers issued by the Royal Yachting Association.

Outboard motors and boats on trailers must be covered by a triptyque or *carnet de passage en douane*, both of which can be obtained from either the AA or the RAC. Further details may be supplied by the French Tourist Office, the Royal Yachting Association, the Cruising Association, etc. (see under guides and publications). The maximum authorised dimensions of vehicle and trailer without special permission and documentation are as follows: height, no restriction; overall width, 2.50m; overall vehicle length, 11m, and overall trailer length, 11m. If trailed boats or outboard motors are placed in bond, it should be borne in mind that these may have to be renewed before returning to France to take the vessel out of bond.

For cruising the French waterways, the former *permis de circulation* is no longer required. Nor is any certificate of competence required for British boatowners (at least for craft up to 20 tonnes), a privilege which arises from the fact that no such certificate exists for inland boating in Britain. All French nationals in charge of boats of more than 10hp must be in possession of a *permis de navigation*, obtained by means of stiff practical and theoretical tests based on the waterway code (*Code Vagnon Fluvial*, published by Les Editions du Plaisancier). This requirement is supposed to be abolished for French nationals cruising on inland waterways in boats of less than 20 tonnes, but as often happens in France, pronouncement of the reform is followed by a long period of gestation during which civil servants study, at their own pace, the practical application. It is as well to remember that exemption from these tests is a privilege, and to exercise all due caution, especially on the larger waterways.

Boats that have cleared the French customs (or using the 6-month temporary importation allowance) are free to explore the French coasts and inland waterways, and can be moved from place to place in France without any further formality, subject to the new licence fees and tolls to be announced in 1991.

The formalities indicated above are a small price to pay for the freedom enjoyed while cruising through the French waterways. Occasionally, boatowners will be asked for basic details, usually only the boat's name and port of registration, by lock-keepers who are also responsible for collecting statistical information on waterway traffic.

HIRING IN FRANCE

A more convenient way of discovering France through its waterways is to hire a comfortable river cruiser, better-suited to inland navigation than most motor yachts. The number of hire bases operating on the French waterways has increased regularly in recent years, and it is now possible to plan a week's cruise virtually anywhere on the network. Only the waterways between the Seine basin and north-eastern France remain poorly represented. Listing all hire firms is a high-risk enterprise, for changes tend to occur from one season to the next, but it is thought worth while to set out all the details, for hire bases are such an important part of development of tourism on the French waterways.

Bases are listed in alphabetical order by region, except for a few relay bases operated mainly to allow clients to cruise one way only. In such cases, the one-way possibility is indicated.

There is no point in contacting the individual bases of the bigger firms for reservations, which are all centralised. These companies, which all have bases throughout France, are listed under the first heading 'Central reservation offices', together with the main UK agencies, Blakes and Hoseasons. The bases which can be booked through these agencies are identified in the regional lists by the letters (B) and (H) after the name.

Many of the individual firms listed have developed successfully, and can offer high-quality boats at reasonable prices. Generally speaking, wherever lower prices can be obtained, for a boat with the same number of berths, clients will get proportionately less for their money (older, smaller, less well equipped and less comfortable boats).

Given the very considerable choice of cruising areas, the sensible approach is to decide first of all where you want to spend your holiday, which waterway and which region appeal to you most, and then to send for the brochures of the various firms operating in the area. Study carefully the characteristics of the boats, their equipment and their internal fittings, and compare the dimensions of boats rather than just taking for granted the spaciousness apparent in the wide-angle photographs. Prices should only be compared once you are sure that the comparison is fair.

Central reservation offices

		Telephone	Fax	Agents for
Blakes Holidays	Wroxham, Norwich, NR12 8DH	0603/782141	0603/782911	Connoisseur Crown Blue Line Rive de France
Hoseasons Holidays	Sunway House, Lowestoft, NR32 3LT	0502/500555	0502/500532	Connoisseur Crown Blue Line
Crown Blue Line	BP 21, 11400 Castelnaudary	68 23 17 51	68 23 33 92	11 bases
Locaboat Plaisance	Quai du Port au Bois, 89300 Joigny	86 91 72 72	86 62 42 41	6 bases
Rive de France	172 boulevard Berthier, 75017 Paris	1/46 22 10 86	1/43 80 65 75	9 bases

Northern and eastern France

Ardennes Nautisme	1 rue de la Rochefoucauld, 08200 Sedan	24 27 05 15	base at Pont-à-Bar at junction of Meuse and C des Ardennes
Autres Horizons	53 Digue de mer, BP 35, 59941 Dunkerque	28 59 20 44	low-price cruising from base in port of Dunkerque
Base de pleine air et de loisirs des Prés du Hem	5/7 av Marc Sangnier, 59280 Armentières	20 77 43 99	on the river Lys, one of the first bases in northern France

Bouchery Plaisance	BP 384, 08106 Charleville Mézières	24 59 35 23	on the Meuse
Canal Evasion	3 rue du Port, 57930 Mittersheim	87 07 62 04	on C des Houillères de la Sarre
CCNB Lorraine Fluvial	21 rue de la Fédération, 54530 Pagny-sur-Moselle	83 81 52 48	on the Moselle between Nancy and Metz
Champagne Navigation	Route Nationale, 02190 Berry-au-Bac	23 79 95 01	Ardennes, Reims and Aisne
Chemins Nautiques d'Alsace (B)	Péniche l'Espérance, 67300 Schiltigheim	88 81 39 39	on Marne-Rhine C. near Strasbourg + relay base on Houillères de la Sarre
Connoisseur Cruisers	Port Saint-Mansuy, 54200 Toul	83 64 61 07	Marne-Rhine and Moselle
Croisières Plus	Ecluse de Cantimpré, 59400 Cambrai	20 24 55 09	canalised Escaut and St Quentin
Crown Blue Line	Pont du Canal, Hesse, 57400 Sarrebourg	87 03 61 74	Marne-Rhine canal through the Vosges to relay base south of Strasbourg
Crown Blue Line Vosges	Port de plaisance, 88240 Fontenoy-le-Château	29 30 43 98	Saône, Canal de l'Est and one-way cruises to Hesse
Meuse Nautic	1 rue de l'Eglise, 55110 Dun-sur-Meuse	29 80 94 17	Meuse (Canal de l'Est)
Nautic 80	191 rue de Verdun, 80000 Amiens	22 92 47 47	Somme
Nautipont	924 r. Bois le Prêtre, 54700 Pont-à-Mousson	83 82 40 93	Moselle
Navi Plaisance	Pont de la Somme, 80450 Camon	22 46 30 83	Somme
Navilor Plaisance	102 rue du Canal, 57820 Lutzelbourg	87 25 37 07	Marne-Rhine + one-way cruises
Navilor Plaisance	20 rue de Pont-à-Mousson, 57000 Metz	87 65 44 14	Moselle + one-way cruises
Rive de France	Port de plaisance, 67150 Krafft		Rhône-Rhine (+ one-way)
Rive de France	Port de plaisance, 57810 Lagarde	87 86 65 01	Marne-Rhine (+ one-way)

Seine basin

Marine-Oise Plaisance	Place du 14 juillet, 60880 Jaux	44 83 70 30	Oise and various circular routes
Marne Loisirs	Chemin de Halage, 77360 Vaires-sur-Marne	1/64 72 97 87	Marne and Canal de l'Ourcq
Seine et Loing Rivières	1 rue du Port de Valvins, 77210 Avon	1/60 72 74 00	base on Seine at Fontainebleau and relay base on Loire latéral

Burgundy and central France

Amicatours	Port des Poujats, 58800 La Collancelle	86 38 90 70	former Saint Line base at Nivernais summit
Aquarelle Sarl	Quai St Martin, 89000 Auxerre	86 46 96 77	Nivernais and river Yonne
Arc en ciel	BP 36, 01990 St Trivier-sur-Moignans	74 55 88 27	attractive base at St Romain-des-Iles on river Saône
Au Fil de l'Eau	Les Tilleuls, 89660 Merry-sur-Yonne	86 29 50 53	low-price cruising in Nivernais
Berry Plaisance	45360 Châtillon-sur-Loire	38 31 10 71	near Briare on Loire latéral
BIPE	Route de Paris, 89140 Pont-sur-Yonne	86 67 14 60	on the river Yonne
Briare Nautique	La Lancière, 89220 Rogny-les-Sept-Ecluses	86 74 54 98	on Canal de Briare
Burgundy Cruisers (BH)	Accolay, 89460 Cravant	86 53 54 55	base on the Nivernais
Canal Plaisance	La Marina, rue Carnot, 21500 Montbard	80 89 44 04	on Canal de Bourgogne
Les Canalous	Port de plaisance, 45250 Briare	38 31 28 98	Briare and Loire latéral
Les Canalous	Le Grand Mardiaugue, 71160 Digoin	85 53 01 63	Centre, Loire latéral, Roanne
Champvert Plaisance	Port de la Copine, BP37, 58300 Décize	86 25 00 35	on the Nivernais
Connoisseur Cruisers	30 rue des Champoulains, 89000 Auxerre	86 46 75 55	Nivernais and Yonne
Connoisseur Cruisers	03230 Gannay-sur-Loire	70 43 49 27	on the Loire latéral
Connoisseur Cruisers	Ile Sauzey, Rue Val de Saône, 70100 Gray	84 65 44 62	on the upper Saône

Connoisseur Cruisers	52 rue Pierre Curie, 89400 Migennes	86 80 08 60	C. de Bourgogne and Yonne
Croisières Eiffel-CNG Vacances	Quai au Bois, 89500 Villeneuve-sur-Yonne	86 96 55 55	on the lower river Yonne
Croisières du Saussois	21 rue des Récollets, 58000 Clamecy	86 24 41 37	Nivernais
Croizur	Rue du Port, 71500 Louhans	85 76 04 96	
Croizur	Port de Plaisance, 71350 Verdun-sur-le-Doubs	85 91 57 08	
Crown Blue Line Bourgogne	Port de Plaisance, 21170 St-Jean-de-Losne	80 29 12 86	Saône and choice of canals
Crown Blue Line Nivernais	Bassin de la Jonction, 58300 Décize	86 25 46 64	Loire latéral and Nivernais
Crown Blue Line Loire	18320 Marseilles-les-Aubigny	48 76 48 01	Loire latéral
Flot'home	Ecluse de Fleury, Biches, 58110 Châtillon-en-Bazois	86 84 02 70	Connoisseur agents with base on the Nivernais
Force 3 (B)	Bassin du Canal, 21360 Pont d'Ouche	80 33 09 91	C. de Bourgogne and relay base at Tonnerre
Lepori Marine	Port de Passavant, 70210 Demangevelle	84 92 87 28	C. de l'Est and upper Saône
Liberty Line (H)	Levée du Canal, 58340 Cercy-la-Tour	86 50 56 12	Nivernais, with second base at Coulanges for one-way cruises
Locaboat Plaisance	Quai du Port au Bois, 89300 Joigny	86 62 06 14	Yonne, Nivernais, Bourgogne, and reservations for all bases
Locaboat Plaisance	Port de plaisance, 70500 Corre	84 92 59 66	upper Saône, Canal de l'Est
Locaboat Plaisance	Port de plaisance, av J. Jaurès, 21000 Dijon	80 41 74 30	Bourgogne
Locadif	Gissey-sur-Ouche, 21410 Pont-de-Pany	80 49 04 76	Bourgogne
Loch 2000	Port de Plagny, 58000 Sermoise-sur-Loire	86 37 64 42	Loire latéral near Nevers
Loisir Nautic de France	Port de plaisance, 70170 Port-sur-Saône	84 68 17 85	upper Saône
Marine-Diesel	Chitry-les-Mines, 58800 Corbigny	86 20 14 80	Nivernais
Nouvelle Vogue (B)	39 avenue Eisenhower, 39100 Dôle	84 82 56 01	Rhône-Rhin (Doubs valley)
Pro-Aqua	89000 Auxerre	86 46 96 77	Yonne and Nivernais
Rive de France	Le Port, 89600 Saint-Florentin	86 43 44 00	Yonne and Bourgogne
Rive de France	Montbard		Bourgogne (one-way cruises)
Rive de France	9 rue St Eloi, 21270 Pontailler	80 36 16 58	
Rive de France	Port de plaisance, 21320 Pouilly-en-Auxois	80 90 74 54	Bourgogne (one-way cruises)
SLM Navigation	45250 Briare	38 31 28 73	Briare and Loire latéral
Tourisme Fluvial du Centre	Montbouy, 45230 Châtillon-Coligny	38 62 04 88	Briare
Vincelles Nautique	Rue de l'Yonne, 89290 Vincelles	86 42 34 61	Nivernais

Midi and South-West

Ancas Away (B)	Quai Général de Gaulle, 30300 Beaucaire	66 58 66 71	Rhône-Sète and Camargue
Aquitaine Navigation	47160 Buzet-sur-Baïse	53 84 72 50	Garonne latéral and Baïse
Au Fil de l'Eau	34440 Colombiers	67 37 14 23	low-price cruising on the Midi
Babou Marine	Port de St Mary, 46000 Cahors	65 30 08 99	inflatables on the Lot
Bateaux Safaraid	46330 Bouziès	65 31 26 83	light cruisers on the Lot
Bateliers du Midi (H)	11120 Port de la Robine	67 93 38 66	English-style canal boats
Camargue Plaisance	105 allée des Goélands, 34280 La Grand Motte	67 56 53 84	Rhône-Sète
Caminav	Base Fluviale, 34130 Carnon	67 68 01 90	Rhône-Sète

Connoisseur Cruisers	Quai de la Paix, 30300 Beaucaire	66 59 46 08	Rhône-Sète
Connoisseur Cruisers	7 quai d'Alsace, 11100 Narbonne	68 65 14 55	La Robine branch of the Midi
Croisières du Soleil	Homps, 11200 Lézignan	68 91 38 11	Midi
Crown Blue Line Aquitaine	Port du Canal, 47160 Damazan	53 79 77 47	near the Garonne latéral/Baïse junction
Crown Blue Line Camargue	Quai du Canal, 30800 Saint-Gilles	66 87 22 66	for Rhône-Sète, Camargue and one-way cruises to Midi
Crown Blue Line Lot	Le Moulinat, 46140 Douelle	65 20 08 79	attractive river port on the Lot
Crown Blue Line Midi	Le Grand Bassin, 11400 Castelnaudary	68 23 17 51	base on the Midi, also head office for reservations
Crown Blue Line Midi	Port-Cassafières, 34420 Portiragnes	67 90 91 70	at eastern end of Midi
DNP France	20 quai du Canal, 30800 Saint-Gilles	66 87 27 74	Rhône-Sète
Europe Yachting	Poilhes, 34310 Capestang	67 93 39 32	on the long pound of the Midi
Locaboat Plaisance	Port de Plaisance, Gare du Pin, 47000 Agen	53 66 00 74	Garonne latéral
Locaboat Plaisance	Homps, 11200 Lézignan	68 91 38 08	in wine country on the Midi
Locaboat Plaisance	Cévenne de Caïx, 46140 Luzech	65 30 71 11	at downstream end of the Lot
Midi Marine	Route de Nissan, 34310 Poilhes	67 93 39 32	on the long pound of the Midi
Rive de France	Port de plaisance, 34440 Colombiers Le Ségala	67 37 14 60	on the long pound of the Midi relay base
Rive de France	Ecluse 44, 47430 Le Mas d'Agenais	53 20 97 17	Garonne latéral
Saintonge Rivières	Canal du Midi, 11150 Bram	68 76 56 18	Midi

Anjou rivers, Charente and Sèvre

Anjou Croisières	Quai des Carmes, 49000 Angers	41 87 93 50	Mayenne
Anjou Plaisance	Route de l'Ecluse, 49220 Grez Neuville	41 95 68 95	Mayenne
Charente Croisières	Le Port, 17610 Chaniers	46 91 04 81	Charente
Charente Plaisance	1 place du Solenon, 16100 Cognac	45 82 79 71	Charente
Compagnie Angevine de Tourisme Fluvial	10 boulevard Henri Arnault, 49000 Angers	41 87 78 11	Mayenne
Espace Europe Loisirs	Quai Pierre de Coubertin, 53200 Château-Gontier	43 70 34 41	Mayenne
Féerives	Route de Grez-Neuville, 49220 Chenillé-Changé	41 95 64 78	Mayenne
Fluvia-Laval	Quai Paul Boudet, 53000 Laval	43 53 66 36	Mayenne
France Anjou Navigation	Quai National, 72300 Sablé-sur-Sarthe	43 95 14 42	Sarthe
France Mayenne Fluviale	53630 Daon	43 70 13 94	Mayenne
Holiday Charente (B)	Les Gabariers, 16120 Saint Simeux	45 62 56 98	Charente
Intercroisières (B)	Pont de Sireuil, 16440 Sireuil	45 90 58 18	Charente
Maine Anjou Rivières (B)	Le Moulin, 49220 Chenillé-Changé	41 95 10 83	Mayenne and Sarthe, with other bases at Châteauneuf, Angers and Mayenne
Mayenne Navigation (H)	Port Rhingeard, 53260 Entrammes	43 98 06 71	Mayenne, and secondary base at Noyen-sur-Sarthe
Jacques Renaud	ZI du Port, 17230 Marans	46 01 17 16	Sèvre Niortaise
SAGEM	Port l'Houmeau, 16730 Fléac	45 38 43 77	upstream limit of Charente
Saintonge Rivières	Base fluviale, 17350 Saint-Savinien	46 32 00 16	downstream end of Charente
Sarthe Evasion	116 quai Amiral Lalande, 72000 Le Mans	43 23 21 31	upstream limit of Sarthe

Brittany

Air et Soleil Mutualité	Quai St Georges, 44390 Nort-sur-Erdre	40 29 56 29	for Erdre and Nantes-Brest C.
Argoat Nautic	35830 Betton	99 55 70 36	C. d'Ille-et-Rance near Rennes
Argoat Plaisance	Port de plaisance, 29119 Châteauneuf-du-Faou	98 81 72 11	on river Aulne (isolated section of Nantes-Brest C.)
Aulne Loisirs	29150 Châteaulin	99 86 30 11	on the tidal river Aulne
Bretagne Fluviale (B)	Quai de l'Erdre, 44240 La Chapelle-sur-Erdre	40 77 79 51	for Erdre and Nantes-Brest C.
Bretagne Plaisance	Quai Jean-Bart, 35600 Redon	99 72 15 80	at the Brittany cross-roads
Chemins Nautiques Bretons	Quai Lyvet, 22690 La Vicomte-sur-Rance	96 83 28 71	on the Rance
Crown Blue Line Brittany	Port de Guipry, 35480 Messac	99 34 60 11	river Vilaine, and one-way cruises to base at Dinan
Comptoir Nautique Redonnais	2 quai Surcouf, 35600 Redon	99 71 46 03	at the Brittany cross-roads
Finistère Canal	Pont Coblant, 29190 Pleyben	98 73 35 20	on isolated Nantes-Brest C.
Leray Loisirs	14 rue de Caradec, 56120 Josselin	97 75 60 98	Nantes-Brest
Rohan Plaisance (H)	Ecluse de Rohan, 56580 Rohan	97 38 98 66	Nantes-Brest (for lockaholics), and relay base at Saint-Grégoire on the Vilaine

Canal du Nivernais lock keeper
on the Sardy flight near the
summit level.
Hugh Potter

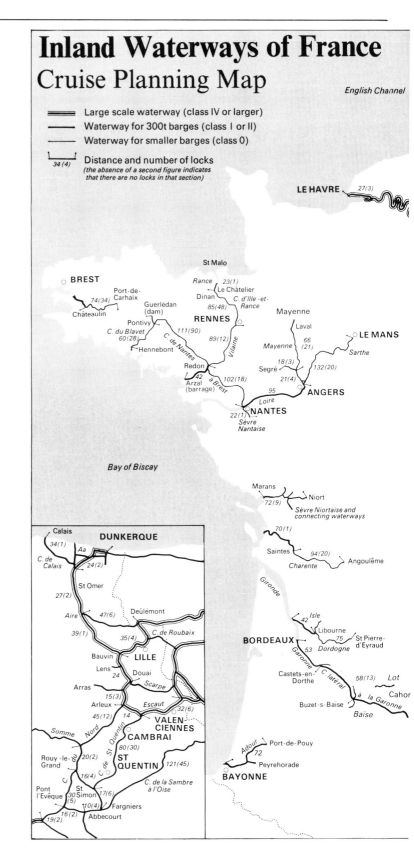

Inland Waterways of France
Cruise Planning Map

English Channel

▬▬▬▬ Large scale waterway (class IV or larger)
───── Waterway for 300t barges (class I or II)
───── Waterway for smaller barges (class 0)

⌐34 (4)⌐ Distance and number of locks
(the absence of a second figure indicates that there are no locks in that section)

LE HAVRE 27(3)

St Malo

○ BREST

Port-de-Carhaix 74(34)
Châteaulin

Rance 23(1)
Le Châtelier
Dinan
C. d'Ille-et-Rance
85(48)

Guerlédan (dam)

Pontivy
C. du Blavet 60(28)
Hennebont

RENNES

Mayenne
Laval

○ LE MANS

111(90)
89(12)

Vilaine

Mayenne 66 (21)
Segré 18(3)

Sarthe

Redon
42
Arzal (barrage)
102(18)

à Brest

21(4) 132(20)
95
Loire ANGERS

22(1)
Sèvre Nantaise
NANTES

Bay of Biscay

Marans
72(9)
Niort
Sèvre Niortaise and connecting waterways

70(1)

Saintes 94(20)
Charente Angoulême

Gironde

Isle 42
Libourne
75 St Pierre-d'Eyraud

BORDEAUX
53 Dordogne
Garonne
Castets-en-Dorthe
C. latéral
58(13) Lot
à la Garonne Cahors
Buzet-s-Baïse
Baïse

Adour Port-de-Pouy
72
Peyrehorade

○ BAYONNE

Calais
34(1) Aa
DUNKERQUE
C. de Calais
27(2)
24(2)
St Omer

Aire 47(6)
39(1)
Deûlémont
C. de Roubaix
35(4)

Bauvin LILLE
Lens Douai
24
Arras
Scarpe
15(3)
Arleux Escaut
45(12) 14
32(6)
VALENCIENNES
Somme Nord CAMBRAI
80(30)
Rouy-le-Grand 20(2) C. de St Quentin
16(4) ST QUENTIN 121(45)
Pont l'Evêque St Simon 17(6)
30(5) C. de la Sambre à l'Oise
16(2) 10(4) Fargniers
19(2) Abbecourt

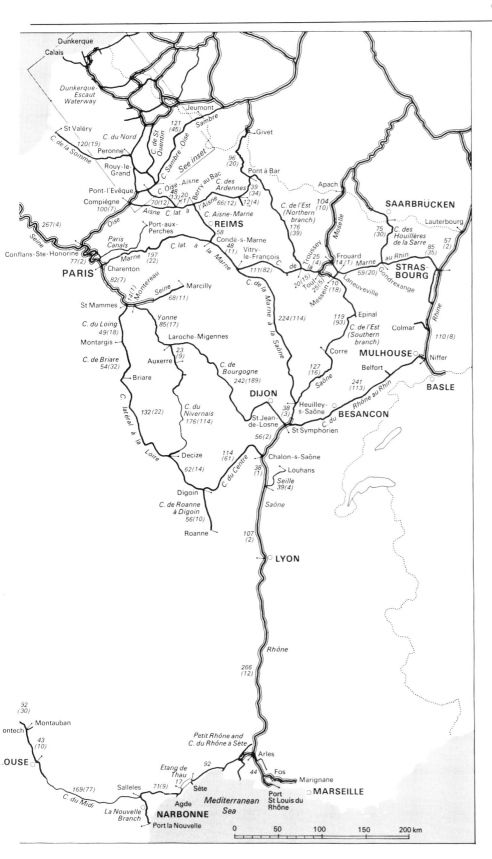

Dunkerque
Calais

Dunkerque-
Escaut
Waterway

Jeumont

St Valéry
C. du Nord
120(19)
C. de la Somme
Peronne
Rouy-le-
Grand
Pont-l'Evêque
Compiègne
100(7)

121
(45)
Sambre
Givet

96
(20)
Pont à Bar
Apach

C. de St
Quentin
C. Sambre. Oise
See inset

C. Oise - Aisne
48
(13)
70(12)
20
(1)
66(12)
39
(34)
72(4)

C. des
Ardennes
Berry au Bac
C. de l'Est
(Northern
branch)
176
(39)

SAARBRÜCKEN

104
(10)

Lauterbourg

Aisne
C. lat à
l'Aisne
C. Aisne-Marne

REIMS
58
Condé-s-Marne
Vitry-
le-François
48
(11)

Moselle

75
(30)
C. des
Houillères
de la Sarre

85
(35)
57
(2)

267(4)
Seine
Conflans-Ste-Honorine
77(2)

PARIS

Paris
Canals
Port-aux-
Perches
Charenton
82(7)

C. lat. à la Marne
Marne
197
(22)
Montereau
Marcilly
Seine
68(11)

111(82)
C. de la Marne à la Saône

Troussey
25
(4)
20(15)
Toul
25(5)
Messein
10
(18)

Frouard
14(1)
Marne
au Rhin
59(20)
Gondrexange
Laneuveville

STRAS-
BOURG

Rhin

St Mammes
C. du Loing
49(18)
Montargis
Yonne
85(17)
Laroche-Migennes

C. de Briare
54(32)
23
(9)
Auxerre
Briare

224(114)

119
(93)
Epinal
C. de l'Est
(Southern
branch)
Corre
Colmar
110(8)

MULHOUSE
Niffer

C. latéral à la Loire
132(22)
C. du
Nivernais
176(114)

C. de
Bourgogne
242(189)

DIJON

127
(16)
Saône
241
(113)
Belfort

Rhône au Rhin

BASLE

38
(3)
Heuilley-
s-Saône
St Jean-
de-Losne
St Symphorien
C. du
BESANCON

Decize
114
(61)
62(14)
C. du Centre
56(2)
Chalon-s-Saône
38
(1)
Louhans
Seille
39(4)

Digoin
C. de Roanne
à Digoin
56(10)
Saône

Roanne
107
(2)

LYON

Rhône

266
(12)

92
(30)
Montauban
ontech
43
(10)
OUSE

Petit Rhône and
C. du Rhône à Sète
Arles
92
44
Fos
Marignane

Etang de
Thau
17
Sète
MARSEILLE

169(77)
Salleles
71(9)
Agde
C. du Midi
La Nouvelle
Branch
NARBONNE
Port la Nouvelle

Mediterranean
Sea

Port
St Louis du
Rhône

0   50   100   150   200 km

GETTING AFLOAT

Owners of trailed craft will find it much easier than in the past to 'get afloat' on the French waterways. Facilities for boats have mushroomed, and all *ports de plaisance*, as well as many of the other facilities to which the French have given sophisticated names – *haltes*, *relais* and *bases* – are equipped with a slip-way or crane suitable for most trailed boats. Hire firms may also be prepared to allow private boatowners to make use of their facilities, except at week-ends when they are busy turning round their own boats. Generally speaking, boat harbours with slipways are encountered much more frequently on river navigations than on canals, but the situation is improving year by year. Most facilities are indicated in the distance tables, but reference may also be made to the individual waterway guides listed under 'Guides and publications'.

NAVIGABLE DIMENSIONS

From the point of view of navigable dimensions, the waterways of France may roughly be divided into three categories, which are clearly differentiated on the cruise planning map.

Conflans-Ste-Honorine. The annual *Pardon de la Batellerie*. *Hugh Potter*

Large-scale waterways (European Class IV or larger)

These are essentially the Seine and Oise, the Dunkerque–Escaut waterway and lower Escaut, the Moselle, the Rhine, the Rhône and the lower Saône, as well as the maritime navigations in the Loire and Gironde estuaries. Navigable dimensions obviously present no constraint for boats and barges on these waterways, which offer lock dimensions of at least 144m by 12m, a minimum navigable draught of 2.50m and a minimum air draught of 4.50m (generally much more).

'Freycinet' waterways, plus Canal du Nord and lower Yonne (Classes I and II)

Most of the waterways come into this category, offering standard dimensions established in 1879 by the Minister of Public Works Freycinet. Here too, the dimensions are ample for most boats, with minimum lock dimensions of 38.50m by 5.10m, minimum navigable draught of 1.80m and a minimum air draught of 3.40m (generally 3.50m).

Smaller waterways, used by boats only (Class 0)

Here dimensions are far more critical, especially for owners of barges or deep-keeled yachts. A glance at the following table of maximum authorised dimensions in metres will show whether or not the proposed itinerary is feasible.

Route	Length	Beam	Draught	Air draught
1. English Channel to Atlantic	25.00	4.60	1.40	2.40
2. Canal de Nantes à Brest	26.50	4.60	1.40[1]	2.40
3. Rivers of Anjou (Mayenne, Oudon, Sarthe)	30.85	5.15	1.40	3.40[2]
4. Sèvre Niortaise	31.50	5.10	1.20[3]	2.20
5. Charente	34.00	6.30	1.00	3.55
6. Canal du Midi (central section)	30.00	5.50	1.60	3.00
7. Lot	30.00	5.00	1.00	4.40
8. Baïse (upstream of Lavardac)	31.00	4.30	1.20	5.50
9. Seille	30.40	5.20	1.50	3.90
10. Canal du Nivernais	30.15	5.10	1.20	3.00
11. Canal de l'Ourcq (Paris canals)	58.80	3.20	0.80	2.40

[1] Reduced to 1.20m on the western section from Châteaulin to Port-de-Carhaix
[2] Reduced to 2.80m above Laval on the Mayenne
[3] Less during periods of drought, especially on the connecting waterways.

RULES OF THE ROAD

The rules of the road are relatively easy to comply with, and the ability to handle one's boat precisely and confidently is just as important as theoretical knowledge of the waterway code. The main rules to be observed by boaters are summarised in the following paragraphs.

Priority to commercial traffic and other barges

Smaller boats must at all times leave room for barges to proceed on their course and to manoeuvre. Barges must never be forced by small boats to steer clear. Skippers of boats must constantly bear in mind this priority to working boats, including trip boats. They must also steer well clear of all craft under way, dredgers and other maintenance vessels, and any work sites on the waterways.

Meeting other craft (*croisement*)

Boats may pass each other only when the channel is wide enough, taking into account local circumstances and other traffic movements. Boats whose respective courses are such that there is no risk of collision must not alter their course or their speed in a manner likely to cause a risk of collision. Boats meeting must normally keep to the right (passing port to port). There is an exception to this rule (more important for barges than for small boats) on wider river navigations, where it is normal practice for boats heading upstream to keep to the inside of the channel in bends to take advantage of the slacker water, while boats heading downstream keep to the middle of the channel. This practice is covered by the international 'blue flag' rule, under which the upstream-bound barge wishing to keep to the left makes its intention clear by displaying a blue flag or panel on the right-hand side of the wheelhouse (or by night, a flashing white light). The barge heading downstream acknowledges by displaying its blue flag or flashing white light, and adopts the corresponding course. If the skipper of the first barge fears his intention has not been understood, he sounds two short blasts (to pass on the left), and this signal must be acknowledged. (Similarly, one short blast confirms the intention to pass normally on the right, and must be acknowledged.) Boats are not bound to observe this rule, but being aware of it makes it that much easier to comply with the number one rule of priority to commercial craft.

On French river navigations, there are certain sections where all craft are forced by the conventional signs B2(a), B3(a) or B4(a) to pass on the left (starboard to starboard). Here too, the blue flag is normally displayed. At points where the prescribed course changes sides (sign B4) it is the boat heading downstream which has priority, the upstream-bound boat slowing down or stopping as necessary. Where there is insufficient width for two barges to pass abreast, the prohibition sign A4 is often displayed. On encountering this sign, a boat must not proceed until the skipper has satisfied himself that the channel in the restricted section is not occupied. (Barge skippers communicate by radio at such locations; boaters should proceed cautiously, sounding a long blast on their horn as appropriate.) Generally speaking, it is the boat heading downstream which has priority over that heading upstream. On some canals, the direction conventionally considered to be downstream is 'up' towards the summit level, at least on one side of the summit. In such cases, and wherever there might be ambiguity (as on summit levels themselves), the distance tables indicate which direction is conventionally 'downstream'.

Overtaking (*dépassement* or *trématage*)

Overtaking normally takes place on the left. Only on wide river navigations may overtaking on the right be envisaged, and the skipper of the overtaking boat must strictly indicate his intention by displaying a blue flag at the bow. Boaters must not accelerate momentarily for the exclusive purpose of passing another boat or barge, and should bear in mind that it is forbidden to overtake (a) whenever it is not certain that the manoeuvre can be effected safely, (b) within 500m from a lock and (c) wherever the prohibition sign A2 is displayed. Generally speaking, never try to overtake a barge on the 'Freycinet' canals unless invited to do so by the barge skipper, since this can be a dangerous manoeuvre. If no such invitation is forthcoming, and the boat skipper is certain that there is time to get far enough ahead of the barge before the next lock is reached not to cause any delay (in practice, this means that the

NAVIGATION SIGNS

The signs most commonly encountered are given here.

Follow direction indicated

Passage forbidden

Stop

Sound horn

Speed limit (km/h)

Attention—danger

Restricted width

Restricted headroom

Channel is 50m from bank

Overtaking forbidden

Traffic one-way only—no meeting or overtaking

Change to left-hand side

No mooring

It is forbidden to cause wash (reduce speed)

Do not pass   Pass this side

(signs on dredgers, etc)

End of prohibition, obligation or restriction

Stop

Proceed

On river navigations

Bridge arch navigable in both directions

Bridge arch navigable in this direction only

Keep within these limits

next lock must be at least 2 or 3 kilometres away), he may signal his intention to overtake by sounding one long blast and two short (to overtake normally on the left). It is then permitted to overtake unless the barge skipper sounds one short blast, meaning that he would prefer to be overtaken on the right, or five short blasts, meaning that he considers it unsafe or inappropriate to be overtaken at this point. However, only experienced navigators with loud horns should indulge in such dialogue; it is simpler, especially on a heavily-locked canal, to moor when the opportunity arises and let the barge get well ahead.

Turning (*virement*)

When a boat wishes to turn to head in the opposite direction, notice of the intention is to be given by one prolonged blast on the horn, followed by one short blast if swinging to the right and two short blasts if swinging to the left.

Navigation signs

The most common navigation signs are shown on the page opposite.

SPEED LIMITS

The special regulations for each waterway (*règlement particulier de police de la navigation intérieure*) lay down speed limits, and the owner of any boat exceeding the authorised limit renders himself liable to prosecution. Throughout the smaller canal network, the limit is 6km/h (3.7 miles/hour) for barges and pleasure boats displacing more than 20 tonnes, reduced to 4km/h for the passage of movable bridges and navigation at night (where allowed). The limit is eased to 8km/h and in some cases 10km/h for boats of less than 20 tonnes. One of the uses of the tables, with distances precise to within 100m, is to allow speed to be checked. In practice, however, speed in the smaller canals should constantly be adapted to local conditions, the basic rule being to ease off whenever the boat causes wash to break on the banks, as well as when passing moored boats and anglers, thus avoiding damage in the first case and unpleasantness in the second.

On canalised rivers, higher speeds are authorised in river sections than in lock-cuts or canal sections. For example, the limits are respectively 15km/h and 6km/h on the Marne, on the Saône above Auxonne and on the Yonne, while the maximum on the smaller river navigations is 10km/h.

On the large-scale waterways, much higher limits are applied, generally 15km/h in canals or lock-cuts and up to 35km/h in open river sections. Speeds higher still, up to 60km/h, are allowed on specified short reaches for the practice of water-skiing and small power boating only. It must be underlined that local restrictions may be applied on any waterway, and indicated by the conventional speed limit sign shown in the section on navigation signs.

LOCKS

Different recommendations must be given for negotiation of locks according to the four main types of lock encountered on the network.

Large-scale waterways

The big locks on these waterways (as defined under navigable dimensions) are all controlled by lockkeepers, and the automatic lock filling or emptying sequences (and corresponding light displays for navigators) are subordinated to the lock-keepers' decisions, based on the observed or announced traffic situation. A boat navigating singly may thus be kept waiting for 20 minutes

Lock keeper's cottage on the
Canal de Bourgogne.
Hugh Potter

or even longer if the lock is ready for a barge announced from the other
direction. This is allowed for by the regulations, so do not be surprised if the
double red light display persists for that time. In case of doubt, moor at one
of the dolphins providing access to the bank and approach the lock-keeper to
announce your arrival. A single red or red and green lights side by side mean
that the lock is being prepared for you. Wait until the double green light is
displayed before entering the lock. If there are barges or other craft queuing
at the lock, take your place in the queue, but in any event when the double
green light shows, allow all barges to enter the lock first. When traffic is
heavy, the lock-keeper will generally wave or use a loud-hailer to call boats
into the spaces remaining in the lock chamber. Avoid coming close to a
barge's stern until she has stopped in the chamber, in case there is an un-
expected last-minute use of reverse at high revs causing pronounced tur-
bulence for some distance behind the prop. The deepest locks have floating
bollards. Otherwise, a certain amount of juggling with the bow and stern
lines may be required, possibly using the rungs of a ladder between two sets
of bollards; it is often more convenient to come alongside a barge (with the
skipper's permission) and make fast to her bollards.

Canal du Centre. Lock control
ropes.
Derek Bowskill

Typical French waterways
sign, indicating that the lock
ahead is automatic.
Hugh Potter

Automated locks on smaller waterways

To reduce operating costs on the smaller canals and canalised rivers (for example, the Canal latéral à la Garonne, the Canal du Centre, the Canal de la Marne au Rhin and the upper Saône), a large number of locks have been equipped for fully automated or semi-automatic operation. These locks are equipped with lights, with the same meanings as above: red = wait, red plus green = lock in preparation and green = proceed into lock. A system of advanced detection registers the boat's arrival some distance before the lock, and a flashing orange light means that the boat has been detected. This system may itself be automatic (radar) or may involve turning a pole suspended above the water. When the green light is displayed, proceed slowly into the lock. The more recently equipped locks have a chamber entry/exit detector, which is either a horizontal pole to be pushed forwards by your boat for at least 5 seconds, or a photoelectric sensor. Once the boat is safely moored in the chamber, pull on the blue cord situated on the edge of the lock, to start the automatic lock filling or emptying sequence. The red cord may be pulled to stop the sequence in a case of emergency only. At the end of the cycle, the gates open automatically. It is important to clear the chamber promptly, actuating the chamber entry/exit detector if there is one. It should be noted that a group of boats locking together should pass the radar detector in close file, and that only the last boat must actuate the chamber entry/exit detector.

Locks operated by lock-keepers

Most locks on the 'Freycinet' network are still operated by lock-keepers. On approaching a lock it is usual to warn the lock-keeper by giving a single prolonged blast on the horn. This is obviously not necessary if other traffic is moored up waiting to lock through. In any event, it is advisable to make a complete stop at a distance of not less than 50m from the lock, to wait until the lock-keeper signals permission to enter. While waiting, if it is preferred not to moor up to the bank, care should be taken not to obstruct the passage of any boat which may emerge from the lock when the gates are opened. On entering the lock (at low speed), arrange for one of the crew to land on the side opposite the lock-keeper, to attend to the lines and to assist in working the lock (closing one of the gates when the boat has entered the lock, possibly working the gate paddles and opening the gate on the same side when the lock is ready). Some of the older locks on the Seine and Yonne have sloping sides, requiring particular caution, especially when descending. Be ready to bear off with boat-hooks, preferably one forward and one aft.

A recent development which is changing the practical arrangements for pass locks on considerable lengths of canal is the complete reorganisation of waterway personnel, the numbers of permanently-posted lock-keepers being drastically reduced (though natural wastage or transfers to maintenance staff). Locks on designated sections are thus attended by mobile teams, which follow boats through successive locks, in some cases only two but perhaps as many as 20. This makes the boater a little less free to move as he pleases, for the teams' movements obviously have to be programmed, and a spontaneous decision to stop between two locks will create confusion and perhaps even delay commercial traffic. Boaters are thus requested to cooperate by giving reasonable notice of their movements and stops.

Finally, it is worth noting that tipping the lock-keepers is not normal practice. Lock-keepers are State employees and are paid a fair salary for their job. On the other hand, they often do more than is strictly required of them, and in such cases the navigator should use his discretion and imagination in judging the best way of showing appreciation. In some cases a few francs may be accepted, for example when water is supplied from the lock-keeper's private tap.

Unmanned locks on the smaller waterways

'Do-it-yourself' lock operation has been instituted on a number of waterways that are used only by tourist traffic. This is the case on the Canal de Bourgogne, the western section of Canal de Nantes à Brest, the Charente, the Seille and the Lot, for example. In all cases the lock operating gear is already installed, and a leaflet of instructions on lock operation is issued to navigators.

HOURS OF NAVIGATION

It is as well when planning a cruise to realise that for all practical purposes there is no navigation after dark or, during the lighter months of the year, after 1930. Locks are generally open between 0630 and 1930 in high summer,

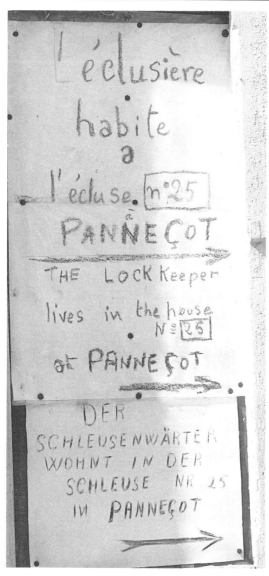

Left:
Lock side directions!
Hugh Potter

Above right:
Ecluse No. 1 at Berry-au-Bac
on the Canal de l'Aisne à la
Marne.
Hugh Potter

Bottom right:
Péniche owners at Conflans
Ste-Honorine.
Hugh Potter

and the working hours progressively shorten as the nights close in. While it is possible to run between locks during the dark hours (the proper navigation lights being shown and the regulation reduction in speed being observed), there is little advantage for boats in doing so, except in an emergency.

TIME OF YEAR

Although the French show an unusual obstinacy in taking their holidays in July and August, the season suitable for pleasure cruising is much longer, extending from April to October. The weather in France, being of the continental type, tends to be more settled than that of the British Isles, and long periods of high temperature are not infrequent in the summer. Before about the end of April, cold weather and night frosts may occur. Moreover, it is always colder on the water than on the land and, owing to the higher humidity, it feels colder apart from the probability of the boat not having really adequate heating arrangements. The weather is often fine in September and October, when the autumn colours make the scenery particularly beautiful. In the late autumn and winter, the intrepid navigator must be prepared for floods (November to March) and also for icing (December to February); for it must be remembered that some of the canals rise to a considerable height above sea level, and with the increase in altitude the fall in temperature is accentuated. Such severe conditions do not usually extend beyond the month of March.

PLANNING A CRUISE

This map is designed to give the maximum information for planning a cruise, notably distances and numbers of locks between junctions and waterway categories (see under 'Navigable dimensions'), in the minimum space. Although the print is necessarily rather small, it is thought that this map will be more convenient to use than a larger-scale map which would have to be unfolded. Several such maps exist, notably Imray's *Map of the Inland Waterways of France, Belgium and the Netherlands* (see under 'Guides and publications'). The following through routes are commonly used:

Calais to Paris via Canal de Saint-Quentin, 470km, 60 locks

This route carries heavy traffic, but presents much of the interest, notably the tunnels on the summit level of the Canal de Saint-Quentin, where boats have no choice but to be towed through. Between the industrial towns the countryside is often pleasant, especially in the Escaut valley above Cambrai and in the lower reaches of the Oise.

Calais to Paris via Canal du Nord, 425km, 37 locks

This alternative is recommended for navigators in a hurry, for the Canal du Nord was built specifically to provide a shorter route from northern France to the Paris region, and to relieve saturation on the Canal de Saint-Quentin. On the other hand, this route is less attractive in terms of scenery and tourist interest than the Saint-Quentin route.

Calais to Lyon via Saint-Quentin and Reims, 897km, 218 locks

This is the most direct route from Calais to Lyon. It joins the Marne route from Paris at Condé-sur-Marne. For those who take the short Channel crossing and who do not wish to visit Paris, this is a useful alternative.

Paris to Lyon via Bourgogne, 629km, 219 locks

This is the shortest of the three main routes, but also the slowest on account of the large number of locks. On the other hand, it is little used by commercial traffic, so no delays at locks need be anticipated, and the Canal de Bourgogne passes through some very beautiful country.

Paris to Lyon via Bourbonnais (Loire), 643km, 157 locks

This is only slightly longer than the Burgundy route, but has much fewer locks. It passes through unspectacular agricultural countryside, with some industrialised sections, notably in the mining region of Montceau-les-Mines. This route is used by most of the barges on hauls between the Seine and Saône basins. There may occasionally be delays at locks.

Paris to Lyon via Nivernais, 706km, 196 locks

This alternative route combines parts of the Bourgogne and Bourbonnais routes, linked by the Canal du Nivernais. This is the slowest route, but it is strongly recommended for navigators with time to spare, for the Nivernais is one of the most remote and attractive waterways in France.

Paris to Lyon via Marne, 713km, 155 locks
This is the longest route, but that with the least number of locks. In practice, it will take only slightly longer to cover than the Bourbonnais route, while the scenery is much more attractive, both on the river Marne and on the Canal de la Marne à la Saône. The level of traffic is slightly higher than on the Bourbonnais route.

Givet to Lyon via Canal de l'Est, 804km, 193 locks
This is the direct route to the south for navigators from the Netherlands and Belgium who enter the French waterway network from the Belgian Meuse at Givet.

Apach to Lyon via Moselle and Canal de l'Est, 638km, 133 locks
This route is used by many German boatowners, who avoid the difficult navigation conditions in the Rhine gorges by turning up the Moselle to enter the French waterways at Apach.

Strasbourg to Lyon via Canal du Rhône au Rhin, 552km, 126 locks
This is the route to the Mediterranean for boatowners who have braved the dangers of the Rhine to reach Strasbourg. For much of its length, the Canal du Rhône au Rhin follows the course of the river Doubs, which can be difficult in times of flood, but which offers spectacular scenery.

Lyon to Mediterranean (Port-Saint-Louis-du-Rhône), 310km, 12 locks
This route continues the six preceding routes, running from Lyon to the Mediterranean (Gulf of Fos) at Port-Saint-Louis-du-Rhône. Navigable conditions are much easier following completion of all the development schemes on the Rhône, and it is no longer necessary to take on a pilot (use the *Guide du Rhône* indicated under 'Guides and publications'). This route also gives access to the Canal du Rhône à Sète and Canal du Midi by turning into the Petit Rhone a short distance above Arles.

Paris to Strasbourg, 564km, 190 locks
This is the direct route from Paris to the Rhine, which is reached at Strasbourg. The Marne is attractive, as is the Canal de la Marne au Rhin where it crosses the Vosges. Elsewhere the scenery is less impressive, and there is much industrial activity. This is a busy route, and some delays at locks may be expected.

English Channel (Saint-Malo) to Atlantic via Vilaine, 239km, 61 locks
For boats drawing little more than 1.00m, this is a useful short cut through Brittany to the west coast of France, avoiding the long open sea passage and strong tides round the iron-bound coast of Ushant. At Redon the Vilaine is crossed by the Canal de Nantes à Brest, which offers two alternative routes to the Atlantic, (a) via Nantes and the Loire estuary (total route length 344km, 78 locks), (b) via Pontivy and the Canal du Blavet (total route length 370km, 178 locks).

Bordeaux to Sète via Canal du Midi, 503km, 139 locks
This route joins the Atlantic Ocean to the Mediterranean Sea, and is formed east of Toulouse by the famous Canal du Midi, the tercentenary of which was celebrated in 1981. This has become the most popular cruising waterway in France, the climate no doubt being a significant factor, and delays at locks are to be expected during the summer season.

Note In calculating route lengths, it should be borne in mind that Paris, denoted here by the junction with the Canal Saint-Martin which has a large new marina just beyond the entrance lock from the Seine, is 72km upstream of the Oise confluence at Conflans-Sainte-Honorine and 5km downstream of the Marne confluence at Charenton.

GUIDES AND PUBLICATIONS

Much of the basic data for the distance tables was taken from the *Guide de la Navigation Intérieure*, a comprehensive two-volume guide published by Berger-Levrault in Paris. Unfortunately, this guide is no longer available, the last edition having been printed in 1965. The *Voies Navigables de France (VNF)* publishes annually a supposedly more attractive but in practice less useful *Annuaire du Tourisme Fluvial*, which gives distances and indicates tourist sites and curiosities, but the relatively cheap publication (90F in 1991) is no substitute for the old Berger-Levrault.

Several publications in Britain usefully complete the information provided in the present work. The titles listed here give a wealth of practical advice based on the authors' individual experience.

A general map of the waterways of France and the more important waterways of Belgium and the Netherlands, scale 1:1,500,000, is published by Imray, Laurie, Norie & Wilson. This is useful for cruise planning and for the comprehensive view it gives of the main waterways in the three countries. In France, equivalent maps are published by the two specialised firms indicated below. Guides Vagnons are available from Imray, Laurie, Norie and Wilson Ltd, Wych House, The Broadway, St Ives, Huntingdon PE17 4BT ☎ 0480 62114 *Fax* 0480 496109.

Other maps which should be acquired for the ship's library are the well-known Michelin series at scale 1:200,000. These maps, reasonably priced, up-to-date and widely available, are useful for details of the country through which the selected route passes; however, it is also possible to obtain in Britain the 1:100,000 series of topographical maps produced by the French equivalent of the Ordnance Survey, the Institut Géographique National (IGN), and these are far more informative. They clearly show the waterways and locks, as well as contours (useful if not indispensable when planning cycle excursions to nearby points of interest), wooded areas, villages with population to the nearest hundred, etc.

It is strongly recommended to have on board the individual waterway guides for the planned itinerary, bearing in mind that such guides are now available for most waterways. The titles produced by the two main publishers are as follows:

Guides Vagnon, Les Editions du Plaisancier (BP 27, 69641 Caluire Cedex, France)

No.1 *Mini Atlas et Carte de France des Voies Navigables* (1:1,175,000)
No.2 *Doubs et Canal du Rhône au Rhin* (1:20,000 and 1:50,000)
No.3 *Canal de Bourgogne* (1:100,000)
No.5 *Rhône, de Lyon à la mer* (1:20,000)
No.6 *Saône et Seille* (1:25,000)
No.7 *Canaux du Midi et Canal du Rhône à Sète* (1:100,000)
No.8 *Meuse et Canal de l'Est, de Maastricht à Corre* (1:100,000)
No.10 *Canaux Bretons et Loire* (1:100,000)

Navicarte series, Grafocarte (64 rue des Meuniers, 92220 Bagneux)

No.21 *Cartes de France, itinéraires fluviaux* (1:1,500,000)
No.1 *La Seine aval: de Paris à la mer par le Canal de Tancarville* (1:50,000–1:15,000)
No.2 *La Seine amont: de Paris à Marcilly-sur-Seine* (1:25,000)
No.3 *La Marne: de Paris à Vitry-le-François* (1:50,000–1:25,000)
No.4 *L'Yonne: d'Auxerre à Montereau* (1:25,000)
No.5 *Canal de Bourgogne: de Laroche à Saint-Jean-de-Losne* (1:50,000)

No.6   *Canaux du Centre: de Saint-Mammès à Chalon-sur-Saône, Roanne-Digoin* (1:50,000)
No.7   *Canal du Nivernais: de Decize à Auxerre* (1:50,000)
No.8   *Champagne-Ardennes: de Namur à la Bourgogne* (1:50,000)
No.10   *La Saône: de Corre à Lyon* (1:25,000)
No.11   *Canal du Midi: de l'Atlantique à la Méditerrannée* (1:50,000)
No.12   *Bretagne: de Saint-Malo à Arzal, de Lorient à Nantes* (1:50,000)
No.13   *Pays de la Loire: Bassin de la Maine, la Loire, l'Erdre* (1:50,000–1:25,000)
No.14   *Nord-Pas-de-Calais: voies navigables* (1:50,000)
No.16   *Le Rhône: de Lyon à la Méditeranée*
No.17   *Canal de la Marne au Rhin: de Vitry-le-François à Strasbourg* (1:50,000)
No.18   *Atlas de Bourgogne: Yonne, Nivernais, Bourgogne* (1:50,000–1:25 000)
No.24   *Picardie: rivières et canaux* (1:50,000–1:25,000)
No.25   *La Charente: de l'Océan à Angoulême* (1:25,000)
No.26   *Canal de l'Est: de Liège à Corre* (1:50,000)
No.27   *Le Lot: de Luzech à Saint-Cirq-Lapopie* (1:16,000)
No.41   *Paris-Bourgogne* (regional map at 1:350,000)

All the above guides have English (most of them German, and some Dutch) texts alongside the French. They are available from specialised bookshops. The ANWB publish a *Map of Belgium and northwest France* (1:300,000). Available from Imray.

The Touring Club de France at 178 Piccadilly, London WlV 0AL, ☎ 071-491 7622 issues a useful pamphlet entitled *Yachting in French Waters*, the annual list of stoppages (*chômages*) on the waterways and cruising guides (without maps) for a number of routes.

Several other publications in Britain may usefully complete the ship's library, generally giving more personal accounts of holiday cruising on the French waterways.

France – the quiet way, John Liley (Stanford Maritime)
Cruising French waterways, Hugh McKnight (Stanford Maritime)
Waterways in Europe, Roger Pilkington (John Murray)
Notes on French inland waterways, Vernon Marchant (Cruising Association)
Through France to the Med, Mike Harper (Cadogan Books)
Through the French canals, Philip Bristow (Nautical)
The Canal du Midi and Canal du Rhône à Sète, Tony Paris (Enterprise Publications)
The Yonne and the Nivernais, Tony Paris (Enterprise Publications)
The Canal de Bourgogne, Tony Paris (Enterprise Publications)

A comprehensive atlas of the Rhine and Moselle (1:10,000 and 1:25,000) is published by Editions de la Navigation du Rhin, Strasbourg.

Finally, the Touring Club de France at 178 Piccadilly, London WlV 0AL, issues a useful pamphlet entitled *Yachting in French Waters*, the annual list of stoppages (*chômages*) on the waterways and cruising guides (without maps) for a number of routes.

Part II Distance Tables and Maps

USING THE DISTANCE TABLES

The distance tables and their accompanying maps are designed to be of use both for planning a holiday and during the actual cruise. Distances precise to within 100m are given in both directions, locks are clearly identified in the middle column, and all possible mooring places are picked out in bold type. The approximate distance from the waterway to the centre of the town or village is also indicated. Such indication is not to be interpreted as a guarantee that mooring will be practicable at this point, but in emergency situations it is reassuring to know that virtually all localities thus identified have at least a public telephone (with direct dialling to most countries). Junctions are readily identifiable by the use of italic type.

The abbreviations u/s and d/s are used for upstream and downstream, and r/b and l/b for right bank and left bank. These abbreviations are also used on canals, the downstream direction being implicit in relation to the summit level or parallel river. (On summit levels geographical directions are used instead, to avoid confusion.)

The index map shows the position of the waterway in the network, and the strip map, which is precise despite the relatively small scale, enables immediate identification of the boat's position in relation to the overall route, and to the towns and villages where it is proposed to stop. Partial distances on these maps are shown by italic figures, with the number of locks in brackets.

Most junctions and locations where alternative routes are possible are covered by detailed plans at a scale of 1:20,000. The topographical detail of the base maps, adapted from the IGN 1:25,000 series, is completed by outlining of water areas, route indications, positions of moorings and other useful information as appropriate.

Addresses and telephone numbers of the subdivisional engineers responsible for each waterway are given, and in case of specific enquiries or difficulties en route, these are the people to contact, rather than the regional waterway authorities to whom most of them are responsible. Details of these regional authorities are as follows:

Direction Régionale de la Navigation, Nord-Pas-de-Calais, 37 rue du Plat, 59034 Lille Cedex
☎ 20 30 85 77, fax 20 57 96 41

Service de la Navigation de la Seine, 2 quai de Grenelle, 75732 Paris Cedex 15
☎ (1) 45 78 61 92 , fax (1) 45 78 08 57

Service de la Navigation de Nancy, 28 bd Albert 1er, 54037 Nancy Cedex
☎ 83 95 30 01, fax 83 98 56 61

Service de la Navigation de Strasbourg, 25 rue de la Nuée Bleue, 67081 Strasbourg Cedex
☎ 88 32 49 15, fax 88 23 56 57

Service de la Navigation de Rhône-Saône, 2 rue de la Quarantaine, 69321 Lyon Cedex 05
☎ 78 42 55 83, fax 78 42 88 43

Service Maritime et de Navigation de Languedoc-Roussillon, 7 r Richard de Belleval, 34210 Montpellier Cedex
☎ 67 14 12 00, fax 67 14 12 10

Service de la Navigation de Toulouse, 2 port Saint-Etienne, 31079 Toulouse Cedex
☎ 61 36 24 24, fax 61 80 97 68

Port Autonome de Nantes, Arrondissement Maritime et de Navigation, 2 rue Marcel Sembat,
44100 Nantes
☎ 40 73 82 00, fax 40 73 30 97

LIST OF RIVERS AND CANALS

Aa

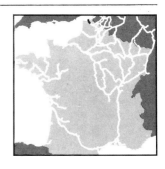

The canalised river Aa extends over just under 29km from Saint-Omer to the North Sea harbour of Gravelines, half way between Calais and Dunkerque (the last 0.7km of this distance is officially in the Port of Gravelines). It used to connect in Saint-Omer with the Canal de Neuffossé (formerly the Canal d'Arques à Saint-Omer), but the waterways in the area were completely transformed when the high-capacity Dunkerque–Escaut waterway was built in the 1960s. Saint-Omer was by-passed, and part of the former through route has been closed to navigation, with the result that access to the centre of Saint-Omer is from upstream (see Dunkerque–Escaut waterway).

The first 2.1km section of the Aa from Saint-Omer to the junction with the main line of the Dunkerque–Escaut waterway is closed to navigation. The lock at Haut-Pont has been closed for years, and the whole section has silted up badly. It is to be hoped that the regional authorities will recognise the value of the old waterway through Saint-Omer for tourism, and find the means to restore this disused section.

From the junction at km 2.1, over a distance of 8km, the Aa is incorporated in the main waterway, and it is the kilometre distances of this waterway that are materialised by the posts on the right bank. For the sake of clarity, the distance table is continued here throughout from Saint-Omer to Gravelines, with official distances on the left and actual distances on the right. The difference of 0.3km is due to the shortening of the original course by the works for the Dunkerque–Escaut waterway. Further downstream, the Aa retains its identity as a tranquil fenland river, connecting with the Canal de Calais and the Canal de Bourbourg. There is also an attractive lock-free branch, the river Houlle, extending 4km from the Aa at km 118.1 to the village of Houlle. For details of navigation between Gravelines and the North Sea (4km from Gravelines sea lock to the seaward limit of the moles forming the entrance channel), reference should be made to the *North Sea Passage Pilot* – Brian Navin.

Locks The lock (Haut Pont) at Saint-Omer is now out of use. Navigation is lock-free from here to Gravelines, where a complex system of tide sluice gates ensures automatic discharge of the river flow to the sea and protection against high water. To proceed through these sluices to enter the Aa or return to the Channel, one day's advance notice must be given to the port authority (address and telephone number below).

Depth The maximum authorised draught is 3.00m in the section which has been upgraded (km 2 to km 10.5), then 2.00m down to the junction with the Canal de Calais, and 1.80m from here down to Gravelines. The maximum authorised draught on the Houlle is 1.20m.

Bridges All the fixed bridges leave a minimum headroom of 4.20m above the highest navigable water level, increased to 5.25m in the improved section, and 5.40m between km 15.1 and Gravelines (respectively 4.45m, 5.55m and 5.65m above normal levels).

Towpath There is a good towpath throughout, at first along the right bank, changing to the left bank at Le Guindal.

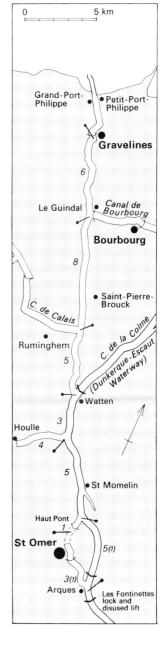

Authority

Direction Régionale de la Navigation, Lille.
Subdivisions:
– Rue de l'Ecluse St. Bertin, BP 353, 62505 **Saint-Omer**, ☎ 21 98 22 00 (km 0-9)
– Terre-plein du Jeu de Mail, BP1008, 59375 **Dunkerque**, ☎ 28 24 34 78 (9-28 4)
– Port de Gravelines, 20 bassin Vauban, 59820 **Gravelines**, ☎ 28 23 13 42 (28 4 to
Channel)

Distance table

	km	lock	km
Saint-Omer basin, former junction with Canal de Neuffossée, closed to navigation	0.0	-	28.8
Lock (Haut Pont), disused	1.2	-	27.6
Junction with Saint-Omer diversion canal, at km 112.6, r/b, beginning of section incorporated in Dunkerque–Escaut waterway, possible mooring for Saint-Omer in basin r/b	2.1/ 112.6	-	26.7
Confluence of Moerlack, r/b (entrance to Wateringues canals used by small unpowered craft)	114.3	-	25.0
Saint Momelin bridge, small village r/b	114.5	-	24.8
Cutoff (bypassing bend in river) r/b	117.7	-	21.6
End of cutoff, junction with river Houlle l/b, navigable 4.0km to the village of **Houlle** (see below)	118.1	-	21.2
Watten bridge, quay d/s r/b, entrance to Watten diversion canal l/b	120.0	-	19.3

Disused Haut-Pont lift bridge
on the river Aa at Saint-Omer.
Author

	km	lock	km
Boat moorings (relais fluvial) on La Bombe river, l/b	120.1	-	19.2
End of diversion canal, Dunkerque–Escaut waterway	120.9/		
continues straight on, Aa branches off left	10.7	-	18.4
Road bridge	10.9	-	18.2
Bridge (Ruth)	11.6	-	17.5
Junction with Canal de Calais, l/b (Pont du West)	15.1	-	14.0
Lift bridge (Bistade), private quays d/s l/b	17.4	-	11.7
Lift bridge (Saint Nicolas)	20.5	-	8.6
Junction with Canal de Bourbourg, r/b (Le Guindal)	22.9	-	6.2
Saint Folquin lift bridge, small village 2000m l/b	23.6	-	5.5
Junction with Canal de Mardyck l/b (small craft only)	24.5	-	4.6
Gas pipeline crossing	24.7	-	4.4
Automatic lift bridge (N1)	27.5	-	1.6
Railway lift bridge, private quays u/s	28.1	-	1.0
Gravelines quay and boat moorings r/b, village 500m	28.5	-	0.6
Bridge	28.6	-	0.5
St Folquin tide sluice gates and fixed bridge	28.7	-	0.4
Bassin Vauban, yacht harbour, 15 visitors' berths	28.9	-	0.2
Gravelines tide sluice gates, swing bridge,			
access to harbour and North Sea	29.1	1	0.0

River Houlle

	km	lock	km
Old mill (Moulin de Lafoscade), limit of navigation but			
inaccessible on account of silting	0.0	-	4.0
Camp site, r/b, mooring possible	0.3	-	3.7
Former cereal loading basin, r/b	0.4	-	3.6
Houlle moorings l/b, village with shops, café, restaurant 300m	0.5	-	3.5
Camp-site l/b	0.7	-	3.3
Disused basin serving brick factory, l/b	1.9	-	2.1
Road bridge	2.1	-	1.9
Café l/b, moorings	2.7	-	1.3
Junction with river Reninghe (unpowered boats only) l/b	3.5	-	0.5
Junction with river Muissens (unpowered boats only), r/b	3.6	-	0.4
SNCF railway bridge	3.9	-	0.1
Lowestel bridge, *junction with Dunkerque–Escaut waterway*			
at km 118.1	4.0	-	0.0

Adour and tributaries

Until the early 1980s, the river Adour was officially navigable from Port de Pouy, 6km upstream of the town of Dax, to its mouth in the Bay of Biscay near Bayonne, a distance of 72km. However, in view of the uncertainty of navigable conditions above the limit of tidal influence, the river has been downgraded over the first 40km, which means that navigation is here at the risk and peril of users. Free-flow navigation formerly continued up the Adour and its tributary, the Midouze, to ports at Saint-Sever and Mont-de-Marsan respectively, but the channel in these sections has long been abandoned, and the river almost completely dries out in exceptionally dry summers. From Port de Pouy to the confluence with the Luy great care is necessary to avoid shoals and the numerous groynes which extend out into the channel. From the Luy to the confluence with the Gaves Réunis depths are greater, but it is advisable to follow the outside of the bends. From the Gaves Réunis to Bayonne there are no obstructions. This navigation is tidal throughout much of its length, and spring tides are felt as high up as Dax. The passage between Bayonne and Dax is much easier if the tidal stream is properly worked. It is best to leave Bayonne about two hours after low water, but local advice should be sought. On account of the shifting banks in the Adour estuary below Bayonne, use of the appropriate marine charts is recommended.

Several tributaries of the Adour are also navigable for a short distance upstream from their confluence. These are the Gaves Réunis, navigable for 9km to the town of Peyrehorade, the Bidouze and a short length of its tributary, the Lihoury, giving access to the hilltop village of Bidache (16km), the Aran (6km), the Ardanavy (2km) and the Nive, which is navigable through the centre of Bayonne and upstream over a distance of 12km. Like the Adour, these are all tidal rivers, and navigation is easier if the tidal stream is used.

Depth Upstream of Dax, the depth is as little as 0.70m. Between Dax and the Luy, it is normally about 1.00m. From the Luy to the Gaves Réunis the mean depth is 1.50m, depending on the state of the tide. From the Gaves Réunis to Bayonne the mean depth is 2.00m. The mean depths of each of the tributaries, and the tidal rise and fall in centimetres, are as follows: Gaves Réunis 1.60m (±40), Bidouze 2.90m (±90), Lihoury 0.90m (±60), Aran and Ardanavy 1.20m (±60) and Nive 1.75m (±75).

Bridges The minimum headroom under the fixed bridges at high spring tides is as follows (the figures in brackets indicate the increased headroom available at low tide): Adour 4.00m (6.50m), Gaves Réunis 3.00m (5.00m), Bidouze 3.50m (5.30m), Lihoury 4.70m (6.00m), Aran 3.60m (4.80m), Ardanavy 3.00m (4.20m) and Nive 0.40m (4.20m). The only problem for most boats is on the Nive at Bayonne, where the bridges should be cleared at low tide before proceeding upstream.

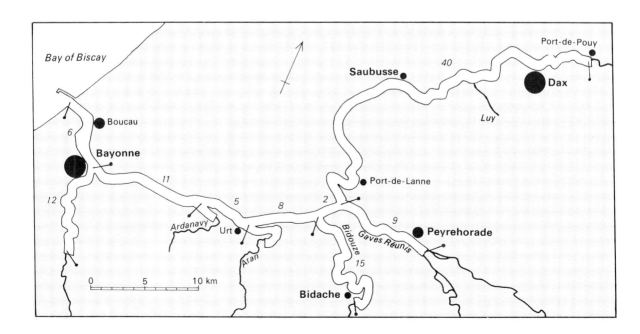

Towpath There is no longer a continuous towpath. The former towpath has been converted into a public road along the left bank for much of the length of the Adour.

Authority

Direction Départementale de l'Equipement, Landes, boulevard Saint-Médard, 40000 Mont-de-Marsan, ☎ 58 51 30 71 (km 0-40)
Direction Départementale de l'Equipement, Pyrénées Atlantiques Service Maritime, Allées Marines, 64100 Bayonne, ☎ 59 44 76 76 (km 40-72 and tributaries).

Distance table

	km	lock	km
Bridge (Pouy), upstream limit of navigation	0.0	-	72.3
Bridge	5.7	-	66.6
Dax bridge, quay d/s l/b, town centre l/b	6.0	-	66.3
Railway bridge	6.9	-	65.4
Mées quay, village 1000m r/b	10.6	-	61.7
Bridge (Vimport), quay u/s l/b	16.0	-	56.3
Confluence of Luy (unnavigable), l/b	18.0	-	54.3
Quay (Carrère) l/b	20.0	-	52.3
Saubusse bridge, quay and village r/b, water	22.0	-	50.3
Bridge (Lamarquèze), quay u/s r/b	26.0	-	46.3
Quay (Gelez) r/b	30.0	-	42.3
Quay (Rasport) l/b	33.1	-	39.2
Port-de-Lanne quay l/b, village 1000m l/b	35.5	-	36.8
Bridge (N117)	36.7	-	35.6
Bec du Gave castle, *confluence of Gaves Réunis*, l/b	40.0	-	32.3
Bec de la Bidouze, *confluence of Bidouze*, l/b	42.4	-	29.9
Quay (Sainte-Marie-de-Gosse) r/b	43.9	-	28.4
Quay (Saint-Laurent-de-Gosse) r/b	49.3	-	23.0
Confluence of Aran, l/b	49.8	-	22.5
Urt bridge, quay d/s l/b, village 800m l/b	49.9	-	22.4
Quay (Saint-Barthélémy) r/b In r/b arm)	52.5	-	19.8
Confluence of Ardanavy, l/b	54.8	-	17.5
Quay (Urcuit) l/b	55.5	-	16.8
Entrance to Lahonce arm, l/b	57.0	-	15.3
Quay (Lahonce) l/b	58.2	-	14.1
Downstream entrance to Lahonce arm, l/b	58.8	-	13.5
Quay (Mouguerre) l/b	63.0	-	9.3
Motorway bridge (A63)	63.5	-	8.8
New road bridge	64.5	-	7.8
Railway bridge	64.8	-	7.5
Bayonne bridge (Pont Saint-Esprit), quays d/s, town centre l/b	65.6	-	6.7
Confluence of Nive, l/b (access to centre of Bayonne)	65.7	-	6.6
Blancpignon port l/b	68.6	-	3.7
Boucau port and small town r/b	69.7	-	2.6
Semaphore tower (Tour des Signaux) l/b, limit of sea	72.3	-	0.0

Gaves Réunis

	km	lock	km
Confluence with Adour (km 40), Bec du Gave castle	0.0	-	9.4
Railway bridge	3.0	-	6.4
Hastingues quay and village r/b	3.9	-	5.5
Peyrehorade bridge, quay d/s r/b, village r/b	8.0	-	1.4
Confluence of Gave de Pau and Gave d'Oloron, head of navigation	9.4	-	0.0

	km	lock	km
Bidouze and Lihoury			
Confluence with Adour (km 42), towpath bridge	0.0	-	15.5
Railway bridge	0.7	-	14.8
Guiche bridge, quay used by sand barges d/s l/b, small village	1.9	-	13.6
Quay (Cassous) l/b	6.5	-	9.0
Quay (Bidache) l/b	8.2	-	7.3
Bidache bridge, village 500m l/b	11.6	-	3.9
Confluence of Lihoury, l/b (navigation continues on Lihoury)	14.9	-	0.6
Bridge (D936), head of navigation, Bidache 800m l/b	15.5	-	0.0
Aran or Joyeuse			
Confluence with Adour (km 50), towpath bridge	0.0	-	6.2
Railway bridge, quay u/s r/b	4.4	-	1.8
Bridge (Larroque), head of navigation, quay d/s l/b	6.2	-	0.0
Ardanavy			
Confluence with Adour (km 55), towpath bridge	0.0	-	2.4
Private quay (Hayet) r/b	2.0	-	0.4
Railway bridge, head of navigation	2.4	-	0.0
Nive			
Confluence with Adour, **Bayonne** (km 66)	0.0	-	12.3
Bridge (Pont Mayou)	0.3	-	12.0
Bridge (Pont Marengo)	0.4	-	11.9
Bridge (Pont Pannecau)	0.6	-	11.7
Bridge (Pont du Génie), **Bayonne** quay l/b, town centre l/b	0.7	-	11.6
Bridge	0.9	-	11.4
Railway bridge	1.4	-	10.9
Quay (Compaïto) r/b, **Villefranque** 2000m r/b	11.1	-	1.2
Weir (Haïtze), head of navigation	12.3	-	0.0

Aisne

The canalised river Aisne extends 57km from its connection with the Canal latéral à l'Aisne at Celles (about 15km east of Soissons) to its confluence with the Oise at Bouche d'Aisne, a short distance upstream of Compiègne. Before the lateral canal was built, navigation extended upstream on the river as far as the connection with the Canal des Ardennes. It is proposed to upgrade the waterway to the European 1350-tonne barge standard as part of the projected high-capacity link between the Seine basin and eastern France.

Locks There are 7 locks, with dimensions slightly larger than the Freycinet standard: 46.00 by 7.95m.

Depth The maximum authorised draught is 2.00m at normal water level.

Bridges All fixed bridges leave a clear headroom of 4.70m above normal water levels, reduced to 3.70m above the highest navigable water level.

Towpath There is a towpath throughout.

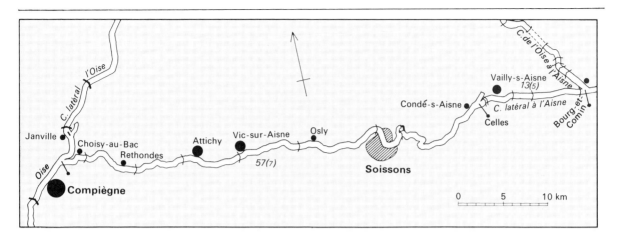

Authority

Service de la Navigation de la Seine, Arrondissement Picardie, Compiègne.
Subdivisions:
– Rue de Mayenne, 02209 Soissons, ☎ 23 53 00 11 (km 0-36)
– 79 Barrage de Venette, 60200 Compiègne, ☎ 44 83 21 12 (km 36-57)

Distance table

	km	lock	km
Connection with Canal latéral à l'Aisne (downstream of Celles double staircase lock)	0.0	-	57.0
Navigation enters river Aisne, navigable upstream 1km to public quay (Couvailles) r/b	0.1	-	56.9
Condé-sur-Aisne bridge, quay d/s l/b, village 500m r/b	0.7	-	56.3
Confluence of Vesle l/b	1.5	-	55.5
Missy-sur-Aisne bridge, quay d/s r/b, village 700m r/b	3.7	-	53.3
Paper mill quay l/b	4.9	-	52.1
Vénizel bridge, quay upstream r/b, village 300m l/b	7.8	-	49.2
Island, navigation in l/b arm	8.0	-	49.0
Entrance to lock-cut, l/b	12.2	-	44.8
Lock 1 (Villeneuve-Saint-Germain), water	12.8	1	44.2
Navigation re-enters river, navigable upstream 1500m to private quay r/b (Bucy arm)	12.9	-	44,1
Railway bridge, private quays downstream l/b	13.7	-	43.3
Bridge (Pont Gambetta)	15.1	-	41.9
Footbridge (Passerelle des Anglais)	15.3	-	41.7

	km	lock	km
Soissons quay r/b, town centre 400m l/b over bridge	15.5	–	41.5
Bridge (Pont du Mail), private quays downstream	15.7	–	41.3
Entrance to lock-cut l/b	16.6	–	40.4
Lock 2 (Vauxrot), water, navigation re-enters river	16.9	2	40.1
Bridge (Pasly)	18.4	–	38.6
Pommiers bridge, quay downstream r/b, village 400m r/b	21.4	–	35.6
Private quays	22.8	–	34.2
Quay (Pernant) l/b	23.7	–	33.3
Island, navigation in l/b arm	24.2	–	32.8
Quay (Osly-Courtil) r/b	26.2	–	30.8
Lock 3 (Fontenoy) in short lock-cut l/b, water	27.3	3	29.7
Fontenoy bridge, quay downstream l/b, village 1300m r/b	29.3	–	27.7
Vic-sur-Aisne bridge, quay downstream r/b, village r/b	34.1	–	22.9
Lock 4 (Vic-sur-Aisne) in short lock-cut l/b, disused railway bridge	34.4	4	22.6
Private quays l/b	34.8	–	22.2
Jaulzy l/b	37.3	–	19.7
Attichy bridge, quay downstream r/b, village 500m r/b	39.3	–	17.7
Lock 5 (Couloisy) in short lock-cut l/b, water	41.0	5	16.0
Berneuil-sur-Aisne bridge, quay l/b, village 800m r/b	42.5	–	14.5
Lock 6 (Hérant) in short lock-cut l/b, water	46.6	6	10.4
Rethondes bridge, quay downstream l/b, village 300m r/b	48.1	–	8.9
Bridge (Francport), quay downstream l/b, Armistice clearing and memorial 700m l/b	51.6	–	5.4
Lock 7 (Carandeau) in short lock-cut l/b, water	53.8	7	3.2
Choisy-au-Bac bridge, quay downstream r/b, village 200m r/b	54.6	–	2.4
Confluence with Oise (km 38.3)	57.0	–	0.0

Canal latéral à l'Aisne

The Canal latéral à l'Aisne forms a 51km link between the Canal des Ardennes at Vieux-lès-Asfeld and the canalised river Aisne at Celles. It also connects with the Canal de l'Aisne à la Marne at Berry-au-Bac and with the Canal de l'Oise à l'Aisne at Bourg-et-Comin. It is an important waterway, carrying east–west and north–south traffic flows in its central section. Commercial traffic is thus over 1 million tonnes per year, while pleasure traffic is also regularly increasing.

Locks There are 8 locks, with a length of 38.50m and a width of 5.20m. The last two at Celles form a double staircase. All locks are equipped for automatic operation, with radar detection, although the suspended pole alternative is being tested at lock 1 (Pignicourt).

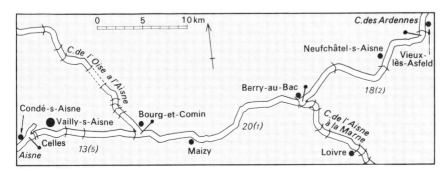

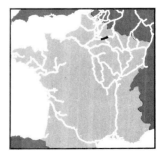

Depth The maximum authorised draught is 1.80m.

Bridges The maximum authorised air draught is 3.50m.

Towpath There is a towpath throughout.

Authority

Service de la Navigation de la Seine, Arrondissement Champagne, Reims.
Subdivision: Quai Valmy, 08300 Rethel, ☎ 24 38 44 10 Fax 24 38 29 90

Distance table

	km	*lock*	*km*
Junction with Canal des Ardennes (d/s of Vieux-lès-Asfeld)	0.0	-	51.3
Quay (Evergnicourt) r/b	4.2	-	47.1
Neufchâtel-sur-Aisne bridge, quay u/s l/b, village 500m r/b	5.5	-	45.8
Lock 1 (Pignicourt), bridge	6.9	1	44.4
Pignicourt quay, small village l/b	7.2	-	44.1
Variscourt bridge, quay and small village d/s l/b	10.5	-	40.8
Sand loading quay l/b	11.8	-	39.5
Railway bridge	12.7	-	38.6
Guignicourt bridge, quay u/s l/b, village 1000m r/b	12.9	-	38.4
Lock 2 (**Condé-sur-Suippe**), bridge, aqueduct u/s, village l/b	13.9	2	37.4
Upstream end of Berry-au-Bac basin, quays l/b	17.7	-	33.6
Junction with Canal de l'Aisne à la Marne, l/b	18.3	-	33.0
Lock 3 (**Berry-au-Bac**), bridge, village 600m r/b	18.5	3	32.8
Feeder enters r/b	18.7	-	32.6
Berry-au-Bac basin r/b	19.0	-	32.3
Gernicourt bridge, small village 400m l/b	21.0	-	30.3
Bridge (Cauries)	23.4	-	27.9
Pontavert bridge, quay d/s r/b, village 700m r/b	24.6	-	26.7
Bridge (Canards)	25.8	-	25.5
Concevreux bridge, quay u/s r/b, village l/b	28.1	-	23.2
Maizy bridge, quays u/s and d/s r/b, village l/b	32.7	-	18.6
Bridge (Aventure)	34.5	-	16.8
Villers-en-Prayères bridge, quays u/s, village 1000m l/b, Oeuilly 1000m r/b	35.9	-	15.4
Bridge (Moulin de Villers)	36.7	-	14.6
Bridge (Bourg)	37.5	-	13.8
Bourg-et-Comin basin (500m long)	37.9	-	13.4
Junction with Canal de l'Oise à l'Aisne, r/b	38.3	-	13.0
Bourg-et-Comin quay r/b, village 800m r/b	38.4	-	12.9
Lock 4 (Cendrière), bridge, quay d/s l/b	38.5	4	12.8
Pont-Arcy bridge, small village 300m r/b	40.5	-	10.8
Bridge (Saint-Mard)	43.6	-	7.7
Lock 5 (Cys), bridge	44.5	5	6.8
Presles bridge, village 200m l/b	45.3	-	6.0
Lock 6 (Saint-Audebert), bridge	46.7	6	4.6
Upstream end of Vailly basin	47.4	-	3.9
Private quays l/b	48.2	-	3.1
Downstream end of Vailly basin	48.5	-	2.8
Vailly-sur-Aisne bridge, quay d/s r/b, small town 800m r/b	48.9	-	2.4
Bridge (Chassemy)	49.9	-	1.4
Double staircase lock 7/8 (Celles), bridge	51.2	8	0.1
Canal joins canalised river Aisne, r/b	51.3	-	0.0

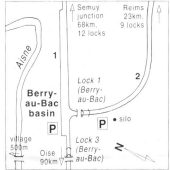

1 Canal latéral à l'Aisne
2 Canal de l'Aisne à la Marne

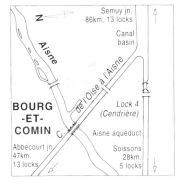

Canal de l'Aisne à la Marne

The Canal de l'Aisne à la Marne runs from the Canal latéral à l'Aisne at Berry-au-Bac to the Canal latéral à la Marne at Condé-sur-Marne, a distance of 58km. The canal rises through the cathedral city of Reims to a summit level at an altitude of 96m, including a 2300m long tunnel at Mont-de-Billy, and then drops down towards the Marne valley.

The maximum authorised dimensions for vessels passing through the tunnel are: draught 2.20m, beam 5.00m and air draught 3.70m.

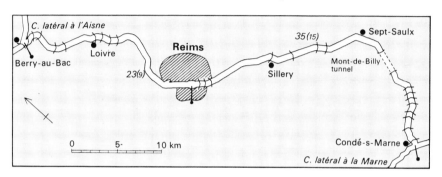

The towage service which used to operate in this tunnel was abandoned in the 1970s, when the tunnel's ventilation system was installed, and all boats proceed through the tunnel under power, respecting the lights controlling the one-way traffic.

Locks There are 24 locks, 16 rising from the Aisne to the Mont-de-Billy summit, the remaining 8 falling towards the Marne. All have effective dimensions of 38.50 by 5.20m. Since 1990, all locks on the canal are equipped for autmatic operation, with radar detection on locks 1 to 9, and poles to be manoeuvred on the approaches to all the other locks (see Introduction).

Depth The maximum authorised draught is 1.80m.

Bridges The maximum authorised air draught is 3.50m.

Towpath There is a good towpath throughout.

Authority
Service de la Navigation de la Seine, Arrondissement Champagne, Reims.
Subdivision: 11 boulevard Paul-Doumer, 51110 Reims, ☎ 26 47 44 61.

Distance table

1 Canal latéral à l'Aisne
2 Canal de l'Aisne à la Marne

	km	lock	km
Junction with Canal latéral à l'Aisne (at Berry-au-Bac basin, km 18.3)	0.0	-	58.1
Lock 1 (Berry-au-Bac), bridge, quay u/s l/b	0.1	1	58.0
Lock 2 (Moulin de Sapigneul)	1.2	2	56.9
Lock 3 (Sapigneul)	2.3	3	55.8
Bridge (Neuville), quay u/s l/b, turning basin, **Cormicy** 2000m l/b	3.8	-	54.3
Lock 4 (Alger)	4.7	4	53.4

	km	lock	km
Le Gaudart, sugar beet loading quay l/b	5.4	-	52.7
Lock 5 (Gaudart)	5.9	5	52.2
Lock 6 (**Loivre**), bridge, water, quay u/s l/b, village l/b	9.4	6	48.7
Lock 7 (Fontaine), bridge	10.1	7	48.0
Lock 8 (Noue-Gouzaine)	11.2	8	46.9
Lock 9 (Courcy), bridge	12.0	9	46.1
Courcy bridge (Pont de Brimont), quay u/s l/b, turning basin, village 800m l/b	12.5	-	45.6
Bridge (Bétheny)	14.5	-	43.6
Quay l/b	15.5	-	42.6
Le Neuvillette bridge, basin d/s, quay l/b, village r/b (suburb of Reims)	17.5	-	40.6
Bridge (Saint-Thierry)	18.8	-	39.3
Bridge (Courcelles)	20.3	-	37.8
Entrance to Reims basin (Port Colbert), 700m long, r/b	20.4	-	37.7
Bridge (Saint-Brice), quay d/s r/b, private quays u/s	21.0	-	37.1
Footbridge (Saint-Charles)	21.7	-	36.4
Skew railway bridge	22.3	-	35.8
Railway bridge and footbridge (Bienfait)	22.5	-	35.6
Bridge (Maréchaux)	22.7	-	35.4
Bridge (Pont de Vesle) over narrow section	22.9	-	35.2
Bridge (Pont de Gaulle)	23.3	-	34.8
Reims basin (Vieux Port), moorings, city centre 500m r/b	23.4	-	34.7
Bridge (Venise)	23.8	-	34.3
Lock 10 (Fléchambault), bridge, private quays u/s r/b	24.4	10	33.7
Lock 11 (Château d'Eau), road bridge, private quays u/s r/b	25.2	11	32.9
Bridge (Rouillat)	25.3	-	32.8
Lock 12 (Huon), bridge, private quays u/s	25.8	12	32.3
New road bridge	27.2	-	30.9
Bridge (Vrilly)	27.5	-	30.6
Bridge (Saint-Léonard)	29.3	-	28.8
Bridge (Couraux)	32.0	-	26.1
Lock 13 (Sillery), Vesle aqueduct u/s, private quay d/s r/b	33.4	13	24.7
Sillery bridge (Pont du Petit-Sillery), basin u/s, quay l/b, village 400m l/b	33.6	-	24.5
Bridge (Sillery)	34.0	-	24.1
Bridge (Moulin de Sillery)	34.6	-	23.5
Footbridge (Sillery sugar mill), quay u/s l/b	34.8	-	23.3
Skew road bridge (Sillery bypass)	35.4	-	22.7
Lock 14 (Espérance), bridge	35.6	14	22.5
Bridge (Prunay)	36.5	-	21.6
Lock 15 (**Beaumont-sur-Vesle**), bridge, turning basin and quay u/s l/b, village 200m l/b	38.4	15	19.7
Lock 16 (Wez), bridge, beginning of summit level	39.5	16	18.6
Courmelois bridge, basin u/s, small village 300m r/b	40.6	-	17.5
Sept-Saulx bridge, basin d/s, village 300m r/b	43.3	-	14.8
Bridge (Issus)	44.4	-	13.7
Northern entrance to Mont de Billy tunnel	46.5	-	11.8
Southern entrance to Mont de Billy tunnel	48.8	-	9.3
Bridge (Vaudemanges)	50.3	-	7.8
Vaudemanges basin, quay l/b, village 800m r/b (over bridge)	50.9	-	7.2
Lock 17 (Vaudemanges), bridge, end of summit level	51.4	17	6.7
Lock 18 (Champ Bon-Garçon)	52.0	18	6.1
Lock 19 (Longues-Raies)	52.5	19	5.6
Lock 20 (Saint-Martin), bridge	53.2	20	4.9
Lock 21 (Fosse-Rodé)	53.9	21	4.2
Lock 22 (Isse)	54.6	22	3.5
Isse bridge, small village 100m r/b	54.8	-	3.3

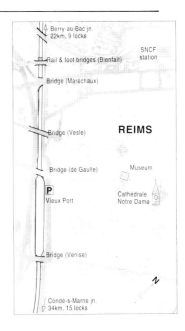

	km	lock	km
Lock 23 (Coupé)	55.9	23	2.2
Lock 24 (Condé-sur-Marne), bridge	57.7	24	0.4
Condé-sur-Marne basin, quay and village r/b	57.9	-	0.2
Junction with Canal latéral à la Marne (km 48)	58.1	-	0.0

Canal des Ardennes

The Canal des Ardennes, opened in 1833, branches off from the canalised river Meuse, forming the northern branch of the Canal de l'Est, at Pont-à-Bar, a short distance upstream from Charleville-Mézières, and after crossing the watershed between the rivers Meuse and Aisne drops down the Aisne valley to connect with the Canal latéral à l'Aisne at Vieux-lès-Asfeld. The distance from the Meuse to the Canal latéral à l'Aisne is 88km. There is a 12km long branch from Semuy to the small town of Vouziers, further up the Aisne valley. Officially the canal is divided into two lengths, with distances counted separately on the watershed link, from Pont-à-Bar to Semuy, and on the canal following the Aisne valley, from Vouziers to Vieux-lès-Asfeld. It is thought more convenient here to carry the distance through from one end to the other, and to treat the section from Semuy to Vouziers as a branch.

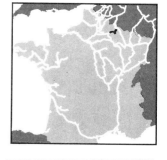

At Saint Aignan there is a tunnel, 197m in length, allowing one-way traffic only. The order of passage is that of arrival at the basin at the downstream end of the tunnel, or at the mooring posts placed at the upstream end, at which points mooring is only authorised pending entry into the tunnel. There is no traffic control at this tunnel, hence the importance of carrying the usual lights, to be clearly visible to boats arriving at the opposite tunnel entrance.

Locks There are 44 locks between Pont-à-Bar and Vieux-lès-Asfeld, of which 7 fall towards the Meuse and the remaining 37 towards the Aisne. There are 4 locks on the branch to Vouziers. All have standard dimensions of 38.50 by 5.20m. The first 7 locks are still manually operated, although mechanisation for automatic operation is expected to be implemented by 1993. Locks 1 to 26 on the Aisne side are all automatic. Note that the sequence of operation of this flight assumes that a boat entering the first lock will continue throughout the flight without interruption. This does not mean that

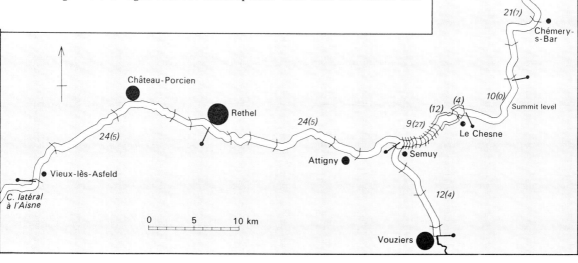

boaters are not free to stop at will, but to avoid disrupting the operating cycle of the entire flight, it is essential in this case to advise the control centre of your intention (or walk back to the lock you have just left and use the telephone beside the control cabin). Lock 27 (Rilly) and all four locks on the Vouziers branch are manually operated (advance notice is to be given for navigation on Sundays).

Depth The maximum authorised draught is 1.80m.

Bridges The maximum authorised air draught is 3.50m.

Towpath There is a towpath throughout.

Authority
Service de la Navigation de Nancy. Subdivision:
– 2 av. de Montcy Notre Dame, 08000 Charleville-Mézières, ☎ 24 33 20 48 (0-39).
Service de la Navigation de la Seine, Arrondissement Champagne, Reims.
– Quai Valmy, 08300 Rethel, ☎ 24 38 44 10 (km 39–88 and branch).

Distance table

	km	lock	km
Junction with Canal de l'Est (river Meuse) (km 96)	0.0	-	88.0
Lock 7 (Meuse), bridge	0.1	1	87.9
Lock 6 (Pont-à-Bar), bridge (D964), quay and Ardennes Nautisme hire base d/s r/b,	0.9	2	87.1
Footbridge	2.3	-	85.7
Hannogne-Saint-Martin bridge, village 500m l/b	3.0	-	85.0
Lock 5 (Saint-Aignan)	6.0	3	82.0
Lock 4 (**Saint-Aignan**), bridge, turning basin and quay d/s r/b, village 800m r/b	6.1	4	81.9
Saint-Aignan tunnel (length 196.50m)	6.3	-	81.7
Omicourt bridge, quay d/s l/b, small village l/b	8.3	-	79.7
Lock 3 (Malmy), bridge, quay u/s, r/b, **Chémery-sur-Bar** 1000m r/b	12.0	5	76.0
Turning basin l/b	13.0	-	75.0
Bridge (Morteau)	14.7	-	73.3
Ambly-sur-Bar bridge, quays u/s and d/s	15.8	-	72.2
Lock 2 (**Cassine**), bridge, small village l/b	16.9	6	71.1
Lock 1 (**Sauville**), start of summit level, village 1700m l/b	20.6	7	67.4
Footbridge	21.5	-	66.5
Tannay bridge, village 1400m east	23.0	-	65.0
Bridge (Pont-Bar), quay	24.8	-	63.2
Skew bridge	28.4	-	59.6
Le Chesne bridge, quay d/s r/b, turning basin, village l/b	28.5	-	59.5
Lock 1 (Chesne), bridge, water, end of summit level	30.1	8	57.9
Lock 2 (Chesne), turning basin d/s	30.3	9	57.7
Lock 3 (Chesne), bridge	30.5	10	57.5
Lock 4 (Chesne)	30.8	11	57.2
Lock 5 (Montgon)	30.9	12	57.1
Lock 6 (Montgon)	31.3	13	56.7
Lock 7 (Montgon)	31.5	14	56.5
Lock 8 (Montgon)	31.8	15	56.2
Lock 9 (Montgon)	32.1	16	55.9
Lock 10 (Montgon)	32.4	17	55.6
Lock 11 (**Montgon**), bridge, village 600m l/b	32.7	18	55.3
Lock 12 (Montgon)	33.0	19	55.0
Lock 13 (Montgon)	33.1	20	54.9

	km	lock	km
Lock 14 (Montgon), bridge, village 600m l/b	33.4	21	54.6
Lock 15 (Montgon)	33.9	22	54.1
Lock 16 (Montgon)	34.2	23	53.8
Lock 17 (Neuville-Day)	34.3	24	53.7
Lock 18 (Neuville-Day)	34.7	25	53.3
Lock 19 (Neuville-Day)	35.0	26	53.0
Neuville-Day quay r/b, village 800m r/b	35.3	-	52.7
Lock 20 (Neuville-Day), bridge	35.4	27	52.6
Lock 21 (Neuville-Day)	35.8	28	52.2
Lock 22 (Neuville-Day), bridge	36.5	29	51.5
Lock 23 (Semuy), bridge	37.2	30	50.8
Lock 24 (Semuy)	37.5	31	50.5
Lock 25 (Semuy)	37.9	32	50.1
Semuy bridge, village r/b	38.2	-	49.8
Lock 26 (Semuy), bridge	38.5	33	49.5
Lock 27 (Rilly), bridge, *junction with Vouziers branch*			
(downstream of lock 4)	39.2	34	48.8
Railway bridge	40.0	-	48.0
Rilly-sur-Aisne bridge, small village 300m l/b	40.1	-	47.9
Bridge (Forest)	42.0	-	46.0
Lock 5 (Attigny), bridge, private quay u/s r/b	44.0	35	44.0
Attigny bridge, quay d/s l/b, village l/b	44.9	-	43.1
Private bridge (railway siding)	45.8	-	42.2
Lock 6 (Givry), bridge, water	47.2	36	40.8
Givry bridge, quay d/s r/b, small village l/b	48.2	-	39.8
Bridge (Montmarin)	49.1	-	38.9
Private quay r/b	50.3	-	37.7
Bridge (Fleury)	51.8	-	36.2
Ambly-Fleury bridge, quay d/s r/b, small village r/b	52.9	-	35.1
Lock 7 (Seuil), bridge, small village 600m l/b	55.0	37	33.0
Bridge (Trugny)	56.7	-	31.3
Lock 8 (Thugny), bridge	57.7	38	30.3
Thugny-Trugny quay r/b, village 600m l/b over bridge	57.8	-	30.2
Lock 9 (Biermes), bridge	60.5	39	27.5
Biermes quay r/b, village 800m l/b over bridge	60.7	-	27.3
Private quay l/b	61.2	-	26.8
Turning basin r/b	63.1	-	24.9
Railway bridges	63.2	-	24.8
Rethel bridge, quay u/s r/b, small town 800m r/b	63.6	-	24.4
Footbridge (sugar mill)	64.3	-	23.7
Bridge	64.9	-	23.1
Lock 10 (Acy-Romance), bridge	65.6	40	22.4
Lock 11 (Nanteuil), bridge	67.8	41	20.2
Nanteuil-sur-Aisne quay and small village l/b	68.2	-	19.8
Private quay r/b (Port-Arthur)	70.8	-	17.2
Château-Porcien bridge, quay d/s r/b, village 500m r/b	73.0	-	15.0
Lock 12 (Pargny), bridge	75.3	42	12.7
Bridge (Blanzy)	78.3	-	9.7
Balham bridge, quay u/s r/b, small village 400m r/b,			
Blanzy-la-Salonnaise 500m l/b	80.4	-	7.6
Lock 13 (Asfeld), bridge, private quays u/s r/b	83.4	43	4.6
Asfeld bridge, quay d/s r/b, village 700m l/b	85.1	-	2.9
Vieux-lès-Asfeld bridge, quay u/s l/b, village 300m l/b	86.9	-	1.1
Lock 14 (Vieux-lès-Asfeld), bridge	87.9	44	0.1
Junction with Canal latéral à l'Aisne	88.0	-	0.0

	km	lock	km
Vouziers branch			
Vouziers bridge, head of navigation, quays d/s l/b, small town l/b	0.0	-	12.1
Lock 1 (Vouziers), water, weir d/s r/b	0.5	1	11.6
Bridge (Condé-les-Vouziers), quay d/s l/b	1.4	-	10.7
Vrizy bridge, quay d/s l/b, village 700m l/b	3.4	-	8.7
Lock 2 (Vrizy), bridge	4.7	2	7.4
Bridge (Echarson)	6.3	-	5.8
Lock 3 (**Voncq**), bridge, quay u/s l/b, village 1500m r/b	8.1	3	4.0
Bridge (Rilly), quay d/s l/b, **Semuy** 400m r/b	11.3	-	0.8
Lock 4 (Rilly), bridge, *junction with main line* (km 39)	12.1	4	0.0

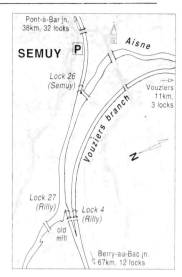

Canal d'Arles à Fos

This canal, which parallels the Rhône over a distance of 31km from the town of Arles, on the left bank, to the point where its course is joined by the new Canal du Rhône à Fos, is virtually disused. It was closed as a through route in the 1970s when a salt barrier was built at the junction with the new cut, and it now serves mainly as a stormwater drain for the land lying southeast of Arles. However, even as a 'dead end', the canal is still of interest for cruising, offering views over the desolate landscape of La Crau. The canal is entered through the large entrance lock from the Rhône at Arles, giving access to the canal basin and a boatyard. At km 2.5, near Montcalde lock, the canal passes through the lift bridge made famous by Van Gogh. From here on, the canal is under the jurisdiction of the Port Autonome de Marseille. Navigation ends at Le Relai, where the salt marshes used to load salt for shipment up the Rhône.

For the location map and further information on the waterway links east of the Rhône, see under the Rhône-Fos-Bouc(-Marseille) waterway.

Locks The entrance lock at Arles, replacing the original lock, which was filled in as part of the Rhône development works, was built to large dimensions, 100 by 12m. It is manned throughout the normal navigation hours. Montcalde lock (km 2.5) offers navigable dimensions of 33.00m by 8.00m. A third lock, at L'Etourneau (km 21), is permanently open, its gates having been removed.

Depth The maximum authorised draught is 1.20m, but this depth cannot be guaranteed and care is required, for there are local obstacles such as wrecked cars and domestic appliances.

Bridges The maximum authorised air draught is 3.50m.

Authority

Service de la Navigation de Lyon.
Subdivision: Quai de Trinquetaille, 13637 Arles, ☎ 90 96 00 85 (km 0-2.5)
Port Autonome de Marseille, Service Travaux de Fos, 13270 Fos-sur-Mer, ☎ 42 05 17 00 (km 2.5-31.3)

Distance table

	km	lock	km
Junction with Rhône on l/b d/s of Arles	0.0	-	31.3
Entrance lock	0.2	1	31.1
Arles canal basin, town centre 500m	0.4	-	30.9
Bridge, boatyard d/s r/b	0.5	-	30.8
Railway bridge	0.9	-	30.4
Lock (Montcalde) and 'Van Gogh' lift bridge	2.5	2	28.8
Bridge (Allen)	4.5	-	26.8
Bridge (Mas de la Ville)	7.0	-	24.3
Bridge (Mollégès)	9.1	-	22.2
Bridge (Beyne)	14.5	-	16.8
Mas-Thibert bridge, moorings, small village l/b	18.5	-	12.8
Former lock (Etourneau), gates removed, no obstacle	21.0	-	10.3
Le Relai salt marshes r/b, effective limit of navigation	31.0	-	0.3
Salt barrier just before junction with the Rhône–Fos canal (no through navigation)	31.3	-	0.0

Baïse

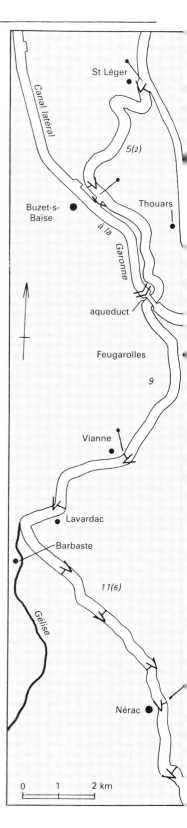

The river Baïse, a canalised left bank tributary of the Garonne, was formerly navigable upstream as far as St Jean-de-Poutge, 86km south in the département of Gers, through 29 locks. Long abandoned, even over the 5km length providing a connection between the Canal latéral à la Garonne (through a double staircase lock at Buzet-sur-Baïse) and the semi-navigable river Garonne at Saint-Léger, the navigation has been restored by the public works department (Direction Départementale de l'Equipement) of Lot-et-Garonne over the first 14km from the confluence up to the village of Vianne. This was in fact the first effectively abandoned waterway in France to be restored for pleasure cruising, which made the re-opening in 1987 something of a milestone in French waterways history. The Direction Départementale de l'Equipement had obtained State funds on the admittedly spurious argument that reopening of this river link, combined with an improvement in conditions of navigation on the Garonne itself, would open up an alternative, faster route for barge traffic between the Baïse and Castets-en-Dorthe, thus helping to maintain the declining commercial traffic on the Garonne lateral canal. In view of the success of this first stage of restoration, the département of Lot-et-Garonne is now securing more conventional finance to proceed with restoration of the section up to Nérac, a historic town where Henri IV was once resident. Accordingly, the distance table is continued up to the first lock above Nérac, expected to be accessible by about 1993.

The cruise on this tranquil shady river, steeped in history, is well worth while, offering a change from the straight pounds of the lateral canal.

Locks The first four locks up to Lavardac have the restricted dimensions of the original locks on the Midi canals: 31.00 by 5.20m. Upstream from this point, the lock chambers are the same length but narrower (4.30m), which effectively excludes Midi barges from the upper sections of the river. Locks are generally operated from 9:00 to 19:00 during the cruising season from Easter to All Saints' Day. See the instructions displayed at the locks down from the canal. A lock-keeper is posted permanently at Buzet from June to September, covering both the staircase locks down from the canal and the lock on the river.

Depth The maximum authorised draught is 1.50m downstream of the junction with the Canal latéral, reduced to 1.20m upstream of the junction.
Bridges The bridges leave a minimum headroom of 5.50m above normal water level (to be confirmed on the as yet unrestored section from Vianne to Nérac).

Towpath The towpath is of varying condition over the first 19km up to Lavardac, and totally impracticable further upstream following sale of the river to riparians between 1956 and 1962.

Authority

Direction Départementale de l'Equipement, Lot-et-Garonne.
Cellule de l'Eau, 2bis rue Jeanne d'Arc, 47000 Agen, ☎53 98 01 26 Fax 53 98 07 60

Distance table

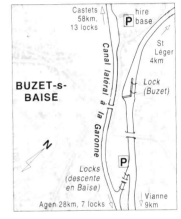

	km	lock	km
Lock 29 (Saint-Léger) and weir, *confluence with the Garonne*	0.0	1	26.4
Lock 28 (Buzet) and weir	4.5	2	21.9
Buzet-sur-Baïse bridge, quay downstream l/b, village 800m beyond lateral canal	4.7	-	21.7
Junction with the Canal latéral à la Garonne, l/b, by a double staircase lock (descente en Baïse)	4.9	-	21.5
Aqueduct (canal latéral crosses over river)	8.7	-	17.7
Motorway bridge (A61, 'Autoroute des Deux Mers')	8.9	-	17.5
Skew road bridge (D119)	9.9	-	16.5
Railway bridge	10.9	-	15.5
Feugarolles quay and boat moorings, r/b, village 600m, restaurant	11.0	-	15.4
Trenquéléon castle, r/b	12.0	-	14.4
Bridge (Vianne)	14.0	-	12.4
Vianne pontoon moorings and turning basin d/s of weir, village l/b, *present limit of navigation*	14.2	-	12.2
Lock 27 (Vianne) r/b, and weir	14.3	3	12.1
Railway viaduct	15.2	-	11.2
Lock 26 (Lavardac)	16.9	4	9.5
Lavardac bridge (Roman arch on r/b)	17.2	-	9.2
Lavardac quay directly below village centre, r/b	17.3	-	9.1
Confluence of Gelise, l/b	18.2	-	8.2
Main road bridge (Pont de Bordes, D930)	18.7	-	7.7
Railway viaduct	19.1	-	7.3
Lock 25 (St Crabary) r/b, and weir	19.5	5	6.9
Castle (Séguinot), l/b	20.6	-	5.8
Lock 24 (Sourbet) l/b, and weir	21.3	6	5.1
Castle (Bournac), l/b	22.0	-	4.4
Lock 23 (Bapaume) r/b, and weir	23.4	7	3.0
Lock 22 (Nérac) l/b, and weir	24.7	8	1.7
Bridge (Vieux-Pont)	24.8	-	1.6
Nérac quay r/b, trip boat departure point, town centre l/b	24.9	-	1.5
Bridge (Pont neuf)	25.0	-	1.4
Lock 21 (Nazareth), *probable limit of navigation pending further restoration*	26.4	-	0.0

Canal de Bergues

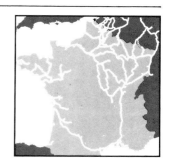

The Canal de Bergues runs from Bergues, where it joins the Canal de la Colme, to the port of Dunkerque, the basins of the port being reached via the short Canal de Jonction (officially a maritime waterway, under port administration). Its length is 8km, although the first 400m is common with the Canal de la Colme. This is one of the oldest canals in Flanders, its course being shown on a map dating from the 9th century. The main interest for boats lies in the possibility of mooring within the medieval walled town of Bergues. The canal is shown on the map of the Dunkerque-Escaut waterway.

Locks There are no locks.

Depth The maximum authorised draught is 1.80m.

Bridges All the bridges are fixed, and leave a minimum headroom of 3.20m above the highest navigable water level (3.50m above normal level).

Towpath There is a good towpath throughout.

Authority

Direction Régionale de la Navigation, Lille. Subdivision:
Terre-Plein du Jeu de Mail, BP 1008, 59375 Dunkerque, ☎ 28 24 38 56

Distance table

	km	lock	km
Junction with Canal de la Colm (disused)	0.0	-	8.1
Bergues basin, boat moorings (relais fluvial), water, town centre 300m	0.2	-	7.9
Junction with the Canal de la Haute Colme (disused, except for boat moorings for Bierne 50m up the canal from the junction), turn right for Dunkerque	0.4	-	7.7
Fort Vallières (fort) r/b	3.2	-	4.9
Bridge (Sept-Planètes), quay upstream l/b	5.0	-	3.1
New road bridge (Dunkerque ring road)	6.3	-	1.8
First bridge (Saint-Georges)	6.7	-	1.4
Second bridge (Saint-Georges)	6.8	-	1.3
Railway bridge	7.0	-	1.1
Flood relief canal, r/b	7.4	-	0.7
Bridge	7.5	-	0.6
Bridge	7.7	-	0.4
Bridge (Pont Rouge)	8.1	-	0.0
Junction with canal de Jonction, turn left for port and **Dunkerque** boat moorings (base fluviale) on north side, and right for the Canal de Furnes and Belgium)	8.1	-	0.0

Canal du Blavet

The Canal du Blavet, which is essentially the canalised river Blavet, is one of the links in the Brittany canal system. It connects with the Canal de Nantes à Brest at Pontivy (km 206) and runs to Hennebont, a distance of 60km. From here the river is tidal and considered as a maritime waterway, giving access to the seaport of Lorient and the Atlantic Ocean (a further 14km beyond Hennebont).

Locks There are 28 locks, with minimum dimensions of 26.30 by 4.70m.

Depth The original maximum authorised draught of 1.40m has been restored thanks to a substantial programme of dredging works on the lock approaches.

Bridges The least headroom under the fixed bridges is 2.40m above normal water level.

Towpath The towpath is practicable throughout most of the length of the canalised river.

Authority

Service de la Navigation de Lorient, Boulevard Adolphe-Pierre, 56322 Lorient, ☎ 97 64 11 36. Subdivisions:
– 1 rue Henri Dunant, 56300 Pontivy, ☎ 97 25 55 21 (km 0-24)
– Rue du Port, 56700 Hennebont, ☎ 97 36 20 82 (km 24-59.8)

Distance table

	km	lock	km
Pontivy basin (Bassin du Champ de Foire), *junction with Canal de Nantes à Brest* (km 205.9), moorings, town centre 300m	0.0	-	59.8
Lock 1 (Récollets), navigation enters river Blavet, quay l/b	0.1	1	59.7
Bridge (Pont de l'Hôpital), quay d/s l/b, town centre 100m	0.3	-	59.5
Bridge (Pont de la Caserne)	0.7	-	59.1
Bridge (Pont Neuf)	1.4	-	58.4
Railway bridge, quay l/b	1.6	-	58.2
Lock 2 (Lestitut)	2.4	2	57.4
Bridge	2.7	-	57.1
Bridge, private quay downstream l/b	3.2	-	56.6
Lock 3 (Signan or Saint-Michel)	4.3	3	55.5
Bridge (Rhin-Danube)	4.5	-	55.3
Lock 4 (Roch)	7.2	4	52.6
Loch 5 (Divit)	9.6	5	50.2
Lock 6 (Rimaison)	11.8	6	48.0
Bridge	11.9	-	47.9
Lock 7 (Kerbecher)	13.9	7	45.9
Lock 8 (Guern)	15.8	8	44.0
Railway bridge	16.5	-	43.3
Railway bridge	17.3	-	42.5
Lock 9 (Saint-Nicolas-des-Eaux)	17.5	9	42.3
Saint-Nicolas-des-Eaux bridge, quay u/s l/b, small village	17.8	-	42.0
Lock 10 (Couarde)	19.6	10	40.2
Railway bridge	20.2	-	39.6
Lock 11 (Camblen)	21.1	11	38.7

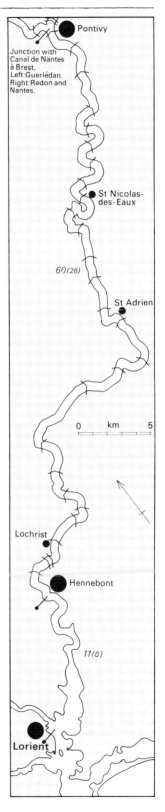

Junction with
Canal de Nantes
à Brest,
Left:Guerlédan.
Right:Redon and
Nantes.

Pontivy

St Nicolas-
des-Eaux

60(28)

St Adrien

0   km   5

Lochrist

Hennebont

11(0)

Lorient

	km	lock	km
Lock 12 (Moulin-Neuf), bridge	23.0	12	36.8
Lock 13 (Boterneau), quay l/b	25.0	13	34.8
Saint-Rivalain bridge, village 1500m r/b	25.2	-	34.6
Lock 14 (Tréblavet)	26.6	14	33.2
Lock 15 (Talhouët)	28.6	15	31.2
Saint-Adrien bridge, small village 300m l/b	30.5	-	29.3
Railway bridge	30.6	-	29.2
Lock 16 (Saint-Adrien), quay r/b	30.9	16	28.9
Lock 17 (Trémorin)	34.2	17	25.6
Railway bridge	34.4	-	25.4
Lock 18 (Sainte-Barbe)	36.4	18	23.4
Pont-Augan bridge, quay downstream l/b, small village r/b	37.0	-	22.8
Railway bridge (disused)	37.5	-	22.3
Lock 19 (Minazen)	39.4	19	20.4
Lock 20 (Manerven)	44.6	20	15.2
Bridge (Pont Neuf), quay downstream r/b	46.5	-	13.3
Lock 21 (Rudet)	47.2	21	12.6
Lock 22 (Trébihan)	49.3	22	10.5
Lock 23 (Kerousse)	50.9	23	8.9
Lock 24 (Quellenec), private quay upstream l/b	52.3	24	7.5
Lock 25 (Lochrist) in l/b arm	54.3	25	5.5
Lochrist bridge, quays downstream, village r/b, Langroix l/b	54.6	-	5.2
Railway bridge (disused)	55.0	-	4.8
Lock 26 (Grand Barrage)	56.0	26	3.8
Lock 27 (Gorets)	56.3	27	3.5
Lock 28 (Polhuern), private quay upstream r/b	57.3	28	2.5
Railway bridge (disused)	59.5	-	0.3
Hennebont bridge, junction with Blavet maritime, moorings downstream r/b, village l/b	59.8	-	0.0

Note The Blavet maritime, a tidal estuary covered by nautical charts and guides, gives access to Lorient, 11km from Hennebont and to the Atlantic at the Citadelle of Port-Louis, a further 3.5km.

Canal de Bourbourg

The Canal de Bourbourg is a 21km link between the river Aa and the Canal de Jonction, officially a maritime waterway within the port of Dunkerque. It used to be a key link between the port and its hinterland, extending to the Paris region, but it has now been superseded by the large-scale Dunkerque-Escaut waterway, except for a 1.6km section which has been upgraded and incorporated into the waterway between the Colme division canal (dérivation de la Colme), km 9.3, and the Mardyck diversion canal (dérivation de Mardyck), km 10.9. For further details (and map) see under the Dunkerque-Escaut waterway.

Locks There are three locks. The two situated on the section between the river Aa and the upgraded length have dimensions of 38.50 by 5.20m. The third lock situated near the end of the canal in Dunkerque has larger dimensions, 110 by 12m. There are no locks on the upgraded length.

Depth The maximum authorised draught is 1.80m up to km 9.3, 3.00m on the upgraded length and 2.20m from km 10.9 to Dunkerque.

Bridges The fixed bridges leave a minimum clear headroom of 3.20m above the highest navigable water level (3.50m above normal level). There are no bridges on the upgraded section.

Towpath There is a towpath throughout.

Authority

Direction Régionale de la Navigation, Lille. Subdivision:
Terre-Plein du Jeu de Mail, BP 1008, 59375 Dunkerque, ☎ 28 24 38 56

Distance table

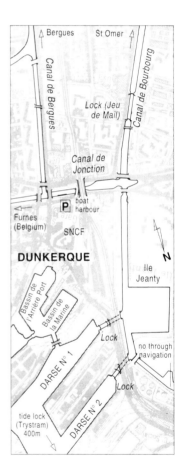

	km	lock	km
Junction with river Aa	0.0	-	21.0
Lock (Guindal), bridge	0.1	1	20.9
Industrial quays	2.8	-	18.2
Lift bridge (Saint-Antoine), private quays	3.1	-	17.9
Lift bridge (Pont-Rouge)	3.7	-	17.3
Bourbourg quay and boat moorings (halte fluviale), on bypassed section of old canal, small town r/b	3.9	-	17.1
Lock (Bourbourg)	4.0	2	17.0
Road bridge	5.7	-	15.3
Coppenaxfort bridge, quay upstream l/b, private quays downstream	8.3	-	12.7
Junction with Colme diversion canal (Dunkerque–Escaut waterway), r/b	9.3	-	11.7
Junction with Mardyck diversion canal (Dunkerque–Escaut waterway), l/b	10.9	-	10.1
Gas pipeline crossing	11.2	-	9.8
Spycker bridge, quay u/s l/b, village 2500m r/b	13.1	-	7.9
Water pipeline crossing	14.7	-	6.3
Old line rejoins canal, l/b (access to Usine des Deux-Synthes)	15.2	-	5.8
Motorway bridge	15.6	-	5.4
Petite-Synthe bridge, public quay upstream l/b	16.0	-	5.0
Turning basin l/b, private basin through bridge r/b	18.8	-	2.2
Railway bridge, public quay downstream l/b	19.1	-	1.9
Road bridge (Dunkerque bypass)	19.2	-	1.8
Private footbridge	19.3	-	1.7
Private basin and public quay (Petite-Synthe), l/b	20.0	-	1.0
Lock (Jeu de Mail), public quay downstream r/b	20.6	3	0.4
Bridge, *junction with maritime waterways of the port of Dunkerque* (turn right along Canal de Jonction for boat moorings and Autres Horizons hire base)	21.0	-	0.0

Canal de Bourgogne

The Canal de Bourgogne connects the river Yonne at Laroche-Migennes with the river Saône at Saint Jean-de-Losne, a distance of 242km. It provides the most spectacular and heavily-locked route between the Seine and the Mediterranean, rising to a summit level at an altitude of 378m, the highest in France. This pound includes a tunnel at Pouilly-en-Auxois, 3337m in length, extended by one-way cuttings on either side. A towage service used to operate, with an electrically-powered tug and a ballasted caisson, for barges with an air draught greater than 3.10m, but this little-used and costly service had to be withdrawn. Boats proceed through the tunnel under their own power, provided that they have a suitable light. Authorisation must be requested at lock 1Y (Pouilly-en-Auxois) for boats arriving from the Yonne and at lock 1S (Escommes) for boats arriving from the Saône. When the tunnel-keeper has ensured that the pound is clear, he will give the go-ahead. Proceed at 6km/h, without stopping, so as to clear the summit level quickly.

There is little commercial traffic on the Canal de Bourgogne, which is considered by many to be the most beautiful waterway in central France. Navigators should not be discouraged by the large number of locks. There is ample compensation for the effort in the splendid scenery, with numerous sites of tourist interest to visit on or near the canal.

Locks There are 189 locks, of which 113 fall towards the Yonne and 76 towards the Saône. Lock dimensions are 39.00 by 5.20m. Two of the locks on the Yonne side have double numbers (106/107 and 114/115). These were originally built as staircase locks, but were replaced by single deep locks when the canal was upgraded to 'Freycinet' standards. On the Saône side of the summit level 10 locks (2S to 8S and 10S to 12S) are equipped for do-it-yourself operation, with a complex safety device to avoid incorrect operation and the wastage of water which may ensue. A leaflet of instructions (in French, English or German) is handed to users at lock 1Y (if heading for Dijon) or 15S (if heading for the Yonne). Four locks on the Yonne side (84Y to 81Y) and two on the Saône side (53S and 63S have been equipped for automatic operation.

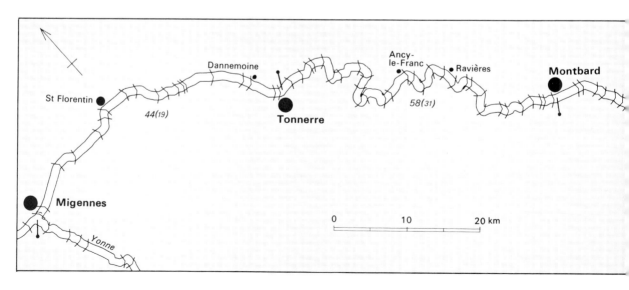

Depth The maximum authorised draught is 1.80m.

Bridges There are many fixed bridges, about half of them sited at locks. They all leave a clear headroom of 3.40m above normal water level.

Regulations The maximum authorised speed is now 6km/h for all boats throughout the length of the canal.

Towpath There is a good towpath throughout, except along the summit level and through the tunnel.

Authority
Direction Départementale de l'Equipement, 57 rue de Mulhouse, Dijon,
☎ 80 66 81 18. Subdivisions:
– Avenue Alfred Grévin, 89700 Tonnerre, ☎ 86 55 05 17 (km 0-137).
– 16 avenue Jean-Jaurès, 21000 Dijon, ☎ 80 45 05 45 (km 137-242).

Distance table

	km	lock	km
Junction with canalised river Yonne (at km 22.7)	0.0	-	242.1
Bridge	0.2	-	241.9
Deep lock 114/115Y (Laroche)	0.3	1	241.8
Migennes basin, moorings, Connoisseur Cruisers hire base, dry dock, slipway, water and fuel points, town centre 400m	0.5	-	241.6
Footbridge (access to station)	0.8	-	241.3
Lock 113Y (Cheny), bridge, basin d/s r/b	1.7	2	240.4
Esnon bridge, quay d/s r/b	6.5	-	235.6
Lock 112Y (Moulin-Neuf), quay d/s r/b	7.9	3	234.2
Brienon-sur-Armançon bridge, basin d/s, village r/b	9.2	-	232.9
Brienon sugar refinery, quay l/b	9.6	-	232.5
Lock 111Y (Boutoir), bridge, Créanton aqueduct u/s	10.2	4	231.9
Bridge (Crécy), quay d/s r/b	12.5	-	229.6
New railway bridge (TGV)	14.1	-	228.0
Lock 110Y (Duchy), bridge, quays d/s r/b	15.1	5	227.0
Lock 109Y (Maladrerie), bridge, quay d/s r/b	17.2	6	224.9
Lock 108Y (Saint-Florentin), bridge, Armance aqueduct u/s	18.6	7	223.5

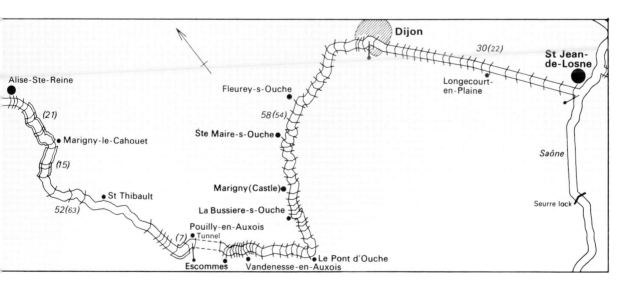

	km	*lock*	*km*
Saint-Florentin basin, Rive de France hire base, services and moorings, town centre 700m r/b	18.8	-	223.3
Bridge (Saint-Florentin, N77) and railway bridge	19.1	-	223.0
Quay r/b (for tanker barges)	19.3	-	222.8
Lock 106/107Y (**Germigny**), bridge, quays u/s and d/s r/b, village 1000m r/b	21.8	8	220.3
Lock 105Y (Egrevin), bridge	23.4	9	218.7
Butteaux bridge, quay u/s r/b, small village 700m	25.2	-	216.9
Lock 104Y (Percey), bridge	26.8	10	215.3
Percey quay r/b, small village 300m	27.5	-	214.6
Lock 103Y (Chailley), bridge	27.8	11	214.3
Lock 102Y (Villiers-Vineux)	29.4	12	212.7
Lock 101Y (Flogny)	30.5	13	211.6
Lock 100Y (Flogny), basin d/s	30.9	14	211.2
Flogny bridge, boat moorings d/s r/b, village 500m	31.4	-	210.7
La Chapelle bridge, quay d/s r/b, village 900m	32.8	-	209.3
Lock 99Y (Charrey), bridge, quay d/s r/b	34.9	15	207.2
Tronchoy bridge, village r/b	37.9	-	204.2
Lock 98Y (Cheney), bridge	39.1	16	203.0
Dannemoine quay r/b, village 400m	40.0	-	202.1
Lock 97Y (Dannemoine), bridge, water	40.3	17	201.8
Footbridge (Epineuil)	42.8	-	199.3
Lock 96Y (Tonnerre), bridge	44.1	18	198.0
Tonnerre basin, moorings, water and fuel points, town centre 1000m l/b	44.3	-	197.8
Lock 95Y (Tonnerre), bridge	44.6	19	197.5
Bridge (D905)	45.1	-	197.0
Lock 94Y (Arcot), bridge	46.5	20	195.6
Lock 93Y (Arthe)	48.7	21	193.4
Bridge (Arthe)	49.9	-	192.2
Lock 92Y (Saint-Martin)	50.4	22	191.7
Lock 91Y (Commissey), bridge	50.8	23	191.3
Commissey bridge, small village r/b	51.6	-	190.5
Lock 90Y (Tanlay)	52.7	24	189.4
Bridge (Tanlay)	52.2	-	189.9
Tanlay basin r/b, boat moorings, village with castle r/b	52.4	-	189.7
Lock 89Y (Moulin de Saint-Vinnemer), bridge	55.2	25	186.9
Saint-Vinnemer bridge, quay u/s r/b, small village	56.4	-	185.7
Lock 88Y (Saint-Vinnemer)	56.7	26	185.4
Lock 87Y (**Argentenay**), bridge, small village 300m l/b	59.6	27	182.5
Lock 86Y (**Ancy-le-Libre**), bridge, small village 400m r/b	61.4	28	180.7
Railway bridge (main line Paris-Dijon)	63.0	-	179.1
Lock 85Y (Lézinnes), bridge, water, basin u/s r/b, village 600m l/b	63.4	29	178.7
Lock 84Y (Batilley), automatic, cement works u/s l/b	65.1	30	177.0
Lock 83Y (Pacy), automatic	66.3	31	175.8
Quay (Pacy-Varennes) r/b	66.9	-	175.2
Bridge (Pacy)	67.5	-	174.6
Lock 82Y (Argenteuil), automatic, bridge	69.7	32	172.4
Railway bridge (main line Paris–Dijon)	70.2	-	171.9
Lock 81Y (Rapille), automatic, bridge	71.2	33	170.9
Bridge (Cusy)	73.7	-	168.4
Ancy-le-Franc basin, moorings r/b, water, electricity, village with castle 800m r/b	73.8	-	168.3
Lock 80Y (Ancy-le-Franc), bridge	74.4	34	167.7
Lock 79Y (**Chassignelles**), bridge, village r/b	75.4	35	166.7
Fulvy bridge, basin d/s, small village 700m l/b	77.1	-	165.0
Lock 78Y (Fulvy)	77.8	36	164.3

	km	lock	km
Lock 77Y (Papeterie), bridge	80.1	37	162.0
Lock 76Y (Huilerie), bridge	81.8	38	160.3
Railway bridge	82.1	-	160.0
Bridge (Ravières)	82.3	-	159.8
Ravières basin, village r/b	82.6	-	159.5
Bridge (Nuits-sur-Armançon), private quay u/s r/b	82.9	-	159.2
Lock 75Y (Nuits), bridge	84.1	39	158.0
Lock 74Y (Arlot), bridge	86.5	40	155.6
Lock 73Y (Cry), bridge, quay d/s r/b, small village 400m l/b	87.2	41	154.9
Lock 72Y (Perrigny), bridge	89.3	42	152.8
Lock 71Y (Forge d'Aisy), bridge, basin u/s	91.5	43	150.6
Aisy-sur-Armançon bridge, quay u/s l/b, village 400m	92.4	-	149.7
Bridge (Rougemont)	93.0	-	149.1
Lock 70Y (Rougemont), bridge	94.0	44	148.1
Lock 69Y (Buffon)	95.0	45	147.1
Bridge (Grande-Forge), quay u/s r/b	95.5	-	146.6
Buffon bridge, small village r/b	96.4	-	145.7
Former bridge-hole (Petite-Forge), restricted passage	96.9	-	145.2
Lock 68Y (Buffon)	97.6	46	144.5
Saint-Rémy bridge, quay u/s l/b, village 300m, castle opposite	98.5	-	143.6
Lock 67Y (Saint-Rémy), bridge	99.3	47	142.8
Lock 66Y (Fontenay)	100.6	48	141.5
Lock 65Y (Montbard), aqueduct u/s	101.4	49	140.7
Montbard lower basin, marina, Canal Plaisance hire base and Rive de France relay base, moorings, water, electricity, showers, near town centre	101.7	-	140.4
Lock 64Y (Montbard), bridge, water	102.2	50	139.9
Bridge (Gare)	102.3	-	139.8
Montbard upper basin l/b, moorings	102.5	-	139.6
Railway bridge (main line Paris–Dijon)	102.9	-	139.2
Lock 63Y (Nogent)	105.3	51	136.8
Nogent bridge, quay d/s l/b, small village	106.0	-	136.1
Lock 62Y (Moulin de Nogent)	106.3	52	135.8
Lock 61Y (**Courcelles**), bridge, water, small village l/b	108.2	53	133.9
Lock 60Y (Benoisey)	109.3	54	132.8
Bridge (Benoisey)	109.9	-	132.2
Lock 59Y (Seigny)	111.1	55	131.0
Bridge (Grignon)	111.4	-	130.7
Lock 58Y (Grignon)	112.2	56	129.9
Lock 57Y (Granges), bridge	112.8	57	129.3
Les Granges-sous-Grignon bridge, small village l/b	113.2	-	128.9
Lock 56Y (Venarey)	114.5	58	127.6
Venarey-les-Laumes bridge, quay d/s l/b, slipway, Connoisseur Cruisers hire base, village 400m l/b, remains of Gallo-Roman town 5km r/b	115.3	-	126.8
Lock 55Y (Venarey)	116.0	59	126.1
Bridge (Venarey)	116.3	-	125.8
Lock 54Y (Venarey)	116.6	60	125.5
Lock 53Y (Mussy)	116.9	61	125.2
Lock 52Y (Mussy), bridge	117.5	62	124.6
Lock 51Y (Pouillenay)	118.2	63	123.9
Lock 50Y (Pouillenay)	118.6	64	123.5
Lock 49Y (Pouillenay), basin u/s	118.9	65	123.2
Lock 48Y (Pouillenay)	119.1	66	123.0
Lock 47Y (Pouillenay)	119.3	67	122.8
Lock 46Y (Pouillenay)	119.6	68	122.5
Pouillenay bridge, basin u/s l/b, village 800m r/b	119.7	-	122.4

Venarey-les-Laumes. Canal de Bourgogne.
Hugh Potter

	km	lock	km
Lock 45Y (Pouillenay)	119.9	69	122.2
Lock 44Y (Pouillenay), basin upstream l/b	120.2	70	121.9
Lock 43Y (Pouillenay)	120.4	71	121.7
Lock 42Y (Pouillenay)	120.7	72	121.4
Lock 41Y (Pouillenay), bridge	121.0	73	121.1
Lock 40Y (Pouillenay)	121.3	74	120.8
Lock 39Y (Pouillenay)	121.5	75	120.6
Lock 38Y (Pouillenay)	121.8	76	120.3
Lock 37Y (Pouillenay), basin (Dos de la Camme), upstream	122.1	77	120.0
Lock 36Y (Chassey)	122.3	78	119.8
Lock 35Y (Chassey), bridge	122.7	79	119.4
Lock 34Y (Chassey)	122.9	80	119.2
Lock 33Y (Chassey)	123.3	81	118.8
Chassey bridge, small village 700m l/b	123.4	-	118.7
Lock 32Y (Chassey), basin upstream l/b	123.6	82	118.5
Railway bridge	123.9	-	118.2
Lock 31Y (Chassey), bridge	124.0	83	118.1
Lock 30Y (Marigny)	124.4	84	117.7
Lock 29Y (Marigny)	124.7	85	117.4
Lock 28Y (Marigny)	125.1	86	117.0
Marigny, lock 27Y, bridge	125.4	87	116.7
Lock 26Y (Marigny), basin upstream l/b	125.8	88	116.3
Lock 25Y (Marigny)	126.0	89	116.1
Lock 24Y (Marigny), bridge	126.4	90	115.7

	km	lock	km
Lock 23Y (Marigny), bridge	127.0	91	115.1
Lock 22Y (Marigny)	127.3	92	114.8
Lock 21Y (Marigny)	127.7	93	114.4
Lock 20Y (Marigny), bridge	128.4	94	113.7
Lock 19Y (Marigny)	128.8	95	113.3
Lock 18Y (Marigny)	129.2	96	112.9
Lock 17Y (Charigny)	129.5	97	112.6
Lock 16Y (Charigny), bridge	129.9	98	112.2
Bridge (Villeneuve-sous-Charigny)	131.0	-	111.1
Lock 15Y (Braux), bridge	132.3	99	109.8
Cutting (La Croisée), one-way traffic for 470m	132.6	-	109.5
Braux bridge, basin downstream r/b, small village 700m r/b	134.0	-	108.1
Bridge (Pierre-My)	134.8	-	107.3
Lock 14Y (Braux)	135.3	100	106.8
Cutting (Saucy), one-way traffic for 280m	135.5	-	106.6
Bridge (Saucy)	136.3	-	105.8
Pont-Royal bridge, basin downstream r/b, small village r/b	137.1	-	105.0
Lock 13Y (Pont Royal)	137.5	101	104.6
Beginning of Creuzot cutting (1130m in length), one-way traffic only	137.8	-	104.3
Bridge (Creuzot)	138.5	-	103.6
End of Creuzot cutting	139.0	-	103.1
Saint-Thibault bridge, basin upstream r/b, village 600m r/b	140.0	-	102.1

The village of Courcelles-lès-Montbard and lock 61 on the Canal du Bourgogne, a few kilometres from Montbard and the Cistercian abbey at Fontenay.
Hugh Potter

	km	lock	km
Cutting (Saint-Thibault) 145m long, with bridge	141.0	-	101.1
Bridge (D970)	142.9	-	99.2
Beurizot bridge, basin downstream r/b, village 400m r/b	143.8	-	98.3
Bridge (Gissey-le-Vieil), basin downstream r/b	145.9	-	96.2
Bridge	146.5	-	95.6
Lock 12Y (Gissey-le-Vieil), bridge	147.9	102	94.2
Basin (Grandchamp)	148.1	-	94.0
Bridge (Garreau)	148.9	-	93.2
Bridge (Eguilly), castle l/b	149.4	-	92.7
Lock 11Y (Eguilly)	149.7	103	92.4
Lock 10Y (Croix-rouge)	150.5	104	91.6
Lock 9Y (Morons)	151.3	105	90.8
Lock 8Y (Carrons)	151.7	106	90.4
Lock 7Y (Chailly), bridge	152.6	107	89.5
Lock 6Y (Argilas)	153.1	108	89.0
Lock 5Y (Pelleson)	153.4	109	88.7
Lock 4Y (Cercey), bridge	153.7	110	88.4
Lock 3Y (Champ-Roger)	154.0	111	88.1
Lock 2Y (Lochère)	154.3	112	87.8
Lock 1Y (Pouilly), bridge, beginning of summit level	154.6	113	87.5
Pouilly-en-Auxois basin r/b, Rive de France relay base, dry dock, water, village 1500m	154.7	-	87.4
Railway bridge, beginning of Pouilly cutting (narrow)	155.1	-	87.0
Pouilly tunnel, northern entrance	156.0	-	86.1
Pouilly tunnel, southern entrance	159.4	-	82.7
Bridge (Lochère)	160.1	-	82.0
End of Créancey cutting	160.3	-	81.8
Escommes basin l/b, moorings	160.4	-	81.7
Lock 1S (Escommes), end of summit level	160.7	114	81.4
Lock 2S (Sermaize), bridge	161.1	115	81.0
Lock 3S (Rambourg)	161.4	116	80.7
Lock 4S (Grand-Pré)	161.7	117	80.4
Lock 5S (Chevrotte)	162.1	118	80.0
Lock 6S (Chaume)	162.4	119	79.7
Lock 7S (Vachey)	162.7	120	79.4
Lock 8S (Vandenesse), bridge	163.1	121	79.0
Vandenesse-en-Auxois quay l/b, village r/b	163.2	-	78.9
Lock 9S (Fourneau)	163.5	122	78.6
Lock 10S (Mine)	163.9	123	78.2
Châteauneuf bridge, village with castle 1200m l/b	164.2	-	77.9
Lock 11S (Rêpe)	164.4	124	77.7
Lock 12S (Révin), bridge	165.1	125	77.0
Motorway bridge (A6, Autoroute du Soleil)	165.4	-	76.7
Lock 13S (Sainte-Sabine)	165.9	126	76.2
Bridge (Sainte-Sabine), quay downstream r/b	166.4	-	75.7
Lock 14S (Bouhey), bridge	167.6	127	74.5
Lock 15S (Fontenis)	168.4	128	73.7
Lock 16S (Crugey)	169.2	129	72.9
Crugey bridge, basin downstream r/b, small village r/b	169.5	-	72.6
Motorway bridge (A6, Autoroute du Soleil)	169.7	-	72.4
Lock 17S (Rempart)	170.1	130	72.0
Lock 18S (Roche-aux-Fées), bridge	171.4	131	70.7
Lock 19S (Sarrée), bridge	172.0	132	70.1
Bridge (Froideville)	172.5	-	69.6
Pont d'Ouche basin and Force 3 hire base r/b, small village	172.6	-	69.5
Ouche aqueduct	172.8	-	69.3
Lock 20S (Pont d'Ouche)	173.1	133	69.0
Lock 21S (Baugey)	173.8	134	68.3

St Marie-sur-Oude. Canal de Bourgogne.
Hugh Potter

	km	lock	km
Lock 22S (Veuvey)	175.1	135	67.0
Veuvey-sur-Ouche bridge, water, quay u/s r/b, village l/b	175.7	-	66.4
Lock 23S (Antheuil)	176.5	136	65.6
Lock 24S (Angles)	177.4	137	64.7
Lock 25S (Forge), bridge	179.1	138	63.0
Lock 26S (Bussière), bridge, basin u/s l/b, **La Bussière-sur-Ouche** 300m l/b	179.6	139	62.5
Lock 27S (Bouchot)	180.2	140	61.9
Lock 28S (Chaume)	181.3	141	60.8
Lock 29S (Saint-Victor), bridge, **Saint-Victor-sur-Ouche** 200m r/b	182.5	142	59.6
Lock 30S (Dennevy)	183.9	143	58.2
Bridge	184.5	-	57.6
Lock 31S (Barbirey)	185.0	144	57.1
Lock 32S (Gissey-sur-Ouche), basin downstream r/b	186.2	145	55.9
Gissey-sur-Ouche bridge, small village l/b	186.5	-	55.6
Lock 33S (Saint-Eau)	187.5	146	54.6
Lock 34S (Moulin Banet)	189.0	147	53.1
Lock 35S (Champagne)	189.8	148	52.3
Lock 36S (**Sainte-Marie**), bridge, village 300m l/b	190.5	149	51.6
Lock 37S (Roche-Canot)	192.1	150	50.0
Lock 38S (Pont-de-Pany), bridge, basin and Locadif hire base d/s	193.5	151	48.6

	km	lock	km
Skew motorway bridge (N5 Dijon spur)	194.0	-	48.1
Lock 39S (Chassagne)	194.7	152	47.4
Lock 40S (Morcoeuil)	195.4	153	46.7
Lock 41S (Potet)	196.3	154	45.8
Fleurey-sur-Ouche bridge, quay u/s r/b, village r/b	197.4	-	44.7
Lock 42S (Fleurey)	198.0	155	44.1
Lock 43S (Creux-Suzon)	199.6	156	42.5
Lock 44S (Combe-de-Fain)	200.6	157	41.5
Lock 45S (Velars), bridge	201.7	158	40.4
Velars quay r/b, village l/b over bridge	201.8	-	40.3
Lock 46S (Verrerie)	202.6	159	39.5
Lock 47S (Crucifix)	203.8	160	38.3
Lock 48S (Neuvon)	205.0	161	37.1
Lock 49S (Craie)	205.9	162	36.2
Plombières basin l/b, village 400m l/b	206.9	-	35.2
Lock 50S (Plombières), bridge	207.0	163	35.1
Lock 51S (Bruant)	208.4	164	33.7
Lock 52S (Carrières Blanches)	210.2	165	31.9
Lock 53S (Marcs-d'Or), automatic	210.5	166	31.6
New road bridge (Dijon suburbs)	210.8	-	31.3
Lock 54S (Larrey), bridge	211.3	167	30.8
Bridge	212.3	–	29.8
Dijon basin, boat harbour and Locaboat Plaisance hire base (see plan), town centre 1000m l/b	212.4	-	29.7
Lock 55S (Dijon), bridge	212.7	168	29.4
New road bridge (Dijon ring road), former basin r/b	213.3	-	28.8
Railway bridge (main line Dijon–Lyon)	213.5	-	28.6
Footbridge (access to railway yard)	214.1	-	28.0
Lock 56S (Colombière), bridge	214.9	169	27.2
Railway bridge, commercial basin d/s r/b	215.0	-	27.1
Lock 57S (Romelet), new road bridge	215.9	170	26.2
New road bridge (motorway spur)	216.3	-	25.8
Longvic bridge, village (Dijon suburb) 500m l/b	216.7	-	25.4
Lock 58S (Longvic)	217.0	171	25.1
Lock 59S (Beauregard), bridge	217.5	172	24.6
Lock 60S (Préville), quay u/s r/b	218.4	173	23.7
Lock 61S (Grand-Ouges), bridge, quay d/s r/b	219.3	174	22.8
Lock 62S (Petit-Ouges), bridge	220.7	175	21.4
Lock 63S (Vernois), automatic	221.4	176	20.7
Lock 64S (Epoisses), bridge	222.6	177	19.5
Lock 65S (Bretenières), bridge	223.6	178	18.5
Lock 66S (Rouvres), bridge	225.2	179	16.9
Lock 67S (**Thorey**), bridge, small village r/b	226.3	180	15.8
Lock 68S (Combe)	227.1	181	15.0
Lock 69S (Longecourt), bridge	228.2	182	13.9
Longecourt-en-Plaine basin, village r/b	228.3	-	13.8
Lock 70S (Potangey)	229.9	183	12.2
Bridge (Potangey)	230.6	-	11.5
Lock 71S (Aiserey), bridge	231.8	184	10.3
Lock 72S (Bietre)	233.1	185	9.0
Lock 73S (Pont-Hémery), bridge, quay d/s r/b	235.1	186	7.0
Bridge (Chapelle)	236.3	-	5.8
Lock 74S (Brazey). private quay upstream r/b (sugar mill)	236.9	187	5.2
Brazey-en-Plaine bridge (Pont de Montot), basin d/s r/b, village 500m r/b	237.4	-	4.7
Lock 75S (Viranne), bridge (D968)	239.6	188	2.5
Railway bridge	240.2	-	1.9
Saint-Usage bridge, canal basin d/s	241.5	-	0.6

Opposite:
Canal du Bourgogne. Lock No. 32 at Gissey-sur-Ouche.
Hugh Potter

	km	*lock*	*km*
Lock 76S (Saint-Jean-de-Losne), bridge	242.0	189	0.1
Saint-Jean-de-Losne, junction with Saône and entrance to canal basin (Gare d'Eau), boat harbour, slipway, dry dock, chandlery, Crown Blue Line base and several boatyards (see plan)	242.1	-	0.0

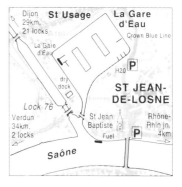

Canal de Briare

The Canal de Briare, completed in 1642, was one of the first 'watershed' canals to be built in Europe. It originally linked the river Loire at Briare to the river Loing at a point 5km north of Montargis. For centuries it was a lifeline for Paris, food produce being brought to the capital by barge from the upper Loire valley. Then the Canal latéral à la Loire was built, with its famous aqueduct crossing from the left bank to the right bank of the Loire at Briare, so the connection with the Canal de Briare was made at La Cognardière, 2.6km and four locks up the canal from its junction with the Loire. The 'by-passed' section of the canal was initially retained as a branch, then abandoned when all commercial traffic had ceased. Recently, it has been restored to allow boats to lock down to the superb canal basin in the middle of the town, where a boat harbour has been developed. The canal thus again

extends 56.7km from the original lock down into the Loire at Briare to its connection with the Canal du Loing at Buges lock, north of Montargis. Connection is made with the Canal latéral à la Loire at km 2.6 (La Cognardière, north of Briare). The canal is part of the 'Bourbonnais' route from Paris to Lyon.

Locks There are 35 locks, of which 11 (3 on the branch up from Briare and 8 on the main line of navigation) rise from Briare to the summit level at an altitude of 165m, the remaining 24 falling towards the Loing. Dimensions of the locks on the main line are 39.00 by 5.20m. Those on the branch to Briare are 30.40 by 5.20m.

Depth The maximum authorised draught is 1.80m (1.40m on the branch).

Bridges All the fixed bridges leave a minimum headroom of 3.50m above the normal water level. There are several lift bridges in the flight of locks between La Cognardière and the summit level.

Towpath There is a metalled towpath throughout.

Authority
Service de la Navigation de Nevers. Subdivisions:
– Usine Elevatrice, 45250 Briare, ☎ 60 01 26 20 (km 0-18).
– Ecluse de la Marolle, 45200 Montargis, ☎ 38 85 37 21 (km 18-54).

Distance table

	km	lock	km
Disused lock 1 down to river Loire (Baraban), limit of navigation	0.0	-	56.7
Bridge (Baraban)	0.1	-	56.6
Briare basin, boat harbour, Les Canalous and SLM Navigation hire bases, good facilities near town centre	0.3	-	56.4
Lock 2 (Briare), bridge	0.7	1	56.0
Lock 3 (La Place), bridge	1.6	2	55.1
Lock 4 (La Cognardière), footbridge	2.6	3	54.1
Junction with Canal latéral à la Loire	2.6	-	54.1
Quay (Belleau) r/b	2.8	-	53.9
Quay (Petit Moulin) r/b	4.5	-	52.2
Lock 5 (Venon), lift bridge	4.7	1	52.0
Lock 6 (Courenvaux), lift bridge, quay downstream r/b	5.9	2	50.8
Turning basin	6.1	-	50.6
Feeder crosses canal on aqueduct	6.6	-	50.1
Ouzouer-sur-Trézée bridge, village r/b	7.6	-	49.1
Lock 7 (Ouzouer-sur-Trézée), quay upstream l/b	7.9	3	48.8
Lock 8 (Moulin Neuf), lift bridge, quay upstream r/b	9.7	4	47.0
Lock 9 (Fées), lift bridge, quay upstream r/b	10.7	5	46.0
Lock 10 (Notre-Dame)	11.0	6	45.7
Site of former railway bridge	11.3	-	45.4
Lock 11 (Petit Chaloy), lift bridge, turning basin, quay u/s l/b	11.4	7	45.3
Lock 12 (Gazonne), lift bridge, beginning of summit level	12.4	8	44.3
Bridge (Rondeau), cereal loading quay	15.3	-	41.4
Bridge (Noue)	16.3	-	40.4
Lock 13 (Javacière), end of summit level	17.0	9	39.7
Lock 14 (Racault), bridge	17.5	10	39.2
Lock 15 (St Joseph)	17.8	11	38.9
Lock 16 (Chantepinot)	18.1	12	38.6

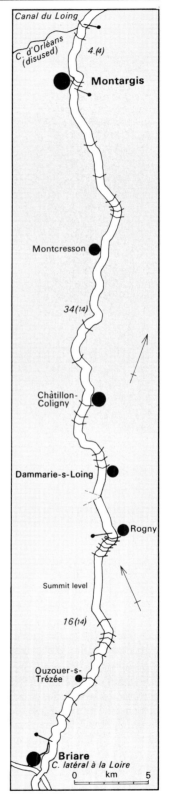

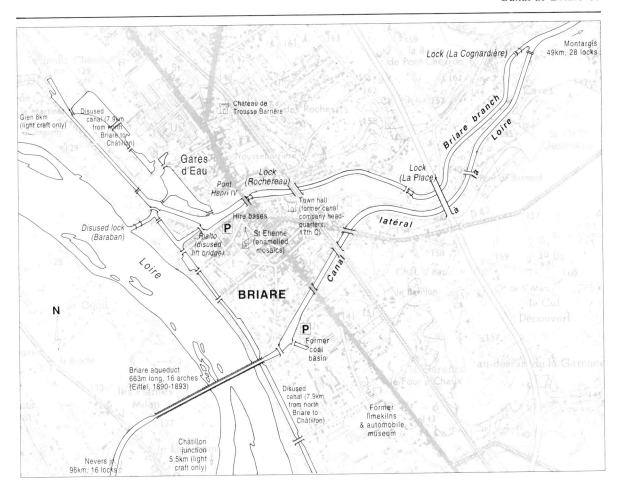

	km	lock	km
Lock 17 (Rogny), bridge, original 17th century flight of seven (staircase) locks, r/b	18.4	13	38.3
Lock 18 (Sainte Barbe), bridge	18.7	14	38.0
Rogny bridge, basin r/b, Briare Nautique hire base, shops, quayside restaurant	18.8	-	37.9
Turning basin r/b	20.0	-	36.7
Bridge (Bruxelles)	22.1	-	34.6
Dammarie-sur-Loing bridge, quay upstream r/b	23.1	-	33.6
Lock 19 (Dammarie-sur-Loing)	23.3	15	33.4
Lock 20 (Picardie)	23.8	16	32.9
Lock 21 (Moulin Brûlé), bridge	24.4	17	32.3
Lock 22 (Briquemault), lift bridge	27.1	18	29.6
Lock 23 (Gazon)	27.6	19	29.1
Turning basin r/b	27.9	-	28.8
Lock 24 (Châtillon)	28.4	20	28.3
Châtillon-Coligny bridge, quay and Tourisme Fluvial du Centre hire base u/s r/b, 12th century castle in village	28.9	-	27.8
Former railway bridge	29.4	-	27.3
Footbridge (Ronce)	30.4	-	26.3
Lock 25 (Lépinoy), bridge	32.0	21	24.7
Bridge (Brangers)	33.2	-	23.5
Lock 26 (Montbouy)	34.3	22	22.4

	km	lock	km
Montbouy bridge, quay d/s l/b,	34.5	-	22.2
Bridge	36.0	-	20.7
Footbridge, castle and gallo-roman ruins l/b	36.9	-	19.8
Bridge (Salles), quay downstream l/b	37.3	-	19.4
Montcresson bridge, quay, turning basin u/s village 400m	40.2	-	16.5
Lock 27 (Montambert)	42.8	23	13.9
Lock 28 (Chesnoy)	43.2	24	13.5
Lock 29 (Moulin de Tours), bridge	43.6	25	13.1
Lock 30 (Souffre-Douleur)	44.1	26	12.6
Lock 31 (Sablonnière), bridge, **Conflans-sur-Loing** 800m	46.0	27	10.7
Lock 32 (Tuilerie), bridge, oil terminal d/s l/b, restaurant	48.0	28	8.7
Railway bridge	49.4	-	7.3
Bridge (Moulin Bardin)	50.3	-	6.4
Road bridge (Montargis by-pass)	50.6	-	6.1
Bridge (St Roch), basin downstream l/b	51.8	-	4.9
Montargis footbridge, town centre l/b	52.3	-	4.4
Lock 33 (Marolle), water, dry dock u/s l/b	52.4	29	4.3
Lock 34 (Reinette), bridge	52.7	30	4.0
Bridge (Loing), N60	52.8	-	3.9
Bridge (Pâtis), N7	53.1	-	3.6
Road bridge, Montargis quays downstream r/b	53.4	-	3.3
Bridge (Ane)	54.5	-	2.2
Private commercial quays	54.8	-	1.9
Railway bridge, basin downstream (commercial quays)	55.7	-	1.0
Lock 35 (Langlée), bridge	57.0	31	0.7
Lock 36 (Buges), bridge, *junction with Canal du Loing* and with disused Canal d'Orleans, upstream of lock l/b)	56.7	32	0.0

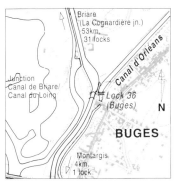

Canal de Calais

The Canal de Calais runs 29.5km from its junction with the river Aa at Le West to the port of Calais. It has three branches, extending to the small towns of Audruicq (2.4km), Ardres (4.8km) and Guînes (6.2km), lying on the edge of the Flanders plain. The main line is still regularly used by commercial traffic, and works to upgrade the canal for 600-tonne barges have been largely completed. These include the reconstruction of Hennuin lock, demolition of the iron swing-bridge at the junction, and automation of lift-bridges. Both the main line of the canal and the branches make attractive cruising waterways.

Locks There is only one lock, situated at Hennuin, with a drop of about 1m in the direction of Calais. The former 38m lock has been replaced by a modern lock for high-capacity barges, 92.00m long and 8.00m wide (opened in 1990). The distance table shows a second lock within the port of Calais, although the official limit of the inland waterway is at the Pont Mollien (km 29.5).

Depth The maximum authorised draught has been increased to 2.00m on the main route. The branches are subject to silting, and offer reduced depths as follows: 1.40m on the Audruicq branch, 1.20m on the Ardres branch and 1.80m on the Guînes branch.

Bridges All the fixed bridges on the main line leave a minimum headroom of 3.17m above the highest navigable water level (3.47m above normal level). The corresponding dimensions for the branches are respectively: Audruicq 3.40/3.70m, Ardres 2.80/3.10m and Guînes 3.10/3.40m. It must also be noted that vessels exceeding 28m in length cannot enter the branch to Ardres on account of the difficulty in turning under the Sans-Pareil bridge at the junction with the main line.

Towpath There is a metalled towpath throughout.

Authority
Direction Régionale de la Navigation, Lille. Subdivision:
Terre-Plein du Jeu de Mail, BP 1008, 59375 Dunkerque, ☎ 28 24 38 56

Above opposite:
Canal de Briare near Rogny.
Derek Bowskill

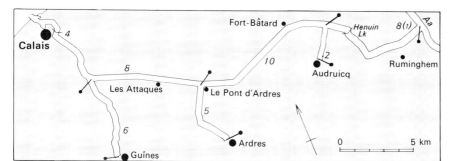

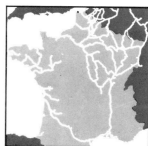

Distance table

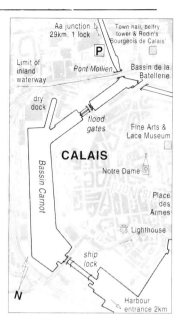

	km	lock	km
Junction with river Aa (km 13.7)	0.0	-	29.8
Public quay l/b, **Ruminghem** 1200 l/b	2.0	-	27.8
New bridge	2.1	-	27.7
New lock (Hennuin), water	6.0	1	23.8
Hennuin lift bridge, quay downstream l/b, small village	6.6	-	23.2
Junction with Audruicq branch, l/b	8.1	-	21.7
Fort-Bâtard bridge, quay upstream r/b	10.8	-	19.0
Motorway bridge (A26)	15.9	-	13.9
Sugar mill and quay, l/b	17.2	-	12.6
Le Pont d'Ardres bridge (Sans-Pareil), *junction with Ardres branch*, l/b, quay downstream r/b	18.1	-	11.7
Les Attaques footbridge and automatic lift bridge, quay u/s r/b	21.1	-	8.7
Turning basin	22.4	-	7.4
Bridge (Pont de Briques)	24.5	-	5.3
Junction with Guînes branch, l/b	25.6	-	4.2
Coulogne automatic lift bridge	26.2	-	3.6
Industrial quays	26.8	-	3.0
Road bridge (Calais bypass)	27.2	-	2.6
Railway bridge	27.4	-	2.4
Lift bridge (Curie), automatic	27.7	-	2.1
Bridge (Saint-Pierre)	28.4	-	1.4
Swing bridge and footbridge (Vic), automatic	28.9	-	0.9
Calais public quay r/b, water	29.3	-	0.5
Bridge (Pont Mollien), limit of inland waterway, moorings d/s	29.5	-	0.3
Lock and bridge, access to inner basin of port of Calais (2400m to Channel)	29.8	-	0.0

Audruicq branch

Audruicq canal basin, limit of navigation, town centre 500m	0.0	-	2.4
Bridge (Pont Rouge)	1.2	-	1.2
Junction with Canal de Calais (km 8.1)	2.4	-	0.0

Ardres branch

Ardres quay, canal ends in cul-de-sac, town centre 500m	0.0	-	4.8
Swinging footbridge (Brêmes), disused, limit of navigation	1.0	-	3.8
Brick works and quay l/b	1.2	-	3.6
Railway and road bridges	4.7	-	0.1
Junction with Canal de Calais (km 18.1) at Sans-Pareil bridge	4.8	-	0.0

Guînes branch

Terminal basin (filled in)	0.0	-	6.2
Guînes public quay, town centre 500m	0.4	-	5.8
Turning basin	1.2	-	5.0
Lift bridge (Banc-Valois)	2.4	-	3.8
Lift bridge (Ecluse Carrée)	4.1	-	2.1
Lift bridge (Planche-Tournoire)	5.1	-	1.1
Junction with Canal de Calais (km 25.6), railway bridge	6.2	-	0.0

Canal du Centre

The Canal du Centre, one of the first watershed links to be built in central France, was opened to navigation in 1790. It rises from the Saône at Chalon-sur-Saône to a summit level at an altitude of just over 300m, in the coal mining and industrial basin of Le Creusot/Montceau-les-Mines, and then drops more gently to connect with the Canal latéral à la Loire at Digoin, a distance of 112km. The original cut through Chalon, entering the Saône at the Port de la Chambre de Commerce, was filled in in the 1950s and obliterated by a modern boulevard, and replaced by a new cut to the north of the town. This cut is 2.1km shorter than the original line, which explains the discrepancy between the distances in the table below and those which may be observed along the route. A 3km length of the old line is retained as a branch serving the Saint-Gobain factory. It connects with the main line at km 5.7 (3.7 in the revised distance table below).

Locks There are 61 locks, of which 35 (numbered 1 to 35M for Mediterranean) fall towards Chalon and 26 (numbered 1 to 26O for Océan) fall towards Digoin. Dimensions are 39.00 by 5.20m, except for lock 35M on the new cut at Chalon, which is 40.00 by 6.00m. This lock replaces three on the original line, hence its exceptional depth of 10.75m. All the locks on the Mediterranean side of the summit are equipped for automatic operation, with the lock entrance controlled by lights and the actual locking cycle actuated by pulling on the blue cord set in a steel pillar at the lock side. In case of emergency, the cycle is interrupted by pulling on the red cord (see also the section on automatic locks in the Introduction).

Depth The maximum authorised draught is 1.80m.

Bridges The bridges leave a nominal minimum headroom of 3.50m, but boats approaching this height must pay particular attention at Saint-Léger-sur-Dheune bridge (km 31), which is reported to offer a few centimetres less headroom.

Towpath There is a metalled towpath throughout, serving as a public road (D974) between Paray-le-Monial and Saint-Léger-sur-Dheune. Elsewhere, the towpath is in reasonable condition.

Authority
Direction Departementale de l'Equipement, Saône-et-Loire.
Subdivision: 9e écluse Océan, 71300 Montceau-les-Mines, ☎ 85 57 21 98

Distance table

	km	lock	km
Chalon-sur-Saône, *junction with Saône*	0.0	-	112.1
Turning basin and industrial quays	1.2	-	110.9
New lock 35 (difference in level 10.76m)	1.5	1	110.6
Bridge (D5)	1.7	-	110.4
Railway bridge	2.1	-	110.0
Bridge (industrial estate)	2.4	-	109.7
Bridge (D19)	3.2	-	108.9
Junction with St Gobain factory branch (former main line)	3.7	-	108.4
Quay l/b	4.5	-	107.6
Lock 34, bridge, **Fragnes** l/b	5.9	2	106.2

	km	lock	km
Motorway bridge (A6)	6.3	-	105.8
Lock 33, bridge, **La Loyère** l/b	7.5	3	104.6
Bridge (Gauchard), trunk road N6	9.1	-	103.0
Lock 32	9.3	4	102.8
Bridge (**Fontaine**), quay downstream l/b, village 2000m	10.8	-	101.3
Lock 31, bridge (Gué de Niffette)	11.7	5	100.4
Lock 30	12.4	6	99.7
Lock 29	13.1	7	99.0
Lock 28	13.6	8	98.5
Lock 27	14.1	9	98.0
Lock 26, bridge, quay downstream r/b, **Rully** 2000m	14.5	10	97.6
Lock 25	15.1	11	97.0
Lock 24	15.7	12	96.4
Chagny basin, boat moorings, town and main line railway station l/b	17.3	-	94.8
Bridge (Chagny) and aqueduct over main line railway	17.4	-	94.7
Bridge (Bouzeron)	18.0	-	94.1
Remigny bridge, quay, village below canal l/b	20.3	-	91.8
Bridge (Fontaine Beaunoise), D974	21.4	-	90.7
Santenay quay l/b, village 1000m	22.5	-	89.6
Bridge (Corchanut)	22.8	-	89.3
Cheilly-lès-Maranges bridge, quay l/b, village 1000m	24.3	-	87.8
Saint-Gilles bridge, quay and village r/b	26.3	-	85.8
Lock 23	26.9	13	85.2
Lock 22	27.4	14	84.7
Dennevy bridge, quay l/b, village r/b	28.3	-	83.8
Lock 21	28.7	15	83.4
Bridge (Planche-Tapois, D148)	29.6	-	82.5
Lock 20	29.9	16	82.2
Saint-Léger-sur-Dheune bridge, boat moorings u/s, village r/b (warning: very low bridge)	30.7	-	81.4
Lock 19	31.9	17	80.2
Bridge (Lochères)	32.4	-	79.7
Lock 18, bridge	33.6	18	78.5
Lock 17, bridge, **Saint-Bérain-sur-Dheune** r/b	34.8	19	77.3
Quay l/b	35.0	-	77.1
Lock 16	35.8	20	76.3
Lock 15	36.2	21	75.9
Bridge (Motte)	36.5	-	75.6
Lock 14, quay downstream l/b, **Perreuil** 1500m	37.6	22	74.5
Lock 13	38.5	23	73.6
Lock 12, bridge	39.1	24	73.0
Lock 11 (Villeneuve)	40.7	25	71.4
Lock 10 (Chez-le-Roi), bridge	41.2	26	70.9
Lock 9 (Moulin de Saint-Julien)	41.7	27	70.4
Saint-Julien-sur-Dheune bridge, quay downstream r/b	42.3	-	69.8
Lock 8 (Abbaye)	42.6	28	69.5
Lock 7 (Rocher)	43.0	29	69.1
Lock 6 (Motte) canal museum and restored lock 9 of original canal, l/b	43.7	30	68.4
Lock 5 (Forge), bridge, Ecuisses, 1500m r/b	44.6	31	67.5
Lock 4 (Ravin), bridge	45.3	32	66.8
Lock 3 (Fourneau)	45.6	33	66.5
Lock 2 (Charmois)	45.9	34	66.2
Lock 1 (Méditerranée), bridge, quay d/s r/b, beginning of summit level	46.1	35	66.0
TGV railway viaduct (Paris-Lyon high speed line)	46.4	-	65.7
New road bridge (N80)	46.9	-	65.2

Péniche and small cabin cruiser on the Canal du Centre at Génelard.
Author

	km	lock	km
Overhead power lines	47.1	-	65.0
Bridge (D18)	47.5	-	64.6
Bridge (Jeanne-Rose)	47.7	-	64.4
Montchanin bridge (D28), café-restaurant 400m, town centre 1800m	49.7	-	62.4
Connoisseur Cruisers hire base on short branch, east bank	49.9	-	62.2
Lock 1 (Océan), end of summit level	50.2	36	61.9
Lock 2 (Brenots), bridge	51.3	37	60.8
Lock 3 (Favée)	51.7	38	60.4
Lock 4 (Parizenot), bridge	53.3	39	58.8
Lock 5 (Planche-Calard), bridge	55.7	40	56.4
Lock 6 (Brûlard)	56.3	41	55.8
Lock 7 (Roche), bridge (Saint-Gelin)	57.2	42	54.9
Railway bridge	57.9	-	54.2
Blanzy bridge, quay upstream r/b, village r/b	58.9	-	53.2
Lock 8 (Mireaux)	59.9	43	52.2
Lock 9 (Montceau), bridge, freight office	61.7	44	50.4
Footbridge (Centre Culturel)	62.0	-	50.1
Montceau-les-Mines basin, moorings l/b, large town	61.9		50.2
Footbridge, adjacent to swing bridge (Montceau)	62.5	-	49.6
Bridge	62.7	-	49.4
Railway bridge	63.1	-	49.0
Bridge (Lucie), service station r/b, basin downstream l/b	64.0	-	48.1
Railway bridge	64.4	-	47.7
Bridge (Chavannes)	65.0	-	47.1
Lock 10 (Chavannes)	65.2	45	46.9
Lock 11 (Vernois)	65.6	46	46.5

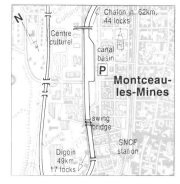

	km	lock	km
Railway bridge	66.1	-	46.0
Bridge (Galuzot), restaurant, service station downstream r/b	66.7	-	45.4
Bridge (Maison Morin)	68.0	-	44.1
Bridge (Pont des Vernes)	69.3	-	42.8
Lock 12 (Four)	69.9	47	42.2
Bridge (Four)	70.5	-	41.6
Lock 13 (Azy)	71.8	48	40.3
Ciry-le-Noble bridge, basin downstream l/b, village r/b	72.7	-	39.4
Lock 14 (Ciry), bridge, quay downstream r/b	73.5	49	38.6
Lock 15 (Ciry), bridge	76.8	50	35.3
Quay l/b (Vernizy), service station r/b	78.7	-	33.4
Bridge (over entrance to Génelard cutting), one-way traffic	78.8	-	33.3
Lock 16 (Génelard)	79.4	51	32.7
Génelard bridge, basin downstream l/b, moorings, village 400m over level crossing	79.5	-	32.6
Lock 17 (Montet)	80.4	52	31.7
Bridge (Montet)	81.4	-	30.7
Palinges bridge, quay upstream l/b, village l/b	83.0	-	29.1
Bridge (Corbary)	83.8	-	28.3
Lock 18 (Thiellay)	84.6	53	27.5
Lock 19 (Digoine), bridge, basin d/s l/b, Digoine castle 1500m	86.1	54	26.0
Bridge (Montceau)	87.7	-	24.4
Bridge (Gravoine), quay upstream l/b	89.1	-	23.0
Lock 20 (Gravoine)	89.5	55	22.6
Lock 21 (Haillers), bridge	92.3	56	19.8
Volesvres bridge, village 600m r/b	93.7	-	18.4
Lock 22 (Volesvres)	93.9	57	18.2
Bridge (Bord), basin downstream r/b	95.8	-	16.3
Quay l/b (Corneloup)	96.9	-	15.2
Railway bridge	97.2	-	14.9
Bridge (Romay)	97.7	-	14.4
Lock 23 (L'Hyron)	99.0	58	13.1
Paray-le-Monial quays and turning basin r/b, boat moorings, town centre 400m	99.3	-	12.8
Bridge (Faubourg), service station l/b	99.7	-	12.4
Bridge (Quatre-Chemins)	100.0	-	12.1
Bridge (Quarrés)	101.3	-	10.8
Lock 24 (Quarrés)	101.8	59	10.3
Lock 25 (Mont)	102.4	60	9.7
New road bridge (N70)	102.7	-	9.4
Colaillot quay l/b (commercial)	103.5	-	8.6
Bridge (Colaillot)	103.9	-	8.2
Lock 26 (Bessons)	105.6	61	6.5
Bridge (Paradis), quay upstream r/b	108.2	-	3.9
Junction with Arroux feeder canal (rigole de l'Arroux), formerly navigable 13km to Gueugnon	109.6	-	2.5
Bridge (Blattiers)	110.4	-	1.7
Commercial quays	110.9	-	1.2
Railway bridge	111.1	-	1.0
Digoin basin, moorings, Les Canalous hire base, fuel, town centre 800m but boats may moor closer to the centre (see plan)	112.0	-	0.1
Bridge (Digoin ring road), *junction with Canal latéral à la Loire*	112.1	-	0.0

Charente

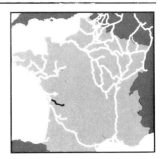

The Charente, one of the most beautiful cruising waterways in France, is navigable over a distance of no less than 164km from Angoulême to the sea. The last 24km from the small coasting port of Tonnay-Charente is tidal estuary, and above this point the waterway is officially unnavigable, having been 'struck from the list of navigable waterways' following disappearance of the last commercial traffic in the 1940s. This legal nicety means that navigation is at the boater's risk and peril, but is otherwise irrelevant, for the départements of Charente and Charente-Maritime, to whom the waterway was conceded partly in 1952 and partly in 1963, have restored navigation throughout, and are effectively committed to maintaining the channel and the structures in navigable condition. Convenient and attractive moorings have been provided at many towns and villages. Several hire firms operate on the river, in addition to trip boats at the main towns, and pleasure cruising is gradually developing, despite the disadvantage of the river's isolation from the rest of the waterway network.

An attractive tributary, the Boutonne, is navigable over a distance of 29km from its confluence with the Charente at km 128 to the small town of Saint-Jean-d'Angély, with four locks. These locks were restored in the 1980s, and one of the passes of the Carillon tide barrier (near the confluence) was provided with a raised footbridge to allow boats to pass when the levels of the two rivers permit. The cumbersome procedure is dissuasive, and few boats have taken advantage of this possibility (about a dozen in 1990). However, construction of a new lock is projected to bypass this barrier, and the Boutonne will doubtless then attract many more boats.

From the sea to km 134 the river is considered as an entrance channel to the ports of Rochefort and Tonnay-Charente. Boats must leave the main channel clear for ships, and anchoring in the channel is forbidden.

Upstream from Tonnay-Charente, speed is limited to 12km/h in Charente-Maritime (up to km 67) and to 10km/h in Charente. There are local restrictions to 6km/h.

Locks There are 21 locks, the minimum dimensions of which are 34.00 by 6.30m. Saint-Savinien lock (48.50 by 8.00m) was built in 1968 as part of a multi-purpose river improvement and flood control scheme. Most of the other locks are unattended, and users have to lock through themselves, using the straightforward paddle winding gear and gate winches. A clear instruction leaflet in English is issued by the waterway authority (addresses below). The locks on the Boutonne are 30.50m by 5.50m. To pass through the Carillon tide barrier on the Boutonne, advance notice is to be given to the authority at Rochefort, for manual operation of the gates. Passage is possible whenever the tide coefficient is greater than or equal to 70. The authority will send an itinerant lock-keeper to lock boats through the first two locks (Bel-Ebat and l'Houmée), while the other two are manned normally.

Depth In the tidal estuary, the least depth available at low tide is 3.00m. Upstream as far as Cognac, the least depth is 1.50m at low water, but during the summer, when the gates of the barrages at Saint-Savinien and La Baine are closed, the minimum water levels maintained are such that 2.50m may be counted on. The available depth decreases progressively working upstream, with 1.50m around Jarnac, and 0.80 to 1.00m between Châteauneuf and Angoulême.

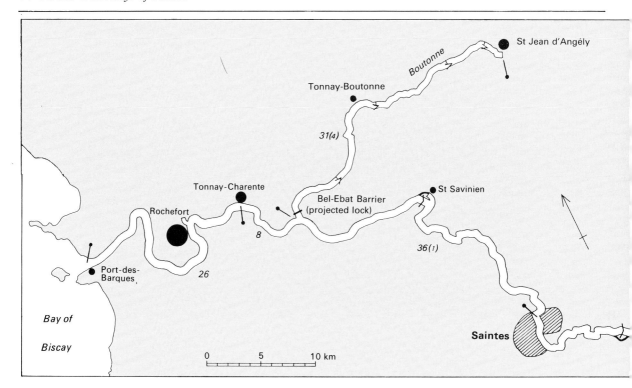

Bridges The fixed bridges offer a minimum headroom of 3.55m above the highest navigable water level. This is the headroom under the railway bridge (Pont de la Cèpe) at km 133, where the mobile span is now no longer in operation. The second lowest bridge is at Vibrac (km 32), with a headroom of 3.72m.

Towpath The towpath has long fallen into disuse.

Authority

Direction Départementale de l'Equipement de la Charente.
Subdivision: Hydrologique, 46 rue de Québec, 16017 Angoulême, ☎ 45 61 06 44 (km 0-67).
Direction Départementale de l'Equipement de la Charente-Maritime.
Subdivision: Maritime et Hydrologie, BP125, Bassin No. 3, 17301 Rochefort-sur-Mer, ☎ 46 99 01 47 (km 67-163).

Distance table

	km	lock	km
Angoulême quay l/b (Port l'Houmeau), SAGEM hire base, town centre 1000m, river may be navigated 2.7km upstream to Chalonne mill	0.0	-	163.5
Lock (Saint-Cybard) r/b (against island)	1.1	1	162.4
(U/s boats) river divides, take l/b arm	1.3	-	162.2
Saint-Cybard bridge	1.5	-	162.0
Island navigation l/b	2.8	-	160.7
New road bridge (Angoulême bypass)	3.2	-	160.3
Bridge	3.8	-	159.7
Lock (Thouérat), r/b, opposite gunpowder factory	4.5	2	159.0

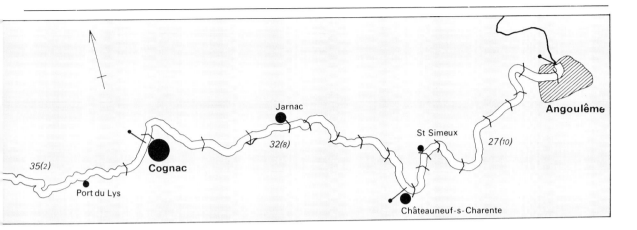

	km	lock	km
(U/s boats) river divides, keep to r/b	5.6	-	157.9
Islands, navigation l/b, **Fléac** r/b	6.3	-	157.2
Bridge, island d/s, take r/b arm	7.7	-	155.8
Lock (Basseau) r/b, weir	7.9	3	155.6
Lock (Fleurac) r/b	9.6	4	153.9
D/s end of Fleurac islands (u/s boats keep to r/b)	10.0	-	153.5
Islands, navigation l/b	10.9	-	152.6
Lock (La Mothe) l/b	12.1	5	151.4
Bridge, **Nersac** 1000m l/b, islands d/s, navigation r/b	13.2	-	150.3
Islands, navigation r/b	16.0	-	147.5
Sireuil bridge, Intercroisières hire base	17.5	-	146.0
Lock (Sireuil) l/b	17.8	6	145.7
D/s end of island (u/s boats keep to l/b)	18.6	-	144.9
River divides, navigation in r/b arm	20.5	-	143.0
Lock (La Liège)	21.4	7	142.1
(U/s boats) river divides, take r/b arm	21.6	-	141.9
Lock (**Saint-Simeux**) l/b, access to village and Holiday Charente hire base via weir stream r/b	23.1	8	140.4
Bridge (u/s boats turn into l/b arm above bridge)	23.8	-	139.7
Entrance to lock-cut r/b (visible at last minute)	24.1	-	139.4
Lock (Malvy)	24.3	9	139.2
(U/s boats) river divides, take r/b arm	24.6	-	138.9
Island (Ile des Groles), navigation r/b	25.8	-	137.7
Lock (Châteauneuf) in short lock-cut r/b, weir l/b	27.0	10	136.5
End of lock-cut (u/s boats take r/b arm)	27.2	-	136.3
Châteauneuf-sur-Charente bridge, quays both banks, small town 200m l/b	27.5	-	136.0
Island (Ile Muguet), navigation r/b	28.9	-	134.6
Entrance to backwater (Brassour) l/b	29.8	-	133.7
River divides, navigation in l/b arm	31.0	-	132.5
(U/s boats) river divides, navigation in l/b arm	31.5	-	132.0
Entrance to lock-cut (middle of three channels), bridge	31.9	-	131.6
Lock (Vibrac), one side slopes, the other has a step	32.1	11	131.4
End of lock-cut	32.2	-	131.3
Saint-Simon quay and village r/b (u/s boats take l/b arm)	33.9	-	129.6
Juac bridge, small village r/b	34.6	-	128.9
Former lock-cut l/b, keep to river	34.8	-	128.7
Lock (Juac) l/b, weir	35.0	12	128.5

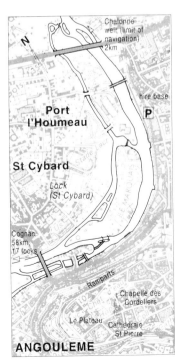

	km	*lock*	*km*
(U/s boats) former lock-cut l/b, keep to river	35.2	-	128.3
Entrance to lock-cut r/b (visible at last minute)	37.8	-	125.7
Lock (Saintonge), **Bassac** 1000m r/b	38.1	13	125.4
End of lock-cut	38.2	-	125.3
Bridge (Vinade), **Bassac** 1000m r/b	39.0	-	124.5
Weir (Gondeville) l/b, keep to r/b	41.6	-	121.9
Lock (Gondeville)	41.7	14	121.8
Weir streams l/b, keep to r/b	42.1	-	121.4
Island, navigation l/b	43.0	-	120.5
Entrance to lock-cut l/b	43.9	-	119.6
Lock (Jarnac), end of lock-cut	44.1	15	119.4
Jarnac bridge, quay and small town r/b	44.3	-	119.2
Entrance to lock-cut r/b	47.6	-	115.9
Lock (Bourg-Charente)	47.9	16	115.6
End of lock-cut	48.0	-	115.5
Bourg-Charente bridge, village l/b	48.7	-	114.8
Lock (Garde-Moulin) l/b, weir	52.5	17	111.0
Island, navigation l/b	53.7	-	109.8
Bridge (D15), **Saint-Brice** village and castle 600m r/b	54.0	-	109.5
Small island, navigation l/b	54.8	-	108.7
Island, navigation l/b	55.6	-	107.9
Island, navigation l/b	56.0	-	107.5
Entrance to Solençon backwater r/b (not navigable)	56.6	-	106.9
Bridge	57.3	-	106.2
Entrance to lock-cut r/b (mill stream l/b)	59.0	-	104.5
Lock (Cognac)	59.1	18	104.4
End of lock-cut (u/s boats take l/b arm)	59.3	-	104.2
Cognac bridge, quays d/s, Charente Plaisance hire base, town centre and distilleries l/b	59.4	-	104.1
Bridge	60.7	-	102.8
Island, navigation l/b	61.3	-	102.2
Island, navigation r/b	61.8	-	101.7
Lock (Crouin) in short lock-cut r/b	62.8	19	100.7
Merpins bridge, small village 1000m l/b	66.0	-	97.5
Limit of Charente and Charente Maritime départements l/b	67.2	-	96.3
Quay (Port-du-Lys) l/b, boat club moorings, slipway	67.5	-	96.0
Limit of Charente and Charente Maritime départements r/b	67.2	-	95.3
Brives-sur-Charente bridge, quay, small village 800m l/b	72.2	-	91.4
Rouffiac boat moorings and slipway, l/b	76.7		86.8
Dompierre-sur-Charente ferry, boat club moorings with fixed and floating pontoons, slipway, village 500m r/b	77.4	-	86.1
Bridge (D134) and railway bridge (Beillant)	80.5	-	83.0
River divides, navigation in r/b arm	82.0	-	81.5
Entrance to lock-cut l/b	82.4	-	81.1
Lock (La Baine)	82.7	20	80.8
End of lock-cut (u/s boats take middle of 3 channels)	82.8	-	80.7
Chaniers ferry, moorings and Charente Croisières hire base u/s r/b, small village 300m r/b	83.6	-	79.9
Port-Hublé slipway, r/b	86.8	-	76.7
Saint-Sorlin r/b	89.8	-	73.7
Railway bridge (Lucérat)	91.8	-	71.7
Road bridge (Saintonge), quay l/b (Quai des Roches)	93.5	-	70.0
Footbridge	94.1	-	69.4
Saintes bridge (Pont de Palissy), quay u/s r/b, town centre l/b, railway station 1000m r/b	94.4	-	69.1
Pontoon moorings (Saintes boat club) l/b	95.2	-	68.3
Courbiac castle l/b, race track r/b	97.0	-	66.5
Bussac castle r/b	99.2	-	64.3

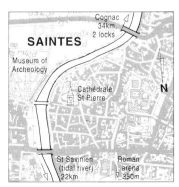

	km	lock	km
Quay (Port-la-Pierre) r/b	104.9	-	58.6
Taillebourg bridge, quay and village r/b	106.8	-	56.7
Port-d'Envaux quay and village l/b (former ferry)	109.5	-	54.0
Navigation enters lock-cut l/b, straight on for			
Saint-Savinien boat harbour and Saintonge Rivières hire			
base, 500m d/s on river, pontoons and slipway, village r/b	116.1	-	47.4
Lock (Saint-Savinien), bridge	116.7	21	46.8
End of lock-cut	117.1	-	46.4
Bridge (Pont de l'Houmée), **Bords** 2000m r/b	127.0	-	36.5
Confluence of Boutonne r/b, navigable to St Jean-d'Angély	128.0	-	33.5
Railway bridge (Pont de la Cèpe)	133.4	-	30.1
New road bridge (N137 Tonnay-Charente bypass)	136.1	-	27.4
Tonnay-Charente suspension bridge, quays for coasters and			
small town d/s r/b	137.7	-	25.8
Saint-Gobain factory, quay r/b	139.0	-	24.5
Junction with Canal de la Charente à la Seudre (disused) l/b	140.2	-	23.3
Commercial port basin through lock r/b	143.6	-	19.9
Rochefort basins 1 (commercial) and 2 (reopened and			
developed as a marina in 1989) through lock, r/b,			
town centre 300m (see plan)	144.1	-	19.4
Quay (Quai de l'Artillerie) with pontoon moorings, r/b	144.2		19.3
Former transporter bridge (Martou)	147.5	-	16.0
Road bridge (with lifting span)	147.9	-	15.6
New road bridge (Viaduc de la Charente, opened 1990)	148.1	-	15.4
Soubise l/b, former ferry, restaurant	151.7	-	11.8
Entrance to Canal de Charras r/b (not navigable)	157.5	-	6.0
Port-des-Barques l/b, limit of sea	163.5	-	0.0

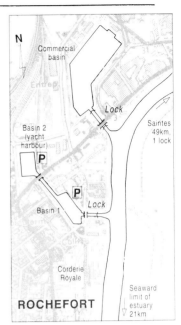

Boutonne

	km	lock	km
Confluence with Charente (km 128)	0.0	-	30.7
Bridge (Carillon)	0.2	-	30.5
River divides, arm leading to future lock l/b, in the meantime			
keep to r/b arm to pass through tide barrier	0.4	-	30.3
Carillon tide barrier	0.7	1	30.0
Railway bridge	1.1	-	29.6
Overhead power lines	3.6	-	27.1
Entrance to lock-cut, l/b	5.8	-	24.9
Lock (Bel-Ebat)	6.0	2	24.7
Sharp bend	10.5	-	21.2
Footbridge	13.2	-	18.5
Tonnay-Boutonne bridge, village r/b	14.0	-	17.7
Junction with Canal Sainte-Julienne (drain), r/b	15.1	-	16.6
Lock (L'Houmée) in short cut, l/b	15.7	3	16.0
Sharp bend	18.4	-	13.3
Torxé bridge, small village r/b	21.2	-	10.5
Lock (Voissay) in short cut, l/b	24.0	4	6.7
Overhead power line	26.4	-	4.3
Motorway bridge (A10)	27.0	-	3.7
Entrance to lock-cut, l/b	28.1	-	2.6
Lock (Bernouet)	28.2	5	2.5
Bridge (Les Granges), effective limit of navigability,			
boat club and moorings d/s r/b, slipway	29.2	-	1.5
Saint-Jean-d'Angély bridge (Saint-Jacques),			
limit of waterway, town centre 600m r/b	30.7	-	0.0

Cher and Canal du Berry

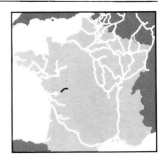

The river Cher was canalised in the 1830s over a distance of about 130km from the confluence with the Loire west of Tours up to Vierzon. After completion of the Canal de Berry, the northern branch of which runs parallel to the river Cher from Vierzon down to Noyers-sur-Cher, the river was no longer maintained for navigation in this section. This left 75.6km of river navigation, although the last 16km down to the Loire was effectively bypassed by a short junction canal running east of Tours from the Cher to the Loire (obliterated years ago by the Paris–Bordeaux motorway).

Projects for restoration of the river were for several years blocked by opposition of the owners of the remarkable early 16th century Chenonceau castle, which strides the river on five arches, and a solution has still to be defined to reconcile the conflicting interests of tourist visits to the castle and navigation on the river, the possible indecorous behaviour of a minority of boat crews being difficult to control. In the meantime, however, the Syndicat du Cher Canalisé in the *département* of Loir-et-Cher, to whom the river was conceded in the 1950s, has gone ahead with restoration of its section, and in summer 1991 a 29km length of the river, with 8 locks, is being opened to navigation. In early 1992, the interest of this isolated length of waterway will be greatly increased by the planned reopening of the entrance lock to the Canal du Berry, giving access to the canal basin and village of Noyers-sur-Cher. Further restoration up to the village of Selles-sur-Cher should follow in the short term, adding a further 12km to the waterway.

The Cher flows gently through a broad valley bordered by gentle hills, making a most attractive landscape, with cultural and historic interest added not just by Chenonceau, just 1.6km beyond the present limit of navigation, but by several other castles and monuments in the valley.

Locks There are 8 locks on the reopened length of the river Cher, offering navigable dimensions of 35m by 5.20m. Locks are worked by boat crews, using the paddle gear installed on the gates. On the Canal de Berry, the locks are narrow, allowing boats up to 2.50m wide only (27.80m long).

Depth The maximum authorised draught is 0.80m (although the depth over the lock sills is between 1.20 and 1.30m).

Bridges The lowest bridge, at Saint-Aignan, offers a headroom of 3.90m above the normal water level; the other bridges offer a minimum headroom of 4.50m.

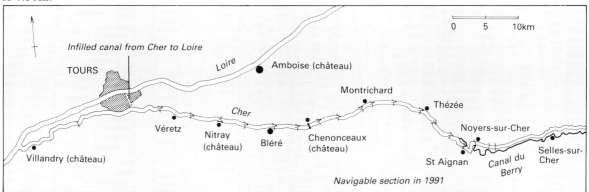

Towpath None

Authority

Direction Départementale de l'Equipement du Loir-et-Cher, Blois
Subdivision: Route du Blanc, 41110 Saint-Aignan, ☎ 54 75 14 41 (km 0-28)

Distance table

	km	lock	km
Canal du Berry			
Noyers-sur-Cher bridge at u/s end of canal basin, probable limit of navigation in 1992, village r/b	0.0	-	0.5
Lock (Noyers), bridge, *junction with river Cher*	0.5	1	0.0
Cher			
Junction with Canal du Berry, limit of navigation on the Cher	0.0	-	75.6
Saint-Aignan bridge	2.5	-	73.1
Lock (Saint-Aignan)	2.6	1	73.0
Lock (La Méchinière)	6.0	2	69.6
Lock (Talufiau)	9.3	3	66.3
Bridge	11.1	-	64.5
Thésée bridge	11.6	-	64.0
Lock (Thésée)	12.9	4	62.7
Lock (Ange)	16.7	5	58.9
Bridge	17.1	-	58.5
Lock (Bourré)	19.2	6	56.4
Montrichard bridge	21.3	-	54.3
Lock (Montrichard)	22.1	7	53.5
Overhead power line	23.9	-	51.7
Bridge	25.6	-	50.0
Lock (Saint-Georges)	25.8	8	49.8
Limit of Indre-et-Loire département, r/b	27.6	-	48.0
Limit of Indre-et-Loire département, l/b	28.6	-	47.0
Lock (Chisseaux), present limit of navigation	28.9	9	46.7
Distance table continued for reference only, pending a decision on navigation past Chenonceau castle			
Bridge	29.5	-	46.1
Chenonceau castle	30.5	-	45.1
Lock (Civray)	32.6	10	43.0
Bridge (la Canardière), camp site r/b	33.0	-	42.6
Lock (Bléré) r/b, weir	36.4	11	39.2
Bléré bridge, small town l/b	36.7	-	38.9
Lock (Vallet) r/b, weir (disused mill on l/b channel)	40.3	12	35.3
Bridge, **Saint-Martin-le-Beau** 1800m r/b	43.3	-	32.3
Lock (Nitray) l/b, weir, mill r/b	44.3	13	31.3
Azay-sur-Cher bridge, village l/b	47.8	-	27.8
Lock (Roujoux) r/b, weir	49.4	14	26.2
Véretz bridge, village l/b	51.6	-	24.0
Overhead power lines	52.8	-	22.8
Lock (Granges) r/b, weir	54.4	15	21.2
Overhead power lines	55.3	-	20.3
Bridge	59.3	-	16.3
Motorway bridge (former junction with link canal to Loire)	59.3	-	16.3
Footbridge (Honcré de Balzac park on l/b)	59.6	-	16.0
Bridge (Bordeaux), main line railway	60.2	-	15.4
Bridge (Sanitas), N10 trunk road	61.7	-	13.9
Tours bridge (Pont Saint-Sauveur), town centre 2km r/b	62.2	-	13.4
U/s tip of island, mill stream l/b	68.8	-	6.8
Mill (Le Grand Moulin), no through navigation	69.0	16	6.6
Confluence with river Loire (Bec de Cher)	75.6	-	00

Dordogne

The Dordogne was formerly navigable from Bergerac weir to its confluence with the Garonne at Bec d'Ambès. However, navigation is now impossible over the first 14km below the weir, and officially begins at Saint-Pierre-d'Eyraud, 12km upstream of the small town of Sainte-Foy-la-Grande. This is a free-flow navigation, with the difficulties that entails, down to Castillon-la-Bataille (km 39). From here, the river is tidal. The length of the river from Saint-Pierre-d'Eyraud to the confluence with the Garonne is 118km. It is to be noted that the possibility of mooring at most of the 'quays' indicated in the distance table depends on the state of the tides. Moorings for boats have been established at the more important towns and villages on the river.

Depth The depth of water to be found in the river is variable. Upstream of Branne (km 56), the bed is very irregular, and the depth may fall to 0.30m at low flow periods, making navigation virtually impossible. Below Branne there is generally ample depth for navigation. The tidal range increases progressively downstream, with 2.00m below Libourne at low water neaps and as much as 4.80m at high water neaps. Local advice should be sought if it is planned to proceed far up the river.

Bridges Above Libourne the fixed bridges leave a minimum headroom of 10m above mean water level, reduced to 5.50m above the highest navigable water level. The bridges below Libourne leave a minimum headroom of 19.85m above the highest water level.

Authority

Service Maritime et de Navigation de la Gironde, Bordeaux.
Subdivision: 61 cours des Girondins, 33500 Libourne, ☎ 57 51 06 53.

Distance table

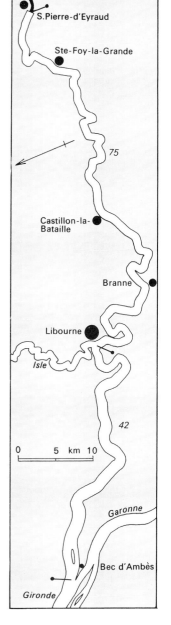

	km	lock	km
Saint-Pierre-d'Eyraud, head of navigation (limit of département of Gironde, l/b), village r/b	0.0	-	117.6
Le Fleix bridge, quay downstream r/b, village r/b	6.9	-	110.7
Sainte-Foy-la-Grande quay l/b, small town	11.9	-	105.7
Port-Sainte-Foy bridge, quay downstream r/b, village r/b	12.3	-	105.3
New road bridge (Sainte-Foy bypass)	12.6	-	105.0
Railway bridge	12.9	-	104.7
Eynesse quay and small village l/b	18.3	-	99.3
Saint-Aulaye quay and small village r/b	20.8	-	96.8
Quay (Saint-Avit) l/b	22.2	-	95.4
Pessac-sur-Dordogne bridge, quay and village l/b	27.2	-	90.4
Flaujagues quay and village l/b	30.8	-	86.8
Lamothe-Montravel quay and village r/b	33.7	-	83.9
Confluence of Lidoire, r/b	38.5	-	79.1
Castillon-la-Bataille bridge, quay and village upstream l/b	39.3	-	78.3
Bridge	40.1	-	77.5
Islands, navigation in middle arm	42.6	-	75.0
Civrac-de-Dordogne quay and village l/b (access from d/s)	43.2	-	74.4
Island, d/s tip, access to Civrac in l/b arm	43.8	-	73.8
Sainte-Terre, mooring possible on r/b, village 500m	45.7	-	71.9
Saint-Jean-de-Blaignac bridge, quay and village u/s l/b	49.5	-	68.1
Cabara quay and village l/b	50.5	-	67.1
Vignonet quay and village r/b	52.7	-	64.9

	km	lock	km
Branne bridge, quay upstream l/b, village l/b	56.1	-	61.5
Moulon quay l/b, village 500m	59.7	-	57.9
Slipway (Carré) r/b, poor condition	64.5	-	53.1
Quay (Génissac) l/b	69.4	-	48.2
Railway bridge (Libourne)	74.0	-	43.6
Libourne bridge, quay u/s and landing stage			
d/s r/b, slipway, town centre r/b	75.0	-	42.6
Confluence of Isle r/b	75.3	-	42.3
Fronsac quay and slipway (poor condition), village r/b	77.7	-	39.9
Arveyres l/b	82.7	-	34.9
Vayres quay and village l/b	84.0	-	33.6
Saint-Pardon quay and village l/b (access delicate)	85.6	-	32.0
Asques slipway, village r/b	96.0	-	21.6
Slipway l/b (Cavernes)	98.3	-	19.3
Motorway bridge (A10, l'Aquitaine)	100.9	-	16.7
Cubzac-les-Ponts bridge, village 1500m r/b	101.9	-	15.7
Railway bridge	102.8	-	14.8
Slipway r/b (Plagne)	105.3	-	12.3
Ambès slipway, village l/b	110.6	-	7.0
Overhead power lines	111.7	-	5.9
Bourg quay and slipway, village r/b, castle	113.9	-	3.7
Ambès oil terminal and refinery, industrial quays l/b	117.0	-	0.6
Confluence with the Gironde, Bec d'Ambès lighthouse l/b	117.6	-	0.0

Dunkerque–Escaut waterway

including the Bauvin–Lys waterway

The Dunkerque–Escaut waterway was completed in the late 1960s to provide a route for high-capacity barges and push-tows between the busy North Sea port and the industrial areas of Denain and (later) Valenciennes on the Escaut. The waterway (*la liaison* in barge skippers' terms) extends over a distance of 143km from its junction with the Escaut (conventionally considered to be at Pont-Malin lock, 500m from the actual junction) to Mardyck lock, which leads into the basins of the port of Dunkerque. An important branch (Bauvin-Lys) leads from the main line at km 54 to the inland port of Lille and the river Lys. The length of this waterway is 35km. Between Quesnoy lock and Deûlémont works are likely to be encountered, this section remaining to be upgraded to high-capacity standards.

The large-scale waterway and its branch incorporate a number of earlier canals, widened, realigned and linked by new cuts (dérivations) as necessary. These canals retained their separate identities in previous editions of this work, but it is now thought more useful to users of the waterway (and a truer reflection of the actual situation) to present the entire route in detail under this single entry. Accordingly, there are no longer separate entries for the following canals:

– Canal de la Sensée (km 0–23.6 of the Dunkerque-Escaut waterway).
– Scarpe diversion canal bypassing Douai (km 23.6-31.5)
– Canal de la Deûle (km 31.5-54 and Bauvin-Lys waterway).
– Canal d'Aire (km 54-93)
– Canal de Neufossé and St Omer diversion canal (km 93-112.6).
– Aa (separate entry maintained, see p33) (km 112.6-121)
– Canal de la Colme (km 121-136)
– Mardyck diversion canal (km 137-143)

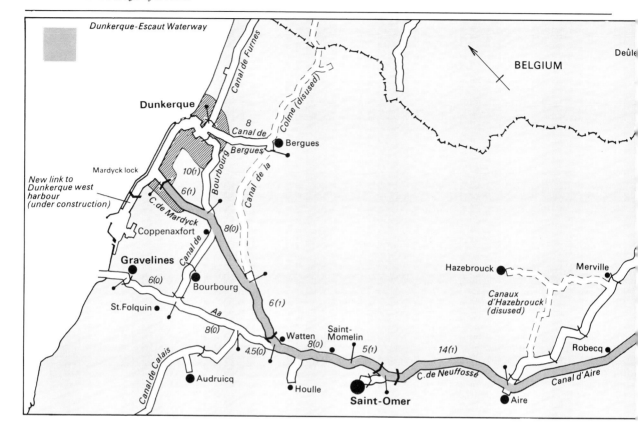

The way in which these canals have been incorporated in the new waterway is made clear by the map, which also shows the numerous other connections and branches.

Barge traffic remains quite heavy on the main line and the Bauvin-Lys waterway, and since some sections remain relatively narrow, particular care should be taken when meeting or overtaking the the bigger barges and pushtows which operate on the waterway. Advantage should be taken of the opportunities to moor in wash-free water off the main line.

At the beginning of the Dunkerque–Escaut waterway, the **old course of the Canal de Sensée** is of interest. It extends over a distance of 3.7km from the canalised river Escaut to join the main canal at km 3.0. It includes the remarkable Bassin Rond, a canal basin which no longer serves any industrial purpose, and is wide enough to allow dinghy sailing and other water sports. The quay along the left bank side of the basin makes an ideal mooring.

The most important branch is the **Canal de Lens**, in a highly industrialised area and no longer meriting a separate entry as in previous editions. Since the upper sections were infilled for new roads and a motorway interchange, the canal no longer even reaches the town of Lens. The canal thus extends 8.6km from its junction with the main line (km 44) to an ignominious end at a vast road interchange east of Lens. It serves a number of industrial quays in this coal-mining area, and is of no interest for pleasure cruising, except for the pontoon moorings established for boats alongside the municipal park of Courcelles.

The **old canal through La Bassée** offers another opportunity to escape into calmer waters, branching off from the main line at km 58.6 and rejoin-

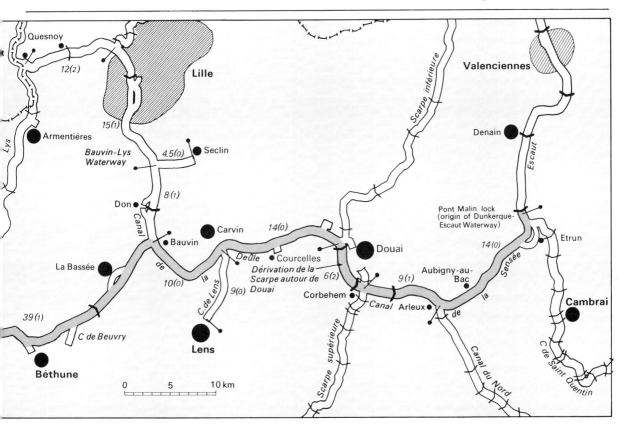

ing it at km 61.0. The bypassed length of the old canal is 2.6km, and includes boat moorings conveniently located near the centre of the small town.

The **Canal de Beuvry** is another attractive branch canal, remarkably rural in character since coal mining ceased in the area. Originally 2.5km long, it could potentially be navigated from the junction with the main canal at km 66.9 through to the culverted bridge at Beuvry, 200m short of the terminal basin, were it not for the lift bridge at km 1.9, which is no longer in working order. This leaves a navigable length of 0.6km, which is well worth exploring, with a bar conveniently located just beside the lift bridge at the end.

Finally, the **Canal de Seclin** is a branch of the Bauvin-Lys waterway (former Canal de la Deûle), which it joins at km 8.4. It is officially no longer navigable, and is highly popular with anglers, for it receives fresh spring water at the terminal basin in the small town of Seclin. This take-over by the angling community seems to be the only obstacle to navigation, and the narrow canal, with its shady banks, cutting straight through the beet fields, is ideal for cruising. Exploration is at the boater's risk, and speed should of course be kept very low.

Locks There are seven locks on the main line, falling towards Dunkerque from an elevation of about 34m at Pont-Malin. Their dimensions are 144.60 by 12.00m. In some cases the original 38.50m lock remains in operation alongside the bigger chamber. The lock-keeper's instructions should be followed. On the Bauvin-Lys waterway, there will be three locks when the current improvement works have been completed, offering the same navigable dimensions as those on the main line. In the 1970s locks of these dimensions were opened at Lille (Écluse du Grand Carré), replacing La Barre lock and allowing elimination of Sainte-Hélène lock, and at Quesnoy, allowing elimination of Wambrechies lock. The lock at Deûlémont remains for the time being, for although the improvement works have been completed on the Lys below the confluence (under a Franco-Belgian agreement), the lock cannot be eliminated until the reach above to Quesnoy has been widened and deepened to 1350-tonne standards. In the meantime, Deûlémont lock restricts through navigation to barges measuring 85.00 by 8.00m. It should be noted that the small barge lock (38.75 by 5.08m) on the old line of the canal at Don has been taken out of service.

There are no locks on any of the branches listed above.

Depth The maximum authorised draught is 3.00m throughout the main line and on the Bauvin-Lys branch down to the port of Lille (km 18). From here to Quesnoy, the maximum draught is 2.50m, while downstream to the Lys it is 2.00m pending completion of the current works. On non-upgraded branches, the maximum authorised draught is 1.80m, except on the Canal de Lens (2.20m) and on the Seclin branch (1.20m).

Bridges In principle, all fixed bridges on the main line and the Bauvin-Lys waterway down to Lille should leave a minimum headroom of 5.25m above the highest navigable water level, but a few bridges offer less, the minimum being 4.30m. The least headroom on the various minor branches is 3.20m (4.20m on the Canal de Lens).

Towpath There is a good towpath throughout the main line.

Authority
Direction Régionale de la Navigation, Lille. Subdivisions:
– 24 chemin du Halage, 59300 Valenciennes, ☎ 27 46 23 41 (km 0-3 and old course of Canal de Sensée),
– 16 route de Tournai, BP 26, 59119 Waziers, ☎ 27 87 12 55 (km 3-54 and Canal de Lens),
– Rue de l'Ecluse Saint-Bertin, BP 353, 62505 St-Omer, ☎ 21 98 22 00 (km 54-123),
– Terre-Plein du Jeu de Mail, BP 1008, 59375 Dunkerque, ☎ 28 24 38 56 (km 123-137),
– Service Maritime, Terre-Plein Guillain, BP 6534, 59386 Dunkerque, ☎ 28 29 70 70 (km 137-143),
– Avenue Max Dormoy, BP 56, 59004 Lille, ☎ 20 92 63 44 (Bauvin-Lys waterway).

Distance table
Dunkerque–Escaut waterway
Canal de la Sensée

	km	lock	km
Connection with canalised river Escaut at upstream end of Pont Malin lock	0.0	–	143.1
Actual junction with river Escaut (see plan)	0.5	–	142.6
Culvert (Pré Piton) for river Sensée	1.9	–	141.2
Bridge (Marlettes)	2.0	–	141.1
Junction with former line of Canal de la Sensée, l/b	3.0	–	140.1
Wasnes-au-Bac bridge (Pont Rade), village 1200m r/b	3.5	–	139.6
Hem-Lenglet village and church l/b, footbridge	5.8	–	137.3
Hem-Lenglet bridge, quay u/s r/b, village 500m l/b	6.2	–	136.9
Fressies bridge, quay d/s r/b, village l/b, Féchain 1500m r/b	7.9	–	135.2

	km	lock	km
Aubigny-au-Bac basin, quay r/b, village 500m r/b	10.8	-	132.3
Main road bridge (N43)	11.0	-	132.1
Railway bridge	11.1	-	132.0
Bridge (Abbaye-du-Verger), quay d/s r/b, **Oisy-le-Verger** 2000m l/b	12.3	-	130.8
Junction with Canal du Nord, l/b	15.1	-	128.0
Arleux bridge, boat moorings u/s l/b, village 1200m l/b	15.5	-	127.6
Public quay r/b	16.5	-	126.6
Industrial quay r/b (cement works)	17.8	-	125.3
Bridge (Moulinet), quay u/s r/b, **Goeulzin** 1200m r/b	18.6	-	124.5
Lock (Goeulzin), two chambers, water	20.2	1	122.9
Férin bridge, quay d/s r/b, village 500m r/b	21.2	-	121.9
Férin basin	22.5	-	120.6
Corbehem bridge	23.3	-	119.8
Junction with river Scarpe, navigation continues in Scarpe diversion canal (Douai bypass)	23.6	-	119.5

Dérivation de la Scarpe autour de Douai

	km	lock	km
Lock (Courchelettes), bridge, water	23.8	2	119.3
Railway bridges	24.2	-	118.9
Road bridge (Douai South bypass)	25.2	-	117.9
Main road bridge (Arras road, N50)	25.6	-	117.5
Quay r/b	26.9	-	116.2
Esquerchin bridge, **Douai** r/b	27.7	-	115.4
Lock (Douai), water	28.0	3	115.1
Footbridge (Ocre)	28.4	-	114.7
Bridge (Ocre)	28.5	-	114.6
Quays	29.7	-	113.4
Junction with Canal de Jonction (link with the Scarpe Moyenne d/s of Douai)	29.8	-	113.3
Bridge (Polygone)	29.9	-	113.2
Boatyard (Polygone), water	30.3	-	112.8
Bridge (Flers)	30.8	-	112.3
Road bridge (Douai North bypass)	30.9	-	112.2
Junction with old line of Canal de la Deûle, r/b (enclosed 1000m long basin with numerous industrial quays), navigation continues in Canal de la Deûle	31.5	-	111.6

Canal de la Deûle

	km	lock	km
Private footbridge with pipeline crossing	32.0	-	111.1
Auby bridge, quay d/s r/b, small town 700m l/b	32.6	-	110.5
Basin r/b	33.8	-	109.3
Footbridge (pipeline crossing), quay l/b	33.9	-	109.2
Entrance to basin l/b	35.5	-	107.6
Courcelles bridge, **Evin-Malmaison** 1500m r/b	36.3	-	106.8
Railway bridge (Houillères)	37.0	-	106.1
Basin (Houillères) r/b	37.1	-	106.0
Railway bridge (SNCF)	38.4	-	104.7
Bridge (Pont-à-Sault), Dourges 1000m l/b	38.8	-	104.3
Motorway bridge (A1, Autoroute du Nord)	41.2	-	101.9
Oignies bridge (Batterie), quay d/s r/b, town centre 1700m r/b (site of the last working mine in northern France, shut down in 1990)	42.2	-	100.9
Junction with Canal de Lens, l/b	43.9	-	99.2
Railway bridge	44.0	-	99.1
Courrières bridge, quay d/s l/b, small town 1500m l/b	44.2	-	98.9
Bridge (Pont Maudit), private quay u/s r/b	46.5	-	96.6
Railway bridge (Houillères)	47.1	-	96.0

	km	lock	km
Annay basin and quays l/b, small town 100m l/b	47.8	–	95.3
Pont-à-Vendin bridge, village r/b	48.6	–	94.5
Railway bridge	48.7	–	94.4
Basin l/b	49.6	–	93.5
Basin (Pont-à-Vendin) and boatyard r/b, quay l/b	49.8	–	93.3
Basin l/b	50.6	–	92.5
Meurchin bridge, quay d/s r/b, village 500m r/b	51.2	–	91.9
Triangular junction with Bauvin-Lys waterway (Canal de la Deûle) navigation continues left in Canal d'Aire	53.9	–	89.2

Canal d'Aire

	km	lock	km
Bauvin bridge (D163), village 1000m r/b	54.0	–	89.1
Billy-Berclau bridge, village 400m l/b	54.8	–	88.3
Road bridge, quay (Douvrin) d/s l/b	57.8	–	85.3
Footbridge (Blanc-Ballot)	57.9	–	85.2
Canal divides, new cut l/b, old line through **La Bassée** r/b	58.6	–	84.5
Bridge	59.3	–	83.8
Bridge	60.2	–	82.9
Skew railway bridge	60.9	–	82.2
New cut rejoins old line, basin d/s l/b	61.0	–	82.1
Bridge (Crêtes), basin u/s l/b (through bridge)	62.5	–	80.6
Basin l/b (through bridge)	63.1	–	80.0
Lock (Cuinchy)	63.6	4	79.5
Cuinchy bridge, quay d/s l/b, village l/b	64.2	–	78.9
Pipeline crossing	65.0	–	78.1
Junction with Canal de Beuvry, l/b	66.9	–	76.2
Gorre quay r/b, small village 400m r/b	67.9	–	75.2
Footbridge (Gorre)	68.4	–	74.7
Bridge (Gorre)	68.7	–	74.4
Basin l/b	69.3	–	73.8
Public quay l/b	70.5	–	72.6
Bridge	71.3	–	71.8
Bridge (Long Cornet)	72.4	–	70.7
Junction with old line through Béthune, l/b, access to **Béthune** boat harbour (Catorive), at end of basin	72.6	–	70.5
Bridge (Avelette)	73.5	–	69.6
Bridge (Hingettes)	74.5	–	68.6
Hinges bridge, village 1500m l/b	75.7	–	67.4
Bridge (Suppli)	78.1	–	65.0
Bridge (Saint-Venant)	79.3	–	63.8
Robecq bridge (Eclemme), quay u/s l/b, village 500m r/b	80.6	–	62.5
Bridge (Biette)	82.1	–	61.0
Bridge (Epinette)	83.7	–	59.4
Railway bridge	85.2	–	57.9
Public basin l/b, u/s entrance	85.3	–	57.8
Public basin l/b, d/s entrance	85.9	–	57.2
Guarbecque bridge, quay u/s r/b, village 500m l/b	86.3	–	56.8
Steel works, private basin l/b (through bridge)	88.2	–	54.9
Footbridge (Bray)	88.5	–	54.6
Railway bridge, basin u/s	88.9	–	54.2
Isbergues bridge, quay u/s l/b, village 1000m l/b	89.2	–	53.9
La Lacque bridge, small village l/b	90.7	–	52.4
Pipeline bridge (private)	91.0	–	52.1
Aire bridge, access to town via former canal, l/b	92.7	–	50.4
Junction with canalised river Lys, navigation continues in Canal de Neuffossé	93.1	–	50.0

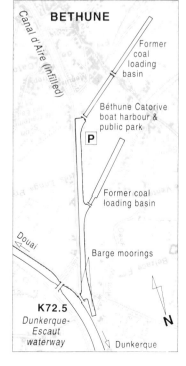

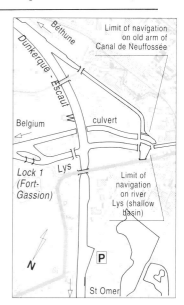

Canal de Neuffossée

	km	lock	km
Bridge	93.2	-	49.9
Pipeline bridge (private)	93.7	-	49.4
Boat moorings at canal widening, l/b (formerly junction with old line of Canal de Neuffossé)	93.6	-	49.5
Bridge (Garlinghem), quay u/s l/b	95.3	-	47.8
Blaringhem bridge, quay d/s l/b, village 800m r/b	98.2	-	44.9
Bridge (Pont d'Asquin), quay u/s l/b	101.2	-	41.9
Bridge (Pont de Campagne)	103.4	-	39.7
Lock (Fontinettes), water	106.0	5	37.1
Railway bridge	106.5	-	36.6
Widening at junction with former cut to Fontinettes lift, r/b	106.6	-	36.5
Arques bridge (Pont de Flandres), small town l/b	107.2	-	35.9
Junction with original line of Canal de Neuffossée, l/b (3km and 1 lock to Saint-Omer), navigation continues in diversion canal	107.3	-	35.8
Lock (Flandres), water	107.9	6	35.2
Railway bridge (Malhove)	108.6	-	34.5
Bridge (Marais Platiau)	108.9	-	34.2
Bridge (D209), quay d/s l/b, **Saint-Omer** 2500m l/b	110.2	-	32.9
End of diversion canal, navigation enters river Aa	112.6	-	30.5

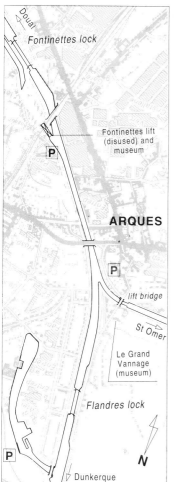

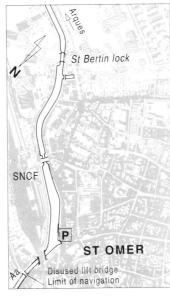

	km	lock	km

Aa

Confluence of Moerlack, r/b (entrance to Wateringues canal system used by small craft)	114.3	-	28.8
Saint-Momelin bridge, small village r/b	114.5	-	28.6
Cutoff (bypassing a bend in the river) r/b	117.8	-	25.3
End of cutoff, *junction with river Houlle*, l/b (navigable 4.0km to the village of **Houlle**, see under Aa)	118.1	-	25.0
Watten bridge, quay d/s r/b, entrance to Watten diversion canal l/b	120.0	-	23.1
End of diversion canal, Aa branches off l/b, navigation continues in Canal de la Colme	121.0	-	22.1

Canal de la Colme

Bridge (D3)	121.0	-	22.1
Lock (Watten)	121.2	7	21.9
Basin	123.0	-	20.1
Millam quay r/b, village 2000m r/b	124.7	-	18.4
Cappelle-Brouck quay l/b, village 2700m l/b	126.2	-	16.9
Bridge (Pont l'Abbesse)	126.5	-	16.6
Entrance to disused branch to Looberghe (former Canal de la Haute-Colme), closed to all traffic, navigation continues in Colme diversion canal, l/b	127.1	-	16.0
Bridge (Lynck)	128.2	-	14.9
Bridge (Looberghe)	130.7	-	12.4
Bridge (Dieppe-Straete)	133.1	-	10.0
Bridge (Coppenaxfort)	134.9	-	8.2
Junction with Canal de Bourbourg, navigation continues in widened section of Canal de Bourbourg	135.6	-	7.5
Entrance to Mardyck diversion canal, l/b	137.0	-	6.1

Mardyck diversion canal

Bridge (Basses-Brouckes)	137.3	-	5.8
Railway bridge (Mardyck)	139.5	-	3.6
Dunkerque canal basin (Port Fluvial), l/b	140.1	-	3.0
Main road bridge (N40)	140.8	-	2.3
Bridge (Fortelet)	142.7	-	0.4
Mardyck maritime lock, navigation terminates in basins of port of Dunkerque	143.1	8	0.0

Bauvin-Lys-waterway

Junction with main line of Dunkerque–Escaut waterway (km 54)	0.0	-	34.8
Bauvin bridge, quay d/s r/b, village 1000m r/b	0.1	-	34.7
Link with main line towards Dunkerque, l/b	0.6	-	34.2
Basin r/b, u/s entrance	1.0	-	33.8
Basin r/b, d/s entrance	1.7	-	33.1
Pipeline bridge (private)	2.6	-	32.2
Railway bridge	2.7	-	32.1
Former canal through Don branches off, l/b	3.0	-	31.8
Lock (Don)	3.5	1	31.3
Bridge (Don)	3.8	-	31.0
Former canal rejoins main line l/b, Don boat moorings, slipway, water, 800m u/s r/b,	4.7	-	30.1
Pipeline crossing	5.5	-	29.3
Ansereuilles power station, former coal unloading quay l/b	5.6	-	29.2
Ansereuilles bridge	6.2	-	28.6
Wavrin bridge, village 2000m l/b	8.0	-	26.8

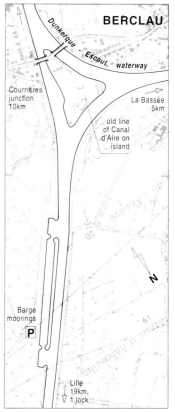

	km	lock	km
Junction with Seclin branch, r/b	8.4	-	26.4
Bridge (Houplin)	9.5	-	25.3
Road bridge (Santes)	11.6	-	23.2
Old line of canal branches off r/b	11.7	-	23.1
Footbridge (Santes)	11.9	-	22.9
Railway bridge	12.2	-	22.6
Old line of canal branches off r/b	12.4	-	22.4
Bridge (Rue du Château)	12.6	-	22.2
Footbridge	12.8	-	22.0
Haubourdin bridge, town centre r/b (Lille suburb)	13.0	-	21.8
Old line of canal branches off, r/b (dead end)	13.4	-	21.4
Motorway bridge	13.7	-	21.1
Railway bridge	13.7	-	21.1

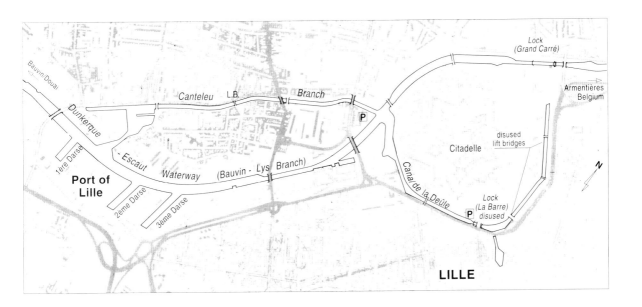

	km	lock	km
Bridge	14.3	-	20.5
Sequedin power station, quay l/b	14.8	-	20.0
Footbridge, numerous industrial quays d/s	15.3	-	19.5
Bridge, navigation enters section officially designated Port of Lille	16.0	-	18.8
Basin r/b (Darse no 1)	16.2	-	18.6
Link with old line of Canal de la Deûle, l/b (Canteleu branch)	16.4	-	18.4
Former basin r/b (infilled)	16.7	-	18.1
Basin r/b (Darse no 3)	17.0	-	17.8
Bridge (Pont de Dunkerque)	17.6	-	17.2
Bridge (Avenue Léon-Jouhaux)	18.3	-	16.5
Lille, junction with old line, l/b (access to city centre via r/b arm, mooring above disused lock, Ecluse de la Barre)	18.5	-	16.3
Footbridge (Colisée)	18.6	-	16.2
Footbridge (République)	19.3	-	15.5
Lock (Grand Carré)	19.7	2	15.1
Road bridge (Royal)	20.0	-	14.8
Railway viaduct (Abattoirs)	20.4	-	14.4
Bridge (Saint-André)	20.8	-	14.0
Railway bridge (Madeleine)	21.6	-	13.2
Private lift bridge and footbridge, industrial quays d/s r/b	21.8	-	13.0
Bridge (Abbaye), numerous industrial quays d/s	22.2	-	12.6
Pipeline bridge	22.3	-	12.5
Private footbridge	22.4	-	12.4
Junction with Canal de Roubaix, r/b	23.1	-	11.7
Marquette-lez-Lille bridge, quay d/s r/b, town r/b (Lille suburb)	23.3	-	11.5
Wambrechies bridge, quay u/s r/b, town l/b	24.9	-	9.9
Private quay (distillery) l/b	25.0	-	9.8
Pipeline crossing (water)	25.9	-	8.9
New lock (Quesnoy)	28.4	3	6.4
Quesnoy bridge, quay d/s l/b, small town r/b	29.9	-	4.9
Railway bridge	30.4	-	4.4
Lock (Deûlémont) to be demolished, with lift-bridge	33.8	4	1.0
Deûlémont quay l/b, village 1500m r/b	33.9	-	0.9
Bridge	34.6	-	0.2
Junction with canalised river Lys	34.8	-	0.0

Branches

Old line of Canal de Sensée (Paillencourt branch)

Junction with the canalised river Escaut at km 12.2	0.0	-	3.7
Bridge (Bassin Rond)	0.3	-	3.4
Beginning of Bassin Rond basin (100m wide); quay l/b	0.4	-	3.3
Entrance to former junction canal on r/b (boatyard)	0.5	-	3.2
End of Bassin Rond widening	1.3	-	2.4
Paillencourt bridge, village 200m l/b	2.0	-	1.7
Junction with Dunkerque–Escaut waterway at km 3.0	3.7	-	0.0

Canal de Lens

Head of navigation at new road interchange 1500m east of **Lens**, industrial quays (2.7km from original terminus)	0.0	-	8.6
Railway bridge, basin upstream r/b	0.6	-	8.0
Noyelles-sous-Lens bridge, quay u/s r/b, town 500m r/b	1.6	-	7.0
Footbridge (former railway bridge)	3.2	-	5.4
Bridge (Fouquières)	3.9	-	4.7
Harnes quay l/b, town centre 300m l/b	4.5	-	4.1

	km	lock	km
Footbridge (Harnes)	4.6	-	4.0
Bridge and footbridge, coal loading quays d/s r/b	5.1	-	3.5
Conveyor bridge (Courrières power station)	6.3	-	2.3
Railway bridge (Vert Gazon)	7.1	-	1.5
Courrières bridge, small town r/b	7.4	-	1.2
Boat moorings alongside public park r/b	8.0	-	0.6
Towpath bridge	8.5	-	0.1
Junction with Dunkerque–Escaut waterway (Canal de la Deûle)	8.6	-	0.0

Old line of Canal d'Aire through La Bassée

Junction with Dunkerque–Escaut waterway at km 58.6	0.0	-	2.6
Disused basin r/b	1.0	-	1.6
Railway bridge	1.1	-	1.5
Basin r/b	1.2	-	1.4
Bridge (Avenue de la Gare)	1.5	-	1.1
La Bassée boat moorings, pontoon, small town, supermarket 200m	1.6	-	1.0
Bridge (D947)	1.6	-	1.0
Junction with Dunkerque–Escaut waterway at km 60.1	2.6	-	0.0

Canal de Beuvry

Beuvry bridge (Planche Wattel), culverted, last 200m of canal inaccessible, small town centre 400m	0.2	-	2.3
Former coal loading quays l/b, camp site r/b	0.4	-	2.1
Disused lift bridge (rue Thomas)	1.1	-	1.4
Large canal basin (150 x 120m) r/b	1.5	-	1.0
Disused lift bridge (rue des Plantes), café	1.9	-	0.6
Boat moorings (pontoon) l/b	2.0	-	0.5
Junction with Dunkerque–Escaut waterway (km 66.9)	2.5	-	0.0

Seclin branch (Canal de Seclin)

Seclin quays, end of navigation, town centre 700m	0.0	-	4.5
Bridge (Postes)	0.8	-	3.7
Turning basin	1.3	-	3.2
Houplin bridge, village 500m r/b	2.0	-	2.5
Footbridge (gas pipeline crossing)	3.0	-	1.5
Bridge (Marais)	3.4	-	1.1
Ancoisne bridge (Pont du Bac), village 1000m r/b	4.2	-	0.3
Junction with main line (km 8.4)	4.5	-	0.0

Former main line paralleled by Port of Lille (Canteleu branch)

Junction with main line (Port of Lille) at km 16.4	0.0	-	2.0
Basin	0.3	-	1.7
Automatic lift bridge	0.5	-	1.5
Footbridge (Bois-Blancs)	1.0	-	1.0
Bridges (Canteleu)	1.3	-	0.7
Bridge (Léo-Lagrange)	1.8	-	0.2
Junction with new cut bypassing Lille Citadelle	2.0	-	0.0

Escaut

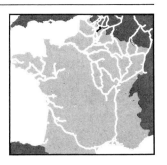

The canalised river Escaut begins at Cambrai, where it connects with the Canal de Saint-Quentin, and runs through the industrial area of Denain and Valenciennes before crossing the Belgian border (in relatively unspoilt countryside) at Mortagne, a distance of 59km. The river subsequently flows past Ghent and Antwerp, two major seaports, before discharging into the North Sea. (In Flemish and Dutch, Escaut becomes Schelde). The river has always carried heavy barge traffic, since it forms part of the route from the Paris region to Northern France, Belgium and the Netherlands, but its importance will now further increase following its upgrading to international waterway standards (navigable by 1350-tonne barges) from its junction with the Dunkerque–Escaut waterway to the Belgian border. The improvement works were carried out progressively, reaching Denain in 1967, Valenciennes in 1975 and the border in 1983.

The Escaut also connects with the Canal de Pommeroeul à Condé (replacing the former Canal de Mons à Condé) on the right bank at km 31.6 and with the canalised river Scarpe on the left bank at km 44.4. The straightening of the river has left numerous minor arms of what is called the Vieil Escaut, and some of these remain open to navigation for access to industrial quays.

In view of the completely different characteristics upstream and downstream of the junction with the Dunkerque–Escaut waterway, the Escaut is divided into two sections, with separate distance tables:
1. the section not upgraded, from Cambrai to Etrun (13km),
2. the upgraded section, from Pont-Malin to the Belgian border (46km).

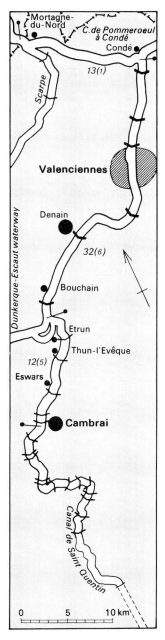

Locks There are 5 locks on the first section, each with twin chambers measuring 40.50 by 6.00m. In the second section there are 6 locks, all of 3000 tonne push-tow dimensions (144.60 by 12.00m).

Depth The maximum authorised draught is 2.20m in the first section 3.00m in the second section down to Trith-Saint-Léger (km 16.5), and 2.50m thereafter to the Belgian border.

Bridges In the first section the headroom under fixed bridges is 3.80m at normal water level. Throughout the second section this is being increased to a minimum of 5.25m above the highest navigable water level (5.55m above normal level), although certain bridges offer slightly less (the minimum is 4.80/5.10m).

Towpath There is a good towpath throughout.

Authority
Direction Régionale de la Navigation, Lille. Subdivision:
– Place Marcellin Berthelot, BP 371, 59407 Cambrai, ☎ 27 81 32 75 (first section),
– 24 chemin du Halage, 59300 Valenciennes, ☎ 27 46 23 41 (second section).

Distance table
Cambrai to junction with large-scale waterway

	km	lock	km
Cambrai bridge (Pont de Marquion), *connection with Canal de Saint-Quentin*	0.0		13.0

	km	*lock*	*km*
Cambrai Cantimpré basin, Croisières Plus hire base and			
moorings l/b	0.1	-	12.9
Lock 1 (Cantimpré), bridge, water, town centre 500m r/b	0.2	1	12.8
Cambrai-Selles basin l/b	0.6	-	12.4
Lock 2 (Selles), bridge	1.0	2	12.0
Bridge (Pont Rouge)	1.4	-	11.6
Railway bridge (Cambrai)	1.5	-	11.5
Lock 3 (Erre), bridge, water, boatyard u/s r/b	3.6	3	9.4
Eswars bridge, quay u/s l/b, small village 600m l/b	6.6	-	6.4
Lock 4 (Thun-l'Evèque), bridge, village 300m l/b	7.9	4	5.1
Quay r/b	8.3	-	4.7
Lock 5 (Iwuy), water, quays u/s r/b, village 1000m r/b	10.0	5	3.0
Motorway bridge (A2)	10.8	-	2.2
Etrun bridge, village 800m l/b	12.0	-	1.0
Junction with original line of Canal de la Sensée, l/b	12.2	-	0.8
Bridge	12.2	-	0.8
Junction with large-scale waterway (Dunkerque–Escaut)	13.0	-	0.0

Upgraded Escaut, from Pont Malin to the Belgian border

	km	*lock*	*km*
Lock (Pont Malin)	0.0	1	45.7
Bouchain bridge, quay d/s r/b, village l/b	2.3	-	43.4
Railway bridge	4.7	-	41.0
Neuville-sur-Escaut bridge, village r/b	5.4	-	40.3
Lourches bridge, town 1200m l/b	6.9	-	38.8
Road bridge	7.2	-	38.5
Junction with Rivière des Moulins l/b, boat moorings 760m			
down branch on r/b	8.1	-	37.6
Lock (Denain), water	8.7	2	37.0
Denain bridge (Pont de l'Enclos), town centre 1000m l/b	9.2	-	36.5
Footbridge	9.6	-	36.1
Bridge (Abattoir), quay d/s l/b	10.2	-	35.6
Railway bridge	11.5	-	34.2
Motorway viaduct (Rouvignies), A2	11.7	-	34.0
Bridge (Rouvignies), N29	12.0	-	33.7
Private footbridge and quay l/b	13.5	-	32.2
Railway bridge (Prouvy)	13.6	-	32.1
Thiant bridge, village 1000m r/b	13.7	-	32.0
Lock (Trith)	15.4	3	30.3
Gas pipeline crossing	15.6	-	30.1
Trith-Saint-Léger footbridge, small town 700m l/b	15.9	-	29.8
Bridge (Pont de la Fontenelle), D59	17.1	-	28.6
Motorway viaduct (Trith), A2	18.8	-	26.9
Railway bridge (Vert Gazon)	18.9	-	26.8
Boat moorings l/b level with dinghy sailing centre on			
adjacent lake (Etang du Vignoble)	19.5	-	26.2
Bridge (Notre Dame)	20.6	-	25.1
Valenciennes bridge (Pont Saint-Waast), quay u/s r/b,			
town centre 500m r/b	21.3	-	24.4
Entrance to Quai des Mines arm, l/b (public quay 300m l/b)	21.8	-	23.9
Bridge (Pont Jacob)	22.0	-	23.7
Lock (Folien), water	22.1	4	23.6
Railway bridge (Bleuse-Borne)	23.1	-	22.6
Railway bridge (Saint-Guillaume)	24.7	-	21.0
Lock (Bruay) in new cut, l/b	24.9	5	20.8
Bridge (Pont des Vaches), **Bruay-sur-l'Escaut** 500m l/b	25.4	-	20.3
Bridge (Marais)	28.7	-	17.0
Bridge (Bellevue), D50, boat moorings d/s r/b,			
Fresnes-sur-l'Escaut 1000m l/b	30.2	-	15.5

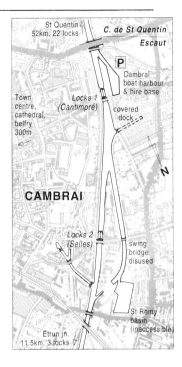

	km	lock	km
Lock (Fresnes)	31.1	6	14.6
Junction with Canal Pommeroeul-Condé	31.6	-	14.1
Bridge (Masys)	32.0	-	13.7
Railway bridge (Moulin)	32.1	-	13.6
Bridge (Sarteau), **Vieux-Condé** 700m r/b	34.2	-	11.5
Boat moorings r/b	36.7	-	9.0
Hergnies bridge, village r/b	37.8	-	7.9
Mortagne-du-Nord bridge, village r/b	44.1	-	1.6
Boat moorings and public park, l/b	44.3	-	1.4
Confluence with canalised river Scarpe, l/b	44.4	-	1.3
Customs office, r/b	44.5	-	1.2
Belgian border	45.7	-	0.0

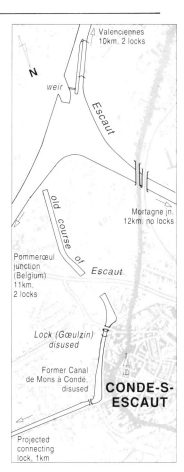

Canal de l'Est (river Meuse)

The Canal de l'Est owes its existence to the French defeat by the Prussians in 1871, for it was built in 1874-1882 to provide a north-south waterway link, west of the occupied regions, serving the industrial areas of Nancy and Toul. It joins the canalised river Meuse in Belgium to the Moselle and the Saône. It is divided into two branches:

1. Northern branch, Givet to Troussey,
2. Southern branch, Neuves-Maisons to Corre.

Northern branch

The northern branch is made up essentially of the canalised river Meuse, offering spectacular scenery where it cuts deep into the Ardennes hills downstream of Charleville-Mézières. The waterway runs south from the Belgian border at Givet to connect with the Canal de la Marne au Rhin at Troussey, a distance of 272km.

Locks There are 59 locks, overcoming a difference in level of almost 150m. The first lock, close to the Belgian border, has a length of 100m and a width of 12m, giving access for the bigger barges to the port of Givet. From Givet to Verdun, lock dimensions are 48.30 by 5.70m. The locks above Verdun have the standard 'Freycinet' dimensions of 38.50 by 5.20m. There are numerous automatic locks, indicated in the distance table. See the general instructions for the passage of such locks in the Introduction (p22).

Depth The maximum authorised draught is 1.80m throughout.

Bridges The minimum headroom is 3.50m above normal water level.

Towpath There is a towpath throughout.

Tunnels There are four tunnels, at Ham, Revin, Verdun and Koeurs. Particulars are presented in the following table:

	Length	Width	Depth	Headroom	Towpath
Ham (km 8)	565.00	5.80	2.20	3.60	No
Revin (km 39)	224.00	5.95	2.20	3.60	Yes
Verdun (km 204)	45.00	5.80	2.20	3.70	Yes
Koeurs (km 250)	50.00	5.80	2.20	3.70	Yes

It should be noted that the headroom indicated above may not be available over the entire navigable width, and boats approaching the maximum authorised air draught of 3.50m should be particularly cautious at Ham tunnel, where difficulties have been reported. As all tunnels only allow of one vessel making a passage at a time, vessels may only proceed under direction to do so.

Authority

Service de la Navigation de Nancy Arrondissement de Verdun. Subdivisions:
– Place du 148e R.I., 08600 Givet, ☎ 24 55 10 02 (km 0-79)
– 2 avenue de Montcy Notre Dame, 08000 Charleville-Mézières, ☎ 24 33 20 48 (km 79-135)
– Ecluse 19 Clair de Lune, 55107 Verdun, ☎ 29 86 02 47 (km 135-239.5)
– 1 rue du Port, 55190 Void-Vacon, ☎ 29 89 84 04 (km 239.5-272)

Southern branch

The southern branch originally connected with the Canal de la Marne au Rhin at Toul, 20km east of the junction at Troussey, but since 1979 it has been superseded by the canalised river Moselle over a distance of 26km to the steel works at Neuves-Maisons, which are now served by Rhine barges and push-tows. The waterway now extends 122km from Neuves-Maisons to the Saône at Corre. The canal follows the Moselle valley to Epinal, then rises sharply to a summit level at an altitude of 360m, the second highest in France after that of the Canal de Bourgogne. The descent towards the Saône, following the steep-sided Coney valley, is most attractive. The canal has two branches:

1. Nancy branch (see below).
2. Epinal branch, extending 3km to the town of Epinal from the main line at the foot of the Golbey flight of locks (km 83).

Locks There 93 locks, of which 47 fall towards the Moselle and 46 towards the Saône. The locks are of standard 'Freycinet' dimensions, 38.50 by 5.20m, except for locks 34 to 47 on the Moselle side, which are slightly longer (41.30m). Most locks are operated by mobile teams of lock-keepers, and a day's notice of passage through the corresponding sections is required. On the Saône side, locks 1 to 18 and 19 to 35 are thus operated as flights, and boaters are invited to call the office at lock 32, ☎ 29 36 31 84.

Depth The maximum authorised draught is 1.80m throughout.

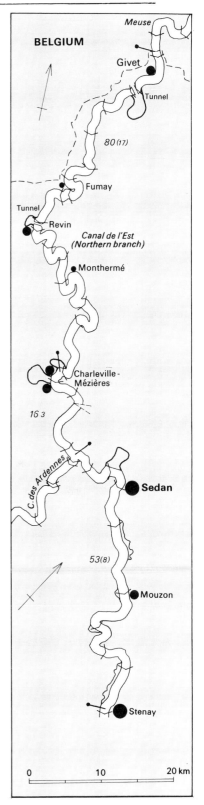

Bridges All the fixed bridges leave a clear headroom of at least 3.70m above normal water level.

Towpath There is a towpath throughout.

Authority
Service de la Navigation de Nancy. Subdivisions:
– 2 bis rue Victor, 54000 Nancy, ☎ 83 32 91 91 (km 26-55)
– 1 avenue de la Fontenelle, 88000 Epinal, ☎ 29 34 19 63 (km 55-147)

Nancy branch (embranchement de Nancy)
The Nancy branch is a 10km long junction canal between the Canal de la Marne au Rhin at Laneuveville, a short distance upstream of Nancy, and the Canal de l'Est, southern branch, at Messein (km 28). It has a short summit level between the Meurthe and Moselle valleys.

Locks There are 18 locks, of which 13 fall towards the Meurthe and the remaining 5 towards the Moselle. They are all 41.30 by 5.20m.

Depth The maximum authorised draught is 1.80m

Bridges The bridges leave a clear headroom of 3.70m.

Towpath There is a towpath throughout.

Authority
Service de la Navigation de Nancy.
Subdivision: 2 bis rue Victor, 54000 Nancy, ☎ 83 32 91 91

Distance table
Northern branch

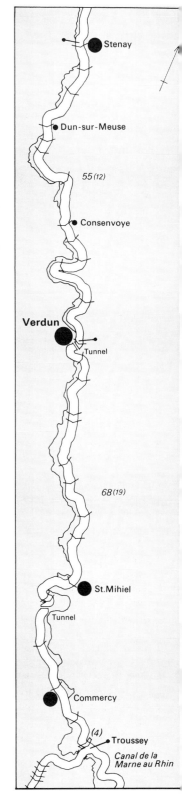

	km	lock	km
Belgian border, junction with Belgian Meuse (just upstream of Heer bridge)	0.0	-	272.4
Lock 59 (Quatre Cheminées), beginning of 2.3km lock-cut, l/b	0.5	1	271.9
Port of Givet, basins l/b	2.2	-	270.2
Flood gate and weir, navigation re-enters Meuse	2.8	-	269.6
Railway bridge, customs post upstream l/b	3.6	-	268.8
Givet bridge, moorings l/b, town spreads on both banks	4.0	-	268.4
Lock 58 (Trois Fontaines), bridge, 2.3km lock-cut, l/b	7.1	2	265.3
Northern entrance to Ham tunnel, length 565m	7.4	-	265.0
Southern entrance to Ham tunnel	8.0	-	264.4
Lock 57 (Ham)	8.4	3	264.0
Flood gate and weir, lift bridge, navigation re-enters Meuse, channel changes to r/b side, Aubrives l/b	9.4	-	263.0
Lock 56 (Mouyon) in 350m lock-cut, r/b	13.1	4	259.3
Vireux bridge, village l/b behind island	14.3	-	258.1
Lock 55 (Montigny), 1.9km lock-cut, r/b	17.1	5	255.3
Bridge (Jean Matine)	17.7	-	254.7
Flood gate and weir, footbridge, navigation re-enters Meuse	18.9	-	253.5
Lock 54 (Fépin) in 380m lock-cut, r/b	22.4	6	250.0
Bridge (Fépin)	22.6	-	249.8
Quay (Moraipré) r/b	23.9	-	248.5
Haybes bridge, quay upstream r/b, town r/b	24.8	-	247.6
Lock 53 (Vanne-Alcorps) in 610m lock-cut, r/b	25.7	7	246.7

An upstream-bound barge
leaves lock 50 on the Canal de
l'Est about to enter the short
tunnel at Revin.
Hugh Potter

The entrance to lock 58,
followed by Givet tunnel, near
the Belgian border on the Canal
de l'Est.
Hugh Potter

	km	lock	km
Fumay bridge, quay upstream l/b, small town, channel changes to l/b side	27.4	-	245.0
Lock 52 (Roche d'Uf) in 130m lock-cut, l/b	30.4	8	242.0
Ferry for slate-works	31.2	-	241.2
Railway bridge	32.9	-	239.5
Lock 51 (Saint-Joseph) in 300m lock-cut, l/b	33.0	9	239.4
Mooring at camp-site l/b	35.8	-	236.6
Lock 50 (**Revin**), automatic, in 420m lock-cut, r/b, mooring on Meuse upstream of lock-cut entrance	39.1	10	233.3
Revin tunnel, length 224m, entrance controlled by lights	39.2	-	233.2
Navigation re-enters Meuse, channel on r/b side	39.5	-	232.9
Footbridge (Orzy)	40.4	-	232.0
Lock 49 (Orzy) in 300m lock-cut, r/b	40.7	11	231.7
Anchamps quay l/b, small village	44.8	-	227.6
Railway bridge	45.0	-	227.4
Lock 48 (Dames de Meuse), automatic, in 2.1km lock-cut, r/b	45.4	12	227.0
End of lock-cut, navigation re-enters Meuse	47.4	-	225.0
Bridge (Laifour)	48.0	-	224.4
Railway bridge	48.5	-	223.9
Lock 47 (Commune), automatic, in 350m lock-cut, r/b	50.0	13	222.4
Quay r/b (Laifour)	50.4	-	222.0
Quay r/b (Grande Commune)	51.8	-	220.6
Mairupt island, pass on r/b side	52.5	-	219.9
Deville quay l/b, village behind railway	53.7	-	218.7
Lock 46 (Deville), automatic, in 3km lock-cut, r/b	54.2	14	218.2
Flood gate, navigation re-enters Meuse	57.1	-	215.3
Monthermé bridge, mooring upstream l/b, water, small town, channel changes to l/b side	58.5	-	213.9
Industrial quay r/b	59.0	-	213.4
Quay (Saint-Rémy) r/b	59.8	-	212.6
Railway bridge	61.0	-	211.4
Private quay l/b	61.6	-	210.8
Château-Regnault bridge, mooring upstream r/b, village dominated by rocky peaks (Rocher des 4 Fils Aymon)	62.4	-	210.0
Lock 45 (Levrézy) in 250m lock-cut, l/b	63.8	15	208.6
Braux bridge, mooring downstream l/b, village l/b	65.1	-	207.3
Joigny bridge, mooring downstream r/b, village r/b	69.4	-	203.0
Lock 44 (Joigny) in 300m lock-cut, l/b	70.1	16	202.3
Nouzonville bridge, quay downstream r/b	72.7	-	199.7
Castle (Château de la Pierronnerie) l/b	74.4	-	198.0
Overhead power lines	76.9	-	195.5
Private quay r/b	79.0	-	193.4
Lock 43 (Montcy) in 400m lock-cut, r/b, bridge	79.1	17	193.3
Bridge (Montcy-Notre Dame), subdivisional engineer	79.4	-	193.0
End of lock-cut, boats may navigate the Meuse 1km downstream to boat harbour, r/b, Bouchery Plaisance hire base and mooring for **Charleville-Mézières**	79.6	-	192.8
Railway bridge	79.7	-	192.7
Private quays l/b	80.4	-	192.0
Railway bridge	81.0	-	191.4
Entrance to Mézières lock-cut, r/b, possible mooring on Meuse 200m upstream, l/b,	81.2	-	191.2
Lock 42 (Mézières), automatic	81.3	18	191.1
Bridge	81.6	-	190.8
End of lock-cut, turn left into Meuse	81.7	-	190.7
Railway bridge	81.9	-	190.5
Charleville steel works, quay l/b	83.0	-	189.4
Quay (Roméry) r/b	84.1	-	188.3

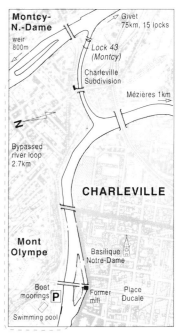

	km	lock	km
Lock 41 (Roméry), automatic, in 1.6km lock-cut, r/b	84.3	19	188.1
Bridge	84.9	-	187.5
End of lock-cut, bridge	85.9	-	186.5
Motorway bridge	86.8	-	185.6
Bridge (**Lumes**), quay upstream r/b, village 600m	86.9	-	185.5
Railway bridge	87.1	-	185.3
Private quay r/b	88.4	-	184.0
Meander cutoff (Ayvelles), l/b	89.2	-	183.2
Flize bridge (railway siding), private quay downstream l/b	92.3	-	180.1
Nouvion bridge, town beyond railway, r/b	93.5	-	178.9
Lock 40 (Dom-le-Mesnil), automatic, in 500m lock-cut, l/b	94.8	20	177.6
Junction with Canal des Ardennes (Pont-à-Bar), l/b	96.3	-	176.1
Confluence of Bar, meander cut-off l/b	97.3	-	175.1
Lock 39 (Donchery), automatic, in 900m lock-cut, l/b	99.6	21	172.8
Donchery bridge, town r/b	100.1	-	172.3
Overhead power lines	101.2	-	171.2
Railway bridge, private quay downstream l/b	102.9	-	169.5
Lock 38 (Villette), in 1.5km lock-cut, motorway bridge	103.3	22	169.1
Bridge (Villette)	103.7	-	168.7
Bridge (Glaire)	104.6	-	167.8
Flood gate, end of lock-cut	104.9	-	167.5
Private quay r/b (textile factory)	105.2	-	167.2

The superb scenery of the river
Meuse (Canal d l'Est) below
Joigny.
Hugh Potter

	km	*lock*	*km*
Bridge (Pont Neuf)	106.6	-	165.8
Entrance to Sedan lock-cut, l/b	106.7	-	165.7
Lock 37 (Sedan), automatic, bridge, water	107.0	23	165.4
Sedan public quay r/b (alternative mooring in Meuse along camp-site), town centre 1000m	107.4	-	165.0
End of lock-cut	107.5	-	164.9
Bridge (Pont de la Gare), private quay upstream l/b	107.7	-	164.7
Road bridge (Sedan by-pass)	108.8	-	163.6
Overhead power line	110.2	-	162.2
Meander cut-off l/b	111.9	-	160.5
Entrance to 5.4km lock-cut, l/b, Meuse navigable 700m upstream to quay (Bazeilles)	112.7	-	159.7
Railway bridge	112.3	-	160.1
Lock 36 (Remilly-Aillicourt), automatic	112.8	24	159.6
Bridge (Aillicourt), private quay upstream l/b	113.7	-	158.7
Remilly bridge, quay upstream l/b, village behind railway	115.1	-	157.3
Bridge (Petit Remilly)	116.5	-	155.9
Flood gate, end of lock-cut	118.0	-	154.4
Villers-devant-Mouzon l/b, ferry, meander cut-off r/b	119.7	-	152.7
Lock 35 (Mouzon), 1.5km lock-cut, r/b	122.5	25	149.9
Bridge (Fourberie)	123.1	-	149.3
Mouzon, quay l/b for short-term mooring (narrow lock-cut)	123.2	-	149.2
Mouzon bridge, private quay upstream r/b	123.6	-	148.8
End of lock-cut	124.0	-	148.4
Lock 34 (Alma), 1.0km lock-cut, r/b, swing bridge	130.8	26	141.6
End of lock-cut	131.7	-	140.5
Létanne quay l/b, meander cutoff r/b	134.6	-	137.8
Entrance to Pouilly lock-cut, l/b, towpath bridge over Meuse	137.4	-	135.0
Lock 33 (**Pouilly**), bridge, water, village 300m r/b	137.9	27	134.5
End of lock-cut	138.1	-	134.3
Meander cut-off l/b	140.3	-	132.1
Entrance to 6.4km canal section, **Inor** quay, village r/b	141.8	-	130.6
Lock 32 (Inor), bridge	142.2	28	130.2
Martincourt-sur-Meuse bridge, basin upstream r/b	143.7	-	128.7
Flood lock (Stenay), bridge, end of lock-cut	148.1	-	124.3
Stenay quays both banks, small town 500m, boat moorings in unnavigable arm r/b	148.6	-	123.8
Lock 31 (Stenay), bridge, water	148.8	29	123.6
Weir l/b	149.5	-	122.9
Entrance to 7.2km canal section, r/b	151.3	-	121.1
Lock 30 (Mouzay), bridge	152.1	30	120.3
Mouzay bridge, quay downstream r/b, village 700m	152.6	-	119.8
Bridge	153.7	-	118.7
Lock 29 (Sep), bridge	155.5	31	116.9
Flood gate (Sassey), bridge	158.4	-	114.0
End of canal section, navigation re-enters Meuse	158.6	-	113.8
Meander cut-off, r/b	160.5	-	111.9
End of cut-off (distance measured on Meuse)	161.8	-	110.6
Dun-sur-Meuse quay, Meuse Nautic hire base, village, r/b	161.9	-	110.5
Lock 28 (Dun), bridge	162.3	32	110.1
Weir r/b	162.6	-	109.8
Entrance to 7.9km canal section, r/b	163.8	-	108.6
Lock 27 (Warinvaux)	164.0	33	108.4
Lock 26 (**Liny-devant-Dun**), bridge, village 700m r/b	165.7	34	106.7
Quay r/b	166.9	-	105.5
Flood lock (**Vilosne**), bridge, village r/b	171.2	-	101.2
Weir l/b, end of canal section	171.7	-	100.7
Lock 25 (Planchette), r/b	172.7	35	99.7

	km	lock	km
Sivry-sur-Meuse basin r/b, village 600m	174.2	-	98.2
Bridge	174.7	-	97.7
Flood gate (Sivry-sur-Meuse), bridge, navigation re-enters Meuse	176.7	-	95.7
Lock 24 (**Consenvoye**) in short lock-cut, r/b (lock chamber with sloping sides), village r/b	179.0	36	93.4
Entrance to 20.8km canal section, r/b	181.1	-	91.3
Lock 23 (Brabant), bridge	181.3	37	91.1
Lock 22 (Samogneux), bridge	184.4	38	88.0
Champneuville bridge, basin upstream r/b	186.5	-	85.9
Lock 21 (Champ), bridge	188.4	39	84.0
Vacherauville bridge, basin upstream r/b (silted up)	194.1	-	78.3
Bras-sur-Meuse bridge, village r/b	195.7	-	76.7
Lock 20 (Bras), bridge, water	196.2	40	76.2
Thierville-sur-Meuse bridge, quay downstream r/b	200.2	-	72.2
Belleville-sur-Meuse basin, D964 along r/b	201.5	-	70.9
Flood gate (Belleville), towpath bridge, navigation re-enters Meuse	201.9	-	70.5
Railway bridge	202.0	-	70.4
Bridge (Galavande), quay upstream r/b	202.6	-	69.8
Verdun bridge (Porte Chaussée), quay further u/s r/b, town spread on both banks	203.3	-	69.1
Bridge (Legay), in bend (danger), Meuse divides immediately upstream, take r/b arm	203.6	-	68.8
Bridge (narrow, followed by bend)	203.8	-	68.6
Quay r/b, close to ramparts	204.1	-	68.3
Lock 19 (Verdun), water, subdivisional engineer	204.4	41	68.0
Tunnel (length 45m) under ramparts	204.4	-	68.0
Weir (Grand Gueulard) l/b, watch our for cross current	204.8	-	67.6
Bridge, quay downstream l/b	205.1	-	67.3
Weir l/b	205.8	-	66.6
Entrance to 30km canal section, r/b	207.0	-	65.4
Lock 18 (Belleray), bridge	207.4	42	65.0
Bridge (Houdainville)	209.5	-	62.9
Lock 17 (Houdainville), bridge	210.4	43	62.0
Motorway bridge (A4 'Autoroute de l'Est')	211.6	-	60.8
Basin l/b (silted up)	212.8	-	59.6
Bridge	213.7	-	58.7
Lock 16 (Dieue-Aval), bridge	214.8	44	57.6
Lock 15 (**Dieue**), bridge, quay upstream r/b, village l/b	216.5	45	55.9
Bridge	219.3	-	53.1
Bridge	220.7	-	51.7
Génicourt-sur-Meuse bridge, quay d/s r/b, village 700m r/b	221.1	-	51.3
Bridge	222.4	-	50.0
Ambly-sur-Meuse bridge, basin downstream r/b	222.8	-	49.6
Lock 14 (Ambly)	222.9	46	49.5
Lock 13 (Troyon), bridge	225.8	47	46.6
Bridge	226.8	-	45.6
Quay (Troyon) r/b	227.9	-	44.5
Bridge	229.7	-	42.7
Lacroix-sur-Meuse bridge, basin u/s r/b, village 400m	230.7	-	41.7
Lock 12 (Lacroix), bridge, water	231.2	48	41.2
Lock 11 (**Rouvrois**), bridge, village r/b	234.1	49	38.3
Maizey bridge, quay downstream l/b, basin r/b	236.2	-	36.2
Flood gate, bridge	236.7	-	35.7
Weir (Maizey), l/b, navigation re-enters Meuse	237.9	-	34.5
Cliffs, r/b	239.0	-	33.4

The wide river Meuse in the Ardennes gorges on the northern branch of the Canal de l'Est.
Hugh Potter

Canal de l'Est. The narrow cut through Fontenay-le-Chitezu on the southern branch.
Author

	km	lock	km
Saint-Mihiel bridge, boat club moorings downstream r/b, small town r/b	240.8	-	31.6
Entrance to lock-cut, r/b	241.5	-	30.9
Lock 10 (Saint-Mihiel), bridge, water, public quay u/s r/b	241.6	50	30.8
Flood gate, bridge	243.0	-	29.4
Weir (Mont-Meuse) l/b, navigation re-enters Meuse	243.2	-	29.2
Meander cut-off r/b	244.4	-	28.0
Bridge (Koeur-la-Grande)	246.3	-	26.1
Entrance to lock-cut, l/b	246.5	-	25.9
Lock 9 (Koeur-la-Petite), bridge	247.0	51	25.4
Lock 8 (Han), bridge	248.0	52	24.4
Railway bridge (no visibility, sound horn)	248.8	-	23.6
Koeur tunnel (length 50m) under D964 and railway, right-angle bends at each end, sound horn	249.6	-	22.8
Bridge	251.4	-	21.0
Sampigny bridge, quay l/b, village l/b beyond railway	252.2	-	20.2
Lock 7 (Vadonville), bridge	254.9	53	17.5
Lérouville bridge, quay downstream r/b, village 800m l/b	256.3	-	16.1
Bridge	256.8	-	15.6
Railway bridges	257.6	-	14.8
Flood lock, bridge, navigation re-enters Meuse	258.1	-	14.3
Entrance to lock-cut, l/b	259.2	-	13.2
Lock 6 (Commercy), bridge, industrial quay upstream l/b	260.8	54	11.6
Commercy bridge, public quay upstream l/b, small town 500m l/b, beyond railway	262.0	-	10.4
Weir (Allemands) r/b, navigation re-enters Meuse	263.1	-	9.3
Entrance to canal section, r/b	265.1	-	7.3
Lock 5 (**Euville**), bridge, village 1000m r/b	266.3	55	6.1
Vertuzey bridge, quay upstream r/b	268.4	-	4.0
Bridge and railway bridge	270.3	-	2.1
Lock 4 (Sorcy), bridge, quay upstream r/b	270.4	56	2.0
Lock 3 (Sorcy), bridge	271.1	57	1.3
Lock 2 (Sorcy)	271.9	58	0.5
Lock 1 (Troussey), footbridge, *junction with Canal de la Marne au Rhin* (km 111.3)	272.4	59	0.0

Southern branch

	km	lock	km
Junction with canalised river Moselle at upstream end of industrial port of **Neuves-Maisons**, turning basin	25.7	-	121.6
Lock 47, bridge	25.9	1	121.4
Turning basin	26.2	-	121.1
Messein bridge, quay u/s r/b, village 200m r/b	26.9	-	120.4
Lock 46, bridge, water	28.2	2	119.1
Junction with Nancy branch, turning basin	28.3	-	119.0
Footbridge	29.6	-	117.7
Lock giving access to gravel pit, l/b	30.0	-	117.3
Richardménil bridge, village 500m r/b	30.2	-	117.1
Lock 45, bridge	31.5	3	115.8
Flavigny quay and turning basin r/b, village 1200m l/b	31.6	-	115.7
Lock 44, bridge	33.0	4	114.3
Lock 43, Moselle aqueduct upstream (length 125m)	33.8	5	113.5
Bridge (N57)	34.6	-	112.7
Bridge, turning basin u/s l/b	36.2	-	111.1
Bridge (N57), disused quay d/s, l/b	38.7	-	108.6
Lock 42, bridge	39.1	6	108.2
Lock 41, bridge, **Crévechamps** 200m l/b	40.9	7	106.4

	km	lock	km
Lock 40, bridge	43.9	8	103.4
Floating footbridge	44.6	-	102.7
Neuviller quay and turning basin l/b, village 500m	45.2	-	102.1
Lock 39, bridge, quay u/s r/b, **Bayon** 1300m r/b	46.8	9	100.5
Lock 38, bridge, **Roville-devant-Bayon** l/b	47.9	10	99.4
Mangonville bridge, small village l/b	49.2	-	98.1
Lock 37, bridge	50.0	11	97.3
Lock 36, bridge, quay d/s l/b, **Bainville-aux-Miroirs** l/b	51.1	12	96.2
Turning basin l/b	52.3	-	95.0
Lock 35, bridge	53.6	13	93.7
Gripport bridge, village 300m l/b	54.5	-	92.8
Lock 34	55.0	14	92.3
Lock 33 (**Socourt**), bridge, quay d/s l/b, village 1000m l/b	56.8	15	90.5
Lock 32 (Plaine de Charmes), bridge	58.2	16	89.1
Basin and private quays l/b	59.3	-	88.0
Lock 31 (Charmes), bridge, water	59.9	17	87.4
Charmes bridge (Grand Pont), quays and small town l/b	60.6	-	86.7
Lock 30 (Moulin de Charmes), bridge, turning basin u/s	61.4	18	85.9
Lock 29 (Vincey), bridge, power station and private quays r/b	63.9	19	83.4
Vincey bridge, quay d/s l/b, village 200m l/b	65.2	-	82.1
Factory and quay l/b	65.4	-	81.9
Skew railway bridge	65.6	-	81.7
Lock 28 (Portieux), bridge	65.8	20	81.5
Lock 27 (Fouys)	67.4	21	79.9
Basin l/b	68.1	-	79.2
Lock 26 (Avière), aqueduct upstream (restricted width 6m)	69.4	22	77.9
Lock 25 (**Nomexy**), bridge, quay u/s l/b, village 500m l/b	70.8	23	76.5
Lock 24 (Héronnière), bridge, turning basin d/s l/b	72.1	24	75.2
Lock 23 (Vaxoncourt), bridge	73.9	25	73.4
Lock 22 (**Igney**), bridge, quay u/s l/b, village 500m l/b	74.8	26	72.5
Lock 21 (Plaine de Thaon), bridge, private quay u/s r/b	76.1	27	71.2
Lock 20 (Thaon), bridge, water	77.5	28	69.8
Thaon-les-Vosges bridge, quay u/s r/b, small town 300m l/b	78.0	-	69.3
Road and railway bridge (private siding)	78.5	-	68.8
Lock 19 (Usine de Thaon), private quays u/s	78.6	29	68.7
Lock 18 (**Chavelot**), bridge, water, village l/b	80.2	30	67.1
New road bridge (Epinal bypass)	81.2	-	66.1
Lock 17 (Prairie Gerard), bridge	81.6	31	65.7
Lock 16, bridge	82.4	32	64.9
Lock 15 (Côte-Olie), bridge (N57)	83.2	33	64.1
Junction with Epinal branch, r/b	83.3	-	64.0
Lock 14 (Golbey)	83.4	34	63.9
Lock 13 (Golbey). basin u/s	83.5	35	63.8
Lock 12 (Golbey), basin u/s	83.7	36	63.6
Lock 11 (Golbey), skew railway bridge d/s, basin u/s	84.0	37	63.3
Lock 10 (Golbey), bridge, water, basin u/s, town 1000m r/b	84.5	38	62.8
Lock 9 (Golbey), industrial quay u/s r/b	84.8	39	62.5
Lock 8 (Golbey), bridge, basin u/s	85.1	40	62.2
Lock 7 (Golbey), basin u/s	85.3	41	62.0
Lock 6 (Golbey), basin u/s	85.4	42	61.9
Lock 5 (Golbey), bridge, water, basin u/s	85.6	43	61.7
Lock 4 (Golbey), basin u/s	85.8	44	61.5
Lock 3 (Golbey), basin u/s	86.0	45	61.3
Lock 2 (Golbey), basin u/s	86.1	46	61.2
Lock 1 (Bois-l'Abbé), bridge, beginning of summit level	86.4	47	60.9
Skew railway bridge and bridge (Bois l'Abbé)	87.0	-	60.3
Les Forges turning basin and quay	88.7	-	58.6
Bridge (Forges)	89.2	-	58.1

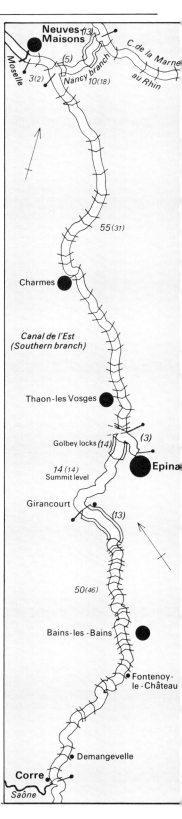

Sanchey bridge, small village	91.1	-	56.2
Aqueduct	92.4	-	54.9
Basin	92.9	-	54.4
Chaumousey aqueduct (over road), basin d/s l/b, village l/b	94.2	-	53.1
Bridge (Gare de Girancourt)	96.8	-	50.5
Lock 1 (Trusey), bridge, end of summit level	97.2	48	50.1
Lock 2 (**Girancourt**), bridge, basin u/s r/b, village l/b	97.8	49	49.5
Turning basin r/b	98.3	-	49.0
Lock 3 (Barbonfoing), bridge	99.0	50	48.3
Lock 4 (Launois), water	99.7	51	47.6
Lock 5 (Void de Girancourt), bridge	100.9	52	46.4
Lock 6 (Void de Girancourt), basin u/s r/b	101.5	53	45.8
Lock 7 (Void de Girancourt), basin u/s r/b	102.3	54	45.0
Lock 8 (Void de Girancourt), basin u/s r/b	102.8	55	44.5
Lock 9 (Void de Girancourt), basin u/s r/b	103.1	56	44.2
Lock 10 (Void de Girancourt), basin u/s r/b	103.4	57	43.9
Lock 11 (Void de Girancourt), basin u/s r/b	103.7	58	43.6
Lock 12 (Brennecôte), basin u/s r/b	104.0	59	43.3
Lock 13 (Thiélouze), basin u/s r/b	104.5	60	42.8
Thiélouze bridge, small village r/b	104.9	-	42.4
Lock 14 (Port de Thiélouze), basin u/s r/b	105.5	61	41.8
Lock 15 (Thillots)	106.1	62	41.2
Lock 16 (**Méloménil**), bridge, small village l/b	106.7	63	40.6
Lock 17 (Reblangotte)	107.7	64	39.6
Lock 18 **Uzemain**), bridge, basin and quay d/s r/b, village 3000m l/b	108.3	65	39.0
Lock 19 (Charmoise-l'Orguielleux)	109.1	66	38.2
Lock 20 (Coney), basins u/s r/b	110.4	67	36.9
Basin r/b	110.8	-	36.5
Lock 21 (Pont Tremblant), bridge, water, basin u/s r/b	111.4	68	35.9
Lock 22 (Thunimont), bridge, water	112.1	69	35.2
Lock 23 (Usine de Thunimont), private quay d/s r/b	112.9	70	34.4
Swing bridge	113.2	-	34.1
Lock 24 (Harsault), bridge, basin u/s r/b	114.2	71	33.1
Basins r/b	115.0	-	32.3
Lock 25 (Colosse), water	115.4	72	31.9
Lock 26 (Forge Quénot), basin u/s r/b	116.3	73	31.0
Basins r/b	116.7	-	30.6
Lock 27 (Basse-du-Pommier), basin d/s r/b	117.3	74	30.0
Lock 28 (Basse Jean-Melin), basin u/s r/b	118.4	75	28.9
Basin r/b	118.8	-	28.5
Bains-les-Bains bridge (Pont du Coney), quay d/s r/b, village 2500m l/b	119.4	-	27.9
Lock 29 (Pont du Coney)	119.6	76	27.7
Lock 30 (Montroche)	120.7	77	26.6
Lock 31 (Manufacture des Bains), bridge, quay d/s l/b	121.3	78	26.0
Lock 32 (Grurupt), bridge, quay d/s l/b	122.3	79	25.0
Footbridge (Pipée), quay u/s l/b	123.8	-	23.5
Lock 33 (Pipée), basin d/s r/b	124.0	80	23.3
Lock 34 (Fontenoy-le-Château)	124.6	81	22.7
Fontenoy-le-Château bridge, boat harbour and Crown Blue Line hire base u/s l/b, village 300m l/b	125.6	-	21.7
Lock 35 (Fontenoy-le-Château), bridge	125.8	82	21.5
Footbridge	126.1	-	21.2
Bridge (D434)	126.2	-	21.1
Lock 36 (Montmotier), bridge	127.7	83	19.6
Lock 37 (Gros-Moulin), bridge, basin u/s r/b	129.9	84	17.4
Basin r/b	130.2	-	17.1

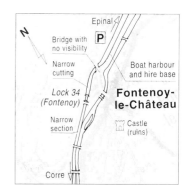

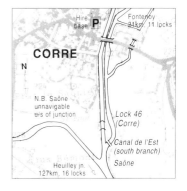

	km	lock	km
Lock 38 (Ambiévillers)	130.8	85	16.5
Freland castle swing bridge, quay d/s r/b	132.5	-	14.8
Footbridge	134.0	-	13.3
Pont-du-Bois bridge, quay d/s r/b, small village 1200m r/b	134.2	-	13.1
Lock 39 (Pont-du-Bois), water	134.4	86	12.9
Lock 40 (Bois de Selles)	136.2	87	11.1
Lock 41 (Carrières de Selles), bridge, quay u/s r/b	136.7	88	10.6
Selles swing bridge, village r/b	137.4	-	9.9
Lock 42 (Village de Selles), bridge, dry dock and basin u/s r/b	138.6	89	8.7
Bridge	140.1	-	7.2
Bridge	140.9	-	6.4
Passavant-la-Rochère basin r/b, Lepori Marine hire base, village 3000m r/b	141.5	-	5.8
Lock 43 (Basse-Vaivre)	142.6	90	4.7
Lock 44 (**Demangevelle**), bridge, village 700m l/b	143.6	91	3.7
Private quay r/b	144.1	-	3.2
Lock 45 (Vougécourt), bridge, private quay d/s r/b	145.9	92	1.4
Bridge	146.6	-	0.7
Corre bridge, quay and Locaboat Plaisance hire base d/s r/b, village r/b	146.9	-	0.4
Lock 46 (Corre), water, *junction with canalised river Saône*	147.3	93	0.0

1 Canal de la Marne au Rhin
2 Canal de l'Est (Nancy branch)

Nancy branch

	km	lock	km
Junction with Canal de la Marne au Rhin (km 169)	0.0	-	10.2
Lock 13 (versant Meurthe), bridge, **Laneuveville-devant-Nancy** 200m r/b	0.2	1	10.0
Lock 12, railway bridge u/s, private quay u/s r/b	0.4	2	9.8
Lock 11, bridge	2.5	3	7.7
Lock 10, basin u/s r/b	3.9	4	6.3
Lock 9, bridge	4.2	5	6.0
Lock 8, bridge (D71)	4.5	6	5.7
Lock 7, basin u/s r/b	4.7	7	5.5
Lock 6, basin u/s r/b	4.9	8	5.3
Lock 5, basin u/s r/b	5.1	9	5.1
Lock 4, footbridge, basin u/s r/b	5.3	10	4.9
Lock 3, basin u/s r/b	5.4	11	4.8
Lock 2, basin u/s r/b	5.6	12	4.6
Lock 1 (versant Meurthe), bridge, beginning of Mauvais Lieu summit level	5.8	13	4.4
Motorway bridge (A33)	6.0	-	4.2
Railway bridge (siding)	7.1	-	3.1
Motorway bridge (B33)	8.2	-	2.0
Lock 1 (versant Moselle), bridge (N57), end of summit level	8.5	14	1.7
Lock 2	9.2	15	1.0
Railway bridge	9.3	-	0.9
Lock 3	9.6	16	0.6
Lock 4	9.9	17	0.3
Lock 5, bridge	10.1	18	0.1
Junction with Canal de l'Est, southern branch, turning basin	10.2	-	0.0

Epinal branch

	km	lock	km
Junction with main line at bottom of Golbey flight (km 83)	0.0	-	3.3
Bridge (N57)	0.2	-	3.1
Moselle aqueduct, narrow passage	0.3	-	3.0
Footbridge (destroyed)	1.2	-	2.1
Bridge (D166)	2.2	-	1.1
Epinal basin, quay r/b, town centre 800m	3.3	-	0.0

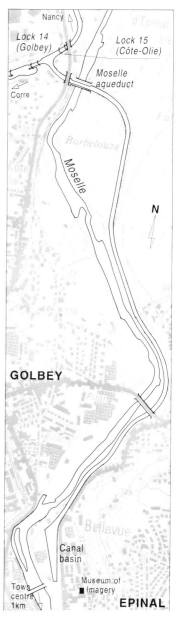

Canal de Furnes

The Canal de Furnes runs 13km from the short Canal de Jonction, officially a maritime waterway within the port of Dunkerque, to the Belgian border, from which point it is called the Canal de Nieuport à Dunkerque. At Nieuport, connection is made with the Belgian waterway network. The canal is shown on the map of the Dunkerque-Escaut waterway.

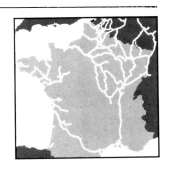

Locks There is only one lock, situated at the entrance to the canal from the Canal de Jonction. Its dimensions are 38.50 by 5.20m.

Depth The maximum authorised draught is 1.80m.

Bridges All the fixed bridges leave a clear headroom of 3.20m above the highest navigable water level (3.50m above normal level).

Towpath There is a towpath throughout.

Authority
Direction Régionale de la Navigation Lille. Subdivision:
Terre-Plein du Jeu de Mail, BP 1008, 59375 Dunkerque, ☎ 28 24 34 78.

Distance table

	km	lock	km
Lock (Furnes), *entrance to canal from the Canal de Jonction within the port of Dunkerque* (boat moorings just d/s of lock)	0.0	1	13.3
Footbridge (Corderies)	0.6	-	12.7
Bridge (Pont Neuf)	1.5	-	11.8
Road bridge (Maraîchers)	1.8	-	11.5
Railway bridge (Rosendaël)	1.8	-	11.5
Bridge (Chapeau Rouge)	2.4	-	10.9
Bridge (Leffrinckoucke)	4.8	-	8.5
Private basin, Usine des Dunes, quays	6.0	-	7.3
Zuydcoote lift bridge, village north bank	8.5	-	4.8
Road bridge	9.7	-	3.6
Ghyvelde lift bridge (automatic), village 1200m south, **Bray-Dunes-Plage** 2000m north	10.5	-	2.8
Customs post	10.6	-	2.7
Belgian border, *connection with Belgian Canal de Nieuport à Dunkerque*	13.3	-	0.0

Garonne and Gironde

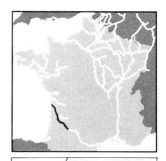

The Garonne rises in the Pyrenees and drains a large part of the Aquitaine basin. Navigation formerly extended upstream of Toulouse, but the river was never canalised, and free-flow navigation is now effectively limited to the part of the river lying downstream of the confluence with the Baïse, on the left bank. However, from here to Castets-en-Dorthe, a distance of 78km, the shifting channel often presents obstacles to navigation, and depths vary considerably, although local improvements are planned. The river becomes fully navigable, as a tidal stream, at its junction with the Canal latéral à la Garonne at Castets-en-Dorthe. It is here that the distance table begins, since from this point downstream the river forms part of the main waterway route across southern France from the Atlantic to the Mediterranean. From the Pont de Pierre in Bordeaux the river is a maritime waterway, but the distance table is continued for convenience. At Bec d'Ambès the Dordogne enters on the right bank, the river widens considerably and changes its name to Gironde. The distance from Castets-en-Dorthe to Bordeaux is 54km, Bec d'Ambès is a further 25km downstream and the length of the Gironde from Bec d'Ambès to the sea is 71km. Navigating the tidal stream presents no exceptional difficulty, but careful attention is required, and use of one of the waterway guides covering this river is recommended. It should further be noted that a bore (mascaret) sometimes forms during low flow periods over a distance of up to 40km upstream from Bordeaux.

Locks None.

Depth Depths are variable and subject to the tides. Local advice should always be obtained, but if the tidal stream is properly worked, vessels drawing up to 1.80m (the maximum authorised draught on the lateral canal) are generally able to make the passage between Bordeaux and Castets-en-Dorthe.

Bridges The bridges leave a minimum headroom of 6.50m above the highest navigable water level.

Towpath There is no towpath.

Authority

Service Maritime et de Navigation de la Gironde, Bordeaux.
Subdivision: Quai Sainte-Croix, face Hangar B, 33000 Bordeaux, ☎ 56 92 81 41.

Distance table

	km	lock	km
Castets-en-Dorthe, *junction with Canal latéral à la Garonne*			
(moorings in canal)	0.0	-	149.8
Bridge	0.3	-	149.5
Quay (Mondiet) r/b	2.0	-	147.8
Saint-Macaire quay r/b, village 800m	5.4	-	144.4
Langon quay and small town l/b	7.6	-	142.2
Former bridge piers	7.7	-	142.1
New road bridge	7.8	-	142.0
Railway bridge, quay d/s l/b	7.9	-	141.9
Quay (Garonnelle) r/b	11.2	-	138.6
Preignac quay l/b, village 500m	12.6	-	137.2
Barsac quay l/b, village 1500m	14.1	-	135.7

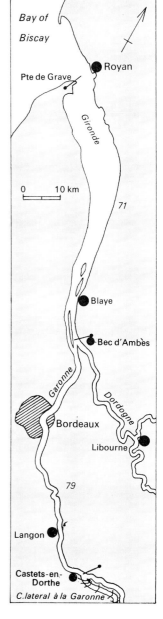

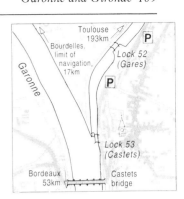

	km	lock	km
Cadillac bridge, quay u/s r/b, village 500m r/b	18.8	-	131.0
Quay (Cérons) l/b	19.8	-	130.0
Podensac quay and village l/b	22.2	-	127.6
Quay (Lestiac) r/b	26.4	-	123.4
Quay (Arbanats) l/b	27.6	-	122.2
Bridge, quay d/s r/b, **Langoiran** 300m r/b	31.0	-	118.8
Portets quay l/b, village 700m	32.3	-	117.5
Quay (Baurech) r/b	36.8	-	113.0
Cambes quay r/b, village 300m	38.3	-	111.5
Quay (Esconac)	39.6	-	110.2
River divides (Ile de la Lande), navigation in r/b arm	40.6	-	109.2
Downstream tip of island	42.2	-	107.6
Private quay (Camblanes) r/b	45.6	-	104.2
Quay (Port Neuf) d/b			
Quay (Port de l'Homme) r/b	46.5	-	103.3
Upstream tip of island (Ile d'Arsins), navigation l/b	47.2	-	102.6
Downstream tip of island, u/s limit of Port of Bordeaux, numerous quays and wharves from this point	48.8	-	101.0
New road bridge	51.2	-	98.6
Railway bridge	52.7	-	97.1
Bordeaux bridge (Pont Saint-Jean), wharves, moorings and waterway authority d/s l/b, water, fuel	52.8	-	97.0
Bridge (Pont de Pierre), limit of inland waterway	53.8	-	96.0
Entrance lock to docks, l/b	57.4	-	92.4
Lormont quay and village (Bordeaux suburb) r/b	59.3	-	90.5
Lormont viaduct (motorway spur), yacht harbour u/s l/b	59.6	-	90.2
Bassens wharves r/b	63.3	-	86.5
Oil refineries and power station r/b, wharves	74.0	-	75.8
Tip of island, channel r/b side (danger, submersible dyke)	75.2	-	74.6
Bec d'Ambès, *confluence of Dordogne*, river changes name to Gironde	79.3	-	70.5
Lamarque ferry terminal l/b beyond tip of island, village 800m	88.6	-	61.2
Blaye ferry terminal and small town r/b (wharves u/s)	90.8	-	59.0
Pauillac quays and small town l/b, moorings	100.3	-	49.5
Oil refinery, tanker berths l/b	103.6	-	46.2
Saint-Estèphe quay l/b, village 1000m	108.3	-	41.5
Saint-Christoly l/b (former quay)	119.9	-	29.9
Mortagne-sur-Gironde quay r/b, (accessible high tide), village 1200m	129.0	-	20.8
Lighthouse (Phare de Richard) l/b	132.4	-	17.4
Merschers-sur-Gironde quay and village r/b (accessible high tide)	142.8	-	7.0
Le Verdon-sur-Mer new port l/b	144.8	-	5.0
Port-Bloc ferry terminal l/b	148.7	-	1.1
Royan ferry terminal r/b, tourist resort, marina, opposite the Pointe de Grave l/b, limit of sea	149.8	-	0.0

Canal latéral à la Garonne

The Canal latéral à la Garonne was opened in 1856 to bypass the unpredictable river Garonne over a distance of 194km from Toulouse, where it connects with the Canal du Midi, to Castets-en-Dorthe, where it falls into the tidal river. It thus forms an important link in the 600km route across southern France from the Atlantic to the Mediterranean, as well as becoming a cruising waterway in its own right, thanks to the installation of five hire bases.

Four branches remain open to navigation. The first is the Canal de Brienne, 1.6km in length, from the diversion weir of Bazacle on the Garonne to the Port de l'Embouchure in Toulouse. This branch is in effect the canal's feeder, but is a dead end for navigation, since the lock giving access to the Garonne is not operated for pleasure boats. There is no basin below this lock, and boats longer than 8m will have difficulty in turning here. The second and most important branch, 11km in length, extends from the main line at Montech to the town of Montauban, where it used to connect with the river Tarn (now unnavigable). The other 'branches' are simply double staircase locks leading down from the main line to the river Tarn at Moissac and to the river Baïse at Buzet-sur-Baïse. The former branch giving access to the Garonne at Agen has been filled in. The canal was boldly designed by Vauban, and has some impressive structures, notably the aqueducts over the Tarn near Moissac and over the Garonne at Agen. More recently, in 1974, the world's first water slope was built to bypass the flight of five locks at Montech.

Locks There are 53 locks, falling towards Castets-en-Dorthe, overcoming a difference in level of 128m. There are 9 locks on the Montauban branch, falling towards Montauban. The five locks at Montech are bypassed by a water slope, 6m wide and designed for barges 38.50m long (boats continue to use the old locks). All the other 48 locks on the main line were enlarged in the 1970s to allow navigation by barges loading 240 tonnes, and their navigable dimensions are 38.50 by 5.80m. The locks in all the branches, and the five at Montech, are of restricted length (30.65 by 5.80m). Most of the locks are equipped for automatic operation and controlled by lights. There is usually a vertical pole suspended above the water some distance before the lock, level with a first set of lights. When the combination red/green appears, the pole is to be given a quarter turn to the right (see also the section on automatic locks in the introduction).

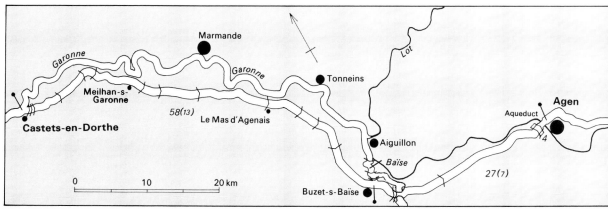

Depth The maximum authorised draught is 1.80m, but this may be reduced on the branches. Local advice should be obtained.

Bridges All the fixed bridges leave a minimum headroom of 3.60m above normal water level.

Towpath There used to be a good towpath throughout, but following years of insufficient maintenance, it has become virtually impracticable over much of the length west of Valence d'Agen. On foot one can always manage, but cyclists be warned!

Authority
Service de la Navigation de Toulouse. Subdivisions:
– 65 allée des Demoiselles, 31400 Toulouse, ☎ 61 52 53 22 (km 0-24).
– Delbessous-Sud, 82200 Moissac, ☎ 63 04 02 41 (km 24-90).
– 107 avenue Général de Gaulle, 47000 Agen, ☎ 53 47 31 15 (km 90-194).

Distance table

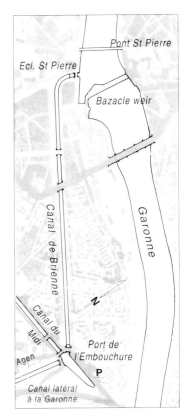

	km	lock	km
Toulouse, *junction with the Canal du Midi*	0.0	-	193.6
Former oil terminal, quay r/b, residential barge moorings	0.2	-	193.4
Road bridge (motorway spur)	1.4	-	192.2
Road bridge	2.5	-	191.1
Bridge (Béziat)	2.6	-	191.0
Lock 1 (Lalande), bridge	3.9	1	189.7
Bridge (motorway spur)	4.1	-	189.5
Motorway bridge (A61, Autoroute des Deux Mers)	4.5	-	189.1
Bridge (Ruppé)	5.1	-	188.5
Lock 2 (Lacourtensourt), bridge	6.5	2	187.1
Lock 3 (Fenouillet), bridge	7.6	3	186.0
Bridge (Latournelle)	8.6	-	185.0
Lock 4 (Lespinasse), bridge	11.4	4	182.2
New road bridge	11.6	-	182.0
Lock 5 (Bordeneuve)	13.3	5	180.3
Lock 6 (**Saint-Jory**), bridge, village 200m r/b	15.2	6	178.4
Bridge (Pont de l'Hers)	18.3	-	175.3
Hers aqueduct	18.4	-	175.2
Lock 7 (Hers)	18.5	7	175.1
Lock 8 (**Castelnau**), bridge, village 1000m r/b	19.4	8	174.2
Bridge (Bordeneuve)	21.1	-	172.5
Lock 9 (Embalens), bridge	22.5	9	171.1

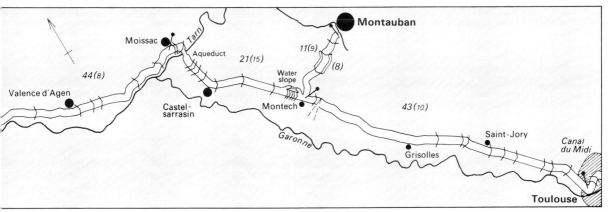

	km	lock	km
Bridge (Saint-Rustice)	23.7	-	169.9
Pompignan bridge, small village r/b over railway	24.9	-	168.7
Bridge (Grisolles)	25.9	-	167.7
Grisolles bridge (Laroque), basin u/s l/b, village 500m l/b	26.7	-	166.9
Bridge (N113)	27.6	-	166.0
Bridge (Saint-Jean)	28.0	-	165.6
Bridge (Villelongue)	29.4	-	164.2
Dieupentale bridge, quay downstream l/b, village 500m l/b	31.1	-	162.5
Bridge (Bessens)	33.4	-	160.2
Bridge (Lapeyrière)	4.4	-	159.2
Bridge (Montbéqui)	35.4	-	158.2
Bridge (Montbartier)	36.6	-	157.0
Bridge (Tourret)	38.2	-	155.4
Bridge (Forêt), Montech forest r/b	39.3	-	154.3
Lock 10 (Lavache), bridge	41.0	10	152.6
Montech bridge, basin d/s l/b, water, village 500m	42.7	-	150.9
Junction with Montauban branch, r/b, and with water slope approach canal	43.0	-	150.6
Lock 11 (Montech), entrance to disused branch serving former paper mills, d/s l/b	43.1	11	150.5
Lock 12 (Peyrets), bridge, level with upstream end of water slope	43.8	12	149.8
Lock 13 (Pellaborie), level with bottom of water slope	44.2	13	149.4
Lock 14 (Escudiés)	44.6	14	149.0
Lock 15 (Pommiès), bridge	45.3	15	148.3
Junction with water slope downstream approach canal, r/b	45.4	-	148.2
Bridge (Escatalens)	47.0	-	146.6
Lock 16 (Escatalens), bridge	47.5	16	146.1
Saint-Porquier bridge, village 600m l/b	49.2	-	144.4
Bridge (Lavilledieu)	49.8	-	143.8
Bridge (Saint-André)	50.6	-	143.0
Lock 17 (Saint-Martin), bridge	51.9	17	141.7
Bridge (Danton)	52.6	-	141.0
Railway bridge	53.5	-	140.1
Bridge (Gaillau)	53.7	-	139.9
Lock 18 (Prades)	55.4	18	138.2
Bridge (Briqueterie)	56.0	-	137.6
Footbridge	56.3	-	137.3
Castelsarrasin basin, moorings, water, town centre 200m l/b	56.4	-	137.2
Bridge (Castelsarrasin)	56.6	-	137.0
Bridge (Gandalou)	57.5	-	136.1
Lock 19 (Castelsarrasin)	57.6	19	136.0
Motorway bridge (A61, Autoroute des Deux Mers)	58.2	-	135.4
Bridge (Saint-Jean-des-Vignes)	58.6	-	135.0
Lock 20 (Saint-Jean-des-Vignes)	59.0	20	134.6
Lock 21 (Verriès), bridge	59.4	21	134.2
Lock 22 (Artel)	59.9	22	133.7
Bridge (Caussade)	60.5	-	133.1
Tarn aqueduct (length 356m)	62.2	-	131.4
Lock 23 (Cacor)	62.6	23	131.0
Lock 24 (Grégonne)	63.2	24	130.4
Lock 25 (Moissac)	63.8	25	129.8
Junction with locks down to the Tarn l/b (extensive reservoir)	63.9	-	129.7
Moissac basin, moorings r/b, water, town centre 300m	64.0	-	129.6
Bridge (Marronniers)	64.2	-	129.4
Swing bridge (Saint-Jacques)	64.4	-	129.2
Footbridge, quay downstream r/b	64.5	-	129.1
Bridge (Sainte-Catherine)	64.6	-	129.0

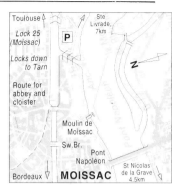

Opposite:
Swing bridge in the middle of Moissac on the Canal latéral à la Garonne.
Author

Opposite:
Canal latéral à la Garonne. The impressive Moissac aqueduct over the Tarn.
Author

	km	lock	km
Bridge (Saint-Martin)	65.0	-	128.6
Lock 26 (Espagnette), bridge	67.4	26	126.2
Bridge (Coudol)	69.2	-	124.4
Lock 27 (Petit-Bezy), bridge	71.2	27	122.4
New road bridge	73.1	-	120.5
Bridge (Malause)	73.6	-	120.0
Bridge (Palor)	74.6	-	119.0
Bridge (Capitaine)	76.2	-	117.4
Lock 28 (Braguel)	76.9	28	116.7
Pommevic bridge, village 400m r/b	77.6	-	116.0
Bridge (EDF)	81.1	-	112.5
Lock 29 (Pommevic)	78.5	29	115.1
Bridge (Gauge)	79.1	-	114.5
Lock 30 (Valence d'Agen)	80.3	30	113.3
Bridge (Auvillar)	81.0	-	112.6
Bridge (EDF)	81.1	-	112.5
Valence d'Agen bridge, quay u/s r/b, town centre 400m	81.5	-	112.1
Bridge (Roux), N113	83.0	-	110.6
Railway bridge (main line Toulouse-Bordeaux)	83.1	-	110.5
Bridge (Coupet)	83.8	-	109.8
Bridge (Golfech)	84.6	-	109.0
Barguelonne aqueduct	85.4	-	108.2
Bridge (Barguelonne)	85.5	-	108.1
Lock 31 (Lamagistère), bridge, water	86.7	31	106.9
Lamagistère quay l/b	87.5	-	106.1
Bridge (Lasparières)	87.7	-	105.9
Bridge (Saint-Pierre)	88.5	-	105.1
Bridge (Laspeyres), N113	90.3	-	103.3
Bridge (Durou)	91.8	-	101.8
Lock 32 (Noble), bridge	93.6	32	100.0
Bridge (Guillemis)	94.7	-	98.9
Bridge (Carrère)	95.6	-	98.0
Lock 33 (Saint-Christophe), bridge	96.7	33	96.9
Bridge (Sauveterre)	97.6	-	96.0
Bridge (Ostende or Lafox)	98.8	-	94.8
Séoune aqueduct	99.4	-	94.2
Bridge (Lascarbonnières)	99.8	-	93.8
Bridge (Saint-Marcel)	100.8	-	92.8
Private quays l/b	101.5	-	92.1
Bridge (Pourret), private quay downstream l/b	102.0	-	91.6
Bridge (Coupat), N113	103.6	-	90.0
Boé oil terminal, quays l/b	104.5	-	89.1
Bridge (Bonde)	104.8	-	88.8
Railway bridge	105.6	-	88.0
Bridge (Cahors)	105.9	-	87.7
Footbridge	106.3	-	87.3
Bridge (Villeneuve), basin downstream	107.0	-	86.6
Agen basin, boat harbour and Locaboat Plaisance hire base l/b, moorings, water, fuel, showers, l/b, town centre 400m	107.1	-	86.5
Bridge (Courpian)	107.6	-	86.0
Moorings along quay l/b (Agen yacht club)	107.8	-	85.8
Bridge (Saint-Georges)	108.5	-	85.1
Railway underbridge	108.6	-	85.0
Agen aqueduct over the Garonne (length 539m)	108.9	-	84.7
Lock 34 (Agen), bridge	109.3	34	84.3
Lock 35 (Mariannettes)	109.7	35	83.9
Lock 36 (Chabrières)	110.1	36	83.5
Lock 37 (Rosette), bridge	110.5	37	83.1

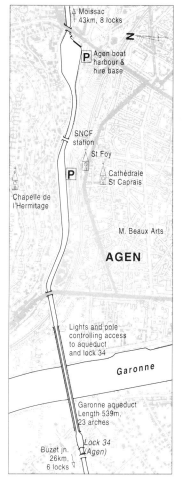

	km	lock	km
Junction with feeder canal (disused) l/b	110.6	-	83.0
Bridge (Fressonis)	111.3	-	82.3
Bridge (Nodigier)	113.5	-	80.1
Bridge (Colomay), quay downstream r/b	115.3	-	78.3
Bridge (Plaisance)	116.8	-	76.8
Bridge (Chicot)	118.1	-	75.5
Sérignac-sur-Garonne bridge, basin d/s r/b, projected marina and hire base, village 500m l/b	119.1	-	74.5
Bridge (Madone)	121.1	-	72.5
Bridge (Frèche)	122.5	-	71.1
Bridge (Lapougniane)	123.9	-	69.7
Bridge (Pages)	124.4	-	69.2
Lock 38 (Auvignon), bridge, basin downstream r/b, **Bruche** 1500m l/b	125.1	38	68.5
Bridge (Saint-Martin)	126.6	-	67.0
Bridge (Thomas)	127.6	-	66.0
Bridge (Castelviel)	128.8	-	64.8
Feugarolles bridge, basin upstream r/b, village 1000m l/b	129.7	-	63.9
Railway bridge	130.4	-	63.2
Bridge (Thouars)	130.7	-	62.9
Baïse aqueduct	132.0	-	61.6
Lock 39 (Baïse)	132.2	39	61.4
Lock 40 (Lardaret), bridge	132.4	40	61.2
Junction with canalised river Baïse via double staircase lock (descente en Baïse) r/b	135.2	-	58.4
Buzet-sur-Baïse bridge, boat harbour and Aquitaine Navigation hire base d/s r/b, village 700m l/b	135.7	-	57.9
Bridge (Burrenque)	137.5	-	56.1
Bridge (Doux)	138.4	-	55.2
Road bridge (Damazan by-pass)	139.7	-	53.9
Damazan bridge, boat harbour and Crown Blue Line hire base in basin d/s r/b, village l/b	139.9	-	53.7
Bridge (Lompian)	141.9	-	51.7
Lock 41 (Berry), bridge	142.8	41	50.8
Bridge (Maurin)	143.6	-	50.0
Bridge (Vigneau)	144.3	-	49.3
Bridge (Monheurt)	145.2	-	48.4
Bridge (Lafallotte)	146.2	-	47.4
Lock 42 (Gaule), bridge	147.5	42	46.1
Bridge (Labarthe), quay downstream r/b, **Tonneins** 4500m	148.4	-	45.2
Lock 43 (Gaulette), bridge	150.2	43	43.4
Bridge (Jeanserre)	151.1	-	42.5
Bridge (Ladonne)	152.2	-	41.4
Lagruère bridge, moorings u/s r/b, small village l/b	153.3	-	40.3
Le Mas d'Agenais bridge, quay and Rive de France hire base downstream l/b, village l/b	155.4	-	38.2
Lock 44 (Mas d'Agenais), bridge	155.8	44	37.8
Bridge (Larriveau)	156.8	-	36.8
Bridge (Larroque)	158.6	-	35.0
Caumont-sur-Garonne bridge, quay d/s r/b, village l/b	160.3	-	33.3
Bridge (Eglise de Fourques)	161.2	-	32.4
Fourques-sur-Garonne bridge, village l/b	162.2	-	31.4
Bridge (Marescot)	163.6	-	30.0
Bridge (Sables), quay upstream r/b, **Marmande** 5000m r/b	164.4	-	29.2
Avance aqueduct	165.6	-	28.0
Lock 45 (Avance), bridge	165.7	45	27.9
Railway bridge	166.1	-	27.5
Bridge (Laronquière)	166.5	-	27.1

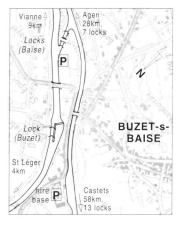

	km	lock	km
Bridge (Rayne)	167.4	-	26.2
Bridge (Baradat)	168.4	-	25.2
Marcellus bridge, village 1000m l/b	169.2	-	24.4
Bridge (Campot)	170.4	-	23.2
Lock 46 (Bernès), bridge, quay downstream r/b	170.9	46	22.7
Bridge (Tersac)	171.7	-	21.9
Bridge (Cantis)	172.5	-	21.1
Lock 47 (Gravières), bridge	173.4	47	20.2
Meilhan-sur-Garonne bridge, basin with moorings and slipway downstream r/b, village 400m l/b	175.2	-	18.4
Bridge (Pimayne)	176.5	-	17.1
Bridge (Lisos)	177.7	-	15.9
Hure bridge, village l/b	179.0	-	14.6
Bridge (Julian)	179.6	-	14.0
Lock 48 (Auriole), bridge	180.8	48	12.8
Bridge (Tartifume)	181.3	-	12.3
Bridge (Berrat)	182.3	-	11.3
Fontet bridge, basin u/s, village l/b, **La Réole** 2500m r/b	182.8	-	10.8
Lock 49 (Fontet), bridge	183.5	49	10.1
Bridge (Loupiac)	184.3	-	9.3
Bridge (Gravilla)	185.5	-	8.1
Bridge (Puybarban)	186.6	-	7.0
Lock 50 (Bassanne), bridge	187.6	50	6.0
Bridge (Castillon)	188.7	-	4.9
Bridge (Noël)	189.5	-	4.1
Bridge (Hillon)	190.3	-	3.3
Bridge (Mazerac)	191.3	-	2.3
Lock 51 (Mazarac), bridge	192.0	51	1.6
Lock 52 (Gares)	192.7	52	0.9
Castets-en-Dorthe basin, moorings, village l/b	193.0	-	0.6
Lock 53 (Castets), double lock down to Garonne	193.3	53	0.3
Junction with river Garonne	193.6	-	0.0

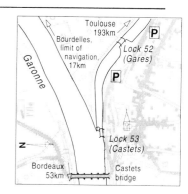

Montauban branch

	km	lock	km
Junction with main line at Montech (km 43), bridge	0.0	-	10.6
Bridge (Rat)	1.1	-	9.5
Motorway bridge (A61, Autoroute des Deux Mers)	2.5	-	8.1
Lacourt-Saint-Pierre bridge, small village l/b	3.4	-	7.2
Lock 1a (Noalhac)	4.5	1	6.1
Bridge (Noalhac)	4.7	-	5.9
Lock 2a (Lamothe)	5.0	2	5.6
Lock 3a (Fisset)	5.4	3	5.2
Lock 4a (Brétoille)	6.2	4	4.4
Lock 5a (Mortarieu), bridge	6.6	5	4.0
Lock 6a (Terrasse)	6.9	6	3.7
Lock 7a (Rabastens)	7.3	7	3.3
Lock 8a (Verlhaguet), bridge	7.6	8	3.0
Lock 9a (Bordebasse), bridge	9.2	9	1.4
Montauban basin, limit of navigation (locks down to river Tarn disused), town centre 1000m	10.6	-	0.0

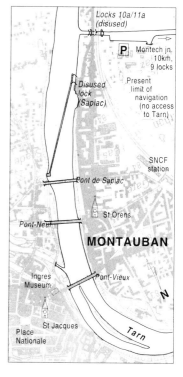

Canal du Havre à Tancarville

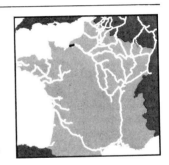

The Canal du Havre à Tancarville was built originally as a ship canal, and opened in 1887. It bypasses what was then still a difficult section of the Seine estuary over a distance of 27km from just below the Tancarville suspension bridge to the basins of the port of Le Havre. It is obligatorily used by barges, but is of little interest for boats, which will generally prefer to proceed up the Seine estuary, except in rough weather. Specific guides should be consulted for cruising on the Lower Seine and the Canal du Havre à Tancarville. See also *North France Pilot* by T. & D. Thompson and *The Seine* by Derek Bowskill.

Locks There are two entrance locks to the canal at Tancarville, accommodating push-tows up to 185m by 23m (new lock) or 14m (old lock). These are opened from three-and-a-half hours before to two-and-a-half hours after high tide. There are also two locks to be negotiated within the port of Le Havre, the Sas de Vétillart and the Sas de la Citadelle.

Depth The maximum authorised draught is 3.50m.

Bridges The maximum authorised air draught is 55m, but above 7m the Pont du Hode (km 7.8) has to be opened, the corresponding request being made by 4 p.m. the day before passage (the bridge is not operated on Sundays and public holidays). There are numerous movable bridges between Harfleur and Le Havre.

Authority
Port Autonome du Havre, Terre-plein de la Barre, BP 1413, 76067 Le Havre, ☎ 35 21 74 00.

Distance table

	km	lock	km
Entrance locks from Seine d/s of Tancarville suspension bridge	0.0	1	27.0
Bridge (Pont du Hode)	7.8	-	19.2
Ferry (Oudalle)	13.0	-	14.0
Gonfreville refinery south bank	16.0	-	11.0
Bridge No. 8	19.0	-	8.0
Harfleur basin north bank	19.2	-	7.8
Bridge No. 7a	19.4	-	7.6
Canal de Jonction (link to new basins of port of Le Havre)	20.0	-	7.0
Bridge No. 7	20.6	-	6.4
Bridge No. 6	22.0	-	5.0
Bridge No. 5 (Bassin Vétillart)	22.9	-	4.1
Bridge No. 4, lock (Vétillart)	23.8	2	3.2
Bridge No. 3 (Bassin Bellot)	24.0	-	3.0
Turn north into Bassin de l'Eure	25.2	-	1.8
Bridge No. 2 (Pertuis de la Citadelle)	25.8	-	1.2
Lock (Citadelle)	26.2	3	0.8
Inner basin of port of **Le Havre**	27.0	-	0.0

Canaux d'Hazebrouck

The Canaux d'Hazebrouck are a system of small canals, with a total length of 23km, which used to connect the small town of Hazebrouck with the canalised river Lys at Thiennes (km 5) and at Merville (km 19). The entire system has been closed to navigation and conceded to the local authorities. The entry is nevertheless maintained for reference, for there is talk of at least partial restoration for pleasure cruising (and the other leisure activities associated with inland waterways). The situation of these canals is shown on the map of the Dunkerque-Escaut waterway (p.81-2).

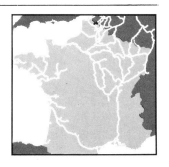

Hérault

The river Hérault is navigable over a distance of 12km from Bessan to the Mediterranean at Le Grau d'Agde. It is a river navigation over a distance of 7km upstream of Agde, part of its course being used by the Canal du Midi. Downstream of Agde, it is a maritime waterway. The weir at Agde is bypassed by a short length of the Canal du Midi, the round lock at Agde and the branch to the Hérault maritime (see plan of Agde, below).

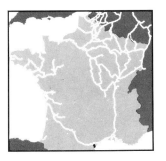

Locks None. The weir at Agde is bypassed by the round lock on the Canal du Midi.

Depth There is a substantial depth in the river, normally at least 2.90m, but this is reduced to 1.60m in the Canal du Midi and its branch to the Hérault maritime.

Bridges The bridges on the Hérault leave a minimum headroom of 5.70m above normal water level. The railway bridge over the branch of the Cana¹ du Midi has a headroom of 4.20m.

Towpath None.

Authority
Service de la Navigation de Toulouse.
Subdivision: Pont Rouge, 34500 Béziers, ☎ 67 76 26 38.

Distance table

	km	lock	km
Bessan bridge, head of navigation, village 700m r/b	0.0	-	12.0
Backwater l/b	5.6	-	6.4
Junction with Canal du Midi (towards Sète), l/b	6.0	-	6.0
Junction with Canal du Midi (towards Toulouse), r/b (to be used by all boats to bypass Agde weir)	6.8	-	5.2
Railway bridge (on Hérault)	7.0	-	5.0
Weir (Barrage du Moulin)	7.2	-	4.8
Junction with Hérault maritime branch of Canal du Midi, r/b	7.4	-	4.6
Agde bridge, quay and town centre d/s l/b	7.5	-	4.5
New road bridge (Agde bypass)	9.2	-	2.8
Le Grau d'Agde, river reaches the Mediterranean	12.0	-	0.0

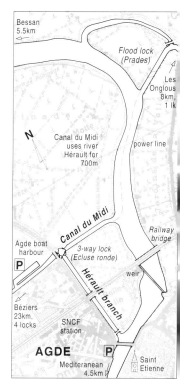

Canal des Houillères de la Sarre

The Canal des Houillères de la Sarre branches off from the Canal de la Marne au Rhin near Gondrexange (km 227), and after cutting through a vast forest strewn with lakes, runs down the Sarre valley to enter the river at Sarreguemines. Navigation continues down the canalised river to the German border, a short distance upstream of Saarbrücken. The canal is 63km long, and the French portion of the canalised river Sarre is 12km long, making a total of 75km. Despite its name, accounted for by the fact that the canal's main function was to carry coal from the Saarbrücken area, the waterway is pleasantly rural throughout most of its length. Its importance as a commercial waterway will be increased when the Saar canalisation project in Germany has been completed throughout the 90km between Saarbrücken and the Moselle, making the industrial centre accessible to Rhine push-tows. The through route will also offer attractive possibilities for pleasure cruising.

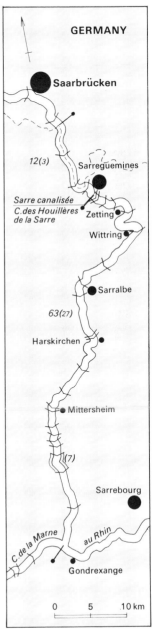

Locks There are 27 locks on the canal, falling towards the Sarre, and 3 locks on the French portion of the canalised river Sarre. The least dimensions are 39.00 by 5.15m.

Depth The maximum authorised draught is 1.80m.

Bridges The fixed bridges on the canal leave a minimum headroom of 3.65m above normal water level. The least headroom on the canalised river is 4.17m, reduced to 3.42m above the highest navigable water level.

Towpath There is a good towpath throughout.

Authority
Service de la Navigation de Strasbourg.
Subdivision: 57930 Mittersheim, ☎ 87 07 67 12.

Distance table

	km	lock	km
Junction with Canal de la Marne au Rhin (km 228), near **Gondrexange**	0.0	-	75.6
Restricted passage	0.1	-	75.5
Bridge (Houillon), quay u/s l/b	2.3	-	73.3
Flood gate, bridge	3.1	-	72.5
Diane-et-Kerprich bridge, small village 200m r/b	3.9	-	71.7
Lock 1, bridge, auberge	5.5	1	70.1
Stock aqueduct, Etang du Stock extends beyond both banks	6.7	-	68.9
Restricted passage	8.7	-	66.9
Bridge (Albeschaux), quay u/s l/b	10.4	-	65.2
Lock 2	11.0	2	64.6
Lock 3	11.5	3	64.1
Lock 4	11.9	4	63.7
Lock 5	12.4	5	63.2
Lock 6	12.8	6	62.8
Lock 7	13.2	7	62.4
Lock 8, bridge, quay (Vorbusch) d/s r/b, auberge	13.6	8	62.0
Lock 9	14.3	9	61.3
Lock 10	15.2	10	60.4
Lock 11	16.1	11	59.5

	km	lock	km
Lock 12	17.4	12	58.2
Railway bridge	18.1	-	57.5
Lock 13, bridge	19.5	13	56.1
Junction with Canal des Salines (abandoned), l/b	20.0	-	55.6
Mittersheim basin, quay and Canal Evasion hire base r/b, village 400m	20.1	-	55.5
Lock 14, bridge	20.3	14	55.3
Lock 15, bridge, quay (Pont-Vert) u/s l/b	22.6	15	53.0
Quay (Burlach) l/b	23.9	-	51.7
Lock 16, bridge, private quays (Schlumberger) u/s and d/s l/b	271	16	48.5
Bridge (Neuweyerhof)	28.3	-	47.3
Bridge (Muller), restricted width	29.5	-	46.1
Bridge (Freywald), restricted width, **Harskirchen** 500m r/b	32.1	-	43.5
Lock 17, bridge	32.8	17	42.8
Bissert-Harskirchen basin, quay and Chemins Nautiques d'Alsace relay base l/b, village 300m l/b	33.0	-	42.6
Lock 18, bridge	33.5	18	42.1
Bridge (Haras)	37.4	-	38.2
Skew railway bridge, turning basin and private quay d/s l/b	37.9	-	37.7
Lock 19	38.8	19	36.8
Bridge (Rech)	39.2	-	36.4
Albe aqueduct	39.8	-	35.8

Canal des Houillères de la Sarre at Sarreguemines.
Author

	km	lock	km
Lock 20, bridge	40.8	20	34.8
Sarralbe quay l/b, small town 300m r/b over bridge	41.1	-	34.5
Towpath bridge (towpath changes from r/b to l/b)	41.3	-	34.3
Private footbridge	41.6	-	34.0
Solvay works, private quay r/b	41.7	-	33.9
Private footbridge	42.0	-	33.6
Railway bridge	42.3	-	33.3
Bridge (Niederau), restricted width	43.0	-	32.6
Motorway bridge (A34)	44.8	-	30.8
Herbitzheim bridge, quay u/s r/b, village 800m r/b	45.2	-	30.4
Lock 21, bridge	45.6	21	30.0
Skew railway bridge	51.4	-	24.2
Lock 22, bridge, boatyard u/s l/b	51.8	22	23.8
Wittring quay, village l/b	52.0	-	23.6
Railway bridge (Dieding)	53.6	-	22.0
Skew railway bridge (Zetting)	57.2	-	18.4
Lock 23, bridge, **Zetting** l/b	57.6	23	18.0
Lock 24, bridge, **Sarreinsming** 400m r/b	60.2	24	15.4
Remelfing quay l/b, turning basin, village 500m d/s l/b	61.1	-	14.5
Lock 25, bridge	61.5	25	14.1
Lock 26, bridge and railway viaduct, moorings d/s r/b	63.0	26	12.6
Lock 27	63.4	27	12.2
Navigation enters canalised river Sarre	63.4	-	12.2
Quays l/b (Grand Port de Sarreguemines)	63.7	-	11.9
China works, landing stage r/b	64.4	-	11.2
Sarreguemines bridge (Pont des Alliés), quay d/s l/b, town centre l/b	64.6	-	11.0
Bridge	64.8	-	10.8
Lock 28 and weir	64.9	28	10.7
Confluence of Blies r/b (r/b in Germany from this point)	65.0	-	10.6
Skew railway bridge	65.7	-	9.9
Entrance to Welferding lock-cut, l/b	66.2	-	9.4
Footbridge	66.3	-	9.3
Welferding bridge, village l/b	66.4	-	9.2
Lock 29	66.8	29	8.8
Navigation re-enters Sarre	66.9	-	8.7
Loading quay for Auersmacher quarries (Germany) r/b	69.5	-	6.1
Quay for Grosbliederstroff power station l/b	70.6	-	5.0
Entrance to Grosbliederstroff lock-cut, l/b	71.1	-	4.5
Grosbliederstroff footbridge, village l/b	71.6	-	4.0
Turning basin	72.3	-	3.3
Lock 30, bridge	72.7	30	2.9
Navigation re-enters Sarre	72.7	-	2.9
French–German border l/b (**Saarbrücken** 6km downstream)	75.6	-	0.0

Ill

The river Ill, a left-bank tributary of the Rhine, is canalised over a length of 10.4km through the Alsace plain and the city of Strasbourg, providing a link from the northern branch of the Canal du Rhône au Rhin at km 33.9 to the Canal de la Marne au Rhin north of Strasbourg at km 311.6. This link is 4.6km long, and the section through Strasbourg, where the Ill divides into two arms flowing round the historic centre, is probably the most attractive urban waterway in France. The 'dead end' sections of the canalised Ill upstream and downstream of this cross-Strasbourg link are respectively 5.3 and 0.4km long, leading to the suburb of Ostwald to the south, where two factories and a large gravel extraction undertaking formerly made use of water transport, and to the suburb of La Robertsau to the north. The southern section, which gave access to the disused Canal de la Bruch, is now navigated at the users' risk, while navigation on the cross-Strasbourg link is not encouraged by the Strasbourg Port Authority (which is concerned to put as many tourists as possible on its trip-boats).

Locks There are three locks, A, B and C. Locks A and B are on the alternative routes through the Strasbourg, the first being on the Ill in the heart of the Petite France district, while the second is on the Canal des Faux Remparts. The latter was re-opened a few years ago, to allow the popular Strasbourg trip-boats to make the round cruise through the city. Lock C is of less interest, since it gives access to the 400m long 'dead end' section of the river north of the level junction with the Canal de la Marne au Rhin. Lock dimensions are 34.85m by 5.32m. Trip-boats of course have priority at the locks.

Depth The maximum authorised draught is 1.80m, but silting may have occurred on the upper reaches towards Ostwald, so caution is required when heading upstream from the junction with the Canal du Rhône au Rhin.

Bridges The least headroom on the cross-Strasbourg link is 3.90m, reduced to 3.50m above highest navigable water level. On the upper reaches, headroom is reduced to 3.15m (2.60m above highest navigable water level).

Towpath There is no towpath, but attractive riverside walks have been developed through much of the navigable ring in Strasbourg.

Distance table

	km	lock	km
Ostwald former quay l/b limit of navigation	0.0	-	10.4
U/s end of Ile des Pêcheurs, navigation in r/b arm	0.2	-	10.2
D/s end of Ile des Pêcheurs	0.8	-	9.6
Gelatine factory and quay r/b, entrance to Gerig lake l/b	1.6	-	8.8
U/s tip of island, navigation in r/b arm	2.7	-	7.7
D/s tip of island	3.0	-	7.4
Railway bridge	3.2	-	7.2
Confluence of river Bruche, l/b	3.4	-	7.0
Junction with Canal de la Bruche, l/b (disused)	3.6	-	6.8
Footbridge	3.7	-	6.7
Bridge	4.5	-	5.9
Motorway bridge (A35)	4.9	-	5.5
Railway bridge	5.3	-	5.1

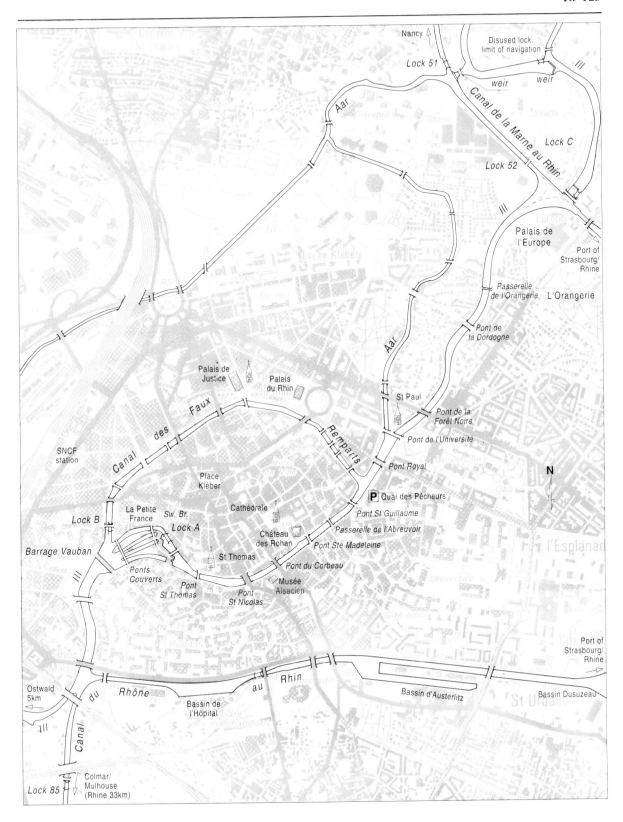

Nancy

Disused lock,
limit of navigation

Lock 51

weir   weir

Canal de la Marne au Rhin

Lock C

Lock 52

Aar

Palais de
l'Europe

Port of
Strasbourg/
Rhine

*Passerelle
de l'Orangerie* L'Orangerie

*Pont de
la Dordogne*

Aar

Palais de
Justice

Palais
du Rhin

St Paul

*Pont de la
Forêt Noire*

Pont de l'Université

Canal des Faux

Remparts

Pont Royal

SNCF
station

P Quai des Pêcheurs

Place
Kléber

Cathédrale

Pont St Guillaume

Lock B

La Petite
France

Sw. Br.

Lock A

Passerelle de l'Abreuvoir

Château
des Rohan

Pont Ste Madeleine

Barrage Vauban

*Ponts
Couverts*

St Thomas

Pont du Corbeau

*Pont
St Thomas*

*Pont
St Nicolas*

Musée
Alsacien

N

l'Esplanade

Port of
Strasbourg/
Rhine

Rhin

Ostwald
5km

Canal du Rhône au Rhin

Bassin de
l'Hôpital

Bassin d'Austerlitz

Bassin Dusuzeau

St Urbain

Colmar/
Mulhouse
(Rhine 33km)

Lock 85

	km	lock	km
Canal du Rhône au Rhin enters, r/b	5.3	-	5.1
Canal du Rhône au Rhin leaves Ill, r/b	5.4	-	5.0
Bridge (Pont Louis Pasteur)	5.5	-	4.9
Bridge (Pont des Abattoirs)	5.8	-	4.6
Barrage Vauban (part of former fortifications), 13 arches, navigation through left-bank arch	6.0	-	4.4
Junction with Canal des Faux Remparts, l/b, Quartier des Moulins, take l/b channel	6.1	-	4.3
Swing bridge (Faisan)	6.3	-	4.1
Lock A (drop 1.90m)	6.4	1	4.0
Bridge (Pont Saint-Martin)	6.5	-	3.9
Bridge (PontSaint-Thomas)	6.7	-	3.7
Bridge (Pont Saint-Nicolas)	7.0	-	3.4
Bridge (Pont du Corbeau)	7.2	-	3.2
Bridge (Pont Sainte-Madeleine)	7.4	-	3.0
Footbridge (Passerelle de l'Abreuvoir)	7.5	-	2.9
Bridge (Pont Saint-Guillaume)	7.7	-	2.7
Downstream junction with Canal des Faux Remparts, l/b	7.8	-	2.6
Bridge (Pont Royal)	8.0	-	2.4
Bridge (Pont de l'Université), river Aar (not navigable) l/b	8.1	-	2.3
Bridge (Pont de la Forêt Noire)	8.3	-	2.1
Bridge (Pont de la Dordogne)	8.8	-	1.6
Footbridge (Passerelle de l'Orangerie)	9.0	-	1.4
Junction with Canal de la Marne au Rhin, in front of Palais de l'Europe, turn left for Paris, right for Port of Strasbourg and Rhine	9.9	-	0.5
La Robertsau weir and lock C, bridge	10.0	2	0.4
Weir and disused lock, limit of navigation	10.4	-	0.0

Canal des Faux Remparts

	km	lock	km
Upstream junction with river Ill (below the Barrage Vauban)	0.0	-	2.0
Lock B (drop 1.90m)	0.1	1	1.9
Bridge	0.25	-	1.75
Bridge	0.35	-	1.65
Bridge	0.5	-	1.5
Bridge	0.7	-	1.3
Bridge	0.8	-	1.2
Bridge	1.0	-	1.0
Bridge	1.2	-	0.8
Bridge	1.5	-	0.5
Bridge	1.6	-	0.4
Bridge	1.7	-	0.3
Bridge	1.8	-	0.2
Bridge	1.9	-	0.1
Downstream junction with river Ill	2.0	-	0.0

Canal d'Ille-et-Rance

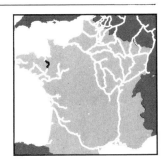

The Canal d'Ille-et-Rance crosses the watershed between the Vilaine and the Rance in Brittany, thus forming part of the English Channel/Atlantic Ocean link which has long been used by yachtsmen, but has also become increasingly popular as a cruising waterway in its own right, with several hire firms based on the canal or its connecting waterways. It extends 85km from Rennes to Le Châtelier lock, north of Dinan. Navigation continues in the tidal Rance estuary (see under Rance maritime). The canal has a summit level 7km in length, at an altitude of 65m, and in times of drought some restrictions may have to be imposed on the use of locks. Tides on the Rance are felt as far up as lock 46 (Pont-Perrin), when both Le Châtelier and Léhon weirs are submerged.

Locks There are 48 locks, of which 20 fall towards the Vilaine and the other 28 towards the Channel. Their dimensions are 27.10 by 4.70m. The tide lock at Le Châtelier has larger dimensions, 30.80 by 8.00m. Locks are manual and worked by the resident lock-keepers, except for lock 2 (Saint-Martin) which is electrically operated and controlled by lights.

Depth The maximum authorised draught is 1.40m.

Bridges The lowest fixed bridges offer a headroom of 2.75m in the centre of the arch and 2.30m at the sides.

Towpath There is a towpath throughout, of variable condition.

Authority
Administration: Institution Interdépartementale pour la Gestion du Canal d'Ille-et-Rance, Hôtel du Département, 1 av. de la Préfecture, 35026 Rennes
Operation: Direction Départementale de l'Equipement d'Ille-et-Vilaine
Subdivision: 1 avenue du Mail, 35000 Rennes, ☎ 99 59 20 60.

Distance table

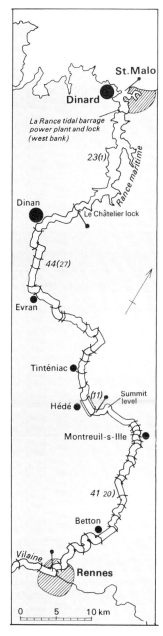

	km	lock	km
Junction with canalised river Vilaine	0.0	-	84.8
Lock 1 (Mail), bridge, water	0.1	1	84.7
Rennes basin (Port du Mail), quay l/b close to town centre	0.2	-	84.6
Bridge (Bagoul or Saint-Etienne)	0.3	-	84.5
Bridge (Legravérend)	0.9	-	83.9
Lock 2 (Saint-Martin), bridge, quays upstream	1.4	2	83.4
Road bridge (Rennes by-pass)	2.8	-	82.0
Railway viaduct	4.6	-	80.2
Lock 3 (Saint-Grégoire), bridge, quay upstream l/b, village 400m r/b	5.6	3	79.2
Lock 4 (Charbonnière)	7.2	4	77.6
Lock 5 (Gacet)	9.9	5	74.9
Bridge (Rennais)	10.3	-	74.5
Lock 6 (Haut-Châlet)	12.6	6	72.2
Betton bridge, Argoat Nautic hire base, moorings and slipway, water and sanitary building d/s r/b, village r/b	13.7	-	71.1
Lock 7 (Brosses), bridge, water	15.7	7	69.1
Chevaigné bridge (Moulin du Pont), village 800m l/b	17.8	-	67.0
Lock 8 (Grugedaine)	18.0	8	66.8
Bridge (Motte)	19.3	-	65.5

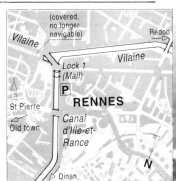

	km	lock	km
Lock 9 (Cours)	20.4	9	64.4
Lock 10 (Fresnay), bridge	21.8	10	63.0
Lock 11 (**Saint-Germain-sur-Ille**), water point, bridge, quay u/s l/b, village 700m l/b	23.9	11	60.9
Lock 12 (Bouessay)	24.8	12	60.0
Railway viaduct (Bois Marie)	25.7	-	59.1
Railway viaduct (Euzé)	26.3	-	58.5
Railway viaduct (Saint-Médard)	27.2	-	57.6
Lock 13 (**Saint-Médard-sur-Ille**), bridge, water, village 300m l/b	27.3	13	57.5
Lock 14 (Dialay)	28.1	14	56.7
Railway viaduct (Bablais)	29.0	-	55.8
Lock 15 (Ille), bridge	30.5	15	54.3
Lock 16 (Haute-Roche)	31.1	16	53.7
Lock 17 (Lengager), bridge (D12), quay and turning basin upstream r/b, **Montreuil-sur-Ille** 1100m l/b	32.0	17	52.8
Lock 18 (Chanclin)	32.8	18	52.0
Lock 19 (Courgalais), bridge	33.5	19	51.3
Lock 20 (Villemorin), beginning of summit level	34.2	20	50.6
La Plousière bridge (D82) and quay, **Guipel** 1500m south	35.5	-	49.3
La Guénaudière bridge	40.9	-	43.9
Lock 21 (Ségerie), end of summit level	41.4	21	43.4
Lock 22, moorings downstream	41.6	22	43.2
Lock 23 (Pêchetière)	41.8	23	43.0
Lock 24, water	42.0	24	42.8
Lock 25 (Parfraire), bridge	42.2	25	42.6
Lock 26	42.3	26	42.5
Lock 27	42.5	27	42.3
Lock 28 (Madeleine), bridge, quays d/s, **Hédé** 1200m l/b	42.7	28	42.1
Lock 29 (Petite-Madeleine)	43.0	29	41.8
Lock 30 (Guéhardière)	43.2	30	41.6
Lock 31 (Dialais)	43.5	31	41.3
Lock 32 (Moucherie), bridge	45.4	32	39.4
Turning basin r/b	46.5	-	38.3
Lock 33 (Tinténiac), bridge	47.1	33	37.7
Tinténiac quay l/b, water and fuel, village l/b	47.2	-	37.6
Lock 34 (Gromillais), bridge	48.9	34	35.9
Lock 35 (Gué Noëllan)	49.9	35	34.9
Lock 36 (Pont-Houitte), bridge	50.8	36	34.0
La Chapelle-aux-Filzméens bridge, quay and turning basin upstream r/b, small village 1200m r/b	53.3	-	31.5
Lock 37 (Calaudry), bridge	54.6	37	30.2
Lock 38 (Couadan)	56.6	38	28.2
Saint-Dominieuc bridge, quay d/s l/b, village 700m l/b	57.3	-	27.5
Bridge (Richeville)	58.8	-	26.0
Lock 39 (Gacet), bridge	60.5	39	24.3
Lock 40 (Butte Jacquette)	60.9	40	23.9
Trévérien bridge, quay and turning basin upstream r/b, water point and sanitary building, village l/b	61.7	-	23.1
Lock 41 (Islots)	62.4	41	22.4
Footbridge (St. Judoce)	65.1	-	19.7
Evran quay r/b, water point, sanitary building and public telephone, village l/b	66.3	-	18.5
Lock 42 (Evran), bridge	66.4	42	18.4
Lock 43 (Roche), bridge	67.8	43	17.0
Bridge (Pont des Planches)	68.2	-	16.6
Lock 44 (Mottay), bridge	70.0	44	14.8
Bridge (Grand Boutron)	71.6	-	13.2

	km	lock	km
Lock 45 (Boutron), swing bridge	71.8	45	13.0
Quay (Vaugré) r/b	73.1	-	11.7
Lock 46 (Pont-Perrin), bridge,	74.1	46	10.7
Léhon bridge (Vieux Pont), quays, village l/b	76.3	-	8.5
Lock 47 (Léhon)	76.8	47	8.0
Dinan viaduct	78.5	-	6.3
Dinan bridge (Vieux Pont), upstream limit of tidal influence boat harbour d/s l/b, restaurant, town 75m above river	78.6	-	6.2
Lanvallay quay r/b	78.8	-	6.0
Quay (Etra or Asile du Pêcheur) l/b	81.5	-	3.3
Taden quay l/b, village 700m	82.4	-	2.4
Le Chatelier quay r/b	83.4	-	1.4
Quay (Petit-Livet) l/b, **Saint-Samson-sur-Rance** harbour	83.8	-	1.0
Quay (Livet) r/b, **Vicomté-sur-Rance** harbour, Chemins Nautiques Bretons hire base	84.2	-	0.6
Tide lock 48 (Chatelier), submersible weir, *navigation continues in tidal Rance (Rance maritime)*	84.8	48	0.0

Isle

The Isle was formerly canalised over a distance of about 144km upstream from its confluence with the Dordogne at Libourne to the town of Périgueux. However, all the structures fell into disuse many years ago, and only the tidal river is now navigable, over a distance of 31km from Libourne to the first lock (lock 40) at Laubardemont. It should be noted that the possibility of mooring at most of the quays indicated in the distance table depends on the state of the tide.

Locks None.

Depth There is a depth of 0.30m at low water neap tides rising to between 0.80 and 1.60m at high water neap tides (at the limit of navigation at Laubardemont).

Bridges The fixed bridges leave a clear headroom of 8.20m at low water neaps, reduced to 3.80m at high water neaps.

Towpath There is no towpath.

Authority
Service Maritime et de Navigation de la Gironde, Bordeaux.
Subdivision: 61 cours des Girondins, 33500 Libourne, ☎ (57) 51 06 53.

Distance table

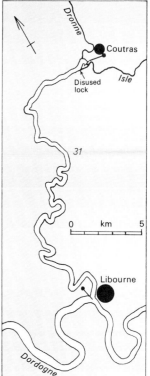

	km	lock	km
Lock 40 (Laubardemont), disused, head of tidal navigation			
Coutras 2500m u/s on Dronne (light craft only)	0.0	-	31.1
Guîtres bridge, quay and village r/b	2.5	-	28.6
Railway bridge	3.0	-	28.1
Quays l/b (Fleix)	9.0	-	22.1
Saint-Denis-de-Pile bridge, quay and village l/b	10.4	-	20.7
Savignac-de-l'Isle bridge, quay d/s r/b, village 400m r/b	14.5	-	16.6
Bridge (D18)	19.8	-	11.3

	km	*lock*	*km*
Saillans r/b, village 1200m	23.5	-	7.6
Libourne bridge, quay u/s l/b, town centre 700m	30.4	-	0.7
Confluence with Dordogne (km 75)	31.1	-	0.0

Canal du Loing

The Canal du Loing, one of the series of waterways forming the 'Bourbonnais' route from Paris to Lyon, connects with the Canal de Briare below Buges lock, north of Montargis, and runs down the Loing valley (using the bed of the river at two places) to enter the Seine at Saint-Mammès, a distance of 49km.

Locks There are 18 locks, with uniform dimensions of 39.10 by 5.20m, plus a flood lock at Fromonville (no 13), which is normally open. Lock 20 at Saint-Mammès has been taken out of service and the adjacent weir demolished, since the downstream level has been raised as a result of reconstruction of the navigation works on the Upper Seine.

Depth The maximum authorised draught is 1.80m.

Bridges All bridges leave a minimum headroom of 3.50m above the normal water level.

Towpath There is a good towpath throughout.

Authority
Service de la Navigation de Nevers.
Subdivision: Ecluse de la Marolle, 45200 Montargis, ☎ 38 85 37 21.

Distance table

	km	*lock*	*km*
Junction with Canal de Briare (downstream of lock 36, Buges)	0.0	-	49.4
Railway bridge	0.5	-	48.9
Lock 1 (Cépoy)	2.2	1	47.2
Cépoy bridge, village l/b	2.3	-	47.1
Quay l/b	3.0	-	46.4
Lock 2 (Vallées), water	5.1	2	44.3
Bridge (Vallées)	5.3	-	44.1

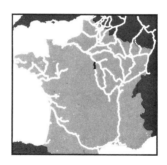

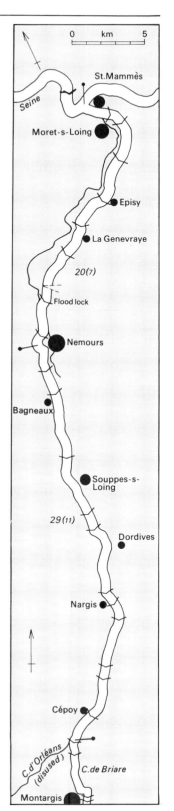

	km	lock	km
Lock 3 (Montabon)	5.9	3	43.5
Bridge (Vaux)	8.1	-	41.3
Lock 4 (Retourné)	8.9	4	40.5
Lock 5 (Nargis), bridge	10.4	5	39.0
Nargis quay and village l/b	10.5	-	38.9
Lock 6 (Brisebarre)	11.1	6	38.3
Bridge (Toury)	12.8	-	36.6
Dordives bridge, quay upstream l/b, village r/b 1000m	14.3	-	35.1
Lock 7 (Néronville), bridge	15.9	7	33.5
Lock 8 (Egreville), bridge, basin downstream l/b, restaurant	17.0	8	32.4
Railway bridge	18.3	-	31.1
Souppes-sur-Loing, quays l/b, town 900m r/b	18.8	-	30.6
Turning basin r/b	20.4	-	29.0
Railway bridge	20.7	-	28.7
Lock 9 (Beaumoulin), bridge, quay downstream l/b	21.3	9	28.1
Bridge (Glandelles), quay downstream l/b	22.4	-	27.0
Bagneaux-sur-Loing bridge, village 600m l/b	24.4	-	25.0
Quay for Pyrex factory, l/b	25.2	-	24.2
Lock 10 (Bagneaux), bridge	25.7	10	23.7
Quay (Fromonceau) l/b	26.0	-	23.4
Lock 11 (Chaintreauville), bridge	27.4	11	22.0
Quay (Fontaines), l/b	28.2	-	21.2
Nemours bridge (Récollets), town centre r/b	28.8	-	20.6
Bridge (Paris)	29.4	-	20.0
Nemours quay l/b, water, fuel	29.8	-	19.6
Lock 12 (Buttes), bridge, restaurant, navigation enters river Loing	30.1	12	19.3
Private quays l/b	30.7	-	18.7
Motorway bridge (A6 Paris-Lyon)	31.7	-	17.7
Flood lock 13 (Fromonville), navigation leaves river	32.6	-	16.8
Montcourt-Fromonville bridge, village r/b, quay d/s l/b	34.7	-	14.7
Lock 14 (Bordes)	36.4	13	13.0
La Genevraye bridge, quay downstream l/b, village r/b	38.1	-	11.3
Lock 15 (Berville)	38.7	14	10.7
Quay (Launay) r/b	39.6	-	9.8
Private quay l/b	40.9	-	8.5
Lock 16 (**Episy**), quay upstream l/b, restaurant r/b	41.2	15	8.2
Quay l/b	41.8	-	7.6
Lock 17 (Ecuelles), bridge	44.1	16	5.3
Ecuelles r/b	44.8	-	4.6
Private quays r/b	45.6	-	3.8
Road bridge (Moret-sur-Loing by-pass)	46.4	-	3.0
Aqueduct crosses canal	46.6	-	2.8
Lock 18 (Bourgogne), bridge (N6), **Moret-sur-Loing** town centre 600m	46.9	17	2.5
Lock 19 (Moret), bridge, navigation enters river Loing (navigable upstream 400m, moorings for **Moret-sur-Loing**)	47.7	18	1.7
Railway bridge	48.4	-	1.0
Boatyard and slipway, l/b	49.1	-	0.3
Saint-Mammès, *confluence with Seine*, mooring quays	49.4	-	0.0

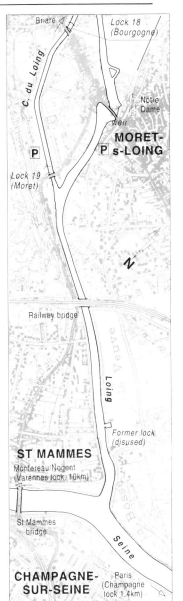

Loire

The Loire, the longest river in France, used to be navigated upstream as far as La Noirie, level with Saint-Etienne, 880km from the sea, but its extreme flow regime makes it the least navigable of all France's major rivers. The flow is relatively small throughout much of the year, and wanders about over a wide bed. In many reaches the depth drops to no more than 0.25m. During floods, the river rises rapidly, and the fast current makes navigation dangerous as soon as depths of about 2.00m have been reached. Thus all navigation has long ceased on the upper and middle courses of the river, except at two places where the water is held back by weirs:

1. Roanne, where there is access to a short navigable length of the river from the Canal de Roanne à Digoin,
2. Decize, where the river is navigable for 1.7km from the Decize branch of the Canal latéral à la Loire to the Canal du Nivernais. This important link is included in the distance table.

The river only becomes fully navigable (with reservations-see below) at its confluence with the river Maine at Bouchemaine. It thus links the Maine and its navigable tributaries (Mayenne, Oudon and Sarthe) to the Canal de Nantes à Brest in Nantes, a distance of 84km. The total distance from the confluence at Bouchemaine to the sea at Saint-Nazaire is 138km. The inland waterway ends at the seaport of Nantes, whence the Loire estuary is officially a maritime waterway, but for convenience the distance table is continued down to Saint-Nazaire. The following indications apply only to the inland waterway section, and for navigation in the estuary reference should be made to nautical works.

Locks None.

Depth From Bouchemaine to Nantes a channel 100 to 150m wide is fixed by means of submersible dykes and groynes. The channel is marked by buoys, red on the left-bank side and black on the right-bank side. At low water, the navigable channel is marked by 4.50m high stakes driven into the sand, those on the left-bank side having their tops partly broken and hanging down. In principle, a depth of 1.50m is maintained at medium low water, but there

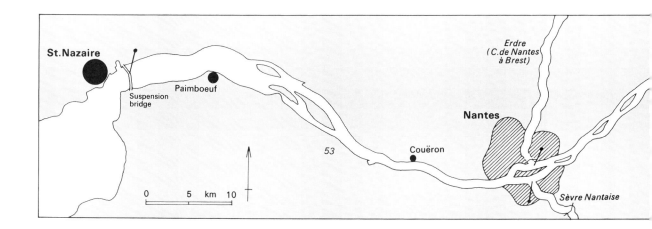

may be marked variations, with as little as 0.35m over certain sills in the channel at exceptional low water levels. It should also be borne in mind that spring tides make themselves felt as far upstream as Champtoceaux. In low water periods enquiries should therefore be made at the offices of the sub-divisional engineers (addresses below) before making the passage. They will indicate the specific dangers to be avoided. Use of the *Guide des Canaux Bretons et de la Loire*, published by Les Editions du Plaisancier (see Introduction) is recommended.

Bridges The bridges on the inland waterway section leave a minimum headroom of 4.50m above the highest navigable water level (7.00m above the mean water level).

Towpath None.

Authority
Service Maritime et de Navigation de Nantes.
Subdivisions:
– 1 quai des Carmes, BP 531, 49035 Angers, ☎ 41 88 58 91 (km 0-43).
– 2 rue Marcel Sembat, 44100 Nantes, ☎ 40 73 30 97 (km 43-84)

Distance table
Link between Decize branch of Canal latéral à la Loire and Canal du Nivernais

	km	lock	km
Decize branch of Canal latéral à la Loire enters river, l/b	0.0	-	1.7
Decize bridge, town r/b	0.5	-	1.2
Quay r/b	1.4	-	0.3
Junction with Canal du Nivernais, r/b	1.7	-	0.0

From Bouchemaine to the sea

	km	lock	km
Confluence of Maine, r/b	0.0	-	138.0
La Pointe Bouchemaine r/b	0.4	-	137.6
Béhuard r/b (on island)	4.6	-	133.4
Bridge (Savennières)	5.1	-	132.9
La Poissonnière quay r/b, village 400m r/b	7.8	-	130.2
Railway bridge (Alleud)	10.9	-	127.1
River divides, navigation in l/b arm	11.3	-	126.7

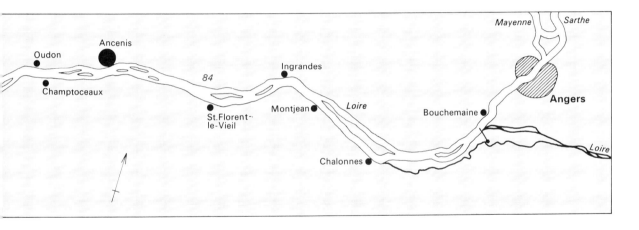

	km	lock	km
Chalonnes-sur-Loire bridge, quay u/s l/b, small town	14.6	-	123.4
Montjean-sur-Loire bridge, quay d/s l/b, village l/b	23.6	-	114.4
Ingrandes bridge, quay u/s r/b, village r/b	28.1	-	109.9
Saint-Florent-le-Vieil bridge (on l/b arm), quay u/s l/b	36.9	-	101.1
Ancenis bridge, quay u/s r/b, small town and castle r/b	49.6	-	88.4
Champtoceaux, mooring in backwater l/b, village 800m	56.1	-	81.9
Bridge (Pont de Champtoceaux)	57.9	-	80.1
Oudon harbour r/b (through railway bridge), village 200m	58.6	-	79.4
Clermont castle r/b	62.4	-	75.6
Mauves-sur-Loire bridge, village 700m r/b	67.8	-	70.2
Bridge (Thouaré)	73.2	-	64.8
New bridge (Bellevue)	78.4	-	59.6
River divides, La Madeleine arm r/b, Pirmil arm l/b	82.0	-	56.0
Railway bridge (extending over both arms)	82.4	-	55.6
Railway bridge (Madeleine arm)	83.6	-	54.4
Junction with Canal de Nantes à Brest (canalised river Erdre), r/b on Madeleine arm	84.0	-	54.0
Nantes bridge (over both arms), town centre r/b	84.3	-	53.7
Bridge (over both arms)	84.9	-	53.1
Confluence of Sèvre-Nantaise, l/b on Pirmil arm	85.3	-	52.7
Bridge (Pont Haudaudine) on Madeleine arm	85.3	-	52.7
Railway and road bridge (Pirmil) on Pirmil arm	85.5	-	52.5
Bridge (Pont Anne-de-Bretagne), mooring d/s r/b (Madeleine arm)	86.1	-	51.9
Port of Nantes, two arms meet	87.3	-	50.7
Rezé boat harbour, l/b	87.8	-	50.2
Quay (Haute-Indre) r/b, downstream limit of port of Nantes	93.0	-	45.0
Basse-Indre quay, village r/b, Indret quay l/b, ferry	95.0	-	43.0
Couëron quay and small town r/b	99.0	-	39.0
Le Pellerin quay and village l/b, ferry	101.0	-	37.0
La Martinière quay l/b (in entrance to former ship canal)	103.5	-	34.5
Cordemaïs power station, coal unloading quay r/b	114.0	-	24.0
Paimboeuf quay and small town l/b	125.0	-	13.0
Donges port, r/b	130.0	-	8.0
Saint-Nazaire suspension bridge, limit of sea (port entrance a further 3km downstream)	138.0	-	0.0

Canal latéral à Loire

The Canal latéral à Loire, opened in 1838, runs down the Loire valley from Digoin, where it connects with the Canal du Centre, to La Cognardière, near Briare, where it connects with the Canal de Briare, a distance of 196km. It is an important waterway, forming part of the 'Bourbonnais' route from the Seine to the Saône, and it has seen some large-scale maintenance works in recent years to restore the original navigable standards (as well as consolidating the fragile banks). Connections are made with the Canal de Roanne à Digoin at km 2, and with the Canal du Nivernais via the branch to Decize and a channel dredged across the river Loire (km 64). The canal also used to connect with the remarkable Canal du Berry system, sadly closed since 1955, at Marseilles-les-Aubigny (km 121). Details of the five branches which remain open to navigation (including the Decize branch mentioned above) are as follows:

1. Dompierre branch (km 25), length 2.7km, no locks (leads to the small town of Dompierre-sur-Besbre),

2. Decize branch (km 64), length 0.5km, 2 locks (including Decize basin, links with the Loire and the Canal du Nivernais),
3. Nevers branch (km 96), length 2.8km, 2 locks (third lock leading down to the Loire has been converted into a swimming pool),
4. Givry-Fourchambault branch (km 115), length 2.4km, 2 locks (links with the Loire),
5. Saint-Thibault branch (km 156), length 0.7km, 1 lock (links with the Loire).

The Lorrains branch (km 108), which serves as a feeder canal from the Allier, is no longer open to navigation.

The canal boasts three fine aqueducts, situated at Digoin (240m, over the Loire), Le Guétin (334m, over the Allier) and Briare (660m, over the Loire). Navigation is one-way only across all these aqueducts. At Digoin and Briare, the first vessel to reach either end of the aqueduct has priority. At Le Guétin, the lights which control passage through the double staircase lock also control passage across the aqueduct.

Locks There are 37 locks, of standard 'Freycinet' dimensions, 38.50 by 5.17m, with the exception of Lock 11 (Gailloux), where the chamber is slightly narrower (5.14m). The locks fall towards Briare, overcoming a difference in level of 98m.

Depth The maximum authorised draught is 1.80m.

Bridges The bridges leave a minimum clear headroom of 3.50m above normal water level.

Towpath There is a towpath throughout the length of the canal, of variable condition.

Authority

Service de la Navigation de Nevers. Subdivisions:
– 1 quai de la Jonction, 58300 Decize, ☎ 86 25 14 75 (km 0-106).
– Saint-Thibault – Saint-Satur, 18300, Sancerre, ☎ 45 54 12 34 (km 106-176).
– Usine Elvatrice, 45250 Briare, ☎ 60 01 26 20 (km 176-196).

Distance table

	km	lock	km
Digoin, *junction with Canal du Centre*	0.0	-	196.0
Footbridge	0.1	-	195.9
Bridge (Charolles), town centre nearby	0.4	-	195.6
Bridge (Perruts)	0.6	-	195.4
Digoin aqueduct over river Loire, 240m long	0.7	-	195.3
Lock 1 (Digoin), bridge	1.0	1	195.0
Chassenard basin, 830m long	1.3	-	194.7
Junction with Canal de Roanne à Digoin l/b	2.1	-	193.9
Bridge (Chassenard)	2.2	-	193.8
Basin (La Broche), r/b	2.7	-	193.3
Bridge (Donjon), N488	3.7	-	192.3
Quay (Fontaine-Saint-Martin) l/b	3.9	-	192.1
Vouzance aqueduct	5.0	-	191.0
Bridge (Péage)	5.5	-	190.5
Bridge (Micaudière)	6.4	-	189.6
Bridge (Mortillon), N488	8.0	-	188.0
Lock 2 (Thaleine), bridge	9.5	2	186.5

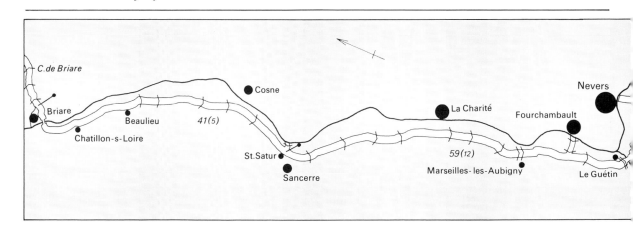

	km	lock	km
Basin (Coulanges) l/b	10.3	-	185.7
Coulanges bridge, small village	10.8	-	185.2
Bridge (Vesvres)	12.3	-	183.7
Lock 3 (Oddes), aqueduct upstream	12.6	3	183.4
Bridge (Oddins)	14.2	-	181.8
Pierrefitte-sur-Loire bridge, basin downstream l/b, village r/b	15.0	-	181.0
Bridge (Enfer), N488	15.6	-	180.4
Lock 4 (Theil)	16.6	4	179.4
Bridge (Theil)	17.2	-	178.8
Lock 5 (Putay), bridge downstream	18.6	5	177.4
Bridge (Cluzeau)	19.5	-	176.5
Railway bridge	20.2	-	175.8
Diou bridge, basin downstream l/b, village 400m	21.4	-	174.6
Bridge (Saligny), Diou 300m	21.8	-	174.2
Bridge (Prats)	22.8	-	173.2
Roudon aqueduct	22.9	-	173.1
Bridge (Ternat)	23.2	-	172.8
Besbre aqueduct, length 86m	24.9	-	171.1
Lock 6 (Besbre), bridge downstream	25.1	6	170.9
Junction with Besbre feeder canal, Dompierre branch, l/b	25.2	-	170.8
Bridge (Abbaye de Sept-Fons)	26.0	-	170.0
Bridge (Taillis)	27.2	-	168.8
Lock 7 (Bessais), bridge downstream	28.7	7	167.3
Bridge (Thiel)	31.0	-	165.0
Bridge (Petrot)	32.7	-	163.3
Lock 8 (**Beaulon**), bridge d/s, basin l/b, village 1000m	33.6	8	162.4
Lock 9 (Clos du May), bridge downstream	35.6	9	160.4
Garnat bridge, basin upstream l/b, restaurant in village r/b	36.6	-	159.4
Bridge (Huilerie)	38.6	-	157.4
Bridge (Saint-Martin), **Paray-le-Frésil** 2000m	40.5	-	155.5
Lock 10 (Rozière)	41.3	10	154.7
Bridge (Rozière)	42.3	-	153.7
Bridge (Boise)	43.8	-	152.2
Lock 11 (Gailloux), bridge downstream	45.3	11	150.7
Bridge (Viviers)	46.7	-	149.3
Gannay basin l/b, Connoisseur Cruisers hire base, village 1000m r/b (across bridge over lock)	48.2	-	147.8
Lock 12 (Vanneaux), bridge downstream	48.5	12	147.5
Bridge (Rue des Gués)	50.8	-	145.2

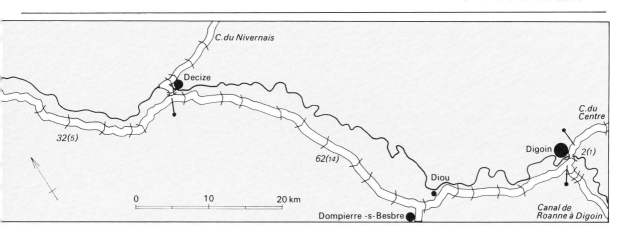

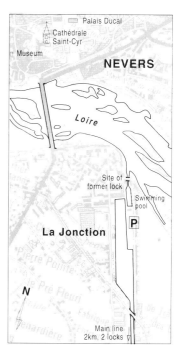

	km	lock	km
Bridge (Nogent)	53.4	-	142.6
Lock 13 (Huilerie)	54.2	13	141.8
Bridge (Cornats), basin upstream l/b	55.6	-	140.4
Lock 14 (Motte)	56.9	14	139.1
Bridge (Motte)	57.4	-	138.6
Bridge (Croix-des-Feuillats)	60.2	-	135.8
Lock 15 (Saulx)	62.8	15	133.2
Bridge (Saulx)	63.2	-	132.8
Junction with Decize branch (connecting with the Canal du Nivernais) r/b, Crown Blue Line base in basin (see plan)	64.4	-	131.6
Bridge (Germany), basin downstream l/b, **Decize** 1400m	64.7	-	131.3
Bridge (Vaux)	66.0	-	130.0
Bridge (Chalons)	66.9	-	129.1
Bridge (Baugy), basin downstream l/b	69.4	-	126.6
Bridge (Réau)	70.2	-	125.8
Lock 16 (Acolin), Acolin aqueduct upstream	70.9	16	125.1
Bridge (Forge-Neuve)	71.6	-	124.4
Lock 17 (Abron), Abron aqueduct upstream, basin d/s	72.0	17	124.0
Avril-sur-Loire bridge, small village r/b	72.8	-	123.2
Bridge (Perrière)	74.9	-	121.1
Fleury-sur-Loire bridge, small village l/b	76.4	-	119.6
Lock 18 (Fleury)	76.7	18	119.3
Bridge (Motte-Farchat), basin upstream l/b, castle 1000m	77.9	-	118.1
Bridge (Vèvre)	79.9	-	116.1
Bridge (Uxeloup)	81.2	-	114.8
Lock 19 (Uxeloup)	81.8	19	114.2
Bridge (Chamond), basin downstream l/b	82.3	-	113.7
Bridge (Planches)	84.5	-	111.5
Lock 20 (Jaugenay), bridge downstream	85.7	20	110.3
Bridge (Atelier)	87.3	-	108.7
Chevenon bridge, village and castle 800m l/b	89.4	-	106.6
Bridge (Crezancy)	91.0	-	105.0
Bridge (Forêt de Sermoise)	93.3	-	102.7
Bridge (Crot de Savigny)	94.7	-	101.3
Bridge (Avenue de Sermoise), **Sermoise-sur-Loire** 1000m	96.2	-	99.8
Junction with Nevers branch	96.4	-	99.6
Bridge (Peuilly)	97.4	-	98.6
Plagny bridge, N7, boat moorings, Loch 2000 hire base in basin u/s l/b, water, electricity, gas, showers, 5-tonne hoist	98.6	-	97.4

	km	*lock*	*km*
Bridge (Pavillon), **Challuy** 500m	99.4	-	96.6
Railway bridge	99.6	-	96.4
Bridge (Seuilly)	100.3	-	95.7
Bridge (Marais)	102.8	-	93.2
Bridge (Colombier), D976, castle 200m	103.9	-	92.1
Gimouille bridge, village l/b	104.8	-	91.2
Bridge (Sampanges), Gimouille basin upstream l/b	105.6	-	90.4
Guétin aqueduct (over river Allier)	106.0	-	90.0
Double staircase lock 21/22 (Guétin), bridge and basin downstream, small village r/b	106.4	22	89.6
Bridge (Caillettes)	107.4	-	88.6
Junction with Lorrains branch (Allier feeder canal), wide basin 700m long	107.5	-	88.5
Bridge (Colombier)	107.8	-	88.2
Cuffy footbridge, village l/b	108.6	-	87.4
Bridge (Presle), castle	109.7	-	86.3
Lock 24 (Laubray)	112.0	23	84.0
Bridge (Laubray)	112.2	-	83.8
Bridge (Mahauts), *junction with Givry-Fourchambault branch*, quay r/b	114.5	-	81.5
Bridge (Crille)	115.2	-	80.8
Cours-les-Barres bridge, village l/b, service station	116.0	-	80.0
Bridge (Dompierre)	117.6	-	78.4
Bridge (Poids de Fer)	120.0	-	76.0
Marseilles-les-Aubigny basin and Crown Blue Line base l/b, small town, *former junction with Canal du Berry* l/b	120.7	-	75.3
Lock 25 (Aubigny), bridge downstream	121.3	24	74.7
Aubois aqueduct and basin l/b	121.4	-	74.6
Lock 26 (Aubois), bridge downstream, freight office	121.6	25	74.4
Loire Line hire base l/b	122.0	-	74.0
Lock 27 (**Beffes**), bridge downstream, village r/b	124.4	26	71.6
Basin l/b	124.9	-	71.1
Bridge (Radis)	126.1	-	69.9
Saint-Léger-le-Petit bridge, village l/b	127.5	-	68.5
Lock 28 (Argenvières), bridge	129.1	27	66.9
Argenvières basin, village r/b	129.5	-	66.5
Quays (Comillons)	130.4	-	65.6
Quay (Charnaye) l/b	130.9	-	65.1
Lock 29 (Rousseaux), bridge	131.6	28	64.4
La Chapelle-Montlinard basin, bridge, **La Charité** 2000m on r/b of Loire, historic sites	133.1	-	62.9
Bridge (Nambault)	134.4	-	61.6
Bridge (Charreau)	135.7	-	60.3
Bridge (Châtillon)	136.9	-	59.1
Lock 30 (**Herry**), bridge, basin and village downstream l/b	138.9	29	57.1
Bridge (Sarrée)	140.9	-	55.1
Lock 31 (Prée), bridge	141.9	30	54.1
Bridge (Champalay)	144.4	-	51.6
Quay (Guillons) l/b	146.3	-	49.7
Lock 32 (Grange), bridge, castle 1000m	146.9	31	49.1
Moule aqueduct	147.9	-	48.1
Saint-Bouize bridge, basin upstream l/b, village 1000m	148.7	-	47.3
Bridge (Rousseaux)	150.5	-	45.5
Lock 33 (Thauvenay), bridge	152.1	32	43.9
Ménétréol-sous-Sancerre bridge, basin downstream l/b, village l/b, track uphill to **Sancerre** 2500m	152.9	-	43.1
Saint-Satur bridge and basin	155.4	-	40.6
Junction with Saint-Thibault branch r/b (connecting with Loire, 600m with one stop lock and one lock, 33a)	155.5	-	40.5

	km	lock	km
Bridge (Mivoie)	156.9	-	39.1
Bridge (Beaufroy)	159.1	-	36.9
Bridge (Ile), quay upstream l/b	160.3	-	35.7
Bannay l/b	161.3	-	34.7
Lock 34 (Bannay), bridge	161.6	33	34.4
Railway bridge	161.8	-	34.2
Bridge (Bussy)	163.2	-	32.8
Bridge (Fouchards), quay downstream l/b, castle 600m	164.0	-	32.0
Bridge (Giraude)	165.0	-	31.0
Lock 35 (Peseau)	165.6	34	30.4
Bridge (Gravereau)	166.4	-	29.6
Bridge (Ménétreau)	167.4	-	28.6
Lock 36 (Houards), bridge	169.5	35	26.5
Léré bridge, basin downstream l/b, village l/b	171.3	-	24.7
Sury-près-Léré bridge, village l/b	172.8	-	23.2
Bridge (Rue)	174.7	-	21.3
Lock 37 (Belleville)	175.2	36	20.8
Belleville-sur-Loire bridge, village and restaurant l/b	175.5	-	20.5
Bridge (Chennevières)	176.7	-	19.3
Lock 38 (Maimbray), aqueduct, bridge downstream	178.3	37	17.7
Bridge (Plessis)	179.1	-	16.9
Beaulieu bridge, basin and village downstream l/b	180.3	-	15.7
Junction with former Châtillon branch (disused) r/b	182.6	-	13.4
L'Etang bridge, flood gates	182.7	-	13.3
Bridge (Gannes)	184.1	-	11.9
Bridge (Folie)	185.1	-	10.9
Bridge (Rabuteloires), flood gates	186.7	-	9.3
Footbridge (Mantelot)	187.4	-	8.6
Châtillon-sur-Loire basin and Berry Plaisance hire base l/b, village 300m	187.5	-	8.4
Bridge (Châtillon)	188.0	-	8.0
Aqueduct	188.1	-	7.9
Bridge (Hautes-Rives)	188.5	-	7.5
Bridge (Chailloux)	189.7	-	6.3
Bridge (Motte), castle r/b	190.9	-	5.1
Saint-Firmin basin l/b	191.6	-	4.4
Bridge (Beauregard), flood gate	191.9	-	4.1
Canal on embankment crosses D951	192.7	-	3.3
Beginning of Briare aqueduct (663m long)	192.9	-	3.1
End of Briare aqueduct, bridge (Saint-Firmin)	193.6	-	2.4
Briare basin, moorings, town centre 300m, restaurant	193.7	-	2.3
Briare bridge (N7)	194.0	-	2.0
Railway bridge	194.2	-	1.8
Bridge (Bléneau)	194.3	-	1.7
Road bridge (Briare by-pass)	194.8	-	1.2
Bridge (Vaugereau)	195.1	-	0.9
Aqueduct (Cognardière)	195.8	-	0.2
Footbridge (Cognardière), flood gate	195.9	-	0.1
Junction with Canal de Briare	196.0	-	0.0

Lot

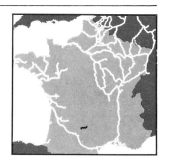

On 30th June 1990, a 64km length of the river Lot in south-west France was officially reopened to navigation by Jacques Delors, president of the European Commission, and a handful of ministers of the French government. The most ambitious waterway restoration project to have been carried out in France, with 13 locks restored and one built from scratch, had thus been completed in less than two years. The findings of the author's feasibility studies for this project have been confirmed by the extraordinary success of the waterway, where two major hire firms have set up bases, as well as a smaller local firm and three trip boats: all this on a navigation unconnected with the other navigable waterways in the south-west! This disadvantage is more than compensated by the exceptional beauty of the river, with its sheer limestone cliffs, attractive narrow lock-cuts, the Cahors vineyards, unspoilt villages and Cahors itself, remarkably located inside a long loop of the river.

The Lot was perhaps the longest canalised river in Europe, navigation extending over no less than 256km from the Garonne near Aiguillon to Livinhac, a small village a few kilometres from the important industrial and mining centre of Decazeville. The natural course of the river, serving as the reference for distances, is 272km long, the difference being explained by the lock-cuts built around 1830-1840 to bypass the extravagant meanders at Luzech, Cajarc, Montbrun and Capdenac, the last three including tunnels with locks at each end. Only the last-mentioned remains intact and could easily be restored. The Cajarc and Montbrun tunnels have been taken over by hydropower plants, while the Luzech lock-cut, which ran through the middle of the village, was infilled from end to end. Any further restoration of the river would thus have to overcome these considerable obstacles, as well as the four large hydropower dams at Luzech, Fumel, Villeneuve and Castelmoron. The author is continuing technical and economic studies of further development of the river, and judging by the motivation of local authorities throughout the course of the river, there is a strong probability that further lengths will be made navigable in the years to come.

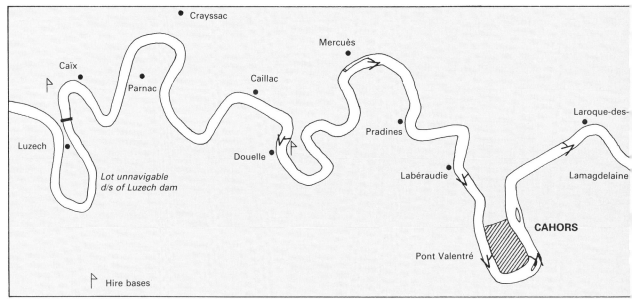

For the time being, navigation starts 500m above the 6m high dam and hydropower plant at Luzech (km 132.5), and continues upstream through Cahors to finish 100m below Crégols weir (km 196.7), near the attractive cliff-top village of St Cirq-Lapopie. In the distance table, the river distances, counted from zero at Nicole on the Garonne, are given on the left, and distances covered from Crégols weir to Luzech dam on the right.

It should be stressed that since the river Lot is not a State-operated navigable waterway, navigation is at the risk and peril of users, who are entirely responsible for checking available headroom and depths according to the stage of the river.

Delicate passages are all in principle marked by buoys, red on the right-bank side of the channel and green on the left-bank side.

Locks There are 14 locks on the restored section, all offering navigable dimensions of 30m by 5.00m, although the actual dimensions of the chambers vary. The maximum authorised length of boat is reduced from 30 to 25m for passage through the Ganil lock-cut, which is not only narrow but has a bend that is impracticable for longer boats. The wider chamber of the lock beneath the Pont Valentré in Cahors was justified in the 19th century by the intense traffic in this section.

Locks may be operated between sunrise and sunset, and are worked by the users, under their own responsibility, with gate paddle and lock-gate winding gear permanently installed. Gate paddles can be a little tiresome to operate, the gearing being somewhat excessive, and there is some curious safety devices, which can be disconcerting when first encountered: firstly, a gate paddle has to be fully opened before opening the corresponding gate; secondly, the gate has to be closed before lowering the gate paddle; finally, a foot lever has to be pressed to start opening or closing a gate. These are minor points, however, and lock operation should be fun for all the crew.

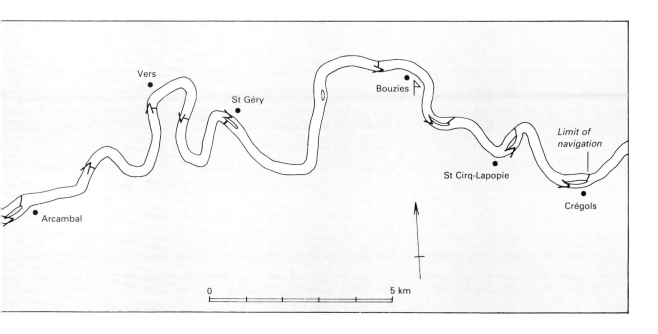

Depth The channel and all structures, especially lock sills, are designed in principle for an effective draught of 1.20m, but as a precaution the maximum authorised draught is limited to 1.00m.

Bridges The maximum authorised air draught (that is the maximum height of the boat's superstructure above the water level, non ballasted) is 4.40m, corresponding to the minimum headroom above the highest navigable water level.

Regulations Speed must not exceed 12km/h in mid-river, and must be reduced to 5km/h in the diversion canals and within 25m of the banks. Care must be taken not to cause wash liable to damage the banks, especially in the narrow lock-cuts. Passenger boats have priority at the locks.

Authority

Direction Départementale de l'Equipement du Lot, Quai Calvaignac, 46009 **Cahors**, ☎ 65 35 20 26

Distance table

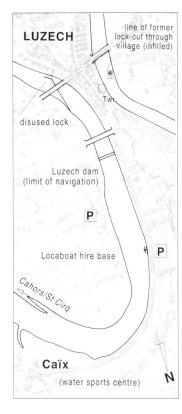

	km	lock	km
Luzech dam and hydropower plant (for reference, not to be approached within 500m)	132.0	-	64.7
Quay r/b and Locaboat Plaisance hire base, limit of navigation, water and fuel, village with all facilities 800m, alternative mooring for village on l/b	132.5	-	64.2
Caïx quay r/b, water sports base, dinghy sailing, canoeing	133.5	-	63.2
Caïx castle, home of Queen Margriet of Denmark, r/b	135.4	-	61.3
Parnac mooring (no facilities) l/b, village and Cahors wine cellars 500m	135.5	-	61.2
Langle castle r/b, former lock, alternative mooring for Parnac l/b	138.1	-	58.6
Caillac mooring (no facilities) r/b, village and restaurants	142.8	-	53.9
Disused railway viaduct (impressive brick arches), moorings and Antinéa trip boat base l/b	144.0	-	52.7
Cessac lock l/b, rise 2.00m, delicate approach from d/s	144.6	1	52.1
Quay r/b and Crown Blue Line hire base (restored tobacco drying shed), water and fuel	144.7	-	52.0
Douelle pontoon mooring beneath quay l/b, attractive village with shops, restaurants	144.8	-	51.9
Douelle suspension bridge	145.0	-	51.7
Cessac r/b	148.0	-	48.7
Outfall of Mercuès hydropower plant, former lock, r/b	150.9	-	45.8
Mercuès lock l/b at end of long narrow channel, rise 4.20m	151.9	2	44.8
Mercuès mooring r/b, village 500m, castle 1200m on hilltop (hotel and restaurant)	152.0	-	44.7
Pradines l/b, shops and restaurant	154.3	-	42.4
Labéraudie lock l/b, rise 0.70m	157.3	3	39.4
Cahors boatyard (Port Saint-Mary) and slipway r/b, Chantier Naval du Lot et de la Garonne, Babou Marine inflatable and small boat hire	158.6	-	38.1
Valentré lock l/b beneath the 14th century **Pont Valentré**, rise 2.75m, Cahors town centre 400m r/b	159.7	4	37.0
Hôtel de la Chartreuse, restaurant on former lock, l/b	160.7	-	36.0
Cahors bridge (Pont Louis-Philippe, or St Georges), D920 main road, camp-site d/s l/b, town centre r/b	160.8	-	35.9
Entrance to Cahors lock-cut, l/b	161.3	-	35.4
Cahors lock (Moulin de Coty), l/b, rise 1.30m	161.4	5	35.3

	km	lock	km
Bridge (Pont de Cabessut), submerged former bridge pier just d/s of the middle of each arch	161.7	-	35.0
Moorings l/b in front of sports grounds, swimming pool, Cahors town centre 1000m over Cabessut bridge	162.3	-	34.4
Cahors rowing club headquarters r/b	162.5	-	34.2
Lacombe lock, l/b, rise 1.40m	164.9	6	31.8
Laroque-des-Arcs quay in centre of village, shops, restaurant, water point on quay	165.8	-	30.9
Lamagdeleine moorings level with sports ground and campsite, r/b, village with café and restaurant 200m	167.3	-	29.4
Arcambal lock, l/b, rise 1.35m	168.8	7	27.9
U/s entrance to Arcambal lock-cut, beware of possible cross-current	169.2	-	27.5
Moorings for Savanac, r/b, **Arcambal**, l/b	170.2	-	26.5
Original Galessie lock taken over by hydropower plant, l/b	171.2	-	25.5
Galessie new lock r/b, rise 2.80m	171.5	8	25.2
Vers lock r/b, rise 0.25m	175.8	9	20.9
Vers bridge, mooring u/s r/b in front of campsite, water, all shops and restaurants in lively village, 200m	175.9	-	20.8
Planiol lock l/b, rise 1.40m	178.0	10	18.7
St Géry lock r/b, rise 3.05m	181.0	11	15.7
St Géry mooring in lock-cut, r/b, village centre 200m	181.2	-	15.5
U/s entrance to St Géry lock-cut	181.6	-	15.1
Masséries lock l/b (disused, pounds level following raising of St Géry weir, keep between buoys towards right bank)	184.2	-	12.5
Railway bridge	184.7	-	12.0
Island, navigation in r/b arm	186.0	-	10.7
Bouziès lock l/b, rise 1.40m	188.3	12	8.4
Bouziès bridge, Hôtel des Falaises, Bateaux Safaraid trip boat, boat hire and canoeing base, swimming pool	189.2	-	7.5
Railway bridge	190.0	-	6.7
Ganil lock, l/b, rise 1.50m	190.5	13	6.2
Confluence of Célé r/b (not visible from lock-cut)	190.8	-	5.9
End of lock-cut, navigation re-enters river, beware of current	191.4	-	5.3
St Cirq lock, l/b, rise 1.85m	193.5	14	3.2
End of lock-cut, navigation re-enters river, beware of current	194.0	-	2.7
St Cirq-Lapopie bridge, camp-site, moorings, famous cliff-top village 1000m up the hill, souvenir shops, art galleries, and several cafés and restaurants (alternative mooring below lock)	194.4	-	2.3
Crégols lock (disused) l/b, village 800m (no facilities)	195.8	-	0.9
Crégols weir (limit of navigation 100m below)	196.7	-	0.0

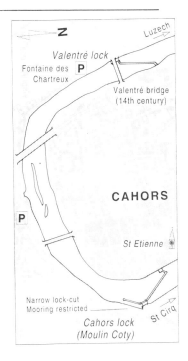

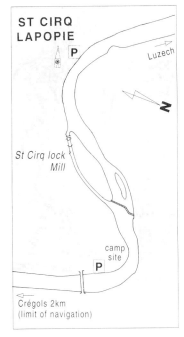

Lys

The canalised river Lys extends from a new junction with the Dunkerque-Escaut waterway (km 93) near Aire-sur-la-Lys to the confluence with the Escaut at Ghent, in Belgium. The length of waterway given in the distance table below is 65km, ending at the point where the river enters Belgium at Halluin/Menin, although it must be noted that the river itself forms the border over a distance of almost 24km downstream from Armentières, the right bank being in France and the left bank in Belgium. The two countries have signed an agreement for upgrading of the common section, to provide a direct high-capacity link with the newly upgraded Canal de la Deûle, forming the Bauvin-Lys branch of the Dunkerque-Escaut waterway. The Deûle joins the Lys at Deûlémont (km 48). The Lys also used to connect with the Hazebrouck canals on the left bank at km 5 and at km 19, but these have been closed to navigation (see Canaux d'Hazebrouck). The secondary arms of the Lys may be navigated at a number of places, as indicated on the general map and in the distance table. Between Aire-sur-la-Lys and Armentières, the river flows quietly through rural Flanders and makes a pleasant cruising waterway, as is testified by the development of a marina on the bypassed loop of the river at Prés Duhem, near Armentières. Downstream of Armentières, an important industrial centre, commercial traffic is heavy.

Locks There are seven locks between Aire-sur-la-Lys and Halluin/Menin, overcoming a difference in level of 11.00m. The first five are of standard 300-tonne barge dimensions, 38.50 by 5.18m. Armentières lock is of Campenois barge dimensions, 85 by 8m. The last lock, at Comines (km 54), comes under Belgian administration, and has been rebuilt to large dimensions.

Depth The maximum authorised draught is 1.80m from Aire-sur-la-Lys to Armentières, increased to 2.00m from this point downstream.

Bridges The fixed bridges offer a minimum headroom of 3.90m above normal water level, reduced to 3.60m above the highest navigable water level.

Towpath The towpath is impracticable in places.

Authority

Direction Régionale de la Navigation, Lille. Subdivisions:
– Rue de l'Ecluse Saint-Bertin, BP353, 62505 Saint-Omer, ☎ 21 98 22 00 (0-34).
– Avenue Max Dorney, Bâtiment 1, BP56, 59004 Lille, ☎ 20 92 63 44 (km 34-65).

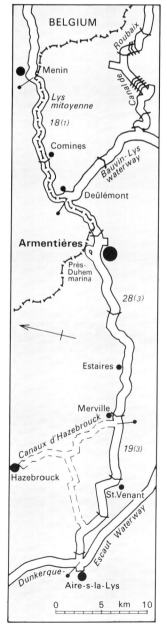

Distance table

	km	lock	km
Aire-sur-la-Lys, *junction with Canal d'Aire and Canal de Neufossé*, river navigable with difficulty for a further 400m upstream to railway bridge (500m from town centre)	0.0	-	65.3
Lock 1 (Fort-Gassion)	0.6	1	64.7
Thiennes lift bridge, quays upstream, village 1000m l/b	3.7	-	61.6
Footbridge (Oxyduc)	4.1	-	61.2
Railway bridge	4.5	-	60.8
Junction with Canal de la Nieppe (disused), l/b	4.6	-	60.7
Houleron quay r/b, small village	5.4	-	59.9
Lock 2 (Cense à Witz) and weir	6.7	2	58.6
Footbridge (Haverskerque)	10.6	-	54.7
Saint-Venant basin and quay r/b, small town 300m r/b	12.5	-	52.8
Lock 3 (Saint-Venant)	12.6	3	52.7
Road bridge (Saint-Venant bypass)	12.7	-	52.6
Saint-Floris village 500m r/b	14.5	-	50.8
Le Sart quay, village 500m l/b	17.4	-	47.9
Railway bridge	18.8	-	46.5
Footbridge (Basse-Boulogne)	19.0	-	46.3
Confluence with Bourre and entrance to lock-cut r/b	19.2	-	46.1
Lock 4 (**Merville**), lift bridges u/s and d/s, small town	19.4	4	45.9
Confluence of Merville arm of Lys, navigable upstream 800m to town	19.9	-	45.4
Swing bridge (private railway siding), quay downstream r/b	20.1	-	45.2
Private quay r/b and private footbridges	22.3	-	43.0
Private railway bridge	22.5	-	42.8
Confluence of Lawe (formerly navigable) r/b	24.4	-	40.9
La Gorgue bridge, village 500m r/b	24.6	-	40.7
Estaires bridge (Pont de la Meuse), quay upstream l/b, small town 300m l/b	25.7	-	39.6
Private footbridge	26.6	-	38.7
Bridge (Pont d'Estaires)	26.7	-	38.6
Sailly-sur-la-Lys bridge, quay downstream r/b, village 400m r/b	30.2	-	35.1
Lock 5 (Bac-Saint-Maur) and weir	32.5	5	32.8
Bac-Saint-Maur bridge, small village r/b	32.9	-	32.4
Entrance to Erquinghem cutoff, r/b	33.9	-	31.4
End of Erquinghem cutoff	35.7	-	29.6
Road bridge	36.1	-	29.2
Entrance to cutoff, l/b	36.2	-	29.1
Motorway bridge (A25), end of cutoff	37.1	-	28.2
Entrance to cutoff, l/b	37.3	-	28.0
End of cutoff	37.7	-	27.6
Railway bridge	37.9	-	27.4
Entrance to cutoff, r/b (Prés-Duhem marina in old course of river, l/b)	38.5	-	26.8
Armentières bridge (D933), town centre 800m r/b	39.1	-	26.2
End of cutoff, Prés-Duhem marina and hire base on old course of river, l/b (see plan)	40.2	-	25.1
Bridge (Bizet)	40.2	-	25.1
Armentières industrial quays	40.4	-	24.9
Bridge (Pont Aristide Briand)	40.6	-	25.7
Footbridge (Bayart)	41.1	-	24.2
Lock 6 (**Armentières**) and weir, beginning of Lys mitoyenne	41.4	6	23.9
Railway bridge (Houplines), entrance to Ploegsteert cutoff, l/b	41.8	-	23.5
Bridge (Ploegsteert)	42.3	-	23.0
End of cutoff	43.6	-	21.7

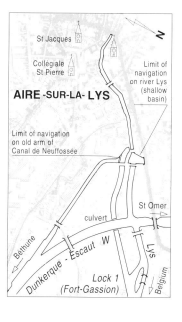

	km	lock	km
Frélinghien bridge, village 200m r/b	44.9	-	20.4
Bridge (Pont Rouge)	47.1	-	18.2
Towpath bridge	47.3	-	18.0
Junction with Bauvin-Lys waterway (Canal de la Deûle) r/b	47.7	-	17.6
Warneton bridge, village l/b (in Belgium)	50.5	-	14.8
Lock 7 (Comines) and weir, quay upstream r/b	54.0	7	11.3
Former junction with disused canal de Comines à Ypres, l/b	54.6	-	10.7
Comines bridge, town centre 200m l/b	55.1	-	10.2
Railway bridge, industrial quay downstream r/b	55.6	-	9.7
Wervicq bridge, quay d/s r/b, town 400m r/b	58.6	-	6.7
Bousbecque r/b	61.6	-	3.7
End of Lys mitoyenne, Belgian border, Menin bridge 1000m further downstream	65.3	-	0.0

Marne

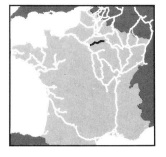

The Marne is navigable from Epernay to its confluence with the Seine at Charenton. However, since the junction with the Canal latéral à la Marne (which extends navigation on the river) is made at Dizy, 5km downstream of Epernay, the main line of navigation is considered as starting here, and the uncanalised length of river up to Epernay is treated as a branch. From Dizy to Charenton, navigation extends over a distance of 178km.

The lower course of the river is bypassed in several places by lengths of canal which are still generally known by their separate names. The Canal de Meaux à Chalifert is entered at Meaux and rejoins the river at Chalifert. It is 12km long, and has three locks. Between the last two, near Chalifert, there is a 290m long tunnel, passage through which is controlled by lights when entering from upstream and by the lock-keeper at lock 14 when entering from downstream. The Canal de Chelles extends 9km from Vaires-sur-Marne (km 155) to Neuilly-sur-Marne (km 164). It has a lock at each end. The Canal Saint-Maur cuts off a long loop of the river between Joinville-le-Pont and Maisons-Alfort. It is 1.2km in length, the first 600m being in tunnel. Passage

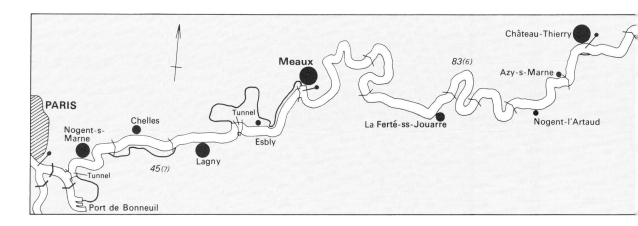

through the tunnel is controlled by lights, situated 50m upstream of the tunnel on the right bank and at the downstream entrance. When both red and green lights are shown (side-by-side), prepare to enter. Warning lights are situated at the upstream end of the Ile Fanac (km 173), to inform masters of vessels heading downstream of the situation likely to be found at the upstream entrance to the tunnel if navigating at normal speed. Green light only: 'at normal speed you will find the green light at the tunnel entrance'. Red and green (vertical): 'prepare to stop upstream of the tunnel entrance'. Downstream of the tunnel there is a large lock.

Apart from the Epernay branch mentioned above, the main branch is made up of the lower 5km of the loop bypassed by the Canal Saint-Maur, giving access to the second biggest port in the Paris region, at Bonneuil-sur-Marne. There is a large lock in this section, which is of little interest for pleasure cruising. The other branches, of minor importance, represented by short lengths of the bypassed river Marne, are indicated on the map and in the distance table.

In the section between Bry-sur-Marne (km 168) and the entrance to the Canal Saint-Maur (km 173), the river twice divides into two navigable channels. Past the Ile d'Amour and the Ile des Loups, the left bank channel is for vessels heading downstream and the right bank channel for vessels heading upstream. Past the Ile Fanac (km 173), the right bank channel is for vessels heading downstream and the left bank channel for vessels heading upstream. Nevertheless, when the gates at Joinville weir are opened on account of the high stage of the river, vessels heading upstream are allowed to use the right bank channel. No overtaking is the general rule in these channels, as well as when passing many of the other islands in the river, the restriction being clearly indicated by the conventional navigation sign. It should be noted that when the level of the river shows 35.32m on the gauge at Joinville bridge, the lock at Saint-Maur functions as a flood outlet and is no longer available to navigation.

Locks There are 18 locks, plus the lock at Créteil on the branch of the river leading to the port of Bonneuil. The first three are situated in short lock-cuts. Locks 4 to 11 are in the main river, set against one of the banks and level with the corresponding weir. The remaining locks are situated in the canals indicated above. The dimensions are 45.00 by 7.80m down to Neuilly-sur-Marne, while the last two locks (and the lock at Créteil) offer much larger dimensions: 125 by 12.00m. (It should be noted, however, that the available width in Saint-Maur tunnel is restricted to 8.60m).

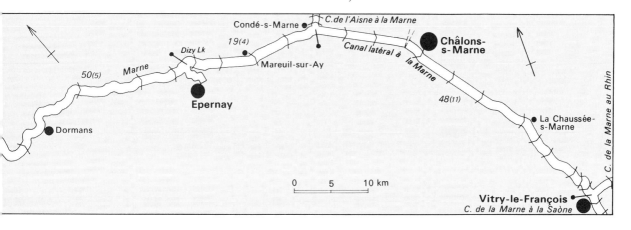

Depth The maximum authorised draught is 1.80m down to Neuilly-sur-Marne (km 165), increased to 3.00m thereafter and on the branch to Bonneuil.

Bridges The maximum authorised air draught is 4.40m from Epernay to Neuilly-sur-Marne, reduced to 4.10m above the highest navigable water level, and 6.40m on the remaining section, reduced to 4.70m above the highest navigable water level.

Towpath There is no towpath.

Authority

Service de la Navigation de la Seine, Paris. Subdivisions:
– Mont-Saint-Père, 02400 Château-Thierry, ☎ 23 70 28 33 (km 0-70).
– Barrage de Meaux, BP 212, 77100 Meaux, ☎ 64 34 04 74 (km 70-134).
– 67 rue de Torcy, 77360 Vaires-sur-Marne, ☎ 60 20 15 94 (km 134-166).
– Quai des Usines, 94340 Joinville-le-Pont, ☎ 48 83 03 11 (km 166-178).

Distance table

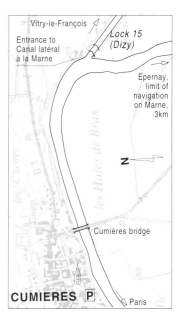

	km	lock	km
Junction with Canal latéral à la Marne (d/s of Dizy lock)	0.0	-	178.3
Cumières bridge, quay and village d/s r/b	1.0	-	177.3
Entrance to lock-cut, r/b, bridge	2.5	-	175.8
Lock 1 (Cumières), bridge	3.2	1	175.1
End of lock-cut	3.3	-	175.0
Daméry bridge, quays u/s r/b, village r/b	5.4	-	172.9
Entrance to lock-cut, r/b, bridge	6.6	-	171.7
Bridge (Port aux Vins)	7.8	-	170.5
Lock 2 (Damery)	8.2	2	170.1
End of lock cut	8.3	-	170.0
Reuil bridge, quay d/s r/b, village r/b	11.8	-	166.5
Port-à-Binson bridge, commercial quays u/s l/b, village l/b	14.8	-	163.5
Island (navigation in both arms)	15.2	-	163.1
Lock 3 (Vandières) in short lock-cut, r/b	17.7	3	160.6
Bridge (Try), quay u/s r/b, **Verneuil** 1000m r/b	22.9	-	155.4
Dormans bridge, quays u/s l/b, village l/b	26.3	-	152.0
Trélou-sur-Marne r/b	28.5	-	149.8
Lock 4 (Courcelles), r/b, weir	30.5	4	147.8
Bridge (Passy)	32.1	-	146.2
Jaulgonne bridge, quay d/s r/b, village r/b	37.5	-	140.8
Bridge (Mont-Saint-Père)	41.5	-	136.8
Charmont-sur-Marne landing stage r/b, village 200m	41.8	-	136.5
Island (follow navigation signs)	42.2	-	136.1
Lock 5 (Mont-Saint-Père), r/b, weir	42.5	5	135.8
Former sugar mill, disused basin l/b	49.5	-	128.8
Entrance to Fausse Marne arm l/b (forbidden to motor boats)	49.8	-	128.5
Château-Thierry bridge, quay and town centre r/b	50.4	-	127.9
D/s entrance to Fausse Marne arm l/b	51.4	-	126.9
New road bridge (Château-Thierry bypass)	52.4	-	125.9
Lock 6 (Azy), r/b, weir	56.2	6	122.1
Azy-sur-Marne bridge, village r/b	56.8	-	121.5

	km	*lock*	*km*
Brick works, quay l/b	62.3	-	116.0
Nogent-l'Artaud bridge, commercial quay and boats moorings u/s l/b, village 400m l/b	63.3	-	115.0
Charly bridge, quay d/s r/b, village 1000m r/b	66.3	-	112.0
Lock 7 (Charly), r/b, weir	66.6	7	111.7
Quay (Pisseloup) l/b	69.0	-	109.3
Nanteuil-sur-Marne, quays u/s, village r/b	74.2	-	104.1
Railway bridge	74.7	-	103.6
Lock 8 (Méry), r/b, weir	75.7	8	102.6
Saacy-sur-Marne bridge, village 500m l/b	76.1	-	102.2
Private quay l/b (brick works)	78.9	-	99.4
Luzancy bridge, quay d/s l/b, village 300m l/b	80.1	-	98.2
Railway bridge (Courcelles)	81.2	-	97.1
Railway bridge (Saussoy)	85.7	-	92.6
Lock 9 (Courtaron), l/b, weir	87.1	9	91.2
La Ferté-sous-Jouarre bridge, quays l/b, town centre r/b	90.4	-	87.9
New road bridge	91.3	-	87.0
Grain loading quay r/b	93.0	-	85.3
Ussy-sur-Marne bridge, village 300m r/b	95.2	-	83.1
Island (Ile de la Fosse-Tournille), channel in r/b arm	96.0	-	82.3
Motorway bridge (Autoroute de l'Est)	97.3	-	81.0
Saint-Jean-les-Deux-Jumeaux bridge, boat club moorings u/s r/b, village 400m l/b	99.4	-	78.9
Lock 10 (Saint-Jean), l/b, weir	100.6	10	77.7
Railway bridge (Armentières)	102.8	-	75.5
Sand unloading quay l/b	109.1	-	69.2
Mary-sur-Marne bridge, village 300m r/b (mooring d/s of railway bridge)	110.6	-	67.7
Railway bridge, quay d/s r/b	110.9	-	67.4
Island (Ile de Cornille), follow navigation signs	111.8	-	66.5
Lock 11 (Isles-les-Meldeuses), l/b, weir	113.1	11	65.2
Bridge (Congis)	113.4	-	64.9
Sand conveyor bridge and quay r/b	115.5	-	62.8
Germigny-l'Evêque bridge, small village l/b	121.2	-	57.1
New road bridge	121.5	-	56.8
Poincy boat harbour in r/b arm, moorings, water, fuel, village 400m	125.1	-	53.2
Railway bridge	126.7	-	51.6
Trilport bridge, quay u/s l/b, village 200m l/b	127.0	-	51.3
Former lock (Basses-Fermes) l/b	128.7	-	49.6
Sand unloading quay r/b	131.6	-	46.7
Entrance to Canal de Meaux à Chalifert, l/b, **Meaux** r/b	133.5	-	44.8
Lock 12 (Meaux), bridge (Saints-Pères), water	133.6	12	44.7
Mareuil-les-Meaux bridge (1), village 200m l/b	136.8	-	41.5
Bridge (Mareuil-les-Meaux 2)	137.0	-	41.3
Bridge (Roizes)	139.0	-	39.3
Condé-Sainte-Libiaire bridge, village and castle r/b	140.8	-	37.5
Condé aqueduct (one-way passage)	141.0	-	37.3
Esbly aqueduct	141.8	-	36.5
Bridge (Esbly 1)	141.9	-	36.4
Grand-Morin feeder canal enters l/b (not navigable)	142.2	-	36.1
Esbly bridge (2), quay d/s r/b, village r/b	142.4	-	35.9
Railway bridge, quay d/s r/b	142.9	-	35.4
Coupvray bridges, village 500m l/b	143.9	-	34.4
Lock 13 (Lesches)	145.1	13	33.2
Chalifert tunnel, upstream entrance, one-way traffic	145.3	-	33.0
Chalifert tunnel, downstream entrance	145.6	-	32.7
Lock 14 (Chalifert)	145.7	14	32.6

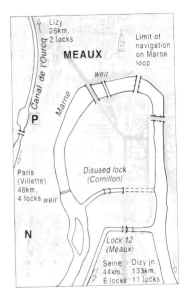

	km	*lock*	*km*
End of Canal de Meaux à Chalifert, navigation re-enters Marne (navigable u/s 6.6km to **Annet-sur-Marne**)	145.9	-	32.4
Touring Club de France harbour l/b (all facilities)	150.3	-	28.0
Lagny bridge (1), quays and town centre l/b	151.5	-	26.8
Bridge (Lagny 2)	151.8	-	26.5
Motorway bridge	154.3	-	24.0
Entrance to Canal de Chelles, r/b, Marne navigable 2.3km d/s to **Noisiel**	155.8	-	22.5
Lock 15 (Vaires), bridge	155.9	15	22.4
Vaires bridge, Marne Loisirs hire base, town centre r/b	156.6	-	21.7
Industrial basin and quay r/b	158.8	-	19.5
Overhead pipeline crossing	159.4	-	18.9
Bridge (**Chelles**)	159.9	-	18.4
Bridge (Moulin), Chelles r/b	160.6	-	17.7
Gournay-sur-Marne bridge, quay d/s r/b, town centre l/b	161.6	-	16.7
Bridges (Chétivet)	162.3	-	16.0
Bridge (Ville-Evrard)	163.6	-	14.7
Lock 16 (Neuilly-sur-Marne), bridge	164.8	16	13.5
End of Canal de Chelles, navigation re-enters Marne	164.9	-	13.4
Neuilly-sur-Marne bridge, town centre r/b	165.1	-	13.2
Private bridge (water works)	165.3	-	13.0
Railway viaduct (SNCF)	165.9	-	12.4
Railway viaduct (RER regional metro), commercial quays r/b	166.7	-	11.6
Footbridge (Bry)	167.5	-	10.8
Bry-sur-Marne bridge, town centre l/b	168.5	-	9.8
U/s tip of islands (Ile d'Amour and Ile aux Loups), follow navigation signs	169.3	-	9.0
Nogent railway viaduct	170.3	-	8.0
Nogent-sur-Marne bridge, d/s tip of islands, town r/b	170.6	-	7.7
Pleasure harbour r/b	170.8	-	7.5
Motorway bridge (Autoroute de l'Est)	172.4	-	5.9
U/s tip of island (Ile Fanac), follow navigation signs	172.8	-	5.5
Joinville-le-Pont bridge, town l/b, d/s tip of island	173.4	-	4.9
Entrance to Canal Saint-Maur and tunnel, r/b	173.6	-	4.7
Saint-Maur tunnel, d/s entrance, basin	174.2	-	4.1
Lock (Saint-Maur), water	174.5	17	3.8
End of Canal Saint-Maur, junction with Bonneuil arm	174.7	-	3.6
Motorway interchange bridges	175.4	-	2.9
Footbridge (Charentonneau), **Maisons-Alfort** l/b	175.8	-	2.5
Lock (Saint-Maurice), r/b, weir	177.2	18	1.1
Charenton bridge, town r/b, **Alfortville** l/b	177.6	-	0.7
Metro bridge	177.7	-	0.6
Railway bridge	177.9	-	0.4
Footbridge (Alfortville)	178.0	-	0.3
Confluence with Seine (km 163.5)	178.3	-	0.0

Epernay branch

Railway bridge, limit of navigation	0.0	-	5.0
Epernay boat harbour l/b, water, slipway	0.8	-	4.2
Epernay bridge, mooring r/b, town centre 500m l/b	1.4	-	3.6
New road bridge (projected)	3.1	-	1.9
Junction with Canal latéral à la Marne, r/b, origin of canalised River Marne	5.0	-	0.0

Bonneuil branch

Bonneuil bridge, u/s limit of inland port of Bonneuil	0.0	-	5.0
Entrance to basins of port of Bonneuil, l/b	1.5	-	3.5

	km	lock	km
Footbridge (Passerelle de la Pie)	1.8	-	3.2
Lock (Créteil), l/b, weir, footbridge, water	2.8	1	2.2
Créteil bridge, town l/b	3.0	-	2.0
Quay (Saint-Maur-Créteil) r/b	3.3	-	1.7
Footbridge (Créteil)	3.6	-	1.4
Bridge (Maisons-Alfort)	4.6	-	0.4
Junction with Canal Saint-Maur, r/b	5.0	-	0.0

Canal latéral à la Marne

The Canal latéral à la Marne extends from a junction with the Canal de la Marne au Rhin north-east of Vitry-le-François to the canalised river Marne at Dizy-Magenta, a distance of 67km. The first 2km section of the canal is a new cut built in the 1960s to bypass the town of Vitry-le-François. Since then, part of the original line of the canal from a three-way junction (with the canals towards the Rhine and the Saône) near the centre of Vitry-le-François has been infilled. The short length which remains open is of little interest for pleasure cruising, and the more convenient mooring for Vitry-le-François is on the Canal de la Marne à la Saône. At Condé-sur-Marne (km 48), the canal connects with the Canal de l'Aisne à la Marne.

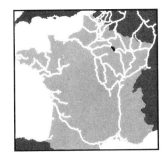

Locks There are 15 locks, falling towards Dizy, with a total difference in level of 34m. They are of standard dimensions, 38.50 by 5.20m.

Depth The maximum authorised draught is 1.80m.

Bridges The bridges leave a minimum clear headroom of 3.70m above normal water level.

Towpath There is a good towpath throughout.

Authority
Service de la Navigation de la Seine, Arrondissement Champagne, Reims.
Subdivision: Chemin du Barrage, 51001 **Châlons-sur-Marne**, ☎ 26 65 17 41.

Distance table

	km	lock	km
Junction with Canal de la Marne au Rhin (km 0.9)	0.0	-	66.7
Bridge (D382)	0.4	-	66.3
Bridge (N44)	1.4	-	65.3
Junction with original line of canal through **Vitry-le-François** (navigable for 0.7km)	1.9	-	64.8
Saulx aqueduct	2.2	-	64.5
Lock 1 (Vitry-le-François), bridge, water	2.3	1	64.4
Disused quay r/b (former cement works), fuel	2.7	-	64.0
Lock 2 (Ermite), bridge, water, turning basin d/s	3.7	2	63.0
Couvrot bridge, quay u/s r/b, village r/b	4.4	-	62.3
Lock 3 (Couvrot)	4.8	3	61.9
Bridge (Villers)	5.4	-	61.3
Quay r/b (cement works)	5.5	-	61.2
Private bridge	5.7	-	61.0
Bridge (Bayarne)	8.0	-	58.7
Soulanges basin, quay and village r/b	8.8	-	57.9

	km	lock	km
Lock 4 (Soulanges), bridge	9.2	4	57.5
Lock 5 (Ablancourt)	11.5	5	55.2
Ablancourt bridge, quay u/s r/b, village r/b	12.0	-	54.7
Bridge (Bois de Marne)	13.5	-	53.2
La Chaussée-sur-Marne bridge, quay u/s r/b, village r/b	14.5	-	52.2
Lock 6 (Chaussée-sur-Marne), water	15.1	6	51.6
Private quay r/b	16.2	-	50.5
Omey bridge, village r/b	16.6	-	50.1
Turning basin l/b	17.1	-	49.6
Pogny bridge, quay d/s r/b, village r/b	17.8	-	48.9
Vésigneul-sur-Marne bridge, small village r/b	20.4	-	46.3
Saint-Germain-la-Ville quay r/b, village 500m r/b	21.4	-	45.3
Lock 7 (Saint-Germain-la-Ville), water	21.6	7	45.1
Bridge (Saint-Germain-la-Ville)	21.8	-	44.9
Bridge (Chepy)	23.7	-	43.0
Bridge (Moncetz), quay d/s r/b	24.8	-	41.9
Lock 8 (Sarry)	26.3	8	40.4
Sarry bridge, quay u/s r/b, village 500m r/b	27.0	-	39.7
Bridge (Allées de Forêts)	30.6	-	36.1
Bridge (Pont Louis XII), cereal loading quay u/s r/b	31.5	-	35.2
Aqueduct	31.6	-	35.1
Footbridge (Passerelle du Jard)	31.7	-	35.0
Island (Ile du Jard), navigation l/b side only	31.8	-	34.9
Châlons-sur-Marne quay and moorings r/b in town centre	32.1	-	34.6
Lock 9 (Châlons-sur-Marne), bridge, water	32.2	9	34.5
Entrance to Canal de Jonction (commercial basin), r/b, turning basin	32.4	-	34.3
Châlons-sur-Marne industrial estate, quay r/b	33.6	-	33.1
Saint-Martin aqueduct and bridge, village r/b	34.8	-	31.9
Turning basin r/b	35.4	-	31.3
Railway bridge	35.8	-	30.9
Bridge (Therme-Brouard)	36.2	-	30.5
Récy bridge, quay u/s r/b, village r/b	37.2	-	29.5
Lock 10 (Juvigny)	39.3	10	27.4
Bridge	40.8	-	25.9
Juvigny bridge, quay d/s r/b, village 1500m r/b	42.6	-	24.1
Lock 11 (**Vraux**), water, village 1000m r/b	44.3	11	22.4
Aigny bridge, village 600m r/b	46.4	-	20.3
Junction with Canal de l'Aisne à la Marne, r/b, turning basin	48.4	-	18.3
Condé-sur-Marne bridge, quay u/s r/b, village r/b	48.7	-	18.0
Tours-sur-Marne quay and village r/b	52.9	-	13.8
Lock 12 (Tours-sur-Marne), bridge, private quay d/s l/b	53.0	12	13.7
Bridge (Bussin)	55.1	-	11.6
Bisseuil swing bridge, village l/b	55.3	-	11.4
Lock 13 (Mareuil-sur-Ay)	58.1	13	8.6
Basin (silted up)	58.2	-	8.5
Mareuil-sur-Ay bridge, quay d/s r/b, village with castle r/b	58.8	-	7.9
Bridge (Cheminets)	60.2	-	6.5
Bridge (Ruets)	61.2	-	5.5
Railway bridge	61.3	-	5.4
Ay bridge (Villemoyer), quay d/s r/b, town centre r/b	61.7	-	5.0
Lock 14 (Ay), bridge, water	62.6	14	4.1
Dizy-Magenta bridge, quay u/s r/b, village 500m r/b	64.7	-	2.0
Bridge (Hautvillers)	66.1	-	0.6
Lock 15 (Dizy)	66.6	15	0.1
Junction with canalised river Marne	66.7	-	0.0

Canal de la Marne au Rhin

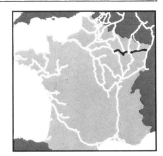

The Canal de la Marne au Rhin, one of the busiest inter-basin canals in France, was completed in 1853. It was also the longest canal in France (313km) until 1979, when a 23km section along the Moselle valley was closed, following completion of the Moselle canalisation works between Frouard and Neuves-Maisons. The route from the junctions with the Canal de la Marne à la Saône and the Canal latéral à la Marne at Vitry-le-François to the port of Strasbourg on the Rhine is now made up as follows:

(a) Canal de la Marne au Rhin, western section (km 0-131); this section connects with the Canal de l'Est, northern branch, at Troussey (km 111), and with a short branch to Houdelaincourt (km 85),

(b) the canalised river Moselle, entered through a new lock, from Toul to Frouard (a distance of 25km, slightly longer than by the original canal),

(c) Canal de la Marne au Rhin, eastern section, from Frouard to Strasbourg (km 154-313); this section makes connections with the Nancy branch of the Canal de l'Est at Laneuveville-devant-Nancy (km 169) and with the Canal des Houillères de la Sarre at Gondrexange (km 228).

The canal has two summit levels, the Mauvages summit (altitude 281m) between the Marne and the Meuse, and the Vosges summit (267m) between the Meurthe and the Rhine.

The first includes the Mauvages tunnel, 4877m in length, while the second has two tunnels within a short distance at its eastern end, Niderwiller (475m) and Arzviller (2307m). There is a fourth tunnel at Foug (867m), cutting through the low watershed between the Meuse and Moselle valleys. There was another tunnel 388m long at Liverdun, on the section now bypassed by the canalised Moselle. There is an obligatory towage service at Mauvages, where boats are placed behind the last barge in the tow. The times of the tows are 0630 and 1330 eastbound from Demange and 0930 and 1630 westbound from Mauvages. The other three tunnels are ventilated, and all craft proceed under their own power when the green light is shown. On entering Foug tunnel from the western end, there is a pole to be pushed forwards for 5 to 10 seconds, to inform the tunnel-keeper (at lock 14).

Locks There are in all 152 locks, to which must be added the transverse inclined plane of Arzviller/Saint-Louis (km 255), opened in 1969. The western section has 97 locks, of which 70 fall towards the Marne and 27 towards the Moselle. The locks are 38.70m long and 5.13m wide, except for the new lock connecting with the Moselle at Toul, which was built to the slightly larger dimensions of 40 by 6m. The eastern section now has only 55 locks (instead of 78). There are 21 up to the summit level from Nancy. The last, at Réchicourt, is a deep lock (15.70m) replacing the flight of six locks on the original canal. East of the summit level and Arzvilles tunnel, a new cut clinging to the side of the Zorn valley leads to the inclined plane, mentioned above, which replaces a flight of 17 locks. From the point where the down stream approach canal rejoins the old line, there are 34 locks down to Strasbourg. The minimum dimensions are the same as on the western section, although the inclined plane (and the new lock at Saverne) were built to the slightly greater width of 5.50m. Many of the locks have been equipped for automatic operation with radar detection.

Bridges The maximum authorised air draught is 3.50m.

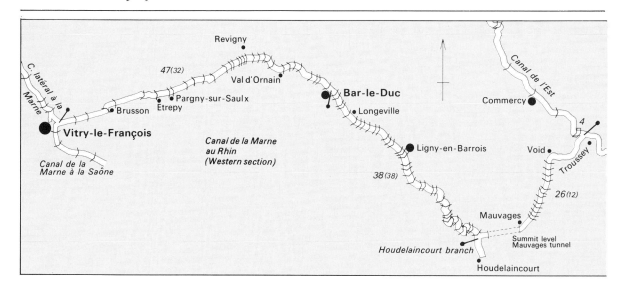

Depth The maximum authorised draught is 1.80m on the western section and 2.20m on the eastern section.

Towpath There is a good towpath throughout.

Authority

Service de la Navigation de Nancy. Subdivisions:
– 1 rue de l'Ormicée, 55012 Bar-le-Duc, ☎ 29 79 12 33 (km 0-68)
– 1 rue du Port, 55190 Void-Vacon, ☎ 29 89 84 04 (km 68-119).
– 2 bis avenue du Colonel Péchot, 54200 Toul, ☎ 83 43 28 39 (km 119-131).
– 2 bis rue Victor, 54000 Nancy, ☎ 83 32 91 91 (km 154-222)

Service de la Navigation de Strasbourg. Subdivisions:
– 57930 Mittersheim, ☎ 87 07 67 12 (km 222-248).
– 12 rue de l'Orangerie, 67700 Saverne, ☎ 88 91 80 83 (km 248-294).
– 46 rue Jacoutot, 67000 Strasbourg, ☎ 88 61 66 01 (km 294-313).

Distance table

Western section, from the Marne to the Moselle

	km	lock	km
Vitry-le-François basin, *junction with Canal de la Marne à la Saône*, town centre 500m	0.0	-	131.7
Commercial quay l/b	0.2	-	131.5
Bridge (Vassues)	0.6	-	131.1
Junction with Canal latéral à la Marne (new cut), r/b	0.9	-	130.8
Bridge (Saint-Jacques)	1.9	-	129.8
Lock 70 (Saint-Etienne), bridge, quay upstream l/b	3.3	1	128.4
Lock 69 (Adecourt), bridge	5.1	2	126.6
Plichancourt bridge, quay and turning basin downstream	5.8	-	125.9
Bridge (Caure)	6.6	-	125.1
Brusson quay l/b, village 300m	7.6	-	124.1
Lock 68 (Brusson), bridge (D395), aqueduct upstream	7.9	3	123.8
Ponthion bridge, small village 300m r/b	9.4	-	122.3
Lock 67 (Ponthion), bridge, quay and turning basin d/s	10.0	4	121.7
Le Buisson bridge, village l/b	12.4	-	119.3
Bridge (Pré-le-Doyen)	13.6	-	118.1

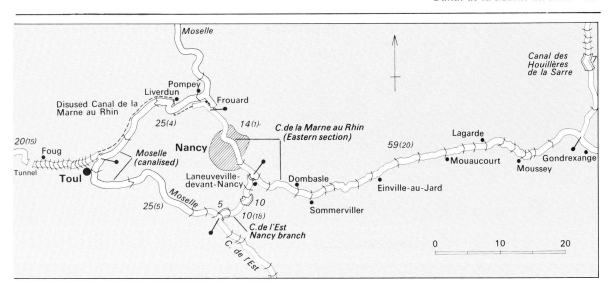

	km	lock	km
Bignicourt-sur-Saulx quay l/b	14.4	-	117.3
Lock 66 (Bignicourt), bridge	14.6	5	117.1
Etrepy quay l/b, village and castle 300m l/b	16.3	-	115.4
Lock 65 (Etrepy), bridge, aqueduct upstream	16.6	6	115.1
Lock 64 (Pargny-sur-Saulx), bridge, water	18.7	7	113.0
Pargny-sur-Saulx basin and quay l/b, village 600m l/b	18.8	-	112.9
Lock 63 (Pargny-sur-Saulx aqueduct), aqueduct upstream	19.1	8	112.6
Bridge (Ajot)	20.9	-	110.8
Lock 62 (Ajot)	21.7	9	110.0
Lock 61 (Chaîne), bridge	23.0	10	108.7
Lock 60 (Sermaize-les-Bains), bridge	24.5	11	107.2
Sermaize-les-Bains basin, quay l/b, small town 600m l/b	24.6	-	107.1
Bridge (Remennecourt)	24.9	-	106.8
Railway bridge, quay upstream l/b	25.2	-	106.5
Lock 59 (Remennecourt), bridge	25.7	12	106.0
Lock 58 (Chevol), bridge	27.4	13	104.3
Contrisson basin, quay l/b, village 400m	28.1	-	103.6
Lock 57 (Contrisson), bridge	28.4	14	103.3
Lock 56 (Braux), bridge, quay downstream l/b	29.1	15	102.6
Railway bridge	29.6	-	102.1
Lock 55 (Haie Herlin)	30.0	16	101.7
Lock 54 (Damzelle), private quays above and below	30.6	17	101.1
Lock 53 (Notre-Dame-de-Grâce), cement works, quay u/s l/b	31.1	18	100.6
Lock 52 (Revigny), bridge	31.7	19	100.0
Revigny quay l/b, small town 1500m r/b	31.8	-	99.9
Overhead power lines	32.0	-	99.7
Lock 51 (Bois l'Ecuyer), bridge	32.8	20	98.9
Lock 50 (Petit-Fraicul)	33.8	21	97.9
Lock 49 (Grand-Fraicul)	34.6	22	97.1
Neuville-sur-Ornain quay l/b, village 1000m r/b	35.3	-	96.4
Lock 48 (Neuville-sur-Ornain), bridge	35.6	23	96.1
Lock 47 (Doeuil), private quay upstream l/b	36.7	24	95.0
Lock 46 (Mussey), lift bridge, basin u/s, Val d'Ornain l/b	38.5	25	93.2
Lock 45 (Chacolée)	39.2	26	92.5

	km	lock	km
Lock 44 (Varney), bridge, quay downstream l/b	40.3	27	91.4
Lock 43 (Rembercourt)	41.2	28	90.5
Fains-Véel quay l/b, village 500m	43.1	-	88.6
Lock 42 (Fains-les-Sources), lift bridge	43.3	29	88.4
Skew railway bridge and new road bridge (D994)	44.5	-	87.2
Lock 41 (Grand-Pré)	44.5	30	87.2
Lock 40 (Pont-Canal de Chanteraines), aqueduct upstream	45.0	31	86.7
Lock 39 (Bar-le-Duc), bridge, water	46.3	32	85.4
Bridge (Triby)	46.8	-	84.9
Bar-le-Duc quay l/b and turning basin, town l/b over railway	47.0	-	84.7
Lift bridge (Marbot), quays upstream	47.5	-	84.2
Lock 38 (Marbot), lift bridge (Cimetière)	47.9	33	83.8
Lock 37 (Popey)	48.6	34	83.1
Railway bridge and main road bridge (N135)	49.2	-	82.5
Lock 36 (Savonnières)	49.9	35	81.8
Lock 35 (Longeville), bridge, aqueduct upstream	50.5	36	81.2
Longeville basin, village 800m	51.5	-	80.2
Lock 34 (Grande-Chalaide), bridge	51.7	37	80.0
Bridge (Petite-Chalaide), Longeville r/b	52.2	-	79.5
Lock 33 (Maheux)	53.3	38	78.4
Lock 32 (Tannois), bridge	54.1	39	77.6
Tannois quay l/b, village 300m	54.4	-	77.3
Lock 31 (Silmont), bridge	54.6	40	77.1
Lock 30 (Guerpont)	55.6	41	76.1
Lock 29 (Bohanne), bridge	56.3	42	75.4
Lock 28 (Tronville), bridge	56.9	43	74.8

Canal de la Marne au Rhin. Lock No. 25 in the Zorn valley.
Hugh Potter

	km	lock	km
Tronville bridge, quays r/b, turning basin, village 300m	57.9	-	73.8
Lock 27 (Chessard), bridge	58.9	44	72.8
Lock 26 (Nançois-le-Petit)	59.5	45	72.2
Lock 25 (Velaines), bridge	60.2	46	71.5
Velaines bridge, quay downstream l/b, village over bridge	60.5	-	71.2
Lock 24 (Maulan), bridge	61.6	47	70.1
Lock 23 (Villeroncourt), bridge	62.2	48	69.5
New road bridge (N4 Ligny-en-Barrois bypass)	62.3	-	69.4
Ligny-en-Barrois basin r/b, town centre 500m	62.5	-	69.2
Lock 22 (Ligny-en-Barrois), bridge, water	62.7	49	69.0
Bridge (Herval)	63.3	-	68.4
Lock 21 (Gainval)	64.1	50	67.6
Lock 20 (Grèves)	64.8	51	66.9
Givrauval quay l/b, village 200m	65.3	-	66.4
Lock 19 (Givrauval), bridge	65.6	52	66.1
Lock 18 (Longeaux)	66.9	53	64.8
Longeaux bridge, quay upstream l/b	67.4	-	64.3
Menaucourt basin l/b	68.0	-	63.7
Main road bridge (Patouillat) and railway bridge	68.2	-	63.5
Lock 17 (Menaucourt), aqueduct upstream	68.5	54	63.2
Lock 16 (Nantois), bridge	69.2	55	62.5
Lock 15 (Naix-aux-Forges), bridge, quay upstream l/b	70.4	56	61.3
Lock 14 (Pont-Canal de la Barboure), aqueduct upstream	71.1	57	60.6
St-Amand-sur-Ornain bridge, quay downstream l/b	72.6	-	59.1
Lock 13 (Saint-Amand)	73.1	58	58.6
Lock 12 (Charmasson)	74.2	59	57.5
Lock 11 (**Trévay**), bridge, water, village 500m l/b	75.5	60	56.2
Turning basin and quay l/b	75.7	-	56.0
Lock 10 (Charbonnières)	76.1	61	55.6
Lock 9 (Petite-Forge), private quay upstream l/b	77.0	62	54.7
Lock 8 (Laneuville-Saint-Joire)	77.9	63	53.8
Saint-Joire bridge, quay downstream r/b, village 500m	78.4	-	53.3
Lock 7 (Saint-Joire)	79.0	64	52.7
Lock 6 (Boeval)	80.2	65	51.5
Lock 5 (Abbaye d'Evaux)	80.8	66	50.9
Lock 4 (Montfort)	82.2	67	49.5
Lock 3 (Bois-Molu)	83.2	68	48.5
Lock 2 (Demange-aux-Eaux)	83.9	69	47.8
Bridge (Croix-des-Morts)	84.1	-	47.6
Demange-aux-Eaux quay r/b, village 700m over bridge	84.6	-	47.1
Lock 1 (Tombois), bridge, water, beginning of Mauvages summit level	84.8	70	46.9
Junction with Houdelaincourt branch, l/b, turning basin	85.1	-	46.6
Bridge	85.3	-	46.4
Mauvages tunnel, western entrance	86.6	-	45.1
Mauvages tunnel, eastern entrance	91.5	-	40.2

N.B. Locks 17 (Menaucourt) to 1 (Tombois) are equipped for automatic operation, with radar detection.

	km	lock	km
Mauvages bridge, village 500m	92.3	-	39.4
Lock 1 (Mauvages), end of Mauvages summit level	94.0	71	37.7
Lock 2 (Villeroy), bridge	94.6	72	37.1
Lock 3 (Chalède)	95.3	73	36.4
Lock 4 (Grand-Charme), bridge	95.9	74	35.8
Lock 5 (Saint-Esprit)	96.8	75	34.9
Lock 6 (Corvée)	97.6	76	34.1
Sauvoy bridge, small village 300m r/b	97.9	-	33.8
Lock 7 (Sauvoy)	98.2	77	33.5
Quay r/b (Sauvoy)	98.6	-	33.1

	km	lock	km
Lock 8 (Varonnes), bridge	98.8	78	32.9
Lock 9 (Biguiottes)	100.0	79	31.7
Lock 10 (Haut-Bois), bridge	100.9	80	30.8
Lock 11 (Vacon), bridge	101.7	81	30.0
Lock 12 (Void), water	102.5	82	29.2
Void quay and footbridge, village l/b	103.9	-	27.8
Void bridge	104.0	-	27.7
Destroyed railway bridge	104.3	-	27.4
Main road bridge (Croix-le-Pêcheur), N4	107.1	-	24.6
Bridge (Naviot)	109.4	-	22.3
Troussey aqueduct (over Meuse)	110.3	-	21.4
Junction with Canal de l'Est, northern branch, l/b	111.3	-	20.4
Pagny-sur-Meuse bridge, village 200m	115.9	-	15.8
Railway bridge	117.5	-	14.2
Cement works and quays, north bank	118.0	-	13.7
Bridge (Lay-Saint-Rémy)	119.9	-	11.8
Bridge (Ugny), beginning of Lay-Saint-Rémy cutting	120.4	-	11.3
Foug tunnel, western portal	120.6	-	11.1
Foug tunnel, eastern portal	121.5	-	10.2
Basin	121.6	-	10.1
Locks 14 and 14A (twin chambers)	121.9	83	9.8
Lock 15, bridge	122.6	84	9.1
Industrial quay, l/b	122.8	-	8.9
Lock 16, water	123.3	85	8.4
Lock 17	124.0	86	7.7
Industrial quay, l/b	124.3	-	7.4
Lock 18, bridge	124.7	87	7.0
Lock 19	125.4	88	6.3
Railway bridges	125.7	-	6.0
Lock 20, bridge	126.1	89	5.6
Lock 21	126.8	90	4.9
Lock 22, bridge	127.4	91	4.3
Railway bridge	127.5	-	4.2
Lock 23	128.2	92	3.5
Lock 24	128.9	93	2.8
Lock 25, bridge, water	129.7	94	2.0
Bridge (Génie)	129.9	-	1.8
Lock 26	129.9	95	1.8
Toul basin (Porte de France), town centre 500m (see plan)	130.2	-	1.5
Bridge (Caponnière), Saint-Mansuy quay d/s r/b, Connoisseur Cruisers hire base, turning basin	130.5	-	1.2
Railway bridge	130.7	-	1.0
Saint-Mansuy lift bridge	130.7	-	1.0
Lock 27, bridge, water	131.2	96	0.5
Entrance to new link to canalised Moselle, r/b	131.4	-	0.3
Lock 27A	131.6	97	0.1
Junction with canalised Moselle	131.7	-	0.0

N.B. Locks 1 (Mauvages) to 12 (Void) are equipped for automatic operation, with radar detection.

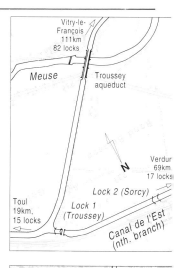

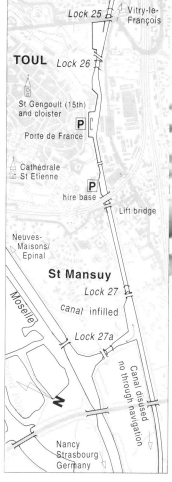

Mauvages tunnel on the Canal de la Marne au Rhin.
Hugh Potter

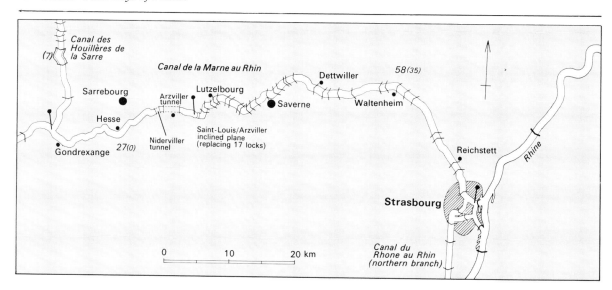

Eastern section, from the Moselle to the Rhine

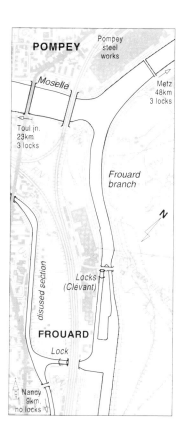

	km	lock	km
Junction with canalised Moselle, port of Nancy-Frouard			
(canal not navigable westward of this point)	154.6	-	158.4
Bridge (access to Frouard railway station), quay	154.7	-	158.3
Motorway bridge (A31)	156.1	-	156.9
Champigneulles bridge (Pont de la Gare), quays d/s l/b, town centre 200m l/b	157.8	-	155.2
Skew railway bridge	158.6	-	154.4
Solvay aerial conveyor, industrial quays downstream l/b	160.3	-	152.7
Maxéville bridge	160.5	-	152.5
Quay (Saint-Sébastien) l/b	161.1	-	151.9
Bridge (Trois-Maisons)	161.8	-	151.2
Malzéville lift bridge and footbridge, quay upstream l/b	162.3	-	150.7
Bridge (Gaz de la Sarre)	162.8	-	150.2
Bridge (Saint-Catherine)	163.5	-	149.5
Footbridge (Pépinière), quays upstream r/b	163.1	-	149.9
Lift bridge (Sainte-Catherine) and footbridge	163.5	-	149.5
Nancy basin (Saint-Catherine), water, fuel, city centre 800m	163.6	-	149.4
Bridge (Pont Saint-Georges), basin upstream	163.7	-	149.3
Bridge (Tiercelins), quays upstream	163.9	-	149.1
Private footbridge	164.4	-	148.6
Tomblaine bridge	164.7	-	148.3
Railway bridge, industrial quays and basin upstream	164.8	-	148.2
Lock 26/26a, bridge	166.4	1	146.6
Jarville-la-Malgrange quays, town (Nancy suburb) l/b	166.5	-	146.5
Bridge	167.3	-	145.7
Barge repair yard l/b	167.9	-	145.1
Laneuveville-devant-Nancy basin, *junction with Canal de l'Est, Nancy branch*, l/b	168.5	-	144.5
Bridge	168.6	-	144.4
Lock 25/25a, water	168.7	2	144.3
Bridge (Noue)	169.5	-	143.5
Lock 24/24a, bridge, industrial quay d/s r/b, basin u/s l/b	171.9	3	141.1
Private viaduct	172.1	-	140.9
Saint-Phlin aqueduct (over Meurthe)	172.5	-	140.5
Chemical factory, quays and conveyor bridge	175.6	-	137.4
Varangéville bridge, quays upstream, town r/b	175.8	-	137.2
Footbridge, basin upstream l/b	176.2	-	136.8

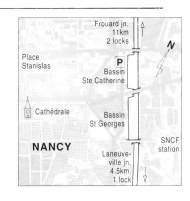

	km	lock	km
Lock 23/23a, water, bridge, industrial quays upstream	177.0	4	136.0
Lift bridge	177.7	-	135.3
Private bridge (Solvay works)	177.9	-	135.1
Footbridge	178.0	-	135.0
Private bridges (Solvay works)	178.1	-	134.9
Dombasle bridge, basin downstream, town 400m l/b	178.6	-	134.4
Lock 22, water	179.2	5	133.8
Sommerviller bridge, quay u/s l/b, village 500m l/b	180.5	-	132.5
Lock 21, bridge, salt works u/s r/b	181.1	6	131.9
Lock 20, bridge	182.6	7	130.4
Crévic bridge, village l/b	183.4	-	129.6
Maixe bridge, quay and village u/s r/b	187.0	-	126.0
Lock 19, bridge	187.5	8	125.5
Salt works, quay r/b	189.3	-	123.7
Lock 18, bridge	189.9	9	123.1
Einville-au-Jard basin l/b, village 300m l/b	190.7	-	122.3
Bridge, private quay u/s r/b	191.1	-	121.9
Bridge (D914)	191.4	-	121.6
Bridge	193.4	-	119.6
Bauzemont basin, quay and small village r/b	194.7	-	118.3

N.B. Locks 21 (Sommerviller) to 7 (Réchicourt) are equipped for automatic operation, with radar detection.

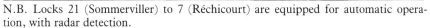

	km	lock	km
Lock 17, bridge	194.9	10	118.1
Bridge	195.2	-	117.8
Hénaménil bridge, quay d/s l/b, village 500m l/b	197.3	-	115.7
Lock 16, bridge	198.7	11	114.3
Bridge	200.1	-	112.9
Parroy bridge, quay d/s r/b, village 500m r/b	201.3	-	111.7
Lock 15, bridge	203.0	12	110.0
Mouaucourt basin l/b, small village 300m l/b	203.2	-	109.8
Xures bridge, basin d/s, quay and small village r/b	205.7	-	107.3
Lock 14, bridge	206.1	13	106.9
Lock 13, bridge	207.8	14	105.2
Lagard bridge, basin u/s r/b, Rive de France hire base	209.2	-	103.8
Lock 12, bridge, water	209.7	15	103.3
Lock 11, bridge	213.0	16	100.0
Lock 10, bridge	215.1	17	97.9
Moussey bridge, basin d/s r/b, village 1000m l/b	215.9	-	97.1
Lock 9, bridge, water	217.0	18	96.0
Lock 8, railway bridge, basin u/s r/b	218.6	19	94.4
Lock 7, bridge, basin (Sainte-Blaise) d/s, quay r/b	219.4	20	93.6
Beginning of new cut (bypassing flight of 6 locks)	219.8	-	93.2
New lock 1 (Réchicourt), bridge, water, beginning of summit level	222.1	21	90.9
Bridge (Col des Français) over cutting	223.1	-	89.9
Stop gate	224.2	-	88.8
Turning basin	225.3	-	87.7
Junction with Canal des Houillères de la Sarre	227.6	-	85.4
Gondrexange bridge, stop gate, village 200m	229.5	-	83.5
Bridge (Prés)	230.2	-	82.8
Skew railway bridge	230.3	-	82.7
Bridge (Hertzing)	232.0	-	81.0
Bridge (N4), basin d/s r/b	232.5	-	80.5
Héming bridge (Pont de Lorquin), quays d/s r/b, village 400m r/b	233.2	-	79.8
Towpath bridge	233.8	-	79.2
Xouaxange bridge over narrow cutting, one-way traffic, quay d/s l/b, small village r/b	236.0	-	77.0

	km	lock	km
Destroyed bridge, narrow passage	237.9	-	75.1
Pipeline crossing	238.2	-	74.8
Laforge aqueduct (length 45m)	238.8	-	74.2
Bridge (Germain)	239.7	-	73.3
Hesse basin and Crown Blue Line hire base r/b, village 300m	240.3	-	72.7
Bridge (Pont du Village)	240.6	-	72.4
Skew railway bridge	240.8	-	72.2
Bridge (Charmenack) over Hesse cutting, 465m long (one-way traffic)	241.0	-	72.0
Bridge (Neuhof)	243.1	-	69.9
Schneckenbusch bridge, small village l/b	243.6	-	69.4
Bridge (Brouderdorff)	244.3	-	68.7
Bridge (Buhl)	244.9	-	68.1
Niderviller-Neubruch bridge, quay d/s l/b, village 1000m	245.5	-	67.5
Bridge (Hombesch)	246.0	-	67.0
Bridge (Niderviller-Altmuhle), basin u/s	247.0	-	66.0
Niderviller tunnel, western entrance	248.0	-	65.0
Niderviller tunnel, eastern entrance	248.5	-	64.5
Basin	249.0	-	64.0
Arzviller tunnel, western entrance	249.3	-	63.7

Arzviller inclined plane.
La Cigogne

	km	lock	km
Arzviller tunnel, eastern entrance	251.6	-	61.4
Arzviller basin	251.8	-	61.2
Entrance to new canal section, r/b, bypassing flight of 17 locks, bridge	251.9	-	61.1
Saint-Louis bridge, village 1000m r/b	252.3	-	60.7
Saint-Louis-Arzviller inclined plane, basin d/s	254.7	22	58.3
Bridge	255.3	-	57.7
New cut rejoins original line of canal below lock 17	255.6	-	57.4
Lock 18, water	256.0	23	57.0
Railway viaduct (Hofmuhle), turning basin d/s	256.1	-	56.9
Lock 19, bridge	256.7	24	56.3
Lock 20, water	257.5	25	55.5
Lock 21, bridge, water	258.5	26	54.5
Lutzelbourg quay, Navilor Plaisance hire base, village l/b	258.7	-	54.3
Lock 22, bridge	259.1	27	53.9
Lock 23	260.3	28	52.7
Lock 24	261.1	29	51.9
Lock 25	262.2	30	50.8
Lock 26, lift bridge	263.0	31	50.0
Lock 27, footbridge	264.3	32	48.7
Lock 28	264.9	33	48.1
Lock 29, bridge (D132)	266.1	34	46.9
Railway viaduct (Haut-Barr)	266.3	-	46.7
Bridge (N4)	268.5	-	44.5
New lock 30/31, bridge	268.6	35	44.4
Saverne basin, moorings, town centre r/b	269.0	-	44.0
Bridge (Orangerie)	269.5	-	43.5
Lock 32, railway bridge u/s	270.1	36	42.9
Lock 33, bridge	271.0	37	42.0
New road bridge	272.0	-	41.0
Lock 34, bridge	272.2	38	40.8
Lock 35	272.5	39	40.5
Lock 36, bridge, quay d/s r/b, **Steinbourg** 800m l/b	273.7	40	39.3
Dettwiller bridge, quay u/s r/b, village 1000m l/b	277.1	-	35.9
Lock 37	277.6	41	35.4
Bridge (D112)	278.0	-	35.0
Lock 38	278.9	42	34.1
Bridge	279.3	-	33.7
Lock 39	279.8	43	33.2
Lupstein bridge, village 500m r/b	280.1	-	32.9
Lock 40, bridge, **Wilwisheim** 700m l/b	281.4	44	31.6
Bridge	281.8	-	31.2
Bridge	283.2	-	29.8
Lock 41, bridge	283.6	45	29.4
Hochfelden bridge, quay d/s l/b, village 1000m l/b	286.2	-	26.8
Lock 42, bridge, quay (Mutzenhouse) d/s r/b	288.0	46	25.0
Schwindratzheim bridge, village 800m l/b	288.8	-	24.2
Lock 43	289.1	47	23.9
Waltenheim bridge, quay d/s r/b, village 200m r/b	290.7	-	22.3
Lock 44, bridge	291.0	48	22.0
Lock 45	292.1	49	20.9
Bridge	293.0	-	20.0
Lock 46, bridge	294.0	50	19.0
Bridge	296.0	-	17.0
Bridge (D30), quay d/s r/b, **Brumath** 2500m l/b	296.8	-	16.2
Bridge (D60)	297.5	-	15.5
Eckwersheim bridge, village 1200m r/b	300.3	-	12.7
Lock 47	300.6	51	12.4

	km	lock	km
Lock 48	301.7	52	11.3
Vendenheim swing bridge, village 500m r/b	302.0	-	11.0
Railway bridge	302.2	-	10.8
Bridge (N63), quay (Vendenheim) d/s r/b	302.4	-	10.6
Bridge	303.9	-	9.1
Motorway bridge (A34)	304.5	-	8.5
New road bridge (motorway access road)	305.0	-	8.0
Bridge	305.2	-	7.8
Lock 49, bridge, **Reichstett** 800m l/b	305.7	53	7.3
Souffelweyersheim quay r/b, village 800m r/b	306.9	-	6.1
Lock 50, bridge	307.0	54	6.0
Railway bridge	307.9	-	5.1
Bridge (D468)	308.0	-	5.0
Hoenheim bridge, village r/b (Strasbourg) suburb)	308.7	-	4.3
Bischheim bridge, quay u/s r/b, town centre 300m r/b	309.5	-	3.5
Schiltigheim bridge, quay d/s r/b, Chemins Nautiques d'Alsace hire base, town centre 800m r/b	310.2	-	2.8
Lock 51	310.6	55	2.4
River Aar crosses on the level (navigable 500m u/s to basin in Schiltigheim)	310.7	-	2.3
Lock 52, bridge	311.3	56	1.7
Junction with river Ill, turn right for access to centre of **Strasbourg** and northern section of Canal du Rhône au Rhin (see under river Ill including plan of Strasbourg)	311.6	-	1.4
Bridge	311.9	-	1.1
Bridge	312.6	-	0.4
Canal terminates in Bassin des Remparts (basin in the port of Strasbourg), *Junction with Rhine 1.2km through northern locks of the port of Strasbourg*	313.0	-	0.0

Lutzelbourg – Canal de la
Marne au Rhin.
Hugh Potter

Strasbourg.
Hugh Potter

Canal de la Marne à la Saône

The Canal de la Marne à la Saône, taken with the canalised river Marne and the Canal latéral à la Marne, provides the third of the main waterway routes across central France between Paris and Lyon (after the Bourbonnais and Burgundy routes). It begins at Vitry-le-François, where it connects with the Canal de la Marne au Rhin (a short distance from the junction of the latter with the Canal latéral à la Marne) and crosses the Langres plateau before dropping down the Vingeanne valley to connect with a lock-cut on the upper Saône at Heuilley-sur-Saône. The length of the canal is 224km. The through route from Paris to Lyon using this canal is the longest of the three, but the least heavily-locked, thanks mainly to its more recent construction (the canal was not completed until 1907) and greater average lock depth than that of the older Canal du Centre and Canal de Bourgogne. It also represents by far the most convenient route from northern France to the Saône. Curiously, it remains little used (except by boats in transit), annual traffic amounting to less than 300 boats in recent years, while barge traffic also on the decline, with about 1000 transits per year.

The canal has a 10km long summit level south of Langres, at an altitude of 340m. This includes the Balesmes tunnel, 4820m in length, extended by narrow approaches to form a one-way only section 7.3km long. Times of passage through this section in each direction follow a fixed schedule:

(a) From the Marne towards the Saône:
   0000–0100 (laden barges)
   1200–1700 (unladen barge and boats)
(b) From the Saône towards the Marne:
   0400–0900
   2000–2100

If the summit level is reached outside these times, and if the traffic situation permits, the tunnel-keepers at the locks at each end of the summit level may be asked for exceptional authorisation to proceed. The Balesmes tunnel offers the rare luxury of being lit.

There is also a 308m long tunnel at Condes (km 106), which is unique in being the only tunnel on the French waterway network (excluding the Paris canals) to allow simultaneous passage in both directions (the width being 18m). There are no special regulations regarding passage.

Locks There are 114 locks, of which 71 fall towards the Marne and 43 towards the Saône. They are of uniform dimensions, 38.50 by 5.20m.

Depth The maximum authorised draught is 1.80m.

Bridges The fixed bridges leave a minimum clear headroom of 3.50m.

Towpath There is a towpath throughout.

Authority

Direction Départementale de l'Equipement de la Haute-Marne (Chaumont).
Subdivisions:
– 4 chaussée St Thiébault, 52100 St Dizier, ☎ 25 05 03 17 (km 3-59)
– 26 avenue du Général-Leclerc, 52000 Chaumont, ☎ 25 03 30 51 (59-148).
– 2 rue Robert-Schuman, 52200 Langres, ☎ 25 85 02 94 (km 148-224).

Distance table

	km	lock	km
Connection with Canal de la Marne au Rhin, turning basin	0.0	-	224.2
Quay (Citadelle) r/b	0.1	-	224.1
Vitry-le-François bridge (Pont de Saint-Dizier), quay u/s l/b, town centre 700m l/b	0.5	-	223.7
Railway bridge	0.9	-	223.3
Lock 71 (Désert), quay u/s l/b	1.1	1	223.1
Bridge	1.4	-	222.8
Frignicourt quay l/b, village 800m l/b	2.7	-	221.5
Lock 70 (Frignicourt), bridge	2.8	2	221.4
Bridge	5.3	-	218.9
Footbridge	5.6	-	218.6
Luxémont basin r/b, village 1000m r/b	6.1	-	218.1
Lock 69 (Luxémont), bridge	6.3	3	217.9
Goncourt bridge, basin u/s l/b (silted up), castle 600m l/b	7.3	-	216.9
Lock 68 (Ecriennes), bridge	8.9	4	215.3
Bridge	9.7	-	214.5
Lock 67 (Matignicourt), footbridge	11.3	5	212.9
Bridge	12.9	-	211.3

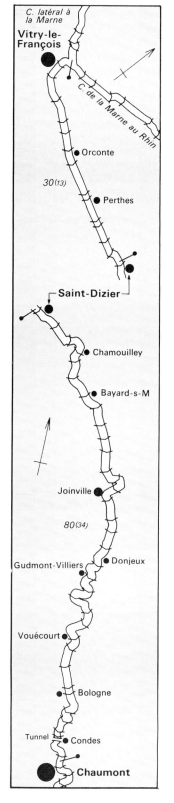

	km.	lock	km
Lock 66 (**Orconte**), bridge, quay d/s l/b, village 400m r/b	13.5	6	210.7
Turning basin	13.8	-	210.4
Bridge	14.3	-	209.9
Lock 65 (Bruyères), bridge	15.4	7	208.8
Lock 64 (Sapignicourt), bridge	18.8	8	205.4
Sapignicourt bridge, small village 300m l/b	19.5	-	204.7
Lock 63 (**Perthes**), quay d/s l/b, village 300m r/b	20.2	9	204.0
Bridge	20.7	-	203.5
Lock 62 (Garenne), bridge	22.6	10	201.6
Lock 61 (**Hallignicourt**), bridge, small village l/b	24.1	11	200.1
Lock 60 (Hoëricourt), bridge (airfield l/b)	26.4	12	197.8
Lock 59 (Noue), right angle turn under bridge (N67)	28.2	13	196.0
Bridge, private quay u/s r/b	28.9	-	195.3
Saint-Dizier bridge, turning basin and quay d/s l/b, town centre 400m l/b	30.0	-	194.2
Lock 58 (Saint-Dizier), water	30.1	14	194.1
Bridge, private basin d/s r/b	30.5	-	193.7
Bridge	30.8	-	193.4
Railway bridge	31.3	-	192.9
Bridge (D384)	31.4	-	192.8
Industrial quays l/b	32.0	-	192.2
Railway swing bridge	33.5	-	190.7
Lift bridge	33.6	-	190.6
Lock 57 (Marnaval)	34.1	15	190.1
Overhead pipeline crossing	35.0	-	189.2
Bridge	35.5	-	188.7
Railway bridge (after right angle bend)	36.1	-	188.1
Lock 56 (Guë)	36.3	16	187.9
Bridge	36.7	-	187.5
Bridge	38.5	-	185.7
Chamouilley bridge, quay d/s r/b, village r/b	38.9	-	185.3
Lock 55 (Chamouilley), water, private quay u/s r/b	39.4	17	184.8
Railway bridge	39.5	-	184.7
Lock 54 (Eurville)	40.7	18	183.5
Eurville lift bridge (automatic), quay d/s r/b, village 300m l/b	41.6	-	182.6
Lock 53 (Bienville), footbridge, aqueduct u/s	43.0	19	181.2
Bienville lift bridge (automatic), turning basin d/s, village 200m r/b	43.2	-	181.0
Lock 52 (Bayard), aqueduct u/s	45.9	20	178.3
Bayard-sur-Marne lift bridge (automatic), quay d/s l/b, village r/b	46.3	-	177.9
Lift bridge	47.2	-	177.0
Lock 51 (Fontaines), bridge	48.2	21	176.0
Lift bridge	48.5	-	175.7
Railway bridge	49.7	-	174.5
Lock 50 (**Chevillon**), bridge, quays u/s and d/s r/b, village 300m r/b	50.6	22	173.6
Lock 49 (Breuil)	52.8	23	171.4
Lock 48 (Curel), footbridge	54.6	24	169.6
Curel lift bridge, quay u/s l/b, village 500m r/b	54.7	-	169.5
Lift bridge (Autigny-le-Petit)	55.6	-	168.6
Autigny-le-Grand lift bridge (automatic), small village r/b	56.5	-	167.7
Lock 47 (Autigny-le-Grand), bridge	57.1	25	167.1
Railway bridge	58.3	-	165.9
Lock 46 (Bussy), bridge, private quay u/s l/b	59.3	26	164.9
Thonnance-lès-Joinville bridge, turning basin and quay u/s r/b, village 600m r/b	60.3	-	163.9
Lock 45 (Rongeant), bridge, aqueduct u/s	61.2	27	163.0

see also Canal latéral à la Marne (jn. 1km)

Canal de la Marne au Rhin

VITRY-LE-FRANÇOIS

Bar-le-Duc 48km, 32 locks

N

SNCF station

Lock 71 (Désert)

Saint-Dizier 29km, 12 locks

	km	lock	km
Joinville bridge, quay d/s r/b, small town 300m l/b	62.5	-	161.7
Lock 44 (Joinville), bridge, water, private quay u/s l/b	63.2	28	161.0
Railway bridge, basin u/s	63.7	-	160.5
Lock 43 (Bonneval), bridge	66.0	29	158.2
Lock 42 (Saint-Urbain), bridge, quay d/s r/b, village 1200m r/b	67.6	30	156.6
Lock 41 (Mussey), bridge, aqueduct u/s	70.4	31	153.8
Mussey-sur-Marne lift bridge, village 1000m l/b	70.5	-	153.7
Donjeux bridge, turning basin and quay d/s l/b, village 500m r/b	71.9	-	152.3
Lock 40 (**Rouvroy**), bridge, aqueduct u/s, village 300m l/b	73.2	32	151.0
Bridge	74.0	-	150.2
Private quay r/b	75.4	-	148.8
Railway bridge	75.9	-	148.3
Lock 39 (**Gudmont**), lift bridge u/s, quay u/s r/b, village 400m l/b	76.0	33	148.2
Railway bridge	77.2	-	147.0
Villiers-sur-Marne bridge, small village 400m l/b	77.9	-	146.3
Lock 38 (Villiers), bridge	78.7	34	145.5
Railway bridge	79.6	-	144.6
Lock 37 (Provenchères), bridge, basin u/s l/b	81.2	35	143.0
Railway bridge	82.5	-	141.7
Lock 36 (Froncles), bridge	84.2	36	140.0
Froncles quay l/b, village 400m l/b	84.4	-	139.8
Turning basin	85.3	-	138.9
Buxières-lès-Froncles bridge, quay u/s r/b, village l/b	85.6	-	138.6
Lock 35 (Buxières), bridge	86.9	37	137.3
Bridge	88.6	-	135.6
Lock 34 (**Vouécourt**), bridge, quay d/s r/b, village l/b	89.7	38	134.5
Lock 33 (Grandvaux), bridge	91.6	39	132.6
Viéville lift bridge (automatic), quay u/s l/b, village 300m r/b	93.2	-	131.0
Lock 32 (Viéville), bridge	94.4	40	129.8
Lock 31 (**Roôcourt**), bridge, turning basin u/s, small village r/b	96.4	41	127.8
Railway bridge	96.9	-	127.3
Lock 30 (**Bologne**), bridge, boat moorings d/s l/b, village 700m l/b	97.4	42	126.8
Bridge, quay u/s r/b	98.0	-	126.2
Lock 29 (**Riaucourt**), bridge, small village r/b	100.9	43	123.3
Lock 28 (Mouillerys)	102.7	44	121.5
Bridge	104.0	-	120.2
Lift bridge	104.5	-	119.7
Lock 27 (Brethenay)	104.6	45	119.6
Brethenay quay and small village l/b	105.1	-	119.1
Lock 26 (Condes), bridge (N67)	105.5	46	118.7
Condes tunnel, northern entrance	105.6	-	118.6
Condes tunnel, southern entrance	105.9	-	118.3
Lift bridge	106.1	-	118.1
Lock 25 (Reclancourt), bridge, quay d/s r/b	108.9	47	115.3
Turning basin	109.5	-	114.7
Chaumont bridge, quay d/s r/b, town centre 2000m l/b	110.0	-	114.2
Lock 24 (Val des Choux)	110.4	48	113.8
Lock 23 (Choignes), bridge, quay u/s r/b	111.9	49	112.3
Bridge	113.0	-	111.2
Lock 22 (**Chamarandes**), bridge, quay u/s l/b, small village 300m l/b	114.9	50	109.3
Lock 21 (Foulon de la Roche), footbridge	116.1	51	108.1
Bridge	117.0	-	107.2

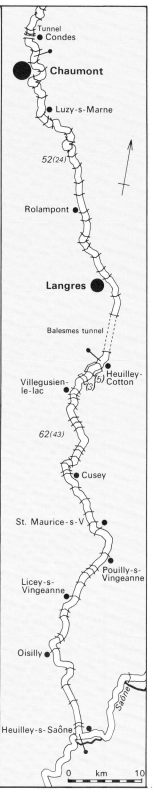

	km	lock	km
Lock 20 (Val des Ecoliers), bridge	117.6	52	106.6
Verbiesles bridge, small village 400m r/b	118.7	-	105.5
Footbridge	119.6	-	104.6
Luzy-sur-Marne lift bridge, quay u/s r/b, village 400m r/b	119.6	-	104.6
Lock 19 (Luzy), footbridge	120.5	53	103.7
Loch 18 (Pêcheux)	122.2	54	102.0
Lock 17 (Foulain), bridge	122.8	55	101.4
Foulain bridge, boat moorings ('halte fluviale') d/s r/b, village l/b	124.3	-	99.9
Lock 16 (Boichaulle), bridge, quay, turning basin d/s r/b	125.9	56	98.3
Railway bridge	127.2	-	97.0
Lock 15 (Pré-Roche)	127.3	57	96.9
Bridge	129.4	-	94.8
Railway bridge	129.7	-	94.5
Lock 14 (Pommeraye)	129.8	58	94.4
Marnay-sur-Marne bridge, village 800m l/b	131.0	-	93.2
Lock 13 (Marnay)	131.1	59	93.1
Vesaignes-sur-Marne quay and small village r/b	132.6	-	91.6
Lock 12 (Vesaignes), bridge	132.9	60	91.3
Bridge	134.0	-	90.2
Lock 11 (Thivet), bridge	134.9	61	89.3
Lock 10 (Prées), bridge	136.5	62	87.7
Rolampont bridge, basin d/s, village l/b	138.8	-	85.4
Lock 9 (Rolampont), bridge	139.2	63	85.0
Lock 8 (Saint-Menge), bridge	140.4	64	83.8
Lock 7 (Chanoy), bridge	142.1	65	82.1
Lock 6 (Pouillot)	143.6	66	80.6
Lock 5 (**Humes**), bridge, quay u/s r/b, village 500m l/b	144.4	67	79.8
Bridge	145.3	-	78.9
Jorquenay swing bridge, small village r/b	145.9	-	78.3
Lock 4 (Jorquenay), bridge	146.3	68	77.9
Railway bridge	147.8	-	76.4
Lock 3 (Moulin-Rouge), bridge	148.1	69	76.1
Langres bridge (D74), basin and quay d/s l/b, town centre 2000m l/b	148.8	-	75.4
Lock 2 (Moulin-Chapeau), bridge	149.8	70	74.4
Bridge	150.2	-	74.0
Skew railway bridge	151.9	-	72.3
Viaduct (N19)	152.4	-	71.8
Lock 1 (Batailles), bridge, beginning of summit level	152.5	71	71.7
Short tunnel under road (D17)	154.9	-	69.3
Balesmes tunnel, northern entrance	155.4	-	68.8
Balesmes tunnel, southern entrance	160.2	-	64.0
Heuilley-Cotton bridge, basin d/s, village l/b	161.7	-	62.5
Bridge	162.1	-	62.1
Lock 1 (Versant Saône), bridge, water	162.6	72	61.6
Lock 2, bridge	163.0	73	61.2
Lock 3, bridge	163.5	74	60.7
Lock 4, bridge (D241)	163.8	75	60.4
Lock 5, bridge	164.2	76	60.0
Lock 6, bridge	164.6	77	59.6
Lock 7, bridge	165.1	78	59.1
Lock 8 (bottom lock of Versant Saône flight)	165.6	79	58.6
Bridge (D67)	165.7	-	58.5
Railway bridge	166.4	-	57.8
Bridge	167.1	-	57.1
Villegusien bridge, basin, quay u/s r/b, village 200m r/b	167.5	-	56.7
Lock 9 (Villegusien), bridge, water	167.8	80	56.4

	km	*lock*	*km*
Lock 10 (Pré-Meunier), footbridge	168.2	81	56.0
Lock 11 (Château), bridge	168.7	82	55.5
Piépape bridge, small village and castle r/b	169.2	-	55.0
Lock 12 (Piépape), footbridge	169.5	83	54.7
Vingeanne aqueduct	171.4	-	52.8
Bridge (D128)	171.6	-	52.6
Lock 13 (Bise l'Assaut), footbridge	171.9	84	52.3
Lock 14 (Croix-Rouge), bridge	172.9	85	51.3
Bridge	173.5	-	50.7
Lock 15 (**Dommarien**), bridge, water, turning basin, quay d/s l/b, village 200m l/b	173.7	86	50.5
Footbridge	175.8	-	48.4
Lock 16 (**Choilley**), bridge, quay d/s l/b, village 200m l/b	176.4	87	47.8
Lock 17 (Foireuse), bridge	177.0	88	47.2
Dardenay bridge (D128), small village l/b	177.7	-	46.5
Lock 18 (Dardenay), footbridge	178.2	89	46.0
Lock 19 (Grand-Côte), footbridge	178.9	90	45.3
Lock 20 (Badin), bridge (D140)	179.6	91	44.6
Aqueduct	179.9	-	44.3
Lock 21 (Montrepelle), footbridge	180.2	92	44.0
Lock 22 (Cusey), bridge, water	180.9	93	43.3
Cusey bridge, turning basin and quay d/s r/b, village 400m l/b	181.5	-	42.7
Lock 23 (Bec), bridge	183.5	94	40.7
Percey-le-Petit bridge, small village 500m l/b	184.6	-	39.6
Lock 24 (**Courchamp**), bridge, turning basin and quay d/s r/b, village 400m r/b	185.6	95	38.6
Bridge	186.6	-	37.6
Lock 25 (Romagne), bridge	187.6	96	36.6
Lock 26 (**Saint-Maurice**), bridge, quay u/s l/b, village 1000m l/b	189.0	97	35.2
Lock 27 (Lavilleneuve), footbridge	190.2	98	34.0
La Villeneuve-sur-Vingeanne bridge, turning basin, quay d/s r/b, small village r/b	192.1	-	32.1
Lock 28 (Pouilly), footbridge	194.0	99	30.2
Bridge	194.8	-	29.4
Pouilly-sur-Vingeanne bridge, small village l/b	195.1	-	29.1
Lock 29 (**Saint-Seine**), bridge, basin u/s r/b, village 1500m l/b	196.7	100	27.5
Lock 30 (Lalau), footbridge	197.3	101	26.9
Lock 31 (Fontaine-Française), footbridge	198.2	102	26.0
Bridge	198.7	-	25.5
Lock 32 (Fontenelle), bridge	199.5	103	24.7
Bridge	200.4	-	23.8
Lock 33 (Licey), bridge	201.8	104	22.4
Licey-sur-Vingeanne bridge, quay u/s r/b, village r/b	202.7	-	21.5
Dampierre bridge, quay u/s r/b, small village 400m r/b	204.1	-	20.1
Lock 34 (Dampierre), bridge	204.4	105	19.8
Lock 35 (Beaumont), bridge, turning basin, quay d/s, r/b	205.2	106	19.0
Bridge, private quay u/s r/b	206.6	-	17.6
Lock 36 (Blagny), bridge	207.9	107	16.3
Blagny-sur-Vingeanne quay and small village r/b	208.5	-	15.7
Lock 37 (Rochette), bridge	208.6	108	15.6
Railway viaduct	210.1	-	14.1
Lock 38 (**Oisilly**), bridge, small village r/b	210.5	109	13.7
Bridge	211.0	-	13.2
Quay r/b	211.4	-	12.8
Bridge, quays d/s	212.4	-	11.8

	km	lock	km
Lock 39 (**Renève**), bridge, turning basin and quay d/s r/b,			
village 500m l/b	214.4	110	9.8
Lift bridge	215.8	-	8.4
Cheuge bridge, small village r/b	216.0	-	8.2
Lock 40 (Cheuge), footbridge	217.4	111	6.8
Lock 41 (**Saint-Sauveur**), bridge, quay d/s r/b,			
village 500m r/b	219.3	112	4.9
Bridge	220.0	-	4.2
Bridge	221.1	-	3.1
Lock 42 (**Maxilly**), bridge, quay u/s r/b, village 400m r/b	222.7	113	1.5
Bridge	222.9	-	1.3
Lock 43 (Chemin de Fer), railway bridge	223.0	114	1.2
Bridge	223.5	-	0.7
Junction with river Saône (Heuilley lock-cut, km 127),			
footbridge	224.2	-	0.0

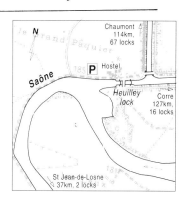

Mayenne-Maine

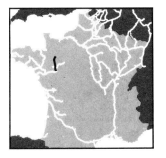

The Mayenne is one of the delightful river navigations of the Anjou region, abandoned by commercial traffic but increasingly popular as a cruising waterway. It was recently conceded by the State to the Pays-de-la-Loire region, allowing development of the river as a cruising waterway and tourist asset. The Mayenne was canalised in the 19th century from Mayenne to its confluence with the Loire at Bouchemaine, a distance of 134km. For many years, the first 26km section from Mayenne was no longer navigable, since the 17 locks in this section were unmanned and in poor condition. An investment programme implemented in 1986-1990 by the region and *département* has resulted in restoration of all 17 locks, and boats are once again be able to reach Mayenne (from 23 March 1991). Note however that only boats with limited air draught can proceed upstream of Laval (see under Bridges).

Just above the town of Angers the Mayenne is joined by the Sarthe, and from this point it takes the name of Maine. The development of pleasure cruising (especially with barges) is hindered by the severely limited draught during summer drought periods on the lower non-canalised sections of both the Mayenne and the Maine. Hence the recently-approve project to build a new weir and lock just downstream of Angers. A secondary channel, known as the Vieille-Maine, forms a cross-link with the Sarthe downstream of Montreuil-Belfroy (see plan). For craft passing from one river to the other, use of this link saves 5km by comparison with the route via the confluence (although most navigators will probably prefer to call at Angers for the facilities offered in the town).

Locks There are 45 locks between Mayenne and Montreuil-Belfroy. The first 37 are 31.00 by 5.20m, the last eight being slightly longer (33m). The top three locks are scheduled to be re-opened to navigation in 1991. Signs have been installed on the locks to distinguish the different situations which boaters will encounter:

- Red disk: lock closed, passage forbidden.
- Yellow disk: lock in operation, and worked by the lock-keeper (whether resident or posted temporarily).
- Blue disk: lock in operation, to be worked by the boat's crew (forbidden at night).

All locks up to Laval are normally worked by lock-keepers, while upstream to Mayenne lock operation is do-it-yourself. During the high season (June to September) a maintenance team will be supervising this section of the river and will be available to provide assistance if necessary. Restrictions may apply outside the cruising season, which in 1991 is defined as March 23 to November 4.

Depth The maximum authorised draught is 1.40m, increased to 1.80m from Angers to the confluence with the Loire.

Bridges Above Laval the air draught is restricted by the limited headroom under the Pont de l'Europe, 2.80m above normal water level and 2.10m above the highest navigable water level. From Laval to the confluence with the Sarthe the bridges offer a minimum headroom of 4.10m above normal water level, reduced to 3.40m above the HNWL. On the Maine the normal headroom is 6.40m.

Authority

Direction Départementale de l'Equipement, Mayenne.
Subdivision: 86 rue du Pressoir Salé, BP860, 53042 Laval, ☎ 43 53 01 37 (km 0-86).
Service de la Navigation Maine-et-Loire, quai Félix Faure, 49000 Angers,
☎ 41 43 61 49 (km 86-134).

Distance table

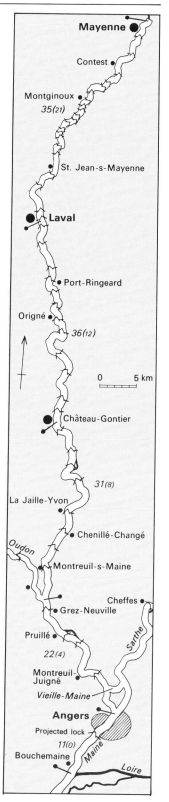

	km	lock	km
Bridge (MacRacken), head of navigation, (from 1991)	0.0	-	133.7
Bridge	0.2	-	133.5
Mayenne, quay and projected moorings, l/b, town with all facilities	0.4	-	133.3
Bridge	0.7	-	133.0
Lock 1 (Mayenne)	0.8	1	132.9
Saint-Baudelle bridge, village 300m r/b	3.4	-	130.3
Lock 2 (Saint-Baudelle)	3.6	2	130.1
Le Val, hamlet and chapel, l/b	5.2	-	128.5
Lock 3 (Grenoux), r/b (limit of navigation until 1991)	7.5	3	126.2
Lock 4 (La Roche)	9.5	4	124.2
Lock 5 (Boussard)	10.5	5	123.2
Lock 6 (Corçu), La Giraudière, small village l/b	13.1	6	120.6
Lock 7 (Bas-Hambert)	14.3	7	119.4
Montginoux bridge, boat moorings with sanitary building, showers, telephone, grocery, **Martigné** 4km l/b, **St Germain d'Anxure** 2.5km r/b	14.5	-	119.2
Lock 8 (Communes), Montginoux castle r/b	14.7	8	119.0
Lock 9 (Port)	15.9	9	117.8
Lock 10 (Nourrière), castle on hillside l/b	17.3	10	116.4
Lock 11 (Verrerie)	18.3	11	115.4
Lock 12 (Richardière)	19.2	12	114.5
Lock 13 (Fourmondière supérieure)	19.8	13	113.9
Bridge (Rochefort), **Andouillé** 3km r/b	20.0	-	113.7
Lock 14 (Fourmondière inférieure)	20.1	14	113.6
Lock 15 (Moulin Oger)	20.9	15	112.8
Lock 16 (Ame)	23.9	16	109.8
Lock 17 (Maignannerie)	24.7	17	109.0
Saint-Jean-sur-Mayenne bridge, quay d/s l/b, village r/b	26.3	-	107.4
Lock 18 (Boisseau), l/b and weir	27.1	1	106.6
Lock 19 (Belle-Poule) l/b and weir	29.9	2	103.8

	km	lock	km
Bridge	30.8	-	102.9
Changé bridge, village r/b	31.0	-	102.7
Lock 20 (Bootz) l/b and weir	33.5	3	100.2
Railway viaduct and footbridge	34.0	-	99.7
Bridge (Pont de l'Europe)	34.3	-	99.4
Laval bridge (Pont Neuf), quay d/s l/b, Fluvia-Laval hire base, town centre spread on both banks	34.7	-	99.0
Lock 21 (Laval) l/b and weir	34.8	4	98.9
Bridge (Pont Vieux)	35.0	-	98.7
Boat moorings ('base nautique') l/b	35.6	-	99.1
Lock 22 (Avenières) l/b and weir	35.9	5	97.8
Bridge (Pont d'Avenières)	35.9	-	97.8
Lock 23 (Cumont) r/b and weir	38.7	6	95.0
Saint-Pierre l/b	39.3	-	94.4
Lock 24 (Bonne) r/b and weir, bridge	42.3	7	91.4
Lock 25 (Port-Ringeard) r/b and weir	43.9	8	89.8
Entrammes bridge (D103), village 1800m l/b	44.0	-	89.7
Boat moorings and Mayenne Navigation hire base l/b	44.1	-	89.6
Lock 26 (Persigand) r/b and weir	45.0	9	88.7
Lock 27 (Briassé) r/b and weir	48.5	10	82.2
Lock 28 (Bénâtre) r/b and weir, picnic area, Origné 800m r/b	51.2	11	82.5
Lock 29 (Fosse) r/b and weir	53.2	12	80.5
La Valette bridge (D4), mooring and picnic area, castle u/s l/b	58.5	-	75.2
Lock 30 (Rongère) r/b and weir, castle u/s r/b	59.4	13	74.3
Boat moorings	62.1	-	74.2
Lock 31 (Neuville) r/b and weir	62.2	14	71.5
Lock 32 (Roche-du-Maine) r/b and weir, picnic area d/s r/b	65.8	15	67.9
Lock 33 (Mirvault) r/b and weir, slipway	68.4	16	65.3
Château-Gontier bridge, quay d/s r/b, Espace Europe Loisirs hire base and moorings u/s l/b, small town spread on both banks	70.5	-	63.2
Bridge	71.1	-	62.6
Lock 34 (Pendu) r/b and weir	71.7	17	62.0
Railway viaduct	71.9	-	61.8
Azé l/b	72.4	-	61.3
Lock 35 (Bavouze) r/b and weir, recommended restaurant	75.9	18	57.8
Entrance to lock-cut, r/b	76.6	-	57.1
Lock 36 (Ménil), moorings u/s r/b, end of lock-cut, weir l/b	77.8	19	55.9
Ménil r/b	77.8	-	55.9
Lock 37 (Fourmusson) in short cut, r/b	82.1	20	51.6
Daon bridge, moorings and France Mayenne Fluvial hire base u/s l/b, village l/b	83.8	-	49.9
Lock 38 (**La Jaille-Yvon**) r/b and weir, small village r/b	88.0	21	45.7
Lock 39 (Chenillé-Changé) in short cut, r/b	90.5	22	43.2
Chenillé-Changé l/b, Maine-Anjou Rivières and Féerives hire bases	90.6	-	43.1
Chambellay bridge, village r/b	92.1	-	41.6
Lock 40 (Roche-Chambellay) in short cut, r/b	93.6	23	40.1
Lock 41 (Montreuil-sur-Maine) r/b and weir	96.8	24	36.9
Montreuil-sur-Maine quay and village r/b	96.9	-	36.8
River divides, keep to r/b arm	98.0	-	35.7
Bridge (Pont de l'Aubinière), **Le Lion d'Angers** 2000m r/b	99.0	-	34.7
Confluence of Oudon, r/b (navigable river)	101.0	-	32.7
Lock 42 (Grez-Neuville) r/b and weir	102.7	25	31.0
Grez-Neuville bridge, quay and Anjou Plaisance hire base u/s r/b, village 200m l/b	102.9	-	30.8
Pruillé r/b (ferry)	106.3	-	27.4

	km	lock	km
Lock 43 (Roussière) r/b and weir	107.3	26	26.4
La Roussière castle and quay r/b	107.4	-	26.3
Entrance to lock-cut, r/b	108.9	-	24.8
Lock 44 (Sautré), end of lock-cut, weir l/b	109.4	27	24.3
Port-Albert quay l/b, **Feneu** 1300m	110.4	-	23.3
Bridge (Juigné-Béné), quay d/s r/b,	113.1	-	20.6
Lock 45 (Montreuil-Belfroy) in cut, r/b, weirs l/b (cruising information available at this lock and at lock 44)	115.6	28	18.1
Cantenay-Epinard bridge (heading u/s take r/b arm), village 700m l/b	118.2	-	15.5
River divides, Vieille-Maine l/b leads to Sarthe	118.9	-	14.8
Bridge	120.7	-	13.0
Confluence of Sarthe, l/b, Mayenne becomes Maine	122.5	-	11.2
Railway bridge	122.6	-	11.1
Bridge (Pont de la Haute-Chaîne), quays l/b	124.4	-	9.3
Angers bridge (Pont du Centre), boat harbour d/s r/b opposite castle and town centre, Anjou Croisières and Compagnie Angevine de Tourisme Fluvial hire bases	125.0	-	8.7
Bridge (Pont de la Basse-Chaîne), quays both banks	125.5	-	8.2
New road bridge (urban expressway)	126.5	-	7.2
Site of proposed new lock (Angers) r/b and weir	126.7	-	7.0
Bridge (formerly rail)	129.4	-	4.3
Railway bridge	131.7	-	2.0
Bouchemaine suspension bridge, village r/b	132.4	-	1.3
Oil tanker quay r/b	132.9	-	0.8
Confluence with Loire, navigable downstream only	133.7	-	0.0

Meuse

The Meuse is one of the great navigable rivers of Europe. It is canalised throughout most of its course in France and Belgium and bypassed by the Juliana Canal in the Netherlands province of Limburg, to continue as a free-flow navigation down to the Rhine delta. It is mentioned here for reference only, since the waterway is designated the Canal de l'Est, northern branch, throughout its course on French soil. See under that canal.

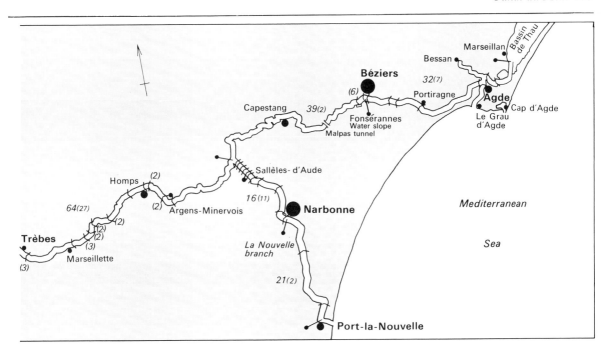

Authority

Service de la Navigation de Toulouse. Subdivisions:
– 65 allée des Demoiselles, 31400 Toulouse, ☎ 61 52 53 22 (km 0-51).
– Port du Canal, 11000 Carcassonne, ☎ 68 25 01 50 (km 51-127).
– 9 bis quai d'Alsace, 11100 Narbonne, ☎ 68 32 02 35 (km 127-174).
– Pont Rouge, 34500 Béziers, ☎ 67 76 26 38 (km 174-240).

La Nouvelle branch

This branch, which leaves the main line at Sallèles (km 168), is in fact made up of three distinct sections. The Canal de Jonction, leading down to the river Aude, is 5km long. The second section is a short length (600m) of the river Aude, whence boats enter the Canal de la Robine (32km long) to reach Narbonne and the Mediterranean at Port-la-Nouvelle. The entire branch was upgraded to the 250-tonne barge standard in the 1980s, in an attempt to maintain the competitiveness of water transport, especially for wine unloaded at Port-la-Nouvelle or produced in the region. However, this policy has been patently unsuccessful, and commercial transport has virtually disappeared, as on the main line.

Locks There are seven locks on the Canal de Jonction (including a deep lock replacing the former staircase at Sallèles) and six on the Canal de la Robine. Their dimensions are 40.50 by 5.85m.

Depth The maximum authorised draught has been increased from 1.60m to 1.80m. However, in periods of exceptional drought this depth may not be available on the crossing of the river Aude.

Bridges The fixed bridges leave a minimum headroom of 3.30m.
Towpath There is a towpath throughout, except for the crossing of the river Aude.

Authority
Service de la Navigation de Toulouse.
Subdivision: 9 bis quai d'Alsace, 11100 Narbonne, ☎ 68 32 02 35.

Descente dans l'Hérault

The descente dans l'Hérault maritime leads from the round lock at Agde (km 231) to the port of Agde on the Hérault. The cut is about 500m long, and includes a railway bridge offering a minimum headroom of 4.22m. The maximum authorised draught is 1.80m. (See also under Hérault).

Distance table

	km	lock	km
Toulouse basin (Port de l'Embouchure), former locks down to Garonne filled in for ring road, moorings, water	0.0	-	240.1
Junction with Canal latéral à la Garonne (Bassin de l'Embouchure)	0.2	-	239.9
Bridge (Pont Jumeau)	0.4	-	239.7
Lock (Béarnais), bridge	1.1	1	239.0
Footbridge (Nymphée), 'Central Park' development	1.5	-	238.6
Deep lock (Minimes)	2.0	2	238.1
Bridge (Minimes)	2.1	-	238.0
Footbridge (Négreneys)	2.6	-	237.5
Footbridge (Raisin)	3.0	-	237.1
Bridge (Matabiau), narrow passage through former lock chambers	3.3	-	236.8
Deep lock (Bayard), bridge, Toulouse station r/b	3.6	3	236.5
Bridge (Riquet)	3.9	-	236.2
Bridge (Constantine)	4.2	-	235.9
Bridge (Colombette)	4.4	-	235.7
Bridge (Guilheméry)	4.9	-	235.2
Basin (Port Saint-Etienne)	5.0	-	235.1
Bridge (Saint-Sauveur or Montaudran)	5.1	-	235.0
Basin (Port Saint-Sauveur), moorings 800m from city centre, water	5.2	-	234.9
Footbridge (Soupirs)	5.6	-	234.5
Railway bridge	6.0	-	234.1
Bridge (Demoiselles)	6.4	-	233.7
Footbridge	7.1	-	233.0
Bridge (university campus)	9.1	-	231.0
New road bridge (motorway spur)	10.5	-	229.6
Footbridge (Ramonville)	11.4	-	228.7
Ramonville new basin r/b, semi-industrial, with dry dock, awaiting development	11.5	-	228.6
Bridge (Madron)	12.1	-	228.0
Port Sud marina, moorings, slipway, crane, services, shops and restaurant in marina, **Ramonville** centre 1000m	12.4	-	227.7
Deep lock (**Castanet**), bridge, village 2000m l/b	15.7	4	224.4
Lock (Vic), bridge	17.4	5	222.7
Bridge (Deyme)	19.8	-	220.3
Bridge (Donneville)	22.7	-	217.4
Bridge (Montgiscard)	24.8	-	215.3
Deep lock (Montgiscard), footbridge	24.9	6	215.2
Montgiscard quay l/b, village 300m beyond main road	25.0	-	215.1
Bridge (Baziège)	26.9	-	213.2
New road bridge (N113)	28.0	-	212.1
Deep lock (Aygues-Vives), footbridge	28.1	7	212.0
Double staircase lock (Sanglier), bridge	29.6	9	210.5

	km	lock	km
Bridge (Enserny)	31.5	-	208.6
Lock (Négra), bridge, **Montesquieu-Lauragais** 1000m l/b	33.3	10	206.8
Bridge (Vieillevigne)	35.0	-	205.1
Double staircase lock (Laval), bridge	37.5	12	202.6
Lock (Gardouch), bridge	38.9	13	201.2
Gardouch quay l/b, village 600m	39.0	-	201.1
Hers aqueduct, **Villefranche-de-Lauragais** 2000m r/b	41.0	-	199.1
Lock (**Renneville**), bridge, small village 400m l/b	43.0	14	197.1
Double staircase lock (Encassan), bridge	45.9	16	194.2
Lock (Emborrel), bridge, **Avignonet-Lauragais** 1500m r/b	47.5	17	192.6
Bridge (Maraval)	49.5	-	190.6
Port Lauragais marina adjacent to motorway service area	50.0	-	190.1
Motorway bridge (A61, Autoroute des Deux Mers)	50.2	-	189.9
Railway bridge (main line Toulouse-Narbonne)	50.6	-	189.5
Lock (Océan), bridge, beginning of summit level	51.6	18	188.5
Feeder enters canal from former octagonal basin, Riquet memorial and commemorative plaques	52.1	-	188.0
Bridge	53.3	-	186.8
La Ségala bridge, quay and Rive de France relay base on south bank, small village	53.8	-	186.3
Lock (Méditerranée), bridge	56.6	19	183.5
Double staircase lock (Roc)	57.5	21	182.6
Bridge	58.2	-	181.9
Triple staircase lock (Laurens), bridge	58.7	24	181.4
Lock (Domergue)	59.7	25	180.4
Lock (Laplanque), bridge	60.9	26	179.2
Bridge (Pont Neuf)	64.5	-	175.6
Castelnaudary quays both banks, mooring, town l/b	64.6	-	175.5
Bridge (Pont Vieux)	64.8	-	175.3
Basin (Grand Bassin), Crown Blue Line hire base r/b	65.2	-	174.9
Bridge (Saint-Roch)	65.4	-	174.7
Quadruple staircase lock (Saint-Roch), water	65.6	30	174.5
Double staircase lock (Gay)	67.1	32	173.0
Triple staircase lock (Vivier), bridge	68.7	35	171.4
Lock (Guilhermin)	69.1	36	171.0
Lock (Saint-Sernin), bridge	69.7	37	170.4
Lock (Guerre), bridge, **Saint-Martin-Lalande** 1000m l/b	70.6	38	169.5
Lock (Peyruque), bridge	71.7	39	168.4
Lock (Criminelle)	72.2	40	167.9
Lock (Tréboul), bridge	73.6	41	166.5
Villepinte bridge, village 1000m l/b	76.0	-	164.1
Lock (Villepinte)	77.4	42	162.7
Lock (Sauzens), bridge	79.0	43	161.1
Lock (Bram), quay and Saintonge Rivières hire base d/s r/b	80.3	44	159.8
Bram bridge, village 1500m r/b	80.8	-	159.3
Railway bridge (main line Toulouse-Narbonne)	83.9	-	156.2
Bridge (Diable)	84.7	-	155.4
Lock (Béteille), bridge	85.9	45	154.2
Bridge (Saint-Eulalie)	89.1	-	151.0
Villesèquelande bridge, village 600m l/b	91.2	-	148.9
Lock (Villesèquelande)	93.4	46	146.7
Bridge (Caux-et-Sauzens)	94.1	-	146.0
Bridge (Rocles), **Pezens** 1500 l/b	95.9	-	144.2
Double staircase lock (Lalande)	98.2	48	141.9
Lock (Herminis), bridge	98.5	49	141.6
Lock (Ladouce)	99.9	50	140.2
Railway bridge	103.6	-	136.5
Bridge (Iéna)	104.4	-	135.7

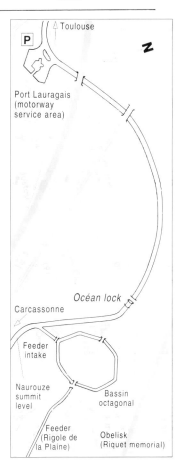

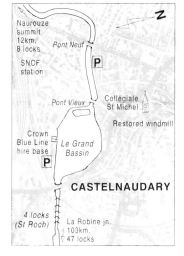

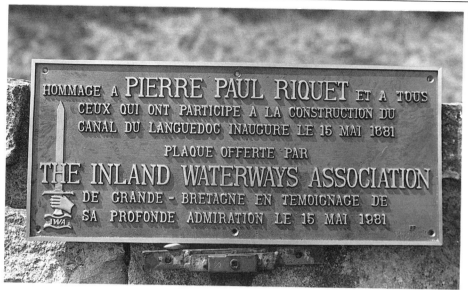

Canal du Midi. Plaque at summit level.

	km	lock	km
Footbridge	104.6	-	135.5
Bridge (Pont de la Paix)	104.8	-	135.3
Carcassonne basin, boat moorings and limited services, close to town centre and 1500m from **La Cité**	105.0	-	135.1
Lock (Carcassonne), bridge	105.3	51	134.8
Railway bridge (main line Toulouse-Narbonne)	105.4	-	134.7
Lock (Saint-Jean), bridge (Friedland)	108.0	52	132.1
Fresquel aqueduct	108.7	-	131.4
Double staircase lock (Fresquel), quay downstream l/b	108.8	54	131.3
Lock (Fresquel)	109.0	55	131.1
Bridge (Conques)	109.3	-	130.8
Bridge (Méjeanne)	110.6	-	129.5
Lock (Evêque), bridge	112.6	56	127.5
Lock (Villedubert)	113.4	57	126.7
Bridge (Rode)	116.2	-	123.9
Orbiel aqueduct	116.7	-	123.4
Trèbes bridge, quay upstream l/b, water, village r/b	117.3	-	122.8
Triple staircase lock (Trèbes)	118.0	60	122.1
Bridge (Saint-Julia)	119.4	-	120.7
Bridge (Millepetit)	121.0	-	119.1
Bridge (Millegrand)	122.2	-	117.9
Marseillette bridge, village 200m r/b	126.2	-	113.9
Lock (Marseillette), bridge	127.2	61	112.9
Triple staircase lock (Fonfile)	130.4	64	109.7
Double staircase lock (Saint-Martin), bridge	131.6	66	108.5
Double staircase lock (Aiguille), bridge	133.4	68	106.7
Bridge (Rieux), **Puichéric** 800m r/b	135.0	-	105.1
Railway bridge (disused)	136.0	-	104.1
Double staircase lock (Puichéric)	136.4	70	103.7
Laredorte bridge (Pont Vieux), restaurant, village 500m l/b	139.5	-	100.6
Aqueduct (Ribassel)	139.6	-	100.5
Bridge (Pont Neuf)	140.5	-	99.6
Aqueduct (Argent-Double)	141.0	-	99.1
Bridge (Métairie du Bois)	141.4	-	98.7
Lock (Jouarres)	142.7	71	97.4
Bridge (Jouarres)	144.0	-	96.1

	km	lock	km
Homps bridge, basin upstream, Locaboat Plaisance and Croisières du Soleil hire bases, moorings, village r/b	145.5	-	94.6
Lock (Homps), bridge	146.4	72	93.7
Double staircase lock (Ognon)	147.1	74	93.0
Stop lock (Ognon), footbridge	147.2	-	92.9
Bridge (Ognon), D11	147.5	-	92.6
Double staircase lock (Pechlaurier)	149.8	76	90.3
Argens-Minervois bridge, village l/b	151.1	-	89.0
Lock (Argens), beginning of long pound	152.3	77	87.8
Roubia bridge, quay downstream l/b, village l/b	154.8	-	85.3
Paraza bridge, quay upstream l/b, village l/b	157.6	-	82.5
Répudre aqueduct	158.8	-	81.3
Ventenac d'Aude bridge, quay upstream l/b, village l/b	160.9	-	79.2
Bridge (Saint-Nazaire)	162.7	-	77.4
Bridge (Pont Neuf), D607	165.4	-	74.7
Le Somail bridge (Pont Vieux), quays d/s, water, village l/b	165.9	-	74.2
Canal narrows, one-way traffic	167.7	-	72.4
Cesse aqueduct	168.0	-	72.1
Bridge (Truilhas)	168.3	-	71.8
La Robine basin l/b, Bateliers du Midi hire base, water, fuel	168.6	-	71.5
Junction with La Nouvelle branch, r/b, moorings	168.7	-	71.4
Railway bridge, end of section with one-way traffic	168.8	-	71.3
Bridge (Pont de la Province)	171.4	-	68.7
Argeliers bridge (Pont Vieux), quay upstream l/b, village 700m l/b	172.6	-	67.5
Bridge (Sériège), quay upstream l/b	176.5	-	63.6
Bridge (Pigasse)	178.3	-	61.8
Bridge (Malveis)	180.6	-	59.5
Capestang bridge, quay and Europe Yachting hire base d/s l/b, water, village r/b	188.3	-	51.8
Bridge	188.5	-	51.6
Bridge (Trézilles), D11	191.7	-	48.4
Poilhes footbridge	194.1	-	46.0
Poilhes bridge, quay and Midi Marine hire base d/s r/b, water, village r/b	194.2	-	45.9
Bridge (Régimont)	196.3	-	43.8
Malpas tunnel (length 161m), Oppidum d'Ensérune ruins 1500m l/b	198.8	-	41.3
Colombiers bridge, marina and Rive de France and Au Fil de l'Eau hire bases, d/s r/b, village r/b	200.5	-	39.6
Canal narrows, one-way traffic	202.0	-	38.1
First passing place	202.7	-	37.4
Second passing place	203.8	-	36.3
End of narrow section	204.0	-	36.1
Bridge (Gourgasse)	204.4	-	35.7
Bridge (Narbonne), N9, commercial quay upstream r/b	205.9	-	34.2
Canal divides, new cut leading to water slope, r/b, six (formerly seven) lock staircase (Fonserannes) l/b	206.5	-	33.6
Water slope (Fonserannes), bridge over staircase	206.6	78	33.5
New cut d/s of water slope rejoins old line of canal	207.0	-	33.1
Orb aqueduct (length 240m)	207.6	-	32.5
Deep lock (Orb), bridge	208.0	79	32.1
Béziers basin, moorings, water, town centre 500m l/b beyond railway	208.1	-	32.0
Deep lock (Béziers), dry dock	208.4	80	31.7
Bridge	208.5	-	31.6
Flood gate (Sauclière), *junction with Canalet du Pont Rouge (disused)*, bridge, quay downstream l/b	208.8	-	31.3

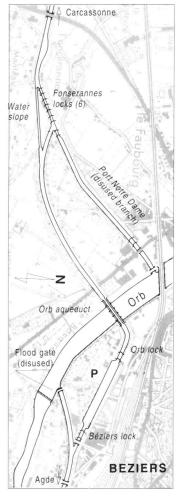

	km	lock	km
Footbridge (Saint-Pierre)	209.5	-	30.6
Lift bridge on industrial railway siding, remains open	210.0	-	30.1
Bridge (Capiscol)	210.5	-	29.6
Lock (Ariège)	212.5	81	27.6
Motorway bridge (A9, Languedocienne)	212.7	-	27.4
Lock (Villeneuve), bridge, **Villeneuve-lès-Béziers** r/b	213.8	82	26.3
Cers bridge, village 800m l/b	215.1	-	25.0
Bridge (Caylus)	216.5	-	23.6
Lock (Portiragne), bridge, **Portiragnes** 400m l/b	218.3	83	21.8
Bridge (Roquehaute)	221.6	-	18.5
Port Cassafières basin r/b, Crown Blue Line hire base, water, fuel, Redoute-Plage 1800m r/b	222.0	-	18.1
Libron crossing, narrow passage, bridge	225.2	-	14.9
Vias bridge (Pont Vieux), village 1200m l/b	226.4	-	13.7
New road bridge (Agde bypass)	228.2	-	11.9
Bridge (Pont Neuf, Vias), N112	229.0	-	11.1
Railway bridge	229.2	-	10.9
Three-arched bridge	229.7	-	10.4
Agde bridge, quay upstream r/b, town centre 800m r/b	231.3	-	8.8
Round lock (three-way), *junction with branch (descente dans l'Hérault)*	231.4	84	8.7
Canal enters Hérault	231.8	-	8.3
Canal leaves Hérault 1km upstream	232.8	-	7.3
Lock (Prades)	233.0	85	7.1
Bridge (Prades)	233.2	-	6.9
Bridge (Saint-Bauzille)	234.1	-	6.0
Lock (Bagnas)	235.3	86	4.8
Bridge (Les Onglous)	238.5	-	1.6
Quay (Les Onglous)	239.8	-	0.3
Les Onglous lighthouse, outfall into the Bassin de Thau	240.1	-	0.0

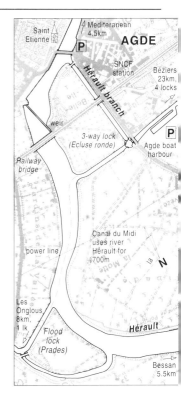

The round lock at Agde, on the Canal du Midi.
Author

Top: Water slope at
Fonserannes.
Below: Narbonne.
Rod Heikell

La Nouvelle branch

	km	lock	km
Junction with main line of Canal du Midi at km168.7	0.0	-	37.3
Footbridge (Cesse), quay downstream r/b	0.1	-	37.2
Lock (Cesse)	0.3	1	37.0
Lock (Truilhas), bridge	1.0	2	36.3
Lock (Empare)	1.6	3	35.7
Lock (Argeliers), bridge	2.3	4	35.0
Lock (Saint-Cyr)	3.0	5	34.3
Sallèles-d'Aude footbridge, quays downstream, village r/b	3.4	-	33.9
Deep lock (Sallèles)	3.7	6	33.6
Bridge (Sallèles)	3.8	-	33.5
Lock (Gailhousty), bridge, dry dock	4.9	7	32.4
End of junction canal, navigation enters river Aude	5.1	-	32.2
Railway bridge	5.4	-	31.9
End of Aude crossing, navigation enters Canal de la Robine r/b	5.7	-	31.6
Lock (Moussoulens), bridge	5.8	8	31.5
Bridge (Pont Vieux, Moussoulens)	6.4	-	30.9
Lock (Raonel), bridge, **Cuxac d'Aude** 1800m l/b	9.8	9	27.5
Lock (Gua), footbridge, quay downstream r/b	14.2	10	23.1
Footbridge, quay downstream l/b	14.6	-	22.7
Footbridge, quay downstream r/b	14.9	-	22.4
Railway bridge	15.1	-	22.2
Bridge (Escoute)	15.1	-	22.2
Bridge (Carmes)	15.2	-	22.1
Bridge (Voltaire)	15.2	-	22.1
Lock (Narbonne)	15.3	11	22.0
Bridge (Marchands)	15.5	-	21.8
Footbridge, Connoisseur Cruisers hire base l/b	15.6	-	21.7
Narbonne quays both banks in town centre	15.7	-	21.6
Bridge (Sainte-Catherine)	15.8	-	21.5
Footbridge	16.1	-	21.2
Lock (Mandirac), bridge, quay downstream r/b	24.1	12	13.2
Bridge	16.3	-	21.0
Motorway bridge (A9, Languedocienne)	17.8	-	19.5
Quay (Gruissan) r/b	25.4	-	11.9
Lock (Sainte-Lucie), quay downstream l/b	34.3	13	3.0
Railway bridge	36.9	-	0.4
Port-la-Nouvelle, canal enters harbour basins, Mediterranean 2500m down entrance channel, town r/b	37.3	-	0.0

Descente dans l'Hérault

	km	lock	km
Junction with main line of Canal du Midi at round lock (km 231.4)	0.0	84	0.5
Railway bridge	0.2	-	0.3
Junction with Hérault maritime	0.5	-	0.0

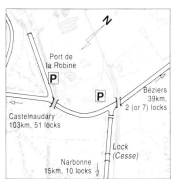

Attractive mooring on the
Canal latéral à la Garonne at
Le Mas d'Agenais. *Author*

Below
Pigasse bridge on the Canal
du Midi near Capestang.
Author

Above A hotel barge moored on the quays of the river Vilaine at Redon.
Below
Verdun-sur-le-Doubs, reached from the Saône 500m to the right. Through the bridge on the left is the Petit Doubs, inaccessible to powered boats. *Author*
Opposite
Cliffs just south of Viviers in the impressive Donzère gorge on the Rhône. *Derek Bowskill*

Above Douelle, a former river
port, is one of the most attractive
villages along the 64km restored
section of the river Lot,
surrounded by the dry *causses*,
contrasting with the fertile plain on
the right bank. *John Riddel*
Opposite Navigation on the Canal
de Beuvry (in the heart of what
used to be coal country, along the
Dunkerque-Escaut waterway) is
interrupted at this disused lift
bridge. *Author*

Barge moored at Lutzelbourg on the Canal de la Marne au Rhin. *John Riddel*

Stop lock 59b and lock cottage on the Canal du Nivernais with Saussois cliffs in the background. *John Riddel*

Above The river
Houlle (a branch of
the river Aa) near
the head of
navigation at the
village of Houlle.
Author

Opposite The imposing
Stella Artois brewery on
the Lys at Armentières.
Author

Sallèles lock, formerly a
staircase, now a single deep
lock, lengthened to 38.50m
and electrified, on the La
Nouvelle branch of the
Canal du Midi. *Author*
Below
Fishing cabins and boats on
the Lez, accessible over a
short length from the Canal
du Rhône à Sète at Palavas.
Author

Above Iron work detail on Eiffel's
aqueduct over the river Lire at Briare.
John Riddel
Above left Entering the cavernous lock on
the Canal du Centre at Chalon-sur-Saône.
Derek Bowskill

Hers aqueduct on the Canal
latéral à la Garonne near St
Jory, with lock 7 in the
background. Part of the
canal's sizeable flow is
routed through the sluices
on the left into a siphon
under the Hers and along
the small bypass canal at the
foot of the embankment
visible beyond the
aqueduct. The French
canals abound in fascinating
engineering details like this.
Author

	km	lock	km
Railway bridge (Nomeny branch line)	49.2	-	344.8
Bridge (Custines 1000m)	49.4	-	344.6
Overhead power line	50.1	-	343.9
Lock (Custines), lift 3.85m, footbridges above and below	50.3	7	343.7
End of diversion canal	51.0	-	343.0
Marbache, l/b	52.0	-	342.0
Motorway bridge (A31 Metz-Nancy)	52.5	-	341.5
Entrance to Belleville diversion canal, l/b, bridge	53.0	-	341.0
Bridge	53.1	-	340.9
Overhead power lines	53.5	-	340.5
End of diversion canal, **Autreville-sur-Moselle** r/b	54.5	-	339.5
Overhead power line	54.7	-	339.3
Motorway bridge (A31 Metz-Nancy)	55.5	-	338.5
Overhead power lines	57.1	-	336.9
Entrance to Blénod-Liégeot diversion canal, l/b	57.5	-	336.5
Flood gate (Liégeot), footbridge	57.9	-	336.1
Overhead power line	58.2	-	335.8
Private quay (Atton) r/b	58.7	-	335.3
Overhead power line	59.5	-	334.5
Dieulouard bridge, small town centre 900m l/b	59.9	-	334.1
Overhead power lines	60.7	-	333.3
Bridge (access to Blénod power station r/b)	61.7	-	332.3
Overhead power line	62.2	-	331.8
Overhead gas pipeline crossing	62.3	-	331.7
Lock (Blénod/Pont-à-Mousson), lift 5.65m, bridge	62.4	8	331.6
End of diversion canal	63.2	-	330.8
Overhead gas pipeline crossing	64.1	-	329.6
Junction with former diversion canal (disused) l/b, possible mooring for Pont-à-Mousson	66.6	-	328.0
Pont-à-Mousson bridge, quay and Nautipont hire base l/b	66.4	-	327.6
Entrance to former canal section, l/b (keep to Moselle)	67.0	-	327.0
New entrance to Pagny/Pont-à-Mousson diversion canal, l/b	68.4	-	325.6
Flood gate (Pont-à-Mousson), bridge, access to grain loading quay l/b	68.6	-	325.4
Bridge (Norroy)	70.3	-	323.7
Overhead power lines	71.3	-	322.8
Vandières public quay l/b, village with shops behind railway line	72.2	-	321.8
Bridge (Chécohée-Vandières)	72.6	-	321.4
Overhead power lines	73.5	-	320.5
Pagny-sur-Moselle basin, CCNB Lorraine Fluvial hire base, town centre 700m l/b	75.5	-	318.5
Lock (Pagny-sur-Moselle), lift 8.50m, bridge	75.9	9	318.1
End of diversion canal	76.6	-	317.4
Overhead pipeline crossings	79.0	-	315.0
Junction with former canal section (disused), l/b	81.4	-	312.6
Corny-sur-Moselle bridge, mooring downstream r/b	81.6	-	312.4
Ancy-sur-Moselle l/b, beyond railway and main road	84.7	-	309.3
Entrance to Ars diversion canal, l/b, and *junction with Canal de Jouy à Metz*, r/b (alternative route to Metz for boats, but restricted operating hours)	85.4	-	308.6
Ars-sur-Moselle bridge, town centre 800m l/b (beyond railway)	86.9	-	307.1
Lock (Ars-sur-Moselle), lift 4.00m	87.3	10	306.7
End of diversion canal	87.9	-	306.1
Railway bridge	88.2	-	305.8
Entrance to Vaux diversion canal, l/b	89.3	-	304.7
End of diversion canal	89.7	-	304.3

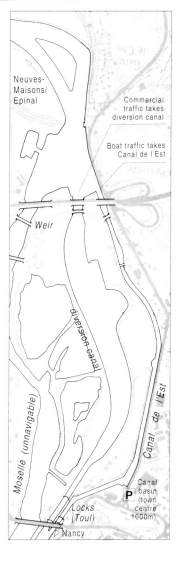

	km	*lock*	*km*
Moulins-lès-Metz bridge, town 1000m l/b	91.3	-	302.7
Railway bridge	93.0	-	301.0
Bridge (Pont de Verdun), **Longeville-lès-Metz** l/b	95.0	-	299.0
Entrance to Metz diversion canal, l/b, Metz town centre and moorings 1500m down Moselle r/b, and junction with *Canal de Jouy à Metz* (see plan)	95.3	-	298.7
Flood gate (Wadrineau)	95.5	-	298.5
Footbridge	95.6	-	298.4
Motorway bridge (A31 Thionville-Nancy)	96.3	-	297.7
Bridge (N3)	96.6	-	297.4
Old port of Metz, basin l/b	96.7	-	297.3
Lock (Metz-Nord), lift 4.60m, parallel large and small chambers	97.1	11	296.9
Bridge (Pont Eblé)	97.3	-	296.7
Bridge	97.5	-	296.5
End of diversion canal	97.7	-	296.3
Railway bridge (Chambières)	98.0	-	296.0
New port of Metz, 900m long basin l/b (biggest cereal port in France)	99.9	-	294.1
Overhead power lines	101.1	-	292.9
Malroy r/b	103.7	-	290.3
Entrance to former Canal des Mines de Fer de la Moselle l/b (now incorporated in canalised Moselle)	105.7	-	288.3
Flood gate (Argancy), bridge	105.9	-	288.1
Railway bridge (branch to Hauconcourt refinery)	106.8	-	287.2
Bridge (Amelange)	107.0	-	287.0
Motorway bridge (A4, cloverleaf interchange l/b)	107.4	-	286.6
Hauconcourt bridge, village 700m r/b, Maizières-lès-Metz 1500m l/b	109.4	-	284.6
Lock (Talange), lift 3.15m, parallel large and small chambers	110.6	12	283.4
Bridge	110.9	-	283.2
Junction with Hagondange branch l/b, 2km long with turning basin (no interest for boats)	111.1	-	282.9
Bridge (Talange)	111.7	-	282.3
Bridge (D55, motorway access road)	112.1	-	281.9
Overhead power line	112.7	-	281.3
Bridge (Hagondange)	112.9	-	281.1
Overhead pipeline crossing	113.2	-	280.8
Industrial quay (Mondelange), l/b	114.0	-	280.0
Mondelange bridge, town 600m l/b (over motorway)	114.3	-	279.7
Richemont industrial basin l/b	116.0	-	278.0
Bridge (Bousse)	116.2	-	277.8
Lock (Orne/Richemont), lift 4.35m, parallel large and small chambers	116.3	13	277.7
Overhead pipeline crossing and power lines	116.7	-	277.3
End of canal section, navigation re-enters Moselle	117.0	-	277.0
Confluence of Orne l/b	117.2	-	276.8
Basse-Guénange r/b	117.6	-	276.4
Motorway bridge (A31 Thionville-Nancy)	117.9	-	276.1
Uckange bridge, town centre 1000m l/b	118.8	-	275.2
Overhead power line	119.0	-	275.0
Overhead pipeline crossing	119.9	-	274.1
Overhead power lines	120.3	-	273.7
Entrance to Thionville diversion canal, l/b	120.7	-	273.3
Flood gate (Uckange), footbridge	121.7	-	272.3
Upstream limit of port of Thionville-Illange, basins l/b	122.0	-	272.0
Overhead power line	123.3	-	270.7
Downstream limit of port	124.0	-	270.0

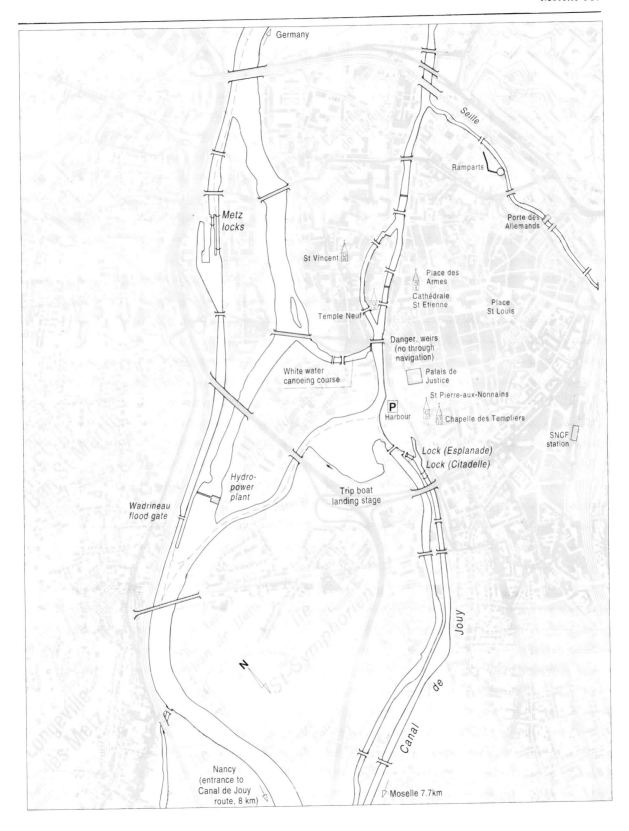

Germany

Seille

Ramparts

Porte des
Allemands

Metz
locks

St Vincent

Place des
Armes
Cathédrale
St Etienne

Place
St Louis

Temple Neuf

Danger, weirs
(no through
navigation)

White water
canoeing course

Palais de
Justice

St Pierre-aux-Nonnains

P
Harbour

Chapelle des Templiers

SNCF
station

Lock (Esplanade)
Lock (Citadelle)

Hydro-
power
plant

Trip boat
landing stage

Wadrineau
flood gate

N

Canal de Jouy

Nancy
(entrance to
Canal de Jouy
route, 8 km)

Moselle 7.7km

	km	lock	km
Lock (Thionville), lift 4.28m, parallel large and small chambers, bridge	124.2	14	269.8
Motorway bridge (A31 Thionville-Nancy) and railway bridge	124.8	-	269.2
End of diversion canal	125.1	-	268.9
Thionville quay l/b, close to town centre	125.5	-	268.5
Bridge (Pont des Alliés)	126.0	-	268.0
Railway bridge (Thionville-Nord)	127.0	-	267.0
Factory r/b, overhead power lines	129.3	-	264.7
Entrance to Koenigsmacker diversion canal, r/b, Cattenom nuclear power station l/b	135.2	-	258.8
Lock (Koenigsmacker), lift 3.90m, bridge (boat lock out of order, all boats use large lock)	135.8	15	258.2
End of diversion canal, **Koenigsmacker** 700m r/b	136.5	-	257.5
Bridge (Malling), destroyed	139.7	-	254.3
Malling r/b	140.0	-	254.0
Meander cutoff r/b	140.9	-	253.1
Berg-sur-Moselle l/b	141.5	-	252.5
Rettel r/b	144.5	-	249.5
Contz-les-Bains l/b	147.0	-	247.0
Bridge (Sierck-les-Bains/Contz-les-Bains)	147.2	-	246.8
Sierck-les-Bains r/b	148.5	-	245.5
Overhead power lines	149.9	-	244.1
Apach r/b, Luxembourg border l/b	150.7	-	243.3
Lock (Apach), lift 4.40m, r/b (all boats use the large lock), customs	151.6	16	242.4
German border r/b (242.2km and 12 locks to Rhine at Koblenz)	151.8	-	242.2

Frouard branch

	km	lock	km
Junction with Moselle (km 346.5)	0.0	-	346.5
Overhead power lines	0.9	-	347.4
Lock (Clévant), one large and one small chamber	1.0	1	347.5
Nancy-Frouard industrial port, basin 400m long, sharp right-hand bend under railway bridge	1.5	-	348.0
Lock	1.6	2	348.1
Junction with Canal de la Marne au Rhin (km 154)	1.7	-	348.2

Canal de Jouy à Metz (with navigable arm of Moselle)

	km	lock	km
Junction with Moselle (km 308.6), Jouy dam on Moselle l/b	0.0	-	10.5
Bridge	0.3	-	10.2
Factory r/b	1.2	-	9.3
Flood spillway l/b, former lock (Polka) permanently open	1.5	-	9.0
Bridge	1.6	-	8.9
Skew railway bridge, 9m passage	2.2	-	8.3
Bridge	2.3	-	8.2
Motorway bridge (A31)	3.2	-	7.3
Bridge (Tournebride)	3.5	-	7.0
Bridge (motorway spur)	4.4	-	6.1
Bridge (Station Hydraulique)	5.6	-	4.9
Railway bridge (8m passage)	5.7	-	4.8
Bridge (rue des Couvents), **Montigny-les-Metz** 700m r/b	6.9	-	3.6
Former industrial basin (La Vacquinière) r/b	7.6	-	2.9
Bridge (rue Saint-Symphorien)	8.1	-	2.4
Bridge (chemin du Port)	8.3	-	2.2
Bridge (motorway spur)	8.4	-	2.1
Lock (Citadelle)	8.5	1	2.0
Lock (Esplanade), bridge	8.6	2	1.9

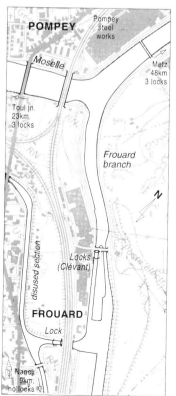

	km	lock	km
End of canal, navigation enters Montigny arm of Moselle	8.7	-	1.8
Bridge	8.7	-	1.8
River widens to form Bassin des Régates, moorings and Navilor Plaisance hire base r/b, navigation continues left upstream in navigable arm of Moselle	8.8	-	1.7
Motorway bridge (A31)	9.3	-	1.2
Wadrineau dam and hydropower plant l/b	9.9	-	0.6
Junction with Moselle (km 298.7), turn right into lock-cut (u/s boats, for Jouy canal turn sharp left on leaving lock-cut)	10.5	-	0.0

Canal de Nantes à Brest

The Canal de Nantes à Brest was built in 1824-1838, to serve essentially as a strategic link between the two seaports. Several rivers were canalised and three canal sections built to cross watersheds, thus forming an inland route no less than 360km long.

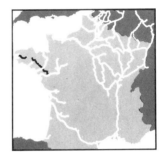

Sadly, this spectacular waterway was closed as a through route in 1920, one section being swallowed up by a reservoir dam and hydroelectric power plant at Guerlédan (km 227), a short distance west of the junction with the canalised river Blavet at Pontivy. The entire length of waterway west of Guerlédan was officially closed in 1957, and the 21km length from Pontivy to Guerlédan has also since fallen into disuse. At the same time, the disappearance of all commercial traffic (in 26m long barges carrying no more than 100-140 tonnes) resulted in the gradual silting up of the canal section between Rohan and Pontivy, so that the available depth in 1983 was only 0.90m.

Fortunately, however, the situation has improved dramatically in recent years. The potential of the Brittany waterways for pleasure cruising is now fully recognised by local authorities throughout the region, as a result of the campaigning efforts of the Breton Canals Committee (Comité de Promotion Touristique des Canaux bretons et des voies navigables de l'Ouest) over the last 25 years. Thus the isolated western section of the canal, made up of the canalised rivers Aulne and Hyères and a short length of canal, has been restored over a distance of 81km from Châteaulin to the limit of the department of Finistère, while the département of Morbihan is at the time of writing restoring the Rohan-Pontivy section to its original condition, offering a greatly increased draught of 1.60m. The main obstacle to re-opening of this section was the shortage of water supply to the summit level. This is being dealt with by building a pipeline from the Blavet to the summit, which will pump up to 450 l/s. Navigation throughout from Nantes to Pontivy should be possible in 1991.

Once restoration of the branch from Pontivy to Guerlédan has also been completed, surely it is not pure fantasy to imagine that one day the impetus will be found to restore the last remaining watershed section between Guerlédan and Port de Carhaix, with a special facility to transfer boats from the canal to the Guerlédan reservoir? In any event, it is with this perhaps not-so-remote prospect in mind, and to pay due respect to the history of this remarkable waterway, that the reopened section in Finistère is included under this entry.

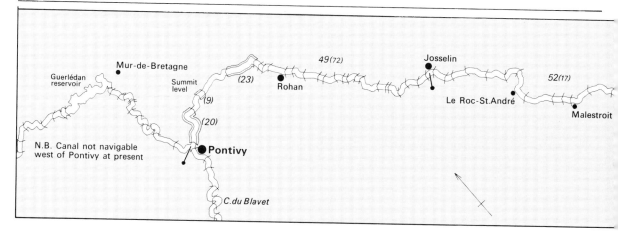

Main section, Nantes to Guerlédan (227km)

The main section of the Canal de Nantes à Brest provides two alternative routes to the Bay of Biscay from the English Channel, in addition to the direct route via the river Vilaine. The navigator reaching the Brittany waterway cross-roads at Redon may turn south-east towards Nantes, a distance of 89km from Bellions entrance lock. Over the last 22km of this distance, navigation is in the river Erdre, which is wide and almost estuarine in character, and considered to be one of the most beautiful rivers in France. From Nantes, the Loire estuary gives access to the sea at Saint-Nazaire. The alternative route is north-west to Pontivy (111km), whence the Canal du Blavet leads down to the sea at Lorient.

Locks From Nantes to Redon there are 18 locks, minimum dimensions 26.50 by 4.70m. The first gives access from the Loire to the river Erdre. Six more lead up to the summit level at an altitude of 19.80m. There are 10 locks down to the Vilaine, this section incorporating the canalised river Isac. The Vilaine must necessarily be entered at Bellions lock (no 17) following closure of the cut which parallels the river between here and Redon. The eighteenth lock is on the river Vilaine (in effect a sluice-gate, called the Grand Vannage, which is raised when water levels above and below are equal; otherwise the canal de Nantes à Brest is re-entered via a lock at the end of Redon canal basin).

From Redon to Pontivy there are 90 locks, of slightly smaller dimensions (25.70 by 4.60m), distributed as follows:

– 35 to Rohan, this section being made up essentially of the canalised river Oust,
– 26 (in a length of 6.6km) to the summit level, at an altitude of 129.60m,
– 29 from the summit down to Pontivy.

From Pontivy to Guerlédan there are 12 locks, although this section is not navigable at present. It is nevertheless included in the distance table in view of its possible future restoration.

Depth The original maximum authorised draught of 1.40m has been restored thanks to a substantial programme of dredging works completed in early 1991. The authorised draught is reduced to 1.20m on the river Erdre branch up to Nort-sur-Erdre.

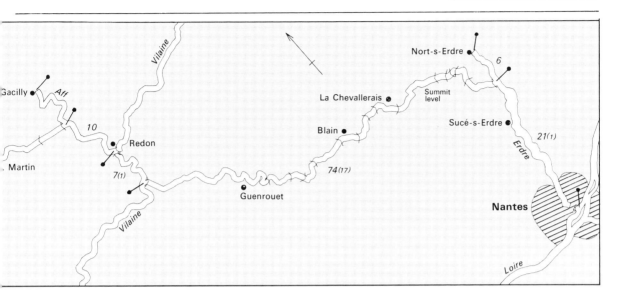

Bridges The maximum authorised air draught is 2.40m (although the normal headroom at most bridges is at least 3.15m).

Towpath There is a towpath along most of the itinerary, but not along the river Erdre nor along the river Vilaine from Bellions lock to Redon.

Authority
Service Maritime et de Navigation de Nantes. Subdivision:
– 2 rue Marcel Sembat, 44100 Nantes, ☎ 40 73 30 97 (km 0-95)
Service de la Navigation de Lorient. Subdivisions:
– 116 rue de Vannes, 35600 Redon, ☎ 99 71 11 45 (km 95-145).
– 1 rue Théodore Botrel, 56120 Josselin, ☎ 97 75 60 60 (km 145-185).
– 1 rue Henri Dunant, 56300 Pontivy, ☎ 97 25 55 21 (km 185-227).

Western section, Goariva to Châteaulin

The western section has been restored throughout its course in the department of Finistère, that is over a distance of 81km from the hamlet of Goariva, near Carhaix-Plouguer, to Châteaulin. However, in practice the first 7km from Goariva to Port-de-Carhaix, a canal section with 11 locks, is not yet opened to navigation, since the waterway authority considers it to be of little interest unless restoration is continued through the department of Côtes d'Armor. From Port-de-Carhaix, navigation follows the canalised river Hyère over a distance of 10km and the canalised river Aulne over the remaining 63km. Downstream of Châteaulin, the Aulne is a maritime navigation, although there is a tide lock at Guily-Glaz, 4km downstream. For convenience, an approximate distance table is given for navigation between Châteaulin and Brest, although nautical works should be consulted for the crossing of the Brest roadstead.

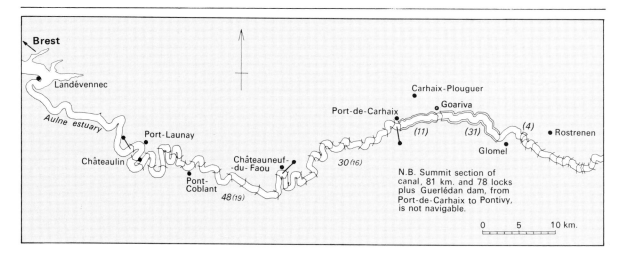

Locks There are 45 locks (numbered 192 to 236 on the original canal), of which 12 are on the canal section down to Port-Triffen, 6 are on the canalised river Hyère and the remaining 27 on the canalised river Aulne. Their dimensions are 25.70 by 4.65m. All these locks are unmanned, and have to be worked by the boat's crew using a windlass, as on the English canals. A leaflet of instructions is issued to all prospective navigators. It should be noted that the tide lock at Guily-Glaz is 40m long and 10m wide, allowing large vessels to reach Châteaulin. Boatowners reaching Châteaulin from the sea and intending to proceed up the Aulne may be supplied with a windlass by the Guily-Glaz lock-keeper.

Depth On the inland waterway down to Châteaulin, the maximum authorised draught is 1.20m. Châteaulin may be reached by vessels drawing as much as 3.00m.

Bridges The fixed bridges leave a minimum headroom of 3.50m.

Towpath There is a towpath throughout the inland waterway.

Authority

Direction Départementale de l'Equipement, Finistère.
Subdivision: 29119 Châteauneuf-du-Faou, ☎ 98 81 76 45.

Distance table

	km	lock	km
Junction with river Loire	0.0	-	226.8
Lock 1 (Saint-Félix), water	0.1	1	226.7
New road bridge	0.2	-	226.6
Entrance to tunnel under boulevards	0.6	-	226.2
Nantes, basin at northern tunnel entrance, moorings close to city centre	1.4	-	225.4
Bridge (Saint-Mihiel)	1.5	-	225.3
Bridge (Général de la Motte-Rouge)	2.3	-	224.5
Bridge (Tortière)	3.1	-	223.7
La Jonnelière quay r/b	5.2	-	221.6
Railway bridge and new road bridge	5.5	-	221.3

	km	lock	km
La Chapelle-sur-Erdre quay r/b, Bretagne Fluviale hire base, village 2500m	9.0	-	217.8
Carquefou quay l/b, village 3000m	10.5	-	216.3
Sucé-sur-Erdre bridge, quay downstream r/b, boats moorings close to village	15.1	-	211.7
Entrance to canal section, r/b, Erdre navigable further upstream to Nort-sur-Erdre (see under Erdre)	21.4	-	205.4
Lock 2 (Quiheix)	21.7	2	205.1
Bridge (Blanchetière)	23.4	-	203.4
Railway bridge	23.6	-	203.2
Bridge (Vive-Eve)	25.1	-	201.7
Lock 3 (Tindière)	26.2	3	200.6
Bridge (Plessis), **Nort-sur-Erdre** 2500m l/b	27.7	-	199.1
Bridge (Rocher), D164	28.8	-	198.0
Lock 4 (Rabinière)	28.9	4	197.9
Lock 5 (Haie Pacoret)	29.9	5	196.9
Lock 6 (Cramezeul)	30.9	6	195.9
Bridge (Rouziou)	31.5	-	195.3
Lock 7 (Pas d'Héric), beginning of summit level	32.3	7	194.5
Bridge (Coudrais), quay	33.0	-	193.8
Bridge (Saffré)	35.9	-	190.9
Bridge (Bout-de-Bois), quay	38.2	-	188.6
Bridge (Remaudais)	39.9	-	186.9
Lock 8 (Remaudais), end of summit level	40.7	8	186.1
La Chevallerais bridge, quay downstream r/b, village 600m l/b	42.3	-	184.5
Bridge (Gué de l'Atelier)	43.4	-	183.4
Lock 9 (Gué de l'Atelier)	43.8	9	183.0
Canal becomes canalised river Isac	43.9	-	182.9
Lock 10 (Terrier)	45.3	10	181.5
Bridge (Terrier)	45.8	-	181.0
Lock 11 (Blain)	48.7	11	178.1
Blain quay r/b, moorings and facilities for boats, town centre 500m	50.2	-	176.6
Bridge (Pont de la Croix Rouge)	50.3	-	176.5
Railway bridge	50.5	-	176.3
Lock 12 (Paudais)	51.5	12	175.3
Lock 13 (Bougard), bridge, quay upstream r/b	56.2	13	170.6
Lock 14 (Barel), bridge	59.5	14	167.3
Lock 15 (Touche)	61.9	15	164.9
Bridge (Pont-Nozay), D3, quay downstream l/b	63.5	-	163.3
Lock 16 (Melneuf)	65.9	16	160.9
Bridge (Melneuf)	66.1	-	160.7
Bridge (Saint-Clair), quay downstream l/b, **Guenrouet** 800m l/b	72.8	-	154.0
Navigation enters Thénot diversion canal, r/b	80.0	-	146.8
Bridge (Catée)	81.7	-	145.1
Bridge (Pont-Miny), quay upstream l/b, **Fégréac** 1500m r/b	83.5	-	143.3
Railway bridge (Trouhel)	85.5	-	141.3
Bridge (Trouhel)	86.0	-	140.8
Bridge (Saint-Jacques)	88.5	-	138.3
Entrance to disused section of Canal de Nantes à Brest, turn left to lock 17	88.6	-	138.2
Lock 17 (Bellions), navigation enters river Vilaine (turn right to rejoin canal at Redon)	88.7	17	138.1
(Navigation in river Vilaine, km 96.1 to km 89.2; note that the course in the river is 0.7km longer than following the original canal)			

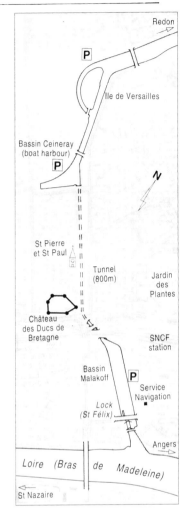

	km	lock	km
Redon, Vilaine crossing, quays, town centre 200m	94.9	-	131.9
Lock 18 (Oust or Redon), bridge	95.0	18	131.8
Road and rail swing bridge, entrance to large basin r/b	95.2	-	131.6
Suspension bridge (Guichardais)	95.6	-	131.2
Bridge (Codilo)	96.3	-	130.5
Railway bridge	96.5	-	130.3
Bridge (Courée)	97.3	-	129.5
Bridge (Marionnette), D764	99.4	-	127.4
Suspension bridge (Potinais)	101.4	-	125.4
Navigation enters river Oust, turning right (u/s), weir left	101.7	-	125.1
Island (Ile aux Pies), beauty spot	103.7	-	123.1
Lock 19 (Maclais, or Painfaut), *confluence of river Aff* l/b	105.3	19	121.5
Bridge (Prévotais)	107.0	-	119.8
Bridge (Bilaire)	108.7	-	118.1
Lock 20 (Limure)	109.8	20	117.0
Navigation re-enters river Oust	109.9	-	116.9
Bridge (Pont-d'Oust), quay, **Peillac** 2000m r/b	112.5	-	114.3
Lock 21 (Gueslin)	116.6	21	110.2
Bridge (Gueslin), quay l/b, **Saint-Martin** 800m l/b	117.5	-	109.3
Lock 22 (Rieux)	120.4	22	106.4
Saint-Congard bridge, quay, small village r/b	123.7	-	103.1
Lock 23 (Beaumont) in short lock-cut r/b	125.5	23	101.3
Lock 24 (Foveno) in short lock-cut r/b	129.6	24	97.2
Malestroit bridge (Pont Neuf), quay d/s r/b, village 300m	132.2	-	94.6

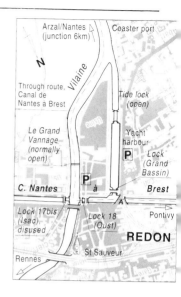

Lock 18, at Redon, giving access from the river Vilaine to the Canal de Nantes à Brest. *Hugh Potter*

Josselin and the imposing castle of the Rohan on the Canal de Nantes à Brest.
Hugh Porter

	km	lock	km
Bridge (Aristide-Briand) over entrance to lock-cut r/b	132.3	-	94.5
Lock 25 (Malestroit), bridge	132.6	25	94.2
Lock 26 (Lanée)	134.4	26	92.4
Lock 27 (Lanée), permanently open, bridge, navigation re-enters Oust	135.4	-	91.4
Railway bridge	137.6	-	89.2
Lock 28 (Ville-aux-Fruglins)	139.7	27	87.1
Roc-Saint-André bridge, mooring d/s r/b, village r/b	141.0	-	85.8
Railway bridge (Hungleux)	141.5	-	85.3
Lock 29 (**Montertelot**), bridge, quay u/s r/b, village l/b	143.7	28	83.1
Railway bridge (Deux-Rivières)	145.0	-	81.8
Lock 30 (Blon)	146.2	29	80.6
Bridge, quay upstream r/b	147.9	-	78.9
Lock 31 (**Guillac**), village 1000m l/b	149.0	30	77.8
Lock 32 (Carmenais)	152.1	31	74.7
Bridge (Saint-Gobrien)	153.7	-	73.1
Lock 33 (Clan)	154.1	32	72.7
Railway bridge (disused)	155.3	-	71.5
Lock 34 (Saint-Jouan), bridge	155.6	33	71.2
Lock 35 (Josselin), communal building for visitors	157.3	34	69.5
Josselin quay, moorings l/b under castle, Leray Loisirs hire base, village 300m l/b	157.4	-	69.4
Bridge (Sainte-Croix)	157.7	-	69.1
Lock 36 (Beaufort) in short lock-cut l/b	158.4	35	68.4

	km	lock	km
Bridge (N24)	159.7	-	67.1
Lock 37 (Caradec) in short lock-cut l/b, bridge	159.8	36	67.0
Lock 38 (Rouvray)	161.4	37	65.4
Lock 39 (Bocneuf)	163.1	38	63.7
Bridge (Bocneuf), D764	164.7	-	62.1
Lock 40 (Pommeleuc) in lock-cut r/b	165.6	39	61.2
Lock 41 (Tertraie), bridge	165.9	40	60.9
Lock 42 (Tertraie), permanently open, bridge, navigation re-enters Oust	167.2	-	59.6
Lock 43 (Cadoret) in short lock-cut r/b, bridge	169.8	41	57.0
Lock 44 (Lié) in lock-cut r/b	170.9	42	55.9
Bridge (Perrin)	172.2	-	54.6
Lock 45 (Griffet) in lock-cut l/b, bridge	172.4	43	54.4
Lock 46 (Grenouillère)	173.3	44	53.5
Navigation enters canal section l/b	174.1	-	52.7
Lock 47 (Trévérend), bridge	174.2	45	52.6
Lock 48 (Penhoët), bridge	175.4	46	51.4
Lock 49 (Lille), bridge	176.4	47	50.4
Lock 50 (Thimadeuc), bridge, Thimadeuc abbey 600m l/b	178.4	48	48.4
Navigation re-enters Oust, weir r/b	179.1	-	47.7
Lock 51 (Quengo)	180.5	49	46.3
Lock 52 (Rohan)	181.4	50	45.4
Rohan bridge (Pont Notre-Dame), boat harbour d/s r/b, Rohan Plaisance hire base, services, village r/b	181.5	-	45.3
Bridge (Pont d'Oust)	181.9	-	44.9
Lock 53 (Saint-Samson) in lock-cut r/b, bridge	183.6	51	43.2
Lock 54 (Guer), bridge	184.8	52	42.0
Navigation leaves Oust for last time, r/b	185.7	-	41.1
Lock 55 (Coëtprat), bridge	185.8	53	41.0
Lock 56 (Kermelin), bridge	186.8	54	40.0
Lock 57 (Sablière)	187.2	55	39.6
Lock 58 (Kériffe)	187.5	56	39.3
Lock 59 (Boju), bridge, quay, Gueltas 1200m r/b	187.8	57	39.0
Lock 60 (Parc-Coh)	188.0	58	38.8
Lock 61 (Goiffre)	188.2	59	38.6
Lock 62 (Goirball)	188.5	60	38.3
Lock 63 (Guernogas)	188.8	61	38.0
Lock 64 (Branguily)	189.0	62	37.8
Lock 65 (Neau-Blanche)	189.2	63	37.6
Lock 66 (Pont-Terre)	189.4	64	37.4
Lock 67 (Forêt), bridge	189.5	65	37.3
Lock 68 (Menn-Merle)	189.7	66	37.1
Lock 69 (Toulhouët)	189.9	67	36.9
Lock 70 (Ville-Perro)	190.1	68	36.7
Lock 71 (Gouvly)	190.2	69	36.6
Lock 72 (**Saint-Gonnery**), bridge, village 1500m l/b	190.4	70	36.4
Lock 73 (Kervezo)	190.6	71	36.2
Lock 74 (Douaren)	190.8	72	36.0
Lock 75 (Grand-Pré)	190.9	73	35.9
Lock 76 (Hilvern), bridge, **Saint-Gonnery** 1500m l/b	191.1	74	35.7
Lock 77 (Pépinière)	191.2	75	35.6
Lock 78 (Bel-Air), beginning of summit level, Hilvern feeder enters canal	191.4	76	35.4
Bridge (Brou)	194.9	-	31.9
Quay (Saint-Gérand)	195.6	-	31.2
Lock 79 (Kéroret), end of summit level, bridge, **Saint-Gérand** 700m l/b	196.3	77	30.5
Lock 80 (Er Houët)	196.4	78	30.4

	km	lock	km
Lock 81 (Kérivy)	196.5	79	30.3
Lock 82 (Parc er Lann)	196.7	80	30.1
Lock 83 (Kerihoué)	196.8	81	30.0
Lock 84 (Parc Lann Bihan)	196.9	82	29.9
Lock 85 (Lann Vras)	197.1	83	29.7
Lock 86 (Parc Buisson)	197.2	84	29.6
Lock 87 (Couëdic), bridge	197.3	85	29.5
Bridge (Kergouët)	198.2	-	28.6
Railway bridge	199.1	-	27.7
Bridge (Saint-Caradec)	199.4	-	27.4
Lock 88 (Joli-Cur)	199.7	86	27.1
Lock 89 (Parc-Lann-Hir)	199.8	87	27.0
Lock 90 (Parc-Lann-Ergo)	199.9	88	26.9
Lock 91 (Parc-Bihan)	200.0	89	26.8
Lock 92 (Kerponer)	200.1	90	26.7
Lock 93 (Restériard)	200.3	91	26.5
Lock 94 (Tri-parc-lann-favilette)	200.4	92	26.4
Lock 95 (Parc-bras)	200.6	93	26.2
Lock 96 (Ros), bridge	200.7	94	26.1
Lock 97 (Guerlaunay)	200.8	95	26.0
Lock 98 (Bohumet)	201.1	96	25.7
Lock 99 (Kervégan), bridge	201.3	97	25.5
Lock 100 (Tren-deur-ros)	202.0	98	24.8
Lock 101 (Kerveno)	202.3	99	24.5
Lock 102 (Parc-Lann-hoarem)	202.8	100	24.0
Lock 103 (Haie), bridge	203.5	101	23.3
Lock 104 (Villeneuve)	204.0	102	22.8
Lock 105 (Kerdudaval)	204.5	103	22.3
Lock 106 (Kervert)	205.1	104	21.7
Lock 107 (Ponteau), bridge	205.5	105	21.3
Pontivy, *junction with Canal du Blavet*, quays, town centre 400m	205.9	-	20.9

(Note: the canal beyond Pontivy to the limit of navigation at Guerlédan is not at present navigable, but the distance table is continued in view of its projected restoration)

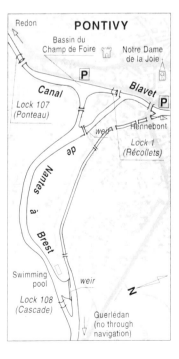

	km	lock	km
Lock 108 (Cascade)	207.1	106	19.7
Lock 109 (Guernal)	209.4	107	17.4
Lock 110 (Porzo)	212.2	108	14.6
Bridge (Lenvos), **Neuillac** 1500m l/b	213.6	-	13.2
Lock 111 (Trescleff)	214.5	109	12.3
Lock 112 (Auquinian)	216.6	110	10.2
Lock 113 (Stumo), bridge	218.7	111	8.1
Lock 114 (Boloré), bridge	220.4	112	6.4
Lock 115 (Saint-Samson)	222.0	113	4.8
Lock 116 (Poulhibet), bridge	222.4	114	4.4
Lock 117 (Kergoric), bridge	223.9	115	2.9
Lock 118 (Quénécan), bridge, quay, Saint-Aignan 1000m r/b, Mur-de-Bretagne 3000m l/b	224.3	116	2.5
Lock 119 (Guerlédan), bridge	226.1	117	0.7
Guerlédan dam, navigation interrupted	226.8	-	0.0

River Erdre branch

	km	lock	km
Junction with Canal de Nantes à Brest downstream of lock 2 (Quiheix)	0.0	-	6.0
Quay (Port Mulan) r/b	5.0	-	1.0
Nort-sur-Erdre bridge, head of navigation, quay d/s r/b, Air et Mutualité hire base, village r/b	6.0	-	0.0

Western section, Goariva to Châteaulin

	km	*lock*	*km*
Goariva bridge (D83), limit of departments of Finistère and Côtes d'Armor and limit of restored section	279.1	-	81.3
Lock 192 (Goariva)	279.4	1	81.0
Lock 193 (Kervoulédic)	280.1	2	80.3
Lock 194 (Prat-ar-Born)	280.5	3	79.9
Bridge	280.8	-	79.6
Lock 195 (Pellerm)	281.0	4	79.4
Lock 196 (Kergoutois)	281.7	5	78.7
Lock 197 (Pont d'Auvlas)	282.4	6	78.0
Bridge, **Carhaix-Plouguer** 3000m r/b	282.6	-	77.8
Lock 198 (Rochaër)	283.2	7	77.2
Lock 199 (Lille)	283.8	8	76.6
Bridge	284.2	-	76.2
Lock 200 (Pont-ar-Brost)	284.3	9	76.1
Former railway bridge	284.8	-	65.7
Lock 201 (Kergaden)	284.9	10	75.5
Lock 202 (Kerdugnès)	285.8	11	74.6
Port-de-Carhaix bridge (D769), quay u/s l/b, beginning of effective navigation	286.3	-	74.1
Bridge	286.4	-	74.0
Lock 203 (Kergoat)	286.7	12	73.7
Navigation enters canalised river Hyère	287.3	-	73.1
Lock 204 (Coz-Castel), bridge (used by footpath GR 37)	287.6	13	72.8
Lock 205 (Kergoff)	289.1	14	71.3
Lock 206 (Stervallen)	291.2	15	69.2
Bridge, **Cléden-Poher** 2300m r/b	292.4	-	68.0
Lock 207 (Le Ster)	293.4	16	67.0
Lock 208 (Lesnévez)	295.7	17	64.7
Lock 209 (Pont-Triffen), bridge (D17), **Landeleau** 2500m r/b	297.2	18	63.2
Confluence with river Aulne (canalised from this point)	297.3	-	63.1
Lock 210 (Pénity)	299.1	19	61.3
Lock 211 (Roz-ar-Gaouen)	301.7	20	58.7
Lock 212 (Méros)	303.3	21	57.1
Lock 213 (Rosily)	305.3	22	55.1
Lock 214 (Lanmeur)	307.3	23	53.1
Bridge (D117)	307.6	-	52.8
Lock 215 (Goaker)	309.9	24	50.5
Bridge, **Saint-Goazec** 1000m l/b	310.2	-	50.2
Lock 216 (Moustoir)	311.8	25	48.6
Lock 217 (Boudrac'h)	314.5	26	45.9
Lock 218 (Bizernic)	316.3	27	44.1
Châteauneuf-du-Faou bridge (Pont du Roy), quay u/s r/b	316.8	-	43.6
Boat harbour l/b, Argoat Plaisance hire base	316.9	-	43.5
Lock 219 (Châteauneuf)	318.0	28	42.4
Lock 220 (Kerboaret)	319.9	29	40.5
Lock 221 (Kersalig)	321.8	30	38.6
Bridge (Pont-Pol-ty-Glas), D72	322.4	-	38.0
Lock 222 (Prat-Pourrig)	325.6	31	34.8
Lock 223 (Ménez)	328.2	32	32.2
Pont-ar-c'hlan quay r/b	329.7	-	30.7
Lock 224 (Rosvéguen)	330.9	33	29.5
Bridge (D41)	331.9	-	28.5
Lock 225 (Buzit)	334.2	34	26.2
Lock 226 (Saint-Algon)	336.3	35	24.1
Pont-Coblant bridge, quay u/s l/b, Finistère Canal hire base, village l/b	336.8	-	23.6
Lock 227 (Stéréon)	338.1	36	22.3
Lock 228 (Coat-Pont)	340.9	37	19.5

	km	*lock*	*km*
Lock 229 (Lothey)	343.4	38	17.0
Lock 230 (Trésiguidy)	345.7	39	14.7
Lock 231 (Le Guillec)	348.7	40	11.7
Lock 232 (Aulne)	350.6	41	9.8
Main road bridge (N165)	351.8	-	8.6
Lock 233 (Prat-Hir)	353.4	42	7.0
Lock 234 (Toularodo)	356.2	43	4.2
Lock 235 (Coatigrac'h)	357.8	44	2.6
Châteaulin bridge, quay d/s r/b, Aulne Loisirs hire base	360.0	-	0.4
Lock 236 (Châteaulin), bridge	360.4	45	0.0

Tidal river Aulne and Brest roadstead, Châteaulin to Brest			
Châteaulin	0	-	51
Port-Launay r/b	2	-	49
Guily-Glaz tide lock	4	1	47
Térénez suspension bridge	23	-	28
Landévennec l/b (outfall into Brest roadstead)	29	-	22
Brest	51	-	0

Canal du Nivernais

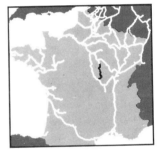

This canal suffered from railway competition shortly after its opening in 1841, and was never a commercial success, but has firmly established its vocation as a cruising waterway over the last 15 years. It extends from the Loire at Saint-Léger-des-Vignes (near Decize) to the canalised river Yonne at Auxerre, a distance of 174km. A short distance up the Loire from Saint-Léger-des-Vignes is the entrance to the Decize branch of the Canal latéral à la Loire, while the Yonne gives access to the Canal de Bourgogne. The Nivernais thus forms a cross link between the Bourbonnais and Bourgogne routes from Paris to Lyon.

The 58km central section of the canal from Cercy-la-Tour (km 15) to Sardy (km 73) was built with 'sub-standard' locks 30m long, thus precluding its use as a through route by 38.50m barges. This was the main reason for its commercial decline and consequent lack of maintenance, and during the 1960s its condition deteriorated rapidly. Thanks largely to the interest aroused by the Saint Line hire base, established on the canal's summit level in 1964, closure was avoided, the central section being conceded by the State to the department of Nièvre in 1972. A 10-year programme of rehabilitation works was started in 1974, financed by the department council with State and regional contributions. At the same time facilities for pleasure cruising are being set up throughout the length of the canal. Hire bases have mushroomed, and offer well over 100 boats for cruising on the canal, which is also regularly navigated by a number of hotel barges.

The canal incorporates numerous river sections or râcles, especially in the descent down the Yonne valley. In these reaches the channel is maintained over a width of only 20m from the bank on the towpath side, and care should be taken to keep within this limit.

The 4.5km summit level, at an altitude of 262m, connects with the Etang de Baye, an expansive reservoir which becomes a hive of dinghy sailing and other recreational activity during the summer. The summit level includes three tunnels, La Collancelle (758m), Mouas (268m) and Les Breuilles

(212m), separated by deep cuttings. The minimum headroom is 3.75m and the minimum width 5.60m. One-way traffic is enforced and controlled by lights.

At Basseville (km 118.5) the canal crosses the Yonne on the level and at right angles. During floods, a cable and winch may be used to assist in the crossing.

There is one branch, extending 3.9km from the râcle du Maunoir (km 154) to the town of Vermenton, on the river Cure.

The Nivernais is an ideal cruising waterway, offering a wide variety of landscapes and numerous places of interest to visit. The difference in character between the Loire and Yonne sides of the watershed is particularly striking. From the Loire to the summit, navigation is almost entirely in man-made cut, following the valley of the river Aron, with broad views across rich pasture-land; the Yonne valley is more spectacular, being compact and wooded, and navigation alternates between canal and river sections.

Locks There are 112 locks, of which 4 are stop locks. From the summit level to the Loire there are 32 locks and 3 stop locks, While on the Yonne side of the summit there are 76 locks and one stop lock (in addition there are five sets of flood gates numbered as locks). There are several double staircase locks and one triple staircase. There were originally 114 locks, but stop lock 47b and lock 48 at Clamecy have been closed, and navigation here follows the river Yonne instead of the former lock-cut. From Auxerre to Sardy-lès-Epiry and from Cercy-la-Tour to Saint-Léger-des-Vignes (as well as on the Vermenton branch), the lock dimensions are 38.50 by 5.30m. The locks on the central section have reduced dimensions of 30.15 by 5.10m.

Depth For the first 3km from Saint-Léger and from Clamecy down to Auxerre, the maximum permissible draught is 1.70m. In between, the canal is open to vessels with a maximum draught of 1.20m only. (The greater draught of 1.70m is also permissible on the Vermenton branch).

Bridges From Saint-Léger to La Copine basin (km 3) the minimum headroom is 3.70m. Onwards, the headroom under the fixed bridges at normal water level is 2.71m as far as Sardy. From Sardy to Auxerre, the headroom is 3.10m, reduced to 2.97m under the bridge at Picampoix (lock 21) and to about 3.00m under the bridge at Mailly-la-Ville (km 146). The fixed bridges on the Vermenton branch leave a minimum headroom of 3.35m.

Towpath There is a good towpath throughout the length of the canal.
Traffic Occasionally a barge ventures up the canal from Auxerre to Chatel-Censoir or Coulanges to load grain, but the Nivernais is now essentially a cruising waterway. Pleasure traffic increased tenfold over the period 1972-1982, to almost 2000 boats per year.

Authority
Service de la Navigation de Nevers.
Subdivision: 2 rue au Loup, 58800 Corbigny, ☎ 86 20 13 23.

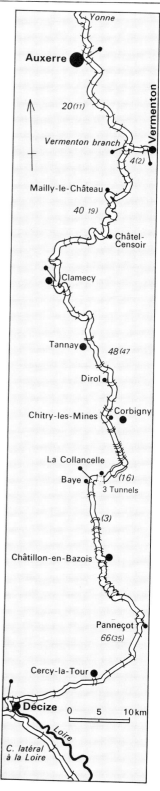

Distance table

	km	lock	km
Saint-Léger-des-Vignes, *junction with the Loire and the Canal latéral à la Loire*, quay r/b	0.0	-	174.1
Lock 35 (Loire)	0.9	1	173.2
Bridge (Saint-Thibault), **Decize** 1000m, quays above and below, r/b	1.4	-	172.7
Lock 34 (Vauzelles), bridge	1.9	2	172.2
Bridge (Copine)	2.9	-	171.2
Railway bridge	3.0	-	171.1
La Copine basin, Champvert Plaisance hire base, r/b	3.1	-	171.0
Bridge (du Port)	3.7	-	170.4
Champvert, quay r/b	4.7	-	169.4
Lock 33 (Champvert), bridge	4.9	3	169.2
Footbridge	6.5	-	167.6
Bridge (Marcou)	7.5	-	166.6
Lock 32 (Roche), Andarge aqueduct	8.2	4	165.9
Bridge (Roche)	8.7	-	165.4
Saint-Gervais bridge and basin, l/b, **Verneuil** 2000m	9.9	-	164.2
Bridge (Vernizy)	12.6	-	161.5
Bridge (Coulangette)	13.7	-	160.4
Stop lock 31 (Cercy-la-Tour), bridge, navigation enters river Aran	15.4	5	158.7
Cercy-la-Tour quay r/b, Liberty Line hire base, slipway, camp-site on l/b of river Aran	15.6	-	158.5
Lock 30 (Cercy-la-Tour), bridge, basin upstream r/b	15.9	6	158.2
Bridge (Martigny)	17.1	-	157.0
Lock 29 (Chaumigny), bridge	18.6	7	155.5
Bridge (Saint-Gratien)	20.1	-	154.0
Lift bridge (Tremblay)	20.9	-	153.2
Isenay quay, l/b	21.5	-	152.6
Lock 28 (Isenay), bridge	21.6	8	152.5
Former lift bridge	22.6	-	151.5
Moulin d'Isenay basin, l/b, **Vandenesse** (village and castle) 3000m	23.2	-	150.9
Lock 27 (Moulin d'Isenay), bridge	23.6	9	150.5
Bridge (Beaudin)	24.6	-	149.5
Bridge (Hâtes de Scia), basin l/b	26.0	-	148.1
Lock 26 (Sauzay), bridge	27.7	10	146.4
Panneçot, mooring r/b d/s of lock, village over bridge	29.5	-	144.6
Stop lock 25 (Panneçot), bridge, navigation enters river Aron	29.6	11	144.5
Panneçot boat harbour, l/b	29.7	-	144.4
Lock 24 (Anizy), navigation leaves river	31.0	12	143.1
Bridge (Anizy)	31.2	-	142.9
Lock 23 (Saigne), bridge	32.1	13	142.0
Bridge (Magny), quay r/b	33.6	-	140.5
Bridge (Prairie)	35.0	-	139.1
Lock 22 (Bernay), bridge	36.4	14	137.7
Lock 21 (Fleury), Flot'home hire base, bridge, **Brienne** 1000m	38.1	15	136.0
Lock 20 (Brienne)	38.8	16	135.3
Lock 19 (Villard), bridge	40.8	17	133.3
Bridge (Romenay)	41.3	-	132.8
Bridge (Cray), **Biches** 500m	41.9	-	132.2
Lock 18 (Meulot), bridge	42.7	18	131.4
Lock 17 (Equilly)	45.9	19	128.2
Bridge (Equilly)	46.3	-	127.8
Bridge (Pont), follow channel on outside of bend, **Alluy** 1500m	47.5	-	126.6
Stop lock 16 (Coeuillon), bridge, navigation enters river Aron, keep to towpath side, r/b	49.1	20	125.0

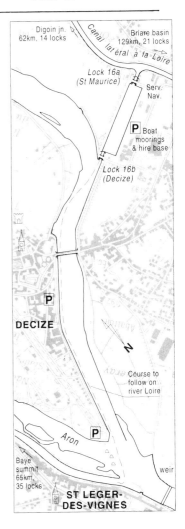

	km	*lock*	*km*
Lock 15 (Châtillon-en-Bazois), bridge, navigation leaves river	50.6	21	123.5
Lock 14 (Châtillon-en-Bazois)	51.0	22	123.1
Châtillon-en-Bazois bridge, moorings upstream r/b, village l/b, castle r/b	51.2	-	122.9
Bridge (Mingot)	53.8	-	120.3
Lock 13 (Mingot), bridge, Aron aqueduct upstream	53.9	23	120.2
Lock 12 (Orgue), bridge	54.6	24	119.5
Lock 11 (Orgue)	56.1	25	118.0
Double staircase lock 10/9 (Mont-et-Marré), bridge	57.1	27	117.0
Double staircase lock 8/7 (Chavance)	59.4	29	115.7
Basin (Chavance)	59.5	-	115.6
Triple staircase lock 6/5/4 (Chavance), bridge	59.7	32	115.4
Bridge (Mougny)	61.8	-	113.3
Lock 3 (Bazolles), bridge, moorings u/s and d/s r/b, **Bazolles** 500m	63.6	33	110.5
Lock 2 (Bazolles)	63.8	34	110.3
Lock 1 (Baye), bridge, beginning of summit level, **Baye** 200m, restaurant	66.0	35	108.1
Quay (Poujats), Amicatour hire base	66.5	-	107.6
Bridge (Poujats), canal narrows, one-way traffic	66.6	-	107.5
Tunnel (Collancelle)	67.2	-	106.1
Tunnel (Mouas)	68.2	-	105.6
Tunnel (Breuilles)	68.6	-	105.3
Bridge (Breuilles)	69.3	-	104.8
Bridge (Port-Brûlé)	70.2	-	103.9
Lock 1 (Port-Brûlé), end of summit level	70.4	36	103.7
Lock 2 (Crain)	70.6	37	103.5
Lock 3 (Patureau)	70.7	38	103.4
Lock 4 (Roche)	70.8	39	103.3
Lock 5 (Demain)	70.9	40	103.2
Lock 6 (Planche de Belin), bridge	71.1	41	103.0
Lock 7 (Gros Bouillon)	71.3	42	102.8
Lock 8 (Mondain)	71.5	43	102.6
Lock 9 (Fussy), moorings downstream r/b	71.7	44	102.4
Lock 10 (Patureau-Volain)	71.9	45	102.2
Lock 11 (Bellevue)	72.2	46	101.9
Lock 12 (Pré Doyen)	72.6	47	101.5
Lock 13 (Doyen)	72.7	48	101.4
Lock 14 (Pré Ardent)	73.0	49	101.1
Lock 15 (Champ Cadoux), last of the 30m locks	73.4	50	100.7
Lock 16 (Sardy), bridge, spring water	73.6	51	100.5
Sardy-les Epiry, former basin l/b, village 500m over bridge	73.8	-	100.3
Lock 17 (Champ du Chêne)	74.4	52	99.7
Lock 18 (Creuzet), bridge	74.8	53	99.3
Lock 19 (Petite Corvée)	75.4	54	98.7
Lock 20 (Bois des Taureaux)	76.0	55	98.1
Picampoix quarries, former loading quay r/b	76.2	-	97.9
Lock 21 (Picampoix), bridge (reduced headroom 2.97m) **Marcilly** 2000m	76.3	56	97.8
Lock 22 (Surpaillis)	76.6	57	97.5
Lock 23 (Pré Colas), quay downstream l/b	77.1	58	97.0
Lock 24 (Yonne), bridge, wide basin downstream	77.6	59	96.5
Beginning of La Chaise cutting, one-way traffic, Yonne feeder with flood gates, r/b	78.2	-	95.9
High bridge (Chaise)	78.6	-	95.5
Bridge (Chaise)	78.8	-	95.3
Bridge (Eugny), D958, **Corbigny** 2500m	79.3	-	94.8

The Canal du Nivernais near
the famous Saussois rocks at
Merry-sur-Yonne.
Hugh Potter

	km	lock	km
End of cutting	79.5	-	94.6
Double staircase lock 25/26 (Eugny)	79.8	61	94.3
Lock 27 (Marcy), bridge	80.2	62	93.9
Marcy basin	80.7	-	93.4
Lock 28 (Chaumot)	81.3	63	92.8
Chitry-les-Mines basin, r/b, village 300m, **Corbigny** 3000m	81.9	-	92.2
Bridge (Chitry), D977 bis	82.0	-	92.1
Chaumot basin, l/b, Marine-Diesel boat hire, repairs, long-term moorings, slipway	82.0	-	92.1
Lift bridge (Germehay)	82.5	-	91.6
Lock 29 (Chitry)	83.2	64	90.9
Lock 30 (Marigny), bridge	84.2	65	89.9
Marigny, l/b	84.4	-	89.7
Lock 31 (Gravier), bridge	84.6	66	89.5
Quay, r/b	84.9	-	89.2
Turning basin	85.5	-	88.6
Lock 32 (Mortes)	85.9	67	88.2
Railway bridge (Mortes)	86.1	-	88.0
Lift bridge (Chazel)	86.3	-	87.8
Canal narrows for 100m, no passing	88.0	-	86.1
Lock 33 (Mont), bridge	88.5	68	85.6
Lock 34 (Dirol), bridge	89.0	69	85.1
Lift bridge (Thoury)	89.4	-	84.7
Lift bridge (Marais)	89.6	-	84.5
Dirol quay, l/b	89.6	-	84.5

	km	lock	km
Canal narrows, one-way traffic for 2000m (with passing places)	90.0	-	84.1
Monceaux-le-Comte bridge, quay upstream r/b, village 1000m	90.7	-	83.4
End of one-way section	92.0	-	82.1
Lock 35 (Châtillon)	92.2	70	81.9
Lock 36 (Laporte), bridge, quay downstream l/b	93.2	71	80.9
Lock 37 (Moulin Brûlé)	93.5	72	80.6
Lift bridge (Saint-Didier)	94.5	-	79.6
Lift bridge (Curiot)	95.5	-	78.6
Cuzy bridge, quay upstream l/b, restaurant, village 400m	95.8	-	78.3
Bridge (Gravelot), **Tannay** 2000m (all shops, wine cellar)	96.8	-	77.3
Double staircase lock 38/39 (Tannay), bridge, **Tannay** 2000m	98.1	74	76.0
Lift bridge (Ane)	99.2	-	74.9
Asnois bridge, village 200m	100.2	-	73.9
Lock 40 (Brèves)	102.3	75	71.8
Brèves bridge, village 300m, turning basin	102.5	-	71.6
Lock 41 (Esselier)	102.8	76	71.3
Canal narrows, one-way traffic for 200m	103.7	-	70.4
Lock 42 (Villiers)	104.6	77	69.5
Villiers-sur-Yonne bridge, village l/b	104.8	-	69.3
Swinging footbridge (Villiers)	105.7	-	68.4
Lock 43 (Cuncy), bridge	106.5	78	67.6
Bridge (Cuncy)	107.2	-	66.9
Lock 44 (Chantenot), bridge	109.3	79	64.8
Chevroches bridge, small village, quay downstream l/b	110.1	-	64.0
Lock 45 (Armes)	110.6	80	63.5
Lock 46 (Maladrerie), bridge	111.7	81	62.4
Flood gate r/b, connection with Yonne (not navigable)	112.0	-	62.1
Bridge (Picot)	112.9	-	61.2
Clamecy, moorings upstream of lock, Croisières du Saussois hire base, toilets and showers, small town l/b	113.6	-	60.5
Lock 47 (Clamecy), swing bridge upstream, navigation enters Yonne	113.7	82	60.4
Bridge (Bethléem), moorings along quay l/b for Clamecy	113.9	-	60.2
Entrance to former lock-cut, l/b (lock 47b Clamecy-Saint-Roch), now disused, navigation follows Yonne	114.5	-	59.6
Island, pass on l/b side	115.9	-	58.2
Flood gates (Forêt) l/b, navigation re-enters canal (boats heading upstream, turn left through these gates)	116.0	-	58.1
Bridge (Presles)	116.6	-	57.5
Lock 49 (Garenne)	117.1	83	57.0
Bridge (Envilliers)	117.7	-	56.4
Lock 50 (Basseville), navigation crosses Yonne on the level, towpath bridge r/b, weir l/b	118.5	84	55.6
Stop lock 51 (Basseville)	118.7	85	55.4
Bridge (Basseville)	119.3	-	54.8
Canal narrows, one-way traffic (with one passing place)	120.0	-	54.1
End of narrow section	120.7	-	53.4
Pousseaux bridge, quay upstream r/b, village 200m, **Surgy** 1000m over bridge	121.1	-	53.0
Lift bridge (Pousseaux)	121.5	-	52.6
Coulanges-sur-Yonne, lock 52, bridge, quay u/s r/b, Liberty Line relay base, village 1000m over bridge	122.8	86	51.3
Lock 53 (Crain), canal joins Yonne for 34m	123.7	87	50.4
Flood gate 53a (Bèze), bridge	124.1	-	50.0
Lock 54 (Bèze), bridge	125.1	88	49.0
Lucy-sur-Yonne, bridge, village r/b	126.1	-	48.0
Lock 55 (Lucy-sur-Yonne)	127.1	89	47.0

	km	lock	km
Bridge (Gué Saint-Martin)	127.9	-	46.2
Railway bridge (La Place)	128.7	-	45.4
Lock 56 (La Place), bridge	130.2	90	43.9
Châtel-Censoir basin l/b, moorings, village over bridge	132.5	-	41.6
Lock 57 (Châtel-Censoir), bridge	132.6	91	41.5
Bridge (Gade)	133.1	-	41.0
Lock 58 (Magny), bridge	134.5	92	39.6
Canal narrows for 235m	135.0	-	39.1
Railway bridge (Terres Rouges)	135.9	-	38.2
Bridge (Terres Rouges)	136.1	-	38.0
Lock 59 (Réchimet), navigation enters Yonne (râcle du Saussois), keep close to towpath on outside of bend	136.5	93	37.6
Entrance to lock-cut, one-way traffic only	137.7	-	36.4
Flood gate 59a (Saussois), bridge, quay and Au Fil de l'Eau hire base l/b, **Merry-sur-Yonne** 500m	138.0	-	36.1
Bridge (Graves)	139.0	-	35.1
Lock 60 (Ravereau), navigation enters Yonne (râcle de Mailly-le-Château)	139.4	94	34.7
Flood gate 61 (Mailly-le-Château)	140.8	-	33.3
Railway bridge	140.9	-	33.2
Canal narrows for 350m	141.2	-	32.9
Mailly-le-Château bridge, quay downstream l/b, village 1000m up hill	141.7	-	32.4
Railway bridge (Parc)	142.4	-	31.7
Lock 62 (Parc), navigation joins Yonne for 600m (râcle du Bouchet)	142.8	95	31.3
Bridge (Mailly-la-Ville)	145.2	-	28.9
Lock 63 (Mailly-la-Ville), navigation enters Yonne (râcle de Mailly-la-Ville)	145.4	96	28.7
Mailly-la-Ville r/b, all shops	145.7	-	28.4
Flood gate 64 (Mailly-la-Ville), bridge (take care when Yonne water level high, headroom less than 3m)	146.0	-	28.1
Quay l/b	146.1	-	28.0
Lock 65 (Sery), bridge	147.5	97	26.6
Sery bridge, small village r/b	147.6	-	26.5
Lock 66 (Saint-Maur), navigation joins Yonne for 640m (râcle des Dames)	148.6	98	25.5
Railway bridge (Dames)	149.9	-	24.2
Lock 67 (Dames), lift bridge downstream, navigation enters Yonne (râcle de Prégilbert)	150.1	99	24.0
Prégilbert bridge, village r/b	151.0	-	23.1
Flood gate 68 (Prégilbert)	151.1	-	23.0
Bridge (Parc de Sainte-Pallaye)	151.5	-	22.6
Sainte-Pallaye bridge (Romains), village r/b	151.9	-	22.2
Lock 69 (Sainte-Pallaye)	152.4	100	21.7
Bridge (Croix Minet), quay d/s l/b, **Bazarnes** 1000m	153.0	-	21.1
Lock 70 (Saint-Aignan), navigation enters Yonne (râcle du Maunoir)	153.7	101	20.4
Railway bridge (Maunoir)	154.0	-	20.1
Junction with Vermenton branch, r/b	154.1	-	20.0
Lock 71 (Maunoir)	154.4	102	19.7
Cravant bridge, quay upstream r/b, service station, village 500m	155.9	-	19.2
Former branch with disused lock, r/b	156.4	-	18.7
Bridge (Colombier)	156.6	-	18.5
Lock 72 (Rivottes), bridge	158.2	103	15.9

	km	lock	km
Lock 73 (Vincelles), bridge, navigation joins Yonne (râcle de Vincelles)	159.5	104	14.6
Vincelles quay l/b, Vincelles Nautique hire base, village l/b	160.1	-	14.0
Vincelottes bridge, village and restaurant 400m	160.6	-	13.5
Lock 74 (Vincelottes), navigation enters Yonne (râcle de Bailly)	161.2	105	12.9
Lock 75 (Bailly) in short lock-cut, followed by râcle de Bélombre	163.4	106	11.7
Railway bridge (Bazine)	163.6	-	11.5
Lock 76 (Bélombre), bridge, **Champs-sur-Yonne** 300m	165.0	107	9.1
Quay (Cour Barrée), l/b	165.3	-	8.8
Lock 77 (Toussac), navigation enters râcle de Vaux	166.2	108	7.9
Vaux bridge, village and restaurant l/b	167.9	-	6.2
Lock 78 (Vaux) in short lock-cut, followed by râcle d'Augy	168.6	109	5.5
Lock 79 (Augy) in short lock-cut, followed by râcle de Preuilly	170.6	110	3.5
Lock 80 (Preuilly) in short lock-cut, followed by râcle du Batardeau	172.5	111	1.6
Railway bridge (Batardeau)	173.6	-	0.5
Lock 81 (Batardeau) in short lock-cut, navigation enters Yonne	173.8	112	0.3
Auxerre bridge (Paul-Bert), large town with all shops and services, *junction with canalised river Yonne*	174.1	-	0.0

Vermenton branch

	km	lock	km
Junction with main canal (râcle du Maunoir, km 154.1)	0.0	-	3.9
Lock (Noue), bridge	0.7	1	3.2
Bridge (Moulin Jacquot)	2.2	-	1.7
Accolay bridge, quay upstream l/b, village l/b	2.5	-	1.4
Lock (Accolay), bridge	3.0	2	0.9
Flood gate (Vermenton), bridge	3.8	-	0.1
Vermenton, quays on river Cure, Burgundy Cruisers hire base	3.9	-	0.0

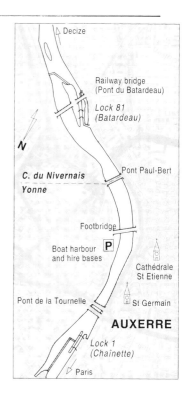

Canal du Nord

Excavation for this canal was started in 1908, when the parallel Canal de Saint-Quentin had already reached saturation, despite its paired locks throughout. By 1914 when war was declared three quarters of the earthworks as well as a number of the locks and bridges had been completed. Following the wartime destruction, several attempts were made to restart the project, but little was achieved in the inter-war period. The rapid economic growth experienced by France in the 1950s saw a marked increase in bulk transport requirements between the Seine basin and the north, and it again became urgent to complete the project. The works were carried out in the early 1960s at an estimated cost of 210 million francs, and the canal opened to navigation in 1966.

The canal extends over a distance of 95km from Arleux, near Douai on the Canal de la Sensée (now the Dunkerque-Escaut waterway) to the junction with the Canal latéral à l'Oise at Pont-l'Evêque. The canal is divided into three sections:

– section 1 extends from Arleux on the Canal de la Sensée to Péronne on the Canal de la Somme (km 45),
– section 2 consists of a borrowed length of the Canal de la Somme from Péronne to a junction near Rouy-le-Petit (km 65),
– section 3 extends from the Canal de la Somme to Pont-l'Evêque on the Canal latéral à l'Oise (km 95).

The first and third sections cross low watersheds, and the respective summit levels incorporate tunnels. The Grand Souterrain de Ruyaulcourt, on the summit level of the first section (km 25-29) has a total length of 4350m. The tunnel is divided into three portions. The first 1600m from each portal is of single barge width (6.30m), while the 1150m middle portion is of double width (12.30m). Thus northbound and southbound barges enter simultaneously at each end, pass each other in the middle portion and exit simultaneously from each end. There is a remote monitoring and traffic control system with red and green lights, ensuring the minimum hindrance to barges on this busy route. The Souterrain de la Panneterie, on the summit level of the third section, is 1100m in length. Its dimensions provide for one-way working only, with entrance controlled by lights as at Ruyaulcourt.

Locks There are 12 locks in the first section (7 falling towards the Sensée and 5 towards the Somme), 2 in the second section and 5 in the third section (one falling towards the Somme and 4 falling towards the Oise). All have the same dimensions, 91.60 by 6.00m, accommodating push-tows made up of two 38.50m barges, as well as a new class of barge loading 700 tonnes, designed specifically to operate on the route between the Seine basin and northern France.

Depth The maximum authorised draught is 2.40m.

Bridges All the bridges leave a minimum headroom of 3.98m above the highest navigable water level (4.28m above normal level).

Authority
Direction Régionale de la Navigation, Lille. Subdivision:
– Place Marcellin-Berthelot, BP371, 59407 Cambrai ☎ 27 81 32 75 (km 0-30).
– Service de la Navigation de la Seine, Arrondissement Picardie. Subdivision:
– 19 route de Paris, BP92, 80200 Péronne, ☎ 22 84 01 14 (km 30-95).

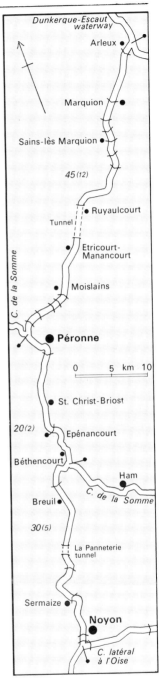

Distance table

	km	lock	km
Junction with Dunkerque-Escaut waterway (Canal de la Sensée), km 15, beginning of 1st section, boat moorings	0.0	-	95.0
Arleux bridge, village 1000m l/b	0.6	-	94.4
Private basin (Malderez) l/b (length 560m)	0.9	-	94.1
Lock 1 (Palluel)	1.4	1	93.6
Palluel bridge (D21), village 400m l/b	1.8	-	93.2
Bridge (Oisy-le-Verger)	3.5	-	91.5
Sauchy-Cauchy bridge, village r/b	5.1	-	89.9
Motorway bridge (A26)	6.6	-	88.4
Turning basin	7.0	-	88.0
Marquion bridge (D939), quay and boat moorings d/s r/b, village 500m r/b	7.7	-	87.3
Lock 2 (Marquion)	8.0	2	87.0
Sains-lès-Marquion bridge, small village 300m r/b	10.0	-	85.0
Lock 3 (Sains-lès-Marquion)	10.7	3	84.3

	km	lock	km
Inchy-en-Artois bridge, quay u/s l/b, village 800m l/b	11.2	-	83.8
Bridge	12.0	-	83.0
Lock 4 (Sains-lès-Marquion)	12.3	4	82.7
Moeuvres bridge, village 500m l/b	13.4	-	81.6
Lock 5 (Moeuvres)	14.0	5	81.0
Bridge	14.3	-	80.7
Bridge (N30)	15.3	-	79.7
Lock 6 (Graincourt-lès-Havrincourt)	15.8	6	79.2
Bridge	16.5	-	78.5
Lock 7 (Graincourt-lès-Havrincourt), beginning of summit level	17.5	7	77.5
Bridge	17.9	-	77.1
Havrincourt bridge (D5), village 1200m r/b	19.8	-	75.2
Turning basin	21.3	-	73.7
Bridge	21.6	-	73.4
Hermies bridge, private quay u/s l/b, village 1200m l/b	22.7	-	72.3
Bridge	23.6	-	71.4
Bridge	24.5	-	70.5
Ruyaulcourt tunnel control post, l/b	25.1	-	69.9
Ruyaulcourt tunnel, northern entrance	25.2	-	69.8
Ventilation shaft	27.4	-	67.6
Ruyaulcourt tunnel, southern entrance	29.6	-	65.4
Bridge (D58)	30.4	-	64.6
Etricourt-Manancourt bridge, village 200m r/b	31.0	-	64.0
Bridge	31.8	-	63.2
Bridge (D72)	32.7	-	62.3
Turning basin	34.2	-	60.8
Bridge	35.5	-	59.5
Bridge	36.8	-	58.2
Moislains bridge (D184), quay d/s l/b, village 400m r/b	37.2	-	57.8
Lock 8 (Moislains), end of summit level	37.6	8	57.4
Turning basin	38.1	-	56.9
Bridge (D43)	38.4	-	56.6
Lock 9 (Moislains)	38.7	9	56.3
Lock 10 (Allaines)	39.7	10	55.3
Allaines bridge, small village 300m l/b	40.0	-	55.0
Bridge, private quay d/s r/b	40.7	-	54.3
Bridge (D944)	41.7	-	53.3
Lock 11 (Feuillaucourt)	42.0	11	53.0
Bridge (D938), quay d/s r/b	43.5	-	51.5
Lock 12 (Cléry-sur-Somme)	43.8	12	51.2
Junction with Canal de la Somme, beginning of 2nd section (common to Canal de la Somme)	45.4	-	49.6
Bridge (N17), quays d/s, **Péronne** 1300m r/b	48.2	-	46.8
Railway bridge	48.6	-	46.4
Lock 13 (Péronne)	49.5	13	45.5
Bridge (Pont-lès-Brie), N336	53.2	-	41.8
Saint-Christ-Briost bridge, quay d/s r/b, village 300m	55.9	-	39.1
Epenancourt l/b	58.9	-	36.1
Lock 14 (Epenancourt)	59.7	14	35.3
Pargny bridge, village l/b	60.9	-	34.1
Béthencourt-sur-Somme bridge, quay d/s r/b	63.7	-	31.3
Junction with Canal de la Somme, end of section common to Canal de la Somme, beginning of third section	65.3	-	29.7
Rouy-le-Petit bridge, small village 400m r/b	67.8	-	27.2
Railway bridge, quay d/s l/b	68.8	-	26.2
Nesle bridge (D930), quays u/s, village 2000m l/b	68.9	-	26.1
Lock 15 (Languevoisin), beginning of summit level	69.6	15	25.4

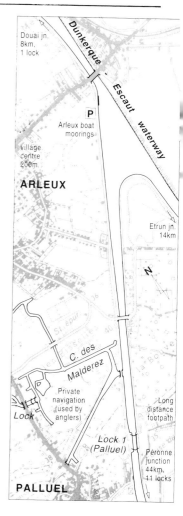

	km	lock	km
Bridge (D89), quay u/s l/b	69.9	–	25.1
Breuil bridge, small village l/b	71.5	–	23.5
Buverchy bridge, small village r/b	72.7	–	22.3
Bridge (D186), quay u/s r/b, Ercheu 2500m l/b	74.6	–	20.4
Libermont bridge, small village 800m r/b	77.1	–	17.9
Tunnel (souterrain de la Panneterie), northern entrance	78.5	–	16.5
Tunnel, southern entrance	79.6	–	15.4
Bridge (Frétoy-le-Château)	81.2	–	13.8
Lock 16 (Campagne), end of summit level	81.9	16	13.1
Campagne bridge, small village l/b	82.9	–	12.1
Catigny bridge, small village r/b	84.3	–	10.7
Bridge (Behancourt)	86.2	–	8.8
Sermaize bridge, village 400m r/b	87.1	–	7.9
Lock 17 (Sermaize-Haudival)	87.7	17	7.3
Beaurains-lès-Noyon bridge, village 500m r/b	89.2	–	5.8
Bridge (D934)	91.2	–	3.8
Noyon quay l/b, town centre 1300m	91.8	–	3.2
Bridge (D938)	93.1	–	1.9
Lock 18 (Noyon)	93.4	18	1.6
Bridge (N32)	93.8	–	1.2
Lock 19 (Pont-l'Evêque)	94.4	19	0.6
Pont-l'Evêque bridge, village 800m l/b	94.7	–	0.3
Railway bridge	94.8	–	0.2
End of third section, *junction with Canal latéral à l'Oise* (km)	95.0	–	0.0

Oise

The canalised river Oise extends 104km from the connection with the Canal latéral à l'Oise at Janville (commune of Longueil-Annel) to its confluence with the Seine at Conflans-Sainte-Honorine (Fin d'Oise). The Oise forms part of the important waterway route from the Seine to Northern France and Belgium, and was the subject of considerable improvement works carried out in the 1960s to make the river navigable by large push-tows. A 2km length of the non-canalised river remains navigable upstream of Janville to serve a boatyard. It should be noted that the kilometre posts along the river are numbered from the upstream end of the Canal latéral à l'Oise. Thus the distance table below starts at 33.8km.

Locks There are seven locks, each with two large chambers side by side (185 by 12m and 125 by 12m) on a short diversion canal at the level of each weir. All locks are electrically-operated and controlled by lights. At Lock 1 (Venette) only the large chamber adjacent to the weir is normally in operation, since the lock-keepers have no clear view of the 125m chamber on the other side of the island. Remote monitoring and control equipment is to be installed, but in the meantime the 125m chamber is used only during floods. The former small locks adjacent to the weirs have been eliminated.

Depth The maximum authorised draught is 2.40m above the confluence of the Aisne, 2.50m down to Creil (km 75) and 3.00m thereafter down to the confluence with the Seine.

Bridges The headroom under the bridges is at least 5.00m above normal water levels, reduced to 4.10m above the highest navigable water level.

Towpath There is a good towpath throughout.

Authority

Service de la Navigation de la Seine, Arrondissement Picardie and Arrondissement Basse-Seine. Subdivisions:
– 79 Barrage de Venette, 60200 Compiègne, ☎ 4 483 21 12 (km 34-96).
– 65 quai de l'Ecluse, 95316 Saint-Ouen-l'Aumône, ☎ 3 464 02 26 (km 96-138).

Distance table

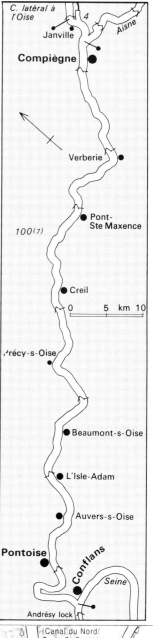

	km	lock	km
Connection with Canal latéral à l'Oise (d/s of lock 4, Janville)	33.8	-	104.4
Canal divides, both branches navigable	34.3	-	103.9
Janville bridge on r/b branch, village r/b beyond railway	34.7	-	103.5
L/b branch joins river Oise (navigable u/s 2km to boatyard)	34.9	-	103.3
R/b branch joins river Oise	35.2	-	103.0
Clairoix bridge, private quay d/s r/b, village 1000m r/b	36.4	-	101.8
Confluence of canalised river Aisne, l/b	38.3	-	99.9
Railway bridge, commercial quays u/s r/b and d/s l/b	39.4	-	98.8
Boat harbour in basin, l/b	39.7	-	98.5
Compiègne bridge, railway station r/b, town centre l/b	40.5	-	97.7
Lock 1 (Venette), one chamber in each arm, weir l/b	42.0	1	96.2
Venette quay r/b, village 400m	42.5	-	95.7
Private quay r/b	43.2	-	95.0
New road bridge (Compiègne bypass)	44.1	-	94.1
Jaux quay, Marine-Oise Plaisance hire base, village r/b	46.0	-	92.2
Lacroix-Saint-Ouen suspension bridge, quay d/s r/b, village 1500m l/b	49.9	-	88.3
Railway bridge, private quay d/s l/b	53.9	-	84.3
Lock 2 (Verberie), parallel chambers, weir l/b	54.8	2	83.4
Verberie bridge, quay u/s l/b, village 500m	55.8	-	82.4
Motorway bridge (A1, Autoroute du Nord)	58.7	-	79.5
Quay (Houdancourt) r/b	62.0	-	76.2
Lock 3 (Sarron), parallel chambers, weir l/b, water	65.8	3	72.4
Pont-Sainte-Maxence bridge, small town l/b, commercial quays d/s	67.2	-	71.0
New road bridge (Pont-Sainte-Maxence bypass)	69.6	-	68.6
Rieux quay r/b, village 400m beyond railway	73.6	-	64.6
Industrial quays r/b (chemicals factory)	74.7	-	63.5
Verneuil suspension bridge (pedestrian), quay d/s l/b, village 800m	75.7	-	62.5
New road bridge (Creil bypass), commercial quays u/s r/b	78.2	-	60.0
Creil bridge, town centre 500m l/b	79.2	-	59.0
Public quay (Long-Boyau) r/b, and industrial quays	79.9	-	58.3
Lock 4 (Creil), parallel chambers, weir l/b	81.9	4	56.3
Skew railway bridge (Laversine)	83.5	-	54.7
Creil power station, coal unloading quay r/b	84.0	-	54.2
Saint-Leu-d'Esserent suspension bridge, railway station and village 400m r/b	86.1	-	52.1
Quay (Gouvieux) l/b	88.0	-	50.2
Précy-sur-Oise suspension bridge, private quays u/s, village r/b	90.2	-	48.0
Public quay r/b	91.0	-	47.2
Boran-sur-Oise suspension bridge, village 400m r/b	94.5	-	43.7
Lock 5 (Boran), parallel chambers, weir l/b	96.5	5	41.7
Entrance to new cut, r/b (bypassing bend in river)	98.3	-	39.9
Bridge (Bruyères-sur-Oise) over new cut	98.9	-	39.3
End of new cut	100.0	-	38.2
Industrial quays r/b	101.4	-	36.8
Beaumont-sur-Oise bridge, quay u/s l/b, small town l/b	103.3	-	34.9
Industrial quays	104.0	-	34.2
Railway bridge	104.6	-	33.6

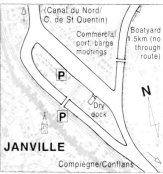

	km	lock	km
Thermal power station r/b, private quay	105.2	-	33.0
Bridge (N1 bypass)	106.0	-	32.2
Island, follow navigation signs	108.3	-	29.9
Lock 6 (Isle-Adam), parallel chambers, weir l/b	109.7	6	28.5
L'Isle-Adam bridge spanning three arms, navigation in central arm, small town 400m l/b, **Parmain** r/b	110.5	-	27.7
Mériel road and railway bridge, village 400m l/b	113.8	-	24.4
Méry-Auvers bridge, private quays l/b	116.5	-	21.7
Railway bridge (Chaponval)	119.9	-	18.3
Industrial quays l/b	121.8	-	16.4
Pontoise bridge, town centre r/b (moor d/s of railway bridge)	123.3	-	14.9
Railway bridge, public quay d/s r/b	123.5	-	14.7
Lock 7 (Pontoise), parallel chambers, weir r/b	124.3	7	13.9
Motorway bridge (A15)	124.7	-	13.5
Skew railway bridge (RER regional metro)	127.1	-	11.1
New road bridge	128.7	-	9.5
Cergy-Pontoise bridge, village r/b	129.5	-	8.7
Marina and water sports centre in former gravel pits, l/b	131.7	-	6.5
Jouy-le-Moutier quay r/b, village 700m	133.2	-	5.0
Neuville-sur-Oise bridge, village l/b	134.8	-	3.4
New road bridge	135.9	-	2.3
Conflans-Fin-d'Oise quay and boatyards r/b, moorings l/b	136.7	-	1.5
Railway bridge (Pont Eiffel)	137.6	-	0.6
Conflans-Sainte-Honorine bridge, barge moorings, town centre 1500m l/b	138.0	-	0.2
Confluence with river Seine (km 71)	138.2	-	0.0

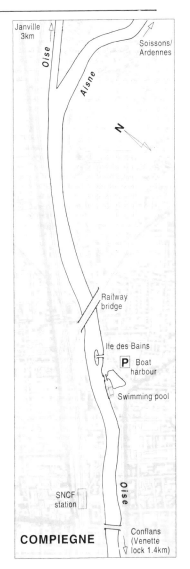

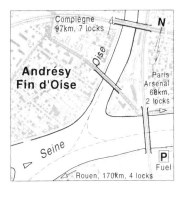

Canal latéral à l'Oise

The Canal latéral à l'Oise connects the Canal de Saint-Quentin at Chauny to the canalised river Oise at Janville, a distance of 34km. Junctions are made with the Canal de l'Oise à l'Aisne (km 3) and with the Canal du Nord (km 19). Forming part of the very busy 'north–south' route between the Seine basin and northern France and Belgium, the canal has seen large-scale improvement works, like the Oise further downstream.

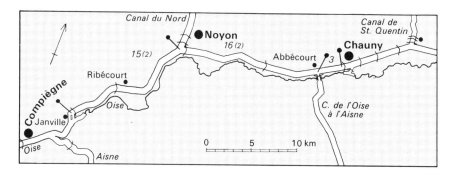

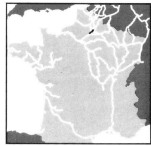

Locks There are four electrically-operated locks. The two downstream of the junction with the Canal du Nord each have two parallel chambers, 125 by 12m and 39 by 6.50m. The two locks above the junction have two chambers of 39 by 6.50m.

Depth The maximum authorised draught is 2.40m.

Bridges The fixed bridges all leave a minimum clear headroom of 4.10m.

Towpath There is a good towpath throughout.

Authority

Service de la Navigation de la Seine, Arrondissement Picardie. Subdivision: 79 Barrage de Venette, 60200 Compiègne, ☎ 44 83 21 12.

Distance table

	km	lock	km
Chauny bridge, *connection with Canal de Saint-Quentin,* quay d/s l/b, town centre 500m r/b	0.0	-	138.2
Abbécourt basin, moorings, boatyard, village 700m r/b	2.6	-	135.6
Junction with Canal de l'Oise à l'Aisne, l/b	2.8	-	135.4
Bridge (Abbécourt)	3.2	-	135.0
Manicamp bridge, quay d/s l/b, village 1000m	4.9	-	133.3
Quierzy bridge, quays l/b, village 1000m	6.6	-	131.6
Appilly bridge, quay u/s l/b, village 700m r/b	8.2	-	130.0
Lock 1 (Saint-Hubert), parallel chambers	9.0	1	129.2
Baboeuf bridge, quay d/s l/b	10.4	-	127.8
Footbridge (Pont-à-la-Fosse)	11.0	-	127.2
Basin r/b, moorings	11.6	-	126.6
Varesnes bridge, quay u/s l/b, village 700m	13.4	-	124.8
Noyon bridge (D934), basin and quays d/s, town centre 2500m r/b	15.3	-	122.9

	km	lock	km
Basin (Pierrot), moorings	17.0	-	121.2
Sempigny bridges, quay u/s l/b, village 400m	17.8	-	120.4
Lock 2 (Sempigny), parallel chambers, quay d/s r/b	18.1	2	120.1
Junction with Canal du Nord, r/b	18.6	-	119.6
Chiry bridge, village 1500m r/b	20.5	-	117.7
Ourscamps bridge, quay u/s l/b, abbey 800m l/b	21.9	-	116.3
Pimprez bridge, village r/b	24.0	-	114.2
Entrance to new cut bypassing bend in old canal	24.6	-	113.6
Bridge (Rouilly)	24.9	-	113.3
End of new cut	25.5	-	112.7
Ribécourt bridge, quay u/s l/b, village 1000m r/b	26.6	-	111.6
Railway bridge (private siding)	26.7	-	111.5
Basin (Ribécourt) r/b, private quay	27.4	-	110.8
Bridge (Bellerive)	27.9	-	110.3
Lock 3 (Bellerive), parallel chambers, basin d/s l/b	28.3	3	109.9
Montmacq bridge, village 400m l/b	30.6	-	107.6
Boatyard l/b	31.3	-	106.9
Thourotte bridge, quay u/s l/b, village r/b beyond railway	31.9	-	106.3
Longueil-Annel bridge, water and fuel d/s, village r/b	32.9	-	105.3
Lock 4 (Janville), parallel chambers, connection with canalised river Oise	33.8	4	104.4

Canal de l'Oise à l'Aisne

The Canal de l'Oise à l'Aisne forms an important link, frequently used by boats heading towards the Mediterranean from Calais, Dunkerque or Belgium. It extends 48km from the Canal latéral à l'Oise at Abbécourt basin (km 3) to the Canal latéral à l'Aisne at Bourg-et-Comin (km 38). The summit level between the two valleys, at an altitude of 66m, incorporates a 2365m long tunnel at Braye-en-Laonnois. The tunnel's width at water level is 6.50m, and the free headroom at least 3.50m. Electric mules haul barge trains through the tunnel, making three or four return trips per day as required by traffic. Towage is not compulsory for powered boats, but times of passage obviously depend on the tows, and must be arranged at the last lock before reaching the tunnel (locks 9 and 10 respectively). There are short aqueducts at each end of the canal, over the rivers Oise and Aisne.

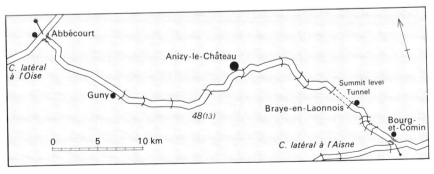

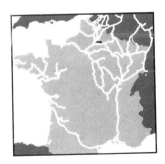

Locks There are 13 locks, of which 9 fall towards the Oise and 4 towards the Aisne. They are of standard 300-tonne barge dimensions, 40.50 by 6.00m.

Depth The maximum authorised draught is 2.20m.

Bridges The fixed bridges offer a headroom of not less than 3.70m.

Towpath There is a towpath throughout.

Authority
Service de la Navigation de la Seine, Arrondissement Picardie. Subdivision:
Rue de Mayenne, 02209 Soissons, ☎ 23 53 00 11.

Distance table

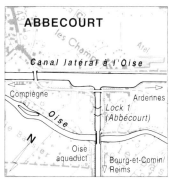

	km	lock	km
Junction with Canal latéral à l'Oise (km 3), basin	0.0	-	47.8
Bridge (Abbécourt)	0.1	-	47.7
Lock 1 (Abbécourt)	0.2	1	47.6
Oise aqueduct	0.3	-	47.5
Bridge (Marizelle), quay u/s r/b	1.4	-	46.4
Bridge (Bac)	2.8	-	45.0
Ailette aqueduct	3.0	-	44.8
Bridge (Manicamp)	3.4	-	44.4
Bridge (Saint-Paul-aux-Bois), quay d/s l/b	4.3	-	43.5
Champs bridge, quay u/s l/b, small village 1200m r/b	7.7	-	40.1
Bridge (Quincy)	9.4	-	38.4
Guny bridge, quay d/s l/b, village 300m	10.8	-	37.0
Bridge (Tempet)	11.4	-	36.4
Lock 2 (Guny), water	11.5	2	36.3
Pont-Saint-Mard bridge, quay u/s l/b, village 1000m	12.3	-	35.5
Bridge (Crécy-au-Mont)	14.1	-	33.7
Lock 3 (Crécy-au-Mont)	14.2	3	33.6
Bridge (Béthancourt), D37	16.0	-	31.8
Basin (Crécy-au-Mont), quay l/b, **Coucy-le-Château** 3000m r/b	16.1	-	31.7
Lock 4 (Leuilly), bridge	17.1	4	30.7
Bridge (Landricourt)	18.1	-	29.7
Bridge (Courson), quay u/s l/b	19.3	-	28.5
Bridge (Folie)	21.2	-	26.6
Lock 5 (Vauxaillon), railway bridge d/s	22.0	5	25.8
Vauxaillon bridge, quay d/s l/b, village 2000m	22.4	-	25.4
Bridge (Locq)	24.4	-	23.4
Pinon bridge, quay d/s and basin u/s l/b, village 1300m, **Anizy-le-Château** 500m r/b	25.4	-	22.4
Lock 6 (Pinon), railway bridge d/s, water	26.0	6	21.8
Lock 7 (Chaillevois), bridge, quay u/s l/b	31.1	7	16.7
Chavignon basin, quay l/b, village 1500m	33.4	-	14.4
Lock 8 (Chavignon), bridge (N2)	33.7	8	14.1
Lock 9 (Pargny-Filain), bridge, turning basin and quay u/s l/b, beginning of summit level	35.0	9	12.8
Chevregny bridge, quay d/s r/b, village 1500m	37.8	-	10.0
Braye tunnel, Oise portal	38.3	-	9.5
Braye tunnel, Aisne portal	40.7	-	7.1
Braye-en-Laonnois bridge, village 500m l/b	40.9	-	6.9
Bridge (Epinettes)	41.4	-	6.4
Bridge (Mont-Saint-Aubeu), quay d/s r/b	41.9	-	5.9
Lock 10 (Moulin Brûlé), end of summit level	42.6	10	5.2
Lock 11 (Metz), bridge	43.3	11	4.5
Quay (Moussy-Soupir) r/b	43.6	-	4.2
Lock 12 (Moussy-Soupir), bridge	43.9	12	3.9
Lock 13 (Verneuil-Courtonne)	44.8	13	3.0

Braye-en-Laonnois tunnel, on the Canal de l'Oise à l'Aisne, equipped with a powerful ventilation system.
Hugh Potter

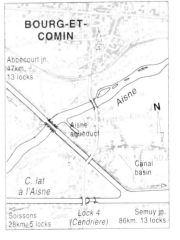

	km	lock	km
Bridge (Verneuil)	45.4	-	2.4
Bridge (Bourg, 9)	46.3	-	1.5
Bridge (Bourg, 10)	46.7	-	1.1
Aisne aqueduct	47.2	-	0.6
Bourg-et-Comin bridge (11), quay d/s r/b, village 700m l/b	47.5	-	0.3
Junction with Canal latéral à l'Aisne (km 38)	47.8	-	0.0

Canal d'Orléans

The Canal d'Orléans was the third watershed canal to be built in France, after the Canal de Briare and the Canal du Midi. It was completed in 1692, to provide a link between the Loire valley near Orléans and the river Loing (hence the Seine) at Montargis. It was 74km long with 28 locks. The original canal joined the river Loire at Combleux, 5.5km short of Orléans, but an extension was later built to give canal traffic direct access to the city, avoiding the river Loire. This extension has been filled in over the last 750m, and a small basin 3.5km from Combleux would be the practical limit of navigation today.

The canal is mentioned here for reference only, since for the time being powered boats are still excluded, but restoration is under way, financed by the *département* of Loiret, and one section has already been opened to allow operation of a hydrojet-powered trip boat between Fay-aux-Loges and Mardié. This 9km length includes one restored lock at Donnery. The canal's tercentenary celebrations may be expected to be accompanied by more ambitious proposals for the canal's future, and despite possible water supply difficulties there are good prospects for restoration throughout from the junction with the Canal de Briare at Buges, over the attractive summit level in the Orléans forest and down to the outskirts of the cathedral city.

Oudon

The river Oudon, a right-bank tributary of the Mayenne, is canalised over a distance of 18km from the Mayenne to the small town of Segré, where a boat harbour has been established near the head of navigation.

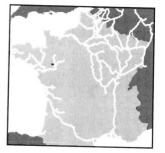

Locks There are three locks, overcoming a difference in level of 3.50m. Their dimensions are 33.00 by 5.20m.

Depth The maximum authorised draught is 1.50m, although in times of drought boats drawing more than 1.00m may have difficulty.

Bridges The least headroom under the bridges is 4.60m above normal water level, reduced to 3.60m above the highest navigable water level.

Towpath There is a rough towpath throughout, with metalled sections near the locks.

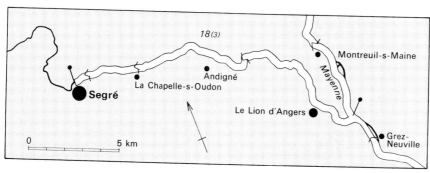

Authority

Service de la Navigation Maine-et-Loire, quai Félix Faure, 49000 Angers,
☎ 41 43 61 49.

Distance table

	km	lock	km
Segré, head of navigation (Moulin de la Tour), boat harbour d/s at former quay	0.0	-	18.0
Railway bridge	0.9	-	17.1
Lock 1 (Maingué) l/b and weir	1.0	1	17.0
Lock 2 (**La Chapelle-sur-Oudon**) l/b and weir, village r/b	4.0	2	14.0
Bridge (Pont du Port-aux-Anglais), **Andigné** 1000m r/b	8.8	-	9.2
Lock 3 (Himbeaudière) l/b and weir	10.0	3	8.0
Le Lion-d'Angers bridge, quay d/s r/b, village r/b	16.0	-	2.0
Confluence with Mayenne (km 101), Bec d'Oudon, bridge	18.0	-	0.0

Paris canals
(canaux de la Ville de Paris)

By contrast with the earlier policy of discouragement to boaters, the municipal canals of Paris (Canal de l'Ourcq, Canal Saint-Denis and Canal Saint-Martin), opened in 1822, are now cruising waterways as well as continuing to serve an important water supply function and some commercial navigation in the industrial section to the north of Paris. The declining commercial traffic and parallel boom in pleasure cruising throughout France brought about the change in attitude on the Paris city council, which thus decided in the early 1980s to open up the entire system, with a total length of 120km. A small due continues to be levied at each of the locks on the Canal Saint-Denis and Canal Saint-Martin, but a couple of pounds is a small price to pay for access to the Canal de l'Ourcq, a unique and charming waterway, where an English narrow boat would not seem out of place. The distance tables are grouped together after the separate descriptions of the three canals.

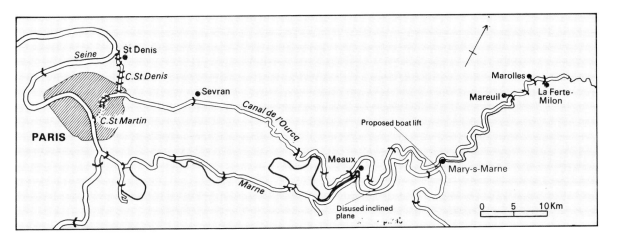

Canal de l'Ourcq

The Canal de l'Ourcq extends 108km from the remote hamlet of Port-aux Perches, on the edge of the Retz forest, to the Bassin de la Villette, in Paris, where it joins the Canal Saint-Denis and Canal Saint-Martin. The waterway is made up of three distinct sections:

- the canalised river Ourcq, over a distance of 11km from Port-aux-Perches to the diversion weir at Mareuil,
- the 'narrow' canal from Mareuil to Pavillons-sous-Bois (86km),
- the widened section from Pavillons-sous-Bois to La Villette (11km).

The widened section is navigable by Seine barges carrying up to 1000 tonnes, but the rest of the waterway is open to special dumb barges, the flûtes or demi-flûtes d'Ourcq. In practice, the narrow canal has been navigated only by maintenance barges for several decades, but 3.20m is wide enough for many boats, and there is no reason why cruising should not develop on this little-known system. Alternative access may eventually be possible from the canalised river Marne at Lizy, where a boat lift if projected, to overcome the 13m difference in level.

No tolls are charged for use of the canal by boats, but a laisser-passer of limited duration must be obtained from the top locks of the Canal Saint-Denis or Canal Saint-Martin or from Sevran lock (km 13.4). Craft with an air draught of less than 1.90m are issued a straightforward déclaration.

The distance table is given in the reverse direction, from La Villette to Port-aux-Perches, for the convenience of navigators entering the canal from the Seine.

Locks There are 10 locks, overcoming a total difference in level of 13.80m. Four of these are on the canalised river Ourcq, and measure 62 by 5.20m. The other six, on the 'narrow' canal, are 58.80m long and 3.20m wide; there are two parallel chambers at five of these locks. At Sevran lock, the first encountered when heading upstream from Paris, a windlass is provided for do-it-yourself operation of all the other locks. A leaflet is also issued, giving all the necessary instructions for lock operation, as well as for mooring on the canal, which is strictly controlled so as to prevent any attempts at residential mooring.

Depth The maximum authorised draught is 2.60m on the widened section to Pavillons-sous-Bois (km 11), and 0.80m throughout the rest of the waterway, although the available depth is 1.30m.

Bridges The fixed bridges offer a minimum headroom of 4.00m on the widened section and 2.40m on the rest of the canal. There are two lift bridges, at Calye-Souilly (km 27) and Congis (km 71), which like the locks must be operated by the users and closed immediately after passage. At Claye-Souilly the bridge offers a headroom of 2.20m in the closed position. As a safety measure for pedestrians and road traffic, this bridge is to be left closed on weekdays from 11.30 to 12.30 and 17.30 to 18.30.

Towpath There is a towpath throughout.

Authority

Services Techniques de la Ville de Paris, Section des Dérivations et Canaux, 6 quai de la Seine, 75019 Paris, ☎ (1) 46 07 34 51.

Lock 5 and iron footbridge on the Canal Saint-Martin in Paris. *Author*

Canal Saint-Denis

The Canal Saint-Denis extends 6.6km from the junction with the Canal de l'Ourcq at the Bassin de la Villette to the Seine at Saint-Denis. It is the busiest of the three canals in Paris, passing through predominantly industrial suburbs, with numerous private quays used by commercial barges. For access to the Canal de l'Ourcq, it is preferable to use the Canal Saint-Martin, entered 30km further upstream on the Seine.

Locks There are seven paired locks, overcoming a total difference in level of 24m. The large chamber is 62.25m long and 8.10m wide, while the small chamber measures 38.90 by 5.20m. A toll of 2.50 francs (in 1983) is payable by boats for the passage of each lock.

Depth The maximum authorised draught is 3.00m from the Seine to lock 3 and 2.60m in the remaining section to the Bassin de la Villette.

Bridges The bridges leave a minimum headroom of 4.60m.

Towpath There is a towpath throughout.

Authority
Section des Dérivations et Canaux, Paris (see under Canal de l'Ourcq).

Canal Saint-Martin

The Canal Saint-Martin, opened to navigation three years after the Canal de l'Ourcq, in 1825, extends 4.5km from the Bassin de la Villette to the Seine at the quay Henri IV, just upstream of the two islands in the heart of Paris. The canal has a certain Parisiam charm, with its elegant iron footbridges, and it has been a tourist attraction for several years, since Quiztour started operating a regular passenger service through the canal with the Patache-Eautobus. Now it will become familiar to boat owners visiting Paris, thanks to the 230-berth marina opened in 1983 in the Bassin de l'Arsenal, immediately beyond the entrance lock from the Seine. The marina is operated by the Association pour le port de plaisance de Paris-Arsenal, founded jointly by the city of Paris and the Chamber of Commerce and Industry. For almost half its length (2069m), the canal is in tunnel (in fact a succession of voûtes or vaults offering varying navigable widths) under two main boulevards and the Place de la Bastille. Vessels are not allowed to meet in the tunnel and passage is controlled by lights. No more than three vessels are allowed to proceed through the tunnel in each direction and in each cycle.

Locks There are 9 locks, of which the first 8 are grouped in 4 double staircases. Their dimensions are 42 by 7.80m. Lock 9, giving access from the Seine to the marina, is remote-controlled from the harbourmaster's office. A toll of 2.50 francs (in 1983) is payable by boats for the passage of each lock.

Depth The maximum authorised draught is 1.90m.

Bridges The fixed bridges leave a minimum headroom of 4.37m. There are two swing bridges.

Towpath There is a towpath throughout.

Authority

Section des Dérivations et Canaux, Paris (see under Canal de l'Ourcq).

Distance table
Canal de l'Ourcq

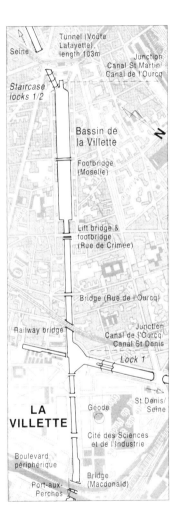

	km	lock	km
Paris			
Junction with Canal Saint-Martin, origin of Bassin de la Villette			
public quays	0.0	-	108.1
Footbridge (Moselle)	0.4	-	107.7
Lift bridge (Rue de Crimée) and footbridge, end of basin	0.8	-	107.3
Bridge (Rue de l'Ourcq)	1.1	-	107.0
Railway bridge	1.3	-	106.8
Junction with Canal Saint-Denis, r/b, turning basin	1.4	-	106.7
Bridge (Abattoirs, d/s)	1.6	-	106.5
Bridge (Abattoirs, u/s)	1.8	-	106.3
Bridge (Macdonald)	2.1	-	106.0
Motorway bridge (Boulevard Périphérique), industrial quays	2.2	-	105.9
Bridge (Mairie de Pantin)	2.6	-	105.5
Bridge (Delizy)	3.3	-	104.8
Bridge (Pantin)	3.5	-	104.6
Bridge (Hippolyte Boyer)	4.3	-	103.8
Railway bridge (main line Gare de l'Est)	5.2	-	102.9
Railway bridge, industrial quays u/s	5.3	-	102.8
Bridge (Folie)	5.7	-	102.4
Railway bridge	7.5	-	100.6
Motorway bridge	7.6	-	100.5
Bridge (Bondy), basin u/s	7.9	-	100.2
Motorway bridge (B3)	8.1	-	100.0
Bridge (Aulnay-sous-Bois)	8.6	-	99.5
Bridge (Forêt)	9.4	-	98.7
Turning basin for barges up to 60m long	9.7	-	98.4
Bridge (Monthyon)	10.5	-	97.6
Bridge (Union)	11.9	-	96.2
Rail and road bridges (Freinville)	12.6	-	95.5
Lock (Sevran), basin u/s	13.4	1	94.7
Sevran bridge, town centre 300m r/b (Paris suburb)	14.1	-	94.0
Private footbridge	14.4	-	93.0
Private bridge	15.1	-	93.0
Bridge (Villepinte)	16.7	-	91.4
Footbridge	16.8	-	91.3
Basin (Moises) l/b	17.5	-	90.6
Private railway bridge (Lambert)	18.6	-	89.5
Bridge (Mitry)	19.3	-	88.8
New bridge (Mitry)	19.6	-	88.5
Overhead power lines	21.1	-	87.0
Overhead power lines	23.3	-	84.8
Bridge (Rosée), D212	24.1	-	84.0
Gressy basin r/b, small village with castle 600m r/b	24.8	-	83.3
Main road bridge (Claye-Souilly bypass)	27.0	-	81.1
Claye-Souilly lift bridge (see above), basin d/s l/b, village l/b	27.4	-	80.7
Main road bridge Claye-Souilly bypass)	28.2	-	79.9
Main road bridge (Marais), N3	29.1	-	79.0
Bridge (Annet)	30.3	-	77.8
Fresnes-sur-Marne bridge, village l/b	31.9	-	76.2
Lock (Fresnes), two chambers, l/b, weir r/b	32.9	2	75.2

	km	lock	km
Bridge (Précy)	34.9	-	73.2
Bridge (Charmentray), basin u/s r/b	36.5	-	71.6
Basin (Trilbardou) l/b	38.5	-	69.6
Bridge (Parc)	38.8	-	69.3
Trilbardou bridge, small village l/b	39.0	-	69.1
Bridge (Vignely)	40.2	-	67.7
Lock (Vignely), two chambers, l/b, weir r/b	40.4	3	67.7
Bridge (Isles-les-Villenoy), D5	42.8	-	65.3
Basin (Bois-Talon) r/b	43.5	-	64.6
Villenoy bridge, village l/b	46.0	-	62.1
Basin (Sucrerie) r/b	47.0	-	61.1
Bridge (Ruellée)	47.3	-	60.8
Lock (Villenoy), two chambers l/b, weir r/b	47.5	4	60.6
Meaux bridge (Saint-Rémy), large basins u/s and d/s, town centre 800m l/b	48.2	-	59.9
Footbridge (Penchard)	48.8	-	59.3
Skew road bridge (N330)	49.3	-	58.8
Grégy-les-Meaux bridge, village r/b	50.4	-	57.7
Basin (Cordeliers) r/b	52.1	-	56.0
Bridge (Justice), D405	53.5	-	54.6
Railway bridge	53.8	-	54.3
Bridge (Saint-Lazare), N3, basin u/s, Meaux centre 1500m l/b	54.6	-	53.5
Lock (Saint-Lazare), two chambers, weir on bypass	54.9	5	53.2
New bridge	55.2	-	52.9
Bridge (Fublaines)	55.5	-	52.6
Upper station of former railway incline (used for transhipment between canal and river Marne below), moorings	57.4	-	50.7
Bridge (Ferme de Beauval)	57.8	-	50.3
Bridge (Beauval-Trilport), N3, basin d/s r/b	58.6	-	49.5
Railway bridge	59.0	-	49.1
Poincy bridge, village 400m l/b, hire base 900m on Marne	60.1	-	48.0
Basin (Poincy) r/b	60.7	-	47.4
Bridge (Voie Blanche), basin u/s r/b	64.1	-	44.0
Lock (Varreddes), two chambers, weir on bypass	64.7	6	43.4
Bridge (Bosse)	64.9	-	43.2
Varreddes bridge (Maladrerie), basin u/s r/b, village 700m l/b	66.4	-	41.7
Congis-sur-Thérouanne lift bridge, basin u/s r/b, village 400m l/b	70.7	-	37.4
Bridge (Congis)	71.5	-	36.6
Bridge (Carreauxs)	71.8	-	36.3
Bridge (Villers-les-Rigault)	73.5	-	34.6
Château de Villers r/b	74.1	-	34.0
Basin (Confluent) r/b, site of projected boat lift connecting with river Marne below	74.7	-	33.4
Lizy-sur-Ourcq bridge, basin d/s r/b, village l/b	76.7	-	31.4
Bridge (Lizy amont), basins d/s r/b and u/s l/b	77.3	-	30.8
Bridge (Vaches d'Echampeu)	79.8	-	28.3
Bridge (Vernelle), hamlet r/b	82.0	-	26.1
Bridge (Marnoue-la-Poterie), basin u/s r/b	83.2	-	24.9
Bridge (May-en-Multien)	85.4	-	22.7
Basin (May) r/b	86.1	-	22.0
Bridge (Ferme de Gesvres), château 700m l/b	87.2	-	20.9
Crouy-sur-Ourcq bridge, large basin d/s, village 1500m l/b	89.2	-	18.9
Bridge (Varinfroy)	90.2	-	17.9
Basin (Beauval) r/b	90.9	-	17.2
Bridge (Beauval)	91.5	-	16.6
Neufchelles bridge, basin u/s, village r/b	92.6	-	15.5

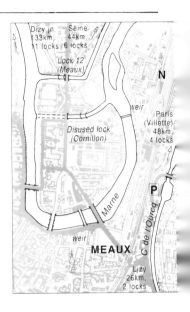

	km	lock	km
Bridge (Clignon)	93.3	-	14.8
Railway bridge	93.9	-	14.2
Basin (Collinance) r/b, former peat bogs	94.0	-	14.1
Bridge (Vaches de Mareuil)	96.1	-	12.0
Mareuil-sur-Ourcq bridge, large basin d/s r/b, weir on Ourcq l/b, navigation enters canalised river Ourcq, village r/b	96.8	-	11.3
Lock (Mareuil) in short cut l/b, weir on river	97.2	7	11.9
Lock (Queue d'Ham) l/b, weir stream r/b	99.7	8	8.4
Marolles bridge, village 400m r/b	102.2	-	5.9
Lock (Marolles) in short cut l/b, weir stream r/b	102.4	9	5.7
Basin (Nimer) r/b	102.9	-	5.2
Weir stream enters l/b	103.8	-	4.3
La Ferté-Milon bridge, basin d/s r/b, village l/b	104.1	-	4.0
Lock (La Ferté-Milon)	104.3	10	3.8
Weir stream l/b	104.4	-	3.7
Railway bridge	105.2	-	2.9
Footbridge (Mosloy)	106.8	-	1.3
Footbridge (Port-aux-Perches)	107.7	-	0.4
Port-aux-Perches hamlet, head of navigation	108.1	-	0.0

Canal Saint-Denis

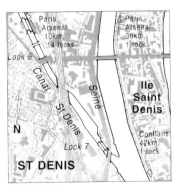

	km	lock	km
Paris			
Junction with Canal de l'Ourcq, turning basin	0.0	1	6.6
Lock 1, two chambers, water	0.1	1	6.5
Bridge (Flandre), basin d/s l/b	0.4	-	6.2
Railway bridge (main line Gare de l'Est)	0.6	-	6.0
Bridge (Macdonald)	0.8	-	5.8
Motorway bridge (Boulevard Périphérique)	0.9	-	5.7
Railway bridge, private basin d/s l/b	1.0	-	5.6
Lock 2, two chambers, water	1.3	2	5.3
Bridge (Stains), private quays d/s	1.8	-	4.8
Lock 3, two chambers	2.2	3	4.4
Swing bridge (Aubervilliers) and footbridge, industrial quays d/s	2.4	-	4.2
Bridge (Landy)	2.7	-	3.9
Lock 4, two chambers, water	3.2	4	3.4
Railway bridges (Soissons)	3.3	-	3.3
Bridge (Pailleux)	3.5	-	3.1
Lock 5, two chambers, water	4.6	5	2.0
Motorway bridge (A1)	4.7	-	1.9
Saint-Denis bridge (Pont de la Révolte), basin u/s, centre and basilica 1000m r/b	4.9	-	1.7
Footbridge (Thiers)	5.3	-	1.3
Lock 6, two chambers, water	5.7	6	0.9
Footbridge (Gare de Saint-Denis)	5.9	-	0.7
Bridge (Rue du Pont)	6.0	-	0.6
Railway bridge (main line Gare du Nord)	6.2	-	0.4
Lock 7, two chambers, water	6.5	7	0.1
Junction with Seine at km 29, bridge (Briche)	6.6	-	0.0

Canal Saint-Martin

Paris	km	lock	km
Junction with Bassin de la Villette (Canal de l'Ourcq), locks 1 and 2 (staircase), water	0.0	2	4.6
Tunnel (Voûte Lafayette), 103m long, 8.10m wide	0.1	-	4.6
Basin (Louis Blanc) with quays	0.4	-	4.2
Bridge (Louis Blanc), basin d/s	0.5	-	4.1
Locks 3 and 4 (staircase), footbridge u/s, water	0.7	4	3.9
Bridge (Pont des Ecluses Saint-Martin)	0.8	-	3.8
Locks 5 and 6 (staircase), footbridge u/s, water	1.3	6	3.3
Swing bridge (Rue de la Grange-aux-Belles)	1.4	-	3.2
Footbridge (Richerand)	1.5	-	3.1
Swing bridge (Rue Alibert/Rue Dieu)	1.6	-	3.0
Footbridge (Rue de la Douane)	1.8	-	2.8
Locks 7 and 8 (staircase), water	1.8	8	2.8
Entrance to tunnel (voûte du Temple, length 276m, width 24.50m)	1.9	-	2.7
End of voûte du Temple, beginning of voûte Richard-Lenoir (length 1510m, width 16m)	2.2	-	2.4
Voûte Bastille (length 180m, width 8.04m)	3.7	-	0.9
Metro bridge (Bastille), 17.60m wide passage, end of tunnel	3.9	-	0.7
Paris-Arsenal marina, moorings for 250 boats, crane, restaurant	4.0	-	0.6
Footbridge (Mornay)	4.2	-	0.4
Lock 9, bridge (Morland), water	4.5	9	0.1
Metro viaduct, *junction with Seine* (Quai Henri IV) at km 168	4.6	-	0.0

Canal de Pommeroeul à Condé

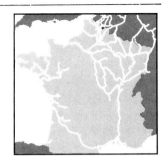

The Canal de Pommeroeul à Condé, replacing the former Canal de Mons à Condé, links the busy commercial waterway networks of Northern France and Belgium. It extends over a distance of 12km from Pommeroeul, on the Nimy–Blaton–Péronnes canal, in Belgium, to Condé, on the canalised river Escaut. It is on French soil over the last 5.5km, but for convenience the whole length is given in the distance table. This is virtually a new waterway, opened to 1350-tonne barges in 1982, and incorporating only 3km of the original Canal de Mons à Condé. Since the Escaut at Condé is now bypassed by a new cut with a large lock at Fresnes, the canal connects with the river downstream of this lock by means of a new cut. The small town of Condé is for the time being no longer accessible, but it is shown on the large-scale plan of the junction, since there are plans to provide a link between the new cut and the old canal at km 9.3.

Locks The canal has two large locks (100 by 12m, with intermediate gates), both on the Belgian section.

Depth The maximum authorised draught is 2.50m, to be increased to 3.00m.

Bridges The fixed bridges offer a minimum headroom of 5.25m above highest water level (5.55m above normal level).

Authority

Direction Régionale de la Navigation, Lille. Subdivision:
24 chemin du Halage, 59300 Valenciennes, ☎ 27 46 23 41 (for French section)

Distance table

	km	lock	km
Junction with Nimy–Blaton–Péronnes canal in Belgium	0.0	-	11.6
Lock (Pommeroeul), bridge	0.5	1	11.1
Railway bridge, basin d/s	0.7	-	10.9
Pommeroeul bridge, village 1000m l/b	1.9	-	9.7
Bridge (Sartis), factory d/s r/b	4.6	-	7.0
Lock (Hensies)	5.4	2	6.2
Border	6.1	-	5.5
Saint-Aybert bridge, small village 200m l/b	6.7	-	4.9
Basin (*planned connection with old cut to Condé, r/b*)	9.3	-	2.3
Bridge (Pont du Bastringue)	10.8	-	0.8
Junction with canalised Escaut d/s of Fresnes lock	11.6	-	0.0

Rance maritime

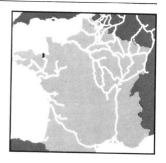

The Rance estuary became famous when the world's first tidal barrage and hydroelectric power station was built near its mouth in the 1960s. For yachtsmen it remains more important as the first section of the series of waterways linking the English Channel to the Atlantic across the heart of Brittany. The seaward limit of the estuary is considered to be level with Dinard, on the left bank, but for practical purposes the waterway route is considered here to start at the entrance to Saint-Malo harbour, a little further seaward on the right bank. Navigation in the estuary extends over a distance of 22.6km from this point to le Châtelier lock, where the Canal d'Ille-et-Rance begins, although high tides are felt up to 2km beyond Dinan. For precise navigational details on the entrance to the estuary and the facilities available at Saint-Malo and Dinard, reference to *North Brittany* by the RCC Pilotage Foundation and nautical charts is recommended.

Locks There are two locks. Le Châtelier lock has dimensions of 30.80 by 8.00m. Its lower sill dries out at low tide, but at high springs the depth is 7.58m and the barrage is completely submerged. Locking through is permitted when the depth over the sill has reached 1.76m. Enquiries may be made at the lock if necessary, ☎ 96 39 55 66. The second lock is situated on the left-bank side of the tidal barrage, and has dimensions of 65 by 13m. The lock is operated every hour on the hour, except one or two hours before and after low tide, depending on the tide coefficient. Enquiries, ☎ 99 46 21 87. There is also a ship lock (160 by 25m) providing access to the inner basins of the port of Saint-Malo.

Depth The river is tidal throughout.

Bridges Apart from the Saint-Hubert suspension bridge, the only fixed bridge is at le Châtelier lock, offering a headroom of 3.50m under normal high tides, reduced to 3.25m under high water springs.

Authority
Service Maritime de Saint-Malo, Quai Pourquoi Pas, 35400 Saint-Malo, ☎ 99 56 07 24.

Distance table
(Note: distances are related to the centre line of the estuary)

	km	lock	km
Saint-Malo harbour entrance, quay, ship lock for access to inner harbour (see *North Brittany Pilot*)	0.0	-	22.6
Dinard point, seaward limit of Rance estuary	0.9	-	21.7
Dinard, l/b, quay, ferry for Saint-Servant/Saint-Malo	1.2	-	21.4
Rocks (Ras de la Mercière)	1.3	-	21.3
Rocks (La Mercière), beacon, Pointe de La Cité	1.8	-	20.8
Prieuré or Dinard bay l/b, Solidor bay r/b, mooring buoys	2.2	-	20.4
La Vicomté point l/b, Bizeux island r/b (beacon)	2.7	-	19.9
Rance tidal barrage, lock on l/b side, bridge	3.8	1	18.8
La Richardais bay l/b, boatyard, moorings, slipway	5.3	-	17.3
Cancaval promontory l/b, beacon	5.7	-	16.9
Tour des Zèbres beacon r/b	5.9	-	16.7

	km	lock	km
Le Montmarin bay l/b	6.1	-	16.5
Slipways (Jouvente l/b, Passagère r/b), ferry	6.7	-	15.9
Pierre et Paul (reef, dries at low water, no beacon)	6.9	-	15.7
Island (Ile Chevret), beacon	7.3	-	15.3
Langronais promontory l/b, L'Ecrais promontory r/b (beacon)	8.3	-	14.3
Island (Ile aux Moines)	8.6	-	14.0
La Landriais bay l/b, boatyard, mooring, slipway	8.7	-	13.9
Promontories (Thon l/b, Bay du Put r/b)	8.9	-	13.7
Promontory (Garel), La Landriais windmill l/b	9.7	-	12.9
Rocky promontories with beacons r/b	10.8	-	11.8
Saint-Suliac jetty and beaching ground r/b	11.1	-	11.5
Langrolay slipway l/b, village 800m	12.1	-	10.5
Promontory (Pointe de Garo) r/b	13.1	-	9.5
Promontory (Pointe de la Haie) l/b	14.4	-	8.2
Overhead power lines	15.4	-	7.2
Saint-Hubert suspension bridge, slipways of former ferry, moorings	15.7	-	6.9
Plouer slipway l/b, village 1200m	16.8	-	5.8
Tower (Chêne-Vert) l/b	18.5	-	4.1
Mordreuc jetty and slipway r/b, moorings	18.9	-	3.7
Rocher des Moulières beacon r/b	19.2	-	3.4
Rocher du Galetier, beginning of stakes marking channel to Le Châtelier	21.2	-	1.4
Lessart railway viaduct	21.5	-	1.1
Le Châtelier lock and submersible weir, bridge, *navigation continues in Canal d'Ille-et-Rance*	22.6	2	0.0

Rhine

The Rhine has its sources in the Swiss Alps southwest of Chur. Passing through Lake Constance, it retains its alpine character along the Swiss–German border down to the Basle region, where navigation begins at Rheinfelden. Just below the busy inland port of Basle the river leaves Switzerland and forms the French–German border over a distance of 184km, down to Lauterbourg. The Rhine then runs north and northwest through Germany and the Netherlands to discharge into the North Sea, 1320km from its source. The Upper Rhine (from Basle down to Bingen in Germany) has always been a difficult and often a dangerous river to navigate. Large-scale training works were carried out between 1840 and 1860, but they had the effect of increasing the current speed and bed erosion. A meandering channel formed within the corrected 250m wide bed, and rocky bars were gradually exposed, the most notorious being at Istein, near Kembs. Further works were required, to fix the channel by means of transverse groynes, but Basle was still only accessible to 600-tonne barges under favourable conditions. A far more effective solution for navigation was already being envisaged before the 1914–1918 war. This was the construction of a lateral canal stretching down the left bank from Basle to Strasbourg, the Grand Canal d'Alsace, designed as a series of hydroelectric power schemes, with benefits for agricul-

ture as well as navigation. France was authorised to undertake the project under the terms of the Treaty of Versailles, and the works were conceded to
Electricité de France. The first section of the canal, avoiding the Istein bar,
was opened in 1932. By 1956 three further pounds had been completed. The
project was then modified under a new agreement between the French and
German governments, to limit the serious environmental impact on the
Rhine itself. Subsequent schemes took the form of diversion canals of varying length, with a barrage on the Rhine and power station and locks towards
the downstream end of the canal. In the 1970s two further schemes were
completed downstream of Strasbourg. As a result, the Rhine is canalised (and
not particularly attractive for cruising) almost throughout its course on the
French border.

Distances on the river are counted from the Rheinbrücke at Constance (under international agreement). The distance table here covers the section of
the river shared by France between km 168.5 and km 352.1. The right-hand
column gives distances working upstream from the French–German border at
Lauterbourg. The Grand Canal d'Alsace extends over a distance of 53km,
from km 173.6 to km 226.6.

There are connections with the Canal du Rhône au Rhin, Niffer branch, at
Niffer (km 185), with the Canal de Colmar (formerly a branch of the Canal
du Rhône au Rhin) at km 226 and with the Canal de la Marne au Rhin at
Strasbourg (km 291 or 295, see plan).

Locks There are 10 locks, all built in the context of important hydroelectric
power schemes. The first four are on the Grand Canal d'Alsace, the remaining six on diversion canals. Each lock comprises two chambers side by side,
one 185 by 24m, the other 185 by 12m. In view of the heavier traffic
downstream of the busy port of Strasbourg (12 million tonnes per year), the
two most recently-built locks, at Gambsheim and Iffezheim, each have two
270 by 24m chambers. The other variations are not significant.

Depth There is a guaranteed depth of 3.00m between Huningue and the
downstream end of the Grand Canal d'Alsace. On the canalised river the
available depth at the normal stage of the river is 2.70m down to Strasbourg
and 2.90m between Strasbourg and Lauterbourg.

Bridges All the fixed bridges offer a clear headroom of 7.00m above the
highest navigable water level between Basle and Strasbourg, 9.10m between
Strasbourg and Lauterbourg.

Authority

Service de la Navigation de Strasbourg. Subdivisions:
– 60 rue du Grillenbreit, BP545, 68021 Colmar, ☎ 89 41 21 53 (km 168-258).
– Route du Rhin, 67760 Grambsheim, ☎ 88 36 85 25 (km 258-352).

Distance table

	km	lock	km
French–Swiss border l/b (**Bâle** centre 2000m u/s)	168.5	-	183.6
Entrance to former Huningue branch of Canal du Rhône au Rhin, l/b (disused), **Huningue** quay and small town l/b	169.7	-	182.4
Port of Basle, Kleinhüningen basin, r/b	169.9	-	182.2
New road bridge (Huningue-Weil), industrial quay d/s l/b	171.3	-	180.8
Navigation enters Grand Canal d'Alsace, Kembs dam r/b	173.7	-	178.4
Kembs locks (lift 13.20m) and power station, bridge	179.1	1	173.0
Junction with Canal du Rhône au Rhun, Niffer branch, l/b	185.4	-	166.7

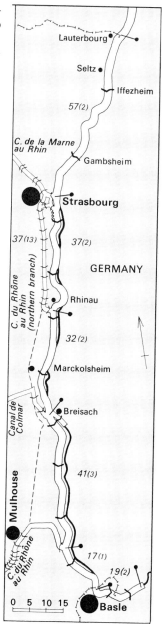

	km	*lock*	*km*
Turning basin (Hombourg), 600 x 200m	191.9	-	160.2
Ottmarsheim locks (lift 14.70m) and power station, bridge	193.7	2	158.4
Motorway bridge (A36)	194.5	-	157.6
Port of Mulhouse-Ottmarsheim l/b	196.0	-	156.1
Industrial quays l/b	197.0	-	155.1
Industrial quay (Rhône-Poulenc) l/b	199.0	-	153.1
Railway and road bridge (Neuenburg-Chalampé)	199.3	-	152.8
Chalampé l/b	199.6	-	152.5
Fessenheim locks (lift 15.10m) and power station, bridge	210.5	3	141.6
Vogelgrün locks (lift 11.80m) and power station, bridge	224.5	4	127.6
Port of Colmar-Neuf-Brisach l/b	225.8	-	126.3
Junction with Canal de Colmar, l/b	226.3	-	125.8
End of Grand Canal d'Alsace, navigation re-enters Rhine	226.6	-	125.5
Breisach harbour with boat club moorings and facilities r/b (Germany)	225.5	-	126.6
Industrial quay (Rhenalu) l/b	228.6	-	123.5
Industrial quay (Kaysersberg) l/b	230.8	-	121.3
Navigation enters diversion canal, l/b	234.3	-	117.8
Marckolsheim locks (lift 13.80m) and power station, bridge	239.9	5	112.2
End of diversion canal, navigation re-enters Rhine	242.5	-	109.6
Navigation enters diversion canal, l/b	248.2	-	103.9
Rhinau-Sundhouse locks (lift 12.30m) and power station, bridge	256.2	6	95.9
Junction with link canal to Canal du Rhône au Rhin, l/b	257.9	-	94.2
End of diversion canal, navigation re-enters Rhine	260.1	-	92.0
Rhinau ferry, village 800m l/b	261.0	-	91.1
Navigation enters diversion canal, l/b	267.5	-	84.6
Gerstheim locks (lift 10.98m) and power station, bridge	272.2	7	79.9
End of diversion canal, navigation re-enters Rhine	274.1	-	78.0
Entrance to gravel loading basin r/b	276.6	-	75.5
Plobsheim compensating basin (used for water sports) l/b	282.5	-	69.6
Entrance to diversion canal, l/b	283.1	-	69.0
Strasbourg locks (lift 10.80m) and power station, bridge	287.4	8	64.7
Port of Strasbourg, basin 4, l/b	288.3	-	63.8
Basin 3	289.1	-	63.0
Basin 2 (Gaston Haelling)	289.8	-	62.1
Basin 1 (Auguste Detoeuf)	290.6	-	61.5
End of diversion canal and *junction with southern entrance to port of* **Strasbourg**	291.4	-	60.7
Bridge (Pont de l'Europe, Strasbourg-Kehl)	293.5	-	58.6
Railway bridge, **Kehl** boat club harbour d/s r/b	293.7	-	58.4
Junction with northern entrance to port of **Strasbourg**	295.6	-	56.5
Entrance to port of Kehl, r/b	297.7	-	54.4
Entrance to gravel loading basin r/b	303.3	-	48.8
Entrance to diversion canal, l/b	307.2	-	44.9
Gambsheim locks (lift 10.35m) and power station, bridge	308.8	9	43.3
End of diversion canal, navigation re-enters Rhine	311.7	-	40.4
Offendorf gravel loading basin l/b	313.7	-	38.4
Drusenheim ferry, village 1500m l/b	318.3	-	33.8
Greffern gravel loading basin and boat club moorings, r/b	321.3	-	30.8
Fort-Louis 1000m l/b (gravel basins u/s and d/s)	326.9	-	25.2
Iffezheim locks (lift 10.30m) and power station, l/b, dam r/b, bridge	334.0	10	18.1
Confluence of Moder, l/b	334.5	-	17.6
Beinheim boat harbour l/b, village 3500m	335.5	-	16.6
Road bridge (formerly railway), Beinheim-Wintersdorf	335.7	-	16.4
Seltz pendulum ferry, village 2500m l/b	340.4	-	11.7
Entrance to gravel basins l/b	341.6	-	10.5

	km	lock	km
Munchhausen 700m l/b, access by river Sauer	344.0	-	8.1
Lauterbourg harbour l/b, restaurant, village 2000m	349.2	-	2.9
Mouth of Vieille-Lauter l/b, French–German border	352.1	-	0.0

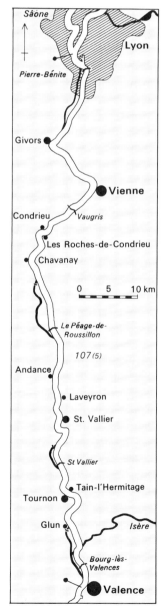

Rhône

Since 1980, when the Vaugris hydroelectric and navigation scheme was brought into use, the Rhône has been fully canalised over a total distance of 310km from its confluence with the Saône at Lyon - La Mulatière to Port Saint-Louis-du-Rhône, whence access to the Mediterranean is via a short ship canal, the Canal Maritime Saint-Louis (the bar formed by the river where it falls into the Mediterranean, 6km further downstream, is impassable for navigation).

The vast programme of works put in hand by the Compagnie Nationale du Rhône in 1933 (pursuant to an Act passed in 1921) has thus been completed between Lyon and the sea, and the navigation, alternating between wide deep river sections and 11 diversion canals, bears no resemblance to that immortalised by Bernard Clavel in Lord of the River; for although the Rhône has been a key communications route since Roman times and earlier, it was always a notoriously difficult river, even after river training works carried out between 1885 and 1905 had increased the low-water navigable draught to 1.60m. The works completed by CNR between Lyon and the Mediterranean have not only made the river navigable throughout the year by 1500-tonne barges and 4500-tonne push-tows; the 12 hydroelectric plants, with a total head of 162m, also produce 13 000 GWh of electricity annually, or 16% of the country's total hydroelectric production (20% if the Upper Rhône schemes are added), and there have been significant benefits for agriculture, especially in the form of new or modernised irrigation networks, throughout the Rhône valley.

The phenomenal engineering works detract only slightly from the beauty of the valley, which runs between the foothills of the Massif Central and the Alps. On the other hand, the navigator can now take his time on the Rhône, visiting numerous towns and sites of historic interest, instead of making a non-stop dash for the Mediterranean, worrying about the dangers of the free-flowing river, with its threatening groynes, or the bill to be presented by the Rhône pilot at the end of the voyage.

At Lyon, the Rhône is joined by the Saône, which connects it with all the waterways of central and eastern France. Upstream of the confluence, the Upper Rhône has also now been partly developed by the CNR, and although the river in practice remains unnavigable over a certain length, the entire route from Lyon to Lake Bourget is covered under the separate entry which follows for the Upper Rhône.

The whole system of connections made by the Rhône downstream of Avignon has been completely altered as a result of the development works. The Canal du Rhône à Sète is inaccessible at Beaucaire (the entrance lock having been rendered unusable by the lowering of the Rhône downstream of the Vallabrègues scheme). Instead, the Petit Rhône (p000), formerly a semi-navigable channel of the delta, has been improved for large-scale navigation (as part of the 'Palier d'Arles' dredging scheme) over a distance of about 20km from Fourques, where it leaves the Rhône, to Saint-Gilles. Here a short length of canal with one lock connects with the Canal du Rhône à Sète.

Similarly, on the left bank, the Canal d'Arles à Fos (formerly the Canal de Marseille au Rhône) has lost its former role as the through route to the Gulf of Fos and the Marseilles region. Large commercial vessels now reach the port of Fos through the newly-opened Canal du Rhône à Fos, entered from the Rhône just upstream of Barcarin ferry, but owners of boats will no doubt prefer to use the existing link through Port-Saint-Louis, if only to take advantage of the facilities offered by this small town.

Note the kilometre markers along the Rhône correspond to the original length of the river, from a point 0.7km upstream of the confluence with the Saône at Lyon to Port-Saint-Louis-du-Rhône. The following distance table gives the actual distances, allowing for the shorter diversion canals.

Locks There are 12 locks, all built by the CNR to the European waterway standard, 195 by 12m. All except Vaugris are situated on diversion canals, adjacent to the hydropower plants. The layout is such that the entrance is not clearly visible until the last few hundred metres. Enter only when a green light is showing. The fall varies between 6.70m (Vaugris) and 22m (Donzère-Mondragon). All locks are fitted with floating bollards. Single boats are locked through if no commercial traffic or other boat appears within 20 minutes of arrival at the lock.

Depth The minimum depth is 3.20m (guaranteed 20m from the channel marker buoys or the diversion canal banks).

Bridges The minimum air draught is 7m above the highest navigable water level, subject to variations dictated by the operating requirements of the power stations. Relatively low bridges have red and white gauges on the piers, the same indication being given by stakes situated a short distance upstream and downstream of the bridges.

Navigation Navigation alternates between the bed of the Rhône, 300 to 500m wide, in which short steep waves may be generated by southerly winds, and 11 diversion canals, in which the locks are generally located towards the downstream end. The mistral (northerly wind) can make lock entry difficult from upstream. The current does not exceed 7km/h, but when combined with the effect of the mistral, it can make progress upstream laborious for low-powered boats. The channel is marked in places by red-and-white buoys or stakes on the right-bank side and (more rarely) by black-and-white markers on the left-bank side. The maximum permitted speed is 35km/h (increased to 60km/h for water sports in certain sections).

Authority

Service de la Navigation Rhône–Saône. Subdivisions:
– 1 place Antonin-Perrin, 69007 Lyon, ☎ 78 72 65 16 (km 0-86).
– Zone Portuaire, 26800 Portes-lès-Valence, ☎ 75 57 00 11 (km 86-158).
– Route de la Courtine, 84021 Avignon, ☎ 90 86 06 70 (km 158-256).
– Quai de Trinquetaille, 13637 Arles, ☎ 90 96 00 85 (km 256-310).

Distance table

	km	lock	km
Lyon-La Mulatière, *confluence with Saône* (tip of peninsula, roughly level with former lock of La Mulatière, r/b)			
Projected Gerland marina l/b	0.0	-	310.0
Port of Lyon-Edouard Herriot, entrance to basins, l/b	2.6	-	307.4

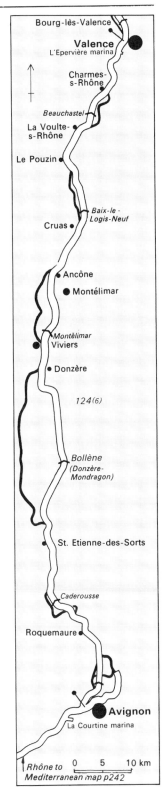

Rhône to Mediterranean map p242

	km	lock	km
Entrance to Pierre-Bénite diversion canal, l/b	3.2	–	306.8
Pierre-Bénite lock (lift 9.25m) and power station	3.4	1	306.6
Motorway bridge (A7)	4.3	–	305.7
Feyzin oil refinery	6.5	–	303.5
Bridge	7.4	–	302.6
Bridge, coal unloading quay d/s l/b	10.3	–	299.7
End of diversion canal	14.3	–	295.7
Arboras railway viaduct	16.5	–	293.5
Givors bridge (oil terminal upstream)	17.2	–	292.8
Confluence of Giers, r/b, mooring	17.6	–	292.4
Suspension bridge	18.2	–	291.8
Fertiliser factory, l/b	19.0	–	291.0
Water intake for power station, r/b	20.3	–	289.7
Entrance to coal unloading basin for Loire-sur-Rhône power station	21.3	–	288.7
Overhead pipeline crossing	21.4	–	288.6
Motorway bridge (B7)	25.7	–	284.3
Backwater, r/b, with small boat harbour	25.8	–	284.2
Vienne bridge	27.9	–	282.1
Suspension bridge	28.3	–	281.7
Mooring, l/b	28.6	–	281.4
Motorway bridge (B7)	32.0	–	278.0
Vaugris lock (lift 6.70m) and power station	33.3	2	276.7
Arenc castle, Ampuis, r/b	34.4	–	275.6
Condrieu meander cut-off (former channel dammed, l/b)	38.8	–	271.2
Les Roches-de-Condrieu boat harbour l/b, all services and comfortable moorings in a sheltered backwater (former meander), restaurant (see plan)	39.7	–	270.3
Condrieu bridge	40.0	–	270.0
Saint-Clair-du-Rhône industrial complex, potash unloading quay, l/b	42.2	–	267.8
Chavanay, r/b	45.8	–	264.2
Chavanay bridge	46.4	–	263.6
Saint-Maurice-l'Exil nuclear power station, l/b	47.0	–	263.0
Entrance to Le Péage-de-Roussillon diversion canal, l/b	49.3	–	260.7
Bridge and public quay, l/b (**Serrières**, 2000m)	54.8	–	255.2
Bridge (N519)	57.8	–	252.2
Sablons lock (lift 14.50m) and power station	58.8	3	251.2
SNCF railway viaduct (Peyraud)	59.4	–	250.6
End of diversion canal	60.2	–	249.8
Champagne, r/b, former ferry, dangerous groyne	62.6	–	247.4
Andance bridge (Andance, r/b, Andancette, l/b)	66.0	–	244.0
Sarrasinière tower (ruin, r/b)	68.6	–	241.4
Nautic Loisirs, harbour and slipway, l/b (Laveyron 600m)	70.0	–	240.0
Confluence of Cance, r/b	70.3	–	239.7
Confluence of Ay, r/b	72.0	–	238.0
Saint-Vallier bridge, town l/b	72.7	–	237.3
Quay l/b	75.3	–	234.7
Serves castle, l/b, and Arras tower, r/b	79.1	–	230.9
Entrance to Saint-Vallier diversion canal, l/b	79.9	–	230.1
Gervans lock (lift 10.75m) and power station	83.3	4	226.7
End of diversion canal	83.7	–	226.3
Table du Roy rock in mid-channel (pass on r/b side)	86.3	–	223.7
Tournon boat harbour and slipway, r/b	88.0	–	222.0
Tournon footbridge, **Tain l'Hermitage** l/b	88.2	–	221.8
Tournon bridge	88.8	–	221.2
Auberge de Frais Matin, quay for clients, l/b	92.8	–	217.2
Entrance to Bourg-lès-Valence diversion canal, l/b	95.4	–	214.6

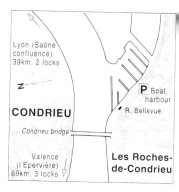

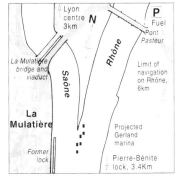

Push-tow. Leaving St-Vallier lock on the Rhône.
Arc Photo

	km	lock	km
Bridge	96.1	–	213.9
Canal enters river Isère	99.1	–	210.9
Canal leaves river Isère (outlet weir, r/b)	100.2	–	209.8
Bourg-lès-Valence lock (lift 11.70m) and power station	102.8	5	207.2
End of diversion canal	105.0	–	205.0
Valence bridge	106.5	–	203.5
Public quay, l/b	106.7	–	203.3
L'Epervière marina, l/b, complete facilities, supermarket 500m	109.0	–	201.0
Soyons, r/b, leaning tower (ruin)	111.7	–	198.3
Portes-lès-Valence quay (commercial) and sub-divisional engineer's office, l/b	113.0	–	197.0
Charmes, entrance to Beauchastel diversion canal, r/b, bridge	116.2	–	193.8
Boat club moorings, r/b	116.4	–	193.6
Beauchastel lock (lift 12.65m) and power station, village 500m, r/b	120.5	6	189.5
End of diversion canal	122.1	–	187.9
Confluence of Eyrieux, r/b	122.5	–	187.5
La Voulte bridge, mooring and town centre r/b	124.0	–	186.0
La Voulte railway viaduct	124.7	–	185.3
Confluence of Drôme, l/b	127.6	–	182.4
Le Pouzin bridge	129.2	–	180.8

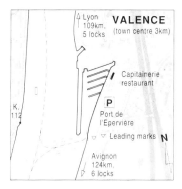

	km	lock	km
Entrance to Baix-Le-Logis-Neuf diversion canal, l/b	131.3	-	178.7
Le-Logis-Neuf lock (lift 13.00m) and power station	138.6	7	171.4
End of diversion canal	140.0	-	170.0
Cruas, quay, r/b, moorings, village 500m	140.9	-	169.1
Cruas nuclear power station, r/b	144.0	-	166.0
Island, main channel on r/b side, boatyard on l/b side (access from d/s)	144.0	-	166.0
Entrance to Montélimar diversion canal, l/b	148.6	-	161.4
Ancône, mooring and village l/b	150.0	-	160.0
Bridge	150.8	-	159.2
Bridge (N540)	153.2	-	156.8
Crossing of river Roubion	153.7	-	156.3
Gournier bridge and chapel	155.4	-	154.6
Montélimar harbour (inconvenient mooring)	155.5	-	154.5
Châteauneuf lock (17.10m) and power station (village 2000m)	159.0	8	151.0
End of diversion canal (Rhône navigable 4km upstream to Lafarge cement works)	161.8	-	148.2
Viviers, public quay and boat harbour, r/b	162.0	-	148.0
Viviers bridge, entrance to Donzère gorge	162.3	-	147.7
Donzère bridge	165.4	-	144.6
Entrance to Donzère-Mondragon diversion canal, l/b	166.4	-	143.6
Bridge with flood gate, quay r/b	166.8	-	143.2
SNCF railway viaduct	170.2	-	139.8
Bridge (N7)	170.3	-	139.7
Bridge (D358)	174.4	-	135.6

Rhône at Tarascon.

	km	lock	km
Bridge (D59)	176.3	-	133.7
Pierrelatte atomic energy centre r/b	178.8	-	131.2
Tricastin nuclear power station r/b	180.3	-	129.7
Bridge (D204)	181.0	-	129.0
Lock approach channel, l/b	182.1	-	127.9
Bollène lock (22.00m) and André Blondel power station	183.1	9	126.9
Bridge (D994), **Bollène** 1000m	185.4	-	124.6
Railway viaduct	188.5	-	121.5
Bridge (N7)	189.2	-	120.8
Bride (D44), Mondragon 500m	190.4	-	119.6
End of diversion canal	193.6	-	116.4
Saint-Etienne-des-Sorts, mooring r/b, former			
boatman's village	196.8	-	113.2
Marcoule nuclear power station, r/b	201.5	-	108.5
Entrance to Caderousse diversion canal, l/b	205.7	-	104.3
Caderousse lock (9.00m) and power station	208.2	10	101.8
End of diversion canal, Rhône navigable 5km upstream to			
port of L'Ardoise	210.5	-	99.5
Montfaucon castle, r/b	212.2	-	97.8
Motorway bridge (A9)	213.1	-	96.9
Bridge (D976)	213.2	-	96.8

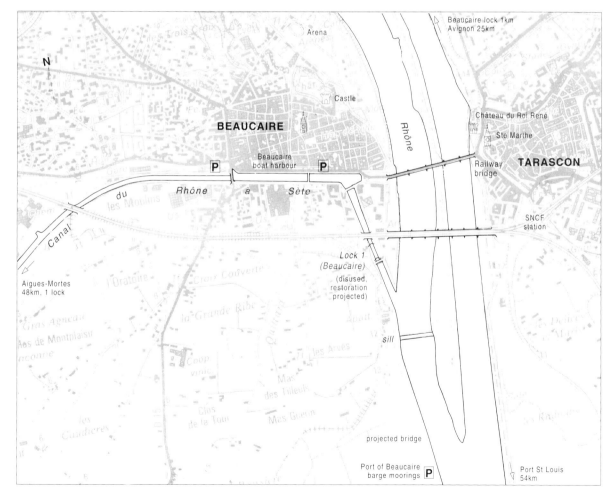

	km	lock	km
Roquemaure quay, castle, r/b, Tour de l'Hers tower, l/b	216.2	-	93.8
Entrance to Villeneuve-les-Avignon diversion canal, r/b	221.4	-	88.6
Villeneuve dam, r/b, and bridge	223.5	-	86.5
Crossing of former Villeneuve arm of Rhône (dammed)	224.4	-	85.6
Avignon lock (10.50m) and power station	225.7	11	84.3
End of diversion canal	226.3	-	83.7
Villeneuve bridge	229.0	-	81.0
Express road bridge	230.0	-	80.0
Junction with Avignon arm of Rhône (see below)	230.6	-	79.4
Railway viaduct	230.8	-	79.2
Confluence of Durance, l/b, access to Courtine marina	234.5	-	75.5
Aramon bridge	239.1	-	70.9
Aramon oil-fired power station and quay for tanker barges, r/b	243.4	-	66.6
Vallabrègues, l/b	248.0	-	62.0
Entrance to Vallabrègues diversion canal, l/b	249.2	-	60.8
Beaucaire lock (12.15m) and power station	251.8	12	58.2
Tarascon bridge, town l/b but no moorings (Beaucaire r/b)	254.2	-	55.8
Railway viaduct	254.6	-	55.4
End of diversion canal (Rhône not navigable, entrance to Canal du Rhône à Sète closed, connection made via Petit Rhône	255.9	-	54.1
Port of Beaucaire, r/b	256.0	-	54.0
Intake of Bas Rhône-Languedoc irrigation canal, r/b	264.1	-	45.9
Junction with Petit Rhône, r/b, and turning basin	265.9	-	44.1
Arles, quay with slipways, convenient mooring, l/b	268.7	-	41.3
Trinquetaille bridge, sub-divisional engineer's office	269.3	-	40.7
New bridge	269.8	-	40.2
Junction with Canal d'Arles à Fos, l/b	270.4	-	39.6
Terrin shoals, fast current	280.0	-	30.0
Junction with Canal du Rhône à Fos, l/b	303.2	-	6.8
Barcarin ferry	303.5	-	6.5
Private ferry serving Salin de Giraud salt marshes	304.1	-	5.9
Port de l'Esquineau, quay, r/b	305.9	-	4.1
Shelter harbour, l/b	309.0	-	1.0
Port-Saint-Louis-du-Rhône, entrance to sea lock and basin, l/b	310.0	-	0.0

(Mouth of Rhône 6km further downstream, not navigable)

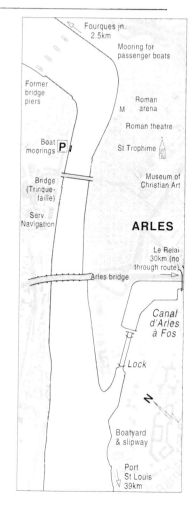

Avignon arm

	km	lock	km
Junction with Villeneuve arm of Rhône (km 231)	0.0	-	9.0
Express road bridge	0.8	-	8.2
Villeneuve bridge	1.6	-	7.4
Saint-Bénézet bridge (the famous 'Pont d'Avignon')	2.0	-	7.0
Avignon boat harbour, near town centre, harbourmaster's office and reception barge with all services: fuel, repairs, showers, information, telephone, VHF call on channels 9/16	2.2	-	6.7
Quai de la Ligne (alternative mooring, l/b)	2.5	-	6.5
Le Pontet, quay, l/b	7.8	-	1.2
Overhead power line	8.4	-	0.6
Limit of navigation, turning basin	9.0	-	0.0

Canal maritime Saint-Louis

This canal provides a passage for vessels between the Rhône and the Gulf of Fos. It includes the entrance lock at Port Saint Louis-du-Rhône, which has a total length 160m with a width of 22m. The minimum depth of water is 5.50m. The port basin is located below the lock. The canal is 3.0km long, extended into the gulf by a dredged channel protected by a breakwater over a further length of 2.0km.

Upper Rhône and Lake Bourget

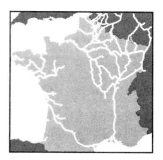

The Upper Rhône, once navigated throughout its length from Lyon to Switzerland, is still theoretically navigable to Seyssel dam, a short distance upstream of the towns of Seyssel (Ain) on the right bank and Seyssel (Haute-Savoie) on the left bank. This dam was built to create a compensating reservoir below the famous Génissiat dam, one of the first high-head hydropower schemes in Europe (completed in 1948). More recent development by the Compagnie Nationale du Rhône, following completion of all their schemes on the river downstream of Lyon, has brought some significant changes, and although the river is still a long way from being fully navigable, substantial sections are now available for cruising. Since there are no facilities for boats at the Chautagne dam, the first downstream from Seyssel, the itinerary presented here is the one followed by the old paddle steamers which ran from Lyon to Belley, then turning right short of Chautagne to pass through the curious Canal de Savières and into Lake Bourget, the biggest natural lake in France, with the important tourist and spa resort of Aix-les-Bains on its eastern shore. The itinerary from the confluence with the Saône at Lyon to the boat harbour at the southern end of Lake Bourget is just over 151km, of which the first 7km up from the confluence and the last 110km from Loyettes can be navigated in safety.

The intermediate section (km 7 to km 41) presents a series of obstacles. The first is the drop and resulting strong current through the Poincaré bridge (km 7.9). Then there are the two disused locks on the Electricité de France Canal de Jonage. Finally, the shifting shoals at the confluence of the Ain downstream of Loyettes make this section impracticable. There are two CNR projects in this section. The first is the Miribel-Saint-Clair scheme, which would incorporate one lock downstream of the Poincaré bridge at Saint-Clair and another in a new cut between the old course of the Rhône and the Canal de Miribel. The decision to go ahead with this scheme depends on industrial development and the need to provide for high-capacity inland shipping to the relatively underdeveloped area east of Lyon. In the meantime, the itinerary here follows the southerly route through the Canal de Jonage. The second scheme cuts through the Ain confluence at Loyettes, a designated area of outstanding natural beauty, hence the State's opposition and shelving of the project. It remains to be seen what kind of development could be envisaged to allow through navigation by pleasure traffic.

Notwithstanding these complications, owners of trailed boats are strongly encouraged to make use of one of the numerous boat harbours to get afloat in the navigable section, for example at Briord (km 76), for the fascinating cruise up the river, with its dramatic Alpine landscapes, and through the Canal de Savières into Lake Bourget. Very few undertake this cruise, for the elevator system at the CNR dams is cumbersome and dissuasive (see following paragraph).

Locks There are 6 structures overcoming a difference in level of 63m between Lyon and Lake Bourget. The first two are the locks built by Electricité de France under the Jonage hydroelectric scheme. These locks, of
substantial dimensions, were rarely operated, and are now out of service. The
following three structures are the hydropower dams completed during the
1980s, at Sault-Brénaz, Brégnier-Cordon and Belley. There are no locks here,
but mobile elevators which are operated on demand, between ramps in the
bank above and below the power plant. These elevators can handle boats up
to 5 tonnes, with a maximum length of 9.50m and maximum beam 3.40m.
There are public telephones at each of these power plants, with the number
of the local mechanic to be called for operation of the elevator. Two hours'
notice is to be given. After these three elevators, boaters will be relieved to
find a conventional lock at Savières, with navigable dimensions of 18m by
5.25m. The lock is operated simply by selecting the direction of passage and
pushing a button on the control cabinet by the lock side. The cycle is automatic.

Depth There is no draught limitation in the regulations for navigation on the
Upper Rhône. The sill depth of Savières lock is 2.50m, and a depth of 2.00m
is available throughout the navigable length of the river and the Canal de
Savières. Between Lyon and Loyettes, on the other hand, the river flows in
its natural state, and there may be as little as 0.30m depth in places.

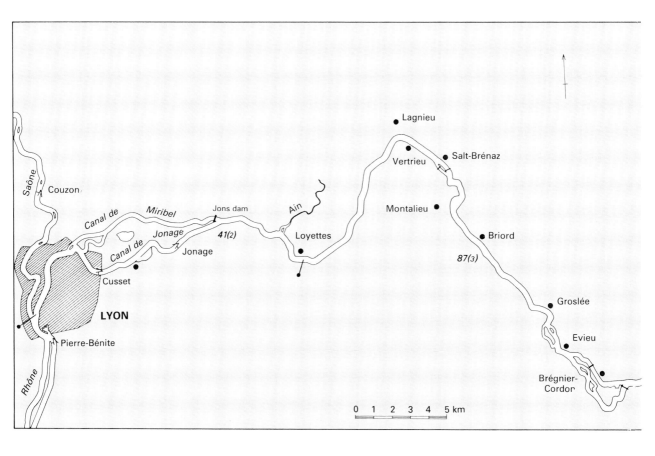

Bridges The lowest bridge is at Portout, on the Canal de Savières, offering a minimum headroom of 3.50m.

Towpath There is no towpath.

Authority

Service de la Navigation Rhône–Saône, Lyon
Subdivision: Place Antonin Perrin, 69007 Lyon, ☎ 78 72 65 16

Distance table

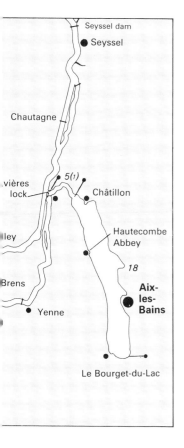

	km	lock	km
Confluence with Saône at La Mulatière/Gerland, Gerland marina projected l/b	0.0	-	151.2
Bridge (Pasteur)	0.6	-	150.6
Railway bridge (Perrache)	2.2	-	149.0
Bridge (Galliéni)	2.5	-	148.7
Bridge (Guillotière)	3.0	-	148.2
Bridge (Wilson)	3.6	-	147.6
Bridge (Lafayette)	4.0	-	147.2
Footbridge (Collège), residential barge moorings l/b	4.8	-	146.4
Bridge (Morand), road with Lyon metro underneath	5.2	-	146.0
Bridge (de Lattre de Tassigny)	5.5	-	145.7
Bridge (Winston Churchill)	6.1	-	145.1
Railway bridge (TGV Lyon-Paris), strong current, dangerous	7.8	-	143.3
Road bridge (Raymond Poincaré)	7.9	-	143.2
D/s tip of island (Ile du Grand Camp), keep to l/b arm	9.3	-	141.9
Bridge (service road giving access to Lyon well field)	10.6	-	140.6
Navigation enters diversion canal l/b, Le Vieux Rhône r/b	10.8	-	140.4
Footbridge	10.9	-	140.3
Bridge (Croix-Luiset)	11.2	-	140.0
Bridge (Cusset)	13.2	-	138.0
Cusset lock r/b, adjacent to hydropower plant, rise 12.20m	13.8	1	137.4
Bridge (Sucrerie), multi-coloured girders	15.7	-	135.5
Décines bridge, town centre 500m l/b	17.2	-	134.0
Opening in breakwater l/b, entrance to 'Le Grand Large' compensating reservoir (sailing clubs)	18.5	-	132.7
Bridge	20.9	-	130.3
Meyzieu bridge, town centre 2100m l/b	22.9	-	128.3
Jonage lock r/b, adjacent to hydropower plant	24.1	2	127.1
Jonage bridge, small town 400m l/b	25.7	-	125.5
Dam (Jons) r/b, end of diversion canal	29.7	-	121.5
Bridge (Jons), campsite r/b	29.9	-	121.3
Confluence of Ain, lower arm, r/b	37.0	-	114.2
Anthon l/b	37.5	-	113.7
Confluence of Ain, upper arm, r/b	37.6	-	113.6
Loyettes bridge, village r/b	41.4	-	109.8
Overhead power lines	46.3	-	104.9
Bugey nuclear power station, cooling water outfall r/b	47.5	-	103.7
Cooling water intake r/b	48.3	-	102.9
Overhead power lines	52.4	-	98.8
D/s tip of island, keep to l/b arm	54.6	-	96.6
Proulieu r/b, castle (Salette) l/b	56.8	-	94.4
Port-Lagnieu bridge (D65), **Lagnieu** 2500m r/b	60.0	-	91.2
Vertrieu castle and village l/b	62.0	-	89.2
Island (Saint-Véran), keep to l/b arm	63.0	-	88.2
Entrance to old lock-cut, leaving Rhône on r/b side and power plant diversion canal on l/b side	65.5	-	85.7

	km	lock	km
Sault-Brénaz bridge, mooring u/s in old lock, village r/b over Rhône bridge (Pont du Saut), Porcieu-Amblagnieu dam and hydropower plant l/b, rise 7.60m	65.7	3	85.5
D/s elevator ramp at end of Sault-Brénaz old lock	65.9	-	85.3
U/s elevator ramp	66.1	-	85.1
Dam (Villebois) r/b, end of diversion canal	67.0	-	84.2
Island	69.0	-	82.2
Montalieu boat moorings and water park ('La Vallée Bleue') l/b in widening	70.6	-	80.6
Bridge (D52, Pont de Briord)	75.6	-	75.6
Briord boat harbour, pontoon moorings r/b, Hors Bord Club du Rhône, boatyards in village, archeological museum	76.1	-	75.1
Creys-Malville nuclear power station and private mooring l/b	78.7	-	72.5
River enters narrow gorge (Défilé de Malarage)	81.4	-	70.8
End of gorge, river widens, small island r/b	82.1	-	69.1
Castle (Mérieu) l/b	82.4	-	68.8
Le Port de Groslée suspension bridge (D60), village r/b	87.1	-	64.1
River divides, take middle channel, keeping towards l/b side	89.0	-	62.2
U/s tip of La Sauge island, navigation in l/b arm	90.3	-	60.9
La Sauge r/b	91.0	-	60.2
Evieu bridge, village 200m r/b	93.3	-	57.9
Navigation enters Brégnier-Cordon diversion canal r/b	93.6	-	57.6
Brégnier-Cordon dam and power plant, rise 11.40m, elevator ramps 200m d/s and 200m u/s	96.1	4	55.1
Bridge (La Bruyère), **Brégnier-Cordon** 1200m r/b	98.8	-	52.4
Bridge (D992),	100.3	-	50.9
Murs-et-Gélignieux boat moorings in canal widening, l/b	100.5	-	50.7
Brégnier-Cordon dam l/b, end of diversion canal	101.4	-	49.8
D/s tip of Chantemerle islands, keep to l/b channel	110.9	-	40.3
Navigation enters Brens-Belley diversion canal, r/b, (canoes and other portable boats continue right on bypassed Rhône, weirs with portage paths)	112.8	-	38.4
Bridge (Brens-Virignin)	113.3	-	37.9
Brens dam and hydropower plant, rise 15,05m, elevator ramps 200m d/s and 300m u/s	114.4	5	36.8
Bridge (La Combe)	115.9	-	35.3
Belley bridge (mooring impracticable), town centre 2000m	117.8	-	33.4
Canal enters narrow gorge	121.5	-	29.7
Bridge (Lit au Roi) at end of gorge	122.0	-	29.2
Canal widens into Lac du Lit au Roi, boat harbour and beaches l/b, island (Ile aux Oiseaux) in middle of lake	122.2	-	29.0
Bridge (Cressin-Rochefort)	124.4	-	26.8
Dam (Lavours) l/b, end of diversion canal	127.6	-	23.6
Savières lock, do-it-yourself, push-button operation, maximum rise 4.25m	128.2	6	23.0
Chanaz boat harbour l/b, campsite, village 500m	128.4	-	22.8

Canal de Savières

	km	lock	km
Turn north from Rhône into Canal de Savières	128.7	-	22.5
Footbridge, access to campsite and boat harbour	129.0	-	22.2
Chanaz boat moorings south bank, small village, restaurants	129.1	-	22.1
Bridge (Chanaz)	129.4	-	21.8
Private mooring north bank	130.7	-	20.5
Private mooring north bank	130.9	-	20.3
Portout bridge and landing stages for trip boats, restaurant	132.4	-	18.8

	km	lock	km
Lake Bourget			

N.B. straight line distances across lake to each point indicated, from the canal entrance south in the left column and from the boat harbour entrance channel (Port des Quatre Chemins) north in the right column

	km	lock	km
Stake marking entrance to Canal de Savières, navigation enters Lake Bourget	133.2	-	18.0
La Châtière boat harbour west shore, **Conjux** 700m south	134.2	-	17.3
Châtillon harbour beneath castle, north-east shore, attractive picnic area, restaurant	134.9	-	17.1
Saint-Gilles private harbour west shore	136.7	-	14.7
Boat harbour west shore (obligatory for visit to abbey)	138.7	-	12.6
Hautecombe royal abbey, west shore, burial place of princes and princesses of Savoy	139.0	-	12.3
Brison harbour east shore beside railway halt, small village	140.2	-	11.7
Pointe de l'Ardre headland, east shore	143.3	-	8.1
Le Grand Port yacht harbour east shore, Aix 3000m	145.0	-	6.5
Aix-les-Bains harbour (le Petit Port) east shore, campsites, town centre 2500m	146.4	-	5.0
Bourdeau castle and village 70m above lake on west shore	147.2	-	4.5
Charpignat boat harbour west shore, **Le Bourget-du-Lac** 2000m south, small town	149.6	-	2.5
Outer mole of breakwater marking channel entrance	150.7	-	0.5
Boat harbour (Port des Quatre Chemins) at southern limit of lake, **Chambéry** 10km	151.2	-	0.0

Petit Rhône and Canal de Saint-Gilles

The Petit Rhône was formerly a narrow shallow channel of the Rhône delta, navigable only by small boats. However, as indicated in the general introduction to the Rhône, the channel has been considerably improved for large-scale navigation over a distance of about 20km from the lower Rhône at Fourques (upstream of Arles) to Saint-Gilles, where a new cut with one lock connects with the Canal du Rhône à Sète. The river thus forms part of the through route from the Rhône to Sète and the Canal du Midi. Only the through route is indicated in the distance table, the distances in the first column being those of the Rhône, counted from Lyon. Small boats may proceed down the Petit Rhône beyond the entrance to the Canal de Saint-Gilles to enter the Mediterranean at Grau d'Orgon, a further 37km winding through the dense vegetation of the Camargue.

Locks There is one lock, of standard Rhône dimensions (195 by 12m, with a sill depth of 4.50m), on the Canal de Saint-Gilles.

Depth The depth of the 30m wide fairway is maintained at 2.20m at low water level.

Bridges There are four bridges. The lowest is the railway bridge at km 294.7, offering a minimum headroom of 4.75m.

Authority
Service de la Navigation de Lyon.
Subdivision: quai de Trinquetaille, 13637 Arles, ☎ 90 96 00 85.

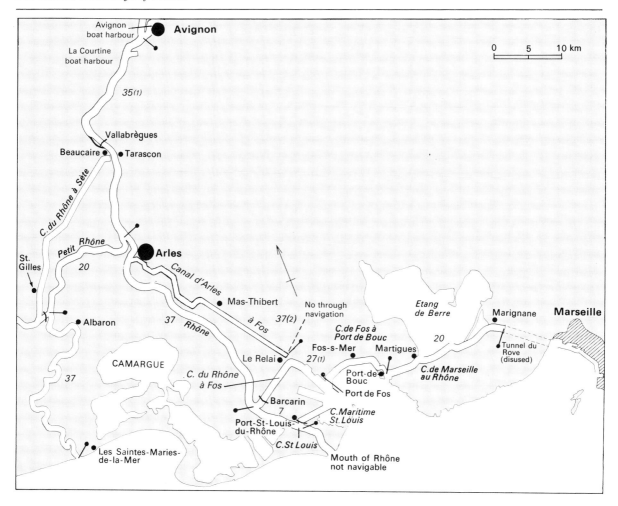

Distance table

	km	lock	km
Entrance to the Petit Rhône from the Rhône at Fourques	279.2	-	22.5
Fourques suspension bridge	281.0	-	20.7
Fourques girder bridge (N113)	281.7	-	20.0
Railway bridge (Cavalet)	294.7	-	7.0
Bridge (Saint-Gilles), N572	297.3	-	4.4
Entrance to Canal de Saint-Gilles, r/b	299.5	-	2.2
Lock (Saint-Gilles)	300.0	1	1.7
Junction with Canal du Rhône à Sète (km 29)	301.7	-	0.0

Rhône-Fos-Bouc (-Marseille) waterway

The system of waterways connecting Marseille to the Rhône has undergone numerous changes over the last 20 years, and a brief recapitulation of the various developments may be helpful. First of all, the former Canal de Marseille au Rhône was closed as a through route after failure of a section of the 7km long Rove tunnel in 1963. In 1970, development of the port of Fos resulted in closure of part of what was then called the Canal d'Arles à Bouc. A new anti-salt lock was built to give access from the canal to one of the basins (Darse 1) of the port of Fos, and the canal changed its name accordingly to Canal d'Arles à Fos. Although the canal remained open to navigation, it continued to carry very little traffic, since the 38.50m barges for which it was designed were unable to navigate on the Rhône. The Canal maritime Saint-Louis (see under Rhône) was the obligatory route for commercial barges and the preferred route for boats. However, with completion of canalisation works on the Rhône in 1980, it became necessary to provide a safe link between the river and Fos (and Port-de-Bouc) for large push-tows, which had to split to negotiate the lock at Port-Saint-Louis, and were often delayed by rough water conditions in the Gulf of Fos. Enlargement of the existing Canal d'Arles à Fos would have been too costly, so a new canal has been opened from the Rhône at km 303 to Darse 1 at Fos. The canal uses the last 2km of the canal d'Arles à Fos, in which the former anti-salt lock has been destroyed. The replacement structure on the canal upstream of the junction with the new cut is an anti-salt barrage, which obstructs navigation. The Canal d'Arles à Fos is therefore closed as a through route. The Rhône–Fos link is not open to boats, which must continue to use the canal maritime Saint-Louis.

The waterway described here is divided into several sections:

1. Rhône–Fos junction canal (km 0-11)
2. Basins of the port of Fos (km 11-18)
3. Fos–Bouc junction canal (km 18-27)
4. Port-de-Bouc roadstead and Canal de Marseille au Rhône (km 27-47).

The waterway is open to push-tows of international dimensions throughout, but the last section will remain a dead end until the (possible) reopening of the Rove tunnel.

It should be noted that traffic through the narrow cutting in Port-de-Bouc is one-way only, controlled by lights.

Locks There is just one lock on the waterway, near the entrance from the Rhône at Barcarin. It has the same dimensions as the locks on the Rhône, 195 by 12m, and overcomes a difference in level ranging between a few centimetres and 2.30m (when the Rhône is in flood).

Depth The maximum authorised draught is 3.20m between the Rhône and Port-de-Bouc. The available depth in the last section to the Rove tunnel is only slightly less.

Authority
Port Autonome de Marseille, Direction des Installations de Fos

Distance table

	km	lock	km
Junction with Rhône (km 316)	0.0	-	47.4
Lock (Barcarin), bridge	1.9	1	45.5
Junction with former Canal d'Arles à Fos (entrance blocked by anti-salt barrage)	9.0	-	38.4
Bridge (N568a)	9.7	-	37.7
Railway bridge	9.8	-	37.6
Navigation enters Darse 1 of port of Fos (end of Rhône-Fos junction canal)	11.3	-	36.1
Navigation enters Darse Sud of port of Fos	16.0	-	31.4
Limit of Darse Sud, navigation enters Fos-Port-de-Bouc junction canal	18.3	-	29.1
Turning basin (Carrefour des Joncs)	20.1	-	27.3
Fos-sur-Mer bridge, village 700m	21.6	-	25.8
Moorings south bank (for vessels waiting to proceed through one-way cutting)	24.5	-	22.9
Railway bridge	25.2	-	22.2
Bridge	25.9	-	21.5
Port-de-Bouc railway and road bridges	26.7	-	20.7
End of one-way cutting, navigation enters Port-de-Bouc basin	27.1	-	20.3
Entrance to Chenal de Caronte	28.1	-	19.3
Railway viaduct (Caronte)	30.3	-	17.1
Motorway bridge	31.7	-	15.7
Martigues swing bridge (Jonquières), navigation enters Etang de Berre	32.9	-	14.5
Cutting (La Mède)	38.1	-	9.3
La Mède quay, access to Etang de Berre opposite, village 700m	38.2	-	9.2
Bridge (Jai)	39.8	-	7.6
Basin (Bolmon)	44.6	-	2.8
Marignane basin, village 1200m north, entrance to Gignac cutting	45.5	-	1.9
Road and railway bridges (Floride)	45.8	-	1.6
Bridge (Toës)	46.6	-	0.8
Northern entrance to Rove tunnel (navigation interrupted)	47.4	-	0.0

Canal du Rhône au Rhin

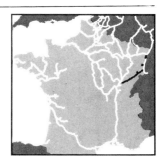

The Canal du Rhône au Rhin, started in 1784 and opened to navigation in 1833, is one of the great watershed links of the French waterway network. It is used by large numbers of boats as one of the main routes between Germany and the Mediterranean, but it is also a cruising waterway in its own right, especially where it follows the valley of the river Doubs. As a commercial route, the canal is used by standard 38.50m barges loading 250 tonnes, but there is a long-standing project to open up a completely new large-scale waterway on the line of the canal, thus providing a continuous route for Rhine shipping from the North Sea to the Mediterranean.

The canal links the Saône at Saint-Symphorien, 4km upstream of the junction with the Canal de Bourgogne at Saint-Jean-de-Losne, to the upper Rhine (in fact the Ottmersheim reach of the Grand Canal d'Alsace) at Niffer (km 185). The length of the canal is 237km. From Saint-Symphorien, a 17km canal section leads to the Doubs. Navigation then uses the course of this river for long sections as far as l'Isle-sur-le-Doubs (km 141). From l'Isle-sur-le-Doubs to Mulhouse (km 224), navigation is almost exclusively in manmade cut, and crosses the Saône–Rhine watershed by a summit level at an altitude of 340m. From Mulhouse to Niffer, navigation follows the former Kembs–Niffer branch of the canal, which was upgraded to the 1350-tonne barge standard as part of the Upper Rhine development works. Officially, the canal starts at the Saône and ends at the Rhine, but the distance table is here presented in the reverse direction, to make it more readable for navigators heading down the Doubs, which requires care in the river sections, where the fixed masonry weirs are difficult to see for boats heading downstream.

Separate descriptions and distance tables are given for the following branches:

– the Belfort branch, 13.5km long, connecting with the main line at km 172,
– the Colmar branch (or Canal de Colmar), 23km long,
– the northern branch, 35km long, extending from the Rhine at Rhinau to the Dusuzeau basin in the port of Strasbourg.

The last two branches are completely separate from the main route from the Saône to the Rhine, and thus do not appear on the general map on these pages. Reference should be made to the general map of the Rhine.

On the main line there are two tunnels, at Thoraise (km 59) and under the citadel at Besançon (km 74), although here boaters will often prefer to cruise through the town, St Paul lock having been reopened for boat traffic. Thoraise tunnel is 185m long, while that at Besançon is 394m long. Both are for one-way traffic only (6m wide). There are also numerous narrow bridgeholes (as little as 5.18m wide), aqueducts and cuttings allowing one-way passage only.

Locks There are 112 locks, of which 72 fall towards the Saône (including two double staircase locks), the remaining 40 towards the Rhine. There are also four flood locks, normally open to navigation, generally situated at the entrances to certain lock-cuts in the Doubs valley. The lock numbers do not tally with these totals, because of various changes made since the canal was first built. At the end of the last century, the summit level was lowered and the first locks on either side eliminated. More recently, locks 12 and 13 at Sochaux were replaced by a single lock at the end of a section upgraded to

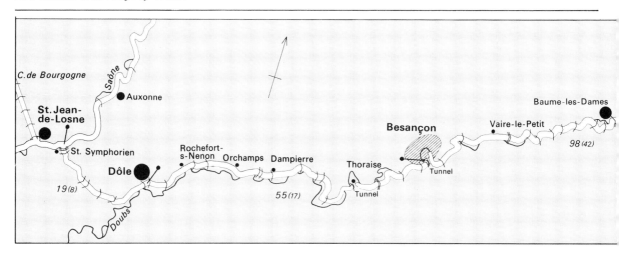

high-capacity standards as part of the future Rhone–Rhine waterway past the Peugeot car factory. The first 68 locks from Saint-Symphorien to km 175 (Allenjoie) are 38.70 by 5.25m. The last five up to the summit level are of larger dimensions (40.70 by 6.28m). The 39 down from the summit level to Mulhouse are 38.80 by 5.10m, while the last lock at Niffer is of Rhine barge dimensions (85 by 12m).

Depth The maximum authorised draught is 1.80m.

Bridges The maximum authorised air draught is 3.50m, reduced to 3.40m above the highest navigable water level when the Doubs is in flood.
Regulations Maximum permitted speed is 10km/h in the river sections and 6km/h in canal sections.

Towpath There is a towpath throughout.

Authority
Service de la Navigation Rhône–Saône, Arrondissement de Besançon, Moulin Saint-Paul, 18 avenue Gaulard, BP 429, 25019 Besançon, ☎ 81 81 10 12.
Subdivisions:
– 2 rue du Général Bethouard, BP 83, 39108 Dôle, ☎ 84 82 01 03 (km 0-57).
– 7 boulevard Tarragnoz, 25000 Besançon, ☎ 81 81 18 55 (km 57-130).
– Port Fluvial, BP207, 25200 Montbéliard, ☎ 81 91 17 32 (km 130-176).
Service de la Navigation de Strasbourg. Subdivisions:
– 6 rue Alfred Engel, 90800 Bavilliers, ☎ 84 21 00 88 (km 176-186 and 214-224).
– 12 rue J.J. Henner, 68100 Mulhouse, ☎ 89 45 65 30 (km 186-214).

Besançon loop

This loop provides an alternative route for boats through the attractive town, bypassing the 500m length of the main line of the canal through the Citadelle tunnel. The loop is 4km long, from the upstream tunnel entrance (flood gate 50a) to the downstream entrance (lock 50, Tarragnoz), and includes lock 51a (Saint-Paul), which has been reopened for pleasure traffic. Navigational characteristics are the same as for the rest of the canal.

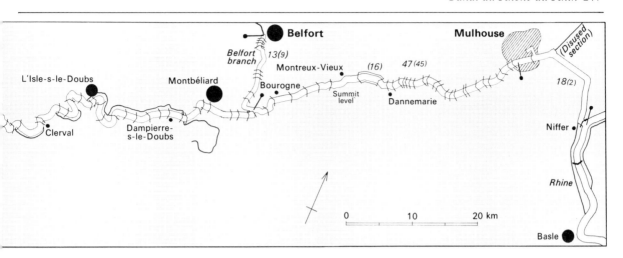

Belfort branch

The embranchment de Belfort leaves the main line at km 172, near Allenjoie, and may be navigated up to km 13.5, where a main road crosses the canal on the outskirts of Belfort. The canal was originally projected to cut through a series of watersheds and connect with the Saône at Port-sur-Saône. Construction was completed up to the main summit level, 14km beyond Belfort, before the project was abandoned. Commercial traffic on the branch has virtually ceased, but increased use by boats may save it from closure. Unfortunately, the branch is accompanied by the A36 motorway over much of its length.

Locks There are 9 locks, with minimum dimensions 38.70 by 5.20m.

Depth The maximum authorised draught is 1.80m.

Bridges The bridges offer a minimum headroom of 3.50m.

Towpath There is a towpath throughout the length remaining open to navigation.

Authority
Service de la Navigation de Lyon, Arrondissement de Besançon.
Subdivision: Port Fluvial, BP207, 25200 Montbéliard, ☎ 81 81 18 55 (km 0-4).
Service de la Navigation de Strasbourg.
Subdivision: 6 rue Alfred Engel, 90800 Bavilliers, ☎ 84 21 00 88 (km 4-135).

Colmar branch (Canal de Colmar)

The original branch of the Canal du Rhône au Rhin, 13km long, is connected to the Rhine opposite Breisach by a 3km length of the former canal maintained for navigation and a 6km link canal (the embranchement de Neuf-Breisach) built as part of the upper Rhine development works. The actual distance from the Rhine to the basin in Colmar is covered by a single distance table for convenience.

Locks There are 3 locks. The new lock on the Neuf-Breisach link canal measures 40 by 6.00m. The second lock (38.80 by 5.10m) is on the former main line of the canal, while the third (38.85 by 5.30m) is at the crossing of the river Ill near Colmar.

Depth The maximum authorised draught is 1.80m.

Bridges The fixed bridges offer a minimum headroom of 3.70m.
Towpath There is a towpath throughout.

Authority
Service de la Navigation de Strasbourg.
Subdivision: 60 rue du Grillenbreit, BP545, 68021 Colmar, ☎ 89 41 21 53.

Northern branch (Friesenheim to Strasbourg)

When the Rhinau diversion canal was built on the upper Rhine, a 3.8km long link canal was also provided, so as to allow standard 38.50m barges to use the original Canal du Rhône au Rhin over the last 31km to Strasbourg. The actual distance from the Rhinau diversion canal (km 258 on the Rhine) to the junction with the Dusuzeau basin of the port of Strasbourg is 35km, given in a single distance table for convenience.

Locks There are 12 locks in this section, plus a flood lock (normally open) at the crossing of the Ill flood diversion canal (km 17). The new lock on the Friesenheim link canal measures 40 by 6.00m. The other locks are 38.80m long and 5.10m wide.

Depth The maximum authorised draught is 1.80m.

Bridges The fixed bridges offer a minimum headroom of 3.70m.

Towpath There is a towpath throughout.

Authority
Service de la Navigation de Strasbourg.
Subdivision: 46 quai Jacoutot, 67000 Strasbourg, ☎ 88 61 66 01.

Distance table
(Note: official distances are those in the right-hand column)

	km	lock	km
Junction with Grand Canal d'Alsace, Ottmarsheim reach	0.0	-	237.1
Niffer lock, bridge downstream, village 1000m	0.3	1	236.8
Junction with former branch to Huningue (disused)	0.4	-	236.7
Bridge	1.5	-	235.6
Bridge	3.3	-	233.8
Bridge (Bouc)	9.5	-	227.6
Motorway bridge (A35), Peugeot factory	11.7	-	225.4
Railway bridge	13.3	-	223.8
Ile Napoleon basin, *junction with former main line*, bridge	13.5	-	223.6
Oil terminal basin, short-term mooring	14.3	-	222.8
Water point and customs post, l/b	14.9	-	222.2
Railway bridge	15.4	-	221.7
Bridge	15.8	-	221.3

	km	lock	km
New Basin l/b (length 1900m, but silted up, mooring not recommended), Shell depot r/b	16.3	-	220.8
Lock 41, bridge	16.4	2	220.7
Lift bridge	17.1	-	220.0
Bridge (Bonnes Gens)	17.9	-	219.2
Tunnel (canal covered for 140m in front of Mulhouse station)	18.1	-	219.0
Mulhouse basin, mooring towards middle of quay, l/b, town centre 500m l/b	18.2	-	218.9
Bridge (Jules Ehrmann)	18.3	-	218.8
Bridge (Noyers)	18.5	-	218.6
Railway bridge, footbridge	19.3	-	217.8
Lock 39	19.4	3	217.7
Lock 38, bridge	20.4	4	216.7
Lock 37, bridge, **Brunstatt** r/b	21.7	5	215.4
Lock 36, bridge	22.7	6	214.4
Turning basin	23.2	-	213.9
Lift bridge	24.3	-	212.8
Lock 35	24.5	7	212.6
Zillisheim lift bridge, village r/b	24.9	-	212.2
Lock 34, bridge	25.8	8	211.3
Lock 33	27.0	9	210.1
Lock 32, bridge, **Illfurth**, 400m r/b	28.3	10	208.8
Lock 31	29.0	11	208.1
Lock 30, bridge, **Heidwiller** r/b	30.2	12	206.9
Lock 29, bridge	31.0	13	206.1
Lock 28	31.7	14	205.4
Bridge (D466)	31.9	-	205.2
Lock 27, bridge	33.3	15	203.8
Lock 26, bridge	34.1	16	203.0
Lock 25, bridge, **Eglingen** r/b	35.3	17	201.8
Lock 24	35.9	18	201.2
Bridge	37.4	-	199.7
Lock 23	37.5	19	199.6
Hagenbach quay r/b	37.7	-	199.4
Lock 22	38.4	20	198.7
Lock 21, footbridge	38.9	21	198.2
Lock 20	39.4	22	197.7
Lock 19, bridge	40.1	23	197.0
Lock 18, bridge	40.8	24	196.3
Lock 17	41.3	25	195.8
Dannemarie bridge, basin d/s, moorings, village 700m r/b	41.6	-	195.5
Lock 16	41.7	26	195.4
Aqueduct	41.8	-	195.3
Lock 15, bridge	42.2	27	194.9
Lock 14, D419 parallel to r/b	42.6	28	194.5
Lock 13, bridge, **Retzwiller** r/b	43.6	29	193.5
Lock 12	44.0	30	193.1
Lock 11	44.4	31	192.7
Lock 10	44.8	32	192.3
Lock 9	45.0	33	192.1
Lock 8	45.2	34	191.9
Lock 7	45.4	35	191.7
Lock 6	45.6	36	191.5
Lock 5	45.7	37	191.4
Lock 4	45.9	38	191.2
Lock 3	46.1	39	191.0
Valdieu bridge (D419) and railway bridge, basin l/b	46.2	-	190.9
Lock 2, beginning of summit level	46.3	40	190.8

	km	lock	km
Bridge	47.5	-	189.6
Montreux-Vieux bridge, village 200m north	49.0	-	188.1
Turning basin	49.9	-	187.2
Lock 3, bridge, end of summit level, **Montreux-Château** 400m	51.6	1	185.5
Lock 4, bridge	53.4	2	183.7
Brebotte bridge, turning basin downstream, village 600m	55.2	-	181.9
Lock 5	55.6	3	181.5
Froidefontaine swing bridge, village l/b	57.7	-	179.4
Lock 6	58.0	4	179.1
Quays l/b	58.7	-	178.4
Railway bridge	59.1	-	178.0
Bourogne bridge (N19), industrial quays downstream l/b, village 800m r/b	59.3	-	177.8
Lock 7	61.0	5	176.1
Navigation enters river Allan (at confluence with Bourbeuse, crossed by towpath on r/b)	61.2	-	175.9
Navigation re-enters canal, Allan weir l/b	62.1	-	175.0
Lock 8 (Fontenelles), bridge, **Allenjoie** 500m r/b	63.0	6	174.1
Disused lock 9 down to Allan, l/b	63.7	-	173.4
Bridge (Allenjoie)	63.9	-	173.2
Towpath bridge (Moulin-de-Boise)	64.5	-	172.6
Junction with Belfort branch, for main line turn sharp left	65.3	-	171.8
Fesches aqueduct over the river Allan	65.3	-	171.8
New lock 9 (Allenjoie)	65.4	7	171.7
Former canal to Fesches, l/b	65.6	-	171.5
Lock 10 (Marivées), bridge	65.8	8	171.3
Lock 11 (Etupes), bridge, village 700m l/b	67.6	9	169.5
Lock 12 (Etupes new lock) leading into 3km section of large-scale waterway (Allan diversion canal)	68.3	10	168.8
Bridge (Exincourt), N437, motorway interchange r/b	69.1	-	168.0
Suspension bridge (Peugeot works)	69.7	-	167.4
Motorway bridge (A36), skew	70.3	-	166.8
Bridge (Ludwigsburg), Sochaux motorway spur, weir r/b	71.3	-	165.8
Flood gate	71.7	-	165.4
Railway bridge, industrial quay upstream l/b, end of large-scale waterway section	71.8	-	165.3
Lock 14 (Montbéliard)	72.3	11	164.8
New road bridge (replacing former lift bridge)	72.6	-	164.5
Montbéliard basin, boat harbour, quay 55m and two perpendicular pontoons 12m, Servie Navigation, slipway, water, town centre 800m r/b	72.8	-	164.3
Diesel fuelling point l/b	73.0	-	164.1
Lock 15 (Côteau Jouvent)	73.4	12	163.7
Courcelles-lès-Montbéliard lift bridge	74.5	-	162.6
Lock 16 (Courcelles-lès-Montbéliard)	75.0	13	162.1
Canal narrows, one-way traffic	75.8	-	161.3
Footbridge (Bart)	75.9	-	161.2
Canal narrows, one-way traffic	76.8	-	160.3
Lock 17 (Voujeaucourt), bridge, quay upstream l/b	77.2	14	159.9
Canal crosses Doubs on the level, keep well to towpath side during floods, strong cross current	77.8	-	159.3
Flood lock 18a (Voujeaucourt), bridge (Moulin)	78.0	-	159.1
Bridge (Berche)	79.0	-	158.1
Lock 18 (Dampierre)	79.7	15	157.4
Bridge (Dampierre-sur-le-Doubs)	80.0	-	157.1
Lock 19 (Plaine de Dampierre)	81.5	16	155.6
Lock 20 (Raydans), bridge (D126)	83.1	17	154.0

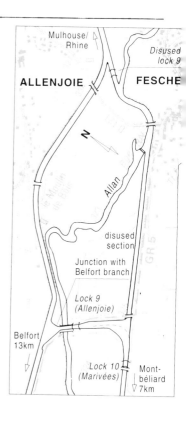

	km	lock	km
Colombier-Fontaine lift bridge, village l/b, commercial quay downstream l/b	84.1	-	153.0
Lock 21 (Colombier-Fontaine)	85.3	18	151.8
Lock 22 (Saint-Maurice), bridge	87.2	19	149.9
Railway bridge	88.7	-	148.4
Lock 23 (Colombier-Châtelot), bridge, basin upstream silted up	89.6	20	147.5
Lock 24 (Blussans), bridge	91.2	21	145.0
Canal narrows, one-way traffic	94.4	-	142.7
Lock 25 (Côteau-Lunans)	94.6	22	142.5
Railway bridge	95.3	-	141.8
L'Isle-sur-le-Doubs lock 26, bridge, mooring in basin upstream r/b, town centre l/b	96.3	23	140.8
Diesel fuelling point l/b	96.7	-	140.4
Bridge (N83)	97.0	-	140.1
Lock 27 (Papeteries), water, navigation enters river Doubs	97.4	24	139.7
Lock 28 and weir (Appenans)	98.6	25	138.5
Lock 29 and weir (Goulisse)	101.1	26	136.0
Entrance to Pompierre lock-cut, r/b, flood lock 30a (Rang), bridge	102.9	-	134.2
Railway bridge	103.4	-	133.7
Lock 30 (Plaine de Pompierre), bridge	105.0	27	132.1
Lock 31 (Pompierre), bridge, navigation re-enters Doubs	106.6	28	130.5
Motorway bridge	107.4	-	129.7
Santoche island (keep to r/b)	108.0	-	129.1
Entrance to Clerval lock-cut, r/b	109.3	-	127.8
Lock 32 (Clerval), bridge	109.9	29	127.2
Navigation re-enters Doubs	110.2	-	126.9
Clerval bridge, mooring upstream r/b, village l/b	110.5	-	126.6
Entrance to Branne lock-cut, r/b, flood lock 33a, bridge	111.7	-	125.4
Lock 33 (Branne)	113.9	30	123.2
Branne towpath bridge, small village r/b	115.3	-	121.8
Lock 34, navigation re-enters Doubs	116.0	31	121.1
Lock 35 and weir (Hermite)	117.5	32	119.6
Lock 36 and weir (Hyèvre-Magny)	118.5	33	118.6
Hyèvre-Magny bridge	118.8	-	118.3
Lock 37 and weir (Grand-Crucifix)	121.0	34	116.1
Lock 38 and weir (Raie-aux-Chèvres)	123.1	35	114.0
Entrance to Grange-Ravey lock-cut, l/b	125.1	-	112.0
Lock 39 (Lonot), navigation re-enters Doubs	125.4	36	111.7
Confluence of Cusancin l/b, towpath bridge	126.4	-	110.7
Entrance to Baume-les-Dames lock-cut, l/b, narrow section, one-way traffic	126.7	-	110.4
Bridge (D492)	127.4	-	109.7
Flood lock 40a (Baume-les-Dames), bridge	127.5	-	109.6
Baume-les-Dames quay l/b, Service Navigation, town centre 1200m r/b	127.8	-	109.3
Bridge (Grange Villotey), canal narrows for 140m	129.1	-	108.0
Lock 40 (Baumerousse), bridge, navigation re-enters Doubs	130.0	37	107.1
Lock 41 and weir (Fourbanne), water	133.5	38	103.6
Lock 42 and weir (Ougney), bridge	135.7	39	101.4
Ougney bridge	136.1	-	101.0
Ougney-la-Roche restaurant l/b, pontoon for shallow draught vessels	137.4	-	99.7
Lock 43 and weir (Douvot), bridge	138.1	40	99.0
Lock 44 and weir (Laissey)	140.4	41	96.7
Laissey bridge	140.6	-	96.5
Lock 45 and weir (Aigremont)	142.4	42	94.7

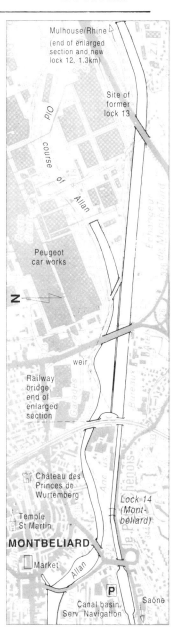

	km	lock	km
Entrance to Deluz lock-cut r/b, flood lock 46a	143.8	-	93.3
Deluz bridge, paper mill, private quay	144.5	-	92.6
Double staircase lock 46/47 (Deluz), electrically operated, bridge, navigation re-enters Doubs	146.7	44	90.4
Bridge (Vaire)	148.8	-	88.3
Footbridge	149.0	-	88.1
Quay for La Rochette-Cenpa paper mill (Novillars), r/b	149.3	-	87.8
Entrance to Roche lock-cut, r/b, flood gate 48a, bridge	151.9	-	85.2
Lock 48 (Chalèze), bridge, navigation re-enters Doubs	154.4	45	82.7
Overhead power lines	157.4	-	79.7
Lock 49 and weir (Malâte)	160.8	46	76.3
Private industrial quays r/b	162.3	-	74.8
Footbridge (Prés-de-Vaux)	162.6	-	74.5
Entrance to tunnel (Souterrain de la Citadelle) l/b, flood gate 50a (Rivotte), keep straight on for access to town centre, passing through lock 51a (Saint-Paul), pleasure traffic only (see plan and distance table for Besançon)	163.0	-	74.1
Lock 50 (Tarragnoz) in downstream tunnel entrance	163.4	47	73.7
Besançon bridge (Tarragnoz), moorings in Doubs arm u/s (and access to town centre, see plan), Service Navigation	163.5	-	73.6
Lock 51 (Tarragnoz), navigation re-enters Doubs	163.6	48	73.5
Bridge (Mazagran)	163.8	-	73.3
Lock 52 and weir (Velotte)	165.1	49	72.0
Bridge (Velotte)	165.5	-	71.6
Floating chandlery l/b opposite island	166.3	-	70.8
Bridge (Beure), N273 Besançon ring road	167.3	-	69.8
Lock 53 and weir (Gouille)	168.7	50	68.4
Entrance to Aveney lock-cut, l/b, flood lock 54a	170.7	-	66.4
Avanne-Aveney bridge, village with restaurant	171.0	-	66.1
Canal narrows for 400m, one-way traffic	173.0	-	64.1
Double staircase lock 54/55 (Rancenay), electrically operated, bridge, navigation re-enters Doubs	174.0	52	63.1
Entrance to Thoraise lock-cut, l/b, flood-lock 56a, bridge	176.8	-	60.3
Thoraise tunnel, length 185m, winding basin at upstream entrance	177.4	-	59.7
Lock 56 (Thoraise), bridge, navigation re-enters Doubs	177.8	53	59.3
Bridge (Torpes-Boussières)	179.4	-	57.7
Entrance to Osselle lock-cut, r/b, flood lock 57a (Torpes)	180.5	-	56.6
Railway bridge	182.2	-	54.9
Bridge (Portail de Roche)	182.3	-	54.8
Lock 57 (**Osselle**), bridge, village 400m	183.2	54	53.9
Bridge (Osselle)	183.7	-	53.4
Bridge (Moulin d'Arenthon), canal narrows for 40m	185.6	-	51.5
New lock 58 (Routelle)	187.3	55	49.8
Bridge (Roset-Fluans)	188.4	-	48.7
Old lock 58 (Roset-Fluans), bridge, navigation re-enters Doubs	188.6	56	48.5
Saint-Vit pontoon moorings r/b (45m long, with 5 catways each 3m long), village 1500m	191.3	-	45.8
Lock 59 and weir (**Saint-Vit**), bridge	191.5	57	45.6
Bridge (Salans-sur-le-Doubs)	191.8	-	45.3
Island, keep to r/b	192.0	-	45.1
Small towpath bridge, r/b	194.0	-	43.1
Entrance to Dampierre lock-cut, r/b	194.2	-	42.9
Flood gate 60a (**Fraisans**), bridge, village 1000m l/b	194.8	-	42.3
Railway bridge (disused)	195.7	-	41.4
Bridge (Dampierre)	195.9	-	41.2
Lock 60 (Dampierre), navigation re-enters Doubs	196.4	58	40.7

	km	lock	km
Entrance to Ranchot lock-cut, r/b, narrow section to lock	197.5	-	39.6
Flood gate 61a, bridge	197.7	-	39.4
Ranchot wooden quay (25m) and village 100m r/b, **Rans** 500m l/b	197.7	-	39.4
Lock 61 (Ranchot)	198.5	59	38.6
Lift bridge (Moulin des Malades)	199.3	-	37.8
Lock 62 (Moulin des Malades), navigation re-enters Doubs	199.5	60	37.6
Entrance to Orchamps lock-cut, r/b, bridge	201.9	-	35.2
Orchamps bridge, moor well upstream for village r/b	203.3	-	33.8
New flood lock 63 (Orchamps), bridge	203.5	-	33.6
Bridge (Lavans)	205.7	-	31.4
Lock 63 (Moulin-Rouge), navigation re-enters Doubs	207.4	61	29.7
Entrance to Audelange lock-cut, r/b, flood gate 64a, bridge	208.5	-	28.6
Lock 64 (Audelange), navigation re-enters Doubs	209.5	62	27.6
Rochefort-sur-Nenon, mooring under cliff r/b, restaurant in village	211.1	-	26.0
Entrance to Rochefort-Dole lock-cut, new flood lock 65, bridge	211.3	-	25.8
Lock 65 (**Baverans**), bridge, village 600m r/b	215.0	63	22.1
Railway bridge	215.3	-	21.8
Bridge (Brevans)	215.9	-	21.2
Railway bridge	217.3	-	19.8
Lock 66 (Charles-Quint), bridge	217.7	64	19.4
Navigation enters small arm of Doubs	217.9	-	19.2
Bridge (Pasquier), towpath crosses to l/b	218.1	-	19.0
Dole basin, boat harbour, Nouvelle Vogue hire base, 60m pontoon, slipway, water and electricity, sanitary building, Service Navigation, town centre r/b	218.5	-	18.6
Bridge (Pont de la Charité)	218.7	-	18.4
Lock 67 (Jardin-Philippe) in short lock-cut l/b, bridge, navigation re-enters Doubs	218.8	65	18.3
Entrance to Doubs–Saône canal r/b, flood lock 68, bridge	220.1	-	17.0
Bridge (Saint-Ylie)	221.3	-	15.8
Choisey bridge, village r/b	222.8	-	14.3
Lock 69 (Bon Repos), bridge (N73), quay downstream r/b	224.4	66	12.7
Railway bridge	225.5	-	11.6
Bridge (Beauregard)	225.7	-	11.4
Tavaux-Cité quay r/b (factory)	226.6	-	10.5
Lock 70 (Belvoye), freight office	226.7	67	10.4
Solvay works, basin l/b	227.2	-	9.9
Private bridge	227.7	-	9.4
Lock 71 (Ronce), bridge	228.8	68	8.3
Lock 72 (**Abergement-la-Ronce**), bridge, shops l/b	230.3	69	6.8
Bridge (Samerey)	232.2	-	4.9
Motorway bridge (A36)	233.3	-	3.8
Basin (silted up)	235.4	-	1.7
Lock 73 (Tuilerie)	236.1	70	1.0
Bridge (Laperrière)	236.2	-	0.9
Lock 74 (Laperrière), basin upstream l/b, **St. Symphorien** 800m	236.7	71	0.4
Lock 75 (Saône), bridge, *junction with Saône* (km 160)	237.1	72	0.0

Besançon loop

	km	lock	km
Upstream junction with main line at km 163.0 (entrance to Citadelle tunnel	0.0	-	4.0
Skew railway bridge (industrial siding)	0.3	-	3.7
Railway bridge	0.5	-	3.5
Bridge (Brégille)	0.8	-	3.2

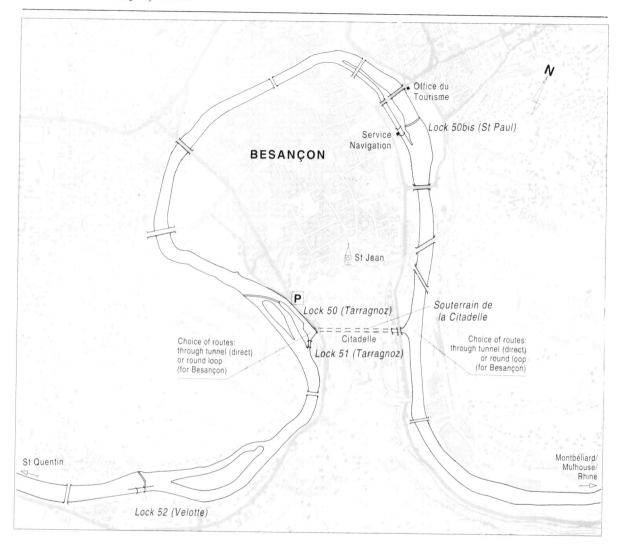

	km	lock	km
Entrance to lock-cut, l/b	1.0	–	3.0
Lock 51a (Saint-Paul) adjacent to mill and Service de la Navigation, private pontoon (15m) d/s l/b, water and electricity	1.1	1	2.9
Bridge (République), quay d/s	1.2	–	2.8
Bridge	1.5	–	2.5
Navigation re-enters Doubs	1.6	–	2.4
Bridge (Battant)	2.0	–	2.0
Bridge (Canot)	2.6	–	1.4
Bridge	3.0	–	1.0
Weir on r/b, keep towards l/b	3.6	–	0.4
Downstream junction with main line between locks 50 and 51	4.0	–	0.0

The beautiful, wooded valley of the river Doubs (Canal du Rhône au Rhin) downstream of Besançon.
Hugh Potter

Belfort branch

	km	lock	km
Junction with main line (km 172)	0.0	-	13.5
Bridge (Jonchets)	0.9	-	12.6
Brognard bridge, small village 300m l/b, motorway r/b	1.8	-	11.7
Lock 1 (Brognard)	2.9	1	10.6
Dambenois bridge, small village 200m l/b	3.6	-	9.9
Lock 2 (Dambenois), bridge	4.1	2	9.4
Bridge (D25)	5.2	-	8.3
Lock 3, bridge, basin d/s r/b, **Trévenans** 400m l/b	6.1	3	7.4
Lock 4, bridge	6.9	4	6.6
Lock 5, bridge	7.7	5	5.8
Bridge (Bermont)	7.9	-	5.6
Bridge (Dorans)	8.5	-	5.0
Botans lift bridge, basin d/s l/b, small village r/b, **Belfort** 4000m l/b	9.7	-	3.8
Motorway bridge	9.9	-	3.6
Bridge	10.8	-	2.7
Railway bridge	12.1	-	1.4
Lock 6	12.2	6	1.3
Lock 7, bridge	12.5	7	1.0
Lock 8	12.7	8	0.8

	km	lock	km
Lock 9 (Bavilliers), bridge, quay d/s l/b	13.3	9	0.2
Bridge, limit of navigation, **Belfort** town centre 1700m l/b	13.5	-	0.0

Colmar branch (Canal de Colmar)

	km	lock	km
Entrance to link canal from Rhine d/s of Vogelgrun locks (Rhine km 226)	0.0	-	23.0
Lock (Rhin), bridge	0.4	1	22.6
Rail and road bridges, **Biesheim** 1500m l/b	2.2	-	20.8
Weir r/b (river Giessen leaves canal)	2.9	-	20.1
Bridge (Boebbels)	3.0	-	20.0
Bridge (D468)	5.3	-	17.7
Kunheim bridge, village r/b	6.2	-	16.8
Junction with former main line of Canal du Rhône au Rhin	6.4	-	16.6
Lock 63, bridge	8.3	2	14.7
Junction with Colmar branch, navigation turns left off main line	9.7	-	13.3
Bridge	10.1	-	12.9
Bridge	11.5	-	11.5
Bridge	12.6	-	10.4
Bridge (D9), **Muntzenheim** 600m south	14.3	-	8.7
Bridge	15.3	-	7.7
Bridge, **Wickerschwihr** 500m north	16.7	-	6.3
Bridge	17.5	-	5.5
Bridge	18.5	-	4.5
Bridge	19.2	-	3.8
Bridge	19.8	-	3.2
Lock (Ill) with flood gate, bridge d/s	20.8	3	2.2
Crossing of river Ill, weir on north side and towpath bridge on south side, navigation enters canalised river Lauch	20.9	-	2.1
Turning basin, industrial quays d/s l/b	22.8	-	0.2
Colmar, basin, head of navigation, town centre 1000m	23.0	-	0.0

Northern branch (Friesenheim to Strasbourg)

	km	lock	km
Entrance to link canal from Rhine d/s of Rhinau locks (Rhine km 258)	0.0	-	35.4
Bridge	0.4	-	35.0
Lock (Rhin)	0.5	1	34.9
Crossing of river Ischert on the level	0.6	-	34.8
Bridge (D468), **Friesenheim** 1000m north	1.5	-	33.9
Junction with former main line of Canal du Rhône au Rhin	3.8	-	31.6
Lock 75, bridge	4.7	2	30.7
Lock 76, bridge (D5)	7.0	3	28.4
Boofzheim quay and Crown Blue Line hire base r/b, village 1200m r/b	7.1	-	28.3
Obenheim bridge, village 1000m r/b	9.6	-	25.8
Lock 77	10.3	4	25.1
Bridge	11.5	-	23.9
Gerstheim quay r/b, village 1200m r/b	12.6	-	22.8
Lock 78, bridge	13.1	5	22.3
Erstein bridge, sugar refinery quay d/s l/b, small town 3000m l/b	15.1	-	20.3
Lock 79, bridge	16.1	6	19.3
Crossing of Ill flood diversion canal on the level, canal navigable 1500m u/s to former quay	16.7	-	18.7
Flood lock 80	16.8	-	18.6

	km	lock	km
Erstein-Krafft bridge, quay and village d/s r/b, Rive de France relay base	17.1	-	18.3
Bridge (D788)	19.0	-	16.4
Lock 81, bridge, aqueduct u/s	20.2	7	15.2
Plobsheim bridge, quay d/s r/b, village 400m r/b	22.4	-	13.0
Lock 82, bridge	23.7	8	11.7
Eschau bridge, quay d/s r/b, village l/b	24.4	-	11.0
Basin (Illkirch-Graffenstaden)	26.3	-	9.1
Lock 83, bridge	26.8	9	8.6
Bridge	28.0	-	7.4
Main road bridge (N83), **Illkirch-Graffenstaden** l/b	29.9	-	5.5
Lock 84, bridge	30.8	10	4.6
Lock 85, automatic, lift bridge, quay u/s r/b	33.4	11	2.0
Rail and road bridges	33.5	-	1.9
Railway bridge	33.8	-	1.6
Junction with canalised river Ill, l/b (navigable through the centre of Strasbourg)	33.9	-	1.5
Flood gate (Heyritz), bridge	34.0	-	1.4
Basin r/b (Bassin de l'Hôpital)	34.4	-	1.0
Lock 86, automatic, bridge, **Strasbourg** centre 800m north	34.9	12	0.5
Bridge	35.2	-	0.2
Bridge	35.3	-	0.1
Junction with Dusuzeau basin of port of Strasbourg	35.4	-	0.0

Canal du Rhône au Rhin (northern section). Lock no. 86.
Author

Canal du Rhône à Sète

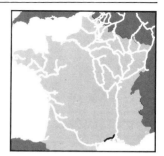

The inland waterway connecting the Rhône to the port of Sète and the Canal du Midi (via the Etang de Thau) was first opened to navigation in 1820. It extends 98km from Beaucaire to Sète. However, canalisation of the Rhône resulted in closure of the entrance lock to the canal at Beaucaire, so that through navigation has to use an improved length of the Petit Rhône and a short length of canal at Saint-Gilles, to enter the Canal du Rhône à Sète at km 29. Accordingly, the through route is now 69km long, and the 29km section to Beaucaire is a dead end. Despite this handicap, the basin in Beaucaire has been attractively developed as a boat harbour and is well worth the detour. There is currently a project to re-establish the direct route, involving not only restoration of Beaucaire lock but also construction of a new lock on the strip of land between the by-passed Rhone and the Beaucaire tailrace canal (see plan).

The canal crosses two rivers on the level, the Vidourle at km 55 and the Lez at km 75. At times of flood, the canal has to be isolated from the river by closure of the movable gates on either side of the crossing, and navigation is interrupted. Both rivers may be used by smaller boats to reach the Mediterranean, although the main points of access to the sea are via the Canal Maritime from Aigues-Mortes (km 51) to the modern resort of Le Grau-du-Roi and via the basins of the port of Sète, reached by crossing part of the Etang de Thau from the western end of the canal. The Canal de la Peyrade, which provides a sheltered route to the port of Sète from the main line at km 96, is crossed by a low road bridge near its junction with the main line, and is in a poor state of maintenance. It is not therefore recommended for through navigation.

Improvements have been made to the canal in recent years, to allow 500-tonne barges to navigate from the Rhône through to the Etang de Thau, and further enlargement is under way so that the port of Sète can derive the maximum benefit from the availability of high-capacity inland shipping on the Rhône–Saône axis. Navigators may thus encounter works along the main route. In particular, new sections have been opened to bypass Aigues-Mortes to the north and Frontignan to the south.

The canal borders the Camargue and crosses expansive sea water lagoons, but views are generally obstructed by the high banks (which nevertheless offer the advantage of protection against the *mistral*).

Locks There is one lock, on the bypassed section of the canal at Nourriguier (km 8). It is 80m long and 12m wide, and automatically operated (follow the instructions for boats). A second lock at Aigues-Mortes (km 50), designed to prevent sea water from penetrating inland, never had to be used and in 1955 the gates were removed. It should be noted that the maximum navigable width is less than the width of Nourriguier lock (see under Bridges).

Depth The maximum authorised draught has been increased by the recent improvement works from 1.80 to 2.20m (except on the dead end section to Beaucaire). This draught is not available on the Vidourle and the Lez, however, and local enquiries should be made by navigators intending to use these links to the Mediterranean.

Bridges The fixed bridges offer a minimum headroom of 4.10m, although this figure is gradually being increased to 5.00m or more on the main line.

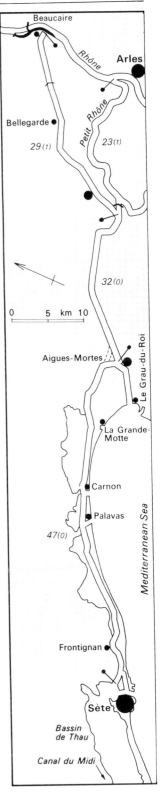

Several bridges offer a reduced width by comparison with the lock at Nourriguier. The least width at the bridges in Beaucaire is 8.70m, the railway bridge at Saint-Gilles is 10.80m wide, the gate structures on either side of the Lez crossing are 10.00m wide and the railway bridge at km 97 offers a navigable width of 9.60m. The bridges on the Lez down to the sea at Palavas offer severely limited headroom: 2.40m above normal water level, reduced to as little as 2.00m when the Lez is in flood. It should be noted that the lift bridge at Frontignan (km 92) is opened for boats at certain times of the day only. For opening times, ring 67 48 65 29.

Authority

Service Maritime et de Navigation du Languedoc-Roussillon, Montpellier.
Subdivisions:
– quai du Canal, 30300 Beaucaire, ☎ 66 59 10 04 (km 0-43).
– 1 quai Philippe-Régy, 34200 Sète, ☎ 67 46 34 00 (km 43-98).

Distance table

	km	lock	km
Beaucaire basin and extensive boat harbour (130 berths), limit of navigation, Ancas Away and Connoisseur Cruisers hire bases (restoration of lock down to Rhône projected), town centre on north side	0.6	–	97.4
Footbridge	0.9	–	97.1
Bridge (Porte Vieille), narrow passage	1.3	–	96.7
Railway bridge and private bridge, narrow passage, industrial quays d/s r/b	2.2	–	95.8
Bridge (Charenconne)	3.4	–	94.6
Lock 2 (Nourriguier), basin d/s r/b	7.7	1	90.3
Bridge (Nourriguier)	7.9	–	90.1
New road bridge (N113)	13.1	–	84.9
Bellegarde bridge (Pont d'Arles), narrow passage, quays d/s, village 1200m r/b	13.2	–	84.8
Bridge (Broussan)	16.6	–	81.4
Footbridge	24.0	–	74.0
Saint-Gilles basin, Crown Blue Line Camargue and DNP France hire bases, water, small town r/b	24.2	–	73.8
Bridge (Saint-Gilles), N572	24.6	–	73.4
Railway bridge, narrow bridge	24.9	–	73.1
Junction with Canal de Saint-Gilles and main line of navigation from the Rhône to Sète	29.0	–	69.0
Bridge (Espeyran)	29.7	–	68.3
Bridge (Franquevaux)	35.1	–	62.9
Gallician bridge, boat harbour d/s r/b, wines, village 400m	39.2	–	58.8
Bridge (Tourradons), narrow passage	43.0	–	55.0
Bridge (Soulier), D58	48.0	–	50.0
Stop lock 3 (permanently open)	49.9	–	48.1
Aigues-Mortes bridge, medieval fortified town l/b	50.8	–	47.2
Railway swing bridge	50.9	–	47.1
Junction with Canal Maritime l/b (access to Aigues-Mortes boat harbour and the Mediterranean at Le Grau-du-Roi, also offering a high-capacity boat harbour at 6km d/s)	51.0	–	47.0
New road bridge (D62)	51.9	–	46.1
Vidourle crossing (river may be navigated by small boats down to Le Grau-du-Roi), footbridges over sluice-gate structures either side of crossing	55.0	–	43.0
New road bridge (D61)	58.9	–	39.1
Junction with Canal de Lunel, r/b (disused)	59.0	–	39.0

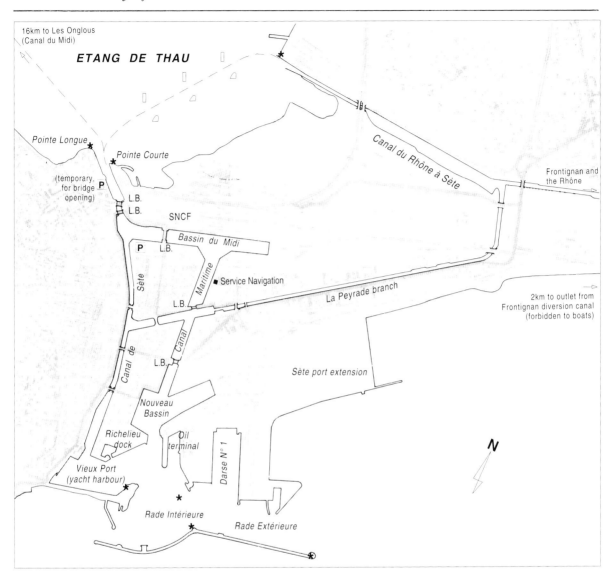

16km to Les Onglous
(Canal du Midi)

ETANG DE THAU

Pointe Longue

Pointe Courte

(temporary,
for bridge
opening)

P

L.B.
L.B.

SNCF

Bassin du Midi

P   L.B.

■ Service Navigation

L.B.

Canal du Rhône à Sète

Frontignan and
the Rhône

La Peyrade branch

2km to outlet from
Frontignan diversion canal
(forbidden to boats)

Sète

Maritime

Canal de

Canal

L.B.

Sète port extension

Nouveau
Bassin

Richelieu
dock

Oil
terminal

Darse Nº 1

Vieux Port
(yacht harbour)

Rade Intérieure

Rade Extérieure

N

	km	lock	km
La Grande-Motte mooring l/b, Camargue Plaisance hire base, resort 1500m l/b	61.7	-	36.3
New road bridge (D62)	70.0	-	28.0
Junction with Grau du Carnon and Canal du Hangar, marina, Caminav hire base, access to Mediterranean for small boats only	70.7	-	27.3
Carnon bridge, resort 1000m	70.7	-	27.3
Lez crossing, footbridges over sluice-gate structures on either side, access to **Palavas** for boats with less than 2.40m air draught	75.2	-	22.8
Bridge (Quatre-Canaux), quays d/s	75.2	-	22.8
Maguelonne Abbey on mound, l/b	78.6	-	19.4
New road bridge (replacing former pedestrian swing bridge)	86.6	-	11.4
Railway bridge	92.1	-	5.9
Frontignan lift bridge, basin d/s, town centre r/b	92.2	-	5.8
Bridge (N108)	96.1	-	1.9
Junction with Canal de la Peyrade, l/b	96.2	-	1.8
Railway bridge, narrow passage (9.60m)	97.3	-	0.7
Bridge (D2)	97.3	-	0.7
Outfall in Etang de Thau (see under Etang de Thau conditions of access to **Sète**)	98.0	-	0.0

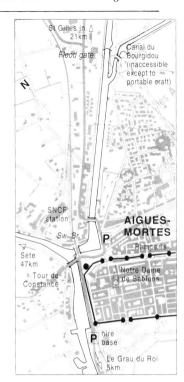

Canal de Roanne à Digoin

The Canal de Roanne à Digoin begins at a large basin in Roanne, connected with a short navigable length of the river Loire, and ends close to the town of Digoin, where it joins the Canal latéral à Loire. The distance from Roanne basin to the junction with the lateral canal is 55.6km. Following the virtual disappearance of commercial traffic, the three départements concerned by the canal, Loire, Saône-et-Loire and Allier, have formed an association to promote its use for tourism, and have provided funding for manning the locks on Sundays (see below). The canal is ideal for pleasure cruising, being a predominantly rural waterway, passing through the unspoilt countryside of the upper Loire valley.

Locks There are 10 locks of standard barge dimensions (39.00 by 5.20m). The total fall is about 37m, towards Digoin. Locks 4, 7 and 8 are among the deepest on the Freycinet network, 6 and 7.19m respectively. From November to March, lock operating times are 0800 to 1200 and 1300 to 1730, Monday to Saturday, but notice of passage has to be given to the canal engineer's office before 1600 the previous day (on Friday for the following Saturday or Monday). From April to October, locks are operated every day of the week, and until 1930 (except in October).

Depth The maximum draught is 1.80m.

Bridges The minimum headroom is 3.45m above normal water level.

Towpath There is a good towpath throughout.

Authority

Direction Départementale de l'Equipement, Loire.
Subdivision: 20 quai Commandant de Foucault, 42300 Roanne, ☎ 77 68 27 28.

Distance table

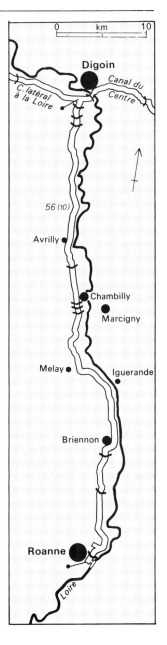

	km	lock	km
Roanne, wide basin 850m long connected to the Loire (navigable for 1km), moorings r/b and l/b, facilities for boats, slipway, trip boats (see plan)	0.0	-	55.6
Lock 1 (Roanne), bridge	0.9	-	54.7
Bridge (Roanne by-pass)	1.8	-	53.8
Bridge (Côtes)	1.9	-	53.7
Oudan basin, l/b, 800m long but silted up	2.2	-	53.4
Oudan aqueduct	2.3	-	53.3
Bridge (Gardet)	3.1	-	53.3
Bridge (Matel)	3.6	-	52.0
Bridge (Vadon)	4.6	-	51.0
Bridge (Aiguilly), D482	5.2	-	50.4
Private quay serving Roanne arsenal, l/b	5.6	-	50.0
Bridge (Bonvert)	6.1	-	49.5
Bridge (Mably)	7.3	-	48.3
Bridge (Escroqué)	8.6	-	47.0
Lock 2 (Cornillon), bridge (castle, l/b, 500m from lock)	9.2	2	46.4
Bridge (Mathérat)	10.3	-	45.3
Bridge (Justices)	11.2	-	44.4
Bridge (Maltaverne)	12.3	-	43.3
Bridge (Rate)	12.9	-	42.7
Lock 3 (Briennon), bridge	13.6	3	42.0
Briennon, boat moorings and village l/b	14.7	-	40.9
Bridge (Briennon), D4, **Pouilly-sous-Charlieu** 2000m and **Charlieu** 7000m	15.0	-	40.6
Bridge (Boutasson)	16.0	-	39.6
Teyssonne aqueduct	18.5	-	37.1
Bridge (Teyssonne)	18.6	-	37.0
Bridge (Ray)	19.6	-	36.0
Bridge (Valendru)	20.2	-	35.4
Bridge (Duplan)	21.1	-	34.5
Iguerande, quay l/b, village 1500m on r/b of Loire	21.2	-	34.4
Bridge (Brivet)	22.8	-	32.8
Bridge (Putenat)	23.3	-	32.3
Bridge (Gallands)	23.9	-	31.7
Bridge (Bagnots)	24.8	-	30.8
Bridge (Corrètes), towpath crosses to l/b	25.5	-	30.1
Melay, boat moorings l/b, village 1500m	26.0	-	29.6
Bridge (Melay), towpath crosses back to r/b	26.1	-	29.5
Aqueduct (Brennons)	26.3	-	29.3
Bridge (Arcelles)	27.4	-	28.2
Bridge (Fanges)	28.2	-	27.5
Artaix, quay l/b	29.0	-	26.6
Bridge (Artaix 1)	29.1	-	26.5
Arçon aqueduct	29.6	-	26.0
Bridge (Artaix 2) and basin l/b, boat moorings and open camp site	29.8	-	25.8
Bridge (Augers)	30.3	-	25.3
Bridge (Narbot)	30.8	-	24.8
Lock 4 (Artaix)	31.8	4	23.8

	km	lock	km
Lock 5 (Montgrailloux), bridge	32.3	5	23.3
Lock 6 (Chambilly), bridge	32.8	6	22.8
Chambilly, quay r/b, **Marcigny** 2500m	33.0	-	22.6
Bridge (Croix-Valentin)	33.3	-	22.3
Bridge (Diens)	34.5	-	21.1
Bridge (Biscot)	34.9	-	20.7
Bridge (Meillerands)	35.5	-	20.1
Bourg-le-Comte quay, boat moorings and Urbise aqueduct, village 300m l/b	35.7	-	19.9
Bridge (Gallay)	36.0	-	19.6
Bridge (Bourg-le-Comte)	36.5	-	19.1
Lock 7 (Bourg-le-Comte)	36.6	7	19.0
Bridge (Bas-du-Riz)	37.3	-	18.3
Bridge (Bouillets)	38.7	-	16.9
Bridge (Thynet)	39.2	-	16.4
Avrilly, quay l/b, small village	40.3	-	15.3
Bridge (Morgat), D210	40.7	-	14.9
Bridge (Bonant)	42.4	-	13.2
Bridge (Lurcy)	44.9	-	10.7
Bridge (Giverdon)	46.5	-	9.1
Bridge (Beaume)	48.2	-	7.4
Bridge (Croix-Rouge), pontoonboat moorings	48.9	-	6.7
Bridge (Séez)	49.7	-	5.9
Bridge (Saint-Léger)	50.9	-	4.7
Bridge (Blancs)	51.7	-	3.9
Lock 8 (Chassenard)	52.3	8	3.3
Lock 9 (Beugnets), bridge	53.4	9	2.2
Lock 10 (Bretons)	54.7	10	0.9
Bridge (Bretons)	55.2	-	0.4
Junction with Canal latéral à Loire (km 2), **Digoin** 2000m	55.6	-	0.0

Canal de Roubaix

The Canal de Roubaix is a watershed canal, the summit level of which passes through the densely built-up area between the industrial towns of Roubaix and Tourcoing, while the lower sections at each end are by comparison almost rural in character. It used to connect the Canal de la Deûle (now the Bauvin-Lys waterway, a branch of the Dunkerque–Escaut waterway) near Lille with the Belgian Canal de l'Espierres, which leads to the Escaut (8.4km and three locks beyond the border). The distance from the junction with the Deûle at Marquette-lez-Lille and the border at Wattrelos is 20km. For several years, however, the canal has been effectively closed as a through route, following mechanical and structural failures on the complex hydraulic lift bridges through Roubaix, compounded by other maintenance and operating problems. This is the archetypal abandoned urban waterway, just waiting to be obliterated from the map and replaced by an urban ring road. The author has been participating in a rearguard action to try to save the canal through Roubaix, and organised a campaigning cruise for a group of members of the Inland Waterways Association in 1988, but the cost of rehabilitation is thought to be prohibitive (perhaps around £3 million). Officially, the canal remains open over a distance of 12 kilometres from the Deûle to the summit level beyond the junction with the Tourcoing branch. In practice, only the lower section following the course of the river Marcq remains in use, giving access to the active boat harbour of Wasquehal, on the Croix branch.

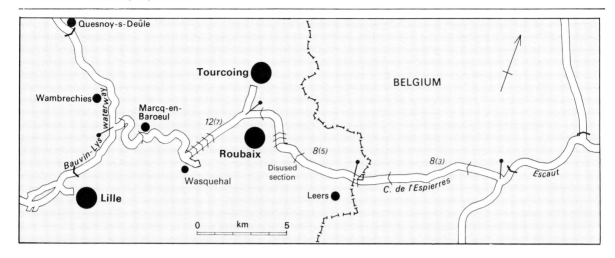

There are two branches, both now with abandoned sections, so that navigation extends from the main line to the boat harbour at Wasquehal (0.6km) and to the disused lift bridge in Tourcoing (0.9km) respectively. It is worth noting that part of the Tourcoing branch has been developed as an urban leisure amenity, but unless funds are made available to restore navigability, it is unlikely to see many boats. On the abandoned section of this branch, there is another hydraulic lift bridge carrying the Lille-Tourcoing tramway over the canal, and this is also not expected to survive the projected upgrading of the tram line.

Locks There are 12 locks, of which seven rise from the Deûle to the summit, the remaining five (now closed) falling towards the Escaut. The lock dimensions are 39.40 by 5.18m. The lock on the Croix branch, just before the Wasquehal boat harbour (Port du Dragon), is now permanently open, following construction of a new weir beyond the harbour and lowering of the intermediate section.

Depth The maximum draught is 2.00m from the Deûle junction up to the junction with the Wasquehal branch, 1.80m over the remaining open length up to km 12.2 and on the Tourcoing branch, and 1.40m on the Wasquehal branch.

Bridges The minimum headroom is 3.30m (3.60m above normal water level). There are numerous swing bridges and lift bridges.

Towpath There is a good towpath, replaced by canalside streets through Tourcoing and Roubaix.

Authority
Direction Régionale de la Navigation, Lille.
Subdivision: Av Marx Dormoy, Bâtiment 1, BP 56, 59004 Lille, ☎ 20 92 63 44.

Distance table

	km	lock	km
Junction with Bauvin-Lys waterway (Canal de la Deûle), bridge	0.0	-	20.0
Bridge (D108)	0.3	-	19.7

	km	lock	km
Lock 1, Marquette	0.4	1	19.6
Bridge	2.1	-	17.9
Bridge (Marcq-en-Baroeul)	2.6	-	17.4
Lock 2, **Marcq-en-Baroeul**, and public quay	3.7	2	16.3
Bridge (Risban)	4.0	-	16.0
New road bridge	4.3	-	15.7
Bridge (Collège)	6.0	-	14.0
Motorway bridge (A1) and overhead power lines	6.2	-	13.8
Bridge (Château-Rouge), N532 Lille-Tourcoing	6.4	-	13.6
Junction with Croix branch, turning basin	7.6	-	12.4
Lock 3 (Trieste), bridge	7.9	3	12.1
Lock 4 (Plomeux), bridge	8.3	4	11.7
Lock 5 (Noir Bonnet)	8.6	5	11.4
Lock 6 (Cottigny), bridge	9.0	6	11.0
Lock 7, (Mazure), beginning of summit level	9.3	7	10.7
Bridge (Mazure)	9.6	-	10.4
Road bridge	9.7	-	10.3
Le Blanc-Sceau, public quay	10.6	-	9.4
Footbridge and swing bridge (Blanc-Sceau)	10.8	-	9.2
Bridge (Fresnoy)	11.7	-	8.3
Junction with Tourcoing branch	11.9	-	8.1
Bridge (Pont de la République), **Roubaix** (centre, 1500m)	12.2	-	7.8
Railway bridges	12.4	-	7.6
Swing bridges (Fontenoy), no longer operated, end of navigable section (distance table continued for reference)	12.6	-	7.4
Lock 8 (Union), bridge, end of summit level	12.9	8	7.1
Lift bridge (Couteaux)	13.6	-	6.4
Footbridge (Hutin)	13.8	-	6.2
Swing-bridge (Daubenton)	14.2	-	5.8
Footbridge and lift bridge (Vigne)	14.3	-	5.7
Lock 9 (Nouveau Monde), bridge	14.7	9	5.3
Lock 10 (Calvaire)	15.0	10	5.0
Footbridge and lift bridge (Wattrelos)	15.1	-	4.9
Lock 11 (Galon d'Eau), bridge	15.2	11	4.8
Footbridge (Soies)	15.6	-	4.4
Railway bridge	16.1	-	3.9
Bridge (Sartel)	16.4	-	3.6
Lock 12 (Sartel)	16.5	12	3.5
Railway bridge	17.2	-	2.8
Footbridge (Sainte-Marguerite)	17.6	-	2.4
Lift bridge (Grimonpont), public quay, customs office	18.7	-	1.3
Frontier, junction with Belgian Canal de l'Espierres	20.0	-	0.0

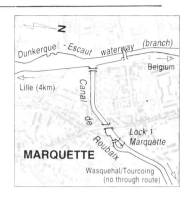

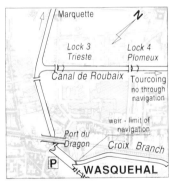

Canal de Saint-Quentin

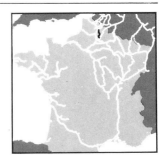

The Canal de Saint-Quentin forms a vital north–south link between the canalised river Escaut at Cambrai and the Canal latéral à l'Oise at Chauny. It is 92.5km long. It connects with the Canal de la Somme by a three-way junction near Saint-Simon (km 68), and with the Canal de la Sambre à l'Oise via the branch to La Fère, which leaves the main line at km 85. The canal crosses the watershed between the Escaut and Somme basins by a 20km long summit level at an altitude of 83m, between locks 17 (Bosquet) and 18 (Lesdins). There are two tunnels on this pound. The first, at Riqueval, also called the Grand Souterrain, is 5670m long (the longest still in use on the French waterways). The second, Lesdins or Tronquoy, is 1098m in length. The tunnels have a navigable width of 6.75m and a headroom of 3.58m. The arrangements for navigation through the summit level were altered in 1985. Between the Riqueval passing basin (km 35.9) and Lesdins lock (km 45.2), the section including the shorter tunnel, all boats proceed under their own power, at a maximum speed of 4 km/h, navigation being one-way only, controlled by lights. Towage remains compulsory for all vessels through the long tunnel, between Riqueval and Bosquet lock. Tows (rames) are made up twice in each direction every 24 hours. The actual departure times must be ascertained locally, but they are approximately:

– Paris towards Belgium (from Riqueval), 0530 and 1500
– Belgium towards Paris (from Vendhuile), 1130 and 1830.

One of the characteristic two chamber locks on the Canal de St Quentin.
Hugh Potter

The service is operated by a special electrically-driven tug, which warps itself along a chain laid on the bed of the canal. The duration of passage through the towage section is about two-and-a-half hours. Boats are joined to the tow behind the last barge. The tariff for towage in 1991 is 91F for boats up to 12m in length, and 125F for boats of 12m or longer. Unladen barges pay 114F and laden barges 290F.

There are plans for construction of a completely new high-capacity canal along the route of the Canal de Saint-Quentin, including water slopes to limit the number of locks and water consumption, but they are unlikely to materialise while this edition remains in print. This busy canal is not unattractive for pleasure cruising, especially the northernmost section following the Escaut valley.

Locks There are 35 locks, of which 17 fall towards Cambrai and 18 towards Chauny. All the locks are paired, with two chambers separated by a central quay. Lock dimensions are 39.30 by 6.00m and maximum vessel dimensions 38.50 by 5.60m. Locks 7 to 12 and 18 to 21 have been equipped for automatic operation, with radar detectors and lock entry lights. By 1991 locks 26 to 30 are also to be equipped.

Depth The maximum authorised draught is 2.20m.

Bridges All the fixed bridges offer a minimum headroom of 3.70m, although it should be noted that Saint-Quentin bridge (km 52) is on a gradient and offers 3.58m on one side and 3.83m on the other. Headroom is reduced by up to 0.30m when the canal drains storm waters.

Towpath There are towpaths on both banks.

Authority
Direction Régionale de la Navigation, Lille. Subdivision:
Place Marcellin-Berthelot, BP 371, 59407 Cambrai, ☎ 27 81 32 75 (km 0-26).
Service de la Navigation de la Seine, Arrondissement Picardie. Subdivision:
44 rue du Gouvernement, 02322 Saint-Quentin, ☎ 23 62 28 56 (km 26-92).

La Fère branch

The branch to La Fère leaves the main line at a junction just below lock 31 (Fargniers) and connects with the Canal de la Sambre à l'Oise between Beautor and La Fère. Its length is 3.8km.

Locks None.

Depth The maximum authorised draught is 2.20m.

Bridges The fixed bridges leave a minimum headroom of 3.70m, as on he main line.

Towpath There is a good towpath throughout.

Authority
Service de la Navigation de la Seine, Saint-Quentin subdivision (as above).

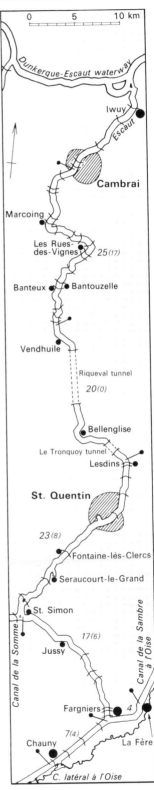

Distance table

	km	lock	km
Junction with canalised river Escaut, **Cambrai** freight office	0.0	-	92.5
Lock 1 (Proville)	2.2	1	90.3
Footbridge	3.2	-	89.3
Lock 2 (Cantigneul), bridge downstream, **Proville** 2000m	3.8	2	88.7
Lock 3 (Noyelles), aqueduct	4.4	3	88.1
Bridge (Râperie), quay, **Noyelles** 700m	5.3	-	87.2
Lock 4 (Talma), quay downstream r/b	7.3	4	85.2
Marcoing bridge, quay downstream l/b, village 700m	7.7	-	84.8
Lock 5 (Marcoing)	7.8	5	84.7
Railway bridge	8.1	-	84.4
Lock 6 (Bracheux)	9.4	6	83.1
Masnières bridge, quays above and below r/b, village 300m	10.7	-	81.8
Lock 7 (Masnières), automatic	11.5	7	81.0
Lock 8 (Saint-Waast), automatic, aqueduct	12.7	8	79.8
Crèvecoeur-sur-l'Escaut, quay r/b, village 500m	13.8	-	78.7
Lock 9 (Crèvecoeur), automatic, bridge downstream	14.1	9	78.4
Lock 10 (Vinchy), automatic, bridge d/s,			
Les Rues-des-Vignes l/b	15.0	10	77.5
Lock 11 (Tordoir), automatic	15.4	11	77.1
Lock 12 (Vaucelles), automatic, bridge d/s,			
Vaucelles abbey 700m	17.9	12	74.6
Bridge (Grenouillère), main road Cambrai-Saint-Quentin	19.3	-	73.2
Private basin l/b	19.8	-	72.7
Lock 13 (Bantouzelle)	20.0	13	72.5
Lock 14 (Banteux), bridge, **Banteux** l/b, **Bantouzelle** r/b	20.5	14	72.0
Lock 15 (**Honnecourt**), bridge, village l/b	23.2	15	69.3
Lock 16 (Moulin-Lafosse)	24.2	16	68.3
Lock 17 (Bosquet), beginning of summit level	24.8	17	67.7
Cereal loading quay in former canal arm	26.6	-	65.9
Vendhuile bridge and village	26.9	-	65.6
Macquincourt basin (formation of southbound tow)	27.6	-	64.9
Grand souterrain, Macquincourt (northern) entrance	29.0	-	63.5
Grand souterrain, Riqueval (southern) entrance	34.7	-	57.8
Basin for formation of northbound tow	35.9	-	56.6
Riqueval bridge	36.0	-	56.5
End of canal widening	37.3	-	55.2
Cereal loading quay	38.0	-	54.5
Bellenglise bridge and village, followed by lay-by	38.2	-	54.3
Bridge (main road Cambrai-Saint-Quentin)	39.5	-	53.0
Le Haucourt bridge, quays either side, village 400m	41.0	-	51.5
Lesdins tunnel, Le Haucourt (northern) entrance	41.9	-	50.6
Lesdins tunnel, Le Tronquoy (southern) entrance	43.0	-	49.5
Basin (originally used for formation of northbound tow)	43.7	-	48.8
Public quay, fuel and water points	44.5	-	48.0
End of summit level, lock 18 (Lesdins)	45.2	18	47.3
Lock 19 (Pascal)	45.5	19	47.0
Lesdins bridge, village 1000m	45.6	-	46.9
Private basin r/b	45.9	-	46.6
Lock 20 (Omissy), bridge, village r/b	46.7	20	45.8
Lock 21 (Moulin-Brûlé), bridge	48.7	21	43.8
Bridge	49.5	-	43.0
Lock 22 (Saint-Quentin)	50.9	22	41.6
Saint-Quentin bridge, freight office, quay r/b,			
town centre 800m	51.7	-	40.8
Road bridge	52.7	-	39.8
Railway bridge, quays r/b	53.0	-	39.5
Bridge (Estres)	54.9	-	37.6

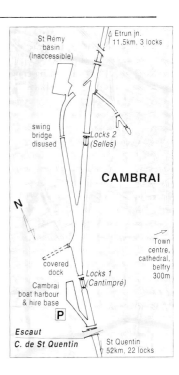

	km	lock	km
Dallon bridge, village r/b	56.9	-	35.6
Lock 23 (**Fontaines-les-Clercs**), bridge, village r/b	58.3	23	34.2
Bridge	60.7	-	31.8
Seraucourt-le-Grand basin in former canal arm l/b, village			
600m	61.1	-	31.4
Bridge	61.7	-	30.8
Lock 24 (Seraucourt-le-Grand)	62.8	24	29.7
Artemps bridge, village l/b	64.4	-	28.1
Entrance to former canal arm r/b (barges' graveyard)	66.1	-	26.4
Pont-de-Tugny bridge	66.3	-	26.2
Lock 25 (Pont-Tugny), downstream entrance to Pont-Tugny			
arm, quays 300m	66.5	25	26.0
Triangular junction with Canal de la Somme, r/b	68.0	-	24.5
Saint-Simon bridge, village l/b	69.0	-	23.5
Jussey basin r/b and quay l/b	74.2	-	18.3
Jussey bridge, village r/b	74.5	-	18.0
Railway bridge (main line Paris-Brussels), footbridge	76.4	-	16.1
Lock 26 (Jussey)	77.1	26	15.4
New road bridge (D53)	78.6	-	13.9
Lock 27 (Mennessis), bridge	79.6	27	12.9
Lock 28 (Voyaux)	80.2	28	12.3
Quessy bridge, quay downstream l/b, village 300m	83.0	-	9.5
Lock 29 (Fargniers I)	83.8	29	8.7
Lock 30 (Fargniers II)	84.1	30	8.4
Fargniers bridge	84.2	-	8.3
Lock 31 (Fargniers III), railway bridge downstream	84.8	31	7.7
Junction with La Fère branch (leading to Canal de la Sambre			
à l'Oise), l/b	84.9	-	7.6
Lock 32 (Tergniers), bridge	85.8	32	6.7
Bridge (D53), public quay upstream l/b, **Condren** 800m	87.1	-	5.4
New road bridge (Chauny by-pass)	88.3	-	4.2
Lock 33 (Viry)	88.4	33	4.1
Viry bridge, railway station 500m, village 1000m	89.7	-	2.8
Bridge (Senicourt)	90.7	-	1.8
Lock 34 (Senicourt)	90.8	34	1.7
Railway bridge	91.8	-	0.7
Junction with Chauny branch, with one lock down to the			
Oise, navigable for 500m, (branch now disused)	92.0	-	0.5
Lock 35 (Chauny)	92.3	35	0.2
Chauny bridge, town r/b, *junction with Canal latéral à l'Oise*	92.5	-	0.0

La Fère branch

Fargniers, *junction with main line of Canal de Saint-Quentin*	0.0	-	3.8
Bridge (Frette)	0.9	-	2.9
Railway bridge, power station and numerous overhead			
power lines, industrial quays	1.5	-	2.3
Bridge (railway siding)	2.4	-	1.4
Beautor bridge	3.1	-	0.7
Railway bridge, quay	3.3	-	0.5
Junction with Canal de la Sambre à l'Oise downstream of			
La Fère bridge	3.8	-	0.0

Sambre

The canalised river Sambre begins at Landrecies, where it connects with the Canal de la Sambre à l'Oise, and ends in Belgium where it has its confluence with the Meuse in the town of Namur. It thus forms an important link in the system of waterways connecting the Seine and Meuse basins. The canalised length from Landrecies to the Belgian border, allowing for various rectification works which have cut almost 2km from the course of the river, is just over 52km. The distance table below retains the original distances, corresponding to the kilometre posts on the river. The places where the course of the river has been shortened by the opening of meander cutoffs are downstream of Sassegnies (km 12-15) and downstream of Berlaimont (km 19).

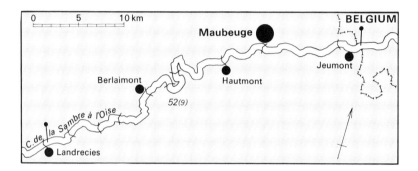

Locks There is a standard 38.50 by 5.20m lock beside each of the nine movable weirs on the river, overcoming a total difference in level of 11.35m.

Depth The maximum authorised draught is 1.80m down to the railway bridge above Hautmont, and 2.00m thereafter down to the Belgian border.

Bridges The fixed bridges leave a minimum headroom of 3.80m, except when the river is in flood.

Towpath There is a towpath throughout.

Authority

Direction Régionale de la Navigation, Lille.
Subdivision: Quai des Hennuyers, 59600 Maubeuge, ☎ 27 64 86 80.

Distance table

	km	lock	km
Junction with Canal de la Sambre à l'Oise (300m d/s of			
Landrecies), turning basin	0.0	-	54.2
Lock 1 (Etoquies) and weir, lift bridge	3.0	1	51.2
Bridge (Hachette)	5.9	-	48.3
Lock 2 (Hachette) and weir	7.7	2	46.5
Lock 3 (Sassegnies) and weir	11.1	3	43.1
Railway bridge	15.7	-	38.5
Railway bridge	17.2	-	37.0
Bridge (Montbard), private quay u/s r/b	17.6	-	36.6
Lock 4 (Berlaimont) and weir	17.8	4	36.4

	km	lock	km
Berlaimont bridge, quay d/s l/b, small town 400m l/b	18.1	-	36.1
Aymeries bridge, small village r/b	19.9	-	34.3
Lock 5 (Pont-sur-Sambre) and weir	21.7	5	32.5
Pont-sur-Sambre bridge, village l/b	22.0	-	32.2
Bachant bridge, village r/b	23.2	-	31.0
Bridge (Quartes)	26.0	-	28.2
Lock 6 (Quartes) r/b and weir	26.2	6	28.0
Boussières-sur-Sambre bridge, village l/b	32.0	-	22.2
Railway bridge and footbridge, numerous industrial quays	34.5	-	19.7
Lock 7 (**Hautmont**) l/b and weir, bridge, town r/b	35.4	7	18.8
Bridge (private railway siding), industrial quays	35.7	-	18.5
Bridges (private railway sidings)	37.5	-	16.7
Bridge (Usinor railway siding)	38.7	-	15.5
Bridge	39.0	-	15.2
Louvroil bridge (Pont Michaux), town r/b	39.5	-	14.7
Railway bridge	39.9	-	14.3
Bridge	41.1	-	13.1
Lock 8 (Maubeuge) r/b and weir	41.4	8	12.8
Maubeuge bridge (Pont Franco-Belge), quays d/s, town l/b	41.5	-	12.7
Road bridge (Maubeuge ring road)	42.2	-	12.0
Bridge	43.5	-	10.7
Assevent bridge, village l/b	45.3	-	8.9
Bridge (private railway siding)	47.0	-	7.2
Boussois bridge, village 200m l/b, Recquignies r/b	47.7	-	6.5
Marpent bridge, small town 400m r/b	50.9	-	3.3
Lock 9 (Marpent) r/b and weir	51.8	9	2.4
Railway bridge, private quays u/s	53.0	-	1.2
Jeumont bridge, quay and customs u/s r/b, small border town r/b	53.2	-	1.0
Private lift bridge	53.9	-	0.3
Private footbridge	54.1	-	0.1
French-Belgian border	54.2	-	0.0

Canal de la Sambre à l'Oise

The Canal de la Sambre à l'Oise is a predominantly rural but unspectacular waterway, forming part of the important route from the Meuse basin in Belgium to that of the Seine. It extends 67km from the canalised river Sambre at Landrecies to La Fère, where it joins the La Fère branch of the Canal de Saint-Quentin. The canal includes a summit level at an altitude of 137.40m, near Landrecies. Throughout most of the descent towards La Fère, the canal follows the upper valley of the river Oise.

Locks There are 38 locks of standard dimensions, 38.50 by 5.20m. Three locks overcome the 5.70m difference in level between Landrecies and the summit level. The other 35 fall towards La Fère (difference in level 86.65m).

Depth The maximum authorised draught is 1.80m.

Bridges The minimum headroom under the fixed bridges is 3.70m, except when the rivers supplying the canal are in flood.

Towpath There is a towpath throughout.

Authority

Direction Régionale de la Navigation, Lille. Subdivision:
Quai des Hennuyers, 59600 Maubeuge, ☎ 27 64 86 80 (km 0-13).
Service de la Navigation de la Seine, Arrondissement Picardie. Subdivision:
44 rue du Gouvernement, 02322 Saint-Quentin, ☎ 23 62 28 56 (km 13-67).

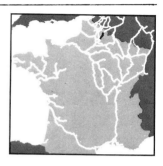

Distance table

	km	lock	km
Junction with the canalised river Sambre, turning basin	0.0	-	67.2
Landrecies bridge, quay downstream r/b, small town	0.2	-	67.0
Lock 3 (Landrecies), weir, quay upstream r/b	0.3	1	66.9
Lock 2 (Ors), bridge, village l/b	5.8	2	61.4
Catillon-sur-Sambre swing bridge, quays, village l/b	8.6	-	58.6
Lock 1 (Bois l'Abbaye), beginning of summit level	12.0	3	55.2
Stop gate (Fesmy)	13.7	-	53.5
Fesmy bridge, village 1300m	13.9	-	53.3
Oisy bridge, village 200m	16.0	-	51.2
Railway bridge	18.6	-	48.6
Lock 1 (Gard), overflow weir, end of summit level, bridge	18.9	4	48.3
Lock 2 (Etreux), overflow weir, quay upstream l/b	19.3	5	47.9
Lock 3 (Etreux), overflow weir	20.1	6	47.1
Lock 4 (Etreux), overflow weir	20.8	7	46.4
Lock 5 (Etreux), overflow weir	21.1	8	46.1
Lock 6 (Etreux), overflow weir, bridge	21.5	9	45.7
Etreux swing bridge, quay upstream r/b, village l/b	21.8	-	45.4
Lock 7 (Etreux), bridge	22.1	10	45.1
Lock 8 (Etreux)	22.5	11	44.7
Lock 9 (Vénérolles)	23.0	12	44.2
Vénérolles bridge, small village l/b	23.2	-	44.0
Lock 10 (Vénérolles), private footbridge	23.8	13	43.4
Lock 11 (Vénérolles)	24.5	14	42.7
Hannapes swing bridge, village r/b	25.0	-	42.2
Lock 12 (Hannapes), quay downstream r/b	25.1	15	42.1
Lock 13 (Hannapes)	26.5	16	40.7
Lock 14 (Tupigny)	27.0	17	40.2
Lock 15 (Tupigny), swing bridge, river Noirrieux enters canal, r/b, quay r/b	27.2	18	40.0
Tupigny swing bridge, village r/b	27.7	-	39.5
Weir (Tupigny) r/b, Noirrieux leaves canal	28.0	-	39.2
Lock 16 (Tupigny)	28.4	19	38.8
Lock 17 (Grand-Verly)	29.2	20	38.0
Lock 18 (Grand-Verly), bridge, village 500m r/b	30.0	21	37.2
Vadencourt swing bridge and railway bridge, turning basin downstream, village 800m r/b	30.9	-	36.3
Vadencourt aqueduct over Oise	31.5	-	35.7
Lock 19 (Vadencourt), quay downstream r/b	31.6	22	35.6
Bridge (Bohéries)	31.9	-	35.3
Lock 20 (Longchamps), bridge, water	33.2	33	34.0
Lock 21 (Noyales), bridge, village 400m r/b	35.2	24	32.0
Macquigny aqueduct over Oise	37.3	-	29.9
Lock 22 (Macquigny), bridge	37.5	25	29.7
Lock 23 (Hauteville), bridge	38.6	26	28.6
Lock 24 (Bernot), bridge, village 700m r/b	40.9	27	26.3
Turning basin l/b	42.4	-	24.8
Neuvillette swing bridge, quay upstream l/b	43.2	-	24.0
Lock 25 (Origny-Sainte-Benoîte), water	43.6	28	23.6
Origny-Sainte-Benoîte bridge (N30), public quay and basin upstream l/b, village 900m l/b	44.1	-	23.1

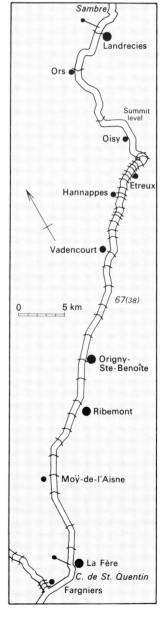

	km	lock	km
Railway bridge (private siding to cement works)	44.1	-	23.1
Private quays both banks	44.2	-	23.0
Lock 26 (Thenelles), bridge	45.9	29	21.3
Lock 27 (**Ribemont**), bridge, quay and turning basin downstream l/b, small town 1200m l/b	48.1	30	19.1
Lock 28 (**Sissy**), bridge, village 600m r/b	49.7	31	17.5
Châtillon aqueduct over Oise	51.3	-	15.9
Lock 29 (**Châtillon**), bridge, small village 600m r/b	51.6	32	15.6
Lock 30 (**Mézières-sur-Oise**), bridge, quay downstream l/b, village 500m r/b	52.9	33	14.3
Railway bridge	53.6	-	13.6
Lock 31 (Berthenicourt), bridge	54.5	34	12.7
Alaincourt bridge, private quay downstream r/b	55.3	-	11.9
Lock 32 (Hamégicourt), bridge, water, quay downstream r/b, **Moÿ-de-l'Aisne** 700m r/b	56.8	35	10.4
Bridge (Brissy)	57.8	-	9.4
Lock 33 (Brissy)	58.4	36	8.8
Vendeuil gravel loading quay r/b	59.3	-	7.9
Vendeuil bridge, quays, village 1200m r/b	60.7	-	6.5
Travecy-Montigny aqueduct over Serre, overhead power line	62.2	-	5.0
Lock 34 (Travecy-Montigny)	62.6	37	4.6
Turning basin and quay l/b	63.5	-	3.7
Travecy swing bridge, quay d/s l/b, village 500m r/b	63.8	-	3.4
Travecy aqueduct over Oise	64.3	-	2.9
Lock 35 (Travecy), bridge, water	65.1	38	2.1
Bridge (N44)	66.1	-	1.1
La Fère bridge, centre 1200m l/b			
Junction with La Fère branch of Canal de Saint-Quentin	67.2	-	0.0

Saône

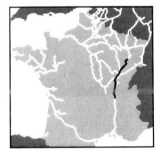

The Saône is one of the great rivers of France, fully canalised over a distance of 365km from Corre, where it is joined by the Canal de l'Est (southern branch), to its confluence with the Rhône at Lyon-La Mulatière. It also forms the 'backbone' of the French waterway network, being joined by four major inter-basin canals along its course: the Canal de la Marne à la Saône (km 127), the Canal du Rhône au Rhin (km 160), the Canal de Bourgogne (km 165) and the Canal du Centre (km 221). For the purposes of navigation, the river may conveniently be divided into two sections, which are completely different in character and in navigational standards:

1. Corre to Auxonne (km 150).
2. Auxonne (km 150) to Lyon (km 365).

Corre to Auxonne

Although forming part of an important link between the Rhine/Moselle basin and Lyon, this section of the waterway is completely unspoilt and ideal for cruising. The river winds lazily through charming pastoral landscapes, the longer meanders being by-passed by lengths of canal incorporating standard 38.50m locks. These canal sections cut almost 30km from the natural length of the river (407km from Corre to Lyon). There are two tunnels: Saint-Albin (km 48) has a length of 681m, a width at water level of 6.55m and a maximum height of 4.10m, while Seveux-Savoyeux (km 76) has a length of 643m, width 6.50m and headroom 3.60m. In both cases, the restricted wetted cross-section of the tunnel is retained for some distance beyond each entrance, and one-way traffic is enforced, controlled by lights. At certain other locations identified in the distance table, passing and overtaking are forbidden. The right-angle junction with the Canal de la Marne à la Saône is controlled by lights from Heuilley lock (17).

Locks In this section there are 19 locks and one flood lock at Cubry-les-Soing, which is normally open. Another flood lock at Ferrières has been closed, and navigation here follows the natural course of the Saône. There are also flood gates protecting most of the lock-cuts. The first 15 locks (Corre to Gray) have a length of 38.50m with a width of 5.20m, while the remaining four are 40 by 8m. Many of the locks are electrified and equipped for automatic operation. Users are handed a leaflet of instructions at the last manually operated lock.

Depth From Corre to Auxonne lock, the maximum authorised draught is 1.80m.

Bridges The minimum headroom in this section is 3.50m.

Towpath There is a good towpath throughout.

Regulations The maximum authorised speed is 15km/h in river sections (although there are some local restrictions), and 6km/h in the lock-cuts. The entrance to the lock-cuts from upstream can be delicate during floods.

Authority
Service de la Navigation Rhône-Saône (Lyon). Subdivisions:
70170 Port-sur-Saône, ☎ 84 91 51 44 (km 0-62).
5 quai Vergy, 70100 Gray, ☎ 84 65 11 02 (km 62-160).

Auxonne to Lyon

Downstream from Auxonne, the Saône becomes wider and loses the rural charm of the upper reaches. In addition, it has been transformed into a high-capacity waterway navigable by barges and push-tows of European standard dimensions. It is along this section that two important routes from the Seine basin join the Saône. The Canal de Bourgogne connects with the Saône at the bargemen's town of Saint-Jean-de-Losne, while the Canal du Centre enters the river at Chalon-sur-Saône. On the left bank is the junction with the Canal du Rhône au Rhin, of particular significance for it is the new waterway planned on this route which justified the upgrading of the Saône, as part of the future high-capacity navigable link between the North Sea and the Mediterranean. The 3km long Mâcon bypass, built for commercial traffic to avoid the low St Laurent bridge at Mâcon, is to be opened to traffic in September 1991.

Locks In 1987, the last of the older locks in this section, at Verdun-sur-le-Doubs, was taken out of service, leaving only five locks over the 216km of

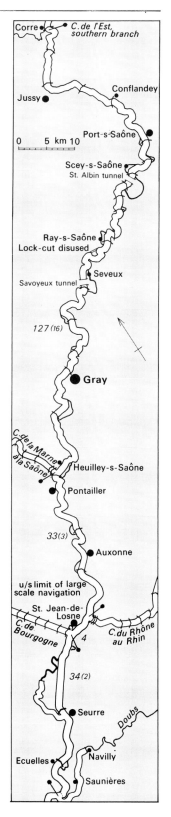

waterway, compared with nine before the modernisation works started. Seurre is the first of the new locks, and is situated at the end of a 10km long diversion canal which cuts almost 11km from the natural length of the Saône. The other new locks are at Ecuelles (replacing Charnay), Ormes (replacing Gigny and Verdun-sur-le-Doubs), Dracé (replacing Thoissey) and Couzon (adjacent to the former lock). The locks at Port Bernalin, Ile Barbe and La Mulatière have all been taken out of service. All the new locks measure 185 by 12m, and are controlled by lights. Boats are locked through after a maximum wait of 20 minutes if no commercial barge has appeared in the meantime. There are several mooring dolphins on the approach to each lock, some of which have gangways for access to the bank. There is no difficulty in negotiating these big locks, which have bollards set into the chamber walls.

Depth When current dredging works between Auxonne and Mâcon have been completed, the navigable depth will be 3.00m throughout this section.

Bridges The lowest bridge in this section is the Pont Saint-Laurent, at Mâcon, with a headroom of 7.20m (over a width of 10m) above the normal level and 3.70m above the highest navigable water level. All other bridges offer a minimum headroom of 6.00m. A 3.7km long by-pass has been built at Mâcon so that commercial traffic can avoid the Pont Saint-Laurent (which is a listed public monument).

Towpath There is no continuous length.

Navigation The channel is marked in places on the right-bank side by red-and-white stakes or red buoys, and on the left-bank side by black-and-white stakes or black buoys (under new international regulations black is to be replaced by green). Care should be taken to avoid the submerged training walls encountered especially downstream of Chalon-sur-Saône, and use of the *Guide de la Saône* (see Introduction, p29) is recommended. The river narrows in Lyon, and during floods alternating one-way navigation is enforced.

Authority
Service de la Navigation Rhône-Saône, Lyons. Subdivisions:
– Port Fluvial, 71100 Chalon-sur-Saône, ☎ 85 43 03 01 (km 160-245).
– Quai des Marans, 71000 Mâcon, ☎ 85 38 07 44 (km 245-341).
– 1 place Antonin-Perrin, 69007 Lyon, ☎ 78 72 65 16 (km 341-365).

Distance table

	km	lock	km
Junction with Canal de l'Est, southern branch, downstream of Corre lock	0.0	-	365.4
Entrance to lock-cut, l/b	2.6	-	362.8
Flood gate	4.0	-	361.4
Ormoy bridge, village l/b	4.3	-	361.1
Footbridge (Devez)	5.1	-	360.3
Ormoy lock (automatic)	5.5	1	359.9
End of lock-cut	5.6	-	359.8
Denon meander cutoff (l/b), bridge	6.9	-	358.5
Rond Pré meander cutoff (l/b)	7.4	-	358.0
Entrance to lock-cut, l/b, flood gate	10.0	-	355.4
Cendrecourt lock (automatic), village 500m	11.9	2	353.5

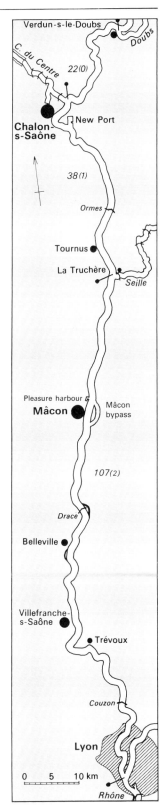

	km	lock	km
End of lock-cut, 25m long wooden quay and slipway 200m up Saône level with campsite, mooring for **Jussey** station 1000m, small town 2000m	12.2	-	353.2
Cendrecourt bridge	12.4	-	353.0
Jussey railway viaduct	13.5	-	351.9
Confluence of Amance, r/b	14.0	-	351.4
La Hang meander cutoff and bridge, passing forbidden	17.9	-	347.5
Montureux-les-Baulay, l/b	18.5	-	346.9
Montureux bridge	20.1	-	345.3
Montureux lock (automatic)	20.5	3	344.9
End of lock-cut	20.6	-	344.8
Fouchecourt, r/b	22.4	-	343.0
Baulay bridge, wooden quay 10m, village 300m l/b	23.1	-	342.3
Port d'Atelier bridge (village r/b)	26.8	-	338.6
Conflandey bridge	30.7	-	334.7
Conflandey lock	30.8	4	334.6
Confluence of Lanterne, l/b	30.9	-	334.5
Tip of island, downstream-bound boats follow r/b arm	31.0	-	334.4
Conflandey footbridge, village r/b	31.3	-	334.1
Tip of island, upstream-bound boats follow l/b arm	31.5	-	333.9
Island (Ile du Cul du Chaudron), keep to l/b side	32.8	-	332.6
Beleau island, overhead power line	34.8	-	330.6
Entrance to lock-cut, l/b	36.6	-	328.8
Port-sur-Saône bridge and flood gate (mooring close to bridge impossible, narrow cut), small town	37.5	-	327.9
Port-sur-Saône basin, Loisirs Nautic de France hire base, moorings, office of sub-divisional engineer	38.0	-	327.4
Bridge (Maladière)	38.3	-	327.1
Port-sur-Saône lock (automatic)	38.8	5	326.6
End of lock-cut	38.9	-	326.5
Gilley island (keep to r/b side)	39.6	-	325.8
Entrance to lock-cut, r/b, bridge	42.3	-	323.1
Chemilly lock (automatic)	42.9	6	322.5
End of lock-cut	43.1	-	322.3
Entrance to lock-cut, l/b, flood gate (proceed down Saône for access to Scey-sur-Saône)	45.5	-	319.9
Quay used by sand-barges, r/b	46.5	-	318.9
Scey-sur-Saône bridge, basin d/s r/b (restaurant, town 1000m)	46.6	-	318.8
Scey lock (automatic)	47.0	7	318.4
End of lock-cut	47.3	-	318.1
Entrance to lock-cut, r/b	47.7	-	317.7
Bridge and flood gate, lights controlling tunnel entrance (canal narrows to one barge's width)	47.8	-	317.6
Saint-Albin tunnel (northern entrance)	48.0	-	317.4
Saint-Albin tunnel (southern entrance)	48.7	-	316.7
Bridge with lights controlling tunnel entrance, end of narrow section	49.2	-	316.2
Rupt lock	49.8	8	315.6
End of lock-cut	50.0	-	315.4
Chantes bridge (village 1000m), **Rupt-sur-Saône** (r/b, 500m)	50.7	-	314.7
Island, channel follows r/b arm	51.2	-	314.2
Entrance to lock-cut, r/b, flood gate	52.4	-	313.0
Chantes lock	52.9	9	312.5
End of lock-cut	53.0	-	312.4
Cubry-les-Soing flood lock, r/b, usually open, village 1500m l/b	55.1	-	310.3
End of lock-cut	55.9	-	309.5

	km	lock	km
Narrow passage, passing and overtaking forbidden	56.9	-	308.5
End of narrow passage	57.9	-	307.5
Entrance to lock-cut, r/b, flood gate	59.9	-	305.5
Soing bridge, village 500m	60.3	-	305.1
Soing lock	61.2	10	304.2
End of lock-cut	61.4	-	304.0
Entrance to lock-cut, l/b (moorings and fuel adjacent to camp-site on l/b of Saône just downstream)	62.3	-	303.1
Charentenay bridge, village and restaurant l/b	62.8	-	302.6
Charentenay lock (automatic)	64.6	11	300.8
End of lock-cut (**Ray-sur-Saône** 1km up the Saône, keep to l/b of island)	64.7	-	300.7
Ray bridge	65.1	-	300.3
Entrance to Ferrières lock-cut, r/b, keep to Saône, l/b	65.4	-	300.0
End of lock-cut, r/b (upstream-bound boats, keep to Saône)	70.2	-	295.2
Recologne, r/b, quay for sand-barges	71.0	-	294.4
Entrance to lock-cut, r/b, flood gate, bridge	73.8	-	291.6
Savoyeux basin, moorings, Snaily hire base	75.0	-	290.4
Seveux bridge, village 1000m l/b, canal narrows, sound horn for Savoyeux tunnel (controlled by lights)	75.2		290.2
Savoyeux tunnel (northern entrance)	76.0	-	289.4
Savoyeux tunnel (southern entrance)	76.6	-	288.8
Railway bridge	76.8	-	288.6
Bridge (with lights controlling tunnel entrance), end of narrow section	76.9	-	288.5
Savoyeux lock	77.3	12	288.1
End of lock-cut	77.3	-	288.1
Quitteur bridge	82.3	-	283.1
Confluence of Salon, r/b	83.0	-	282.4
Entrance to lock-cut, l/b	85.7	-	279.7
Bridge, flood gate	86.5	-	278.9
Véreux lock	87.8	13	277.6
End of lock-cut	87.9	-	277.5
Prantigny bridge	90.1	-	275.3
Carosse island (keep to l/b arm)	92.0	-	273.4
Entrance to lock-cut, l/b, flood gate, bridge	95.5	-	269.9
Rigny lock	96.3	14	269.1
End of lock-cut	96.5	-	268.9
Camp-site, l/b	100.2	-	265.2
Connoisseur Cruisers boatyard and hire base l/b	100.6	-	264.8
Gray lock and bridge	100.7	15	264.7
Gray quays and boat moorings l/b close to town centre	100.8	-	263.9
Bridge (Pont Neuf)	101.6	-	263.8
Cereal loading basin, r/b	101.9	-	263.5
Restaurant and service station, mooring stage, r/b	103.0	-	262.4
Mantoche moorings and village r/b	107.7	-	257.7
Entrance to lock-cut, r/b, flood gate, bridge	108.8	-	256.6
Apremont bridge (basin silted up)	109.8	-	255.6
Apremont lock	112.0	16	253.4
End of lock-cut	112.1	-	253.3
Island (keep to r/b arm), Cecey quay, r/b	113.2	-	252.2
Confluence of Vingeanne, r/b	118.4	-	247.0
Montseugny island (keep to r/b arm)	119.2	-	246.2
Quays for sand-barges, l/b	121.8	-	243.6
Pontoon moorings, l/b, **Broye** 2000m	123.0	-	242.5
River divides, take r/b arm (Ile de Fley)	123.4	-	242.0
Entrance to lock-cut, r/b, flood gate, bridge	124.4	-	241.0
Heuilley basin, silted up	124.8	-	240.6

The hotel barge *Janine* is accompanied by English canal barge *Beecliffe* through Ecuelles lock on the Saône.
Hugh Potter

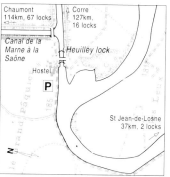

	km	lock	km
Bridge	125.3	–	240.1
Junction with Canal de la Marne à la Saône (controlled by lights)	126.9	–	238.5
Heuilley lock, restaurant	127.0	17	238.4
End of lock-cut	127.1	–	238.3
Entrance to Vieille Saône, r/b, access to Pontailler boat harbour and Rive de France hire base	130.1	–	235.3
Pontailler bridge, mooring downstream r/b, small town r/b	130.2	–	235.2
Confluence of Vieille Saône, r/b	132.1	–	233.3
Vonges, commercial quay, r/b	132.2	–	233.2

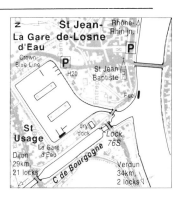

	km	lock	km
Basin, r/b, completely silted up	134.6	-	230.8
Pontoon moorings r/b, Hostellerie de St Antoine hotel and restaurant set back from the river and snack bar/pizzeria beside mooring	135.6	-	229.8
Lamarche-sur-Saône bridge, mooring l/b, village r/b	136.0	-	229.4
Entrance to lock-cut, l/b, bridge	139.2	-	226.2
Poncey lock	140.5	18	224.9
End of lock-cut	140.7	-	224.7
Island (Ile de la Bouillie)	144.7	-	220.7
Auxonne bridge, town centre l/b	146.5	-	218.9
Entrance to lock-cut, l/b, and SNCF railway bridge	147.0	-	218.4
Bridge and flood gate, office of sub-divisional engineer	147.1	-	218.3
Auxonne lock	149.5	19	215.9
End of lock-cut	149.6	-	215.8

Large-scale waterway, Auxonne to Lyon

	km	lock	km
Bridge (des Maillys)	155.8	-	209.6
Confluence of Tille, r/b, shoals	157.0	-	208.4
Quay for sand-barges, r/b	157.6	-	207.8
Island, channel in l/b arm	158.5	-	206.9
Junction with Canal du Rhône au Rhin, l/b	160.4	-	205.0
Saint-Symphorien, l/b	161.6	-	204.8
Saint-Jean-de-Losne bridge, small town r/b	164.4	-	201.0
Junction with Canal de Bourgogne, r/b, large basin (Gare d'Eau) entered at junction, biggest boat harbour on the Saône, with all services: Blanquart, Atelier Fluvial Diesel, H20 and Crown Blue Line hire base (see plan)	164.6	-	200.8
Railway viaduct (Saint-Usage)	165.7	-	199.7
Commercial quays, r/b	166.0	-	199.4
Former entrance to Saint-Jean-de-Losne lock-cut, replaced by a new meander cutoff (river dammed)	166.6	-	198.8
End of meander cutoff (river dammed), H20 barge moorings in former lock-cut, r/b	167.3	-	198.1
Entrance to new lock-cut, l/b (Pagny dam)	170.1	-	195.3
Bridge (Pagny)	172.5	-	192.9
Bridge (Labruyère)	174.6	-	190.8
Motorway bridge (A36)	175.8	-	189.6
Bridge (Chamblanc)	177.3	-	188.1
Seurre lock, lift 3.75m, water on mooring pile d/s	179.4	1	186.0
End of lock-cut and moorings for Seurre, l/b	179.9	-	185.5
Seurre bridge, small town l/b	180.3	-	185.1
Island (Ile aux Princes), new channel on r/b side, Bourgogne-Buissonnière hire base l/b	180.4	-	184.5
Former entrance to Seurre lock-cut (keep to Saône)	182.1	-	183.3
Seurre lock (disused), l/b, and end of lock-cut	183.1	-	182.3
Chivres viaduct (railway converted to road)	184.5	-	180.9
Chazelles, l/b, quay, restaurant	185.7	-	179.7
Entrance to new lock-cut, r/b (**Charnay-les-Chalon** 700m l/b)	188.7	-	176.7
Ecuelles lock (replacing Charnay lock), lift 3.20m	189.9	2	175.5
End of lock-cut	190.2	-	175.2
Ecuelles quay and village r/b	190.9	-	174.5
Former Verdun lock, r/b	197.6	-	167.8
Confluence of Doubs, l/b, access to **Verdun-sur-le-Doubs**	198.4	-	167.0
Bragny bridge	198.6	-	166.8
Chauvort, r/b, (destroyed bridge)	200.2	-	165.2
Chauvort viaduct	200.6	-	164.8
Gergy pontoon moorings and snack bar at campsite, r/b	205.7	-	159.7

	km	lock	km
Gergy bridge	205.9	-	159.5
Fuel depot, quay r/b	208.4	-	157.0
Alleriot, l/b	214.7	-	150.7
Junction with Canal du Centre, r/b	220.5	-	144.9
Chalon-sur-Saône port, r/b	222.2	-	143.2
Yacht Club de Chalon, private moorings, l/b	222.4	-	143.0
Chalon-sur-Saône bridge (Saint-Laurent), town centre r/b boat harbour with all facilities in Génise arm d/s, l/b	223.4	-	142.0
Bridge (Jean-Richard)	224.0	-	141.4
Chalon railway viaduct	224.6	-	140.8
New road bridge (Pont Sud de Chalon)	226.7	-	138.7
New port of Chalon, basin 1500 by 350m, l/b	227.8	-	137.6
Port d'Ouroux, l/b	235.5	-	129.9
Ouroux bridge, moorings and restaurant at campsite d/s l/b	235.6	-	129.8
Confluence of Grosne, r/b	236.8	-	128.6
Thorey bridge	240.6	-	124.8
Gigny lock (disused) and boat harbour r/b	242.2	-	123.2
Ormes lock (in short lock-cut on l/b), lift 2.90m	246.2	3	119.2
Tournus boat club moorings, r/b	252.7	-	112.7
Tournus bridge, quay and town centre r/b	253.2	-	112.2
Tournus bridge	254.2	-	111.2
Junction with Seille, l/b (see under *Seille*)	258.7	-	106.7
Uzichy bridge	262.2	-	103.2
Fleurville bridge (*junction with disused canal de Pont-à-Vaux* l/b), restaurant r/b, village 1500m	267.7	-	97.7
Confluence of Reyssouze, l/b	268.2	-	97.2
Asnières-sur-Saône, restaurant with landing stage, l/b	275.2	-	90.2
Saint-Martin-Belle-Roche, restaurant, r/b	276.3	-	89.1
Vésines, restaurant with landing stage (little water), l/b	277.7	-	87.7
Road bridge (Mâcon by-pass), tip of island (Ile Palme), channel in l/b arm	280.7	-	84.7
Mâcon yacht harbour, entrance to basin, r/b	282.1	-	83.3
U/s entrance to diversion canal, l/b (pleasure traffic continues on Saône except in flood; if using bypass add 0.7km to distance covered)	283.0	-	82.4
Mâcon bridge (Saint-Laurent), mooring downstream r/b	284.8	-	80.6
D/s entrance to diversion canal, l/b	286.0	-	79.4
Port of Mâcon, basin r/b	286.4	-	79.0
Mâcon railway viaduct	287.0	-	78.4
New port of Mâcon, basin r/b	288.0	-	77.4
TGV railway viaduct (high-speed line Paris-Lyon)	290.2	-	75.2
Arciat bridge	292.5	-	72.9
Saint-Romain-des-Iles bridge, small boat harbour d/s r/b, Arc-en-ciel hire base	299.0	-	66.4
Thoissey bridge, mooring downstream l/b	301.8	-	63.6
Dracé lock, r/b, lift 2.90m	303.0	4	62.4
Former Thoissey lock (disused), l/b	304.0	-	61.4
Islands (buoyed channel)	308.0	-	57.4
Belleville island	309.4	-	56.0
Belleville bridge , restaurant r/b (town 800m)	310.1	-	55.3
Northern tip of Montmerle island (channel on l/b side)	310.7	-	54.7
Southern tip of Montmerle island	312.7	-	52.7
Montmerle bridge, small town land restaurant /b	313.0	-	52.4
Port Rivière, r/b	317.7	-	47.7
Fareins boat harbour, l/b (water, petrol, slipway, restaurant)	322.0	-	43.4
Beauregard bridge	322.8	-	42.6
Villefranche industrial port, r/b	323.3	-	42.1

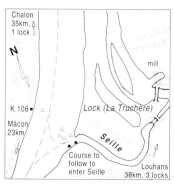

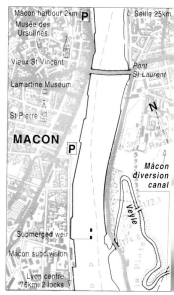

	km	lock	km
Jassans-Riottier boat harbour, l/b, village 400m	324.5	-	40.9
Frans bridge, commercial quays downstream r/b	324.8	-	40.6
Saint-Bernard bridge, castle l/b	330.1	-	35.3
Trévoux suspension bridge, mooring upstream l/b	334.1	-	31.3
New bridge (boatyard and moorings upstream r/b)	334.5	-	30.9
Former Bernalin lock (disused), l/b	338.9	-	26.5
Saint-Germain-au-Mont d'Or, former Yacht Club du Rhône, boat harbour, slipway, crane, r/b	342.5	-	22.9
Neuville-sur-Saône bridge	344.5	-	20.9
Couzon lock, l/b, lift 4.00m (varying with the level in the Rhône at Lyon)	347.9	5	17.5
Couzon suspension bridge	348.1	-	17.3
Fontaines-sur-Saône bridge	350.4	-	15.0
Tip of island (Ile Roy), downstream-bound boats take l/b channel	351.0	-	14.4
Tip of island, upstream-bound boats take r/b channel	352.0	-	13.4
Collonges railway viaduct	353.0	-	12.4
Collonges bridge mooring u/s r/b (Bocuse)	353.1	-	12.3
Island (Ile Barbe), channel in l/b arm	355.0	-	10.4
Bridge (Ile Barbe)	355.4	-	10.0
Former lock, l/b	355.6	-	9.8
Lyon			
Bridge (Mazaryk), beginning of alternating one-way navigation in time of flood	358.1	-	7.3
Bridge (Clémenceau)	358.5	-	6.9
Bridge Général Koenig)	359.1	-	6.3
Bridge (Homme de la Roche)	359.9	-	5.5
Footbridge (Saint-Vincent)	360.4	-	5.0
Bridge (La Feuillée)	360.6	-	4.8
Bridge (Maréchal Juin)	360.9	-	4.5
Former boat harbour, mooring possible in the heart of Lyon, l/b	361.3	-	4.1
Bridge (Bonaparte)	361.5	-	3.9
Footbridge (Saint-Georges)	361.8	-	3.6
Bridge (Kitchener-Marchand)	362.5	-	2.9
Motorway bridge (A6) and railway viaduct (Quarantaine)	362.6	-	2.8
Port Rambaud (commercial quays, l/b)	364.0	-	1.4
Motorway bridge (A7) and railway viaduct (de la Mulatière)	365.1	-	0.3
Lyon-La Mulatière, former lock, r/b, *confluence with Rhône*	365.4	-	0.0

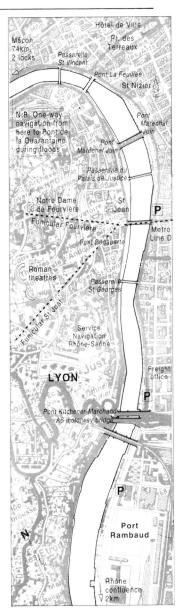

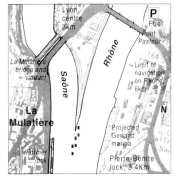

Sarthe

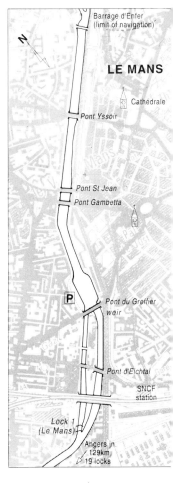

The Sarthe is navigable from the Barrage d'Enfer, a weir situated in the town of Le Mans, to its confluence with the Mayenne upstream of Angers, a distance of 132km. Over the first 113km down to the lock at Cheffes, the river is canalised. The remaining 18km is free flow navigation, offering restricted depths during summer drought periods. This problem may be solved by the construction of a new weir and lock on the Maine downstream of Angers (see under Mayenne-Maine). Together with the Mayenne and Oudon, the Sarthe forms the Anjou river system, a delightful cruising ground where several hire bases have been established.

Locks There are 20 locks. The first 16 (down to the limit of the departments of Sarthe and Maine-et-Loire) are 30.85m long and 5.20m wide. The last four are 33.00m long and 5.15m wide.

Depth The maximum authorised draught is 1.40m, but in practice there is only 1.10m between Le Mans and Sablé during low flow periods, and little more in the free flow section downstream of Cheffes lock.

Bridges From Le Mans to km 86, the bridges offer a minimum headroom of 3.90m (reduced to 3.40 above the highest navigable water level). Over the rest of the waterway the least headroom is 4.40m (4.00m above HNWL). It should be noted that access to the moorings at Malicorne, on the weir stream at km 47, is through a bridge offering very restricted headroom (2.35m).

Towpath There is no regular towpath.

Authority
Direction Départementale de l'Equipement, Sarthe (Le Mans).
Subdivision: 1 rue du Vert Galant, 72000 Le Mans, ☎ 43 24 14 19 (km 0-86).
Service de la Navigation Maine-et-Loire, quai Félix Faure, 49000 Angers,
☎ 41 43 61 49 (km 86-132).

Distance table

	km	lock	km
Weir (Barrage d'Enfer), limit of navigation in Le Mans	0.0	-	131.6
Bridge (Pont Yssoir)	0.5	-	131.1
Bridge (Pont Saint-Jean)	0.8	-	130.8
Le Mans bridge (Pont Gambetta), quay d/s r/b, Sarthe Evasion hire base, water, town centre l/b	0.9	-	130.7
Bridge (Pont du Greffier), weir l/b	1.6	-	130.0
Bridge (Pont d'Eichtal)	1.8	-	129.8
Railway bridge	2.1	-	129.5
Lock 1	2.2	1	129.4
Confluence of Huisne; l/b	3.0	-	128.6
New road bridge (Le Mans bypass)	3.3	-	128.3
Railway bridge	4.0	-	127.6
Entrance to lock-cut, l/b	4.4	-	127.2
Bridge (Pont Rouge)	4.6	-	127.0
Lock 2 (Raterie), end of lock-cut, weir r/b	5.0	2	126.6
Bridge (D147e)	5.2	-	126.4
Lock 3 (Chahoué) l/b and weir	6.1	3	125.5
New road bridge	9.3	-	122.3
Arnage l/b	10.6	-	121.0

	km	lock	km
Entrance to lock-cut, l/b, bridge	13.0	-	118.6
Spay bridge, village 600m r/b	13.3	-	118.3
Lock 4 (Spay), end of lock-cut	14.1	4	117.5
Fillé bridge, village r/b	16.3	-	115.3
Entrance to lock-cut, r/b	16.6	-	115.0
Bridge	16.8	-	114.8
Bridge (Cheneaux)	20.2	-	111.4
Lock 5 (Roëzé), end of lock-cut	22.0	5	109.6
Roëzé-sur-Sarthe bridge, village r/b	23.0	-	108.6
La Suze-sur-Sarthe bridge, quay u/s r/b, village l/b	26.5	-	105.1
Entrance to lock-cut, r/b	26.6	-	105.0
Railway bridge	26.7	-	104.9
Lock 6 (La Suze), end of lock-cut	27.0	6	104.6
Fercé-sur-Sarthe bridge, village 200m r/b	32.5	-	99.1
Lock 7 (Fercé) l/b and weir	33.0	7	98.6
Railway bridge	39.7	-	91.9
Noyen-sur-Sarthe quay, Mayenne Navigation relay base, village r/b, water	40.0	-	91.6
Entrance to lock-cut, l/b	40.0	-	91.6
Bridge	40.1	-	91.5
Lock 8 (Noyen), end of lock-cut	41.0	8	90.6
Entrance to lock-cut, r/b	46.3	-	85.3
Malicorne-sur-Sarthe bridge, village 300m l/b (on weir stream, access from u/s)	46.6	-	85.0
Lock 9 (Malicorne), end of lock-cut	47.0	9	84.6
Dureil, small village with church, l/b	52.0	-	79.6
Castle r/b (Château de Pêcheseul)	53.5	-	78.1
Entrance to lock-cut, r/b	54.6	-	77.0
Lock 10 (Ignères), end of lock-cut	55.0	10	76.6
Entrance to lock-cut, r/b	57.3	-	74.3
Parcé-sur-Sarthe bridge, quay d/s l/b, village 200m	57.8	-	73.8
Lock 11 (Parcé), end of lock-cut	58.0	11	73.6
Avoise r/b	60.5	-	71.1
Entrance to lock-cut, r/b	62.3	-	69.3
Lock 12 (Courtigné)	63.0	12	68.6
End of lock-cut	63.4	-	68.2
Confluence of Vègre, r/b	64.5	-	67.1
Lock 13 (**Juigné-sur-Sarthe**) r/b and weir, village r/b	68.6	13	63.0
Solesmes bridge, quay u/s l/b, village and abbey l/b	69.8	-	61.8
Lock 14 (Solesmes) in short cut, r/b, swing bridge	70.0	14	61.6
Railway bridge (Port-Etroit), quay r/b	71.6	-	60.0
New road bridge (D309 bypass)	72.3	-	59.3
Sablé-sur-Sarthe bridge, quay d/s l/b, France Anjou Navigation hire base, small town r/b	72.7	-	58.9
Lock 15 (Sablé), weir stream enters l/b	73.1	15	58.5
Islands	74.5	-	57.1
Island	75.7	-	55.9
Railway viaduct	77.1	-	54.5
Lock 16 (Beffes) in short cut, r/b, swing bridge	81.3	16	50.3
Lock 17 (Pendu) in short cut, r/b, weir and mill l/b	87.2	17	44.4
Morannes bridge, quay d/s l/b, village l/b	90.5	-	41.1
Entrance to lock-cut, r/b	92.5	-	39.1
Lock 18 (Villechien), weir and hydropower station l/b	93.4	18	38.2
Brissarthe quay and village r/b	97.3	-	34.3
Le Porage, railway station, l/b	99.2	-	32.4
Lock 19 (Châteauneuf-sur-Sarthe) r/b and weir	102.9	19	28.7
Châteauneuf-sur-Sarthe bridge, quay d/s r/b, village r/b	103.3	-	28.3
Juvardeil quay and village r/b	105.8	-	25.8

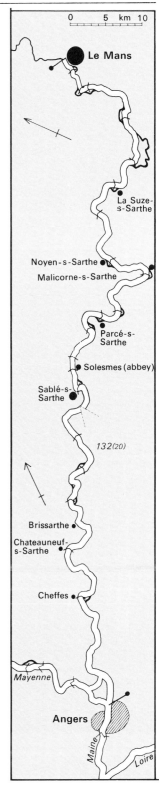

	km	lock	km
River divides, navigation in r/b arm	108.6	-	23.0
(Boats heading u/s) river divides, navigation in r/b arm	110.3	-	21.3
Weir (Cheffes) l/b	112.5	-	19.1
Bridge (D74)	113.0	-	18.6
Lock 20 (Cheffes) l/b and weir	113.3	20	18.3
Cheffes r/b	113.4	-	18.2
Briollay bridge, village d/s l/b	119.9	-	11.7
Confluence of Loir, l/b	121.9	-	9.7
Ecouflant l/b	126.7	-	4.9
Confluence of Vieille-Maine (3km navigable arm connecting with Mayenne), r/b	127.0	-	4.6
Island, pass on r/b side	129.5	-	2.1
Confluence with Mayenne and Maine (3km u/s of Angers)	131.6	-	0.0

Scarpe

The canalised river Scarpe begins at the canal basin in Arras (linked to the river by a short length of canal) and ends at the confluence with the Escaut at Mortagne. For navigation purposes it is divided into three sections:
– Scarpe supérieure, Arras to Corbehem (23km)
– Scarpe moyenne, Corbehem to the lock at Fort-de-Scarpe (7km)
– Scarpe inférieure, Fort-de-Scarpe to Mortagne (36km).

However, most of the second section, through the town of Douai, has been closed following construction of a bypass canal (the dérivation de la Scarpe autour de Douai) as part of the high-capacity Dunkerque–Escaut waterway. This cut branches off from the left bank of the Scarpe opposite the junction with the Canal de la Sensée, passes to the west of the town and joins the Canal de la Deûle on the northern outskirts. Continuity of navigation on the Scarpe is ensured by a short (800m) link canal (Canal de Jonction), leaving the bypass at km 6.2 and joining the Scarpe moyenne downstream of the Pont Vauban in Douai. The distances in the table below are those of the original line of navigation, making a total of 66km from Arras to Mortagne. The line effectively used by navigation, bypassing Douai, is 1km longer (see plan).

Locks There are 9 locks on the Scarpe supérieure, of standard barge dimensions (38.50 by 5.20m), all of which have been equipped for automatic operation. The locks on the Scarpe moyenne have been taken out of use, while those on the bypass canal are of large dimensions. At Courchelettes (écluse sud) and at Douai (écluse nord) there are two chambers 144.60 by 12.00m and 91.60 by 12.00m. There is no lock on the Canal de Jonction. The six locks on the Scarpe inférieure are also of standard barge dimensions (38.70 by 5.20m).

Depth The maximum authorised draught is 1.80m on the Canal Saint-Michel in Arras, 2.20m on the rest of the Scarpe supérieure, 3.00m on the bypass canal and 2.00m on the Scarpe inférieure.

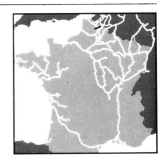

Bridges Below the Pont des Grès in Arras, with a headroom of 3.50m, all fixed bridges offer a clear headroom of 3.95m above normal water level, reduced to 3.75m during flood flows on the Scarpe supérieure and 3.65m on the Scarpe inférieure. The least headroom on the bypass canal is 5.25m.

Towpath There is a towpath throughout.

Authority
Direction Régionale de la Navigation, Lille.
Subdivisions:
– 16 route de Tournai, BP 26, 59119 Waziers, ☎ 27 87 12 55 (km 0-51).
– 24 chemin du Halage, 59300 Valenciennes, ☎ 27 46 23 41 (km 51-66).

Distance table

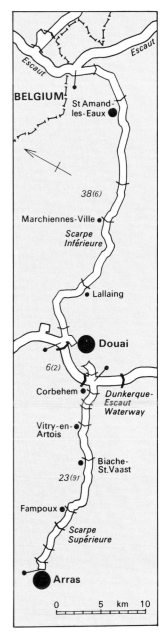

	km	lock	km
Scarpe supérieure			
Arras basin, public quays, town centre 300m	0.0	-	66.1
Bridge (Pont des Grès), boat moorings u/s r/b	0.2	-	65.9
Lock 1 (Saint-Nicholas), automatic, navigation enters Scarpe	0.6	1	65.5
Main road bridge (N25), public quay u/s l/b	0.9	-	65.2
Basin r/b, new port of Arras	1.3	-	64.8
Lock 2 (Saint-Laurent-Blangy) in short cut l/b, bridge	2.3	2	63.8
Railway viaduct	3.9	-	62.2
Chemicals factory r/b, quay	4.0	-	62.1
Lock 3 (Athies), automatic, in short cut l/b, bridge, **Athies** 300m l/b	5.0	3	61.1
Lock 4 (Fampoux), automatic, in short cut r/b, bridge	7.3	4	58.8
Fampoux quay l/b, village 800m l/b	7.9	-	58.2
Railway viaduct	8.1	-	58.0
Motorway viaduct (A1)	8.7	-	57.4
Roeux bridge, quay d/s l/b, village 300m l/b	10.1	-	56.0
Pelves quay r/b, village 400m	11.1	-	55.0
Plouvain basin and boat moorings l/b, village 1700m	11.6	-	54.5
Motorway viaduct (A26)	12.3	-	53.8
Biache-Saint-Vaast quay l/b, small town 400m l/b	14.1	-	52.0
Lock 5 (Biache-Saint-Vaast), automatic, in cut r/b, bridge	14.2	5	51.9
Basin l/b (cement works)	14.3	-	51.8
Vitry-en-Artois bridge, quay u/s l/b, small town l/b	17.3	-	48.8
Bridge (Vitry-en-Artois)	17.7	-	48.4
Lock 6 (Vitry), automatic, r/b, weir	18.0	6	48.1
Lock 7 (Brébières-Haute-Tenue), automatic, in short cut l/b	20.1	7	46.0
Lock 8 (Brébières-Basse-Tenue), automatic, bridge	20.6	8	45.5
Brébières quay l/b, village 400m	21.0	-	45.1
Overhead pipeline and conveyor belt crossings (3)	22.0	-	44.1
Private basins	22.1	-	44.0
Lock 9 (Corbehem), automatic	22.4	9	43.7
Corbehem bridge, village l/b	22.6	-	43.5
Junction with Scarpe diversion canal and Canal de la Sensée (Dunkerque–Escaut waterway) at km 23.6			
Courchelettes boat moorings 700m down bypassed section of Scarpe (see plan)	23.1	-	43.0
Scarpe diversion canal (dérivation autour de Douai)			
Junction with Scarpe supérieure and Scarpe moyenne (navigable 600m only to disused lock)	23.6	-	6.2
Lock (Courchelettes), bridge, water	23.8	10	6.0
Railway bridges	24.2	-	5.6

	km	lock	km
Road bridge (Douai bypass)	25.2	-	4.6
Bridge (Arras, N50)	25.6	-	4.2
Quay r/b	26.9	-	2.9
Esquerchin bridge, **Douai** r/b	27.7	-	2.1
Lock (Douai), water	28.0	11	1.8
Footbridge (Ocre)	28.4	-	1.4
Bridge (Ocre)	28.5	-	1.3
Quay l/b	29.7	-	0.1
Junction with Canal de Jonction (link with the Scarpe moyenne d/s of Douai)	29.8	-	0.0

Canal de Jonction

	km	lock	km
Junction with the Scarpe diversion canal (km 6.2)	0.0	-	0.8
Bridge (Boulevard Lahure)	0.1	-	0.7
Bridge (Chemin Vert)	0.7	-	0.1
Junction with Scarpe moyenne	0.8	-	0.0

Scarpe moyenne

	km	lock	km
Junction with Canal de Jonction (Scarpe moyenne navigable 1100m u/s to former lift bridge in Douai)	29.0	-	37.1
Railway bridge	29.1	-	37.0
Railway bridge	29.2	-	36.9
Basin l/b (former *junction with Canal de la Deûle, disused*)	29.9	-	36.2

Scarpe inférieure

	km	lock	km
Lock 1 (Fort-de-Scarpe)	30.0	12	36.1
Bridge (Pont Rouge)	30.4	-	35.7
Road bridge (Douai north bypass)	31.1	-	35.0
Raches lift bridge, automatic, village l/b	33.3	-	32.8
Lallaing lift bridge, automatic, small town 400m l/b	36.4	-	29.7
Lock 2 (Lallaing), automatic	36.8	13	29.3
Quay l/b	37.6	-	28.5
Lift bridge (Germignies)	37.9	-	28.2
Private railway bridge	38.8	-	27.3
Overhead water pipeline crossing	39.5	-	26.6
Pumping station r/b	40.3	-	25.8
Vred swing bridge, boat moorings d/s l/b, water, village l/b	41.5	-	24.6
Lock 3 (Marchiennes), water	45.3	14	20.8
Marchiennes bridge, public quay d/s r/b, attractive boat mooring d/s l/b, small town with all facilities l/b	45.5	-	20.6
Railway bridge	46.9	-	19.2
Overhead gas pipeline crossing	47.2	-	18.9
Lock 4 (**Warlaing**), lift bridge, village 500m l/b	49.7	15	16.4
Hasnon bridge, village r/b	54.2	-	11.9
Motorway bridge (A23)	54.5	-	11.6
Railway bridge (Saint-Amand)	57.6	-	8.5
Saint-Amand-les-Eaux lift bridge (route de Valenciennes), footbridge u/s, quay u/s l/b, town centre 500m l/b	58.2	-	7.9
Boat moorings for Saint-Amand, l/b	58.6	-	7.5
Lift bridge (route de Condé), footbridge d/s	59.1	-	7.0
Lock 5 (Saint-Amand)	59.3	16	6.8
Road bridge (Saint-Amand bypass)	59.9	-	6.2
Nivelle bridge, village 800m l/b	62.3	-	3.8
Lock 6 (Thun), new lock opening June 1990	63.7	17	2.4
Mortagne lift bridge	65.8	-	0.3
Confluence with Escaut	66.1	-	0.0

Seille

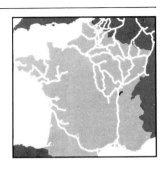

The Seille, one of the most charming cruising rivers in France, extends 39 km from the Saône at La Truchère (downstream of Tournus) to the head of navigation at the picturesque town of Louhans. Canalised, with four locks, the river winds peacefully past lush meadows and wooded slopes, and the constantly changing pastoral landscape contrasts with the monotony of the broad Saône valley. In recent years, the river has become increasingly popular, thanks in part to the establishment of a hire base a few kilometres short of the head of navigation at Branges. Pontoon moorings for boats, with water and electricity, have been installed at Louhans, Cuisery and La Truchère.

Locks There are four locks, all situated in short lock-cuts on the left bank and overcoming a total difference in level of 7.20m. The first lock, at La Truchère, has standard barge dimensions of 38.50 by 5.20m. The other three are 30.40m long and 6.20m wide. There are no longer lock-keepers at locks 2 (Brienne), 3 (Loisy) or 4 (Branges), and users of the waterway are required to work through these locks themselves, using the conventional winding gear fitted to the gate sluices and the less common chain and capstan gear for the gates (the chain sometimes catches, giving the impression that the gate is obstructed; do not be deceived!).

Depth The maximum authorised draught is 1.30m.

Bridges The maximum authorised air draught is 3.50m.

Navigation Maximum speed 10 km/h, and 6 km/h in the lock-cuts. A canalised river, the Seille has very little current and generally offers a good depth throughout its width, so there is no particular problem of navigation in the reaches. Cross-currents may present a difficulty on entering and leaving the lock-cuts in time of flood.

Authority
Direction Departementale de l'Equipement, Saône-et-Loire.
Subdivisions: 9 écluse Océan, 71397 Montceau-les-Mines, ☎ 85 57 21 98.

Distance table

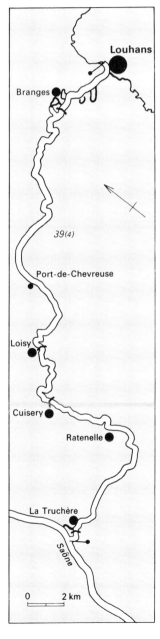

	km	lock	km
Junction with Saône opposite km post 106 (just upstream of wood on left bank)	0.0	-	39.0
La Truchère lock	0.7	1	38.3
La Truchère, quay (restaurant and café), pontoon moorings with water and electricity	1.1	-	37.9
Seille bridge	3.7	-	35.3
Ratenelle, bridge (village 500m r/b)	8.6	-	30.4
Railway bridge (disused)	9.0	-	30.0
Brienne lock	13.2	2	25.8
Bridge (Cuisery)	13.6	-	25.4
Cuisery pontoon moorings level with campsite on r/b, village 500m	13.7	-	25.3
Loisy, destroyed bridge (village 500m r/b)	17.8	-	21.2
Loisy bridge	18.2	3	20.8
Port de Chevreuse, bridge, water l/b	23.4	-	15.6
Bantanges	27.7	-	11.3

	km	lock	km
Junction with weir stream, r/b, navigable 600m u/s to **Branges**, village with boat harbour	34.8	-	4.2
Branges lock	35.5	4	3.5
Louhans quay and pontoon moorings, Croizur hire base, water and electricity, l/b, town centre 300m	38.7	-	0.3
Confluence of Solnan on left bank	38.8	-	0.2
Rail and road bridges (supermarket u/s l/b)	38.8	-	0.2
Head of navigation	39.0	-	0.0

Seine

The Seine rises in the Côte d'Or mountains and discharges into the English Channel near Le Havre after a course of nearly 800km. The Seine has always been the most navigable of the great rivers of France, and is today a major transport artery, navigated by a substantial fleet of high-capacity barges and push-tows throughout most of its navigable length of 412km down to the seaport of Rouen, and from here inland shipping shares the 11m deep channel with ships of up to 120 000 dwt down the tidal estuary to Le Havre, a further 105km.

The river is canalised from its confluence with the Aube (and junction with the disused Canal de la Haute-Seine) at Marcilly. The waterway should strictly be divided into five or six sections, to reflect the successive changes in navigational characteristics, designation and administration, but for the present purposes it is sufficient (and less confusing) to consider just two sections, described separately hereafter:

First section, Marcilly to Paris (Pont de la Tournelle), 169km,
Second section, Paris to Le Havre, 348km.

First section: Marcilly to Paris (Pont de la Tournelle)

Over the first 68km from Marcilly, the river is a 'dead end', but is nevertheless being developed for large-scale navigation up to the busy cereal port of Nogent (km 20). Depending on the exact state of the works, the distances actually navigated in this section may differ slightly from those given in the table. In particular, works are scheduled over the period 1991–1993 to allow 1000-tonne barges to load cereals at Nogent. The river is here called the Petite-Seine. At Montereau (km 68), the river becomes the Haute-Seine, and is joined by the canalised river Yonne on the left bank, forming part of the Bourgogne route from Paris to the south of France. A short distance downstream, at Saint-Mammès (km 81), the Seine connects with the equally important Bourbonnais route to the south, of which the first link is the Canal du Loing. All the works required to open the Haute-Seine to large-scale navigation were completed in the early 1970s, and are presented accurately in the distance table. There are further connections with the canalised river Marne at Charenton (km 163) and the Canal Saint-Martin (one of the Canaux de Paris) in Paris itself at km 168. Despite the volume of commercial traffic, the Seine above Paris remains largely unspoilt and offers some of the most picturesque river scenery in France.

The limit between the first and second sections of the waterway is given as the Pont de la Tournelle, on the left bank arm of the Seine past the Ile Saint-Louis, rather than the Pont Marie (the official zero point for the lower Seine) on the right bank arm, since navigation is obliged to follow the left bank arm. This is of little importance, however, since the two bridges are level with each other on either side of the island.

Locks The total number of locks between Marcilly and Paris is at present 19, of which 11 are situated on the Petite-Seine down to Montereau (overcoming a difference in level of 21m), the remaining 8 on the Haute-Seine (overcoming a difference in level of 20m). The first four locks down to Nogent are 38m long and 7.80m wide. The following five down to Bray-sur-Seine are 121.00 by 10.50m (1000-tonne barge standard), with the exception of lock 8 (Vezoult), 57.40 by 8.00m, to be replaced by a 3000-tonne lock (185m by 12m) by 1992. Subsequent completion of the 3000-tonne scheme up to Nogent will involve construction of a new lock at Melz and elimination of the lock at Jaulnes. The last two locks on the Petite-Seine, Grande Bosse and Marolles, built in the 1970s, are of large dimensions, 185 by 12m. Similar dimensions apply at all the 8 locks on the Haute-Seine below Montereau. All except Varennes have two chambers side by side (one on each side of the weir). All the weirs are of recent construction, with movable gates, and when a certain flood stage is reached one of the gates is lowered to provide a navigable passage. The large locks are electrically-operated and controlled by lights, but navigators of boats must also pay attention to audible instructions give by the lock-keepers.

The Seine above Paris.
Derek Bowskill

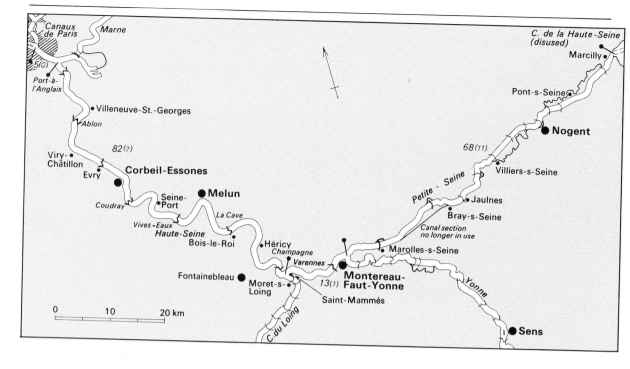

Depth The maximum authorised draught is 1.20m from Marcilly to Nogent bridge (km 20), 1.80m down to Bray-sur-Seine (km 45), 2.20m down to Montereau (km 68) and 2.80m thereafter down to Paris.

Bridges The following table gives the minimum headroom offered by the fixed bridges in the successive sections:

	Normal water level	Highest navigable water level
Marcilly to Nogent	3.40	2.80
Nogent to Grande Bosse lock	4.35	3.40
Grande Bosse to Paris	5.50	3.60

Towpath There is no towpath along the Seine.

Authority

Service de la Navigation de la Seine, Arrondissement Seine Amont.
Subdivisions:
– Chemin de Halage, 10400 Nogent-sur-Seine, ☎ 25 39 86 48 (km 0-68).
– 26 quai Hipollyte Rossignol, 77000 Melun, ☎ 64 39 54 22 (km 68-142).
– 103 quai Blanqui, 94140 Alfortville, ☎ (1) 43 75 32 24 (km 142-165).
Arrondissement Paris Hydrologie.
Subdivision: 2 quai de la Tournelle, 75005 Paris, ☎ (1) 43 25 45 73 (km 165-169).

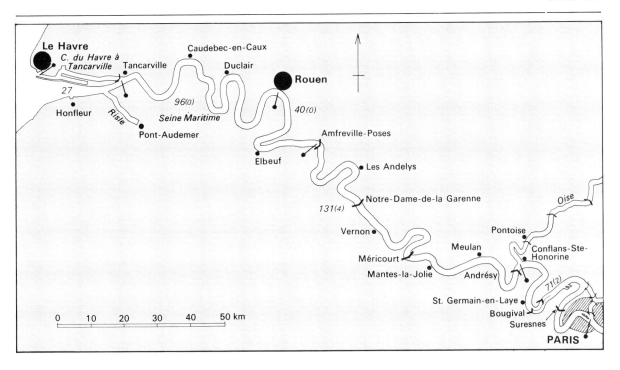

Second section: Paris (Pont de la Tournelle) to Le Havre

As indicated in the general introduction, a single distance table is given for the entire waterway from Paris to the seaward limit of the Seine estuary near Le Havre, a distance of 348km.

Through the city of Paris (down to km 9), the Seine carries very heavy traffic, and navigation is complicated by the numerous bridges and several islands, which generally have to be passed on one side by boats heading downstream and on the other by those heading upstream. The distance table clearly indicates the route to be followed in each case, as well as those arms that are forbidden to navigation. These include the Bras Marie, on the right bank side of the Ile Saint-Louis, which may be used only by bateaux-mouche heading downstream. Passage past the two islands in the centre of Paris (on the left bank side of the Ile Saint-Louis and the right bank side of the Ile de la Cité) is one-way only, the right of way alternating on an hourly cycle. Craft heading upstream are authorised to proceed by two green lights displayed horizontally on the Pont au Change from the hour to 20 minutes past (*00*.00 to *00*.20). From *00*.20 to *00*.00 two red lights are displayed, and boats have to wait. Similarly, boats are authorised to proceed downstream by green lights on the Pont Sully from *00*.35 to *00*.50. Heading upstream, the Bras de la Monnaie may also be used, but great care is required, especially during floods. Other navigation signs displayed on the bridges are conventional, and described in the Introduction.

Shipping becomes even more dense downstream of the city of Paris, with more high-capacity barges and push-tows, to which must be added low-profile coasters; the latter category of vessel, in particular, can create a heavy wash, making life difficult for small boats. Navigation continues in the canalised river Seine down to the last lock at Amfreville-Poses (km 202), the river thereafter being tidal down to the inland waterway limit at Rouen (km 242); in this 40km section, allowance must be made for the rise and fall of the tide when mooring, to avoid the risk of grounding. The port of Rouen marks the beginning of maritime navigation in the Seine estuary, and rules of navigation, as well as lights and marks used, are of the maritime type from this point. The seaward limit of the estuary is 105km further downstream, between the confluence of the Risle and the fishing harbour of Honfleur.

The only navigable connections on the lower Seine are with the Canal Saint-Denis (one of the Paris canals) on the right bank at km 29 and with the canalised river Oise (linking with northern France) at the waterway capital of Conflans-Sainte-Honorine (km 71). Mention should also be made of the Canal du Havre à Tancarville, which offers sheltered access to the port of Le Havre from the northern shore of the estuary at km 338.

For navigation on the Seine estuary between Rouen and Le Havre, the use of a detailed guide is indispensable. The recommendations and regulations for boats are too numerous and important to be even briefly stated here.

Locks There are six groups of locks on the lower Seine. At Suresnes there are two chambers, 187 by 18m and 176 by 17m (12m at the gates). At Bougival the two chambers measure 220 by 17m (12m at the gates) and 112 by 12m. Navigation may bypass Bougival locks by using the Rivière Neuve arm, including a lock overcoming the same difference in level at Chatou (185 by 18m). At Andrésy there are two chambers (185 by 24m and 160 by 12m), at Méricourt three (185 by 12m, 160 by 17m and 141 by 12m), at Notre-Dame-de-la-Garenne two (185 by 24m and 185 by 12m) and at Amfreville-Poses two (220 by 17m and 185 by 12m). All locks are controlled by lights; enter behind the barges.

Depth The channel is dredged to allow coasters drawing 4.00m to reach the port of Gennevilliers. Above here and through Paris the maximum authorised draught is at present 3.00m.

Bridges Below Gennevilliers, all bridges offer a minimum headroom of 7.00m above the highest navigable water level. Above Gennevilliers, the minimum headroom is about 6.00m above normal water level, reduced to 3.70m above the highest navigable water level.

Towpath None.

Authority

Service Navigation de la Seine, Arrondissement Paris-et-Marne. Subdivision:
– 2 quai de la Tournelle, 75005 Paris, ☎ (1) 43 25 45 73 (km 0-9).
Arrondissement Basse-Seine. Subdivisions:
– 27 quai Galliéni, 92150 Suresnes, ☎ (1) 45 06 11 98 (km 9-35).
– Ecluse de Bougival, 78380 Bougival, ☎ (3) 918 23 45 (km 35-67).
– Ecluse d'Andrésy, 78260 Achères, ☎ (3) 911 08 33 (km 67-95).
– 62 route du Hazay, 78520 Limay, ☎ (3) 092 56 00 (km 95-147).
– BP No. 3, 27590 Pitres, ☎ 32 49 80 18 (km 147-225).

Service de la Navigation de la Seine, 4e section
– BP 4075, 34 boulevard de Boisguilbert 76022 Rouen, ☎ 35 88 81 55 (km 225-242)
Port Autnome de Rouen
– BP 4075, 34 boulevard de Boisguilbert 76022 Rouen, ☎ 35 88 81 55 (km 242-348)

Distance table

	km	*lock*	*km*
Petite-Seine			
Junction with Canal de la Haute-Seine (disused)	0.0	-	169.1
Confluence of Aube and Seine	0.4	-	168.7
Marcilly-sur-Seine bridge, quay u/s l/b, village r/b	0.8	-	168.3
Entrance to Conflans-Bernières lock-cut, l/b	3.2	-	165.9
Lock 1 (Conflans), bridge, water	3.3	1	165.8
Pipeline crossing (former railway bridge)	3.7	-	165.4
Bridge (Maugis), **Crancey** 500m l/b	7.9	-	161.2
Crancey aqueduct (length 26m, restricted width)	8.2	-	160.9
Bridge (Pâtures)	8.5	-	160.6
Pont-sur-Seine lift bridge, quay u/s l/b, village r/b	11.0	-	158.1
Bridge (Parc)	11.2	-	157.9
Bridge (Soupirs)	11.8	-	157.3
Lock 2 (**Marnay**), bridge, water, small village r/b	13.8	2	155.3
Bridge (Outres)	14.9	-	154.2
Lock 3 (Bernières), bridge, water	16.3	3	152.8
End of lock-cut, navigation re-enters Seine	16.5	-	152.6
Railway bridge	16.6	-	152.5
Lock 4 (Nogent) in cut, r/b, water, Service Navigation	18.7	4	150.4
Nogent bridge (Pont Saint-Edme), town l/b, quay d/s l/b beyond mill stream outfall	19.6	-	149.5
Grain silos, quays l/b	20.5	-	148.6
Entrance to new meander cutoff (under construction), r/b	21.0	-	148.1
End of new cut	21.5	-	147.6
Entrance to Beaulieu/Villiers-sur-Seine lock-cut, r/b	22.0	-	147.1
Lock 5 (Beaulieu), flood lock, bridge, water, basin d/s l/b	22.2	5	146.9
Bridge (Beaulieu)	22.7	-	146.4
Lock 6 (Melz), bridge, water	25.9	6	143.2
Bridge (Courceroy)	27.8	-	141.3
Bridge (Villiers-sur-Seine)	29.7	-	139.4
Lock 7 (Villiers-sur-Seine), bridge	30.6	7	138.5
End of lock-cut, navigation re-enters Seine	31.1	-	138.0
Noyen-sur-Seine bridge, village 1000m l/b	33.1	-	136.0
Le Port Montain r/b, new cutoff under construction l/b	33.7	-	135.4
Lock 8 (Vezoult) in short cut, r/b, bridge, water, new lock under construction u/s l/b	35.8	8	133.3
Lock 9 (Jaulnes), r/b, weir	41.8	9	127.3
U/s tip of Jaulnes island, navigation in r/b arm	42.0	-	127.1
D/s tip of Jaulnes island, navigation in r/b arm	42.5	-	126.6
Bray-sur-Seine bridge, public quay u/s l/b, small town l/b	44.5	-	124.6
Entrance to former Bray/La Tombe lock-cut, l/b, navigation continues in Seine	45.0	-	124.1
New lock (Grande Bosse) l/b, weir	48.2	10	120.9
Bridge (Roselle)	52.0	-	117.1
Former lock-cut entrance l/b (heading u/s keep to Seine)	56.8	-	112.3
La Tombe bridge, quay u/s l/b, small village	57.2	-	111.9
Entrance to Marolles lock-cut, l/b	59.8	-	109.3
Marolles-sur-Seine bridge, village l/b	61.4	-	107.7
Lock (Marolles), two chambers, water, telephone	61.5	11	107.6
End of lock-cut, navigation re-enters Seine	61.8	-	107.3
Marina in former gravel pit, r/b	62.3	-	106.8

	km	lock	km
Railway bridge	64.4	-	104.7
Railway bridge (new high speed line Paris-Lyon)	66.1	-	103.0
Industrial basin l/b	67.3	-	101.8
Montereau bridge, *confluence of Yonne* l/b, quays, town centre d/s l/b	67.7	-	101.4

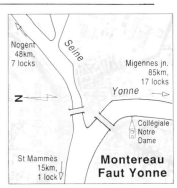

Haute-Seine

	km	lock	km
Railway bridge	70.4	-	98.7
Lock 1 (Varennes) in short cut, r/b, bridge, water	71.2	12	97.9
Private basin r/b	75.4	-	93.7
Former lock (Madeleine) r/b, power station	76.6	-	92.5
Power station cooling water outfall r/b	77.4	-	91.7
Moorings for boats l/b	79.7	-	89.4
Saint-Mammès bridge, quays and town centre l/b	81.1	-	88.0
Confluence of Loing (forming Canal du Loing) l/b	81.5	-	87.6
Aqueduct (Voulzie)	82.5	-	86.6
Lock 2 (Champagne) r/b, two chambers, weir	83.5	13	85.6
Champagne-sur-Seine bridge, Thomery boatyard and slipway u/s l/b	84.2	-	84.9
Quay l/b, Seine et Loing Rivières hire base	89.8	-	79.3
Bridge (Valvins)	90.3	-	78.8
Samois island, navigation in r/b arm	93.0	-	76.1
Bridge (Fontaine-le-Port)	97.7	-	71.4
Lock 3 (La Cave) l/b, two chambers, weir	101.1	14	68.0
Chartrettes bridge, village 1000m r/b	102.0	-	67.1
Railway bridge (Pet-au-Diable), boat club u/s l/b	107.3	-	61.8
U/s tip of Melun island, navigation in l/b arm (r/b arm for boats only, max speed 5 km/h)	109.2	-	59.9
Melun bridge No. 1	109.6	-	59.5
Melun bridge No. 2, quay d/s r/b, town centre 400m r/b	109.7	-	59.4
Melun bridge No. 3	110.0	-	59.1
D/s tip of Melun island, navigation in l/b arm (see above)	110.2	-	58.9
Railway bridge (Mée), public quay u/s r/b, factories l/b	111.0	-	58.1
Boat club l/b	112.9	-	56.2
Lock 4 (Vives-Eaux), l/b, two chambers, weir	115.8	15	53.3
Boissise-la-Bertrand quay and village r/b	116.0	-	53.1
Bridge (Sainte-Assise)	119.4	-	49.7
Former lock (Citanguette) l/b	122.6	-	46.5
Seine-Port boat harbour and village r/b	123.4	-	45.7
Lock 7 (Coudray) and bridge, chambers r/b and l/b, weir between, water	129.7	16	39.4
Boat harbour r/b, petrol, industrial quay (Bas-Vignons) l/b	131.3	-	37.8
Corbeil-Essonnes bridge, quay u/s l/b, town centre l/b	134.4	-	34.7
Confluence of Essonnes, l/b	134.8	-	34.3
Motorway bridge (F6), port of Corbeil-Essonnes l/b	136.0	-	33.1
U/s tip of island, navigation in l/b arm	136.6	-	32.5
D/s tip of island, navigation in l/b arm	137.4	-	31.7
Evry bridge, quay, boat moorings u/s l/b, station 400m l/b	137.7	-	31.4
Lock 8 (Evry), l/b, two chambers, weir	138.7	17	30.4
Ris-Orangis bridge, town 1000m l/b	141.8	-	27.3
Port of Viry-Châtillon, l/b, boat harbour opposite	144.3	-	24.8
Basin (Port Longuet) l/b	145.0	-	24.1
Juvisy-sur-Orge bridge, town l/b, industrial quays d/s l/b	146.0	-	23.1
Railway bridge (Athis-Mons), industrial quays d/s l/b	148.0	-	21.1
Confluence of Orge, l/b	148.9	-	20.2
Lock 9 (Ablon), chambers r/b and l/b, weir	150.0	18	19.1
Villeneuve-Saint-Georges bridge, industrial quay d/s, town centre r/b	152.4	-	16.7

	km	lock	km
Boat harbour r/b (Touring Club de France)	154.7	-	14.4
Railway bridge	155.6	-	13.5
Private basin l/b	156.2	-	12.9
Choisy-le-Roi bridge, quay u/s l/b	157.5	-	11.6
Basin r/b (power station)	158.8	-	10.3
Footbridge and pipeline crossing	159.3	-	9.8
Alfortville industrial quay r/b	159.9	-	9.2
Vitry-sur-Seine suspension bridge	161.0	-	8.1
Lock 10 (Port-à-l'Anglais), chambers r/b and l/b, weir	161.1	19	8.0
Overhead pipeline crossing, industrial quay u/s r/b	162.3	-	6.8
Ivry-sur-Seine bridge	163.3	-	5.8
Confluence of Marne, r/b	163.5	-	5.6
Ivry power station unloading quay l/b	163.6	-	5.5
Charenton pipeline crossing, quay u/s r/b	163.7	-	5.4
Conflans bridges	164.3	-	4.8
Motorway bridge (Boulevard Périphérique), u/s limit of city of **Paris**	165.3	-	3.8
Bridge (Pont National)	165.6	-	3.5
Bridge (Pont de Tolbiac)	166.2	-	2.9
Bridge (Pont de Bercy)	167.0	-	2.1
Metro viaduct (Viaduc d'Austerlitz)	167.8	-	1.3
Bridge (Pont d'Austerlitz)	168.0	-	1.1
Entrance to Canal Saint-Martin, r/b (see Paris canals)	168.2	-	0.9
U/s tip of Ile Saint-Louis, navigation in l/b arm only	168.6	-	0.5
Bridge (Pont Sully)	168.7	-	0.4
Bridge (Pont de la Tournelle)	169.1	-	0.0

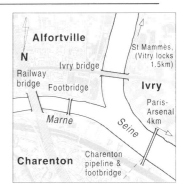

The Seine in Paris. Nôtre Dame. Downstream boats take the Bras St Louis on the right. *Derek Bowskill*

	km	lock	km
Bras de la Tournelle			
Bridge (Pont de la Tournelle)	0.0	-	242.4
U/s end of Ile de la Cité, Bras Saint-Louis r/b (between islands), Bras de la Monnaie l/b, take r/b arm	0.2	-	242.2
Bridge (Pont Saint-Louis)	0.3	-	242.1
D/s end of Ile Saint-Louis, Bras Marie r/b (forbidden to navigation), navigation continues in Bras de la Cité	0.4	-	242.0
Bridge (Pont d'Arcole)	0.6	-	241.8
Bridge (Pont Notre-Dame)	0.7	-	241.7
Bridge (Pont au Change)	0.9	-	241.5
Bridge (Pont-Neuf)	1.3	-	241.1
D/s end of Ile de la Cité, Bras de la Monnaie l/b	1.4	-	241.0
Bras de la Monnaie (upstream only)			
U/s end of Ile de la Cité, Bras Saint-Louis r/b	-	-	242.2
Bridge (Pont de l'Archeveché)	-	-	242.1
Bridge (Pont au Double)	-	-	241.8
Bridge (Petit Pont)	-	-	241.7
Bridge (Pont Saint-Michel)	-	-	241.5
Bridge (Pont Neuf)	-	-	241.2
D/s end of Ile de la Cité, Bras de la Cité r/b	-	-	241.0
Footbridge (Passerelle des Arts)	1.6	-	240.8
Bridge (Pont du Carrousel)	1.9	-	240.5
Bridge (Pont Royal)	2.2	-	240.2
Footbridge (Passerelle de Solférino)	2.6	-	239.8
Bridge (Pont de la Concorde)	3.0	-	239.4
Touring Club de France moorings r/b, all facilities	3.4	-	239.0
Bridge (Pont Alexandre III)	3.5	-	238.9
Bridge (Pont des Invalides), Office National de la Navigation headquarters 200m l/b (2 bd de Latour-Maubourg)	3.7	-	238.7
Bridge (Pont de l'Alma)	4.4	-	238.0
Footbridge (Passerelle Debilly)	4.8	-	237.6
Bridge (Pont d'Iéna)	5.3	-	237.1
U/s end of Ile des Cygnes, navigation continues in Bras de Passy r/b	5.8	-	236.6
Bridge (Pont de Bir-Hakeim) and Metro viaduct	5.9	-	236.5
Railway bridge	6.4	-	236.0
Bridge (Pont de Grenelle)	6.6	-	235.8
D/s end of Ile des Cygnes, Bras de Grenelle l/b	6.7	-	235.7
Bras de Grenelle (upstream only)			
U/s end of Ile des Cygnes	-	-	236.6
Bridge (Pont de Bir-Hakeim) and Metro viaduct	-	-	236.5
Railway bridge	-	-	236.1
Bridge (Pont de Grenelle)	-	-	235.8
D/s end of Ile des Cygnes, Bras de Passy r/b	-	-	235.7
Bridge (Pont Mirabeau)	7.2	-	235.2
Bridge (Pont du Garigliano)	8.2	-	234.2
Bridge (Boulevard Périphérique)	8.7	-	233.7
D/s limit of City of Paris	8.8	-	233.6
U/s end of Ile Saint-Germain, navigation in Bras de Billancourt, r/b (l/b arm for rowing boats only)	9.3	-	233.1
Bridge (Issy-les-Moulineaux)	9.4	-	233.0
Quay (Boulogne-Billancourt), r/b	9.6	-	232.8
Bridge (Billancourt)	10.3	-	232.1

	km	*lock*	*km*
Bras de Meudon (downstream only)			
U/s end of Ile Séguin	10.9	-	-
D/s end of Ile Saint-Germain, Bras d'Issy-les-Moulineaux l/b	11.0	-	-
Private bridge (Renault factory)	11.2	-	-
D/s end of Ile Séguin	11.9	-	-
Bras de Boulogne (upstream only)			
U/s end of Ile Séguin	-	-	231.5
Private bridge (Renault factory), private quays d/s	-	-	231.2
D/s end of Ile Séguin	-	-	230.5
Bridge (Pont de Sèvres)	12.0	-	230.4
Bridge (Pont de Saint-Cloud)	13.5	-	228.9
Motorway bridge	14.2	-	228.2
Footbridge (Passerelle de l'Avre), boat clubs d/s	14.8	-	227.6
Suresnes bridge	16.4	-	226.0
Triple lock (Suresnes) and weir in l/b arm, weir in r/b arm (forbidden to navigation)	16.8	1	225.6
Puteaux bridge	18.1	-	224.3
Neuilly bridge	19.3	-	223.1
D/s end of Ile de Puteaux	19.6	-	222.8
U/s end of Ile de la Grande-Jatte, Neuilly arm r/b forbidden to navigation	19.7	-	222.7
Courbevoie bridge	20.7	-	221.7
Levallois-Perret bridge and d/s end of Ile de la Grande-Jatte	21.8	-	220.6
Railway bridge (Asnières)	22.6	-	219.8
Asnières bridge	22.7	-	219.7
Clichy bridge	23.6	-	218.8
Bridge (Gennevilliers), commercial quay (Asnières) u/s l/b, oil terminals d/s r/b	24.6	-	217.8
Railway bridge	25.1	-	217.3
U/s end of Ile Saint-Denis, navigation continues in Saint-Ouen/Saint-Denis arm, r/b; Gennevilliers arm, l/b, navigable only for access to industrial quays	25.5	-	216.9
Saint-Ouen bridge, numerous industrial quays d/s r/b	26.1	-	216.3
Motorway bridge (A86)	27.0	-	215.4
Bridge (Ile Saint-Denis)	28.3	-	214.1
Junction with Canal Saint-Denis, r/b	28.9	-	213.5
Industrial quay (Epinay-la-Briche) r/b	29.4	-	213.0
Epinay bridge	31.8	-	210.6
Railway bridge	32.2	-	210.2
D/s end of Ile Saint-Denis	32.8	-	209.6
Motorway bridge	33.8	-	208.6
Entrance to port of Gennevilliers basins 5 and 6, l/b	33.9	-	208.5
Entrance to port of Gennevilliers basins 1 to 4, l/b	35.1	-	207.3
Railway bridge (Argenteuil)	35.4	-	207.0
Argenteuil bridge	35.8	-	206.6
Bridge with aqueduct (Colombes)	37.3	-	205.1
Bezons bridge	39.4	-	203.0
U/s end of Ile de Chatou, navigation in Marly arm, l/b, under normal conditions (navigation in Rivière Neuve arm, r/b, during floods only)	40.2	-	202.2

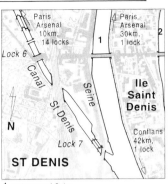

1 main arm of Seine
2 l/b arm of Seine also navigable, entrance 3km u/s and 4.5km d/s

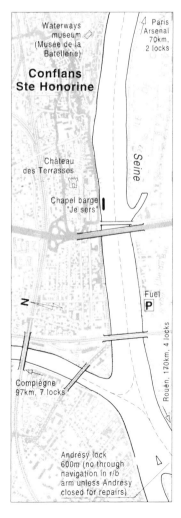

	km	lock	km
Railway bridge (Nanterre), industrial quays l/b	40.9	-	201.5
Railway bridge (Carrières)	41.8	-	200.6
Entrance to private gravel pit, l/b	42.1	-	199.3
Reuil-Malmaison bridge, quay u/s l/b	45.2	-	197.2
Railway bridge (Reuil)	45.5	-	196.9
Bougival bridge	48.2	-	194.2
Triple lock (Bougival) between Ile de la Chaussée and Ile de la Loge, Marly arm l/b unnavigable, Rivière-Neuve arm r/b to be used in time of flood	48.7	2	193.7

Bras de la Rivière-Neuve

	km	lock	km
(upstream and downstream in time of flood)			
U/s end of Ile de Chatou, Marly arm l/b	40.2	-	202.2
Railway bridge (Nanterre)	41.0	-	201.4
Railway bridge (Carrières)	41.7	-	200.7
Lock (Chatou), l/b, weir	44.6	2	197.8
Reuil-Malmaison bridge	45.3	-	197.1
Railway bridge (Reuil)	45.7	-	196.7
Bougival bridge	48.1	-	194.3
D/s end of Ile de la Loge, Marly arm l/b unnavigable	50.8	-	191.6
Le Pecq bridge, quay u/s l/b	52.1	-	190.3
Island (Ile Corbière), downstream r/b arm	52.4	-	190.0
Railway bridge (Pecq)	52.7	-	189.7
Island (Ile Corbière), upstream l/b arm	52.9	-	189.5
Quay r/b	55.1	-	187.3
U/s end of Ile de la Borde, navigation r/b (Maisons-Laffite arm l/b forbidden to navigation)	56.1	-	186.3
Railway bridge (Maisons-Laffitte)	57.9	-	184.5
D/s end of Ile de la Commune, boat harbour in entrance to Maisons-Laffitte arm l/b	58.3	-	184.1
Maisons-Laffitte bridge	58.6	-	183.8
Industrial quay r/b (cement works)	60.1	-	182.3
Herblay r/b, ferry	64.8	-	177.6
U/s end of Ile d'Herblay, Garenne arm l/b for boats only	65.4	-	177.0
D/s end of island	67.1	-	175.3
U/s end of Conflans island (small channel l/b infilled)	68.9	-	173.5
D/s end of island, 'Je Sers' floating chapel r/b	70.3	-	172.1
Conflans-Sainte-Honorine bridges, barge moorings r/b	70.4	-	172.0
Barge fuelling points l/b	70.7	-	171.7
Railway bridge (Conflans)	71.1	-	171.3
Confluence of Oise, r/b, numerous barges moored	71.3	-	171.1
U/s end of Ile de Nancy, navigation in Plafosse arm l/b	71.8	-	170.6
Double lock (Andrésy) l/b, weir	72.7	3	169.7
Boatyards l/b	74.0	-	168.4
Weir (Denouval) r/b in passage between Ile d'en Bas and Ile de la Dérivation)	75.0	-	167.4
D/s end of Ile de la Dérivation, lock (Carrières) in cut, r/b (normally closed)	76.3	-	166.1
U/s end of Ile de Carrières, Saint-Louis arm l/b, main channel r/b	76.4	-	166.0
Car loading quay r/b (Talbot factory)	77.1	-	165.3
D/s end of Ile de Carrières	77.2	-	165.2
Poissy bridge	77.8	-	164.6
U/s ends of Ile des Migneaux and Ilôt Blanc, navigation in central arm, l/b arm forbidden to powered boats	78.1	-	164.3
D/s end of Ilôt Blanc	78.9	-	163.5
Boat harbour (Nauti-Mécanique) in former gravel pit, r/b	81.1	-	161.3

	km	lock	km
U/s end of Ile de Médan, Mottes arm r/b for downstream boats (except the biggest barges and push-tows)	81.7	-	160.7
Private ferry in Médan arm, l/b	82.0	-	160.4
Médan l/b (on Médan arm)	82.5	-	159.9
Small arm (Couleuvre) between Ile de Médan and Ile d'Hernière, impracticable	83.2	-	159.2
Industrial quay l/b (fibre cement factory)	84.2	-	158.2
D/s end of Ile d'Hernière, Médan arm l/b for u/s boats	84.4	-	158.0
Triel-sur-Seine bridge	85.1	-	157.3
Yacht Club moorings l/b	85.8	-	156.6
U/s end of Ile de Vaux, Vaux arm r/b for small boats only, entrance to gravel pit l/b	88.1	-	154.3
D/s end of Ile de Vaux	90.5	-	151.9
U/s end of Ile du Fort, main channel in Mureaux arm l/b, Meulan arm r/b for access to **Meulan** (mooring d/s of bridge r/b)	92.4	-	150.0
Les Mureaux bridge, industrial quay u/s l/b	93.4	-	149.0
Entrance to former lock-cut l/b, keep to r/b side	94.5	-	147.9
D/s entrance to former lock-cut l/b, keep to r/b side	95.2	-	147.2
Car loading and unloading quays l/b (Renault plant)	97.5	-	144.9
D/s end of Ile de Juziers, r/b arm for small boats only	98.6	-	143.8
Industrial quay r/b (cement works)	99.7	-	142.7
U/s end of Ile de Rangiport, Fermettes arm r/b for d/s boats	100.8	-	141.6
Gargenville bridge	101.3	-	141.1
D/s end of Ile de Rangiport, Blanc Soleil arm l/b for u/s boats	102.4	-	140.0
Ile de Porcheville r/b and Ile de l'Etat l/b, main channel between them (islands marked by stakes)	103.4	-	139.0
Porcheville thermal power station, quay r/b	104.5	-	137.9
Industrial port basin (Limay) r/b	106.8	-	135.6
U/s end of Ile de Limay, main channel l/b	107.1	-	135.3
Railway bridge (Mantes)	108.2	-	134.2
Mantes-la-Jolie bridge, town l/b	109.4	-	133.0
Access to Limay arm r/b (moorings for boats) through short arm between Ile aux Dames and Ile aux Boeufs (restricted headroom)	109.9	-	132.5
D/s end of Ile l'Aumône, Limay arm r/b for access only	111.9	-	130.5
Châteaux de Sully l/b (Rosny-sur-Seine)	117.0	-	125.4
Rolleboise quay l/b, fuelling point	119.0	-	123.4
U/s end of Ile de la Sablière, navigation l/b	120.1	-	122.3
Triple lock (Méricourt) l/b, weir	120.7	4	121.7
U/s end of Ile Saint-Martin, r/b arm for d/s boats	124.9	-	117.5
Private ferry in r/b arm	127.6	-	114.8
D/s end of Ile Saint-Martin, l/b arm for u/s boats	128.0	-	114.4
Vétheuil slipway r/b, u/s end of series of islands, small channels r/b unnavigable	128.1	-	114.3
D/s end of Ile de Haute Isle, r/b arm navigable by small boats for access to Haute Isle	132.0	-	110.4
U/s end of Ile de Haute (followed by Grande Ile), main channel l/b	138.8	-	103.6
Bonnières-sur-Seine bridge, industrial quays d/s l/b	139.8	-	102.6
D/s end of Grande Ile, u/s end of Ile de la Flotte, minor channel l/b forbidden to navigation	141.0	-	101.4
D/s end of Ile de Merville, minor channel l/b forbidden to navigation	143.6	-	98.8
Disused lock chamber (Port-Villez) l/b, possible mooring	144.8	-	97.6
Vernon bridge, mooring d/s r/b (Vernonnet), behind small islands	150.1	-	92.3

	km	lock	km
Industrial quays l/b	151.6	-	90.8
U/s end of Ile Souveraine, main channel l/b	153.2	-	89.2
Minor arm r/b between Ile Souveraine and Ile Souquet	154.6	-	87.8
Minor arm r/b between Ile Souquet and Ile Emien	155.6	-	86.8
U/s end of Ile aux Boeufs, Goulet arm l/b unnavigable	157.2	-	85.2
U/s end of Ile Falaise, channel l/b leads to locks, r/b channel leads to weir (may be passable during floods)	160.1	-	82.3
Locks (Notre-Dame-de-la-Garenne), four chambers, l/b	161.1	5	81.3
Courcelles-sur-Seine bridge, industrial quay d/s l/b	164.0	-	78.4
U/s end of Ile du Roule, main channel l/b	165.0	-	77.4
D/s end of Ile du Roule (extended by submerged dyke)	167.4	-	75.0
U/s end of Ile Bouret, minor arm l/b unnavigable	168.3	-	74.1
D/s end of Ile de la Tour, boatyard in minor arm l/b	170.9	-	71.5
Bridge (Port Morin)	173.4	-	69.0
Les Andelys yacht harbour r/b, Château Gaillard and small town r/b	173.6	-	68.8
U/s end of Ile du Château, l/b arm for d/s boats	174.0	-	68.4
D/s end of Ile du Château, r/b arm for u/s boats	174.6	-	67.8
Yacht harbour (Val Saint-Martin) r/b	175.7	-	66.7
Small island (Ile Motelle) r/b, followed by Ile de la Roque, minor channel r/b unnavigable	178.3	-	64.1
U/s end of Ile du Port, main channel l/b, **Muids** r/b	182.7	-	59.7
D/s end of Ile du Port, ferry	183.4	-	59.0
Entrance to private basin l/b (former gravel pits)	184.0	-	58.4
U/s end of Ile des Grands Bacs/Ile de la Cage, main channel r/b	184.1	-	58.3
Minor arm l/b between Ile de la Cage and Ile de Lormais	186.1	-	56.3
D/s end of Ile de Lormais, main channel r/b	187.8	-	54.6
Quay for sand barges r/b	188.8	-	53.6
Piers of former railway bridge	189.0	-	53.4
U/s end of Ile du Héron, followed by Ile du Bac, main channel l/b	189.6	-	52.8
Saint-Pierre-de-Vauvrey bridge, village l/b	190.9	-	51.5
Minor arm r/b between Ile du Bac and Ile Brunel	191.3	-	51.1
Minor arm r/b between Ile Brunel and Ile du Martinet	191.8	-	50.6
Minor arm r/b between Ile du Martinet and Ile du Moulin	192.2	-	50.2
D/s end of Ile du Moulin, main channel l/b	193.2	-	49.2
Porte-Joie l/b	193.7	-	48.7
U/s end of Ile de Port Pinché, r/b arm for d/s boats	193.9	-	48.5
R/b arm divides (Ile de Connelle), minor channel r/b	194.3	-	48.1
D/s end of Ile de Port Pinché, l/b arm for u/s boats	195.4	-	47.0
U/s end of Ile de Pampou, minor channel l/b	196.3	-	46.1
D/s end of Ile de Pampou	196.7	-	45.7
Tournedos-sur-Seine l/b	197.4	-	45.0
Entrance to Poses lake l/b (recreational and water sports area)	198.3	-	44.1
D/s end of Ile de Tournedos, minor channel r/b	198.6	-	43.8
U/s end of Ile du Noyer, main channel r/b	198.9	-	43.5
Minor channel l/b between Ile du Noyer and Ile du Trait	199.7	-	42.7
U/s end of Ile d'Amfreville, r/b arm for d/s boats	200.1	-	42.3
D/s end of Ile d'Amfreville, l/b arm for u/s boats	200.7	-	41.7
U/s end of Grand Ile, r/b arm leads to locks	200.8	-	41.6
Locks (Amfreville), two chambers, weir (Poses) l/b (warning: the river is tidal from this point)	202.0	6	40.4
Railway bridge (Manoir)	204.7	-	37.7
Pont-de-l'Arche bridge	207.7	-	34.7
Confluence of Eure (unnavigable) l/b	207.9	-	34.5
Motorway bridge (A13)	211.1	-	31.3
Entrance to Freneuse arm (unnavigable) r/b	215.2	-	27.2

	km	lock	km
Second confluence of Eure (unnavigable) l/b	216.8	-	25.6
Entrance to r/b arm leading to former locks (Saint-Aubin)	218.2	-	24.2
Elbeuf bridge (Pont Jean Jaurès), mooring d/s l/b, water, town l/b	218.9	-	23.5
Suspension bridge (Pont Guynemer)	219.4	-	23.0
Railway viaduct (Orival)	221.4	-	21.0
Commercial quay (Elbeuf) r/b	222.8	-	19.6
U/s limit of Ile Légarée, main channel l/b	225.2	-	17.2
Submerged dyke between islands r/b	226.9	-	15.5
Motorway bridge (A13)	228.0	-	14.4
U/s end of Ile aux Boeufs, main channel l/b	229.4	-	13.0
Oissel bridge and railway viaduct, keep l/b side of all islands in d/s reach	229.7	-	12.7
Private quay l/b (paper mill)	233.4	-	9.0
Private quay l/b (iron foundry)	235.7	-	6.7
D/s end of last island before Rouen, main channel l/b	235.9	-	6.5
Amfreville/Saint-Etienne ferry	237.6	-	4.8
Fuelling points for commercial barges r/b	238.5	-	3.9
U/s end of Ile Lacroix, r/b arm (Pré au Loup) may only be entered on rising tide (against the current)	240.4	-	2.0
Railway viaduct (Eauplet)	240.5	-	1.9
Bridge (Pont Mathilde)	241.2	-	1.2
Yacht harbour l/b (in Pré au Loup arm)	241.7	-	0.7
Boatyard and fuel l/b (in Pré au Loup arm)	241.8	-	0.6
Bridge (Pont Corneille)	241.9	-	0.5
D/s end of Ile Lacroix, r/b arm (Pré au Loup) may only be entered on falling tide (against the current)	242.0	-	0.4
Bridge (Pont Boïeldieu), quays both banks	242.2	-	0.2
Rouen bridge (Pont Jeanne d'Arc), city centre r/b	242.4	-	0.0

Seine estuary (maritime navigation)

	km	lock	km
Bridge (Pont Guillaume le Conquérant)	243.0	-	104.7
Entrance to Bassin aux Bois l/b	244.9	-	102.8
Entrance to Bassin Saint-Gervais r/b, pontoon mooring for masted yachts only 600m into basin on l/b side	245.5	-	102.2
Entrance to oil terminal (Bassin aux Pétroles), l/b	246.7	-	101.0
Ferry (Dieppedalle)	248.1	-	99.6
Basin l/b (dry docks)	251.3	-	96.4
Basin l/b (Petit Bassin)	252.9	-	94.8
La Bouille ferry, village l/b	259.7	-	88.0
D/s limit of port of Rouen	260.1	-	87.6
Yacht club r/b (l'Anerie)	276.4	-	71.3
Duclair ferry, village r/b	278.0	-	69.7
Ferry (le Mesnil-sous-Jumièges)	286.0	-	61.7
Ferry (Jumièges)	295.2	-	52.5
Ferry (Yainville), power station and factory d/s r/b	298.6	-	49.1
Shipyard r/b (le Trait)	301.2	-	46.5
La Mailleraye-sur-Seine l/b	303.1	-	44.6
Brotonne suspension bridge	308.2	-	39.5
Caudebec-en-Caux r/b	309.6	-	38.1
Villequier r/b	313.5	-	34.2
Aizier l/b	323.3	-	24.4
Vieux-Port l/b	324.5	-	23.2
Quilleboeuf-sur-Seine ferry, town l/b opposite oil refinery	331.8	-	15.9
Tancarville suspension bridge	338.2	-	9.5
Entrance to Canal de Tancarville r/b (old lock)	338.2	-	9.5
Entrance to Canal de Tancarville r/b (new lock)	338.6	-	9.1

	km	lock	km
Confluence of Risle, l/b	345.9	-	1.8
Official limit of river Seine	347.7	-	0.0

(**Honfleur** is a further 8km seaward on the south shore)

Sèvre Nantaise

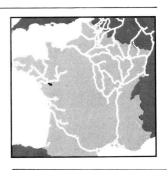

The Sèvre Nantaise is a part-tidal, part-canalised river, navigable over a distance of 21.5km from its confluence with the Loire at Pont-Rousseau (suburb of Nantes) to Monnières bridge. It has been abandoned by commercial traffic, but is maintained for pleasure cruising. Together with its tributary, the Petite Maine, which could potentially be made navigable over a distance of 5.5km from the confluence to Chateauthébaud, the Sèvre Nantaise is featured in the *Guides des Canaux Bretons et de la Loire*, published by Les Editions du Plaisancier, which describe the river as being most attractive, especially in its upper reaches. For convenience, the distance table is presented working upstream from its confluence.

From 1992, the river is entered through a modern tide sluice with three 21m-wide sector gates at Pont-Rousseau. This new structure maintains a constant level up to Vertou lock, with benefits for navigation as well as for the environment and maintenance of this section of the river, previously subjected to tides and to extensive silt deposition from the Loire. The sluice is opened for roughly two hours before and after each high tide. The gates are remote-controlled by the lock-keeper at St Félix (at the entrance to the Canal de Nantes à Brest), to whom enquiries may be made by using the phone link at the pontoon moorings above and below the sluice. Passage is controlled by lights.

Locks There is just one lock, situated at Vertou, with a length of 31.50m and a width of 5.50m.

Depth The maximum authorised draught is 1.20m, although the available depth up to Vertou lock will generally be much greater following completion of the Pont-Rousseau tide sluice. The minimum depth on the sill of Vertou lock is 1.80m.

Bridges There are several fixed bridges. Those above Vertou leave a headroom of not less than 5.50m above the normal water level; those below the lock, and the Pont-Rousseau tide sluice, leave a headroom of 4.00m above the normal high water level.

Towpath There is no towpath.

Authority
Service Maritime et de Navigation de Nantes.
Subdivision: 2 rue Marcel Sembat, 44100 Nantes, ☎ 40 73 66 66

Distance table

	km	lock	km
Confluence with the Loire (km 84.5)	0.0	-	21.5
Pont-Rousseau tide sluice and footbridge	0.1	1	21.4
Pont-Rousseau quay l/b	0.2	-	21.3

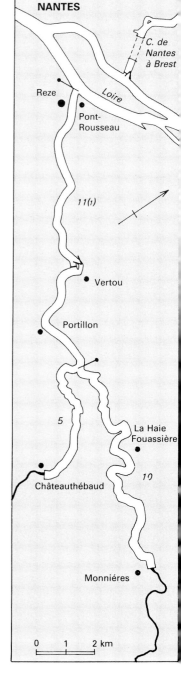

	km	lock	km
New bridge (Pont-Rousseau)	0.3	-	21.2
Old bridge (Pont-Rousseau), landing stages upstream l/b	0.3	-	21.2
Bridge (Morinière)	2.0	-	19.5
Overhead power lines	3.0	-	18.5
Beautour quay r/b	3.5	-	18.0
Overhead power lines	4.5	-	17.0
Castle l/b (Château de Portereau)	5.2	-	16.3
Vertou lock and weir (lock in r/b arm)	6.7	1	14.8
Le Chêne bridge, quay downstream l/b, Vertou 1000m r/b	7.1	-	14.4
Portillon bridge, quay downstream l/b	9.2	-	12.3
Confluence of Petite-Maine l/b, theoretically navigable upstream 5.5km to Chateauthébaud	11.1	-	10.4
Bridge (Ramée)	11.6	-	9.9
La Haie Fouassière bridge, quay downstream r/b, village 1000m	16.1	-	5.4
Port Domino quay r/b	21.0	-	0.5
Monnières bridge, head of navigation	21.5	-	0.0

Sèvre Niortaise and connecting waterways

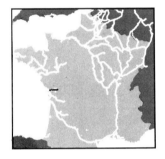

The Sèvre Niortaise is navigable from Niort to its estuary in the Atlantic Ocean at Aiguillon bay (north of La Rochelle), a distance of 72km. Much of its course lies in the regional park of the 'Marais Poitevin', a fenland area ideal for cruising in smaller boats. The waterway may be divided into two distinct sections. The first, extending 54km from Niort to Marans, is canalised river navigation. Connection is made in this section with the canalised rivers Vieille Autise, Mignon and Jeune Autise. The second section, 18km from Marans to the sea, is maritime, and part of its length is by-passed by a ship canal, the Canal maritime de Marans au Brault, by which coasters gain access to the small seaport of Marans. The situation is made clear by the accompanying map. For convenience, the connecting waterways are also described under this entry. These are:

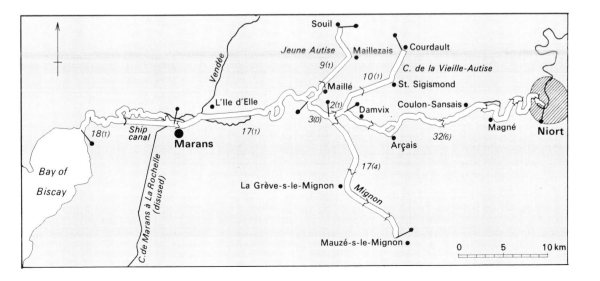

a) Canal de la Vieille Autise

The Canal de la Vieille-Autise is made up essentially of the canalised river Autise, and is navigable over a distance of almost 10km from the Sèvre-Niortaise near Damvix (km 32) to the head of navigation in a small basin at the village of Courdault.

b) Mignon

The canalised river Mignon, generally known as the Canal du Mignon, is the longest of the Sèvre tributaries. It is navigable for boats with limited draught from its confluence with the Sèvre-Niortaise at km 34.3 to the small town of Mauzé-sur-le-Mignon, a distance of 17km.

c) Autise (Jeune)

Although officially designated a river navigation, the Jeune-Autise is essentially a man-made cut, which receives part of the natural flow of the river Autise through a 4.5km feeder canal. It extends almost 9km from a junction with the main line of navigation on the Sèvre-Niortaise at Maillé (km37.3) to a basin in the village of Souil, the first 1.2km being in a navigable loop of the Sèvre. Regrettably, the very small dimensions of its only lock at Maillé make the navigation inaccessible to all but the smallest boats.

The main purpose of the navigation was to carry to the seaports of Marans or La Rochelle the timber produced in the Marais Poitevin, and two tugs still operate on the river, hauling timber rafts downstream. Pleasure traffic amounts to no more than 150 to 200 boats per year, one important limiting factor being the draught and headroom in the upper reaches, another being the hostility of the local population to any form of powered boats. Careful navigation is called for, so as not to worsen the situation, and depending on the boat's size and hull shape it may be advisable to cruise at below the maximum permitted speed of 10km/h, especially when passing the countless flat-bottomed river boats which ply the river.

Locks In the first section from Niort to Marans there are 8 locks, dimensions 31.50 by 5.20m (minimum), overcoming a total difference in level of 8m. Their use is controlled during the low flow period, which unfortunately corresponds to the pleasure cruising season (June to October). The maritime section has one lock (Enfreneaux), measuring 40 by 7m, a short distance downstream of Marans. There is also a ship lock, 126 by 11m, at the seaward end of the Canal maritime de Marans au Brault.

The lock on the *Vieille-Autise* has a length of 31.50m and a width of 5.20m. On the *Mignon*, there are four locks, offering minimum dimensions of 31.50 by 5.10m. They overcome a difference in level of 4.65m. On the *Jeune-Autise*, there is just one lock, at Maillé. It has severely restricted dimensions (designed for small river boats and timber rafts) of 7.00 by 3.00m.

Depth From Niort to lock 7 (Bazoin), the mean water depth is 1.60m, reduced to 1.40m during periods of drought. However, there are shoals downstream of locks 3 (Tiffardière) and 4 (Marais-Pin) and at La Barbée (km 32), where the guaranteed depths are further reduced to 1.20m (mw) and 1.00m (lw). From Bazoin to Marans depths are greater: 2.50m (mw) and 2.00m (lw). On the tidal Sèvre below Enfreneaux lock, the depth ranges between 1.00m at low tide and 5.50m at high tide. The port of Marans and the ship canal offer depths of 5.35m (mw)/4.50m (lw). Depths in the various by-passed sections of the river between lock 7 (Bazoin) and Marans are 1.50m (mw)/1.00m (lw).

Vieille-Autise The normal depth of water is 1.20m, but this drops to 0.80m during the summer low water period. *Mignon* From the confluence to a short distance upstream of La Grève-sur-Mignon, the normal depth of water is 1.20m, falling to 0.60m at low water. In the upper reaches, no more than 0.60m may be counted upon in normal conditions, reduced locally to 0.40m at times of low water. It should be mentioned that these depths, although insufficient for large cruisers, are adequate for the local flat-bottomed river boats which ply the Sèvre-Niortaise and its tributaries. On the Jeune-Autise, from the Sèvre to the lock at Maillé, the normal depth of water is 2.20m, reduced to 1.70m during the summer low water period. Similar depths are available above the lock, but the lock itself has a very shallow sill, offering a depth of only 0.50m at normal water level, reduced to 0.20m at low water.

Bridges Craft aiming to reach Niort should not be higher than 2.20m, which is the least headroom offered at mean water level in the section above lock 5 (Sotterie). At the highest navigable water level the headroom is reduced to 1.10m, but this would be an exceptional occurrence during the cruising season. From lock 5 to Marans the minimum headroom is 2.40m (mw)/1.70m (lw). The new bridge downstream of Brault offers ample headroom.

The minimum headroom under the bridges above normal water levels is 3.05m on the *Vieille-Autise*, 3.30m on the *Canal du Mignon* and 2.40m on the *Jeune-Autise*

Towpath There is officially a rough towpath throughout, but conditions probably vary widely according to local usage, and towpath access should not be counted upon.

Authority
Direction Départementale de l'Equipement des Deux-Sèvres, 39 avenue de Paris, 79022 Niort, ☎ 49 28 16 11.
Subdivisions:
– Cale du Port, 79000 Niort, ☎ 49 09 00 59 (km 0-35).
– Le Port, 17230 Marans, ☎ 46 01 10 35 (km 35-72).

Distance table
Sèvre-Niortaise

	km	lock	km
Niort canal basin, head of navigation, moorings, town centre across river	0.0	-	72.0
Lock 1 and weir (Comporté), take care, sloping sides	0.9	1	71.1
New road bridge (Niort by-pass)	1.5	-	70.5
Tellouze castle r/b	2.5	-	69.5
Saint-Liguaire slipway, moorings, village l/b	6.0	-	66.0
Lock 2 and weir (Roussille), bridge	6.8	2	65.2
Lock 3 and weir (Tiffardière), take care, sloping sides	7.6	3	64.4
La Tiffardière bridge, village r/b	8.1	-	63.9
Railway bridge	8.3	-	63.7
Sevreau arm l/b (navigable by small boats 500m to Sevreau bridge)	10.1	-	61.9
Magné lift bridge, slipway, village l/b	10.9	-	61.1
Lock 4 and weir (Marais-Pin)	13.6	4	58.4
Coulon-Sansais bridge, moorings and slipway d/s r/b, small boats for hire, village r/b	16.0	-	56.0
Footbridge	16.4	-	55.6
Junction with canal to La Garette, l/b (small boats only)	16.6	-	55.4

Map labels: Courdault 9km; C. de la Vieille Autise; Niort 32km, 6 locks; Sèvre; N; Sèvre Niortaise; Marais de l'Océan; Drainage canal, not navigable; **Bazoin**; Lock (Bazoin); Mauzé 17km; C. du Mignon; Lock 4 (Bazoin); Marans 19km

	km	lock	km
Lock 5 and weir (Sotterie)	19.1	5	52.9
Irleau bridge, village 1000m l/b	21.2	-	49.8
Footbridge (Cabanes de la Sèvre)	23.7	-	47.3
Entrance to Arçais arm, l/b (navigation uses r/b arm)	25.6	-	46.4
End of Arçais arm, l/b	27.5	-	44.5
Lock 6 and weir (Bourdettes), lift bridge	28.7	6	43.3
Confluence of Vieille Sèvre, r/b	29.2	-	42.8
Damvix bridge, moorings and slipway u/s r/b, village r/b	30.1	-	41.9
Les Loges, r/b	31.3	-	40.7
La Barbée, r/b	32.0	-	40.0
Junction with Canal de la Vieille Autise, r/b	32.5	-	39.5
Lock 7 and weir (Bazoin), bridge, take care, sloping sides	34.0	7	38.0
Junction with Canal du Mignon, l/b	34.3	-	37.7
Bridge (Croix des Maries)	35.0	-	37.0
Rabatière diversion canal, l/b (no interest for navigation)	36.2	-	35.8
Junction with Canal de la Rabatière, l/b (not navigable)	36.4	-	35.6
Entrance to meander cutoff (Fossé du Loup), l/b, navigation in by-passed loop (Contour de Maillé) for access to **Maillé** and *junction with Canal de la Jeune Autise*	37.3	-	34.7
End of meander cutoff	38.2	-	33.8
Bridge (Sablon)	38.9	-	33.1
Entrance to meander cutoff (Canal du Sablon) r/b, navigation possible in by-passed section (Contour des Combrands)	41.3	-	30.7
End of meander cutoff	42.7	-	29.3
Short meander cutoff, l/b (downstream of yacht club)	45.1	-	26.9
Entrance to Canal de Pomère, r/b, navigation possible in by-passed section (Contour de Pomère)	45.9	-	26.1
L'Ile d'Elle bridge, village 1200m r/b	50.6	-	21.4
End of Canal de Pomère	50.7	-	21.3
Railway bridge	50.8	-	21.2
Confluence of Vendée, r/b (unpowered boats only)	50.9	-	21.1
River divides, take l/b arm	52.2	-	19.8
Entrance to outlet drain, r/b (not navigable)	53.2	-	18.8
Marans bridge, town l/b	53.9	-	18.1
Lock 8 and weir (Carreau d'Or)	54.2	8	17.8
Port of Marans, beginning of maritime waterway, moorings	54.4	-	17.6
Junction with former Canal de Marans à La Rochelle, l/b (disused)	55.0	-	17.0
Entrance to ship canal (Canal maritime de Marans au Brault), l/b	55.2	-	16.8
Lock (Enfreneaux) r/b, to tidal Sèvre, bridge	55.6	9	16.4
Bridge (Pont du Brault)	64.8	-	7.2
Junction with ship canal (Brault lock), l/b	64.9	-	7.1
(Note: the ship canal is 5.2km long, while the tidal section of river it by-passes is 9.7km in length)			
New road bridge	65.6	-	6.4
Le Corps de Garde moorings l/b, limit of sea	67.9	-	4.1
Port du Pavé causeway l/b, moorings, estuary opens into Aiguillon bay	72.0	-	0.0

Vieille-Autise

	km	lock	km
Courdault basin, head of navigation, village 300m	0.0	-	9.7
Bridge (Chanceau), Liez 1500 r/b	2,2	-	7.5
Saint-Sigismond bridge, village 200m l/b	3.3	-	6.4
Lock (Saint-Arnault)	6.8	1	2.9
Bridge	7.5	-	2.2
Bernegoue bridge, village 700m r/b	8.4	-	1.3

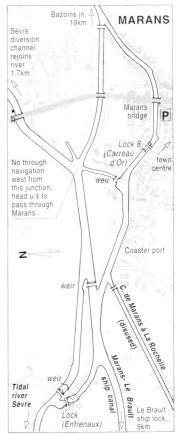

	km	lock	km
Footbridge (Ouillete), *confluence with Sèvre-Niortaise* (km 32)	9.7	-	0.0

Mignon

Mauzé-sur-le-Mignon basin, head of navigation, village 1000m	0.0	-	17.1
Bridge (Moulin-Neuf)	1.0	-	16.1
Lock 1 (Chaban) and weir	2.7	1	14.4
Quay (Chaban) l/b	3.6	-	13.5
Footbridge	4.0	-	13.1
Lock 2 (Sazay) and weir	5.6	2	11.5
Bridge (Port des Gueux), quay l/b	6.4	-	10.7
Bridge (former railway)	8.6	-	8.5
La Grève-sur-Mignon bridge, village 700m l/b	8.7	-	8.4
Lock 3 (Grève-sur-Mignon) and weir	9.9	3	7.2
Lidon r/b	12.4	-	4.7
Rigole de la Garette drain enters r/b	14.9	-	2.2
Entrance to Dérivation de la Rabatière (not navigable) l/b	16.4	-	0.7
Lock 4 (Bazoin) and weir	17.0	4	0.1
Confluence with Sèvre-Niortaise (km 34)	17.1	-	0.0

Jeune-Autise

Souil basin, small village 200m	0.0	-	8.9
Feeder enters, l/b	0.5	-	8.4
Bridge	1.8	-	7.1
Maillezais bridge, abbey ruins, village 800m l/b	3.3	-	5.6
Lock (Maillé), aqueduct upstream	7.5	1	1.4
Maillé bridge (Saint-Nicolas), village 400m l/b	8.0	-	0.9
Bridge	8.5	-	0.4
Confluence with Sèvre-Niortaise in Maillé loop (main line of navigation a further 1.2km)	8.9	-	0.0

Canal de la Somme

The Canal de la Somme, built in 1770–1843 to provide an outlet to the sea from Saint-Quentin, is in effect the canalised river Somme throughout the greater part of its course. It is one of the most attractive waterways of northern France, passing through a marshy valley dotted with lakes and gravel pits, and in view of its declining commercial importance its use for pleasure cruising must be actively encouraged. It extends 156km from Saint-Simon, on the Canal de Saint-Quentin, to the sea lock at Saint-Valéry-sur-Somme, where navigation enters the Somme estuary. It thus provides an alternative approach route from the English Channel to the waterways of central France. The canal may be divided into three sections: from Saint-Simon to below lock 11, Froissy (km 54), it runs parallel to the river Somme (over a 20km length within this section, the canal also forms the second section of the Canal du Nord); from Froissy to downstream of Abbeville (km 142), navigation is mainly in the river Somme, with occasional lock-cuts; from Abbeville to the estuary the navigation is designated the Canal maritime d'Abbeville à Saint Valéry-sur-Somme. The section shared with the Canal du Nord has been upgraded to the standards of that canal.

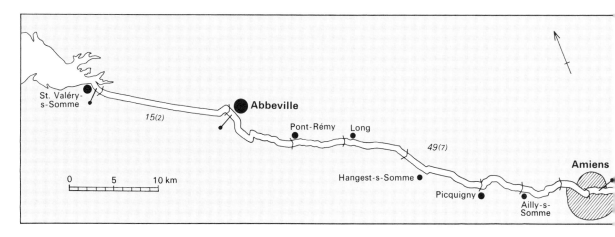

Locks There are 25 locks, including the sea lock at Saint-Valéry. They fall continuously from the Saint-Simon pound of the Canal de Saint-Quentin (65m above sea level) towards the sea. Lock dimensions vary, but the smallest are 38.50 by 6.35m.

Depth The maximum authorised draught is 1.80m from Saint-Simon to Abbeville. This is increased to 3.20m in the canal maritime, allowing small coasters to trade up to Abbeville.

Bridges The normal headroom under the numerous fixed bridges is 3.70m, but the bridge upstream of lock 17 in Amiens may present a reduced headroom of 3.43m. The swing bridge at Feuillères (km 43) is equipped for automatic operation, with radar detection, and it is advisable for small boats to have a radar reflector. There are four swing bridges and one lift bridge on the canal maritime.

Towpath There is a towpath throughout.

Authority

Direction Départementale de l'Equipement de la Somme.
Subdivision: Boulevard du Port, BP 2612, 80026 Amiens, ☎ 22 91 15 15.

Distance table

	km	lock	km
Saint-Simon, *triangular junction with the Canal de Saint-Quentin*	0.0	-	156.4
Lock 1 (Saint-Simon), bridge	0.1	1	156.3
Bridge (D56 Dury-Ollezy)	1.6	-	154.8
Sommette-Eaucourt, l/b	3.1	-	153.3
Former railway bridge (destroyed)	5.1	-	151.3
Ham basin l/b, large village, alternative mooring above lock r/b	6.1	-	150.3
Lock 2 (Ham), bridge	6.6	2	149.8
Lock 3 (Ham), bridge	7.2	3	149.2
Quays l/b	7.9	-	148.5
Footbridge	8.3	-	148.1
Footbridge	10.0	-	146.4

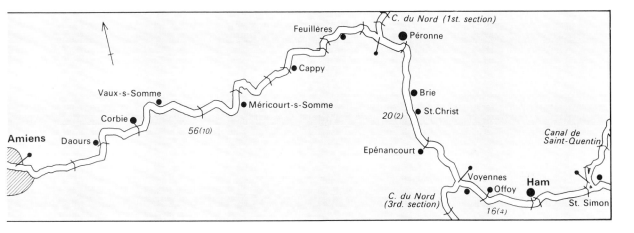

	km	lock	km
Canizy l/b (windmill)	11.2	-	145.2
Lock 4 (Offoy), bridge, quay downstream l/b, **Offoy** 300m	12.5	4	143.9
Voyennes bridge, village 300m	14.8	-	141.6
Junction with Canal du Nord l/b, beginning of common section (upgraded)	16.4	-	140.0
Béthencourt-sur-Somme bridge, quay downstream r/b	17.9	-	138.5
Pargny bridge, quay upstream l/b	20.7	-	135.7
Lock 5 (Epénancourt)	22.2	5	134.2
Epénancourt l/b	22.7	-	133.7
Saint-Christ-Briost bridge, quay and turning basin d/s r/b	25.7	-	130.7
Bridge (Pont-lès-Brie)	28.4	-	128.0
Lock 6 (Péronne)	32.9	6	123.5
Railway bridge	33.1	-	123.3
Bridge (N17), quays d/s, Péronne 300m	33.5	-	122.9
Junction with Canal du Nord r/b, end of common section	36.7	-	119.7
Bridge (Bazincourt)	36.9	-	119.5
Lock 7 (Sormont), bridge, quay r/b	39.1	7	117.3
Motorway bridge (A1)	39.9	-	116.5

	km	lock	km
Feuillères lift bridge (automatic, with radar detection), quay upstream l/b	41.3	-	115.1
Lock 8 (Frise), bridge, quay upstream r/b	43.6	8	112.8
Lock 9 (**Frise**)	44.7	9	111.7
Quay l/b	46.0	-	110.4
Eclusier-Vaux lift bridge	46.9	-	109.5
Cappy lift bridge, quay upstream r/b	50.4	-	106.0
Lock 10 (Cappy)	51.0	10	105.4
Froissy bridge, quays downstream	52.8	-	103.6
Lock 11 (Froissy), quay downstream r/b	52.9	11	103.5
Navigation enters Somme (Bray arm r/b)	54.1	-	102.3
Etinehem arm r/b (no longer used)	57.1	-	99.3
Lock 12 (**Méricourt-sur-Somme**), bridge, village 1300m	58.6	12	97.8
Cerizy/Chipilly bridge, quay upstream r/b	62.4	-	94.0
Bridge (Cerizy l/b)	63.7	-	92.7
Lock 13 (**Sailly-Laurette**), bridge, village 600m r/b	65.3	13	91.1
Sailly-le-Sec r/b (track to village, 600m)	66.8	-	89.6
Bridge (Vaire-sous-Corbie)	70.7	-	85.7
Lock 14 (**Corbie**), bridge, quay upstream l/b, small town r/b	74.5	14	81.9
Railway bridge	77.2	-	79.2
Bridge (Daours/Vecquemont)	79.3	-	77.1
Lock 15 (Daours)	79.7	15	76.7
Railway bridge	80.1	-	76.3
Private quay r/b	80.5	-	75.9
Lock 16 (Lamotte-Brebière) in short lock-cut r/b	84.3	16	72.1
Railway bridge	85.6	-	70.8
Bridge (Longueau), boat harbour and Navi-Plaisance hire base u/s r/b, **Camon** r/b	88.7	-	67.7
Bridge (Camon)	90.1	-	66.3
Amiens bridge (Beauvillé), quay and Nautic 80 hire base d/s l/b, large town l/b (see plan)	92.4	-	64.0
Bridge (Célestins)	93.4	-	63.0
Bridge (Saint-Pierre)	93.6	-	62.8
Bridge (Maulcreux), lowest on the Somme	93.8	-	62.6
Lock 17 (Amiens), bridge	94.0	17	62.4
Footbridge (Saint-Maurice), quay downstream l/b	94.3	-	62.1
Bridge (Cagnard), private quay upstream l/b	95.0	-	61.4
Bridge (Blanc)	95.8	-	60.6
Railway bridge	97.1	-	59.3
Lock 18 (Montières), bridge	97.7	18	58.7
Bridge (**Dreuil**), village l/b	100.0	-	56.4
Lock 19 (**Ailly-sur-Somme**), bridge, village l/b	102.5	19	53.9
Lock 20 (**Picquigny**), bridge, village l/b	108.0	20	48.4
Bourdon bridge, quay upstream l/b	115.0	-	41.4
Lock 21 (Labreilloire)	117.5	21	38.9
Railway bridges	117.9	-	38.5
Bridge (Etoile)	120.6	-	35.8
Longbridge, village r/b (mooring in basin 500m u/s l/b)	124.7	-	31.7
Lock 22	124.8	22	31.6
Bridge (Cocquerel)	127.5	-	28.9
Towpath bridge	130.3	-	26.1
Pont-Rémy quay r/b	130.6	-	25.8
Bridge (D901)	131.0	-	25.4
Lock 23	131.3	23	25.1
Bridge (Eaucourt-sur-Somme)	133.0	-	23.4
Bridge (Epagne)	134.2	-	22.2
Bridge (Epagnette)	136.0	-	20.4
Railway bridge (Béthune)	139.5	-	16.9

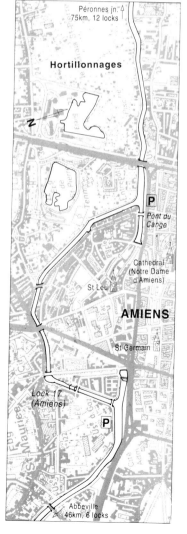

	km	lock	km
Bridge (Boulevard des Prés)	140.6	-	15.8
Bridge (Portelette), entrance to lock-cut, l/b	140.7	-	15.7
Abbeville, bridge (Gare), railway station l/b, town centre r/b	141.0	-	15.3
Lock 24	141.7	24	14.7
Bridge (Hocquet)	142.0	-	14.4
Towpath bridge, end of lock-cut, Somme navigable a few hundred metres upstream towards the town centre	142.1	-	14.3
Railway bridge (Boulogne), beginning of canal maritime	142.3	-	14.1
Private quay l/b	142.9	-	13.5
Swing bridge (Sursomme)	143.1	-	13.3
Swing bridge (Laviers)	145.2	-	11.2
Swing bridge (Petit-Port)	148.2	-	8.2
Swing bridge (**Boismont**), village 1000m l/b	153.0	-	3.4
Lift bridge (D940)	155.6	-	0.8
Lock 25, railway swing bridge downstream, end of canal maritime, **Saint-Valéry-sur-Somme** harbour in estuary below lock	156.4	25	0.0

Etang de Thau

The Etang de Thau is a large sheltered sea water lake which forms a link between the Canal du Midi and the Canal du Rhône à Sète. The through route across the lake is 17km in length, from the lighthouse on the mole at Les Onglous, marking the outfall of the Canal du Midi, to the point where the Canal du Rhône à Sète falls into the eastern part of the lake, known as the Etang des Eaux Blanches. There are two navigable outlets to the Mediterranean, at the western end, through the canal de Pisse-Saumes, 2km long, and especially at Sète, through the Canal Maritime (see plan), giving access to this busy port. There is no buoyed channel, the safe course with ample depths being straight across the lake from Les Onglous to the Roquérols lighthouse, situated about midway between two promontories (Pointe de Barrou to the south and Pointe de Balaruc to the north). Both Les Onglous and Roquérols lighthouses show a white occulting light at night. There are harbours on the northern shore of the lake at Marseillan and Mèze. The crossing of the lake should be avoided in bad weather. Conditions are particularly dangerous when a strong north-westerly wind is blowing.

Depth A minimum of 2.00m may be counted on at all times.

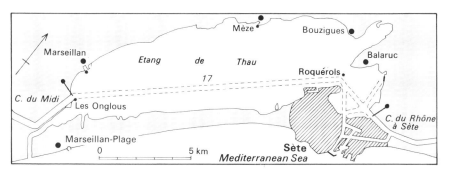

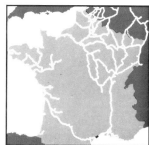

Distance table

	km	lock	km
(Note: distances relate to the straight line across the lake)			
Les Onglous lighthouse, outfall of Canal du Midi	0.0	-	17.0
Marseillan harbour, north shore	1.0	-	16.0
Mèze harbour, north shore	10.5	-	6.5
Roquérols lighthouse	14.7	-	2.3
Navigation crosses dredged shipping channel serving industrial quays on eastern shore	16.7	-	0.3
Outfall of Canal du Rhône à Sète	17.0	-	0.0

Vilaine

The canalised river Vilaine forms a link in the waterway route across Brittany from Saint-Malo to the Bay of Biscay, an inland route regularly used by yachtsmen long before the current boom in inland cruising. The river is navigable from Rennes, where it is joined by the Canal d'Ille-et-Rance, to below La Roche-Bernard, where it flows into the Atlantic, a distance of 137km. It is crossed by the Canal de Nantes à Brest at Redon (km 89), below which point it used to be tidal, until a barrage was built at Arzal, 6km inland, incorporating a large lock. This has transformed the estuary into a wide freshwater lake of more or less constant level and more attractive for yachting and inland cruising. Despite this scheme, the large sluice-gate on the river at Redon (the 'Grand Vannage') is often closed, offering protection against exceptionally high tides, and since there is no lock here the structure has to be bypassed. Proceeding downstream on the Vilaine, the route to be followed (if the Grand Vannage is closed) is right through lock 18 (Oust) of the Canal de Nantes à Brest, then immediately left through another lock into the large basin at Redon (360 by 60m), which has been developed as a yacht harbour (Port de Plaisance). The basin is linked to the Vilaine downstream of the Grand Vannage through a short length of canal, in which the former tide lock has been eliminated. It is thus a clear run from Redon basin to the lock at Arzal, a distance of 42km.

It should further be noted that the junction with the Canal de Nantes à Brest in the direction of Nantes is no longer made at the Redon 'cross-roads', but 7km downstream through the lock at Bellions, the section of the canal between Bellions and Redon having been closed.

Locks There are 12 locks on the Vilaine between Rennes and Mâlon (km 52), with dimensions of 26.60 by 4.70m. In the distance table, the Grand Vannage sluice at Redon (km 89) is counted as a lock insofar as it represents an obstacle to navigation, although the route by which it is bypassed in fact involves negotiating two locks on the canal de Nantes à Brest (of similar dimensions to the above). The lock at the Arzal barrage is of large dimensions (85 by 13m), allowing big yachts and passenger boats to navigate up the river to Redon basin. There is an intermediate gate which allows a shorter length of the chamber to be used when sufficient. A lift bridge spans the lock.

Depth In the days of commercial navigation, the depth was maintained at 1.50m, but this is far from being guaranteed today, especially in the reach downstream of Mâlon. Dredging works are planned, but in the meantime, the maximum authorised draught can be assumed to be 1.20m between Rennes and Redon. Downstream of Redon depths are substantially greater.

Bridges The bridges leave a minimum clear headroom of 3.20m above normal water level, reduced to as little as 1.80m above the highest navigable water level between lock 13 (Mâlon) and Redon. During floods, local enquiries should therefore be made.

Towpath The towpath has fallen into disuse.

Authority

Direction Départementale de l'Equipement d'Ille-et-Vilaine. Subdivisions:
– 1 avenue du Mail, 35000 Rennes, ☎ 99 59 20 60 (km 0-52).
– 116 route de Vannes, 35600 Redon, ☎ 99 71 10 66 (km 52-131).

Distance table

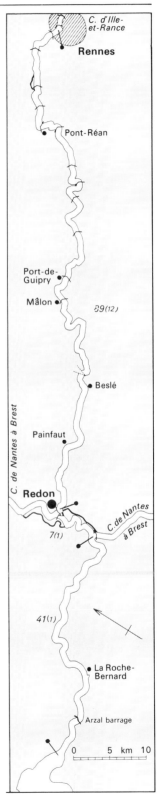

	km	lock	km
Rennes bridge (boulevard de la Tour d'Auvergne), limit of navigation (Vilaine covered through the town)	0.0	-	137.0
Junction with Canal d'Ille-et-Rance, r/b	0.1	-	136.9
Quays, water, fuel, town centre 500m (better mooring above lock 1 on Canal d'Ille-et-Rance)	0.2	-	136.8
Bridge (Abattoir)	0.7	-	136.3
Bridge	0.9	-	136.1
Confluence of Ille, r/b	1.0	-	136.0
Railway bridge, former industrial quays downstream	1.3	-	135.7
Lock 2 (Comte) in short lock-cut l/b, swing bridge	1.9	1	135.1
New road bridge (Rennes bypass)	2.6	-	134.4
Meander cutoff r/b	4.2	-	132.8
Lock 3 (Apigné) in short lock-cut l/b, bridge	5.5	2	131.5
Bridge (Chancors), weir r/b, entrance to lock-cut l/b	9.3	-	127.7
Lock 4 (Cicé), lift bridge, navigation re-enters Vilaine	11.0	3	126.0
Confluence of Meu, r/b	13.9	-	123.1
Bridge (Mons), quay downstream l/b, **Bruz** 2000m l/b	14.1	-	122.9
Lock 5 (Mons) and weir	14.3	4	122.7
Lock 6 (Pont-Réan), l/b, and weir	17.8	5	119.2
Pont-Réan bridge, quay downstream r/b, hire base, village r/b	18.0	-	119.0
Confluence of Seiche, l/b	20.3	-	116.7
Railway viaduct (Cahot), moorings downstream l/b	20.5	-	116.5
Lock 7 (Boël), r/b, and weir	21.0	6	116.0
Laillé bridge, quay upstream r/b, village 2500m l/b	23.7	-	113.3
Lock 8 (Bouëxière), r/b, and weir	26.8	7	110.2
Bridge (Glanret), quay downstream r/b, **Bourg-des-Comptes** 1800m l/b	28.5	-	108.5
Lock 9 (Gailieu), r/b, and weir	30.2	8	106.8
Lock 10 (Molière), r/b, and weir	33.8	9	103.2
Bridge (Charrière), **Pléchâtel** 1000m l/b	35.3	-	101.7
Railway viaduct (Cambrée)	37.3	-	99.7
Bridge (Macaire), moorings downstream l/b	39.9	-	97.1
Lock 11 (Macaire), r/b, and weir	40.6	10	96.4
Lock 12 (Guipry), r/b, and weir, Crown Blue Line hire base upstream l/b, **Messac** 1300m l/b	47.9	11	89.1
Guipry bridge, quay downstream r/b, village 1500m r/b	48.0	-	89.0

	km	lock	km
Railway viaduct (Guipry)	48.5	-	88.5
Lock 13 (Mâlon), r/b, and weir, shoals downstream	52.0	12	85.0
Bridge (Saint-Marc), entrance to gorge	55.0	-	82.0
Railway viaduct (Corbinières)	56.7	-	80.3
Port de Roche bridge, quay upstream r/b, end of section in gorge, small village r/b	62.2	-	74.8
Confluence of Chère, l/b	66.4	-	70.6
Railway viaduct (Droulin)	67.6	-	69.4
Beslé bridge, quay upstream l/b, water, fuel, village 500m l/b	69.3	-	67.7
Brain-sur-Vilaine island, navigation in r/b arm, quay, village r/b	71.3	-	65.7
Ferry	73.0	-	64.0
Bridge (Ilette), quay upstream r/b	74.3	-	62.7
Lake (Lac de Murin) beyond left bank	76.5	-	60.5
Painfaut bridge, small village 300m r/b	79.3	-	57.7
Bridge (Grand-Pas)	84.0	-	53.0
Railway viaduct (Redon)	88.8	-	48.2
Redon bridge (Pont de Saint-Nocholas), quay upstream r/b, town centre r/b	89.1	-	47.9
Crossing of Canal de Nantes à Brest, enter canal through lock 18 (Oust), r/b, when downstream barrage closed	89.2	-	47.8
Quays r/b, Bretagne Plaisance and Comptoir Nautique Redonnais hire bases	89.3	-	47.7
Barrage (Grand Vannage), open when upstream and downstream levels equal (see plan), limit of tides	89.4	13	47.6
Redon basin (Grand Bassin, boat harbour) r/b	89.7	-	47.3
Commercial quays r/b	90.1	-	39.9
Confluence of Oust, r/b	90.9	-	46.1
Junction with Canal de Nantes à Brest, l/b, through Bellions lock (see plan)	96.1	-	40.9
Rieux quay r/b, former ferry	96.7	-	40.3
Confluence of Isac, l/b	100.0	-	37.0
Bridge (Cran) with swinging span l/b, pontoon moorings d/s l/b, restaurant	101.8	-	35.2
Ferry (Passage Neuf)	103.8	-	33.2
Foleux boat harbour r/b, water	114.9	-	22.1
Boat moorings l/b	121.2	-	15.8
Suspension bridge	122.0	-	15.0
La Roche-Bernard harbour (Port du Rhodoir) l/b, moorings and boatyard (Atelier Naval de la Couronne), village 500m up hill l/b	122.6	-	14.4
Arzal-Camoël yacht harbour l/b	130.8	-	6.2
Arzal dam, lock r/b	131.0	14	6.0
Slipway (Vieille Roche) l/b	131.2	-	5.8
Tréhiquier quay and boat harbour l/b, former ferry	136.6	-	0.4
Discharge into the Atlantic, Pointe du Moustoir r/b, Pointe du Scal l/b	137.0	-	0.0

Opposite. Top:
Redon on the Vilaine; with the
normally open Grand Vannage
sluice in the background.
Hugh Potter
Bottom: The Arzal barrier and
lock on the Vilaine estuary,
from the upstream side.
Hugh Potter

Yonne

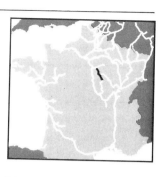

The canalised river Yonne extends from Auxerre, where it joins the Canal du Nivernais, to its confluence with the Seine at Montereau, a distance of 108km. Over the first 22km, down to the junction with the Canal de Bourgogne, it forms part of the Nivernais route, a cross link between the Bourgogne and Bourbonnais routes from Paris to Lyon. The rest of the waterway forms part of the Bourgogne route, the shortest but most heavily locked of the three main routes across central France. The Yonne is an attractive cruising river, with huge locks but little commercial traffic (except in the lower reaches). The river is avoided by lock-cuts at three places: Gurgy, Joigny and Courlon.

Locks There are 26 locks. The nine between Auxerre and Laroche-Migennes (junction with Canal de Bourgogne) are 93m long and 8.30m wide. The next 14 down to Port-Renard are 96 by 8.30m, while the last three are slightly wider (10.50m). Many of the locks have sloping sides, which are particularly awkward for boats proceeding downstream. The crew should be at the ready to fend off with boathooks.

Depth The maximum authorised draught is 1.80m.

Bridges The lowest bridges are the Pont de la Tournelle in Auxerre and Courlon bridge (km 87). The first offers a headroom of 4.40m above normal water level, reduced to 4.20m above the highest navigable water level (over the navigable width of 8.30m). The corresponding dimensions at Courlon are 4.80 and 4.40m.

Towpath There is a good towpath throughout.

Authority

Service de la Navigation de la Seine, Arrondissement Haute-Seine.
Subdivision: 60 quai de la Fausse-Rivière, 89106 Sens, ☎ 86 65 26 92.

Distance table

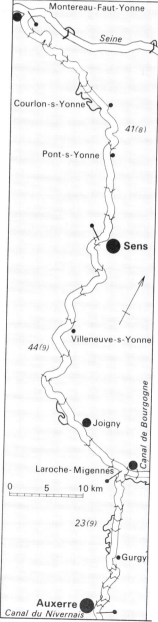

	km	lock	km
Connection with Canal du Nivernais (Pont Paul-Bert in Auxerre)	0.0	-	108.0
Auxerre footbridge, boat harbour r/b, Aquarelle, Connoisseur and Pro-Aqua hire bases, city centre and cathedral l/b	0.3	-	107.7
Bridges (Pont de la Tournelle and new road bridge)	0.8	-	107.2
Lock 1 (Chaînette), l/b, weir	1.0	1	107.0
Lock 2 (Ile Brûlée), l/b, weir	2.5	2	105.5
Lock 3 (Dumonts), l/b, weir	4.3	3	103.7
Lock 4 (Boisseaux), l/b, weir	5.9	4	102.1
Monéteau bridge, mooring r/b	6.8	-	101.2
Lock 5 (Monéteau), r/b, weir	7.5	5	100.5
Motorway bridge (Autoroute du Soleil)	8.9	-	99.1
Gurgy quay, r/b, Navig-France hire base	10.1	-	97.9
Entrance to Gurgy lock-cut, r/b	10.5	-	97.5
Bridge (Gurgy) and flood gate	10.6	-	97.4
Bridge (Chaumes)	12.0	-	96.0
Skew bridge (**Appoigny**), quay u/s l/b, village 1500m l/b	12.9	-	95.1
Lock 6 (Néron), bridge	14.0	6	94.0
Lock 7 (Raveuse), bridge	15.4	7	92.6

	km	lock	km
End of Gurgy lock-cut, navigation re-enters Yonne	15.6	-	92.4
Lock 8 (Bassou), r/b, weir	17.0	8	91.0
Bassou bridge, village 400m l/b, **Bonnard** r/b	17.9	-	90.1
Lock 9 (Gravière), l/b, weir	21.1	9	86.9
Confluence of Armançon, r/b	21.4	-	86.6
Bridge (Migennes)	21.8	-	86.2
Bridge (Charmoy)	22.2	-	85.8
Railway bridge (Laroche)	22.6	-	85.4
Junction with canal de Bourgogne, r/b	22.7	-	85.3
Quay (Coches), r/b, **Migennes** 500m	22.9	-	85.1
Laroche-Saint-Cydroine bridge, village r/b	23.8	-	84.2
Lock 1 (Epineau), l/b, weir, boat club with slipway d/s r/b	24.8	10	83.2
Lock 2 (Pêchoir), l/b, weir	28.7	11	79.3
Joigny bridge, quay and town centre r/b	31.1	-	76.9
Quay l/,b, Locaboat Plaisance hire base	31.6	-	76.4
Entrance to Joigny lock-cut, r/b	32.6	-	75.4
Bridge (Epizy) and flood gate	32.7	-	75.3
Lock 3 (Saint-Aubin) with sloping sides, bridge	35.4	12	72.6
End of Joigny lock-cut, navigation re-enters Yonne	36.0	-	72.0
Saint-Aubin-sur-Yonne quay and village r/b	36.1	-	71.9
Villecien r/b	37.0	-	71.0
Lock 4 (Villevallier), r/b, weir	40.3	13	67.7
Villevallier bridge, mooring r/b	41.8	-	66.2
Lock 5 (Armeau) with sloping sides, r/b, weir	44.9	14	63.1
Villeneuve-sur-Yonne bridge, Croisières Eiffel hire base d/s l/b, small town r/b	50.0	-	58.0
Lock 6 (Villeneuve-sur-Yonne) with sloping sides, r/b, weir	50.5	15	57.5
Quay (Passy) r/b, private quay l/b	54.1	-	53.9
Lock 7 (Etigny) with sloping sides, r/b, weir	56.0	16	52.0
Etigny bridge, village 400m l/b	57.0	-	51.0
Quay (Rosoy) r/b	59.5	-	48.5
Lock 8 (Rosoy), sloping sides, r/b, weir	60.5	17	47.5
Lock 9 (Saint-Bond), sloping sides, r/b, weir	65.3	18	42.7
River divides, navigation in r/b arm	66.5	-	41.5
Sens bridge, boat harbour u/s l/b, town centre r/b	66.8	-	41.2
(Boats heading u/s river divides, navigation in r/b arm	67.3	-	40.7
Road bridge (Sens bypass)	67.6	-	40.4
Commercial quays r/b	68.0	-	40.0
Lock 10 (Saint-Martin), r/b, weir	69.5	19	38.5
Saint-Denis quay and village r/b	71.0	-	37.0
Lock 11 (Villeperrot), sloping sides, r/b, weir	74.5	20	33.5
Vanne aqueduct	76.1	-	31.9
Pont-sur-Yonne bridge, quay d/s l/b, BIPE hire base, village 100m	78.6	-	29.4
Lock 12 (Champfleury), r/b, weir	80.2	21	27.8
Serbonnes castle r/b	84.4	-	23.6
Serbonnes r/b	85.0	-	23.0
Courlon-sur-Yonne r/b	86.9	-	21.1
Entrance to Courlon lock-cut, r/b	87.0	-	21.0
Bridge (Courlon) and flood gate	87.1	-	20.9
Bridge (Morlaix)	88.6	-	19.4
Bridge (Gain)	89.1	-	18.9
Lock 13 (Vinneuf), sloping sides, bridge	90.1	22	17.9
Lock 14 (Port-Renard), end of lock-cut, navigation re-enters Yonne	91.8	23	16.2
Misy-sur-Yonne bridge, mooring d/s r/b, village 300m	93.8	-	14.2
Lock 15 (Barbey), sloping sides, r/b, weir	96.2	24	11.8
Lock 16 (Brosse), sloping sides, r/b, weir	100.6	25	7.4

St Etienne cathedral towering above the Yonne above Auxerre. On the far right is the tower of St Germain abbey.
Hugh Potter

	km	lock	km
Pipeline crossing	102.3	-	5.7
Cannes-Ecluses bridge, quay for boats u/s l/b, village 200m	104.4	-	3.6
Lock 17 (Cannes), sloping sides, r/b, weir	104.7	26	3.3
Railway bridge (Pont de Moscou), private quay u/s l/b	106.7	-	1.3
Montereau-Faut-Yonne bridge, moorings and town centre l/b	107.9	-	0.1
Confluence with Seine (km 68)	108.0	-	0.0

Appendix

I. GLOSSARY

French – English

acajou (m), *mahogany*; okoume, *Gaboon mahogany*.

accoster, *to come alongside*.

affaler, *to lower, to overhaul*.

affluent (m), *tributary*.

agréner, *to pump (water from a boat)*.

aiguilleter, *to seize*.

aiguillot (m), *pintle (of rudder)*.

alternat (m), *alternating one-way traffic*.

amarrage (m), *lashing*; amarrage en portugaise, *racking seizing*; faire un amarrage, *to lash, to seize*.

amarrer, *to make fast, to belay*.

amount (en), *upstream*; en amont du pont, *above bridge*.

ancre (f), *anchor*; bras, *arm*; pattes (F), *flukes*; jas, *stock*; cigale, *ring*; chasser sur l'ancre, *to drag the anchor*.

anse (f), *cove, small bay*.

arborer, *to hoist (a flag)*.

arbre (m), *shaft*; arbre à cames, *camshaft*.

assureur (m), *underwriter*.

aube (f), *paddle wheel*.

aval, *downstream*; en aval du pont, *below bridge*.

avalant (m), *boat heading downstream*.

avant (m), *bow (of a vessel)*.

bac (m), *ferry*.

bâche (f), *canvas cover, hood*.

bague (f), *hank, grummet*.

balise (f), *beacon, stake*.

bande (f), *list, heel*; donner de la bande, *to have a list*.

barrage (m), *weir*; barrage éclusé, *weir and lock*.

bas-fonds (m), *shallows, shoals*.

bâtiment (m), *ship, vessel (either man-of-war or merchantman)*; vaisseau, *man-of-war*; navire, *merchantman*.

banquière (f), *shelf (of ship)*.

ber (m), *launching cradle*,

berceau (m), *cradle, engine-bed*.

berge (f), *bank (of canal)*.

bief (m), *'pound' or reach of canal*.

bief de partage, *summit level*.

bielle (f), *connecting rod*.

bitord (f), *spun yarn*.

bitte (f), *bollard*.

bosse (f), *painter (of boat)*.

boucle (f), *mooring ring*.

bouée (f), *buoy*.

boujaron (m), *tot*; boujaron de rhum, *tot of rum*.

buse (m), *sill (of lock)*.

cale (f), (i) *slipway*, (ii) *hold (of ship)*.

calaison (f), *draught (of ship)*.

calanque (f), *cove, fiord*.

calfatage (m), *caulking*.

calfater, *to caulk*.

caréner, *to careen*; basin de carénage, *basin for careening*.

carlingue (f), *keelson*.

carreau (m), *sheer stake*.

chaland (m), *lighter, barge*.

chatterton (m), *insulation tape*.

chaumard (m), *fairlead*.

chavirer, *to capsize*.

chemin de halage, *towpath*.

chignole (f), *hand-drill*.

chômage (m), *stoppage, closure of canal for repairs*.

choquer, *to check, to surge*; choquer les amarres, *to check the mooring ropes*.

cigale (f), *anchor ring*.

clayonnage (m), *facines, wicker-work, training mattress*.

clin (m), *clinker*; construit à clin, *clinker-built*.

cloison (f), *bulkhead*; cloison étanche, *watertight bulkhead*.

connaissance (des temps) (f), *the Nautical Almanac*.

contre-étrave (f), *apron (at stern)*.

contre-plaqué (m), *plywood*.

convoi poussé (m), *push-tow*.

cordage (m), *rope*.

cosse (f), *thimble, eyelet*.

cote (f), *height above datum, spot height*.

couple (m), *frame, timber*.

courbe (f), *knee*.

courtier maritime (m), *ship broker*.

crépine (f), *strainer*.

croisement (m), *meeting (two ships)*.

dalot (m), *scupper*.

dames (f), *crutches (for oars)*.

darse (f), *tidal basin, dock*.

déclinaison (f), *variation (magnetic)*.

décommettre, *to unlay (a rope)*.

démarrer, *to unmoor*.

démarreur (m), *starter (motor)*.

dérive (f), *drift, leeway*; aile de dérive, *leeboard*; quille de dérive, *centre-board*.

désarmer, *to lay up (vessel)*.

déversoir (m), *weir*.

déviation (f), *deviation (compass)*.

digue (f), *dike, embarkment, training-wall*.

drisse (f), *halliard*.

écluse (f), *lock*; élusier (m), *lock-keeper*.

écueil (m), *reef, shelf*.

élingue (f), *sling, strop*.

élinguer, *to sling*.

enter, *to scarf, to joint*.

épi (m), *training wall (river)*.

épisser, *to splice*.

epissoir (m), *fid, marline-spike*.

épissure (f), *splice*; épissure à oeil, *eye splice*.

épuisette (f), *bailer*.

équiper, *to fit out (ship)*.

erse (f), *strop, becket*; erse en bitord, *selvagee stro*.

éscope (f), *bailer*.
étambot (m), *sternpost*.
étampe (f), *punch*.
étoupe (f), *oakum*.
étrave (f), *stem*.

fanal (m), *mast-head light*.
faubert (m), *swab*.
faux-bras (m), *tow-rope, warp*.
femelots (m), *gudgeons (rudder)*.
feu (m), *light*; feu-de-position, *riding light*; feux de route, *navigation lights*.
fil (m), *wire, twine*; fil de cuivre rouge, *copper wire*; fil de fer, *iron wire*; fil de laiton, *brass wire*; fil de caret, *rope yarn*; fil de voile, *sail twine*; fil de bougie, *ignition wire*.
filer, *to pay out, to veer*.
filière (f), *stocks and dies*.
fleur à d'eau, *awash*.
franc-bord (m), *freeboard*; à franc-bord, *carvel built*.
fond (m), *bottom*; bas-fonds, haut-fonds, *shallow water*; à fond plat, *flat-bottomed*.
fortune (f), *jury*; mât de fortune, *jury mast*.
fraiser, *to ream out, to countersink*.
franchir, *to freshen*; le vent franchit, *the wind freshens*.

gabare (f), *lighter*.
gabarit (m), *mould, gauge*.
galbord (m), *garboard strake*.
garants (m), *falls of a tackle*.
genoper, *to belay, to seize*.
gicleur (m), *jet*; gicleur bouché, *choked jet (carburettor)*.
gisement (m), *bearing (compass)*.
godiller, *to scull (over stern of boat)*.
goudron (m), *tar*; goudron à bois, *Stockholm tar*; brai (m), *pitch*.
goupille (f), *pin*; goupille fendue, *split-pin*; goupille conique, *taper-pin*.
grau (m), *channel connecting salt lake to the sea*.
grelin (m), *warp, hawser*.
guidon (m), *burgee, pennant*.
guipon (m), *mop*.

habitacle (m), *binnacle*.
halage (m), *towage*; chemin de halage, *tow-path*.
hausse (f), *rising water (river)*.
haut-fonds (m), *shoal*.
hélice (f), *propeller*; pas de l'hélice, *pitch of propeller*.

hermétic (m), *jointing compound*.
herminette (f), *adze*.
hiloire (f), *coaming*.

instructions (f), *sailing directions*.
interrupteur (m), *switch (electric)*.

jas (m), *stock (of anchor)*.

kiosque (m), (de timonerie), *wheelhouse*; kiosque des cartes, *charthouse*.

laiton (m), *brass*.
largeur (f), *beam, breadth of beam*.
larguer, *to let go*; larguer les amarres, *to let to the mooring ropes*.
levier (m) (du rupteur), *contact-breaker arm*.
liège (m), *cork*.
ligne (f) (de foi), *lubber's line*.
limander, *to parcel (a rope)*.
lisse (f), *ribband, stringer, moulding*.
louvoyer, *to tack (under sail)*.
lover, *to coil down*.
lusin (m), *houseline, marline*.

manchon (m), *collar, bush*.
mandrin (m), *mandrel (for lathe)*.
manille (f), *shackle*.
mascaret (m), *bore, tidal wave*.
mèche (f), *drill, bit, heart (of rope)*.
mélèze (f), *larch*.
minium (m), *red lead*.
montant (m), (i) *stanchion*, (ii) *vessel heading upstream*.
mouillage (m) (i) *anchorage*, (ii) *channel depth*.
mouiller, *to anchor, to moor*.

nable (m), *plug-hole (of boat)*.
noeud (m), *knot, bend, hitch*; noeud d'arret, *figure of 8*; noeud de vache, *granny*; noeud d'anguille, *running bowline*; noeud de chaise, *bow-line*; noeud plat, *reef*; noeud de grappin, *fisherman's bend*; noeud d'écoute, *sheet bend*; demi-clef, *half-hitch*; deux demi-clefs à capeler, *clove hitch*; noeud de fouet, *rolling hitch*; noeud de bois, *timber hitch*; gueule de loup, *Blackwall hitch*.
nouer, *to hitch*.

oeil (m) (de pie), *eyelet*
ordre (m) (d'allumage), *firing order (motor)*.
organeau (m), *mooring ring*.
orin (m), *buoy rope*.

palan (m), *tackle*; palan à croc, *luff tackle*; palan à chaine, *chain block*; palan de dimanche, *handy-billy*; gréer un palan, *rig a tackle*.
palier (m), *bearing (machine)*; palier à billes, *ball-bearing*; palier de butée, *thrust bearing*.
papillon (m), *wing nut*.
pas (m), *pitch (of screw propeller)*.
passoire (f), *strainer, filter*.
patte (f), *cringle*; patte d'une ancre, *flukes of an anchor*; pattes d'araignée, *oil-grooves*.
paumelle (f), *palm (and needle)*.
péniche (f), *lighter, barge, pinnace*.
pin (m), *pine wood*; pitchpin, *pitchpine*.
plat-bord (m), *gunwale*.
plot (m), *contact-point (motor)*.
pointeau (m), *centre-punch, needle of carburettor*.
poinçon (m), *pricker, bradawl*.
pomme (f), *truck (of mast)*.
pompe (f), *pump*; pompe de cale, *bilge-pump*; alumer une pompe, *prime a pump*; la pompe est eventée, *the pump sucks*.
poulie (f), *block, sheave*; poulie simple, *single block*; poulie double, *double block*; poulie coupée, *snatch block*.
poussage (m), *push-towing*.
pousseur (m), *push-tug*.
pont-canal (m), *aqueduct*.
prélart (m), *tarpaulin*.
presse-étoupe (m), *suffing-box or gland*.

queue (f), *tang (of file or tool)*; queue d'aronde, *dovetail*; queue de rat, *pointing (rope's end)*, *rat-tail file*.

rabattre, *to clench (a nail)*.
râblure (f), *rabbet*.
rabot (m), *plane (for wood)*; passer le rabot sur, *to plane*.
radeau (m), *raft*.
radouber, *to refit (a vessel)*; cale de redoub, *graving slip*.
ras (m), (de marée), *tidal wave, bore*.
raté (m), *misfire (motor)*.
réa (m), *sheave (of block)*.
récif (m), *reef (of rocks)*.
relâche (f), *port of call*; relâcher à, *to call at*.
relèvement (m), *bearing (compass)*; relèvement croisé, *cross-bearing*.
remorquer, *to tow*.
remorqueur (m), *tugboat*;

remorqueur à aubes, *paddle-wheel tug*; remorquer à couple, *to tow alongside*.

remous (m), *backwash, eddy*.

rive (f), *bank (of river)*.

rondelle (f), *washer*; rondelle à ressort, *spring washer*.

rose (f) (de vent), *compass rose*.

roulement (m) (à billes), *ball-bearing, ball-race*; roulement de butée, *ball-bearing thrust*.

rupteur (m), *contact-breaker*.

sapin (m), *fir, deal, spruce*.

sas (m), *lock chamber*.

scaphandrier (m), *diver*.

semence (f), *tacks, fine nails*.

souder, *to weld, to solder*; souder à l'etain, *soft solder*; souder à l'autogène, *oxyacet weld*.

surbau (m), *coaming*.

surlier, *to whip (rope)*.

surliure (f), *whipping (of rope)*.

taquet (m), *cleat, kevel*.

tarière (f), *auger*.

tirant (m) d'air, *air draught*.

tirant (m) d'eau, *draught*.

tolletière (f), *rowlock*.

tonture (f), *sheer (of vessel)*.

toron (m), *strand (of rope)*.

touage (m), *towage (on rivers and canals)*.

touer, *to tow* .

toueur (m), *tow-boat (esp. operated by chain in river or canal bed)*.

tour (m), *turn*; tour mort, *round turn*.

trait (m), *tow-rope (on river)*.

trématage (m), *overtaking (canal)*.

treuil (m), *winch*.

vanne (f), *sluice*.

versant (m), *one side of a watershed*.

vibord (m), *sheer strake*.

vilebrequin (m), *brace*; vilebrequin à cliquet, *ratchet-brace*.

virement (m), *turning, turn*.

virure (f), *strake (of vessel)*.

visser, *to thread, to screw*.

voie (f) (d'eau), *leak*; faire une voie d'eau, *spring a leak*; aveugler une voie d'eau, *stop a leak*.

vrille (f), *gimlet*.

English – French

air draught, *tirant d-air (m)*.

alongside, *bord à bord*; to come alongside, *accoster*.

anchor, *ancre (f)*; anchorage, *mouillage (m)*.

anchor (to), *mouiller*.

apron, *contre-étrave (f)*.

auger, *tarière (f)*.

awash, *à fleur d'eau*.

backwash, *remous (m)*.

bailer, *épuisette (m), éscope (f)*.

ball-bearing, *roulement à billes (m)*; ball-thrust, *roulement de butée*.

bank (of river), *rive (f)*; (of canal), *berge (f)*.

barge, *péniche (f), chaland (m)*.

basin (tidal), *darse (f)*.

bay (small), *anse (f)*.

beacon, *balise (f)*.

beam (breadth of), *largeur (f)*.

bearing (of machine), *palier (m)*; ball-bearing, *palier à billes*; thrust bearing, *palier butée*.

bearing (compass), *relèvement (m)*.

becket, *erse (f)*.

belay (to), *amarrer*.

binnacle, *habitacle (m)*.

block, *poulie (F)*; single block, *poulie simple*; double block, *poulie double*; snatch block, *poulie coupée*.

bollard, *bitte (f)*.

bore (river), *mascaret (m), ras de marée (m)*.

bottom, *fond (m)*; flat-bottomed, *à fond plat*.

bow, *avant (m)*; on the port bow, *par babord avant*.

bowline (knot), *noeud de chaise (m)*; running bowline, *noeud d'anguille*.

brace, *vilebrequin (m)*; ratchet-brace, *vilebrequin à cliquet*.

bradawl, *poinçon (m)*.

brass, *laiton (m)* .

bulkhead, *cloison (f)*; watertight bulkhead, *cloison étanche*.

buoy, *bouée (f)*; mooring-buoy, *bouée de corps mort*; buoy-rope, *orin (m)*.

burgee, *guidon(m)*.

bush (of machine), *manchon (m)*.

capsize (to), *chavirer*.

carburettor (needle), *pointeau (m)*; float, *flotteur (m)*; jet, *gicleur (m)*.

careen (to), *caréner*; careening-basin, *bassin de carénage*.

carvel (built), *à franc-bord (m)*.

caulk (to), *calfater*; caulking, *calfatage (m)*.

chart-house, *kiosque des cartes (m)*.

check (to), *choquer*; to check the mooring ropes, *choquer les amarres*.

cleat, *taquet (m)*.

clench (a nail), *rabattre*.

clinker, *clin (m)*; clinker-built, *construit à clin*.

coil (to), *lover*.

coamings, *hiloire (f)*; *surbau (m)*.

collar (machine), *manchon (m)*.

compass, *compass (m)*; compass bearing, *relèvement (m)*; *gisement (m)*; cross-bearing, *relèvement croisè*; compass rose, *rose des vents (f)*.

confluence (rivers), *confluent (m)*.

connecting-rod, *bielle (m)*.

contact-breaker, *rupteur (m)*; contact-breaker arm, *levier du rupteur*; contact-point, *plot (m)*.

cotter, *groupille (f)*.

countersink (to), *fraiser*.

cove (small), *anse (f), clanque (f)*.

cradle (for vessel), *berceau (m)*; launching cradle, *ber (m)*.

cringle, *patte (f)*.

crutches (for oars), *dames (f)*.

deviation (compass), *déviation (f)*.

dike, *digue (f)*.

diver, *scaphandrier (m)*.

dock (no gates), *darse (f)*.

dovetail, *queue d'aronde (f)*.

draught (of vessel), *calaison (f), tirant d'eau*.

drift, *dérive (f)*, leeboard, *aile de dérive*; centre-board, *quille de dérive*.

drill, *mèche (f)*; hand-drill, *chignole (f)*.

eddy, *remous (m)*.

embankment, *digue (f)*.

eyelet (canvas), *oeil de pie (m)*.

fairlead, *chaumard (m)*.

ferry, *bac (m)*.

figure of 8 (knot), *noeud d'arrêt (m)*.

fiord (cove), *calanque (f)*.

fir, *sapin (m)*.

firing order (motor), *ordre d'allumage (f)*.

fisherman's bend, *noeud de grappin (m)*.

fit out (to), *équiper*.

flukes (of anchor), *pattes (f)*.

frame (of hull), *couple (m).*
freeboard, *franc-bord (m).*
freshen (to), *franchir;* the wind
   freshens, *le vent franchit.*

garboard (stake), *galbord (m).*
gauge, *gabarit (m).*
gimlet, *vrille (f).*
gland (suffing), *press-étoupe (m).*
granny (knot), *noeud de vache (m).*
grummet, *bague (f).*
gudgeons (of rudder), *femelots (m).*
gunwale, *plat-bord (m).*

halliard, *drisse (f).*
hank (sail), *bague (f).*
heart (of rope), *mèche (f).*
heel (to), *donner de la bande (f).*
hitch (to), *nouer.*
hitch (rolling), *noeud de fouet (m);*
   clove hitch, *deux demi-clefs à*
   capeler; half-hitch, *demi-clef;*
   timber hitch, *noeud de bois;*
   Blackwall hitch, *gueule de loup.*
hoist (to), *arborer.*
houeseline, *lusin (m).*

insulation tape, *chatterton (m).*

jet (carburettor), *gicleur (m);* choked
   jet, *gicleur bouché.*
jointing (compound), *hermétic (m).*
jury, fortune (f); jury mast, *mât de*
   fortune.

keelson, *carlingue (f).*
knee, *courbe (f).*
knot, *noeud (m);* figure of 8, *noeud*
   d'arret; granny, *noeud de vache;*
   bow-line, *noeud de chaise;* running
   bow-line, *noeud d'anguille;* reef,
   noeud de plat; fisherman's bend,
   noeud de grappin; sheet bend, *noeud*
   d'écoute.

larch, *mélèze (m).*
lashing, *amarrage (m).*
lay up (to), *désarmer.*
leak, *voie d'eau;* spring a leak, *faire*
   une voie d'eau; stop a leak, *aveugler*
   une voie d'eau.
leeway, *dérive (f);* leeboard, *aile de*
   dérive; centre-board, *quille de*
   dérive.
let go (to), *larguer;* to let go the
   mooring ropes, *larguer les amarres.*
lights (navigation), *feux de route;*
   riding-light, *feu de mouillage.*
lighter, péniche (f), chaland (m),
   gabare (f).

lock, *écluse (f);* lock sill, *buse (m);*
   lock chamber, *sas (m) .*
lower (to), *affaler.*
lubber's line, *ligne de foi.*

mahogany, *acajou (m);* Gabon
   mahogany, *okoume (m).*
mandrel (for lathe), *mandrin (m).*
marline, *lusin (m).*
meeting (on river or canal), *croisement*
   (m).
misfire (motor), *raté (m).*
moor (to), *mouiller;* mooring,
   amarrage (m); mooring ring, *boucle*
   (f); mooring buoy, *bouée de corps*
   mort.
mop, *guipon (m).*
mould, *gabarit (m);* moulding, *lisee*
   (f).

nails (fine), *semence (f).*
oil-grooves, *pattes d'araignée (f).*
overtaking (on river or canal),
   trématage.

paddle-wheel, *aube (f).*
painter (of boat), *bosse (f).*
palm (sewing), *paumelle (f).*
parcel (to), *limander.*
pay out (a rope), *filer.*
pennant, *guidon (m).*
pin (machine), *goupille (f);* split-pin,
   goupille fendue.
pine, *pin (m);* pitche-pine, *pitch-pin*
   (m).
pintle (of rudder), *aiguillot (m).*
pitche (tar), *brai (m).*
pitche (of screw), *pas (m).*
plane (for wood), *rabot (m).*
plug-hole (of boat), *nable (m).*
plywood, *contre-plaqué (m).*
pointing (rope's end), *queue de rat (f).*
port (of call), *relâche (f);* to call at,
   relâcher à.
pound (of canal), *brief (m).*
pricker, *poinçon (m).*
propeller, *hélice (f);* pitch of
   propeller, *pas de l'élice.*
pump, *pompe (f);* bilge-pump, *pompe*
   de cale; to prime a pump, *allumer*
   une pompe; the pump sucks, *la*
   pompe est eventée.
punch (tool), *etampe (f.*
push-tow, *convoic poussé (m).*
push-towing, *poussage (m).*
push-tug, *pousseur (m).*
rabnbet, *râblure (f).*
raft, *radeau (m).*
reach (of canal), *bief (m).*

ream (to ream a hole), *fraiser.*
red lead, *minium (m).*
reef (of rocks), *récif (m), écueil (m).*
reef-knot, *noeud de plat (m).*
refit (to), *radouber;* graving-slip, *cale*
   de redoub.
ribband, *lisse (f).*
rising water (river), *hausse (f).*
rope, *cordage (m);* hemp rope, *cordage*
   en chanvre.
rope-yard, *fil de caret.*
rowlocks, *tolletières (f).*

sailing directions, *instructions (f).*
scarf (to), *enter.*
screw (to) (thread), *visser.*
scull (to) (over stern), *godiller.*
scupper, *dalot (m).*
seize (to), *aiguiller, genoper.*
seizing, *amarrage (m);* racking-
   seizing, *amarrage en portugaise.*
shackle, *manille (f).*
shaft (machine), *arbe (m);* crankshaft,
   vilebrequin (m); camshaft, *arbre à*
   cames.
sheave, *poulie (f); réa (m).*
sheer (of vessel), *tonture (f);* sheer-
   strake, *carreau (m), vibord (m).*
sheet-bend, *noeud d'écoute (m).*
shelf (of ship), *banquière (f).*
shelf (reef), *écueil (m).*
ship, *bâtiment (m);* man-of-war,
   vaisseau (m); merchantman, *navire*
   (m).
ship-broker, *courtier maritime (m).*
shoals, *haut-fonds (m), bas-fonds (m).*

sill (of lock), *buse (m).*
sling (to), *élinguer*
sling, élingue (f).
slipway, *cale (f).*
sluice, *vanne (f).*
solder (to), *souder;* soft-solder, *souder*
   à l'etain.
spice (to), *épisser;* eye-splice, *épissure*
   à oeil.
spun-yarn, *bitord (m).*
stanchion, *montant (m).*
starter, *démarreur (m).*
stem (of ship), *étrave (f).*
stern-post, *étambot (m).*
stock (of anchor), *jas (m).*
stock (and die), *filière (f).*
strainer, *crépine (f); passoire (f).*
strake, *virure (f);* garboard-strake,
   galbord (m).
strand (of a rope), *toron (m).*
stringer, *lisse (f).*
strop, *erse (f), élingue (f);* selvagee
   strop, *erse en bitord.*

stuffing-box, *presse-étoupe (f)*.

summit level (of canal), *bief de partage (m)*.

swab, *faubert (m)*.

switch (electrical), *interrupteur (m)*.

tack (to), *louvoyer*.

tacks (fine nails), *semence (f)*.

tackle, *palan (m)*; falls of tackle, *garants (m)*; luff tackle, *palan à croc*; handy-billy, *palan de dimanche*; chain-block, *palan à chaine*; to rig a tackle, *gréer un palan*.

tang (of a file), *queue (f)*.

tar (coal), *goudron (m)*; Stockholm tar, *goudron à bois*; pitch, *brai (m)*.

tarpaulin, *prelart (m)*, *bâche goudronnée (f)*.

thimble, *cosse (f)*.

tidal wave (river), *mascaret (m)*, *ras de marée (m)*.

timber (frame of ship), *couple (m)*.

timber-hitch, *noeud de bois (m)*.

tot, *boujaron (m)*; toto of rum, *boujaron de rhum*.

tow (to) (by boat), *remorquer*.

towage, *halage (m)*; tow path, *chemin de halage*; tow-rope, *faux-bras (m)*; tow-rope (on river), *trait (m)*.

training-wall (river), *digue (f)*, *épine (f)*; facines, wickerwork, *clayonnage (m)*.

tributary, *affluent (m)*.

truck (of a mast), *pomme (f)*.

tug-boat, *remorqueur (m)*; paddle-wheel tug-boat, *remorqueur à aubes*; to tow alongside, *remorquer à couple*.

turn (of rope), *tour*; a round turn, *un tour mort*.

turn (or turning), *virement (m)*.

twine, *fil (m)*; sail twin, *fil à voile*.

underwriter, *assureur (m)*.

unlay (to), *décommettre*.

upstream, *amont*; above bridge, *en amont du pont*.

variation (of compass), *déclinaison (f)*.

veer (to), *filer*.

vessel (ship), *bâtiment (m)*; man-of-war, *vaisseau (m)*; merchantman, *navire (m)*.

wall (training in river), *digue (f)*, *épine (f)*, facines, wickerwork, *clayonnage (m)*.

warp (to), *touer*; warping, *touage (m)*.

warp, *faux-bras (m)*; *grelin (m)*.

washer, *rondelle (f)*.

watershed, *ligne de partage (f)*.

weir, *barrage (m)*, *déversoir (m)*.

weld (to) (oxyacet), *souder à l'autogène*.

wheel-house, *kiosque de timonerie (m)*.

whip (to) (a rope), *surlier*.

whipping, *surliure (f)*.

winch, *treuil (m)*.

wire (metal), *fil (m)*; iron wire, *fil de fer*; brass wire, *fil de laiton*; copper wire, *fil de cuivre rouge*; ignition wire, *fil de bougie*.

yard (rope), *fil de caret (f)*.

CONVERSION TABLES

metres–feet

m	ft/m	ft
0·3	1	3·3
0·6	2	6·6
0·9	3	9·8
1·2	4	13·1
1·5	5	16·4
1·8	6	19·7
2·1	7	23·0
2·4	8	26·2
2·7	9	29·5
3·0	10	32·8
6·1	20	65·6
9·1	30	98·4
12·2	40	131·2
15·2	50	164·0
30·5	100	328·1

centimetres–inches

cm	in/cm	in
2·5	1	0·4
5·1	2	0·8
7·6	3	1·2
10·2	4	1·6
12·7	5	2·0
15·2	6	2·4
17·8	7	2·8
20·3	8	3·1
22·9	9	3·5
25·4	10	3·9
50·8	20	7·9
76·2	30	11·8
101·6	40	15·7
127·0	50	19·7
254·0	100	39·4

metres–fathoms–feet

m	fathoms	ft
0·9	0·5	3
1·8	1	6
3·7	2	12
5·5	3	18
7·3	4	24
9·1	5	30
11·0	6	36
12·8	7	42
14·6	8	48
16·5	9	54
18·3	10	60
36·6	20	120
54·9	30	180
73·2	40	240
91·4	50	300

kilometres–statute miles

km	M/km	M
1·6	1	0·6
3·2	2	1·2
4·8	3	1·9
6·4	4	2·5
8·0	5	3·1
9·7	6	3·7
11·3	7	4·3
12·9	8	5·0
14·5	9	5·6
16·1	10	6·2
32·2	20	12·4
48·3	30	18·6
64·4	40	24·9
80·5	50	31·1
120·7	75	46·6
160·9	100	62·1
402·3	250	155·3
804·7	500	310·7
1609·3	1000	621·4

kilograms–pounds

kg	lb/kg	lb
0·5	1	2·2
0·9	2	4·4
1·4	3	6·6
1·8	4	8·8
2·3	5	11·0
2·7	6	13·2
3·2	7	15·4
3·6	8	17·6
4·1	9	19·8
4·5	10	22·0
9·1	20	44·1
13·6	30	66·1
18·1	40	88·2
22·7	50	110·2
34·0	75	165·3
45·4	100	220·5
113·4	250	551·2
226·8	500	1102·3
453·6	1000	2204·6

litres–gallons

l	gal/l	gal
4·5	1	0·2
9·1	2	0·4
13·6	3	0·7
18·2	4	0·9
22·7	5	1·1
27·3	6	1·3
31·8	7	1·5
36·4	8	1·8
40·9	9	2·0
45·5	10	2·2
90·9	20	4·4
136·4	30	6·6
181·8	40	8·8
227·3	50	11·0
341·0	75	16·5
454·6	100	22·0
1136·5	250	55·0
2273·0	500	110·0
4546·1	1000	220·0

Index

Imray publications

Also available

Cruising Guide to the Netherlands Brian Navin
A guide to a selection of through routes in the Netherlands which can be used by yachts without demasting. This guide also contains details of the sea ports of entry.

North Sea Passage Pilot Brian Bavin
Covers the ports of entry into the French canal system in northwest France.

North France Pilot T. & D. Thompson
A guide to the French coast from Calais to Cherbourg which also contains details of the French channel ports for those interested in entering the canal system.

The Seine Derek Bowskill
A guide to the navigable waters above and below Paris.

North Brittany RCC Pilotage Foundation K. Adlard Coles, revised by Nick Heath.
A guide for the north coast of Brittany which also covers ports connecting with the Brittany canals.

South France Pilot. West – Spanish Border to Cap Sicié Robin Brandon
Covers the ports of Languedoc and Golfe de Fos which connect with the canals associated with the Rhône and the Midi.

Mediterranean France and Corsica – A sea guide Rod Heikell
This contains a section devoted to the inland waterways of France which is also of interest to inland waterway users on passage to the Mediterranean.

The Danube – A river guide Rod Heikell
A guide to the river from southern Germany to the Black Sea for river users and travellers.

Map of the Inland Waterways of France Compiled by K. Nussbaum 1:500,000
A good general map of the waterways of France, Belgium and the Netherlands. A useful companion to *Inland Waterways of France*, this is invaluable for route planning.

Imrays also distribute maps and guides to the waterways of central Europe and a full list is available on request.

Cartes et Guides Vagnon de Navigation

Published in France by les Editions du Plaisancier. Each with English translation, Vagnon guides are being redesigned to improve clarity and detail. They are regarded by many to be the best series of guides to the canals in France.

1 Carte de France des voies navigables
2 Guide du Doubs & Canal Rhône au Rhin
3 Guide de Canal de Bourgogne
4 Canaux de la Loire et Canal du Centre
5 Guide du Rhône
6 Guide de la Saône, avec la Seille
7 Guide des Canaux du Midi
8 Guide de la Meuse et du Canal de l'Est
10 Guide des Canaux Bretons et de la Loire

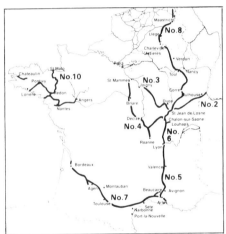

	Guide N°
Aulne	10
Baise	7
Blavet	10
Bourgogne (canal de)	3
Briare (canal de)	4
Centre (canal du)	4
Doubs	2
Erdre	10
Est (canal de l')	8
Garonne	7
Garonne (canal lateral a la)	7
Ille et Rance (canal d')	10
Loing (canal du)	4
Loire	10

	Guide N°
Loire (canal lateral a la)	4
Meuse (belge et française)	8
Midi (canal du)	7
Nantes a Brest (canal de)	10
Rance	10
Rhône	5
Rhône (petit)	7
Rhône - Fos - Bouc (liaison)	5
Rhône au Rhin (canal du)	2
Rhône a Sete (canal du)	7
Roanne a Digoin (canal de)	4
Saône	6
Seille	6
Vilaine	10

Imray, Laurie, Norie & Wilson Ltd

Wych House The Broadway St Ives Huntingdon Cambridgeshire PE17 4BT England

☎ St Ives (0480) 62114
Telex 329195 IMRAYS G
Fax (0480) 496109

les Cartes touristiques locales